Seventh Edition

In Our Times
America Since World War II

Norman L. Rosenberg
Emily S. Rosenberg
Macalester College

Prentice
Hall

Upper Saddle River, New Jersey 07458

Library of Congress Cataloging-in-Publication Data

Rosenberg, Norman L., (date)
  In our times : America since World War II / Norman L. Rosenberg, Emily
S. Rosenberg.— 7th ed.
    p. cm.
Includes bibliographical references and index.
  ISBN 0-13-099648-3
  1. United States—History—1945- I. Rosenberg, Emily S., 1944- II.
Title.
  E741 .R667 2003
  973.92—dc21

                                                    2002029286

VP, Editorial Director: Charlyce Jones Owen
Sr. Acquisitions Editor: Charles Cavaliere
Editorial Assistant: Adrienne Paul
Associate Editor: Emsal Hasan
Sr. Managing Editor: Jan Stephan
Production Liaison: Fran Russello
Project Manager: Rosie Jones/
  Clarinda Publication Services
Prepress and Manufacturing Buyer:
  Sherry Lewis

Cover Designer: Bruce Kenselaar
Art Director: Jayne Conte
Permission Specialist: Cindy Miller
Cover Image Specialist: Karen Sanatar
Image Permission Coordinator:
  Charles Morris
Photo Researcher: Elaine Soares
Marketing Manager: Claire Bitting

Cover Art: (*bottom left*) *U.S. 99, "There's no way like the American Way"* Credit: Courtesy of
  the Library of Congress; (*top left*) *Civil Rights March*, 1960's. Credit: Courtesy of the
  Library of Congress; (*top right*) *Gas station closed (out of gas)*. Credit: Irene Springer/
  Pearson Education/PH College; (*bottom right*) *Fast food service*. Credit: Laima
  Druskis/Pearson Education/PH College.

This book was set in 10/11 New Baskerville by The Clarinda Company and printed and
bound by Courier Companies, Inc. The cover was printed by Phoenix Color Corp.

© 2003, 1999, 1995, 1991, 1987, 1982, 1976
by Pearson Education, Inc.
Upper Saddle River, New Jersey 07458

Printed in the United States of America

10 9 8 7 6 5 4

ISBN 0-13-099648-3

Pearson Education LTD., London
Pearson Education Australia Pte, Limited, Sydney
Pearson Education Singapore, Pte. Ltd
Pearson Education North Asia Ltd, Hong Kong
Pearson Education Canada, Ltd., Toronto
Pearson Educacion de Mexico, S.A. de C.V.
Pearson Education–Japan, Tokyo
Pearson Education Malaysia, Pte. Ltd
Pearson Education, Upper Saddle River, New Jersey

*To the memories of Joseph and Dorothea Rosenberg
and of Albert A. and Helen Griggs Schlaht*

*Also to our children,
Sarah, Molly, Ruth, Joseph*

Contents

Preface

In Our Times, like the period of U.S. history it seeks to represent, remains a work in progress. We began writing the first edition of this book in the mid-1970s, when only thirty years had elapsed since 1945. In this seventh, 2002 edition, the book now wears twice as many years as when we began—and so do we. We continue to be gratified that this book—one of the first texts designed for "1945 to present" courses—remains a favorite among history teachers and students. We have again undertaken the kind of reorganization and updating that those who use *In Our Times,* and we ourselves, expect.

We strive to provide students and instructors with an interesting, readable, and coherent historical framework. We have streamlined the narrative, integrated new scholarship, and entirely reorganized most chapters. New, and more numerous, pictures, charts, and maps enhance the book's visual dimension. Updated bibliographies, along with suggested websites, provide additional resources for teaching and learning. Users will find that our new introductions to chapters and to sections bring major themes into focus while enhancing the text's narrative quality.

In this seventh journey through "our times," we have incurred many debts of gratitude. Our greatest goes to the anonymous reviewers, some of whom suggested the reorganizations and additions that we have undertaken for this new edition. We trust that they will see many of their fine recommendations reflected in these pages: more discussion, for example, of the soldier's experience in Vietnam and of cultural diplomacy; greater consistency in chapter size; improved organization in the coverage of politics, diplomacy, and culture; significant expansion of material on the 1980s and 1990s. We have, of course, revised and updated our strong treatment of mass culture, a feature that has appealed to students over the years.

We also extend our special thanks to our editors. Charles Cavaliere enthusiastically imparted a new vision and a special commitment to *In Our Times.* Emsal Hasan has skillfully carried this book forward through the last two editions; his enthusiasm, good sense, and attention to detail has made him a true collaborator. Rosie Jones provided vital expert assistance on the finishing touches of the book. Joelle Blomquist, a senior history major at Macalester College, has provided meticulous and thorough assistance in the tasks of research and revision. Herta Pitman, department coordinator at Macalester, has also contributed her expertise. Finally, of course, we are indebted to all of the scholars whose books and essays make doing the history of "our times" meaningful and exciting.

In Our Times, like our teaching career at Macalester College, remains a joint production. Although we continue to split the primary responsibility for re-reviewing and rewriting specific sections, the computer remains community property. One of us will often complete the paragraph or sentence that the other had begun or had once thought, mistakenly, to be complete. For any errors of fact or judgment, each of us can offer the ready excuse that it was surely committed by "the other Professor Rosenberg." Yet we will also be happy to take joint credit for whatever positive features this book offers.

Norman L. Rosenberg
Emily S. Rosenberg

1

The World's Superpower

The Second World War was over! Japan had surrendered! On August 14, 1945, at 7:00 P.M., President Harry S. Truman made the official announcement. Across the country, people began to celebrate. In Washington, outside the White House, a crowd that had been waiting all day struck up the chant, "We want Harry, we want Harry!" The president appeared, said a few words, and left, only to be called back twice by repeated shouts. Finally, he sank into a chair and sighed, "I'm glad that it's over."

Pressing problems and hard decisions, Truman knew, would likely not end with the war. Indeed, postwar reconstruction and the development of a "cold war" between the United States and the Soviet Union kept international affairs in perpetual crisis.

COLLAPSE OF THE OLD ORDER, RISE OF THE NEW

Before World War II, Europeans believed they occupied the center of progress, civilization, and world power. London and Paris set cultural trends, held the reins of government for colonial peoples throughout the globe, and provided financial institutions for the business of distant empires. But World War II, coming only two decades after the trauma of World War I, dramatically altered Europe's position. The costs of the long struggle left the nations of Europe—both the victors and the vanquished—exhausted. As Europeans spent their military and economic resources, their grasp over colonial areas weakened. Global warfare strengthened local nationalist movements and their desires for independence and self-determination. Anticolonial revolutionary movements were

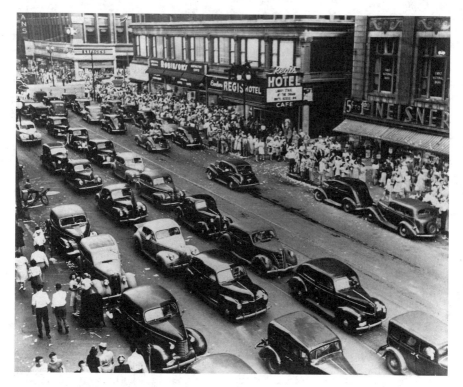

FIGURE 1–1 V-J Day in Omaha.

All across the country, people celebrated victory over Japan, the end of World War II.
Source: Nebraska State Historical Society.

poised to dismember the European empires and to create new nations throughout Asia and Africa.

With European economies in ruin and colonial institutions disintegrating,
U.S. policymakers feared what might happen. Secretary of State Cordell Hull
warned that "the people of many countries will be starving . . . homeless . . .
their factories and mines destroyed; their roads and transport wrecked. . . . Disease will lurk everywhere. In some countries confusion and chaos will follow the
cessation of hostilities." Hull advised that "victory must be followed by swift and
effective action."

One of the architects of U.S. policy, Undersecretary of State Dean
Acheson (later Truman's secretary of state), entitled his memoirs of this
period *Present at the Creation.* Hull, Acheson, and others believed that the
United States needed to help draft a blueprint for a postwar order. Its territory untouched by battle, enriched by wartime profits, and free from political instability, the United States emerged as the victor of victors, the
undisputed superpower. U.S. leaders tried to imagine how to use this power
in the postwar world. The supposed folly of isolationism and appeasement
during the 1920s and 1930s had turned many American policymakers into

internationalists. During World War II, they were already laying the basis for postwar international reconstruction.

How did American policymakers envision the postwar world? Two articles of internationalist faith—maintenance of open access for trade and investment and creation of an international organization—provided the cornerstones of their plan.

Reconstructing an International Economic System

A trading nation with a dynamic, expanding economy, the United States had always opposed restrictions on the free flow of its overseas trade and investment. During the depression decade of the 1930s, policymakers watched uneasily as economic restrictions threatened to close large parts of the world to U.S. businesses. Japan's expansionist leaders had threatened to create a closed economic sphere in Asia. Fascist Germany had reached out to control sources of raw materials. Even Great Britain, America's ally, had moved toward an "imperial preference" system, which placed nations outside the British Empire at a commercial disadvantage. As a condition for receiving lend-lease assistance from the United States on the eve of American entry into World War II, Britain and other Allied nations had to promise to work toward the "elimination of all forms of discriminatory treatment in international commerce."

U.S. leaders hoped to call in these promises in the postwar world. They believed that unhampered commerce brought peace, whereas economic restrictions—such as unequal tariffs, preferential commercial arrangements, and currency inconvertibility—bred jealousy and war. "If we could get a freer flow of trade," Cordell Hull wrote, "the living standards of all countries might rise, thereby eliminating the economic dissatisfaction that breeds war." While ushering in prosperity and peace, freer trade would, not incidentally, also enhance U.S. influence worldwide because of its dominant financial position. In planning a postwar world, as in most other endeavors, ideology and self-interest dovetailed.

In July 1944, representatives from forty-four countries gathered at Bretton Woods, New Hampshire, to work out a postwar economic structure. The Soviet Union did not attend. Although the Bretton Woods delegates did not adopt every U.S. proposal, they did formulate a system that generally reflected American goals.

A revised international monetary system seemed essential to free-flowing trade and investment. The delegates consequently created the International Monetary Fund (IMF) and charged it with maintaining a stable international system of exchange in which each national currency was convertible into any other at a fixed rate. A country could alter its exchange rate (i.e., adjust the value of its money in relation to that of other currencies) only by agreement with the IMF. The architects of the IMF hoped that this system would combat the kind of economic nationalism that had grown during the 1930s, maintain relative stability in value among the world's currencies, and forge an interdependent, peaceful world economy.

The delegates to Bretton Woods also created the International Bank for Reconstruction and Development, later called the World Bank. It was to encourage loans for postwar economic recovery. These loans would help both to restore war-ruined economies and to revive pre-war trading patterns. Financial stabilization, it was believed, would also help curb radical political movements that fed on economic discontent. Following its creation, the World Bank became dominated by American capital and headed by a succession of American directors. Perhaps its most prestigious head was Robert McNamara, former secretary of defense under presidents John Kennedy and Lyndon Johnson, who directed the bank between 1968 and 1981.

Policymakers believed that the World Bank served world reconstruction and America's domestic prosperity equally well. It would not only stabilize needy nations but support U.S. trade interests by ensuring that other countries had the money to buy American products. In addition, the World Bank participated in or guaranteed many private American loans made to foreign nations. The United States was by far the richest nation in the postwar world, and the bank indirectly helped American businesses invest excess capital around the globe, particularly in the development of raw materials needed for domestic recovery. The outflow of American investment reduced the pressures toward inflation at home and enhanced the recovery of international trade.

The Bretton Woods agreement stabilized the international economy by helping to revive trade and investment. It helped sustain America's postwar economic predominance, and the U.S. dollar became the lynchpin of international finance. Until 1971, when a system of floating exchange rates replaced the fixed system established at Bretton Woods, the economic agreements of 1944 remained the foundation for global economic activity outside the Soviet bloc. For the developed nations, Bretton Woods provided a structure for nearly three decades of steady growth and global economic integration.

Creating the United Nations

During World War II, Franklin Roosevelt revived President Woodrow Wilson's dream of creating an international organization. The U.S. refusal to join the League of Nations after World War I, many U.S. policymakers came to believe, had contributed to the outbreak of war in 1939. A new representative world assembly, they assumed, would moderate tensions and build a world community under the aegis of the major postwar powers—United States, Britain, France, and the Soviet Union. These powers would become the collective guarantors of postwar peace, substituting "collective security" for the old-style, balance-of-power diplomacy.

At Dumbarton Oaks in Washington, D.C., in August 1944, and at San Francisco in April 1945, the wartime Allies hammered out the structural details for the new United Nations. The basic structure remains today: a General Assembly, in which all member nations have one vote; a Security Council comprising five permanent members (the United States, Great Britain, France, the Soviet Union, and China) and six rotating, temporary members; a Secretariat to handle day-to-day business; and an Economic and Social Council comprising committees for worldwide social rehabilitation and economic development. Eleanor Roosevelt, who had been a tireless advocate for internationalism throughout her husband's presidency, served as a delegate to the first meeting of the General Assembly and also guided the drafting of a Universal Declaration of Human Rights, adopted by the UN in 1948. The Declaration set forth "inalienable" human rights and freedoms as cornerstones of international law.

The Security Council, which according to the UN charter had the "primary responsibility for the maintenance of international peace and security," consisted of the major victors in World War II. The inclusion of China, at American insistence, always seemed incongruous. At war's end, China had an unpopular and corrupt government led by Jiang Jie-shi (formerly spelled Chiang Kai-shek). Few observers believed that Jiang could maintain control at home, much less play an active role in international affairs. But the inclusion of Jiang's China represented the U.S. hope of turning China into a friendly Pacific power that would fill the vacuum left by Japan's defeat. After 1949, Jiang's Nationalist government fled to the small island of Formosa and a Communist regime headed by Mao Zedong (formerly spelled Mao Tse-tung) came to power, but the Nationalist regime continued to sit on the Security Council until 1971. This discrepancy between the realities of world power and Security-Council membership proved to be one weakness of the United Nations.

The UN charter provided that each permanent member of the Security Council could exercise an absolute veto over decisions. None of the great powers would have joined the UN without this means of safeguarding their national interest. But the veto provision meant that the UN could act only when all five permanent members agreed, and unanimity was rare in the postwar world. The UN's strongest action, sponsoring a military force to assist South Korea in 1950, was approved while the Soviet Union's delegate was boycotting sessions of the Security Council.

If the Security Council did not always fulfill the peacekeeping role that its founders envisioned, other UN bodies did serve useful functions. The humanitarian programs of the UN's social and economic agencies boosted its prestige. In addition, the General Assembly provided a forum in which nations could articulate their positions; it provided a barometer of international tensions and a gauge of shifting views on various issues. It also provided a platform for smaller nations whose viewpoints might not otherwise be heard.

American postwar plans sounded selfless and impartial. Nonrestrictive trade and investment policies and an open international forum for debate and collective peacekeeping appeared to set aside narrow nationalism. In the period immediately after World War II few American observers doubted that their country's new internationalism was both realistic and righteous. Critics, however, claimed that American policy would inevitably advance the interests of the nation that was economically and politically the strongest—the United States. Americans used internationalist rhetoric, critics charged, to camouflage self-interest and their own globalist designs. Did U.S. policy serve the world or itself? Could it do both at once?

THE ONSET OF THE COLD WAR

The political and economic order envisioned by U.S. policymakers depended on cooperation among the great powers. But divisions within the wartime Grand Alliance undermined the kind of interconnected world that American policymakers hoped to create. Tensions between the United States and the Soviet Union dated back to the Bolshevik revolution of 1917, which had created a

Communist state. The World War II alliance between the two countries had been more a marriage of convenience than conviction. After cooperating to defeat Germany, Italy, and Japan in World War II, the old distrust returned, and it rapidly grew into a forty-five year rivalry called the cold war.

Mounting Distrust between the United States and the Soviet Union

Throughout World War II, the Soviet Union and the other Allies repeatedly clashed, especially over military strategy. British planners, eventually supported by the United States, favored peripheral campaigns against Germany, first into French North Africa and then up through Sicily and Italy. Soviet Premier Joseph Stalin denounced these Anglo-American offensives because they postponed the opening of a second front to the west of Germany and forced his nation to bear the main thrust of the German war machine. Stalin suspected that his allies were shoring up spheres of influence in North Africa, Italy, and the Middle East, while allowing Germany and the Soviet Union to pound each other into exhaustion on the war's eastern front. The long delay in opening a second front, Stalin reasoned, indicated that the wartime alliance against Nazism had not softened capitalist hostility toward Soviet communism.

The fierce fighting between Germany and the Soviet Union and the Soviet army's tremendous casualties helped shape Stalin's postwar policies. The Soviet leader wanted to eliminate the German threat that had repeatedly menaced his country. He viewed the creation of a pro-Soviet zone in neighboring Eastern Europe as vital to his country's national security. During 1944 and 1945, Stalin believed he had some Allied support for his goal of creating a Soviet sphere of influence. At a meeting in 1944, Britain's Winston Churchill and Stalin secretly reached an informal agreement: Churchill would grant Soviet predominance in Romania and Bulgaria in return for British preeminence in Greece. President Franklin Roosevelt did not protest the arrangement. Publicly, Americans talked of eliminating such spheres of influence; privately, American policymakers seemed to understand their inevitability. At the Yalta Conference in February 1945, Allied harmony reached its high tide with the implicit recognition of spheres of influence: Germany was divided into four zones of occupation; the Soviet Union agreed to sign a treaty of friendship with America's ally in China, Jiang Jie-shi; the Soviets made a vague promise to hold "free elections" in liberated Poland, but Anglo-American negotiators also implied that they understood Stalin's security concerns about maintaining a friendly government there.

In the end, the course of battle helped determine the postwar situation. Soviet troops marched into Berlin from the East as American and British forces advanced through Germany from the West. The separate zones of occupation soon hardened into a divided Germany. The nationality of occupation forces likewise helped shape the destiny of areas outside Germany. Anglo-American influence was strong in France, Italy, Greece, and the Middle East; Soviet power predominated in Eastern Europe. Meanwhile, the United States assumed exclusive control of the Japanese-dominated Pacific islands and of defeated Japan itself.

Stalin largely ignored the Yalta declaration supporting free elections in Poland. Pro-Soviet governments came to power in Romania, Hungary, Bulgaria, Albania, and Poland; Latvia, Lithuania, and Estonia were absorbed completely by the Soviet Union. Stalin refused to include an Anglo-American–sponsored group in the new government of Poland. Stalin justified these moves as a minimal guarantee of the future security of the Soviet Union. Russians had borne the brunt of Germany's force during World War II and lost more than ten times as many soldiers as did the United States. Stalin also noted that Anglo-American commanders had not allowed Soviet participation in governments under their military influence. In Italy after Benito Mussolini's overthrow, for example, Britain and the United States had installed a rightist regime committed to purging any leftist or pro-Soviet elements.

Many people in the United States, however, expressed outrage at Soviet actions. Republicans blamed President Roosevelt, especially, for failing to obtain stronger guarantees for Eastern Europe at the Yalta Conference. They felt that he had betrayed the cause of democracy. Americans of Eastern-European descent, especially the six million Polish-Americans and others who had expected the war to open all Europe to American trade and ideas, also denounced the Soviet Union's postwar moves. Moreover, Stalin's brutal, iron-handed suppression of domestic dissent made him a convincing villain. Accustomed to thinking in terms of an evil and aggressive enemy, a growing number of Americans substituted the Soviet Union for the now defeated Nazi Germany as the new archenemy. A former State Department official, William C. Bullitt, expressed this attitude: "The Soviet Union's assault upon the West is at about the stage of Hitler's maneuvering into Czechoslovakia [in 1938]." This analysis could have only one conclusion—that there should be no appeasement, no compromise with Soviet power.

American-Soviet relations quickly degenerated. The atmosphere of cooperation at Yalta in early 1945 became one of deep distrust by the end of the same year. Stalin's Eastern European policies provided the backdrop to this change, but events in the United States also contributed.

Harry S. Truman, who had become president in April 1945 following the death of Franklin Roosevelt, lacked his predecessor's cool self-confidence, easy affability, and cosmopolitan world view. He had not been close to Roosevelt and knew little of his policies or intentions. In attempting to form guidelines for his own administration, Truman sided with those advisers who advocated a harder line than Roosevelt had taken against the Soviet Union, and he rejected the notion of a Soviet sphere of influence in Eastern Europe. Setting a style for his successors, he began to talk tough to the Russians, especially at the Potsdam Conference of July 1945.

Truman felt that he had two potential weapons in bargaining with Stalin. The first was atomic power. Even before Roosevelt's death, some advisers had suggested that the bomb might be an effective diplomatic lever. After demonstrating the bomb's power at Hiroshima and Nagasaki in order to bring about Japan's rapid and unconditional surrender, some officials believed that Stalin would have to accede to U.S. demands to open Eastern Europe. Truman also hoped that the Soviet's need for postwar economic assistance would bring Stalin into line. After the termination of wartime lend-lease, Stalin requested additional aid to help rebuild Russia's war-damaged economy. But Truman's tough tone meant that assistance would be contingent on a change in the Soviet Union's Eastern-European policy.

Fearful of the strings attached to any U.S. economic aid package, Stalin eased his country's difficulties in other ways: a new Five-Year Plan to rebuild Soviet industry and an expropriation of materials from occupied territories, particularly in Eastern Germany. The Soviet Union carried away whatever it could use—in some cases entire factories—and closed the Soviet-dominated occupation zone to Anglo-American influence.

U.S. officials argued over whether or not Truman's hard line was at least partially responsible for Stalin's growing hostility. Secretary of Commerce and former Vice-President Henry A. Wallace, for example, advocated a more co-operative attitude toward the Soviet Union, claiming that a secure and prosperous Russia would be more accommodating than a frightened and hungry one. Angered by dissent from within his administration, the president demanded Wallace's resignation and moved closer to hard-line advisers. Compromise with Stalin, they argued, would be interpreted as weakness and would only encourage the Soviets to enlarge their imperial vision.

From allies in a hot war, the United States and the Soviet Union became enemies in a cold one. In 1946 Stalin publicly expressed distrust of his old capitalist allies. Their opposition to Soviet policy in Eastern Europe, he claimed, indicated their intention to crush communism and isolate the Soviet regime. On the other side, Britain's Winston Churchill charged that Stalin had dropped an "iron curtain" across Europe, holding Eastern-European peoples captive and denying them self-determination. With the collapse of the wartime alliance, the world entered a period of bipolar politics in which America and the Soviet Union vied for worldwide influence.

Debates about the origins of the U.S.-Soviet cold war have raged ever since the 1940s. The dominant view, adopted by the Truman administration and many later historians, assumed that U.S. policymakers were on the defensive, reacting to contain Soviet aggression and save freedom. A so-called revisionist view, more in line with Henry Wallace's position that U.S. behavior had been unduly provocative, gained substantial credibility during the era of the Vietnam War, when many Americans began to rethink the consequences of U.S. anti-Communist crusading. Revisionists criticized U.S. policy as providing a self-righteous mask for its own global economic interests. The cold war officially ended, of course, in 1989, when the Soviet Union's hold on Eastern Europe (and, later, communism's position in the USSR) suddenly collapsed. These events revived the view, sometimes called "triumphalism," that the United States had consistently been the defender of freedom against a historically doomed Communist system. People could "now know," as one study put it, that cold-war policies represented a justifiable and wise response to the Soviet-Communist threat. Although the debate over the origins of the cold war has continued, recent histories seem more interested in highlighting other important postwar foreign policy trends, such as decolonization, that the emphasis on the cold war had once obscured.

Cold War Aid Programs

In the years following World War II, U.S. leaders faced a dilemma. They had almost completed a rapid military demobilization, and most Americans expected a period of international tranquility and declining military expenditures. At the same time, though, policymakers were looking for ways to check the spread of Communist governments that might ally with the Soviet Union. According to Secretary of State James Byrnes, "We must help our friends in every way and refrain from assisting those who either through helplessness or for other reasons are opposing the principles for which we stand." But would Congress and the American public approve the monetary expenditures that such help required?

In early 1947, the issue seemed urgent. A leftist revolution threatened the conservative regime in Greece, and Great Britain, which had previously considered Greece within its sphere of influence, announced that it could no longer provide economic and military assistance. The U.S. State Department wanted to extend a military aid package to Greece and Turkey, a move that would have established a precedent for U.S. entry, as a replacement for European power, into other areas of the world. But the chances of Congress supporting such commitments seemed slim. As Republican Senator Arthur Vandenberg assessed the situation, Truman "will have to go and scare the hell out of the country."

Truman was equal to the task, and he set out to sell Congress and the public on both the aid package and his broader view of an anti-Communist foreign policy. A leftist victory in Greece, he claimed, would lead to Communist takeovers in other parts of Europe. Before a joint session of Congress in March 1947, the president advanced the Truman Doctrine. He portrayed the struggle in Greece as a conflict between two ways of life—one "distinguished by free institutions, representative government, free elections, guarantees of individual liberty, freedom of speech and religion, and freedom from political oppression"; the other relying on "terror and oppression, a controlled press and radio, fixed elections, and the suppression of personal freedoms." By failing to support freedom in Greece, Truman concluded, "we may endanger the peace of the world—and we shall surely endanger the welfare of our own nation." Truman's formulation, which became popularly known as the "domino theory," saw the "fall" of one country to communism leading to the toppling of other nations. These arguments, casting anticommunism as a global struggle, induced Congress to appropriate $400 million for assistance—primarily military aid—to Greece and neighboring Turkey, strategically located near the Dardanelles.

The Truman Doctrine established the terms of foreign-policy analysis for years to come and formed the core of a policy termed *containment*. The classic definition of containment came in a 1947 article by George Kennan in the journal *Foreign Affairs*. Writing under the pseudonym "X," Kennan, a respected foreign service officer, analyzed the Soviet Union's "expansive tendencies" and advocated a "firm and vigilant" application of counterforce to meet Soviet aggression until internal changes in the Soviet Union moderated the threat to the West. Kennan stressed the importance of ordering strategic priorities; of concentrating strength only in the locations deemed truly critical to national interest; and of seeing the Soviet Union itself, not some vague ideology called international communism, as the threat to be contained. But these subtleties became lost as containment evolved into an ideological, and increasingly militarized, crusade to be pursued in every region of the world.

A harsh winter in 1947 brought severe shortages to Europe. Food riots erupted in some cities; dollar-short governments feared bankruptcy; and moderate politicians warned that local Communist parties were rapidly gaining strength. In response, Truman approached Congress for an extended commitment of economic aid to European nations, including Germany. Initially, Congress balked, but a pro-Communist coup in neutralist Czechoslovakia convinced many people that containment strategies had to be implemented quickly. A new aid program—the Marshall Plan—passed by an overwhelming margin. Although the American government invited the Soviet Union itself to participate as a recipient of Marshall Plan assistance, the program's conditions for receiving aid ensured Soviet refusal.

The Marshall Plan sprang not only from a desire to alleviate human suffering but also from a pragmatic assessment of U.S. interests. The economic and political system that policymakers had constructed during postwar conferences depended on economic revival in Europe. U.S. leaders recognized that American prosperity, in particular, required a prosperous and stable Europe. But European economies were faltering, and Germany remained a divided and defeated nation. As hostility toward the Soviet Union mounted, it seemed necessary to counter Soviet power with a strong, industrialized Western Europe. As one reluctant Republican congressman averred, "We get it from all sides by official speakers, the press and the radio. They all say the same thing—either vote for this aid to Europe or all Europe will go Communist." The Joint Chiefs of Staff, alarmed by the growing political instability, drew up military contingency plans in case Italian Communists won Italy's election of 1948, and the new Central Intelligence Agency began channeling money to bolster non-Communist parties in Italy, France, and elsewhere.

COLD WAR CRISES

Cold war tensions escalated during Truman's second term. Truman and Dean Acheson, who became secretary of state in 1949, confronted a series of foreign-policy crises that fed domestic fears of a Communist threat that then came to justify new anti-Communist measures at home and new techniques for extending U.S. power abroad. Acheson hoped that later generations would recognize the "truly heroic mold" of the Truman administration's cold-war policies, and many later historians have indeed applauded the "wise men" who charted this anti-Communist course. Other historians have suggested that the simplistic mold of an ideological battle between Soviet "evil" and U.S. "freedom" impeded the shaping of effective policies for diverse geographical areas and specific international situations.

The Berlin Crisis

Germany, the Nazi enemy that had once united capitalists and Communists, became the focal point of the cold war, ominously divided between the two competing camps. The United States, Great Britain, and France decided to merge their zones of occupation in Germany into one federal republic and to institute a program of economic rehabilitation. On June 18, 1948, the three powers announced a currency reform for what would become, in 1949, the Federal Republic of Germany, or West Germany. Establishing West Germany as an industrial power and reintegrating it into the European economy seemed essential to the vision of continental recovery set forth in the Marshall Plan. As the Soviet Union changed from ally to enemy, West Germany changed from enemy to ally.

The Soviet Union saw the creation of West Germany as a provocation. Stalin wanted Germany to remain weak and divided. He still wanted German reparations for war damage and sought to dismantle the country's industrial capacity, not to rebuild it. In retaliation for the West's actions, he formed the German Democratic Republic, popularly known as East Germany, and closed off West Berlin, an Anglo-American–controlled sector of the capital city that was wholly within the Soviet zone of occupation.

Only one way remained into the blockaded city—by airplane. Planes began flying around the clock to deliver food, fuel, and medicine to the 2.5 million people in West Berlin. Pilots practiced landings at a flight-training center in Montana that was equipped with an air corridor, runways, and navigational aids exactly duplicating those in Berlin. Operation Vittles, as the pilots dubbed the airlift, could bring as much into Berlin as water and rail had provided before the blockade. To underscore how seriously he viewed the crisis, Truman also reinstated the draft, in order to restaff the armed forces, and sent to Great Britain, two squadrons of B-29s, the planes used to deliver atomic weapons. In the face of these moves, the Soviet Union backed off. In May 1949, Stalin reopened surface travel into West Berlin, but the divided city would remain a point of tension throughout the cold-war era.

During the year-long Berlin crisis, which had closely followed the Communist coup in Czechoslovakia, the nations of Western Europe grew increasingly anxious. With U.S. encouragement, Britain, France, Belgium, the Netherlands, and Luxembourg signed the Brussels Pact, pledging cooperation in economic and military matters. They also appealed for a stronger U.S. commitment to their security. Finally, in the spring of 1949, twelve nations, including the United States and the Brussels Pact countries, established the North Atlantic Treaty Organization (NATO). This collective-security pact provided that an attack against one of the signatories would be considered an attack against all. Furthermore, these nations promised closer economic ties with one another. NATO laid the groundwork for America's long-lasting military presence in Western Europe and provided a pattern for other collective-security pacts—CENTO and SEATO—in other parts of the world. (CENTO and SEATO are discussed in Chapter 3.) NATO, together with the Marshall Plan, brought Western Europe under the economic and military umbrella of the United States.

The Chinese Revolution

Throughout World War II, China had not only battled invading Japanese troops but had also been embroiled in a civil war between the Nationalist government of Jiang Jie-shi and Communist forces under Mao Zedong. The United States supported Jiang's government, providing it with arms, money, and advisers. Throughout the war and into the postwar period, however, many U.S. diplomats in China predicted that Jiang's government was too corrupt and incompetent to prevail. Mao's forces enjoyed greater popularity among China's peasants and had been more effective in fighting the Japanese.

Statistical comparisons made Jiang's victory over the Communists seem inevitable. By 1947, he had twice the number of troops and three or four times the number of rifles. From 1945 through 1948, the United States extended him a billion dollars in military aid and another billion in economic assistance.

Yet these figures only measured his lack of domestic support. Despite American help, Jiang's armies rapidly lost ground; Chinese peasants flocked to the Communist side, which promised land reform and popular government. At the end of 1948, the director of the American military advisory group in China reported that "the military situation [had] deteriorated to the point where only the active participation of United States troops could effect a remedy." And this adviser "certainly [did] not recommend" allying with what he termed "the world's worst leadership" to attempt the impossible: regaining the enormous expanse of Chinese territory that Jiang had lost to the Communists. Although many officials in China predicted Jiang's downfall, the Truman administration continued supporting Jiang, unable to see an alternative.

Early in 1949, the Nationalist government was forced to withdraw to the island of Formosa (Taiwan) and leave Mao Zedong in control of the mainland. To Secretary of State Acheson, the turn of events was disturbing, but in a "White Paper" defending the Truman administration's actions he wrote that the situation in China was "beyond the control of the government of the United States." Still, the U.S. government was trapped by its previous attempt to strengthen Jiang. Not wishing to harm the Nationalist cause, U.S. officials had failed to acknowledge publicly the full extent of Jiang's unpopularity and ineptness. Jiang's defeat, which had seemed nearly inevitable to people knowledgeable about China, looked to other Americans like a U.S. sellout of a "free" China to communism.

The news of China's "fall" to communism rocked American politics. Truman's Republican opponents, especially members of a powerful China lobby financed by conservative business leaders, began charging that Truman and his State Department were responsible for "losing" China. Both policymakers and their opponents pictured a 1949 alliance between China and the Soviet Union as an ideological bond that cemented an "international Communist conspiracy" to conquer the world. For the next twenty years, the United States would refuse to recognize or deal with the Communist Chinese government, even after a bitter split between China and the Soviets totally shattered claims about the monolithic threat called "international communism."

The Communist victory in China had repercussions throughout Asia. U.S. policymakers now looked to Japan to become America's strongest ally in the region. The American occupation government there moved swiftly to curtail Communist influences in Japan's labor movement and political system, while stimulating economic growth linked to the United States. Within five years, Japan (like Germany) had changed from being a wartime enemy into being a crucial cold-war ally.

The Anti-Communist Crusade

Following swiftly on the news from China came word that the Soviet Union had exploded a nuclear device. The United States no longer had sole possession of the ultimate weapon. Publicly, the Truman administration claimed the Soviet breakthrough had been expected and that it necessitated no change in America's own policies. Privately, however, Truman decided to escalate competition in thermonuclear weaponry by developing a hydrogen bomb, a device based on the still-hypothetical concept of nuclear fusion.

The constant crises of 1949—Berlin, China, and Russia's new bomb—unsettled many Americans. The Communist threat appeared to be everywhere; U.S. power seemed in retreat. Many Republicans and some Democrats sought the source of America's problems not in the world at large but in traitors in their midst. (See Chapter 2.) The view gained credibility when a former State Department officer, Alger Hiss, was accused of passing government papers to the Soviet Union. The search for Soviet spy rings became the order of the day. Republican Senator William E. Jenner of Indiana charged that the Truman administration consisted of a "crazy assortment of collectivist cutthroat crackpots and Communist fellow-traveling appeasers." Acheson's assessment regarding China—that the United States could not control all world events—sounded to some like a new form of appeasement, and many Republicans demanded that the secretary of state resign.

The 1949 crises and the criticism from Republican leaders prompted senior officials in the State and Defense departments to draft a report outlining current foreign-policy assumptions and future strategies. This report, called NSC 68 (1950), was approved by the National Security Council and the president. According to NSC 68, the Soviet Union was determined to stamp out freedom and spread its "slavery" to the rest of the world. Negotiation was futile, for the Soviets did not bargain in good faith, and there could be no valid distinction between national and world security. The United States could not, as Acheson put it, "pull down the blinds and sit in the parlor with a loaded shotgun, waiting." The country had to embark on a massive military buildup at home and create "situations of strength" abroad, regardless of cost. NSC 68 provided the blueprint for a "national security state" with overwhelming military power, a wide variety of economic weapons, and an extensive capacity for covert operations. Acheson traveled throughout the country trying to regain his credibility as a tough anti-Communist by preaching the foreign-policy tenets on which NSC 68 was based. The report's logic soon became the conventional wisdom of the cold war.

In his cold-war speeches, Acheson argued that freedom was advanced wherever governments remained non-Communist. Those people who wanted to go from U.S. ally to U.S. ally "with political litmus paper testing them for true-blue democracy" were "escapists." Furthermore, an anti-Communist consensus at home served freedom, whereas differences of opinion aided the enemy. The "fomenters of disunity" who advocated negotiation with the Soviets, Acheson explained, contributed to American weakness. Using this formulation, "freedom" could be invoked to support dictators abroad or to justify illegal surveillance at home, as long as the goal was anticommunism.

The Korean War

Koreans, long dominated by Japan, had looked forward to liberation and independence after World War II. By 1946, however, two zones of military occupation in Korea, as in Germany, had hardened into political jurisdictions. The Communist North, under the dictatorship of Kim Il Sung, allied with China and the Soviet Union to pursue policies toward land and labor based on a Communist model. The South, under the elite-based rule of Syngman Rhee, allied with the United States.

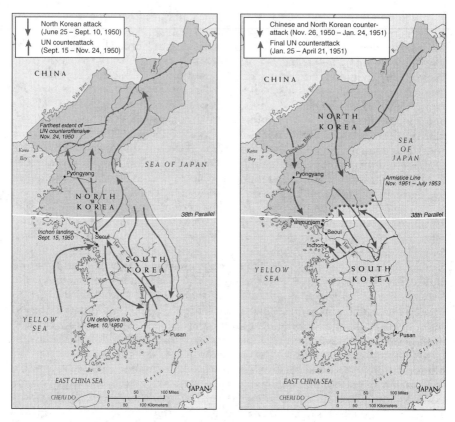

FIGURE 1–2   The Korean War.

U.S.-U.N. military efforts, orchestrated by General Douglas McArthur, criss-crossed the entire Korean peninsula and nearly provoked full-scale war with China.

In June 1950, Communist North Korea attacked South Korea across the thirty-eighth parallel dividing line in an attempt to unify the country. Kim Il Sung, documents now suggest, had gained reluctant support for his action from both Chinese and Soviet leaders by assuring them that a U.S. military response was unlikely. With NSC 68 on his desk, however, Truman viewed the Korean conflict as a showdown with "international communism." Using the logic outlined in his Truman Doctrine for Greece and Turkey and in the new policy paper, the president announced that "if aggression is successful in Korea, we can expect it to spread through Asia and Europe to this hemisphere." One weak spot in the "free world" defense would start the dominoes falling.

Truman responded by increasing defense budgets and shoring up U.S. military capabilities globally. He gained UN support for a U.S.-controlled "police action" defending Syngman Rhee's South Korean regime, announced protection for Jiang Jie-shi's exiled regime in Formosa, and offered aid for

France's effort to hold off a Communist-led nationalist movement in French Indochina. The administration also extended assistance to the Philippine government, which was battling leftist Huk rebels, and accelerated efforts to rebuild Japan into a bastion of anticommunism in the Far East. In Europe, more troops were added to the NATO military force, and a program for rearming West Germany was announced. The front line against communism lay everywhere, and Truman committed U.S. power, prestige, and money around the world.

U.S. policymakers were torn between two goals during the Korean War: containment, which would leave Korea divided, and "rollback," which would unite it under U.S. influence. As long as South Korean and U.S. troops were retreating southward early in the war, restoration of a boundary at the thirty-eighth parallel seemed victory enough. But after a regrouped UN force under the command of U.S. General Douglas MacArthur made a daring landing at Inchon behind enemy lines and drove the North Koreans back to the thirty-eighth parallel, decisions became more complicated. Could MacArthur "liberate" North Korea? Would the Soviet Union and China intervene if he tried to do so? The president allowed MacArthur to pursue the war northward as long as he did not ignite a wider war with China, but the general underestimated Chinese reaction. After crossing the thirty-eighth parallel, U.S. soldiers began to encounter Chinese "volunteers." Then, as American forces pressed further into North Korea and approached its border with China, China could not ignore the provocation. Chinese troops streamed into North Korea and sent MacArthur's armies reeling southward across the thirty-eighth parallel once again. After MacArthur regrouped and once more pushed northward, Truman ordered him to seek a negotiated settlement.

Truman's order sparked a clash between civilian and military authority. MacArthur publicly opposed Truman's "limited war" and sought a full-scale commitment to victory over North Korea, even over China. He claimed that this was America's chance to "roll back" communism in Asia. Truman, however, insisted that a lengthy conflict in Korea would weaken the U.S. defense posture in other, more vital, areas. He viewed the Soviet Union as the real enemy and believed an Asian land war would only play into Stalin's hands. In light of MacArthur's challenge to presidential authority, Truman had only one choice: He removed the general from command.

The "Asia-firsters," who had denounced Truman following Jiang Jie-shi's defeat in China, now had new ammunition and a popular martyr. They condemned the "no-win policy" against communism, and MacArthur returned home a hero. Telegrams demanding Truman's impeachment flooded Capitol Hill. Huge crowds greeted the general in San Francisco, Washington, D.C., and New York. A parade in New York on his behalf attracted 7.5 million people (compared with 4 million for Dwight Eisenhower at the end of World War II). The Gallup Poll reported that only 29 percent of its sample supported President Truman's action against MacArthur.

This outpouring of support, which included a brief MacArthur-for-president boomlet, subsided. Senate hearings showed that most military strategists opposed a wider conflict in Asia, and few Americans wanted full-scale war. MacArthur, a vain and imperious personality, quickly spent his political capital. Admiration for his military achievements remained, but most people welcomed

FIGURE 1–3 U.S. Infantrymen in Korea.

One soldier comforts another while a third methodically fills out casualty tags.
Source: National Archives and Records Administration, Records of the Office of the Chief Signal Officer. Photo by Sfc. Al Chang.

some negotiated settlement in Korea. When the 1952 Republican nominee for president, General Dwight D. Eisenhower, promised to go to Korea and lend his personal prestige to ending the struggle, he received applause and votes. By the end of Truman's presidency in January 1953, the war in Korea had grown less intense, and combatants had gathered around a conference table. Hammering out the details of a negotiated settlement (which eventually reestablished the thirty-eighth parallel as a dividing line between North and South Korea) would fall to a new administration.

SHIFTS IN POLICY MAKING

With the rise of U.S. global power and the decline of European influence in the Middle East, India, Africa, and Southeast Asia, U.S. officials had to develop policies toward areas they formerly considered unimportant. Significantly, decisions were forged less from experience, which was scant, than out of the bipolar, cold-war assumptions of NSC 68.

Foreign Policies in New Areas of Concern

During World War II, U.S. policymakers had formed loose ties to anticolonial movements and encouraged their European allies to plan for decolonization. Given the anticommunism of the late 1940s and early 1950s, however, the United States increasingly turned a cold shoulder to popular nationalist movements, many of which had Communist support or sought neutrality. In Indochina, the United States severed its wartime contacts with the Vietnamese leader Ho Chi Minh, who was both a Communist and a strong nationalist, and supported French efforts to maintain the old colonialist order. In India, U.S. policymakers confused Jawaharlal Nehru's nationalist policy of nonalignment with sympathy toward the Soviet Union. Both policymakers and the media pictured Nehru, a widely respected leader of Third World nationalist aspirations, as a befuddled mystic who lacked the clarity of vision to recognize the Soviet threat. Dean Acheson, after meeting Nehru during his goodwill trip to the United States in 1949, wrote, "I was convinced that Nehru and I were not destined to have a pleasant personal relationship. . . . He was one of the most difficult men with whom I have ever had to deal."

Issues of race and international politics emerged with special clarity during the late 1940s in South Africa. The white, Afrikaner-based Nationalist party came to power in 1948 and began erecting apartheid—an elaborate system of racial separation and systematic, legally sanctioned discrimination against non-whites, who made up more than 80 percent of the South African population. Although some U.S. policymakers, fresh from fighting Nazi ideas of a "master race," questioned the wisdom and morality of such a racially based governmental system, the desire to open South Africa to U.S. trade and investment and to maintain friendly access to South Africa's copious store of strategic raw materials took precedence. The South African government also garnered U.S. support by portraying black aspirations as Communist-inspired and casting its own white, minority rulers as stalwart defenders of capitalism in Africa. In addition, strong criticism of South Africa seemed difficult in light of America's own system of racial segregation in the states of the old Confederacy.

America's growing economic presence in South Africa, attracted by the cheap labor supply that apartheid guaranteed, provided the basis for close ties between the United States and the white South African government. Within the next two decades, nearly fifty African nations became independent, and U.S. policy toward these states—nearly all black-ruled and determinedly hostile to South Africa's repressive regime—took shape within the context of the close South African-U.S. alliance.

The Middle East also presented new issues. Only in Saudi Arabia, largely through oil investments, had the United States maintained a substantial presence before World War II. During that war, strategic and economic bonds with this desert kingdom increased dramatically, and U.S. interests expanded into other areas as well. When, in 1946, the Soviet Union attempted to extend its economic and political influence into northern Iran, for example, the United States made it clear that Britain's postwar weakness in this traditional zone of British influence should not mean gains for the Soviets. The Soviets retreated, leaving Iran and its rich oil fields within the perimeter of Anglo-American power and interest. Policies in this area would continue to be based both on anticommunism and U.S. access to oil.

Marshall-Plan "Freedom Trains" circulated with banners proclaiming "Prosperity Makes You Free." Voice of America radio transmissions proliferated, issuing broadcasts in almost every language in the world, including the twenty spoken in the Soviet Union. Radio, which could easily cross borders, seemed the central weapon in the Campaign of Truth.

While promoting its own informational programs, the Truman administration also worked to build an "open" world order through which America's private commercial culture could easily flow. In the postwar period, many foreign countries sought to restrict entry of Hollywood films to protect their own national film industries. In the late 1940s, however, Washington insisted on satisfactory access for American films in return for providing desperately needed economic assistance. Hollywood films, after all, seemed to be one of America's most successful weapons against communism. If officials sometimes worried that Hollywood purveyed unflattering stereotypes of American life as violent and gangster-ridden, still the lavish lifestyles depicted by Hollywood's dream machine spilled out images of capitalist abundance that attracted crowds of ordinary citizens.

Before the cold war, Americans had never in peacetime operated offices of information or propaganda targeting other nations. As in so many other areas of foreign policy, however, Truman's anti-Communist cultural crusade brought significant changes upon which his successors would build.

A FOREIGN POLICY ESTABLISHMENT

The Second World War had revolutionized the U.S. government bureaucracy. Before the war, the federal government had employed about 800,000 civilians, 10 percent of whom were involved with war-related issues. By the end of the war, the figure had risen to nearly 4 million, with 75 percent working for agencies that dealt with the newly named arena of "national security." Although the new government bureaus had been designed to increase the efficiency of wartime operations, their sheer size and complexity often complicated decision making.

The State Department, traditionally responsible for foreign policy, had been transformed during the war. The department and its related agencies outgrew old quarters and, during the 1950s, expanded into twenty-nine buildings throughout Washington, D.C. When all of these offices were finally brought together in 1961, it took eight stories, covering a four-block area, to house them. Before the war, a few assistant secretaries could meet in the secretary of state's office, discuss world problems, and set policy. By the end of the war, this kind of cozy familiarity and easy communication had given way to bureaucratic routine. Dean Acheson once asked Cordell Hull, Franklin Roosevelt's secretary of state, to come by the department and meet the assistant secretaries. Hull declined, wryly commenting that he had never done well in crowds.

After 1949, the crisis atmosphere of the cold war delivered strong blows to the State Department. Mao's victory in China outraged people who claimed that communism could never triumph on its own merits. The China lobby, with its close ties to the media, pressed an effort to purge the department's experts on Asia and other regions, who supposedly had "sold out" Jiang Jie-shi and showed a toleration for communism. Throughout the 1950s, many seasoned diplomats lost influence to people who took a hard anti-Communist line, and the immediate suspicion of anyone who questioned cold-war verities quashed healthy differences of opinion. The State Department became inclined to interpret events according to a preestablished cold-war viewpoint. The anti-Communist atmosphere of the early and mid-1950s, combined with the attacks on experienced diplomats, damaged the effectiveness, and ultimately the prestige and power, of the State Department.

Other agencies challenged the state department's primacy in foreign policy making. Before the war, nearly all foreign-policy functions had been centralized at State. After the war, other departments and agencies assumed major responsibilities. Policy making became a complex process involving many different bureaucracies, each with its own experts and point of view. The military establishment became the department's most powerful rival. During the war, Roosevelt had increasingly turned to the military for advice, and the Joint Chiefs of Staff, created in 1941, challenged the state department's position as the preeminent body in foreign policy. In 1947, the National Security Act reorganized the military establishment and also created a new National Security Council to advise the president. This reorganization boosted the prestige of the military, housed in the huge new Pentagon building, and its input into the policy making process.

The Central Intelligence Agency (CIA) also rivaled the State Department. The CIA grew out of the Office of Strategic Services (OSS), a wartime intelligence-gathering agency. After the war, the State Department, the armed services, and the FBI all hoped to assume the functions of the OSS. As a compromise in 1947, the CIA was created as an independent agency under the new National Security Act. The CIA, under its activist director Walter Bedell Smith, became preoccupied with anticommunism. (Smith reportedly once confided that even General Eisenhower might be a Communist.) Although the CIA's appropriations and operations remained secret, scholars have estimated that the agency rapidly surpassed the State Department both in number of employees and in budget. Most CIA work involved intelligence collection and analysis, but the agency also delved into covert operations, secret activities carried out in foreign lands.

Some elements of postwar foreign policy were altogether external to the government. Although private businesspeople abroad had always influenced international affairs, the giant U.S.-based multinational corporations of the new era exerted an unparalleled impact. For example, the great oil giants—the so-called seven sisters—profoundly affected the world's economy through their agreements that set the world price of oil and divided up spheres of production and distribution. Many companies with distant investments began to view themselves as wholly new forces in international relations; corporate interests could sometimes even rival national loyalties.

Only a few years after the United States had celebrated victory in World War II, Americans were once again being asked to mobilize against a foreign threat. The years immediately after World War II set the patterns of foreign policy making for the next half-century. Policymakers embraced internationalism as never before, helping to forge the UN, global economic institutions, multilateral defense pacts, foreign-aid programs, new military commitments, and enlarged foreign-policy bureaucracies. Rivalry with the Soviet Union and fear of communism both shaped and was shaped by this new superpower role.

Anticommunism came to dominate U.S. foreign-policy priorities and, increasingly, affected domestic life as well.

SUGGESTED READINGS

The relationship between the cold war and U.S. foreign policy remains one of the most bitterly contested issues in American history. See Marc Trachtenberg, *A Constructed Peace: The Making of the European Settlement 1945–1963* (1999); David Reynolds, *One World Divisible* (2001); Thomas G. Paterson, *Meeting the Communist Threat: Truman to Reagan* (1988); Thomas J. McCormick, *America's Half-Century: United States Foreign Policy in the Cold War and After* (2nd ed., 1995); Warren I. Cohen, *America in the Age of Soviet Power* (1993); Fraser J. Harbutt, *The Iron Curtain: Churchill, America, and the Origins of the Cold War* (1986); John Lewis Gaddis, *Strategies of Containment: A Critical Appraisal of Postwar American National Security Policy* (1982), his *The Long Peace: Inquiries into the History of the Cold War* (1987), and his *We Now Know: Rethinking Cold War History* (1997); Lawrence S. Kaplan, *The Long Entanglement: NATO's First Fifty Years* (1999); Robert A. Pollard, *Economic Security and the Origins of the Cold War, 1948-1950* (1985); Thomas Paterson, *On Every Front: The Making and Unmaking of the Cold War* (rev. ed., 1992); Walter LaFeber, *America, Russia, and the Cold War, 1945–1992* (8th ed., 1996); Stephen Ambrose, *Rise to Globalism: American Foreign Policy Since 1938* (8th ed., 1997); H. W. Brands, *The Devil We Knew: Americans and the Cold War* (1993); Melvin Leffler, *The Specter of Communism* (1994); Randall Bennett Woods and Howard Jones, *Dawning of the Cold War: The United States Quest for Order* (1991); Deborah Welch Larson, *Anatomy of Mistrust: U.S.-Soviet Relations during the Cold War* (1997); Fraser J. Harbutt, *The Cold War Era* (2001); and Ronald E. Powaksi, *The Cold War: The United States and the Soviet Union, 1917–1991* (1998).

For the history of specific issues and incidents of the early cold-war era, see Michael J. Hogan, *The Marshall Plan: America, Britain, and the Reconstruction of Western Europe, 1949–52* (1987); Gary B. Ostrower, *The United States and the United Nations* (1998); Chester Pach, *Arming the Free World* (1991); Louis Liebovich, *The Press and the Origins of the Cold War, 1944–1947* (1988); Sallie Pisani, *The CIA and the Marshall Plan* (1991); Lawrence S. Wittner, *One World or None: A History of the World Nuclear Disarmament Movement through 1953* (1993); Richard Rhodes, *Dark Sun: The Making of the Hydrogen Bomb* (1995); Gregg Herken, *The Winning Weapon: The Atomic Bomb in the Cold War, 1945–1950* (1980); Justus D. Doenecke, *Not to the Swift: The Old Isolationists in the Cold War Era* (1979); Richard Freeland, *The Truman Doctrine and the Origins of McCarthyism* (1971); Michael S. Sherry, *Preparing for the Next War* (1977); Fred J. Block, *The Origins of International Economic Disorder* (1977); Lawrence Kaplan, *The United States and NATO* (1984); Robert A. Divine, *Since 1945: Politics and Diplomacy in Recent American History* (3rd ed., 1985); Erik Beukel, *American Perceptions of the Soviet Union as a Nuclear Adversary* (1989); and Thomas W. Zeiler, *Free Trade, Free World: The Advent of GATT* (1999).

On national security policy during the late 1940s and early 1950s, consult Daniel Yergin, *Shattered Peace: The Origins of the Cold War and the National Security State* (1977); Melvyn Leffler, *A Preponderance of Power: National Security, the Truman Administration, and the Cold War* (1992); Michael S. Sherry, *In the Shadow of War: The United States since the 1930s* (1995); and Michael J. Hogan, *A Cross of Iron* (1998).

On U.S. national security policy for specific geographical areas, see Geir Lundestad. *"Empire" by Integration: The United States and European Integration, 1945–1997* (1998); John Killick. *The United States and European Reconstruction, 1945–1960.* (1997); Terry H. Anderson, *The United States, Great Britain and the Cold War, 1944–1947* (1981); Bruce Kuklick, *American Policy and the Division of Germany* (1972); William Roger Louis and Hedley Bull, eds., *The Special Relationship: Anglo-American Relations since 1945* (1986); Frank Ninkovich, *Germany and the United States: The Transformation of the German Question since 1945* (1988); E. Timothy Smith, *The United States, Italy, and NATO, 1947–52* (1991); Michael D. Haydock, *City Under Siege: The Berlin Blockade and Airlift, 1948–1949* (1999); James Edward Miller, *The United States and Italy, 1940–50* (1987); Ronald L. Filippelli, *American Labor and Postwar Italy, 1943–1953: A Study of Cold War Politics* (1989); Frank Costigliola, *France and the United States: The Cold War Alliance since 1945* (1992); Akira Iriye, *The Cold War in Asia* (1974); Robert J. McMahon, *Colonialism and Cold War: The United States and the Struggle for Indonesian Independence* (1981); Nancy B. Tucker, *Patterns in the Dust: Chinese-American Relations and the Recognition Controversy, 1949–1950* (1983); Mark Gallicchio, *The Cold War Begins in Asia: American East Asian Policy and the Fall of the Japanese Empire* (1988); June M. Grasso, *Harry Truman's Two-China Policy* (1987); Steven Hugh Lee, *Outposts of Empire: Korea, Vietnam, and the Origins of the Cold War in Asia, 1949–84* (1995); Robert Accinelli, *Crisis and Commitment: United States Policy toward Taiwan, 1950–55* (1996); John Dower, *Embracing Defeat: Japan in the Wake of World War II* (2000); Michael Schaller, *The American Occupation of Japan* (1985); Howard Schonberger, *Aftermath of War: America and the Remaking of Japan, 1945–1952* (1989); Gary Hess, *The U.S. Emergence as a Southeast Asia Power* (1986); Ronald McGlothlen, *Controlling the Waves: Dean Acheson and U.S. Foreign Policy in Asia* (1993); Gordon Chang, *Friends and Enemies: The United States, China, and the Soviet Union, 1948–1972* (1989); W. Michael Weis, *Cold Warriors & Coup d'Etat: Brazilian-American Relations, 1945–1964* (1993); Thomas M. Leonard, *The United States and Central America, 1944–1949* (1984); Michael L. Krenn, *The Chains of Interdependence: U.S. Policy toward Central America, 1945–1954* (1996); Thomas Noer, *Cold War and Black Liberation: The United States and White Rule in Africa, 1948–1968* (1985); Thomas Borstelmann, *Apartheid's Reluctant Uncle: The United States and Southern Africa in the Early Cold War* (1993); Howard Jones, *A New Kind of War: America's Global Strategy and the Truman Doctrine in Greece* (1989); Bruce R. Kuniholm, *The Origins of the Cold War in the Near East: Great Power Conflict and Diplomacy in Iran, Turkey, and Greece* (1980); David Painter, *Oil and the American Century* (1986); and Nathan Godfried, *Bridging the Gap between Rich and Poor* (1987).

There are excellent histories of the Korean War. Burton I. Kaufman, *The Korean War* (1986), is a brief synthesis. A more detailed analysis may be found in several volumes by Bruce Cumings: *The Origins of the Korean War* (1981); *Child of Conflict* (1983), a series of essays that he edited; and, coauthored with Jon Halliday, *Korea: The Unknown War* (1988). See also William S. Stueck, Jr., *The Road to Confrontation* (1981) and *The Korean War: An International History* (1995); Stanley Sandler, *The Korean War: No Victors, No Vanquished* (1999); Chen Jian, *China's Road to the Korean War: The Making of the Sino-American Confrontation* (1994); Qiang Zhai, *The Dragon, the Lion, and the Eagle: Chinese-British-American Relations, 1949–1958* (1994), and Paul G. Pierpaoli, Jr., *Truman and Korea: The Political Culture of the Early Cold War* (1999). For more specific topics, see Katharine

H.S. Moon, *Sex Among Allies: Military Prostitution in U.S.-Korea Relations* (1997); William T. Bowers, William H. Hammond, and George L. MacGarrigle, *Black Soldier, White Army: The 24th Infantry Regiment in Korea* (1996); and Sherie Mershon and Steven Schlossman, *Foxholes and Color Lines: Desegregating the U.S. Armed Forces* (1998).

Biographical studies include Ronald Steel, *Walter Lippman and the American Century* (1980); Robert Ferrell, *Harry Truman and the Modern American Presidency* (1983); Walter Issacson and Evan Thomas, *The Wise Men: Six Friends and the World They Made: Acheson, Bohlen, Harriman, Kennan, Lovett, McCloy* (1986); Evan Thomas, *The Very Best Men: Four Who Dared; The Early Years of the CIA* (1995); Mark A. Stoler, *George C. Marshall* (1989); Walter Hixson, *George F. Kennan* (1989); Anders Stephanson, *Kennan and the Art of Foreign Relations* (1989); Townshend Hoopes and Douglas Brinkley, *Driven Patriot: The Life and Times of James Forrestal* (1992); Thomas Schwartz, *America's Germany: John J. McCloy and the Federal Republic of Germany* (1991); Howard B. Schaffer, *Chester Bowles: New Dealer in the Cold War* (1993); Steve Neal, *Harry and Ike: The Partnership that Remade the Postwar World* (2001); and John T. McNay, *Acheson and Empire: The British Accent in American Foreign Policy* (2001).

2

Postwar Adjustments, 1946–1953

THE RECONVERSION FROM WAR TO PEACE

A mood that oscillated between unlimited optimism and deep pessimism marked the years between 1945 and 1953. The motion picture industry captured, and helped to create, this frame of mind. Postwar Hollywood turned out many films that celebrated happiness, innovation, and prosperity. *Singin' in the Rain* (1952) invoked Hollywood's own transition from the days of silent films to the early era of talking pictures to show how vigorous, flexible people could adjust to perilous times. This musical became both a popular and a critical success. Yet the film industry also produced motion pictures that looked into the dark corners of American life. This group of movies, later called *film noir*, mocked the optimism of pictures like *Singin' in the Rain* by portraying flawed people who fell victim to sinister forces, stumbled while pursuing their goals, and often failed to survive. In *film noir*, the pursuit of the American Dream seemed a futile, dangerous obsession. *Noir* films such as *The Asphalt Jungle* (1950) suggested that only a fool would find rain-soaked city streets a place in which to sing.

This oscillation between optimism and pessimism touched most aspects of postwar life. Anywhere one looked, the postwar era seemed riddled with contradictory hopes and fears. Which vision of the future would prevail?

Wartime Tensions, Postwar Fears

The government's informational agencies and the advertising industry had presented World War II as a struggle to preserve the "American way of life." When the global conflict dragged into 1945, however, more and more people

FIGURE 2–1   A Postwar Saturday Afternoon in a West Virginia Town.

As the nation moved from war to peace, famed photographer Russell Lee portrayed shoppers and movie-goers filling a small-town street in 1946.
Source: National Archives and Records Administration, Records of the Solid Fuels Administration for War. Photo by Russell Lee.

suspected, despite their desire to preserve the familiar, that their lives had entered uncharted waters.

Wartime mobilization had affected most areas of American life. During World War II, for instance, millions of women entered the labor force, sometimes filling traditionally male jobs and sometimes even receiving equal pay with men. "Latchkey children," who returned home from school while their parents were still at work, became a familiar sight, and Washington, under the Latham Act (1944), provided limited federal financing for day-care centers. Some observers blamed working women for discontented husbands and an alleged surge in juvenile delinquency. Although wartime publicists portrayed labor-market changes as temporary, women workers overwhelmingly hoped, surveys suggested, to retain their wartime positions and wages.

These surveys portended postwar debate over gender roles. Many policymakers expected that women would abandon the workplace in order to restabilize family relations and maximize employment prospects for men. Returning servicemen, they argued, needed jobs that paid a "family wage." Despite pressure from the Department of Labor's Women's Bureau and women's groups within labor unions, men hostile or indifferent to the future of female workers dominated policy making for reconversion. For many women, consequently, the decision of whether or not to center their postwar lives around the home involved no meaningful choice at all. For those who remained in the labor market, opportunities narrowed to lower-paying jobs rather than the family-wage positions that men could find elsewhere in the economy.

The process of converting from war to peace also involved racial and ethnic issues. The nearly 120,000 people of Japanese descent who had been stripped of their property and forcibly relocated from their homes to internment camps during World War II needed to rebuild their lives and their once-prosperous communities. Other people of Asian descent, however, particularly those of Chinese and Filipino heritage, made gains during the war. Similarly, many African Americans, American Indians, and Mexican Americans pursued new opportunities, even though this often meant moving from rural to urban-industrial areas. Between 1939 and 1945, the average income of families of African descent roughly doubled, and Filipinos became eligible for U.S. citizenship during the war. These kinds of rapid demographic and social changes stirred some hostility, and tension flared into conflict in many parts of the country during and immediately after World War II. A number of cities, particularly Detroit and Philadelphia, experienced significant racial violence.

These conflicts prompted renewed protest against discrimination. During the war, civil rights leaders postponed a planned March on Washington, on behalf of greater job opportunities, after President Franklin Roosevelt pledged that his Fair Employment Practices Committee would fight racially discriminatory hiring practices in the war-production sector. But smaller-scale, grass-roots protests against discrimination continued. The so-called zoot-suiters, young Mexican American and African American men, adopted a style of dress that featured excessive yards of elaborately draped pants and jackets. By flaunting wartime calls for rationing the amount of fabric used in clothing, the zoot suit could serve as a symbolic, sartorial protest against mainstream culture. The mere appearance of zoot-suiters sparked conflict in West Coast cities such as San Diego and Los Angeles. At the same time, African American women who worked outside of their homes protested discriminatory practices by public transportation systems in the Deep South, where, even during a war for democracy, racial segregation remained the law. If the nation were to attack discrimination, it seemed the federal government in Washington would need to play a much more active role.

President Harry S. Truman and his advisers obviously desired peace but worried about the problems it threatened to produce. They recognized that the massive governmental spending for a war overseas, not the domestic programs of Franklin Roosevelt's New Deal, finally ended the depression of the 1930s. Remembering the economic downturn that had followed the first Great War—and the bitter social conflicts that the postwar depression of 1919 had brought—many leaders dreaded the transition from war to peace. What would happen when production for World War II ended? Only a few weeks after Japan surrendered, almost 100,000 defense workers in Detroit alone lost their jobs. Could production for civilian consumption eventually pick up the slack and keep people at work?

A related question concerned Washington's role in economic policy making. Economists who had worked in wartime agencies argued that the national government should expand the domestic programs of the depression and war eras. Government spending measures should continue and become a permanent part of the postwar political economy. Increased spending for social welfare programs would pump money into the economy, easing the problem of reconversion and providing a cushion against social conflict. Unless Washington took decisive action, some forecasters claimed, more than 10 million workers might face unemployment.

Only three weeks after war's end, President Truman sent twenty-one domestic spending programs to Congress. These included an increased minimum wage; money for hospital construction; funds for small businesses; permanent government price supports for farmers; and, most controversial, legislation for governmental measures to ensure full employment. The Truman administration faced congressional opposition from the "conservative coalition," a group of Republicans and southern Democrats that opposed New-Deal style domestic programs. Still, this Seventy-Ninth Congress did pass a number of Truman's proposals: a Hospital Construction Act; the Veterans Emergency Housing Act; funds for power and soil conservation projects; and, eventually, a modified version of the much-discussed Full Employment Bill of 1945.

The Full Employment Bill produced fierce, prolonged debate. Its drafters hoped to "establish a national policy and program for assuring continuing full employment," largely through economic planning and generous spending by the national government. Washington would take responsibility for ensuring that the "free enterprise" system would produce employment opportunities. The specter of a permanent system of governmental planning and massive spending in peacetime frightened conservatives, both Republicans and Democrats. They saw the Full Employment Bill as a giant leap toward a centrally planned economy, if not socialism.

This measure and similar planning proposals drew their inspiration not from advocates of socialism but from the Keynesian economists who adapted theories first offered during the 1930s by Britain's John Maynard Keynes. A complex capitalist economy, postwar American Keynesians argued, required constant governmental management. Whenever consumer spending declined, for example, increased spending by government would supposedly take up the slack, maintain employment, and prevent recession. Funds for public housing, hospitals, schools, and social welfare programs would provide assistance for low-income people while promoting general economic growth. In addition, governmental officials could use taxation as an economic tool. In times of slow growth, they could lower personal and business taxes to stimulate buying power and investment; when inflationary pressures developed, they could raise taxes as one way to reduce the amount of spending and hold down prices. Keynes's postwar American disciples did not follow all of these ideas. Political realities could wreak havoc with academic theories about the economic benefit of suddenly raising taxes or boosting governmental expenditures. Most academic economists, however, embraced the broad outlines of the Keynesian-inspired "new economics".

Many other Americans came to support some type of continuing economic role for the federal government, and in 1946 Congress passed a modified, and retitled, version of the Full Employment Bill. Although it did not satisfy advocates of centralized planning or promise full employment, the Employment Act of 1946 provided the institutional framework for ongoing governmental involvement in economic affairs. Congress created a new executive-branch body, the Council of Economic Advisers, and charged it with counseling the president and with developing policies to "promote free competitive enterprise, to avoid economic fluctuations . . . and to maintain employment, production, and purchasing power."

Most legal historians view the Employment Act of 1946 as nothing less than an informal amendment to the Constitution. This law sketched the outlines of a new constitutional order called "the positive state," one in which the national government, especially agencies in the executive branch, would take positive action to promote economic growth, maintain high levels of employment, and stabilize prices. Economic oversight and substantial spending by Washington, especially for national defense, would become prominent features of political life during the rest of the twentieth and into the twenty-first century. The free enterprise system, it seemed, had become too important to be left to marketplace mechanisms. If advocates of the new economics could not directly plan and manage the economy, they could oversee and advise.

1946: Inflation, Black Markets, Strikes, and a National Election

The United States faced numerous economic issues during the immediate postwar period. Consumers drained their savings accounts, tapping funds that wartime rationing and production controls had prevented them from spending, and went on a buying spree. They bought up items that had been scarce or unavailable during the war—refrigerators, new-model cars, nylon stockings, cameras and film, rubber-centered golf balls, wire coat hangers, and toy trains. With greater supplies of gasoline becoming available, vacationers took to the highways. Hotels and motels complained that they could not handle the crush of tourists.

Soon, demand outstripped supply, and an inflationary spiral set in. As prices soared, supplies further dwindled. Buyers could not find enough meat, cars, or housing. In June 1946, a delivery truck in Denver lost its entire load of bread to a crowd that overpowered its driver outside a grocery store. Rumors of a shipment of meat produced an angry, shoving crowd of over 2,000 people in front of a Brooklyn store, and a Detroit supermarket served coffee and doughnuts in hopes of placating angry shoppers who had to wait in line just to enter the store. A thriving "black market" quickly developed. To obtain a new car or a T-bone steak, a buyer might have to tip an automobile dealer or butcher. Some people tried a barter system. A meat cutter in Atlanta offered steaks and roasts in exchange for nails, flooring, and plumbing fixtures for his home. Everywhere, people found it difficult to find homes or apartments.

Harry Truman received much of the blame for these postwar economic problems. While Republicans berated him for rising prices and black-market conditions, labor unions, firm supporters of Roosevelt's New Deal, also clashed with the new president.

Bitter labor disputes rocked major industries during 1946. The Congress of Industrial Organizations (CIO) launched "Operation Dixie," an attempt to organize workers throughout the largely nonunion South.

Meanwhile, more than five million workers throughout the country were involved in nearly 5,000 work stoppages. Approximately one-quarter of the CIO's entire membership was on strike in early 1946. A walkout against General Motors by the United Auto Workers (UAW) lasted almost four months. The UAW's leader, Walter Reuther, wanted GM to agree not to raise the price of cars. Inclusion of such a clause in any new contract, Reuther argued, would prevent GM from using the union's wage gains as an excuse for price hikes that would affect the entire economy. GM stoutly resisted, claiming that such a provision would impinge on its "managerial prerogatives." GM bitterly denounced another of the UAW's demands, that GM allow the union to inspect its books in order to prove that the auto giant's profits could absorb its wage request.

The UAW's aggressive stance antagonized the business community and drew little support from President Truman. *Business Week*, the widely read bible of American industry, expressed a common theme. The "time had come," it argued, to beat back "further encroachment into the province of management." A GM attorney used even stronger terms. To accept the UAW's position "would mean the end of free enterprise and efficient management." Walter Reuther's claim that his position actually bolstered Truman's own desire for price stability failed to convince the president to put White-House pressure on GM. In the end, the UAW obtained a wage increase, but Reuther's hope of winning organized labor a broader role in determining political-economic decisions collapsed.

As the November 1946 elections neared, Truman seemed to be losing support within his own party. While labor leaders were questioning his commitment to their cause, other Democrats who hoped to revive the New Deal at home were dismissing Truman as an inept politician who could not lead their party.

Truman did stumble over the reconversion process. Seeking popularity by promising the rapid discharge of armed-forces personnel, his administration mishandled the demobilization process. At one point, the navy found it lacked the ships to transport the large number of troops scheduled to return to the United States. By Truman's own admission, the process "was no longer demobilization . . . it was disintegration." Although he did face difficult economic decisions, Truman made things even worse by failing to develop clear and consistent policies. He vacillated for more than a year, for example, over whether or not to extend the authority of the Office of Price Administration (OPA), an executive-branch agency that had regulated war-time wages and prices. Suddenly, in November 1946, Truman proclaimed an end to virtually all controls. Even many Democrats saw Truman, who seemed indecisive and beholden to old political cronies from Missouri, offering little consistent or effective leadership on domestic problems.

Republicans hardly lacked campaign issues in 1946: soaring prices, black-market economic conditions, labor strikes, and an unpopular president. By October, the Gallup polling organization reported that only 32 percent of their sample approved of Truman's performance as president, compared with a figure of 87 percent a little over a year earlier. After years as the minority party, Republicans found themselves almost back in control of Congress. Summing up the anti-Democratic campaign of 1946, GOP billboards simply asked, "Had Enough? Vote Republican!"

In the November 1946 elections Republicans gained control of the new Eightieth Congress and captured twenty-five governorships. Jersey City's venerable Democratic political boss, Frank Hague, expected these results. "The Republicans would have won even had they put up a German," an aide quoted Hague. 1948 promised to be a banner year for Republicans.

Truman Under Fire

Under siege by Republicans and many Democrats, Truman refused to go quietly. In foreign affairs, he launched a vigorous anti-Communist crusade (see Chapter 1) and warmed up for the domestic battles of 1947–1948 by thrashing John L. Lewis, the pugnacious leader of the United Mineworkers Union, and by battling the Republican-dominated Congress.

Lewis wanted to go beyond wage issues and confront the coal industry over the questions of safety and health conditions in the mines. He denounced both the mine owners and the Truman administration in equally harsh terms. If Truman were really pro-labor, Lewis argued, he would aggressively support his miners. In response to Lewis's decision to send mine workers out on strike, Truman obtained a federal court injunction in late November 1946 against the union and its officers. Lewis initially defied the injunction, which he claimed was unconstitutional, but he ultimately backed down and ordered miners back to work.

The Truman-Lewis confrontation proved significant. First, Truman's action provided another sign that labor unions lacked enough political clout to push labor-management negotiations into new areas, even health and safety. In the end, even most Democrats agreed with management's broad view of its prerogatives. Second, many Democrats saw Truman's stand against Lewis as a sign that the president might become a political force. "There was a big difference in the old man from then on," one aide remembered. "He was his own man at last."

Truman attacked the Republican-controlled Eightieth Congress, which had generally supported his foreign policy, for its approach to domestic issues. He demanded Republicans pass legislation to which they were inalterably opposed and refused to seek common ground on other measures, such as a higher minimum wage. At the same time, the president gave congressional Democrats confusing indicators of his domestic priorities. One Democratic senator grumbled that working with Truman was like playing a night baseball game in the dark. "I'm supposed to be the catcher and I should get the signals. I not only am not getting the signals, but someone actually turns out the light when the ball is thrown." While proposing costly social-welfare programs, for example, Truman also urged unspecified spending reductions in order to achieve a balanced federal budget. The president's confrontational approach ruffled relations with Capitol Hill but helped him to build the image of a reactionary Republican Congress against which he could run in 1948.

The Eightieth Congress, ridiculed by Truman as a do-nothing body, actually passed several significant pieces of domestic legislation. In response to

Franklin Roosevelt's four successful presidential bids, it approved and sent to the states the popular Twenty-second Amendment, which prohibited anyone from being elected to the presidency for more than two terms. In addition, Congress created a special commission to study reorganization of the federal bureaucracy. Under the leadership of former Republican President Herbert Hoover, the commission submitted a plan that became the basis of the Reorganization Act of 1949. By clarifying lines of authority and reducing the number of executive-branch agencies, the Hoover Commission hoped to streamline governmental operations.

Robert Taft, Republican majority leader in the Senate, dominated the Eightieth Congress. Son of President William Howard Taft, this shy, middle-aged Ohioan seemed uncomfortable in the glare of national politics. His unofficial title, "Mr. Republican," signified both his appeal within the GOP and his lack of support outside it. In hopes of broadening his political base and gaining the White House in 1948, Taft touted what he called "modern Republicanism." To conservatives, he argued that positive-state Democrats were abandoning Roosevelt's New Deal and moving toward socialism. They would bankrupt the country, he charged, and place individual liberties at the mercy of an overbearing federal bureaucracy. At the same time, to attract a wider constituency, Taft moderated his earlier anti-New Deal views. He now backed federal aid to education, a limited program of public housing, and moderate funding for many social-welfare programs.

Passage of the landmark Taft-Hartley Labor Act of 1947 demonstrated Taft's legislative skills. The law, which Republicans hoped would further reduce the power of organized labor, outlawed the closed shop (the practice of hiring only union workers), prohibited the use of union dues for political activities, and authorized presidential back-to-work orders whenever labor strikes threatened national security. The law, Taft claimed, would not destroy unions and, by curbing the abuses of allegedly corrupt labor bosses, would actually help rank-and-file workers. Labor leaders denounced the bill as "a slave-labor act" and the "Tuff-Heartless Act." Pro-union demonstrators even appeared at the wedding of Taft's son. Taft adroitly steered the bill through the Senate and worked out a compromise with House Republicans, who wanted an even stronger antiunion law. Truman vetoed the measure, another act that helped to convince his Democratic critics that he might become a more assertive president, but Taft collected the votes needed to override Truman's action.

Taft-Hartley underscored the position of organized labor in the postwar political economy. On the one hand, the act successfully rolled back powers that unions had gained during the 1930s and early 1940s. On the other, Taft-Hartley implicitly acknowledged that labor unions would retain greater influence than die-hard conservatives considered desirable. In time, with the support of the courts and the National Labor Relations Board, an informal labor-management arrangement began to emerge. Management expected labor unions to bargain aggressively on wage issues, including cost-of-living increases, and other compensation questions, such as pension plans and fringe benefits. In exchange, labor would become more productive—that is, turning out more products in the same unit of time—and would concede management's prerogatives over a wide range of basic decisions, including how to organize the work process and where to locate plant facilities.

Union leaders divided over how to respond to this emerging, postwar labor-management arrangement. Many urged resistance. Nearly 100,000 people joined a march against Taft-Hartley in New York City, and more than 500,000 participated in a brief work stoppage in Detroit. If this new balance of power offered union members the promise of higher wages and more benefits, it also removed many crucial issues from the process of labor-management bargaining and assigned them solely to the prerogatives of industry. Eventually, though, middle-of-the-road union leaders accepted the arrangement and pushed aside more militant unionists, especially those aligned with the Communist party of the United States. The CIO eventually expelled about one-quarter of its membership and nearly a dozen unions. In 1950, negotiations between the UAW and the auto industry focused solely on compensation issues, rather than the broader questions that Walter Reuther had earlier sought to raise, and established a pattern that structured labor-management relations until the 1970s.

1948: "Truman Beats Dewey!"

Robert Taft, despite efforts to remake his political image, lost the 1948 presidential nomination to Governor Thomas E. Dewey of New York, the GOP's standard-bearer in 1944. Taft's reputation as a poor vote getter overshadowed his work in Congress. Republicans, who had not nominated a winning presidential candidate in twenty years, desperately wanted a victory in 1948. Dewey had run well against FDR in 1944, had won a smashing victory in the 1946 New York gubernatorial race, and enjoyed the support of the party's "eastern establishment." These Republicans argued that Taft's modern Republicanism still smacked of knee-jerk opposition to Democratic programs, even popular ones like Social Security, and doomed the GOP to remain as a minority, oppositional party. This pragmatic attitude prevailed among younger Republicans, particularly those who came from large northern cities or held state offices. Dewey and his running mate, Governor Earl Warren of California, appeared to be shoo-ins.

But the victor in 1948 was not Tom Dewey. Harry Truman surprised most political observers of the era, and the entire Republican party, by narrowly winning the presidency in his own right. "You've got to give the little man credit," said Republican Senator Arthur Vandenberg. "Everyone had counted him out, but he came up fighting and won the battle. That's the kind of courage the American people admire." To the extent that the presidential sweepstakes was a "beauty contest" between competing images, Truman did emerge as the clear winner. Dewey could not match Truman's mercurial personality. "I don't know which is the chillier experience—to have Tom ignore you or shake your hand," joked one of his detractors. "You have to get to know Dewey to dislike him," another quipped. Overconfident and overly cautious, the Republican candidate earned the title of "Thomas Elusive Dewey" by making far fewer personal appearances than Truman. And when Dewey did speak, he seemed wedded to platitude-filled, overly bland rhetoric about the need for national unity.

In contrast, Harry Truman slashed away at the Eightieth Congress. His arms in perpetual motion, Truman denounced Republican representatives as "errand boys of big business" and bragged that he had vetoed more legislation

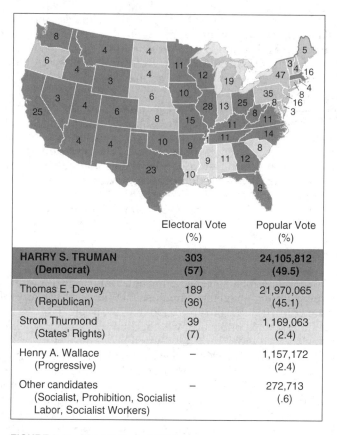

	Electoral Vote (%)	Popular Vote (%)
HARRY S. TRUMAN (Democrat)	**303 (57)**	**24,105,812 (49.5)**
Thomas E. Dewey (Republican)	189 (36)	21,970,065 (45.1)
Strom Thurmond (States' Rights)	39 (7)	1,169,063 (2.4)
Henry A. Wallace (Progressive)	–	1,157,172 (2.4)
Other candidates (Socialist, Prohibition, Socialist Labor, Socialist Workers)	–	272,713 (.6)

FIGURE 2–2 The Election of 1948.

"Give 'Em Hell Harry" Truman emerged victorious in a presidential election featuring three other major candidates.

than any other president of the twentieth century. During the brief interval between the Democratic convention and the November election, Truman called Congress into special session and submitted a list of "must-pass" legislation. When the Republican-controlled body adjourned after passing only a few minor measures, Truman linked his attack on Dewey to his denunciation of the Eightieth Congress. The president's seventeen-car, armor-plated campaign train whistle-stopped across the country to shouts of "Give 'em hell, Harry."

In addition to roasting the "no-account, do-nothing" Republican Congress, Truman touted his version of the positive state. He called for a higher minimum wage, repeal of Taft-Hartley, more public housing, and higher farm prices. During the final week of the campaign, he became the first president to appear in Harlem, where he told a crowd of 35,000 African Americans that he supported the "goal of equal rights and equal opportunities" for all Americans.

The civil-rights question did cost Truman some normally Democratic votes in the South. The president's advisers had hoped the party convention would adopt a mild statement in support of civil rights, but urban Democrats from the North, whose political coalitions included black voters, pushed through a stronger proposal. Following the vote, segregationist delegates from Alabama and Mississippi stalked out and eventually formed the States Rights, or "Dixiecrat," party. Its platform denounced "totalitarian government" and advocated "segregation of the races." The Dixiecrats, with Strom Thurmond (then the Democratic governor of South Carolina) as their presidential nominee, hoped to gain at least one hundred electoral votes in the South—enough ballots, they imagined, to throw the presidential election into the House of Representatives. Thurmond's campaign, however, lacked the money to run an effective effort, and the Dixiecrat strategy failed. A majority of southern Democrats stayed with Truman, and Thurmond's thirty-nine electoral votes, from four states in the Deep South, fell short of his early goal.

Another potentially more serious Democratic revolt against Truman also fizzled. Henry Wallace, whom the president had dismissed as secretary of commerce for criticizing the administration's hard-line, anti-Soviet foreign policy, ran as the candidate of the hastily constructed Progressive party. Endorsed by numerous groups on the political left, including the Communist party, Wallace urged greater cooperation with the Soviet Union, an end to the military draft, more federal money for social and economic programs at home, and American support for a UN Reconstruction Fund to promote economic recovery worldwide. By avoiding conflict with the USSR, Wallace argued, the United States would not only revive the New Deal's domestic agenda but also export its positive-state vision to the entire world. A rally of the Progressive party resembled a left-wing folk-music festival, or "hootenanny," as singers such as Pete Seeger and Woody Guthrie campaigned for Wallace and his running mate (another guitar player), Senator Glen Taylor of Idaho. One of Guthrie's songs, sung to the tune of "The Wabash Cannonball," expressed the class-based appeal of Wallace's left-leaning supporters.

> There's lumberjacks and teamsters and sailors from the sea,
> And there's farming boys from Texas and the hills of Tennessee,
> There's miners from Kentucky and there's fishermen from Maine,
> Every worker in the country rides that Wallace-Taylor train.*

The Wallace-Taylor special derailed well short of the White House. Highlighting his role as the nation's commander-in-chief, Truman allowed subordinates to link Wallace with the enemy in Moscow. "A vote for Wallace," the Democratic National Committee claimed, "is a vote for the things" for which Stalin stood. Wallace's refusal to renounce the support of the Communist party, opposition from anti-Communist labor leaders, defection of anti-Communist Democrats to Truman, and the insurmountable problems of any new political effort hampered the Progressive insurgency. In December 1947, a poll showed that 13 percent of likely voters favored Wallace's candidacy. By election day, the Wallace campaign had virtually collapsed and received less than 3 percent of the popular ballots and not a single electoral vote. The four-way presidential contest also apparently confused some voters, and 1948 became what political scientists call a "decline election." Only 53 percent of the

---

The Farmer-Labor Train by Woody Guthrie © Copyright 1947 by Woody Guthrie Publications, Inc. All rights reserved. Used by permission.

eligible electorate bothered to turn out on election day, the lowest percentage since 1924.

Looking back at November of 1948, most historians, freed from the partisan passions and primitive poll data of that moment, now see Truman's victory as a less than stunning surprise. The election confirmed the staying power of the Democratic-New Deal political coalition and the broad popular support for its positive-state programs, especially Social Security. From this perspective, a win for Dewey in 1948 would have been a greater surprise than Truman's victory. The president's energetic campaign did not suddenly convince great numbers of people, who were planning to vote for Dewey and Warren, to support the Democratic ticket instead. Rather, it shored up party loyalty among long-time Democrats and rekindled the fear that the GOP's conservative wing, even with the pragmatic Dewey in the White House, might try to mount a general assault on measures such as Social Security. Midwestern farmers, urban ethnic voters, organized labor, African Americans, and even most southerners continued to support the Democratic party. The Democrats not only won the presidency, but they regained control of Congress in 1948. The election of 1948, then, maintained the basic political configuration that had taken shape during the 1930s. It left unsettled, though, the question of whether or not Truman and the Democratic party enjoyed a mandate for a new domestic agenda, the vision of the positive state that had been outlined in the Employment Act of 1946.

THE FAIR DEAL

After their victory, Truman and his advisers offered an extensive set of domestic proposals. Collectively known as the "Fair Deal," these measures looked beyond the New Deal. Roosevelt's programs of the 1930s had been designed to end a depression and restore prosperity. Truman's Fair Deal aimed at sustaining the productive output of the war years and building an ever-expanding economy for the postwar era.

Truman's Domestic Program

Truman's economic advisers claimed to have solved the mysteries of policy making. Economic adviser Leon Keyserling predicted that well-designed federal spending programs could guarantee full employment, higher wages, and greater profits. The United States had no need to take from the rich to care for the poor. Properly monitored, its capitalist economy could out-produce any socialist or centrally planned system. In 1948, nearly two-thirds of all American families lived on incomes of less than $4,000 a year. By 1958, Keyserling predicted, economic growth would make $4,000 the minimum income for every family. "The people of America need to be electrified by our limitless possibilities," he proclaimed.

The Fair Deal promised new programs to stimulate economic growth and improve social welfare. Charles F. Brannan championed an ambitious proposal that he claimed would simultaneously give farmers higher prices and consumers cheaper food. Under Brannan's program, the government would lift New Deal restrictions on the number of acres planted and would maintain farm income through direct price supports. Truman also proposed the expansion of Social

Security, generous federal funding for public housing projects, a national plan for medical insurance, federal aid to education, and civil rights legislation. Truman touted the Fair Deal as America's version of a "middle way" between socialism and fascism. "Between the reactionaries of the extreme left with their talk about revolution and class warfare, and the reactionaries of the extreme right with their hysterical cries of bankruptcy and despair, lies the way of progress," he declared.

The Truman administration enacted some of its domestic Fair Deal. Congress extended Social Security benefits; raised the minimum wage (to seventy-five cents an hour); and appropriated federal funds for soil conservation, flood control, and public power. In 1952, Congress passed perhaps the most significant domestic legislation of the Truman era, the Veterans Readjustment Assistance Act or "GI Bill of Rights." This measure extended to veterans of the Korean conflict benefits that had been voted for World War II vets in the 1944 GI Bill—financial assistance for college and vocational-training programs, generous terms for home loans, and medical coverage at a separate system of military hospitals.

At the same time, the U.S. economy generally performed well. It never matched Leon Keyserling's optimistic predictions, but real income—what workers took home in salaries and wages after they were adjusted for inflation—did rise. People who had remained economically afloat during the Great Depression of the 1930s, with help from the New Deal, did even better during the era of the Fair Deal.

The Fair Deal: An Assessment

Sandwiched between Franklin Roosevelt's New Deal of the 1930s and Lyndon Johnson's Great Society of the 1960s, the Fair Deal of Harry Truman suffers by comparison. For many years, historians dismissed it as a grab bag of social-economic programs left over from the 1930s or as a prelude to the burst of legislation enacted during LBJ's presidency. But most historians now credit the Fair Deal for establishing the broad public-policy paradigm, which lasted until the late 1970s, on the relationship between the economy and the national government. The Fair Deal also established a pattern in which the legislative policy proposals of Democratic administrations outstripped the support they could ultimately attract.

The Fair Deal expressed the faith that the U.S. economic system, so severely criticized during the 1930s, would outshine any centrally planned economic order. Capitalism, not democratic socialism or Soviet communism, represented the wave of the future. Classical defenders of the free enterprise system, of course, had always argued that a marketplace economy maximized individual freedoms and efficiently allocated resources and finished products. But during the cold-war era, capitalism's less conservative defenders also claimed that it could advance the cause of social justice, the banner under which the political left, including much of the Democratic party, marched. The U.S. economic system could generate apparently unlimited economic growth, something that economists could measure by a relatively new statistical gauge, the gross national product (GNP). A steadily rising GNP—the total dollar value of all goods produced and services rendered—would prove that the economic collapse and widespread poverty of the 1930s would not recur. Indeed, given the economic wisdom now available, it could not!

Visions of economic growth bedazzled postwar economic and social policymakers. Able to monitor the economy and accurately diagnose its health, economists promised to administer the kind of remedies—including measures to adjust interest rates, levels of taxation, and amounts of government spending—that could cure an ailing economy or pep up a sluggish one. This ever-expanding economy, Truman's advisers promised, would ensure economic security for the people and organized interests that had already benefited from the New-Deal legislation of the 1930s. At the same time, a larger economic pie offered hope to those, estimated by Franklin Roosevelt to be one-third of the population, who had been largely untouched by New-Deal social programs. In seeking to advance the cause of social justice, the United States could deftly sidestep difficult issues involving redistribution of wealth, income, or political power. As long as the capitalist economy generated growth, it could provide the material basis for aiding people who were lagging behind in the race for success. As later explained by Walter Heller, a Keynesian economist who began his distinguished career during the Truman era, economic growth was both the pot of gold and the rainbow.

The confidence of the Fair Dealers in the future of U.S. capitalism and their own expertise encouraged them to think beyond the New Deal's primary goal of economic recovery. Blessed with programs and bureaucratic institutions that would ensure economic growth, policymakers could now hope to use the tax dollars gained from this growth to address social problems, such as unequal access to medical care. Truman's domestic proposals, more than anything envisioned by Franklin Roosevelt, remained the basic aims of the Democratic party for the following four decades. The postwar generation of Democratic leaders, including John F. Kennedy and Hubert Humphrey, entered politics during the Fair Deal, and most never questioned its basic assumptions about the promise of the positive state.

Despite the optimistic vision of the Fair Deal, its ambitious agenda died in a Democratic-controlled Congress. Lobbying by the American Medical Association, which raised the cry of "socialized medicine," and disinterest among voters who were benefiting from the expansion of private medical plans like Blue Cross, helped kill Truman's proposal for national health insurance. Opposition from other pressure groups encouraged conservative Republicans and southern Democrats to block general federal aid to state school systems and the Brannan plan for agricultural subsidies. More important, the relatively affluent people who participated most actively in politics wanted to enjoy the benefits of expanding economic production themselves—in the form of larger homes, second cars, new consumer goods, and greater recreational opportunities. These people showed little enthusiasm for letting Washington spend their tax dollars to finance new domestic programs.

The Truman administration itself spent most of its political capital on foreign rather than on domestic issues. America's national security and its economic well-being, Truman and his internationalist advisers believed, depended on the successful conduct of a global foreign policy. Preoccupied with foreign affairs and always clumsy in dealing with Congress, the Truman administration provided relatively little leadership on domestic issues and focused the bulk of its attention on matters overseas. (See Chapter 1.)

Civil Rights during the Truman Era

The fight over civil-rights legislation provided an important test of the Fair Deal's commitment to domestic change. Revulsion against Nazi racism had helped to produce a backlash against racial discrimination at home; wartime economic gains had encouraged civil-rights groups to mount new attacks on discrimination; and scattered outbreaks of racial violence immediately after the war had intensified efforts to calm tensions. Meanwhile, the cold war itself seemed to demand improvements in race relations at home. With the United States proclaiming that it, not the Soviet Union, offered the model for other nations, continued legal discrimination in the United States proved increasingly difficult to excuse. Still, the Fair Deal moved cautiously in its antidiscrimination effort.

Truman had seemingly endorsed an ambitious civil-rights program. He proposed a ban on poll taxes; legislation to guarantee equal employment opportunities; and a federal law against lynching, an acknowledgment that southern states could still not, at the mid-point of the twentieth century, control white lynch mobs. During the 1948 presidential campaign, the president issued executive orders that ended (at least on paper) discrimination in federal employment. Truman consistently used nationwide radio addresses, in an age

FIGURE 2–3   Racial Segregation in the Rural South.

A store for "colored only," 1945.
Source: National Archives and Records Administration.

when few people had TV sets, to appeal for civil-rights measures. Most important, he began the process of actually desegregating the armed forces, "the greatest thing that ever happened to America," he later claimed. He appointed a committee to study civil-rights issues, and it issued a dramatic report, entitled "To Secure These Rights" (1948), which called for new federal legislation to attack racial discrimination along a broad front.

African Americans themselves constantly pressed for change during the late 1940s and early 1950s. The modern civil rights movement, in this sense, did not suddenly emerge in the middle 1950s, in the wake of the *Brown* decision. Earlier pressure during the Truman presidency created the climate for that ruling and for broader initiatives against discrimination. Local activists, such as E.D. Nixon and Rosa Parks in Montgomery, Alabama, organized voter registration drives and began protesting segregated bus facilities during the 1940s.

Thurgood Marshall, legal strategist for the National Association for the Advancement of Colored People (NAACP), orchestrated a legal offensive that yielded several important Supreme-Court victories. In *Shelly v. Kraemer* (1948), the Court unanimously ruled that states could not enforce restrictive covenants, legal agreements that prevented real estate from being sold to "non-whites." In two other cases—*Sweatt v. Painter* (1950) and *McLaurin v. Oklahoma Board of Regents* (1950)—the Court found that a separate law school for African Americans violated the Fourteenth Amendment's requirement for equality in education and that graduate schools could not segregate students according to race. Although these cases did not abolish all segregated educational facilities, they did point the way toward the broader school-desegregation decision in *Brown v. Board of Education* (1954), which declared educational segregation "inherently unequal." (See Chapter 3.) In all of these cases, the Truman administration filed legal briefs in support of Marshall's campaign.

While Marshall and the NAACP were winning cases such as *Sweatt* and *McLaurin*, some grassroots activists opposed their nationally orchestrated strategy. Rather than seeking racially integrated schools across the South, a course that local strategists accurately predicted would mean a loss of jobs for middle-class African-American teachers, they pressed southern states to provide truly equal funding for the existing system of segregated schools. With additional money, they argued, the schools already located in African-American neighborhoods could provide better educational opportunities and cultural support than integrated institutions promised by the NAACP's approach.

Many local activists saw national civil-rights policy as an example of the gap between the Fair Deal's promise and its performance. Truman did try to avoid a direct stand on civil rights. The threat of African-American voters in the North defecting to Henry Wallace in 1948 seems to have speeded his executive orders on the military and on federal hiring. Still, Truman could not act on his own. Some activists blamed Truman for giving the fight against discrimination too low a priority and for deferring too much to white southern Democrats. The conservative coalition in Congress bottled up legislation, and some military officials worked to delay desegregation of the armed forces. Similarly, the president's initiatives in ending job discrimination ultimately depended on the commitment of other officials, often white southerners, in the federal bureaucracy. No executive order could be self-enforcing.

The moves that Truman did make prompted considerable opposition. Segregationists made the old Confederate flag a symbol of resistance. One flag company boasted that Virginians were flying more Confederate banners in 1951 than had been flown during the Civil War, and a New York City firm reported that the demand for rebel flags exceeded orders for the Stars and Stripes. Throughout the nation, racists violently opposed the drive for integration. When an African-American couple attempted to move into an apartment in Cicero, Illinois, a mob of about 5,000 whites broke through National Guard lines and set the building ablaze. In the same year, 1951, a black civil-rights leader died when explosives destroyed his Miami home on Christmas Day. Decrying the increased use of explosives in racial attacks, Walter White of the NAACP claimed that "the bomb has replaced the lynchers' rope" as the main weapon of racist resistance. This upsurge in violence constituted one more impediment to national action against racial discrimination.

If promise exceeded performance, Truman's record on civil rights still looked better than that of any previous twentieth-century president. He was the first to make civil rights a national issue, and his administration at least proposed a comprehensive legislative program. During the mid-1950s, of course, the issue of racial desegregation would inexorably move to the center of the national political stage and dramatically alter politics in the United States.

ANTICOMMUNISM AT HOME

Truman faced his most intensive criticism on another emotional domestic issue, Communist "subversion." In time, despite an extensive "internal security" program of its own, the Truman administration would attract the wrath of anti-Communist crusaders.

The "Age of Surveillance"

In 1947, Truman rushed to uncover "security risks" in the federal bureaucracy. Employing a broad definition of disloyalty, agencies purged people with "subversive" political ties. The president opposed suggestions for more Draconian measures, such as abolition of the Fifth Amendment in national security cases, but the White House sometimes failed to restrain its own Justice Department. J. Edgar Hoover's FBI illegally peered into the private lives and the political beliefs of many ordinary citizens. Extending a practice that had begun during the Roosevelt years, it used wiretaps in violation of the Federal Communications Act of 1934. In 1949, Truman rejected suggestions of a special investigation of the FBI. "Hoover has done a good job," the president insisted.

In pursuit of Communist activity in the United States, the CIA, the FBI, military intelligence, and other surveillance agencies broadened their oversight of domestic life. People on the political left, who might be casually linked to a Communist "conspiracy," faced intense scrutiny. Phones were tapped, dossiers collected, innuendos spread. The FBI's Hoover insisted that "the ignorant and the apologists and the appeasers of Communism in our country" consistently minimized the "danger of these subversives in our midst." After cataloging activities by the FBI and other agencies, the civil liberties lawyer Frank J. Donner called the postwar period "the age of surveillance."

Did the threat of subversion justify such broad surveillance? Did the White House and the Justice Department overstate the danger? Certainly, the Communist party itself attracted relatively few members and enjoyed little influence, and there is scant evidence that pro-Communists actually influenced specific U.S. policies in ways that directly harmed the United States. Recently declassified documents, however, show that the government did possess credible information about the activities of Communist agents, both at home and overseas, and convincing evidence of the passing of classified military secrets to Soviet agents operating in the United States.

Debating the Threat of Communist Subversion

Both U.S. intelligence information, kept secret until the 1990s, and documents from archives in the former USSR and Eastern Europe have recently provided historians with a clearer view of Soviet espionage. During World War II, a U.S. Army unit began secretly monitoring transmissions between Moscow and the United States. The results of this surveillance, collected by the National Security Agency as the "VENONA Files," revealed a Soviet espionage network that extended into several wartime agencies and showed that information on U.S. nuclear weapons research did reach Moscow. Espionage, in other words, was a matter of legitimate concern in cold-war Washington. Ironically, though, a special commission on governmental secrecy concluded, in a 1997 report, that the U.S. surveillance bureaucracy protected its operations so tightly that Truman's own administration, perhaps the president himself, likely lacked full access to information collected in the VENONA files.

This evidence, which has generated much new scholarship, documents extensive Soviet espionage activities. A 1997 book entitled *Bombshell* shows how a young physicist named Theodore Hall began passing atomic secrets to the Soviets as early as 1944. In addition, the evidence now demonstrates that Julius Rosenberg spied for the Soviet Union and that his wife, Ethel, although not a spy herself, may have known about his activities. The federal government secured the conviction of both Ethel and Julius Rosenberg, members of the American Communist party, for espionage and executed the couple in 1953, an action that remains highly controversial.

Recent historical studies have yet, however, to settle other questions. In the case of the longstanding debate over the guilt or innocence of Alger Hiss, a prominent Democratic official who was accused in 1948 of having earlier passed secret documents to the USSR, additional archival evidence has sparked new controversy. Because of legal technicalities, the government could not charge Hiss with espionage, but it did secure his conviction, in 1950, for giving perjured testimony to a congressional committee about his links to Soviet spies. Hiss, who died in 1995 while still proclaiming his innocence, remains a lightning rod for debates about cold-war subversion. Documents made public during the 1990s, many historians agree, show spying activities by Hiss. A dissenting minority, though, has insisted that even the VENONA documents offer inconclusive evidence on this celebrated case because of the difficulty of linking the Soviet's complex system of code names directly to Hiss. Greater access to previously classified material, then, sometimes has only provided new ammunition with which to refight old controversies such as the Hiss case.

Other questions about the nature of Soviet activities in the United States remain open to debate. What, for example, was the effect of the Soviet spy efforts? Some historians insist that secret information about U.S. nuclear weaponry, especially that provided by Hall, accelerated Moscow's bomb program by several years. Many, however, also point out that the information passed by Julius Rosenberg was obtainable elsewhere and of marginal use to the Soviets. Consequently, even scholars who accept the guilt of Julius Rosenberg still raise questions about the larger Rosenberg case. Was execution for espionage the constitutionally appropriate punishment for Julius and (particularly) Ethel Rosenberg or did they become symbols for anti-Communist hysteria? Why did the government prosecute so few cases and never produce the VENONA evidence? Why did the government seek the death penalty *only* in the case of the Rosenbergs?

Anti-Communist Initiatives during the Truman Years

The Truman administration, historian-critics continue to charge, had political reasons for mounting a vigorous anti-Communist crusade at home. Since the late 1930s, anti-New Deal Democrats and conservative Republicans, particularly those on the House Committee on Un-American Activities (HUAC), had been claiming that communists and "fellow travelers" infested the Roosevelt and Truman administrations. Charges of Communist influence in the federal government accompanied broader attacks on "socialistic" domestic welfare programs. By responding vigorously to the taunt of being "soft on communism," critics of Truman's actions claim, the White House hoped to prevent the GOP from capitalizing on the anti-Communist issue.

An aggressive attack on Communist activities within the United States also dovetailed, of course, with the administration's strong anti-Soviet foreign policy. Postwar public-opinion polls revealed that few Americans considered communism a major problem in the immediate postwar period, and Truman's advisers feared that such attitudes, along with the strong popular opposition to costly overseas commitments, might hamstring an activist foreign policy. Truman's tough measures against communism at home and a constant barrage of anti-Communist rhetoric might neutralize domestic resistance to his global foreign policy.

The Truman administration accompanied its measures on internal subversion with a campaign to teach American values. In 1947, Attorney General Tom Clark developed the Freedom Train program, a historical society on rails. This train carried important documents, including a copy of the Truman Doctrine, to more than two-hundred major U.S. cities. When it returned to Washington in the fall of 1947, the government staged a "Week of Rededication." At patriotic rallies, government employees took a "freedom pledge" and sang "God Bless America." In a similar vein, the Office of Education promoted its "Zeal for Democracy" program: Washington encouraged local schools "to revitalize and improve education in the ideals and benefits of democracy and to reveal the character and tactics of totalitarianism."

Others followed the lead of the Truman administration. The U.S. Postal Service banned Communist materials from being transmitted through the mail. Many states adopted laws prohibiting "subversives" from holding government jobs. Bar associations and school boards required prospective attorneys and teachers to sign loyalty oaths. Congressional committees looked for "red webs" that supposedly stretched from Hollywood to Washington, D.C. Members of HUAC, including a young representative from California named Richard Nixon, claimed to have uncovered an extensive list of pro-Communist activities that hindered the conduct of U.S. foreign policy.

The Truman administration, critical historians have argued, thus encouraged a militant anticommunism that eventually veered out of its control. Truman's initiatives and rhetoric, in this view, helped to shift attention from a specific problem, actual Soviet espionage, to wide-ranging fears about an "alien" Communist "invasion" of American life. Truman's policies identified too few security risks and helped to smear too many innocent reputations. The Attorney General's List of Subversive Organizations, first issued in 1947, even provided a model for establishing guilt by association. Non-Communists who happened to belong to legal but left-leaning groups sometimes found that this governmental initiative helped to brand them as "reds," "pinkos," or "fellow travelers." Civil libertarians charged that the attorney general's list too often equated legitimate political dissent with Communist subversion. Partly encouraged by this kind of governmental activity, many anti-Communist activists became less concerned about Soviet agents than about the alleged spread of pro-Communist ideas through an allegedly unsuspecting, overly tolerant society. Overzealous witch-hunters, according to critics of their crusade, pursued perfectly loyal citizens on the political left who merely criticized U.S. foreign policy or who simply favored militantly pro-labor or pro-integrationist policies at home.

Anti-Communists targeted the entertainment industry. In 1947, HUAC sought to uncover Communist infiltration of Hollywood. Its widely publicized hearings, which featured both "friendly" witnesses (who willingly testified about alleged Communist involvement in film making) and "unfriendly" ones (who refused to say anything about anyone's political affiliations), splintered the motion picture community. The "Hollywood Ten," a group of witnesses that included past and present members of the American Communist party, went to prison, after being found guilty of contempt of Congress, for refusing to testify before HUAC about suspected Communists.

Studio heads cooperated with the investigations. Ultimately, hundreds of people—writers, performers, and technical support workers—who were suspected of holding dangerous ideas or having suspicious affiliations, found it difficult, if not impossible, to find jobs in Hollywood. They were "blacklisted" and thus barred from working in the movie industry. Despite overwhelming evidence to the contrary, some participants denied the existence of blacklisting. Ronald Reagan and John Wayne, for example, claimed to know nothing about a blacklist, yet both acknowledged helping to rid Hollywood of people they considered subversives. Reagan served not only as the president of the Screen Actors Guild during the cold-war years, but also as a secret informant for the FBI, known to the Bureau as Agent T-10.

Negotiating the blacklist became a way of life in postwar Hollywood. Screenwriters such as Abraham Polonsky, who could submit scripts under an alias or through a friend who served as a "front," had it easier than once well-known actors, such as Larry Parks and Betty Garrett, who watched their Hollywood careers collapse. Even writers, though, could not receive on-screen credit for their scripts and generally had to work at reduced salaries. Many people on the blacklist, such as Paul Jerrico and Ring Lardner, Jr., would wait until the 1990s before obtaining formal acknowledgment for screenplays that had been filmed nearly a half-century earlier. The only way to escape the blacklist was to appear before an investigative committee, admit political errors, ritualistically condemn communism, and "name names" of alleged subversives. Once "cleared" through this process, which one historian later likened to a "degradation ceremony," a person could again find work. During the 1950s, the search for subversives spread from Hollywood to the radio and television industries. Investigations into the political ideas and affiliations of members of the entertainment industry forced radio and TV artists, much like movie stars, to name names in order to remove their own names from the blacklist.

This anti-Communist initiative remains controversial. Blacklisting and the process of naming names, insist historians who accept the appropriateness of aggressive anti-Communist policies, represented a legitimate effort to root out pro-Soviet elements. The vast majority of "victims," these scholars have claimed, blindly supported the Communist party and betrayed their own artistic independence. In response, historians opposed to blacklisting see the antisubversive effort getting out of hand and praise those Hollywood dissidents, such as Polonsky and screenwriter Lillian Hellman, who resisted. After her companion, the detective novelist Dashiell Hammett, went to jail for defying HUAC, Hellman condemned the other "scoundrels" who did testify about the affiliations and ideas of one-time friends.

The anti-Communist crusade in Hollywood, historian-critics note, involved more than the careers of performers and writers. As civil libertarians have consistently charged, the practice of monitoring ideas in Hollywood may have set in motion a wider impulse for conformity that affected the larger political culture. Rather than risk the ordeal of appearing before a committee and naming names, many writers arguably limited their own expression, a practice that civil libertarians came to call the "chilling," rather than the overt censoring, of speech. The era of blacklisting also coincided with an assault on labor unions and on the progressive political movement that had developed in the movie capitol. In this view, studio executives not only hoped to eliminate left-wing politics from Hollywood but to recast the postwar movie industry as a symbol of the limitless possibilities of free-market capitalism—the same cultural-economic ideal that Ronald Reagan would carry from Hollywood into national politics thirty years later.

The impact of the blacklist, and of naming names, continued to divide Hollywood long after the cold war had moderated. The 1976 motion picture *The Front*, which featured writers and performers who had once been blacklisted, renewed old feuds by portraying an anti-Communist investigative committee recklessly stigmatizing people's beliefs and callously destroying their personal and professional lives. In 1999, a decision by the Academy of Motion Picture Arts and Sciences to honor Elia Kazan, a director who had testified and named names nearly fifty years earlier, ignited the passions of actors and writers who had been infants (or not yet born) during the cold-war years. When the aged, ailing Kazan received his award, one group of Hollywood celebrities stood and applauded while a larger contingent remained seated, with their arms conspicuously folded.

McCarthyism

An overly obsessive concern with internal subversion and the commitment to extreme measures to combat it became known as "McCarthyism," named for Senator Joseph McCarthy. Anticommunism existed before the senator from Wisconsin discovered the issue, and other red-hunters made wilder charges. But McCarthy dominated the headlines. His tactics were disarmingly simple: fling accusations as fast as the media could report them but avoid specific proposals for doing something about concrete issues. When asked how he would change the Voice of America's allegedly ineffectual, anti-Communist programming, one acquaintance reported, "the Senator looked blank; obviously he had never thought about it."

McCarthy rarely documented his sensational charges. His famous Wheeling, West Virginia, speech of 1950, in which he charged the State Department with harboring more than two-hundred Communist sympathizers, rested on a hodgepodge of contestable evidence. Even when the Senate gave him broad investigative power, McCarthy never pursued allegations against the State Department but chased after alleged security threats in other parts of the government.

McCarthy posed as a political rebel. He railed against "establishment Democrats" such as Alger Hiss and Dean Acheson. These "bright young men who were born with silver spoons in their mouths" and all those "striped-pants diplomats," McCarthy charged, were "selling the nation out." As he escalated his attacks, even many anti-Communists began to see McCarthy as a demagogic liability to their cause. The Wisconsin senator, his opponents feared, led a massive right-wing movement that seemed to appeal to large numbers of narrow-minded people.

McCarthyism, in this view, represented the political manifestation of the extremist wing of a widely shared "anti-Communist culture." In support of this claim, cold-war critics of McCarthyism often cited the detective novels of Mickey Spillane, which sold more than 6 million copies by 1950, as primary examples of the movement's cultural base. Although cast in the mold of Dashiell Hammet's Sam Spade, Spillane's fictional Mike Hammer lacked the chivalric code attributed to this earlier hard-boiled detective hero. Hammer pounded away at sexual "perverts," independent women, civil libertarians, and "bleeding-heart" liberals with the same gusto that he smashed Communists. Spillane's series of Hammer novels, which began with *I the Jury* (1947), seemed to express the same, the-ends-justify-any-means approach as political McCarthyism.

Few historians still see McCarthy as directing a broad mass movement or tapping a deep cultural vein. Instead, his rapid rise relied on influential political elites who either supported his attacks or failed to oppose them vigorously. Other Republicans from the Midwest, for instance, gave McCarthy vital political assistance. Political leaders who would not stoop to McCarthy's smear tactics themselves—Robert Taft, for example—tacitly encouraged the Wisconsin senator. Anything that hurt the Democrats, these Republicans reasoned, helped the GOP. McCarthy received assistance from other important sources. Most newspapers, regardless of political leaning, splashed McCarthy's charges across their pages. Sensational scoops about Communist influence provided good copy—and even better sales. Many prominent politicians hoped to avoid the ire of the senator and other McCarthyites for fear of being labeled soft on communism.

Passage of the McCarran Internal Security Act of 1950 demonstrated how political leaders approached anti-Communist measures. Rather than denouncing Senator Pat McCarran's harsh proposal, the White House and congressional Democrats offered competing internal-security bills of their own. In so doing, they implicitly accepted the basic position of the McCarthyites: Members of the Communist party should not expect the same civil liberties as other Americans. In its final form, the McCarran Act required Communist and "Communist-front" organizations to register with the attorney general, barred foreign Communists from entering the United States, and authorized secret prison camps for detention of domestic subversives during wartime. Only seven senators and a handful of representatives voted against the McCarran Act. Truman, after some hesitation, vetoed it as a violation of civil-liberties guarantees, but Congress quickly overrode his action. McCarthyism continued to influence national policy.

Anticommunism and Culture during the Cold War

The postwar cultural elite, while dismissing the exaggerations of McCarthy and McCarran, espoused their own brand of anticommunism. Fears about an invasion by "alien" elements emerged, to one degree or another, in many parts of postwar culture. A wide spectrum of opinion considered communism, defined in different ways, a major threat to the "American way of life" and dismissed Marxism as a pernicious doctrine without any intellectual respectability. As the journalist Tom Braden put it, the cold war was being "fought with ideas instead of bombs." A number of prominent postwar intellectuals consequently joined the Congress for Cultural Freedom (CCF), an international organization pledged to promote liberty and oppose "state-sponsored ideologies," such as Soviet communism. Behind the scenes, however, the CCF received secret funding from the CIA. Although the CIA never told members of the CCF what to publish in their influential journal, *Encounter*, the organization rarely sought out writers who questioned the anti-Communist foreign policy of the United States.

Did this culture of anticommunism narrow the spectrum of debate in the postwar United States and exert a chilling effect on healthy dissent, as civil libertarians claimed about the blacklist? A look at media and academic institutions during this period offers conflicting evidence. Certainly U.S. journalists remained free from direct government censorship, and many vigorously criticized the way in which specific cold-war programs were implanted.

After the collapse of Henry Wallace's Progressive party in late 1948, however, few prominent journalists questioned the anti-Communist assumptions that animated U.S. policy making. Attending Washington cocktail parties, listening to officials' "off-the-record" justifications, and accepting governmental handouts at face value, influential journalists might be seen, in effect, as part of the ideological apparatus by which the cold-war state promoted anticommunism. Journalists such as I. F. Stone, who scrutinized governmental arguments with a critical eye, were the exception. In contrast to his one-person operation, *I. F. Stone's Weekly*, which treated every official statement to be suspect until independently confirmed and which interrogated the premises of cold-war policies, most other media rarely questioned cold-war orthodoxy.

A similarly pattern characterized academic life. By the late 1940s, the horrors of Stalinism, fears about domestic threats on both the right and the left, and the positive performance of postwar capitalism helped to produce an academic culture that generally avoided critical perspectives that might be labeled "radical." Academic leaders proclaimed their anti-Communist credentials. Scientists at university-based research laboratories and professors in the humanities and social sciences enlisted in the cold war. Historians of U.S. foreign relations pictured the policy of containment as the natural continuation of internationalist ideas associated with enlightened "realists" such as Theodore and Franklin Roosevelt. In the social sciences, the dominant trend labelled passionate works of social criticism, such as those of the sociologist C. Wright Mills, as "old-fashioned" and out of step with current scholarly standards. Despite calls for "objective" analysis, a celebratory mood dominated higher education. The United States should be praised for its many virtues rather than criticized for its few vices.

This mood of celebration, according to most prominent intellectuals of the postwar era and many present-day historians, did not compromise academic freedom or scholarly responsibility. While admitting that some left-wing teachers did lose their jobs, the leaders of the postwar academic establishment noted that prominent dissenters, such as Mills, were not arbitrarily silenced as they would have been in totalitarian states such as the USSR. Since the collapse of the Soviet Union in 1989, many historians have underscored this postwar judgment. The few cases of excess, although regrettable, pale in comparison to the Soviet threat. In light of the challenge from a historically doomed Soviet Union, postwar journalists and academics should be seen as both patriots and realists for embracing anticommunism.

Other historians judge postwar cultural leaders more harshly. Cultural figures, in this view, reneged on their responsibility to interrogate, rather than simply confirm, dominant ideas and images. The postwar university, the historian Ellen Schrecker has insisted, was "no ivory tower." The FBI and even the CIA closely monitored campus life. In one notorious case, FBI agents pilfered a draft copy of a law review article that criticized the agency as a threat to civil liberties, a move that enabled J. Edgar Hoover to begin a campaign to discredit the article's authors, even before their work appeared in print. In other cases, anti-Communist agencies worked with prominent academics who covertly named names of suspected subversives at their institutions. The history of higher education, according to critical scholars such as Schrecker, involved more dismissals, a longer blacklist of suspected radicals, and a closer cooperation with surveillance institutions than historians once thought. As a result, more than a half-century later, academic institutions such as Harvard University and Smith College have formally apologized for dismissing professors whose "disloyalty" consisted only of holding ideas considered "dangerous" to overly zealous cold-warriors. Debate over the possible limiting of expression, like that over the impact of internal-security policies, continues to rage.

THE PROMISE AND THE PERILS OF PROGRESS

Publicists for General Electric, who hired Ronald Reagan as their primary spokesperson in 1954, coined a phrase that exemplified postwar optimism: "Progress is our most important product." According to this widely shared vision, a better future, largely defined in terms of the increased consumption of

FIGURE 2–4   Progress Was Every Company's Most Important Product.

This *Look* magazine ad for Western Electric employed the era's characteristic cartoon graphics to illustrate the evolution of the modern telephone.
Source: "How Many of Em Can You Remember?" Item #: R0741. Ad*Access. 1999. Rare Book, Manuscript, and Special Collections Library, Duke University. [http://scriptorium. lib.duke.edu/adaccess/]. Property of AT&T. Reprinted with permission of AT&T.

goods and services, seemed preordained. This future would be a bigger, better, streamlined version of the present. Public-spirited business corporations, employing the latest scientific and technological know-how, would produce an ever-expanding array of improved products for an ever-larger group of contented consumers.

Celebrants of postwar life claimed economic deprivation would soon vanish. Thanks to the miracles of mass production and the mechanics of mass consumption, the lifestyles of the nation's diverse population would ultimately converge. New "communities," based on the mutual consumption of similar products, would emerge. The wealthiest Americans, to be sure, would still have the most, but even people with low incomes could live increasingly comfortable lives. Skilled technocrats, the kind of people who had proved so adept at harnessing science and technology for production during the Second World War, could translate this vision into reality.

Science and Technology

Discussions of science and technology raised both hopes and fears. The atomic explosions that ravaged Japan initially produced terrifying images of worldwide destruction, alongside optimistic pictures of how the nation's nuclear prowess might open a new age in human history. After several years of fierce debate, in which vastly different images of a nuclear future competed against one another, opposition to full-scale nuclear development faded away. Scientists who remained critical of the new nuclear culture found themselves ignored and, in some cases, ostracized by colleagues and the increasingly influential nuclear research lobby.

By the early 1950s, claims about the necessity of more powerful bombs and the domestic value of nuclear technology dominated public discussion. Correctly developed and properly harnessed, atomic energy, it was argued, could power the nation's cities, propel its naval vessels, and even carry astronauts into outer space. In addition, the use of radioactive technology in medicine promised exciting new advances, including victory over cancer.

A new legal framework helped to organize the nuclear industry. The Atomic Energy Act of 1946 gave the president sole authority to order the use of nuclear weapons but vested day-to-day control over nuclear materials in a new executive agency, the Atomic Energy Commission (AEC). Run by civilians, the AEC initially conducted research and made basic policy decisions about nuclear technology. The Atomic Energy Act of 1954, however, modified this system of tight federal control in favor of an arrangement by which the AEC would grant licenses to private users of nonmilitary atomic energy. This new system would allow rapid growth of privately owned but government-regulated nuclear generating plants. Few people questioned the wisdom of this step toward the creation of a private nuclear power industry.

Entry into the nuclear age carried important costs. For years, the government tested nuclear weapons on islands in the South Pacific and in the western United States. And it kept secret, until the 1990s, the devastating, sometimes fatal, effect of radioactive fallout on people—Pacific Islanders, armed-service personnel, workers in the nuclear industry, and anyone who had lived "downwind" of the explosions or who had come in contact with products, including milk, contaminated by radioactive materials. Recently declassified information reveals cold-war research programs in which people, without their consent, became the objects of scientific tests on the effects of radioactivity on humans. During the cold-war era, however, information about these aspects of the nation's atomic energy program remained classified.

The national government also became more involved in a wide range of other, nonnuclear scientific activities after World War II. The wartime experience suggested the need for ongoing support of military research, and advocates of federal aid urged Washington to spend more money on nonmilitary, scientific experimentation. In a report entitled *Science—The Endless Frontier* (1945), Vannevar Bush, who had managed scientific projects for the government during World War II, called for a single national agency to administer grants for scientific research. Scientists, he argued, stood ready to make important discoveries. The cold war provided a hospitable climate for such proposals. In 1950, Congress established the National Science Foundation (NSF), and NSF grants soon allowed scientists to explore subjects that were unknown only a generation earlier. By the 1960s, federal funds underwrote most of the scientific research conducted in the United States.

Scientific activity, encouraged by governmental funds (and by grants from tax-exempt, private foundations), accelerated dramatically in the postwar era.

Ever since the late nineteenth century, the number of scientists and technicians had been growing faster than the general population, and this trend continued during the cold-war era. The new discoveries—in fields such as chemistry, biology, electronics, and nuclear energy—rested on the generous funding of highly sophisticated laboratories, many of them located at or near prominent research universities.

Enthusiasm for scientific and technological innovation knew few bounds. Instead of merely adapting human institutions to the natural environment, scientists celebrated their ability to go beyond the natural to create an artificial world. Knowledge of scientific theories permitted them to rearrange molecular structures and to produce synthetic fibers, high-strength adhesives, synthetic construction materials, and many other new products. In 1944, scientists at Rockefeller Institute had isolated a compound called DNA, which opened the secrets of genetic reproduction. Biochemists subsequently worked to unravel the molecular structure of DNA and, finally in 1953, constructed a model of a DNA molecule. Abstract theoretical knowledge and sophisticated technology were becoming important national resources, like iron and coal. Indeed, scientific know-how and up-to-date technology now seemed the most vital national resources of all.

But some developments, such as those in the computer electronics industry, called into question the dominant, postwar narrative about scientific progress. From management's perspective, the ideal factory seemed one nearly devoid of human labor. In 1946, *Fortune* magazine ran a feature on the "Automatic Factory," including an article entitled "Machines Without Men." By the use of new, computer-assisted technology, it seemed, companies could empty their factory of troublesome workers, and rely on a handful of technocratic managers to watch over the "accurate," "untiring," and highly efficient "electronic gadgets" that produced products. The following year an executive at Ford Motor Company offered a term that has remained, depending on one's point of view, either a threat or a promise—"automation."

What would be the fate of workers in a world of computer-assisted technologies? According to corporate managers and other apostles of progress, the answer seemed obvious. A more efficient production process appeared eminently democratic. Automation, while relieving workers of the burdens of repetitive labor, would allow greater numbers of consumers to obtain more goods and services at lower prices. If one reversed the perspective, however, difficulties appeared. New technologies—developed by management (often with generous governmental subsidies), controlled by management, and explained to the public by corporate publicists—promised to strip workers of a good deal of power and control over the work process and, ultimately, their job security.

A GE publicist-turned-author, Kurt Vonnegut, Jr., tried to open a debate over this "progress-is-our-most-important-product" vision by means of a dystopian novel, *Player Piano* (1952). Loosely based on Vonnegut's experience at GE's complex in Schenectady, New York, *Player Piano* fantasized a future in which automation obliterates the skills, self-confidence, and spirit of workers. It imagined a world in which one-dimensional technocrats preside over a moral and spiritual wasteland. The future, this book warned, might not bring evolutionary progress, as corporate spokespeople predicted.

The dominant story of postwar medicine also portrayed progress as inevitable. Undeniably, the 1940s and 1950s saw stunning medical breakthroughs.

After World War II, the United States experienced a severe, unprecedented epidemic of poliomyelitis. Between 1947 and 1951 this disease, which generally crippled those it did not kill, struck an annual average of 39,000 Americans, mostly children. (Between 1938 and 1942, the annual average had been only 6,400, a figure that rose to 16,800 between 1942 and 1947.) In 1955, Dr. Jonas Salk pioneered the first truly successful vaccine against polio. A nationwide program to inoculate people with this and the later Sabin vaccine resulted in the virtual elimination of polio in the United States by the 1960s.

The medical-pharmaceutical industry made great strides in other areas. Penicillin, an antibiotic that had been discovered in the 1920s and refined during World War II, came into general use after 1945; other powerful antibiotics—Streptomycin, Aureomycin, Terramycin, and Magnamycin—also appeared; and antihistamines, which proved important in the treatment of allergies, became available during the late 1940s. These drugs and improved surgical techniques allowed many Americans to lead longer and more comfortable lives. They also encouraged more determined research into cancer and heart disease, two afflictions that became increasingly common as the United States became more urbanized and industrialized.

The postwar period also brought innovations in mental health care. During World War II, psychiatrists increasingly improved their ability to deal with stress among military personnel; in 1946 hospitals run by the Veterans Administration were still treating more than 100,000 people for neuropsychiatric disorders. Against this backdrop, a new generation of practitioners sought to expand their profession's mission beyond that of caring (in the words of one mental health activist) for "a hopeless and hapless few." Younger activists hoped to treat everyone who suffered, needlessly they argued, from the stresses of an increasingly complex society.

These mental health professionals prevailed within their own ranks and in congressional politics. Battling traditionalists who wanted to retain the emphasis on treatment within mental hospitals, the innovators hoped to introduce the practice of psychiatry into community clinics and educational institutions. Confident of their ability to diagnose mental problems with scientific accuracy and anxious to dispense cures from a variety of different places, they helped to push the National Mental Health Act of 1946 through Congress. This law, which even gained support from conservatives such as Robert Taft, committed Washington to "the improvement of the mental health of the people of the United States" by supporting research into "psychiatric disorders," by training additional personnel, and by encouraging states to fund new types of treatment centers. In 1949, activists secured the establishment of the National Institute of Mental Health (NIMH), which played a vital role in getting both Congress and state legislatures to support community mental health clinics. Within ten years, NIMH's annual budget topped $50 million, and during the early 1960s it increased fourfold.

Postwar medical technology brought significant change in the delivery of health-care. New developments accelerated the disappearance of the family doctor—the general practitioner celebrated in the popular illustrations of Norman Rockwell—and the proliferation of specialists—doctors trained to diagnose accurately and treat effectively a limited number of conditions. Postwar medical innovations meant that the large hospital complex, with its sophisticated equipment and large staff of specialists, replaced the home and the doctor's office as the primary treatment center. Fewer doctors made house calls; more people went to hospital emergency rooms or outpatient centers. In 1946, only one of every ten Americans was admitted to a hospital for inpatient care; twenty years later, the figure had risen to nearly one of every six.

New medical practices did not automatically bring better health-care. Exotic drugs, complicated treatment procedures, and expensive hospital facilities increased costs. Those with low incomes and many elderly people could not afford the new "wonder" cures. Rural areas and small towns, unable to compete with metropolitan areas, often lacked specialists and state-of-the-art hospital facilities. Largely as a result of this maldistribution of medical services, the United States was actually losing ground, compared with other industrial nations, in reducing its infant mortality rate.

A hospital visit did not always result in a cure or, in some cases, even proper treatment. Careful studies suggested that about half of common surgical operations, particularly those performed on women and children, seemed unnecessary. Meanwhile, antibiotics produced new strains of super-bacteria that spawned a search for another generation of super-drugs. An increasingly desperate drugs-versus-bacteria race soon developed. Medical research also pointed to a proliferation of iatrogenic illnesses, ailments brought on by "medical treatment" for some other malady. Many iatrogenic illnesses, studies claimed, resulted from a naive faith in new treatments, from improper testing and regulation of new drugs, and from a faith that medicine possessed a miracle cure for every ache and pain. Assessing the impact of medical technologies was becoming a complex task. Philosophers who specialized in medical issues, as well as the medical community and the general public, would begin to ponder the ethical questions surrounding health-care.

Agriculture

Farmers, supposedly the last people to alter their ways, generally embraced innovations in science and technology. Farming became more scientific and mechanized than ever before. Sophisticated biological research produced new types of seeds. Hybrid corn, which had been introduced in some areas during the 1930s, spread to all parts of the country during the postwar period. Equally important to grain producers, the chemical industry produced less expensive fertilizers and pesticides. Farmers quickly adopted these chemicals in order to boost output. They used three times as much fertilizer in 1950 as ten years earlier. Farmers also began to adopt labor-replacing machines on a massive scale. Between 1940 and 1960, for example, the number of tractors increased by more than 200 percent, and the number of grain combines rose nearly as much. Meanwhile, engineers increased the size of these machines, boosting their horsepower with higher-compression engines, and offering a variety of attachments. New chemicals and machinery drastically reduced the number of farm laborers needed to bring in key crops.

Farm output exploded. For many years, agricultural production had been increasing, but now—with hybrid seeds, better equipment, more affordable fertilizers, and improved irrigation facilities—output rose at a much faster rate than before. Farmers could cultivate hitherto unproductive land and areas once set aside as pastures for horses and mules. (In 1920, farmers had used more than 90 million acres of potential crop lands to graze draft animals; by 1960, less than 10 million acres went for pasturage.) In addition, the new agricultural methods permitted farmers to utilize their land more intensively, and the yield per acre rose substantially.

Change also brought new problems. Irrigation required massive amounts of water, and fertilizers and pesticides created health hazards for both farm workers and consumers. Meanwhile, steadily increasing production yields kept farm prices low, thereby straining the rural economy. Most of the world's people spent almost half their incomes for food, but American consumers could feed a family on only about 20 percent of a paycheck. Many U.S. farmers did not share the rising incomes of other Americans, and only the largest and most efficient operations reaped substantial profits. Although the Fair Deal tried to support farm incomes by updating the programs devised during the 1930s— direct subsidies and various plans for restricting acreage—nothing really succeeded. Low prices and steadily rising costs continually plagued small operators. Taking advantage of their private economic power and their ability to secure federal assistance, larger farming operations gained an increasing share of the agricultural market while the number of small-scale farms declined steadily.

Changes in agriculture affected all parts of the country, but no region felt the impact more than the largely rural South. During the 1940s and 1950s, increased mechanization meant that millions of African Americans who had worked as agricultural laborers, especially in the cotton-growing industry, left the South for the Midwest, the Northeast, and the West Coast. Changes in the nature of farming also forced white farmers out of Appalachia for Dayton, Detroit, Cincinnati, Cleveland, and Chicago. Anyone who tilled their own holding found that small-scale farming could no longer support a family. For millions of people who had once sustained themselves on the land, the postwar era's much-touted "progress" seemed a distant dream.

"Selling Out" and the End of the Truman Era

The promise of the postwar era also seemed marred by signs of spreading corruption. In 1950 and 1951, a Democratic senator from Tennessee, Estes Kefauver, unveiled the shadowy world of organized crime. Skillfully using television, Kefauver brought underworld figures, from top mobster Frank Costello to petty gamblers and prostitutes, into people's living rooms. The Kefauver Hearings rivaled Hollywood's best dramas. "It was difficult at times to believe that it was real," marveled the *New York Times*.

Organized crime's corrupt empire, it appeared, was not unique. In 1950, the U.S. Military Academy, the citadel of gentlemanly honor and patriotic values, expelled ninety West Pointers, including nine starting members of the football team, for cheating on examinations. That same year, prosecutors in New York uncovered a point-shaving scandal in college basketball. Star players on several teams—including City College of New York, which had won the national championship, and the University of Kentucky—had taken bribes in exchange for rigging the scores for the benefit of gamblers. These cadets and athletes seemed to have "sold out," exchanging their integrity for money.

Bernard Malamud's novel *The Natural* (1952) brilliantly captured the cultural narrative of selling out. A talented but naive baseball star, Roy Hobbs, conspires with a corrupt owner and a sinister gambler to sell out his teammates by fixing a crucial game. Hobbs finally realizes his mistake but finds that he cannot escape his past misdeeds. Malamud's novel of the 1950s, in contrast to the film version of the 1980s (which starred Robert Redford as Hobbs), ends on a note of despair. Roy fails to redeem himself, striking out rather than hitting a game-winning home run, and becomes a tragic symbol of the consequences of succumbing to the temptations of corruption.

In time, the search for corruption reached into the White House. Republicans charged that the Truman administration harbored fixers, people selling their political influence by accepting kickbacks to arrange government contracts. During the final years of Truman's presidency, talk of fixers and selling out became widespread. In two of the most celebrated cases, an old friend of the president was accused of accepting illegal gifts for fixing government contracts, and another official with supposedly soliciting an expensive mink coat in lieu of a monetary payoff. Truman, combative to the end, proclaimed that "my house is always clean," but the GOP's constant focus on "the mess in Washington" inevitably tainted his presidency. Even though Truman was not personally linked to any of the corruption, he left Washington with the reputation of having been an ineffectual leader.

Only the passage of time and the uncovering of far greater scandals in subsequent presidential administrations would make Harry S. Truman an American folk hero. Both Republicans and Democrats eventually came to lionize Truman for exhibiting political courage and a feisty independence, especially in pursuing the policy of containment against the Soviet Union. Truman's reputation, among historians of the presidency at least, would eventually surpass that of the popular Republican who succeeded him, Dwight David Eisenhower.

SUGGESTED READINGS

Lary May, ed, *Recasting America: Culture and Politics in the Age of the Cold War* (1989), offers essays on different aspects of postwar life, while William Graebner, *The Age of Doubt* (1991), provides a brief overview. The most comprehensive political history of the cold war era is James T. Patterson, *Grand Expectations: The United States, 1945–1974* (1996).

For broad overviews of cultural politics, see George Lipsitz, *Rainbow at Midnight: Labor and Culture in the 1940s* (1994); Stephen J. Whitfield, *The Culture of the Cold War* (rev ed. 1996); and Tom Englehardt, *The End of Victory Culture: Cold War America and the Disillusioning of a Generation* (1995).

There are a number of biographies of President Truman. The most thorough is Alonso L. Hamby, *Man of the People: A Life of Harry S. Truman* (1995). See also Robert Ferrell, *Harry Truman and the Modern American Presidency* (1983); William Pemberton, *Harry S. Truman: Fair Dealer and Cold Warrior* (1989); and David G. McCullough, *Truman* (1992). Truman's own account can be found in *Memoirs* (2 vols., 1955–1956); Robert H. Ferrell, ed., *Off the Record: The Private Papers of Harry S. Truman* (1980); and Merle Miller, *Plain Speaking* (1974), a series of interviews that helped spark the rehabilitation of Truman's reputation. Michael J. Lacey, ed., *The Truman Presidency* (1989), offers interpretive essays; and

Alonso Hamby, *Beyond the New Deal* (1973), remains a useful look at Truman's Fair Deal, but it should be supplemented by the relevant chapters of the same author's *Liberalism and Its Challenges* (2nd ed., 1992).

The election of 1948 has attracted considerable scholarship. See Fred Kofsky, *Harry S. Truman and the War Scare of 1948: A Successful Campaign to Deceive the Nation* (1993); Gary A. Donaldson, *Truman Defeats Dewey* (1998); Harold I. Gullan, *The Upset That Wasn't: Harry S. Truman and the Crucial Election of 1948* (1998); and Zachery Karball, *The Last Campaign: How Harry Truman Won the 1948 Election* (2000).

Specialized studies on the Truman presidency include R. Alton Lee, *Truman and Taft-Hartley* (1966); Allen J. Matusow, *Farm Policies and Politics in the Truman Administration* (1966); William C. Berman, *The Politics of Civil Rights in the Truman Administration* (1970); Maeva Marcus, *Truman and the Steel Seizure Case* (1977); Monte Poen, *Harry S. Truman versus the Medical Lobby* (1977); Andrew J. Dunar, *The Truman Scandals and the Politics of Morality* (1984); Steven M. Gillon, *Politics and Vision: The ADA and American Liberalism, 1947–1985* (1986); Sean J. Savage, *Truman and the Democratic Party* (1997). Samuel J. Walker, *Prompt and Utter Destruction: Truman and the Use of Atomic Bombs against Japan* (1997); and Michael T. Benson, *Harry S. Truman and the Founding of Israel* (1997).

Economic and labor issues may be traced in Robert Leckachman, *The Age of Keynes* (1966); John Bernard, *Walter Reuther and the Rise of the Auto Workers* (1983); Gerald D. Nash, *The American West Transformed* (1985); Robert H. Zeiger, *American Workers, American Unions, 1920–1985* (1986); Milton Derber et al., *Labor in Illinois: The Affluent Years, 1945–1980* (1989); Mark Friedberger, *Farm Families and Change in Twentieth-Century America* (1989); Kim McQuaid, *Uneasy Partners: Big Business and American Politics, 1945–1990* (1993); and Phyllis K. De Luna, *Public versus Private Power during the Truman Administration: A Study of New Deal Liberalism* (1997).

For cultural interpretations of national security policies, see Paul Boyer, *By the Bomb's Early Light* (1985); the relevant chapters of Richard Slotkin, *Gunfighter Nation: The Myth of the Frontier in Twentieth-Century America* (1992); Robert J. Corber, *In the Name of National Security: Hitchcock, Homophobia, and the Political Construction of Gender in Postwar America* (1993); Guy Oakes, *The Imaginary War: Civil Defense and American Cold War Culture* (1994); Robbie Lieberman, *The Strangest Dream: Communism, Anticommunism, and the U.S. Peace Movement, 1945–1963* (2000); and Ron T. Robin, *The Making of a Cold War Enemy: Culture and Politics in the American Military Complex* (2001).

There has been considerable recent scholarship on espionage activities. See Daniel Patrick Moynihan, *Secrecy: The American Experience* (1998); Joseph Albright and Marcia Kunstel, *Bombshell: The Secret Story of America's Unknown Atomic Spy Conspiracy* (1997); Allen Weinstein and Alexander Vassiliev, *The Haunted Wood: Soviet Espionage in America: the Stalin Era* (1999); Harvey Klehr and John Earl Haynes, *Venona: Decoding Soviet Espionage in America* (1999); Sam Roberts, *The Brother: The Untold Story of Atomic Spy David Greengalss and How He Sent His Sister, Ethel Rosenberg, to the Electric Chair* (2001); and Alexander Feklisov and Sergei Kostin, *The Man Behind the Rosenbergs* (2001).

There are many excellent studies of the postwar red scare. Joel Kovel, *Red Hunting in the Promised Land* (1993), and M. J. Heale, *American Anticommunism*

(1990), take the long view, whereas Fred Inglis, *The Cruel Peace* (1991), offers an international perspective. Richard M. Fried, *Nightmare in Red: The McCarthy Era in Perspective* (1990), and Ellen Schrecker, *The Age of McCarthyism* (2001) and *Many are the Crimes: McCarthyism in America* (1998), are recent syntheses. David Caute's *The Great Fear* (1978), still offers a good, very detailed account.

Specialized studies include Michael Belknap, *Cold War Political Justice* (1971); Frank J. Donner, *The Age of Surveillance* (1980); Peter Steinberg, *The Great "Red Menace"* (1982); Stanley I. Kutler, *American Inquisition* (1982); Larry Ceplair and Steven Englund, *The Inquisition in Hollywood* (1983); David Oshinsky, *A Conspiracy So Immense: The World of Joe McCarthy* (1983); Gerald Horne, *Black and Red: W. E. B. DuBois and the Afro-American Response to the Cold War* (1986); Ellen Schrecker, *No Ivory Tower: McCarthyism & the Universities* (1986); Herbert Mitgang, *Dangerous Dossiers: Exposing the Secret War Against America's Greatest Authors* (1988); Bernard Dick, *Radical Innocence: A Critical Study of the Hollywood Ten* (1989); Robert P. Newman, *Owen Lattimore and the "Loss" of China* (1992); Sigmund Diamond, *The Compromised Campus* (1992); Marjorie Garber and Rebecca L. Walkowitz, eds., *Secret Agents: The Rosenberg Case, McCarthyism, and Fifties America* (1995); John F. Neville, *The Press, the Rosenbergs, and the Cold War* (1995); Allen Weinstein, *Perjury: The Hiss-Chambers Case* (rev. ed., 1997); Ronald Radosh and Joyce Milton, *The Rosenberg File* (2nd ed., 1997); Arthur J. Sabin, *In Calmer Times: The Supreme Court and Red Monday* (1999); and Philip Jenkins, *The Cold War at Home: The Red Scare in Pennsylvania, 1945–1960* (1999).

Athan Theoharis offers several outstanding histories of the culture of surveillance and anticommunism. See, for example, *The Truman Presidency: The Origins of the Imperial Presidency and the National Security State* (1979), *Beyond the Hiss Case* (1982), and *From the Secret Files of J. Edgar Hoover* (1991), three volumes that he edited. See also the relevant chapters of Theoharis and John Stuart Cox, *The Boss: J. Edgar Hoover and the Great American Inquisition* (1988); Richard Gid Powers, *Secrecy and Power: The Life of J. Edgar Hoover* (1988); and Curt Gentry, *J. Edgar Hoover and the Secrets* (1991).

The culture of the cold war era has attracted considerable attention. In addition to the three general studies just cited, see Richard Pells, *The Liberal Mind in a Conservative Age* (1984); Alan Nadel, *Containment Culture: American Narrative, Postmodernism, and the Atomic Age* (1995); and Margot A. Henricksen, *Dr. Strangelove's America: Society and Culture in the Atomic Age* (1997). For more specialized studies, see Robert Booth Fowler, *Believing Skeptics* (1978); Mary Sperling McAuliffe, *Crisis on the Left: Cold War Politics and American Liberals* (1978); Serge Guilbaut, *How New York Stole the Idea of Modern Art: Abstract Expressionism, Freedom, and the Cold War* (1983); Alexander Bloom, *Prodigal Sons: The New York Intellectuals & Their World* (1986); the relevant chapters of Alan Wald, *The New York Intellectuals: The Rise and Decline of the Anti-Stalinist Left from the 1920s to the 1980s* (1987); Lawrence H. Schwartz, *Creating Faulkner's Reputation: The Politics of Modern Literary Criticism* (1988); Robbie Lieberman, *"My Song Is My Weapon": People Songs, American Communism, and the Politics of Culture, 1930–1950* (1989); Thomas Hill Schaub, *American Fiction in the Cold War* (1991); Daniel Horowitz, *Vance Packard and American Social Criticism* (1984); Wendy Kozol, *Life's America: Family and Nation in Postwar Photojournalism* (1994); Alan M. Winkler, *Life Under a Cloud: American Anxiety About the Atom* (1993); Michael

Wreszin, *Rebel in the Defense of Tradition: The Life and Politics of Dwight McDonald* (1994); Gary Wills, *John Wayne's America: The Politics of Celebrity* (1997); Robert Corber, *Homosexuality in Cold War America: Resistance and the Crisis of Masculinity* (1997); and Lary May, *The Big Tomorrow: Hollywood and the Politics of the American Way* (2000).

Science, medicine, and technological issues are discussed in Daniel Ford, *The Cult of the Atom* (1982); George T. Mazuzan and J. Samuel Walker, *Controlling the Atom: The Beginnings of Nuclear Regulation* (1984); David Noble, *Forces of Production* (1984); Bryan Jennett, *High Technology Medicine; Benefits and Burdens* (1986); Howard Ball, *Justice Downwind: America's Atomic Testing Program* (1986); James Patterson, *The Dread Disease: Cancer and Modern American Culture* (1987); Jonathan Liebenau, *Medical Science and Medical Industry: The Formation of the American Pharmaceutical Industry* (1987); Rosemary Stevens, *In Sickness and in Wealth: American Hospitals in the Twentieth Century* (1989); David A. Hounshell and John K. Smith, Jr., *Science and Corporate Strategy: DuPont R&D, 1902–1980* (1989); Brian Balogh, *Chain Reaction: Expert Debate and Public Participation in American Commercial Nuclear Power* (1991); Andrew Polsky, *The Rise of the Therapeutic State* (1991); Gerald N. Grob, *From Asylum to Community: Mental Health Policy in Modern America* (1991); Stephen P. Waring, *Taylorism Transformed: Scientific Management Theory Since 1945* (1991); Daniel M. Fox, *Power and Illness: The Failure and Future of American Health Policy* (1993); Stuart W. Leslie, *The Cold War and American Science* (1993); G. Pascal Zachary, *The Endless Frontier, Vannevar Bush, Engineer of the American Century* (1997); and Eileen Welsome, *The Plutonium Files: America's Secret Medical Experiments in the Cold War* (1999). On the culture of scientific thought, see Jessica Wang, *American Science in an Age of Anxiety: Scientists, Anticommunism, and the Cold War* (1999), and David M. Hart, *Forged Consensus: Science, Technology, and Economic Policy in the United States, 1921–1951* (1998).

3

Eisenhower Republicanism

The broad smile of Dwight David Eisenhower dominated the political culture of the 1950s. During his two terms as president, Eisenhower, whose successful military career had rested on a politician's keen sense of strategy and timing, relied on leadership skills he had learned in the U.S. Army. He radiated down-home common sense rather than political guile. Even his nickname, "Ike," had an old-time, folksy ring. In the face of puzzling domestic and international issues, Eisenhower proclaimed that traditional values remained the key to tapping the full possibilities of postwar life.

DOMESTIC POLITICS

Republican leaders, encouraged by Harry Truman's troubles, anticipated electoral victory in 1952. They wanted to take no chances, however, and their desire to pick a sure winner pointed toward Eisenhower. In 1948, the popular general had rejected political overtures from both Republicans and Democrats. In early 1951, some Democrats were still hoping that Eisenhower might become their standard-bearer in the following year's election. However, while president of Columbia University from 1948 to 1951, Eisenhower formed close ties to the GOP's "eastern establishment" and found he shared its perspectives on foreign and domestic policies.

The Elections of 1952 and 1956

Eisenhower became convinced that the GOP—and the country—needed him to seek the presidency in 1952. The Republicans had not won a presidential election in more than twenty years, and he worried that continued failure might embolden the more conservative and the McCarthyite wings of the GOP. He also believed that the United States must play an active role in Europe and feared that conservative Senator Robert A. Taft, his leading rival for the nomination, lacked a firm commitment to U.S. participation in NATO. After winning a first-ballot victory at the 1952 Republican convention, Ike pacified conservatives by selecting Richard M. Nixon of California as his vice-presidential candidate. Nixon, a strong anti-Communist then only thirty-nine years old, was also expected to attract younger voters. Although Eisenhower announced that "I shall not and will not engage in character assassination, vilification, and personalities," he allowed Nixon and other surrogates to link Democrats with communist influence in Washington, corruption in government, and a "no-win" war in Korea.

Nixon nearly lost his spot on the ticket when allegations of a secret political slush fund surfaced. Nixon's televised response featured insinuations that the "reds" wanted to deny him the vice-presidency and musings about his wife's "Republican cloth coat," (a veiled reference to a "mink-coat scandal" during the Truman presidency), his worn-out Oldsmobile, and his one political payoff—his daughters' little dog, Checkers. The "Checkers speech" saved Nixon's career and earned him a reputation as a skilled television performer.

The Democrats found few bright spots in 1952. Their presidential nominee, Governor Adlai Stevenson of Illinois, impressed liberal journalists and academics with cleverly phrased speeches, but critics complained that his erudite addresses sailed over the heads of most voters. Stevenson's image as an "egghead" intellectual and a recent divorce became frequently noted handicaps. In addition, Stevenson had to outrun the unpopular shadow of Harry Truman, who insisted on taking an active role in the campaign. Political pollsters, who had substantially revised their techniques after the miscalculations of 1948, discovered that many voters simply felt that a Democrat had been in the White House too long. Election-day results corroborated this finding. Eisenhower carried all but nine states, and the Republicans also gained control, by very narrow margins, of both houses of Congress.

Most voters approved Eisenhower's leadership. In 1956, when the presidential contest between Eisenhower and Stevenson was replayed, Ike's popularity remained undiminished. Retaining Nixon as a running mate (after the vice-president ignored hints that he might "prefer" a cabinet post), Eisenhower received almost 10 million more popular votes than Stevenson. This time, however, Ike's personal victory did not help the Republican party as much as it had in 1952. The Democrats had already regained control of Congress in 1954, and they solidified their hold in the 1956 election.

A "Hidden-Hand" Presidency?

Eisenhower promised a "constitutional presidency." Celebrating the virtues of local government and state autonomy, he claimed that Democratic administrations had extended national power too far and spent public tax dollars too freely. Eisenhower felt that Truman, for whom he had little respect, had needlessly embittered relations between the White House and Capitol Hill. Ike immediately reached out to Congress, and his desire for cooperation became a necessity after the Democratic rebound in 1954 and 1956. Eisenhower instructed members of his administration to work with Congress. Leadership, he told one associate, did not mean "hitting people over the head. Any damn fool can do that. . . . It's persuasion—and conciliation—and education—and patience. That's the only kind of leadership I know—or believe in—or will practice."

Eisenhower received considerable help from two cagey congressional Democrats from Texas, Representative Sam Rayburn and Senator Lyndon Johnson. Political centrists themselves, Rayburn and Johnson agreed with many of Eisenhower's policies, especially on foreign affairs. One pundit described their version of "loyal opposition" as "three parts loyal and one part opposition." Although the executive branch and Congress sometimes clashed, most of the bitter personal rancor of the Truman era disappeared.

Eisenhower also sought harmony within his administrative structure. Believing that his Democratic predecessors had ignored sound managerial practices, he filled his first cabinet with Republican business leaders. A pro-Democratic magazine dismissed Eisenhower's appointees as "eight millionaires and a plumber." The plumber was Democrat Martin Durkin, president of the United Association of Plumbers and Steamfitters. Eisenhower hoped that a union leader might smooth relations between his administration and organized labor, but Durkin was gone in less than a year.

Eisenhower drew heavily from business and the military to fill positions on his White House staff and presided over a corporate-style management team. He gave Sherman Adams, his chief aide, whom many people considered an assistant president, broad authority. Adams closely guarded access to the Oval Office, a practice that especially alienated Republicans who sought the president's ear. Adams, who handled many sensitive issues that the president wished to avoid, became notorious for brusque phone calls—he made hundreds every day—in which he barked orders and then hung up without waiting for a reply. This style gained Adams a wide range of enemies but allowed Eisenhower himself to avoid ticklish situations. Eisenhower adopted a similar strategy both in foreign affairs and on economic issues. Secretary of State John Foster Dulles and Treasury Secretary George Humphrey took the political heat, while Ike remained above the day-to-day battle.

This use of subordinates as political lightning rods grew, in part, from a feeling that, after Truman's troubles, Eisenhower needed to reestablish the image of the presidency. Although Eisenhower had formed no formal church ties during his military career, he joined Washington's National Presbyterian Church (where seven previous presidents had been members) and became a Sunday-morning regular. He opened cabinet meetings with a silent devotion and began the tradition of "prayer breakfasts" at the White House. Eisenhower's inaugural parade contained a hastily constructed entry called "God's Float," which was flanked by slogans proclaiming "In God We Trust" and "Freedom of Worship" and topped by a structure that was supposed to resemble a nondenominational church. This curious creation struck one observer as "an oversized model of a deformed molar left over from some dental exhibit."

Eisenhower rarely stumbled in subsequent public relations efforts. Above all, Ike evoked sincerity. Although critics might question the wisdom of his policies or his grasp of complex issues, few doubted his integrity or decency. His much-publicized addiction to golf and bridge, pastimes that millions of other people were avidly pursuing, allowed the former general to project a common touch. While serving in the White House, Eisenhower took up the "paint by

associated with increasing governmental spending and enlarging the federal bureaucracy. Even so, Eisenhower accepted several new domestic spending programs, especially during his first term. In response to an economic downturn in 1953–1954, he permitted some acceleration of spending for public works projects as a way of stimulating the economy. He also endorsed several new projects that did not overly burden the federal budget, especially the Interstate Highway Act of 1956.

The interstate highway program, arguably the largest public works project in human history, attracted broad support. Financed by taxes on gasoline purchases, which were earmarked for a federal highway trust fund that supplemented state expenditures, the act envisioned crisscrossing the nation with controlled access expressways. While surveying the economic situation in Germany after the end of World War II, Eisenhower had admired Germany's system of high-speed highways, and he later claimed that a similar network in the United States could contribute to national defense by accelerating the flow of troops and supplies during any cold-war confrontation. The timing of spending on new highway construction, Eisenhower also suggested, might be used so that it could "have some effect in leveling out peaks and valleys in our economic life."

The interstate highway program proved popular. A major national commitment to Detroit's gas guzzlers, it provided an ongoing governmental subsidy for the trucking industry and for people who could afford long-distance travel in their private vehicles. It also produced a host of spin-offs. Construction companies prospered; gas stations, restaurants, and motel chains sprang up near exit ramps; and the mobile-home industry, symbolized by the sleek, aluminum Airstream trailer, entered an era of mass production. Dizzying mazes of on- and off-ramps, monuments to the increasingly sophisticated ingenuity of highway planners, eventually marked the landscape. In time, enterprises located near many interstate exits flourished, and some economists likened this nationwide economic complex to a "fifty-first state."

The highway-building program also brought new problems, critics claimed. Railroads, a less expensive and less polluting means of transportation, could not compete with truckers who used free interstate highways. Major railway companies headed for deep financial trouble and eventual bankruptcy. In New York City, Los Angeles, and elsewhere, mass-transit facilities decayed and light-rail transit disappeared, part of a conspiracy by the "highway lobby," charged some urban observers. The more people drove, the more there seemed no alternative to driving. Those without cars, especially the elderly and people with low incomes, were obvious losers. The political payoffs, sometimes associated with the purchase of right-of-ways and the award of contracts to construction companies, tainted local government and recalled the corruption that had accompanied the railroad boom of the late nineteenth century.

During the 1950s, according to most estimates, people who were regularly employed, including the majority of blue-collar workers, saw their incomes and lifestyles rise to levels that sociologists called "middle class." As the Pentagon became the center of a military-industrial complex, what might be called an auto-home-electrical-appliance complex developed on the home front. Both home ownership and a host of new consumer products, made available by credit buying, became real possibilities for millions of people. The president and his defenders credited their own cautious economic approach with helping to promote these trends.

FIGURE 3–2   The End of Light-Rail Mass Transit.

Photographers record the 1953 burning of street cars in Minneapolis, part of the nation's embrace of freeways and automobile transportation.
Source: Minneapolis Star–Journal–Tribune, Minnesota Historical Society.

As Eisenhower's presidency wound down, the president became increasingly conservative on fiscal matters. By the spring of 1958, signs of a recession were everywhere, and the official unemployment rate reached 7.5 percent. Although Eisenhower had accepted responsibility for responding to the recession of 1953–1954 by moderately increasing governmental expenditures, he showed no such inclination in 1957–1958, when confronted by a much more severe downturn. Even many business leaders, who had hitherto enthusiastically supported Eisenhower, urged a more energetic response, such as a tax cut, from Washington. Although Eisenhower endorsed the National Defense Education Act (NDEA) of 1958, which created a loan program for college students as a means of promoting instruction in science and mathematics, he blocked efforts by his own secretary of HEW to extend federal funding of classroom construction at the elementary and secondary levels. Spurning the advice of Arthur Burns, who had helped to guide the more vigorous response to the 1953–1954 recession, Eisenhower insisted that the recession of 1957–1958 would eventually cure itself, without either tax cuts or increased domestic expenditures. To speed recovery, he simply advised consumers to spend more money.

Fearful that greater governmental spending would spark an inflationary spiral, Eisenhower remained committed to balancing the federal budget. William McChesney Martin of the Federal Reserve Board (FRB) supported the president's fiscal conservatism. Martin, the first FRB head to use the intricacies of monetary policy, especially control over the amount of money in circulation, shared Ike's fears about inflation and his fondness for balanced federal budgets. More broadly, Eisenhower always reminded himself that he had entered politics to soothe and assure, not to reform and crusade. Many years later, he still proudly remembered his principal presidential accomplishment as having created "an atmosphere of greater serenity and mutual confidence."

All in all, the economy did grow at a generally steady pace during the 1950s. The GNP (measured in constant dollars) expanded nearly 25 percent during Eisenhower's eight years in office, while consumer prices rose by an annual rate of less than 1.5 percent. Unemployment figures, though, also rose, from a rate of about 3 percent in 1953 to more than 6 percent in 1959–1960.

The Critical Culture of the 1950s

By 1960, critics in government, academic life, and the media were beginning to see public policy making as too cautious. Devotees of the new economics wanted more active intervention by Washington. They considered the rate of economic expansion too slow to keep up with population growth. The economic growth rate of the 1950s, they argued, lagged behind that of the Soviet Union. Moreover, Germany and Japan were rebuilding their war-shattered economies, while economic policymakers in the United States seemed to be resting on their laurels, apparently blind to their increasingly outdated industrial plants and deteriorating infrastructure. Activists in both major parties charged that the lack of new federal programs stemmed not from the absence of pressing problems—such as urban and rural poverty, air pollution, central-city blight, and an inequitable system of health-care—but from the Eisenhower's administration's determination to ignore them.

By the end of Eisenhower's presidency, critics were becoming more outspoken. Cautiously breaking with the celebratory tone of the immediate postwar period, they identified sizeable tears in the social fabric. Much of their criticism initially focused on what were said to be the private discontents of the growing middle class: a lack of purpose, a sense of aimlessness, and a restless search for greater peace of mind. The sociologist David Riesman wrote about such issues in *The Lonely Crowd* (1950). Beneath the surface of tranquillity in public life, social critics detected a seething strata of private tensions.

Some shifted the focus from private discontents to public problems. Daniel Bell, who had earlier proclaimed the "end of ideology," gradually became less sanguine about technological expertise being able to solve every problem, especially those related to the organization of the work process. He sympathetically cataloged the discontents of U.S. workers and criticized management's preoccupation with efficiency and workplace control. In *The Affluent Society* (1958), John Kenneth Galbraith denounced the parsimony of public welfare programs and contrasted the personal affluence of most Americans with the lack of decent public services. Galbraith sardonically wrote of the tourists who drove luxurious automobiles through badly paved and littered streets so that they could snack on elaborately packaged foods from a portable refrigerator—by a polluted river in a shabby, public park.

As a remedy for the gap between private comforts and public services, economists such as Galbraith urged higher levels of taxation and greater governmental spending. The important body of critical commentary that emerged during Ike's second term would provide the basis for John F. Kennedy's critique of the Eisenhower presidency during the 1960 presidential campaign.

REPUBLICAN FOREIGN POLICIES

In foreign policy, President Dwight Eisenhower's personal style contrasted with that of his more flamboyant predecessors, Franklin Roosevelt and Harry Truman. For years he had reconciled diverse opinions into consensus, first as commander of the world's greatest amphibious invasion, the D-day attack against occupied France; then as president of Columbia University; and from 1950 to 1952 as leader of NATO's (North Atlantic Treaty Organization) vast military apparatus in Europe. Distrustful of expansive government and its potential for public waste, Ike championed conservative economic principles and scrutinized defense expenditures carefully. This general enjoyed quiet games of golf and, unlike "Give 'em hell, Harry Truman," vowed to "wage peace."

John Foster Dulles, the austere corporation lawyer who became secretary of state, helped chart Eisenhower's foreign policy. A fervent anti-Communist, he extended the position of the 1952 Republican platform that condemned Truman's containment policy as "negative, futile, and immoral" by stridently calling for a psychological and political offensive to "roll back" communism. Dulles saw himself, one biographer wrote, "as the chess master of the free world, daily engaged in a mortal contest against a monolithic adversary."

The New Look

How could the Eisenhower administration reconcile a suspicion of large government with its rhetorical commitment to an open-ended struggle against anything perceived as socialist or Communist? The cost-conscious president, his secretary of state, and Pentagon generals recast America's strategic doctrines into a "New Look" that stressed the deterrent of massive retaliation. They believed that modern technology could increase American military power while reducing its cost: Secretary of Defense Charles Wilson quipped that nuclear weaponry provided "more bang for the buck." Nuclear bombs, together with sophisticated delivery systems, could protect the United States from attack since no nation would risk a second-strike reprisal by Washington.

Determined to stake out the boundaries of the "free world" as broadly as possible, Dulles also dramatically expanded the nation's collective-security arrangements. He spent months traveling around the world, signing up allies. A succession of bilateral defense pacts with Taiwan, Korea, and Japan extended America's nuclear umbrella to the shores of China. New collective security arrangements shored up Britain's weakness east of the Suez Canal. The Southeast Asia Treaty Organization (SEATO) of 1954 linked Australia, the Philippines, Thailand, and Pakistan with the United States, Britain, and France. The next year, Washington sponsored the Central Treaty Organization (CENTO) with Turkey, Iraq, Iran, and Pakistan. Turkey tied CENTO with

FIGURE 3–3 Exercise "Desert Rock," 1951.

Eisenhower's "New Look" placed greater emphasis than ever before on nuclear weapons. Continuation of tests such as this one in Nevada, created plumes of radioactive smoke and exposed onlookers and "downwinders" to dangerous levels of radiation.
Source: National Archives and Records Administration, Records of the Office of the Chief Signal Officer. Photo by Cpl. McCaughey.

NATO; Pakistan connected SEATO with CENTO. Although these multilateral covenants remained weak, in theory they pledged that an attack against one member, either by overt aggression or, as Dulles put it, "by internal subversion," would bring all into consultation to decide common action. Eisenhower, already skeptical about the military value of large American army reserves, thought that local forces, financed partly from Washington and linked to a network of alliances controlled by the United States, could contain regional threats and prevent them from escalating into nuclear cataclysm. Although initially designed to decrease America's obligations, regional pacts could ultimately increase them by involving the United States in local disputes.

The New Look stressed atomic weaponry, but it also brought other tools into what Republicans viewed as a global struggle against communism: an increase in overseas bases; a larger commitment to foreign military aid; economic assistance programs to accomplish political goals; and a stepped-up program of covert action, run by the Central Intelligence Agency (CIA), to subvert unfriendly governments. Aware of how important techniques of psychological warfare had been during World War II, Eisenhower also emphasized more aggressive use of propaganda. He expanded Truman's Campaign of Truth and formed a new agency—the United States Information Agency (USIA)—in 1953.

The USIA disseminated American books, art, music, and films abroad. It instituted and expanded programs of educational exchange, American Studies curricula, magazine publications, and exhibitions. Articles such as "100 Things You Should Know about Communism," written by the USIA but published under local bylines abroad, purveyed the anti-Communist message. Radio programming by the Voice of America and Radio Free Europe broke through the Soviet's attempts to control information in countries they dominated. In 1954 the Voice of America's Willis Conover started "Music USA," a jazz program that would run for thirty-four years and build a larger audience than any other internationally broadcast program. The USIA also sponsored world tours (especially to Africa) by some of jazz's greatest African-American musicians to counteract the negative image of the United States as a segregated society.

The Eisenhower administration talked about limited government, but historians now recognize how thoroughly it expanded and employed new foreign policy techniques. Use of economic, psychological, and covert diplomacy—all fairly well hidden from public view or scrutiny—sharply distinguished Eisenhower's foreign policy from prewar patterns. Ironically, Eisenhower's covert expansion of the United State's global capacities to fight communism, further enlarged by his successors, began to erode the idea of limited government that the president publicly espoused.

Korea

Armistice negotiations with North Korea and China had broken down in October 1952, largely because of a complicated impasse over the issue of prisoners of war. The Communists demanded that the usual international practice of returning all POWs to their homeland be observed. The United States, however, insisted on voluntary repatriation. Since many enemy soldiers wanted to stay in South Korea, voluntary repatriation meant that the South could gain, and the North lose, as many as 50,000 trained soldiers. Stalemates also continued on the battlefield.

True to his campaign promise, Eisenhower toured the front in November 1952 and then, with Dulles, orchestrated an exercise in New Look diplomacy. The president wired General Mark Clark, the UN commander, that the United States might "carry on the war in new ways never yet tried" if the Communists remained intransigent. Dulles dispatched more specific warnings through third parties about using nuclear weapons to terminate the conflict if negotiations failed. Negotiations resumed, and both sides quickly initialed armistice terms. Korea was to stay divided, as before the war; neutral powers were to tackle POW repatriation (an issue eventually settled according to the voluntary formula). On July 27, 1953, a truce—not a peace treaty—ended a war that had killed over 2 million Asians, mostly civilians, and 33,000 Americans.

To American policymakers of the time—and many subsequent historians—the Korean War represented a clear case of Communist expansionism: aggression across an international boundary to take over a free state. In this view, expansionism was successfully contained by a strong military response topped off by an atomic threat. The Korean War seemed to exemplify the cold-war premises of NSC 68 and to require a rapid buildup of American military strength and nonmilitary leverage.

The Korean War, however, was also a civil war. Korea was a deeply divided society—factionalized between right and left and divided since 1946 by an arbitrary border that cut across lines of ethnicity, religion, and political allegiance. The governments of North Korea and South Korea, both dictatorships, were deeply committed to reunification of the country and both appealed to their cold-war allies to assist their efforts. After gaining U.S. support, South Korea's President Syngman Rhee continued to imprison dissenters and consolidate his dictatorship, becoming a questionable symbol of the "free world." Korea was consistent with a predominant theme in Eisenhower's overall foreign policy toward the Third World: support for autocratic regimes who were perceived as the only alternative to communism.

Summitry

Although the New Look assumed that the Soviet Union led an international Communist conspiracy, headed by a Stalinist police state, Soviet communism, in fact, began to mellow after the mid-1950s. On March 5, 1953, Soviet dictator Joseph Stalin died, and his tyranny partially withered. Stalin's theories had proved wrong: World War II had revived liberal capitalism, not doomed it. The troika that replaced Stalin—Foreign Minister Vyacheslav Molotov; Defense Minister Nikolai Bulganin; and Nikita Khrushchev, first secretary of the Communist party—went along with Premier George Malenkov's plan to ease tensions with the United States. Within three years, Khrushchev had triumphed over the others, and the Soviet people, tired of fear and poverty, enthusiastically responded to his promises of peaceful coexistence and more consumer goods. The Soviet Union reduced its armed forces from 4 million to less than 3 million by the mid-1950s. Although primarily an effort to shift economic priorities toward consumer industries, the unilateral gesture did seem to contradict Dulles' hard-line premises. It also calmed European fears of Soviet power. After Khrushchev denounced Stalin's "Gestapo tactics" in 1956, Russians dreamed of less regimentation, less sacrifice, and Eisenhower became interested in refashioning America's relationship with the Soviet Union.

In the midst of the Russian thaw, British leaders urged a conference of heads of state to settle European problems, particularly German reunification. The idea of such a summit meeting intrigued Eisenhower, despite Dulles's pessimistic admonitions. Summitry offered a new forum for long-stalled negotiations over disarmament and cultural exchange. In July 1955, the president traveled to Geneva, where he met with his counterparts from the Big Four: Premier Bulganin and First Secretary Khrushchev, Prime Minister Anthony Eden of Britain, and Premier Edgar Faure of France. Negotiations over Germany's future went nowhere, but the drama of such face-to-face sessions promoted what came to be called a new, more accommodating "spirit of Geneva." Eisenhower proposed that the United States and the Soviet Union exchange blueprints of all military installations and permit reconnaissance flights over each other's territory. The proposal had little chance for practical success because the Soviets were historically suspicious of opening their territory to Western scrutiny. Still, this "open skies" proposal did represent more than a propaganda victory for the United States; it contributed to ideas about disarmament and to a moderation of rhetoric between the two superpowers. Moreover, the summit talks brought agreements on cultural exchanges that increased the flow of U.S. information into the Soviet bloc.

In this spirit of summitry, leaders of both nations embarked on personal diplomacy. In the fall of 1959, Khrushchev visited the United States for twelve days. He addressed the United Nations, talked to Iowa farmers, and met Hollywood film stars. Then premier and president conferred privately at Camp David, Eisenhower's mountain retreat in Maryland. Although it achieved nothing concrete, the "spirit of Camp David" further moderated rancor in both countries. The leaders also launched much-publicized goodwill trips elsewhere. Eisenhower went to Europe, the Middle East, Latin America, and the Far East, although anti-American riots protesting a bilateral defense treaty forced him to cancel a trip to Japan. Khrushchev appeared in Western Europe, Afghanistan, and India. An American exhibition in Moscow in 1959, attended by Vice President Richard Nixon, displayed U.S. consumer products—from modern kitchens to sleek automobiles to lipstick—to large crowds of Soviet citizens, who seemed fascinated by the material abundance enjoyed even in working-class families in America. In the famous "kitchen debates," held in the model home displayed in the exhibit, Nixon and Khrushchev verbally sparred:

> Nixon (pointing to a washing machine): "In America these are designed to make things easier on our women."
> Khrushchev: "A capitalist attitude."
> Nixon: "I think this attitude toward women is universal."
> Khrushchev: "These are merely gadgets."

The dangers of radioactive fallout from atomic tests spurred further efforts toward accommodation. In mid-1958, negotiations between the Soviets and the Americans failed to reach a comprehensive ban on nuclear testing, but both sides did agree to a voluntary moratorium. A limited test ban treaty would be finalized in 1963.

In early 1960, Khrushchev called for another summit meeting, this time in Paris. On May 1, 1960, however, the Soviets shot down an American U-2 spy plane over their territory. Khrushchev trumpeted Russia's injury, demanding both an apology and an end to such spy flights. Eisenhower knew that Khrushchev would use the Paris meeting to embarrass the West, and the summit was cancelled.

The summitry of the Eisenhower years did not narrow fundamental disagreements nor provide diplomatic breakthroughs. Its importance lay less in substance than in media-attracting pageantry. Still, the gains from face-to-face conversations, though small, moderated cold-war tensions.

Challenges to Superpower Dominance

Even as Soviet-American hostilities eased, discontent spread within the alliance systems of both superpowers. The New Look, based on America's strategic superiority, inspired resentment against American dominance among some allies, and the Soviet thaw, which spread throughout its Eastern European empire, created unrest—even outright rebellion.

In America's relationship with Western Europe, its oldest and strongest partner, tensions mounted. Washington was working to create an integrated NATO force armed with conventional weapons. A joint effort would force Europe to finance a larger portion of its defense, increase pressure against the Soviet Union, and bring German power into a regional enterprise. Dulles advocated creation of a European Defense Community (EDC), but many Europeans, particularly the French, opposed its transnational approach and its lack of nuclear weapons. In response, Dulles ruminated at a press conference about "an agonizing reappraisal" of America's relations with Europe if EDC were not supported.

Dulles's tactics to force acceptance of the EDC angered politicians in France and England, who asserted national defense to be the province of their own parliaments, not of foreign leaders. They believed that specialization—an American nuclear force paired with conventional European armies—would continue Europe's second-class status in the NATO alliance. Would the United States risk nuclear war, and likely its own destruction, to save Western Europe? Conversely, might not Washington and Moscow pull back from direct superpower confrontation after mushroom clouds rose over Paris and, say, Warsaw? When the French National Assembly finally refused to ratify the EDC treaty on August 30, 1954, most Europeans happily approved. Britain and France accelerated their own plans for nuclear armament.

Tensions with America's European allies worsened during the 1956 crisis over the Suez Canal. The Suez crisis stemmed from events in Egypt. In 1952, military leaders had overturned King Farouk's corrupt monarchy, intending to modernize the country and escape Britain's economic domination. Two years later, Gamal Abdel Nasser assumed near dictatorial power, intending to make Egypt the chief military power in the Middle East and to cast himself as the leader of pan-Arabic nationalism. At first, Nasser's declared neutrality in the cold war garnered him money and technological aid from both the United States and the Soviet Union. In addition, popular resentment at Israeli statehood and at British control over much of the Middle East's political life had brought him popularity in the Arab world. After an Israeli raid into Egypt's Gaza Strip, however, Nasser signed an agreement to buy advanced weapons from Czechoslovakia. Angry with Nasser's dealing with Communists, Dulles withdrew American support for the construction of Egypt's Aswan Dam, a huge project designed to improve agricultural harvests along the Nile River and provide hydroelectric power for industrialization. In retaliation, Nasser seized the Suez Canal on July 25, 1956, assuming that canal tolls could finance the dam's construction.

Britain, France, and Israel resolved to act against Nasser. Israelis saw the Suez crisis as a pretext for preventive war; Europeans hoped to destroy Arab nationalism in the Middle East. When Eisenhower avoided a clear position on the Suez crisis during the 1956 presidential campaign, the British Foreign Office inferred an endorsement of their intervention in the Middle East. The United States, British officials thought, could not abandon its closest ally once military operations began. On October 29, 1956, Israel attacked Egypt, and several days later Anglo-French forces retook the Suez Canal.

The war ended quickly, partly because Egypt's armies proved surprisingly inept but largely because of superpower reactions. The United States angrily announced opposition to "any aggression by any nation." Eisenhower threatened to support cutting oil shipments to the invaders and to destroy the English pound by opposing renewal of British loans from the International Monetary Fund. The Soviets also condemned the intervention. Under such pressure, Britain and France could only acquiesce in a Canadian-American plan for UN troops to police the Sinai Peninsula.

The affair severely damaged America's prestige in most parts of the world. Egyptians were angry that the "American peace" stationed foreign soldiers in their country but not in Israel, which they perceived as the aggressor. In addition, the Suez crisis interjected the Soviets into Egyptian affairs, especially after they took over financing the Aswan Dam, and ensured Nasser's popularity in the Arab world. Moreover, Washington's actions alienated the Europeans. Most French people believed that the United States had sacrificed their national interest, and the French government became more determined to chart an independent course. Although unwilling to give up their "special relationship" with the United States, the British were also stunned by U.S. threats.

Strains within the Western alliance over nuclear policy and the Suez crisis coincided with more dramatic restiveness within the Soviet bloc. After World War II, Stalin had backed pro-Soviet regimes throughout Eastern Europe. These Soviet "satellites" embarked on industrial programs designed to complement the Soviet Union's own reconstruction. Never content with Stalinist tactics and the distortion of their national economic needs, however, some Eastern Europeans challenged Soviet domination. They began to test how much liberalization Moscow's post-Stalin rulers might allow. In June 1956, over 15,000 factory workers rioted at Poznan in Poland. Their three-day protest set off a popular upsurge of support for Wladyslaw Gomulka, a former minister removed by Stalin when he publicly opposed collectivization and advocated national development. After complicated negotiations, Moscow accepted the return of the unorthodox Gomulka. Events had caught Soviet leaders off guard, but their recognition of Gomulka seemed to indicate that they might allow economic reform that did not threaten the integrity of the Soviet bloc.

Misunderstanding this cue, Hungarians reached for true political independence a few months later. Emboldened by Poland's success, on October

23, 1956, students, workers, intellectuals, and housewives paraded for hours, demanding the return of Imre Nagy, like Gomulka, a former minister banished for his liberal views. As Nagy formed a new government, protests against subservience to the Soviet Union turned into armed rebellion in the countryside and paralyzed Hungary's capital as well. Misled by broadcasts from America's CIA-financed Radio Free Europe, the revolutionaries hoped for U.S. assistance. Nagy pledged free elections and a multiparty system. "No nation," he declared, "can intervene in our internal affairs." The lure of independence and Dulles's talk of "liberating captive peoples" betrayed the Hungarians into tragic illusions. As violence continued, a huge Soviet army entered the country and brutally crushed the Hungarian revolt of 1956. Moscow would not tolerate neutrality on its strategic borders, and Soviet leaders saved face by pointing to the simultaneous British and French intervention against Egypt.

THE THIRD WORLD AND THE COLD WAR

During the 1950s, the focus of international affairs began to shift toward Asia, Africa, and Latin America—the so-called Third World. Many nations in these areas were struggling to overcome a colonial past and to build a new sense of their own national identity in a postcolonial world. Most sought to steer between Russian and Yankee, avoiding an exclusive, neocolonialist reliance on either. Seeking economic as well as political independence, Third-World leaders often sought to gain greater control over their country's national resources and to use an activist state as an instrument in economic planning and development. The Soviets argued that their model of centralized planning was more relevant than the American model for accelerating industrialization, and many Third World leaders agreed. Through such an appeal, the Soviets tried to build ties to anticolonial movements and to advise them on state-directed development. U.S. policymakers under Eisenhower, by contrast, endorsed democracy and self-determination, but they opposed centralized economic planning and state ownership of basic industries. They often equated economic nationalism with communism and were less sympathetic toward Third-World fears of domination by foreign capital. To Eisenhower's advisers, development would come best through attracting, not nationalizing or restricting, foreign enterprise. They advanced "modernization" theories built on free-market capitalism. America's battle against communism, therefore, often seemed to clash with nationalistic aspirations in the Third World.

Vietnam

America's most perplexing involvement in Third-World politics came in Southeast Asia, particularly Vietnam. French colonialism had dominated Indochina for eighty years, but Japan's initial victories throughout the area in 1940 unseated French rule and galvanized nationalist intellectuals into a movement for postwar independence. Ho Chi Minh, a Marxist scholar dedicated to spreading a Communist-nationalist revolution to his country of peasants, assumed leadership of the Viet Minh, a popular front of several revolutionary parties. As Japanese power collapsed at the end of World War II, Ho declared Vietnam's independence (on September 2, 1945) and hoped that he could attract support from the United States, whose leaders were then urging decolonization. France almost immediately launched a war of reconquest, and the United States gradually gave France more and more support. Ho and an exceptionally skillful general, Vo Nguyen Giap, countered with guerrilla tactics, seeking to avoid defeat in the field while winning the people of Vietnam over to their cause. Financed heavily by Washington, French armies struggled against the forces led by Ho Chi Minh for control of Vietnam for nine years.

In 1954, the French had to accept defeat. Giap surrounded 25,000 French troops at a frontier outpost, Dien Bien Phu, while a constant artillery barrage cut off French reinforcements. The Viet Minh slowly advanced, using a complicated system of tunnels and munitions backpacked into the mountains by thousands of peasants. As the French public watched the slow strangulation of its army, the government under Pierre Mendes-France pledged to end the war, even if this meant leaving Vietnam to Communists under Ho Chi Minh. The French prepared for a peace conference in Geneva.

American policymakers were divided in their responses. Shocked that yet another area might "go Communist," John Foster Dulles and some Pentagon figures—notably Admiral Arthur W. Radford, chair of the Joint Chiefs of Staff—proposed an air strike against Giap's army. Some even discussed sending American troops to revitalize the French war effort or the use of atomic weaponry. Eisenhower did not want to "lose" Indochina so soon after the Chinese debacle, but he recognized America's limited power in so distant a place and worried about the federal budget. Congressional leaders refused to authorize intervention unless the United States first secured foreign support, and Britain quickly refused. After the army outlined cost and manpower estimates, Eisenhower concluded that U.S. intervention was impossible. Chief of Staff General Matthew Ridgway predicted that a million men, huge draft quotas, and enormous destruction might win this political-guerrilla war, but he thought that even then most Vietnamese would probably still support the Viet Minh.

Meanwhile, peace negotiations at the Geneva Conference reached a conclusion. France wished only to get out of the war. The Russians and the Chinese urged Ho Chi Minh to accept a compromise. France granted Vietnam, Laos, and Cambodia full independence, although none of the new states could join foreign alliances or permit foreign soldiers on its soil. French troops were to regroup in Vietnam south of the seventeenth parallel; Communist forces were to stay north of it. A nationwide election, to be held within two years, was to provide a single government for the reunified country. This solution provided a graceful exit for the defeated French in exchange for the possibility of an electoral victory for the Communist party in Vietnam.

American policymakers did not support the settlement. Instead, they saw a way to "save" at least some of Vietnam, although it required unilateral action. Dulles, not a party to the Geneva accords, announced that the United States considered North and South Vietnam to be two separate entities. The State Department hurriedly completed plans for SEATO and gratuitously extended its coverage to South Vietnam, Cambodia, and Laos. After Bao Dai, the Vietnamese emperor who supported the French, stepped down in 1955, the Eisenhower administration pledged vast amounts of economic aid to his pro-Western successor, Ngo Dinh Diem. With American backing, Diem called off the scheduled national elections in which a Communist victory appeared certain. The

Republican administration updated the so-called domino theory to justify these maneuvers: If South Vietnam "fell," Thailand would be next, then the rest of Indochina, and perhaps even India, Australia, and Japan. If the West stood firm now, as Britain and France should have done with Hitler in 1939, the supposed Communist advance would falter.

U.S. policymakers desired to forge a democracy in Vietnam that could serve as an example for the Third World. The connection between Washington and the South Vietnamese government in Saigon, however, quickly became so one-sided that South Vietnam became more a colony than a sovereign state. South Vietnam's dependency seemed to require ever-increasing U.S. intervention. Throughout the rest of the 1950s, the United States supplied South Vietnam's pro-West Diem with economic aid, military supplies, and diplomatic protection.

The results at first seemed to vindicate the gamble that a limited commitment might not only stave off a Communist victory but also build a capitalist model for the Third World. Between 1954 and 1957, South Vietnam ended wartime economic controls, initiated reconstruction, and began industrial development. Diem redistributed land confiscated from French landlords to peasants in the Mekong River delta. His steadily improving army brought order in Saigon and forced allegiance from the semi-feudal religious sects in the countryside.

Diem, however, could never really cement a nation together, and his Catholicism alienated the predominately Buddhist population. To ensure at least the appearance of popular support, Diem replaced local officials with his loyalists. A much touted "population relocation" program degenerated into political purges. Land reform ultimately benefited a new kind of absentee owner, the Saigonese bureaucrat. Corruption diluted American aid, so that little of it helped villagers trapped in the war-ravaged countryside or refugees hounded into inflation-ridden cities. Diem retreated more and more into a contracting circle of family members and army generals. His regime's growing isolation and dependence on the United States alarmed South Vietnamese nationalists.

To protest, a coalition of anti-Diem intellectuals, nationalists, harassed politicians, and Viet Minh Communists organized the National Liberation Front (NLF) in 1960. Its platform promised return to village rule, immediate land ownership for the peasants, and a coalition cabinet in Saigon. Discontent in the countryside propelled many recruits into the NLF's makeshift army, which Communist cadres soon dominated, partly because of their experience during the earlier guerrilla struggle against France. The NLF championed the communal traditions of the village rather than the alien dictatorship in Saigon, which relied on U.S. support.

The ensuing Communist-led war for national liberation set in motion a spiral of violence. The renewal of serious fighting panicked Washington into supplying Diem with billions of dollars and a growing corps of American advisers—nine hundred by 1960. In response, the Communist regime in Hanoi aided the insurgents, training recruits in the North. Then, after a five-year plan made their country the most heavily industrialized state in Southeast Asia by 1959, the North Vietnamese shipped large amounts of war material south along the Ho Chi Minh Trail. This primitive line of communication depended as much on human backs as on gasoline engines, and it permitted the NLF to make great progress in the face of America's reinforcements. This cycle of American reinforcement, leading to more aid from Hanoi and then more reinforcement, brought ever-greater American involvement in South Vietnam's survival.

Washington tried to break this cycle by asking Diem to reform his government, but he cared little about generating local popularity as long as he could rely on U.S. support. Despite American dissatisfaction with Diem, he seemed the only practical alternative to the NLF. The more isolated Diem became, the more American support he needed; yet the more aid he received, the more corrupt and unpopular he became.

During the 1950s, the Eisenhower administration was able to avoid decisions about direct military involvement by U.S. troops. The secretary of state suggested during a press conference that "the free world would intervene in Indochina rather than let the situation deteriorate." Having become involved, Dulles thought, American's prestige required victory. But the president demurred. Eisenhower was a charter member of the Never Again Club, a group of generals whose analyses of the Korean War left them resolutely opposed to another land war in Asia. He contradicted his chief adviser on foreign affairs. "I can conceive of no greater tragedy," he said "than for the United States to become engaged in all-out war in Indochina." The next administration would inherit Eisenhower's ambiguous legacy.

Intervention: Iran, Guatemala, Lebanon, Cuba

Vietnam was only one area of American concern. In the Middle East and Latin America, as in Southeast Asia, the decline of European power and the rise of local nationalism brought difficult policy dilemmas for the United States. In these areas, Eisenhower's extensive new foreign policy apparatus—encompassing a mix of economic pressure and covert action, as well as conventional military strength—was tested and refined.

In Iran, American economic interests had always been small; Britain held tightly to its petroleum monopoly in that oil-rich land. But in 1951, Iranian Prime Minister Mohammed Mossadegh nationalized Britain's Anglo-Iranian Oil Company. The State Department feared the precedent of nationalization of strategic raw materials. The CIA, which had previously received explicit orders to make the protection of American-owned supplies of raw materials one of its prime duties, went to work organizing and financing opposition to Mossadegh. Kermit Roosevelt, the grand-nephew of Theodore, orchestrated one of the CIA's most stunning "successes." In a swift operation in 1953, CIA agents brought crowds into the streets, forced Mossadegh out of office, and reinstalled their friend, Shah Reza Pahlevi. Under the terms of a renegotiated oil contract, American companies emerged holding 40 percent of the Iranian oil concession previously held by British Petroleum, and the shah launched a "modernization" program closely wedded to American interests. As the shah became more dictatorial, Iranians who opposed his rule came to blame the United States for installing and keeping him in power.

Events in Iran enabled the major oil companies to convince the Eisenhower administration to drop a large antitrust suit against them. In 1953, Eisenhower told his attorney general that because the giant oil companies supplied an essential commodity to the free world, the enforcement of antitrust laws "may be deemed secondary to the national security interest." Iran's attempted nationalization thus proved timely and doubly beneficial to the American-dominated international oil cartel, a cartel that—at that time—controlled the world price of oil.

The CIA's ability to manipulate politics in Iran encouraged the Eisenhower administration to expand its use of covert action. Headed by John Foster Dulles's brother Allen, the CIA next turned its attention toward Guatemala. President Jacobo Arbenz of Guatemala, who had been legally elected on a reform platform, challenged the United Fruit Company's long-standing dominance in his country by threatening to nationalize lands that the company left idle and unproductive. As in Iran, American business interests and government policymakers viewed economic nationalism as communism. Dulles, himself closely connected with the fruit company, saw Guatemala as one more battle in the global anti-Communist struggle. Eisenhower, who knew little about Latin America, accepted Dulles's assessment that Arbenz was controlled by Communists. Most members of Congress, Republicans and Democrats, backed Senator Lyndon Johnson's sense-of-the-Congress resolution demanding action to "keep Communism out of the Western Hemisphere." A Representative from Texas claimed that, "a Communist-dominated government in Guatemala is only 700 miles from Texas—only 960 miles, or a few hours' bomber time, from the refiners, the chemical plants, and the homes of my own Second District."

Ike authorized and the CIA carried out a covert 1954 operation in Guatemala that included economic strangulation, psychological warfare, and the funding of a pro-U.S. armed force to foment a coup. Under these pressures, the Arbenz government collapsed, and a dictatorship friendly to the U.S. government and to United Fruit entrenched itself. The generals who came into power carried out a systematic campaign of repression, with U.S. aid, that killed thousands of Guatemalans. (In 1999 President Bill Clinton would visit Guatemala and publicly admit that "support for military forces and intelligence units which engaged in violence and widespread repression was wrong, and the United States must not repeat that mistake.")

U.S.-backed repression in Guatemala and U.S. ties to other dictatorial regimes in the hemisphere reaped rising anti-Americanism in Latin America. During Vice President Richard Nixon's tour of Latin America in 1958, thousands of Venezuelans mobbed his motorcade, threatening American officials. This display of enmity against the United States got Eisenhower's attention. The president subsequently supported creation of an Inter-American Development Bank, and the State Department stopped awarding medals to dictator allies and shifted its praises to reformers such as Venezuela's Rómulo Betancourt. Still, American military aid continued to strengthen oligarchs and their military allies, who usually allied themselves against rising popular demands for economic and political change.

In another effort to contain Communist influence, the Eisenhower administration tried to frame a general doctrine covering American security interests in the Middle East, a region still reeling from the aftershocks of the Suez crisis and the Iranian coup. After weeks of dickering during the spring of 1957, Congress authorized the president to defend countries in the Middle East "against overt armed aggression from any nation controlled by international communism." This new Eisenhower Doctrine hardly fit the political realities of the area, in which older imperial tensions, regional and religious distrust, and the rise of fervent nationalism shaped events more than did superpower contests over communism. However, the Eisenhower Doctrine, like the Truman Doctrine before it, forced complex events into simple molds and made it easy to label any local challenge to American interests as Communist aggression.

During the summer of 1958, when rioting broke out in the small country of Lebanon, the doctrine had its first test. Animosity between Christians and Muslims, city and countryside, Nasserites and moderates was turning Lebanon into a tinderbox, and the country's established elements asked the United States to stabilize their power. They blamed growing riots on saboteurs from the newly organized United Arab Republic (Egypt and Syria). Anxious to check Nasserism, the United States and Britain both moved to protect their dangerously exposed oil pipelines in the area. Over 14,000 U.S. marines eventually waded ashore on Lebanese beaches in an intervention notable for its bloodlessness and short-range success. American troops set up a new, strongly anti-Nasser government in Beirut. In neighboring Jordan, the British restored King Hussein's control over Jordan's army.

This Anglo-American intervention provoked new fears of Western imperialism and likely pushed some Arab nationalists toward Moscow. Other Arabs began to turn away from the United States, not because they were pro-Communist, but because they suspected American motives and disliked its close alliance with Israel.

U.S. policy did not contain revolution everywhere. In fact, a leftist revolt succeeded in a place long considered a secure outpost of America's informal empire—Cuba. In 1959, a guerrilla leader named Fidel Castro converted his mountaintop rebellion into an island-wide social revolution that not only deposed Cuba's dictator, Fulgencio Batista, but also ended Cuba's dependence on the United States. The Cuban revolution initially attracted sympathy from many Americans. The rich sugar crop had benefited foreigners and Cuba's upper class, whereas most Cubans had suffered low wages and miserable living conditions. Batista's regime had grown notoriously corrupt. The prospect of honest government, social justice, and land redistribution provided support for the charismatic thirty-two-year-old Castro.

Welcomed by many Americans as an alternative to the repressive Batista, Castro soon encountered hostility as he tried to loosen his country's economic ties to the United States. After a disagreement with some American companies, Castro nationalized their holdings; Eisenhower retaliated by curtailing the amount of Cuban sugar the United States would import; Castro stepped up nationalization and turned toward the Soviet Union for aid. By the time this spiral of deteriorating relations ended, Castro had nationalized over a billion dollars worth of U.S. assets, killed thousands of Cubans as "enemies of the people," and frightened most of Cuba's upper middle class into exile in Florida. During a visit to the United States, Castro appealed to America's racial minorities to follow his example. Later, he joined hands with Nikita Khrushchev at the United Nations and declared himself a Communist.

The Eisenhower administration moved to drive Castro from power. It ended American imports of Cuban sugar, which had maintained the island's prices above world market levels. Under great pressure from Washington, the Organization of American States expelled Cuba, thus cutting off all of its aid to Castro's regime. These measures forced Castro to rely further on the Soviets. Anxious to take advantage of America's lost position, Khrushchev purchased Cuba's sugar crop in 1960 at an inflated price. CIA operatives began training a Cuban invasion force in Guatemala and plotting various kinds of sabotage against Castro's regime, but threats of American intervention only justified a further swing to the left by Castro. Attempted containment in the Caribbean, no less than in the Middle East, produced nationalist reactions often hostile to American goals.

The Eisenhower administration relied on its covert action capabilities to try to thwart potentially pro-Communist movements elsewhere as well. In 1958 the CIA supplied planes, pilots, and encouragement to a rebellion against Achmed Sukarno, the Indonesian president who drew some support from Indonesia's large Communist Party. When the attempted overthrow failed, the United States abandoned its Indonesian allies, and Sukarno tightened his hold on power. The CIA also maneuvered against Patrice Lumumba, a popular black nationalist in the Congo whose leftist leanings threatened the interests of U.S. and European mining companies. Lumumba was killed in 1961, although scholars still debate the extent of direct CIA involvement in his death. The subsequent administrations of John Kennedy and Lyndon Johnson faced nearly continual crises associated with the resultant civil war in the Congo, out of which emerged one of the world's most corrupt and oppressive dictators, Joseph Mobutu Sese Seko, who gained western support because of his staunch anticommunism.

REEVALUATION

On October 4, 1957, the Soviet Union orbited the first space satellite, Sputnik I. A month later Sputnik II, which weighed over 1,300 pounds and carried a live dog, spent several days in space. The accuracy and large payload of the Russian rockets caused alarm throughout America because of the potential military implications. Most military officials, however, recognized that America's manned bombers far outclassed Soviet defense systems. Although spectacular, Sputnik in no concrete way threatened the safety of the United States. Still, the Soviet satellites proved to be powerful symbols. Coming amid a recession, they ended America's easy confidence in its technological ascendance and created new, often exaggerated fears of Soviet strength.

A sense of vulnerability pervaded American life, and pressure built—from many directions—for greater expenditures on armaments. The Sputnik satellites frightened the Pentagon into deploying intermediate-range rockets in Britain, Turkey, and Italy. Meanwhile, the defense department channeled more money into research and development of new weapons systems. Defense intellectuals, gathered into research institutes and universities, supported calls for larger government funding of technological innovation and scientific discovery. Sensing a political advantage, many Democrats also advocated more military spending, hoping that it would stimulate the economy. Powerful business interests in such politically important areas as Long Island, Texas, and Southern California pressed Congress to increase lucrative defense contracts. This combination of American generals, defense intellectuals, politicians, and business leaders coalesced into a powerful group. Gradually, the idea spread that the United States suffered a missile gap vis-à-vis the Soviet Union, a dubious claim that John F. Kennedy used as an election slogan against the Republicans in the election of 1960.

Eisenhower recognized some of the problems he left his successor. He confided to Kennedy that "foreign affairs are in a mess" and warned the American people of "a burgeoning military-industrial complex." Eisenhower had tried to build a cost-conscious domestic program and to pursue peace abroad. He had, however, also endorsed an open-ended ideological crusade to refashion the world into a mold compatible with U.S. interests and had greatly expanded the government's foreign-policy commitments: a chain of anti-Communist military alliances, a proliferation of bases and armaments abroad, a new informational agency, and a large CIA emboldened by covert capabilities. He had helped set the stage for larger defense spending and even more ambitious cold-war crusading during the early 1960s.

SUGGESTED READINGS

Charles Alexander, *Holding the Line* (1975) is an older introduction to the Eisenhower years, and the early portions of Martin P. Wattenberg, *The Decline of American Political Parties, 1952–1980* (1984) set the political background. These can be updated with Chester Pach, Jr., and Elmo Richardson, *The Presidency of Dwight D. Eisenhower* (rev. ed., 1993), the relevant chapters of Gary Reichard, *Politics as Usual: The Age of Truman and Eisenhower* (1988), and Alonso Hamby, *Liberalism and Its Challengers* (1992). Stephen Ambrose's two-volume study, *Eisenhower* (1983, 1984), despite its flaws, will probably remain the standard source for years. See also Fred Greenstein's *The Hidden-Hand Presidency* (rev. ed., 1994); Herbert J. Parmet, *Eisenhower and the American Crusades* (1972); Robert F. Burk, *Dwight David Eisenhower* (1986); William B. Pickett, *Dwight David Eisenhower and American Power* (1993); Geoffrey Perret, *Eisenhower* (1999); William B. Pickett, *Eisenhower Decides to Run: Presidential Politics and Cold War Strategy* (2000); and Steve Neal, *Harry and Ike: The Partnership That Remade the Postwar World* (2001). Ike's own memoirs, *Mandate for Change and Waging Peace* (1963, 1965) are worthwhile.

Specialized studies include Gary Reichard, *The Reaffirmation of Republicanism* (1975); Burton J. Kaufman, *The Oil Cartel Case* (1978); Mark Rose, *Interstate: Express Highway Politics* (1979); Robert F. Burk, *The Eisenhower Administration and Civil Rights* (1984); Duane Tanabaum, *The Bricker Amendment: A Test of Eisenhower's Political Leadership* (1989); R. Alton Lee, *Eisenhower and Landrum-Griffin: A Study in Labor-Management Politics* (1990); Raymond J. Saulnier, *Constructive Years: The U.S. Economy under Eisenhower* (1991); John W. Sloan, *Eisenhower and the Management of Prosperity* (1991); Craig Allen, *Eisenhower and the Mass Media: Peace, Prosperity, and Prime Time TV* (1993); Jeff Broadwater, *Eisenhower and the Anti-Communist Crusade* (1992); Clarence G. Lasby, *Eisenhower's Heart Attack: How Ike Beat Heart Disease and Held on to the Presidency* (1997); and Peter J. Roman, *Eisenhower and the Missile Gap* (1996).

On foreign policy, Robert Divine, *Eisenhower and the Cold War* (1981) and Blanche Wiessen Cook, *The Declassified Eisenhower* (1981) offer differing interpretations. See also Joann P. Kreig, ed., *Dwight D. Eisenhower: Soldier, President and Statesman* (1987); H. W. Brands, *Cold Warriors: Eisenhower's Generation and American Foreign Policy* (1988); Robert R. Bowie and Richard H. Immerman, *Waging Peace: How Eisenhower Shaped an Enduring Cold War Strategy* (1998); Burton F.

Kaufman, *Trade and Aid: Eisenhower's Foreign Economic Policy* (1982); Richard A. Melanson and David Mayers, eds., *Reevaluating Eisenhower: American Foreign Policy in the Fifties* (1987); and Caroline Pruden, *Conditional Partners: Eisenhower, the United Nations, and the Search for a Permanent Peace* (1998).

The Eisenhower administration's emphasis on intelligence agencies and covert operations may be seen in several studies: William Blum, *The CIA: A Forgotten History* (1986); Robin Winks, *Cloak and Gown: Scholars in the American Secret War, 1939–1961* (1987); Stephen Ambrose and Richard H. Immerman, *Ike's Spies: Eisenhower and the Espionage Establishment* (1981); Richard H. Immerman, *The CIA in Guatemala: The Foreign Policy of Intervention* (1982); Michael R. Beschloss, *Mayday: Eisenhower, Khrushchev, and the U-2 Affair* (1986); Rhodri Jeffreys-Jones, *The CIA and American Democracy* (1989); Loch K. Johnson, *America's Secret Power: The CIA in a Democratic Society* (1989); Thomas F. Troy, *Donovan and the CIA: A History of the Establishment of the Central Intelligence Agency* (1981); John Prados, *President's Secret Wars: CIA and Pentagon Covert Operations since World War II* (1986); Scott Lucas, *Freedom's War: The American Crusade against the Soviet Union* (1999); Audrey R. Kahin and George McT. Kahin, *Subversion as Foreign Policy: The Secret Eisenhower and Dulles Debacle in Indonesia* (1995); and Nicholas Cullather, *Secret History: The CIA's Classified Account of its Operations in Guatemala, 1952–1954* (1999).

Specialized works on the Eisenhower era include Douglas Kinnard, *President Eisenhower and Strategy Management: A Study in Defense Politics* (1977); Saki Dockrill, *Eisenhower's New-Look National Security Policy, 1953–61* (1996); Laura McEnaney, *Civil Defense Begins at Home: Militarization Meets Everyday Life in the Fifties* (2000); David L. Snead, *The Gaither Committee, Eisenhower, and the Cold War* (1999); Richard G. Hewlett and Jack M. Holl, *Atoms for Peace and War, 1953–1961: Eisenhower and the Atomic Energy Commission* (1989); Campbell Craig, *Destroying the Village: Eisenhower and Thermonuclear War* (1998); Robert Divine, *Blowing in the Wind: The Nuclear Test-Ban Debate* (1978) and *The Sputnik Challenge: Eisenhower's Response to the Soviet Satellite* (1993); Allan M. Winkler, *Life Under a Cloud: American Anxiety About the Atom* (1993); Stuart W. Leslie, *The Cold War and American Science: The Military-Industrial-Academic Complex at MIT and Stanford* (1993); Ron Robin, *The Making of the Cold War Enemy: Culture and Politics in the Military-Intellectual Complex;* and John Fousek, *To Lead the Free World: American Nationalism and the Cultural Roots of the Cold War* (2000).

Regional studies of Eisenhower's foreign policy include Stephen G. Rabe, *Eisenhower and Latin America: The Foreign Policy of Anticommunism* (1988); Richard E. Welch, Jr., *Response to Revolution: The United States and the Cuban Revolution, 1959–1961* (1985); Thomas G. Paterson, *Contesting Castro: The United States and the Triumph of the Cuban Revolution* (1994); Piero Gleijeses, *Shattered Hope: The Guatemalan Revolution and the United States, 1944–54* (1991); Zachary Karabell, *Architects of Intervention: The United States, the Third World, and the Cold War, 1946–1962* (1999); David F. Schmitz, *Thank God They're On Our Side: The United States and Right-Wing Dictatorships, 1921–1965* (1999); Zhang Shu Guang, *Deterrence and Strategic Culture: Chinese-American Confrontations, 1949–1958* (1992); Robert J. McMahon, *The Cold War on the Periphery: The United States, India and Pakistan* (1994); Kenton J. Clymer, *Quest for Freedom: The United States and India's Independence* (1995); Isaac Alteras, *Eisenhower and Israel: U.S.-Israeli Relations, 1953–1960* (1993); Bonnie F. Saunders, *The United States and Arab Nationalism:*

The Syrian Case, 1953–1960 (1996); Nigel J. Ashton, *Eisenhower, Macmillan, and the Problem of Nasser: Anglo-American Relations and Arab Nationalism, 1955–59* (1997); G. Wyn Rees, *Anglo-American Approaches to Alliance Security, 1955–60* (1996); Cole C. Kingseed, *Eisenhower and Suez Crisis of 1956* (1995); William Rogers Louis, ed., *Suez, 1956: The Crisis and Its Consequences* (1989); Diane B. Kunz, *The Economic Diplomacy of the Suez Crisis* (1991); David W. Lesch, *Syria and the United States: Eisenhower's Cold War Policy in the Middle East* (1993); Herbert Druks, *The Uncertain Friendship: The U.S. and Israel from Roosevelt to Kennedy* (2001). For works on the Korean War, see the Suggested Readings at the end of Chapter 1.

African Americans and foreign policy are discussed in Brenda Gayle Plummer, *Rising Wind: Black Americans and U.S. Foreign Affairs, 1935–1960* (1996); Penny M. Von Eschen, *Race Against Empire: Black Americans and Anticolonialism, 1937–1957* (1997); Azza Salama Layton, *International Politics and Civil Rights Policies in the United States, 1941–1960* (2000); and Mary L. Dudziak, *Cold War and Civil Rights* (2001).

On cultural diplomacy, see Walter L. Hixson, *Parting the Curtain: Propaganda, Culture, and the Cold War, 1945–1961* (1997); Robert H. Haddow, *Pavilions of Plenty: Exhibiting American Culture Abroad in the 1950s* (1997); Richard Pells, *Not Like Us: How Americans Have Loved, Hated, and Transformed American Culture Since World War II* (1997); Naima Prebots, *Dance for Export: Cultural Diplomacy and the Cold War* (1998); Francis Stonor Saunders, *The Cultural Cold War: The CIA and the World of Arts and Letters* (2000); and Arch Puddington, *Broadcasting Freedom, The Cold War Triumph of Radio Free Europe and Radio Liberty* (2000).

On the deepening U.S. involvement in Vietnam during the 1950s, see the opening chapters of George Herring, *America's Longest War* (1986); Andrew J. Rotter, *The Path to Vietnam* (1987); Lloyd C. Gardner, *Approaching Vietnam: From World War II Through Dien Bien Phu* (1988); Melanie Billings-Yun, *Decision Against War: Eisenhower and Dien Bien Phu* (1988); James Arnold, *The First Domino: Eisenhower, the Military, and America's Intervention in Vietnam* (1991); David L. Anderson, *Trapped by Success: The Eisenhower Administration and Vietnam, 1953–1961* (1991); Lloyd C. Gardner and Ted Gittinger, eds., *Vietnam: The Early Decisions* (1997); and Mark Philip Bradley, *Imagining Vietnam and America: The Making of Postcolonial Vietnam, 1919–1950* (2000).

Eisenhower's controversial secretary of state is the subject of several good studies: Townshend Hoopes, *The Devil and John Foster Dulles* (1973); Ronald Pruessen, *John Foster Dulles* (1982); Mark Toulouse, *The Transformation of John Foster Dulles* (1985); and Richard Immerman, ed., *John Foster Dulles and the Diplomacy of the Cold War* (1989).

The 1950s were a period of intense debate over the direction of U.S. foreign policy. Some of the contemporary viewpoints may be found in Henry Kissinger, *Nuclear Weapons and Foreign Policy* (1957); Walt W. Rostow, *The United States in the World Arena* (1960); Maxwell Taylor, *An Uncertain Trumpet* (1960); and Robert Strausz-Hupe, et al., *Protracted Conflict* (1961). Memoirs include George B. Kistiakowsky, *A Scientist at the White House* (1976); Henry Cabot Lodge, Jr., *As It Was* (1976); and George F. Kennan, *Sketches from a Life* (1989).

4

Life during the 1950s

Sandwiched between the tumultuous decades of the 1940s and 1960s, the 1950s is often remembered as an island of tranquility, a time of affluence and social harmony. Fears of communism at home and abroad, however, continually punctured any serenity. Moreover, significant changes in the cultural and social rituals of daily life and important demographic shifts jarred the lives of most Americans.

GENDER AND FAMILY

Between the mid-1940s and 1957, the peak years of the "baby boom," the United States saw an unprecedented increase (nearly 50 percent) in the birthrate. This baby boom seemed especially striking when measured against the relatively low birthrates of the 1930s. Between 1940 and 1960 families had more children sooner and in closer succession. The birthrate for third children doubled and that for fourth children tripled. Economic growth encouraged couples to marry at a young age; during the early 1950s, nearly one-half of all brides were still teenagers. In contrast to the trend during the 1980s and 1990s, the average family size was larger for middle-and-upper-income families than for those with lower incomes. In 1955, a survey revealed that 40 percent of white women from middle-income families considered four to be the ideal number of children. Sheer numbers provided baby boomers with a vague generational identity. As youngsters, this population bulge stimulated school-building; as teenagers, it spearheaded a new consumption-oriented youth culture; in old age it would strain retirement and medical systems.

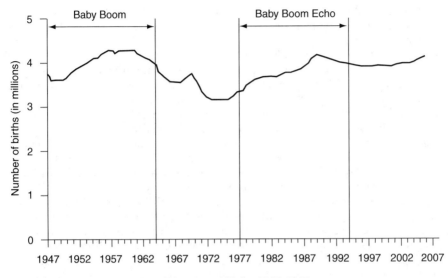

FIGURE 4–1　Baby Boom: Annual Number of Births, 1947–2007

The surge in the number of births after World War II lasted through the early 1960s. The "baby boom echo," children of the baby boom generation, began in the late 1970s and is projected to remain fairly stable for a number of years. What might be some of the causes and consequences of these trends?
Source: U.S. Department of Education, National Center for Education Statistics. Projections of Education Statistics to 2000.

The Baby Boom and the New Family Ideal

During the 1950s, the baby boom became closely associated with a new ideal of family life. Both parents were expected to contribute, ideally in collaboration, to making the home the key element in the social, cultural, and moral development of their children. In 1954, *McCall's,* a popular women's magazine, coined the term "togetherness" to describe the new family ideal. During one survey of middle-class couples, most respondents claimed that they had sacrificed nothing by marrying, and they listed children and security among the things they had gained. More than ever before in American history, family life became the center of popular culture, the place in which both parents amused and entertained, as well as reared and nurtured, their children. According to one approach, advanced by guides like *The Family Fun Book* and *Planning Your Home for Play,* the ideal home would become a kind of good-time, family clubhouse.

Advice manuals and magazines assigned many new, gender-specific tasks to mothers and fathers. Although advertisers hailed "labor-saving devices," such as washers and power vacuums, the amount of time women spent on housework actually increased during the 1950s. Women were expected, for example, to use the new household appliances to keep floors cleaner and linens whiter than ever before. While women's magazines featured recipes and redecorating ideas for mother, men's magazines, such as *Popular Mechanics,* showed dad how to make his home workshop the center of a cottage-based, do-it-yourself enterprise. While mother was sewing new draperies, father could be building their plywood valances.

Many social institutions supported this vision of family life. Following in the footsteps of William Levitt, who had opened his first Levittown home on Long Island in 1947, giant development companies and smaller builders rushed into the home construction business. Washington encouraged the postwar home-buying spree. The Federal Housing Administration (FHA) program, begun during the 1930s, and the Veterans Administration (VA) subsidies, established for veterans of World War II and the Korean conflict, reduced the amount of money required for a down payment on a house to less than 10 percent of the purchase price and guaranteed relatively low-interest (2 or 3 percent), long-term (thirty-year) mortgages. By the mid-1950s, the housing shortage of the immediate postwar period seemed a distant memory. Couples discovered that it was cheaper to buy their own homes than to rent. In the twenty-year period after 1940, the number of families owning their own homes increased by 50 percent; by 1960, fully one-fourth of the U.S. housing stock had been built during the previous decade.

While the government-supported housing industry was providing middle-income families with homes of their own, other financial institutions were helping out with the furnishings. The practice of buying consumer goods on credit was not a postwar invention, but the 1950s saw an unprecedented surge in installment buying. The J.C. Penney department store chain, which had long refused to use charge accounts, finally issued its first credit card in 1957. Financing arrangements and charge accounts allowed homeowners to obtain new appliances, furniture, and decorative items of all kinds. Although the amount of a family's income that was spent on food and clothing rose only modestly during the late 1940s and 1950s, outlays for appliances and furnishings increased by nearly 250 percent.

The New Suburbs

Building a family and buying a home became widely identified with new suburban developments. The population of central cities increased by about 8 percent during the 1950s, whereas surrounding suburban areas grew by nearly 50 percent. Not surprisingly, 85 percent of the housing built in the 1940s and 1950s was located in new suburban areas. Wealth and income, as well as people, came to these suburbs. According to one estimate, less than 20 percent of the U.S. population lived in suburbs, but they accounted for 30 percent of the nation's annual income during the early 1950s.

The new suburbs not only tended to be stratified by wealth and income, they were also segregated by race. Until the Supreme Court declared restrictive covenants unconstitutional in 1948, the standard lease for all homes in Levittown declared that no persons "other than members of the Caucasian race" could live there; it did allow, however, "the employment and maintenance of other than Caucasian domestic servants." Even after such arrangements lost any legal force, families of color represented only a minuscule percentage of the residents. The new, postwar suburbs remained among the most segregated areas in the cold-war United States.

Home planners hailed suburbia's new "ranch style" home as the ideal habitat for consumer-oriented families. In contrast to the boxlike bungalow, which had dominated earlier home-building styles, or even the Cape Cod featured in the earliest Levittown developments, the ranch house expressed the openness and adaptability associated with postwar family life. The kitchen, which had been tucked away as the wife's special domain at the rear of the old bungalow, came to serve as both the point of entry and the center of daily life in most ranch-style homes. Planners still expected women to do most of the meal preparation, but the kitchen was no longer exclusively theirs. The ranch home, generally configured so that living patterns could "flow" into every part of the house, made the kitchen into a gathering place for the entire family. *Tomorrow's House: A Complete Guide for the Home-Builder* (1946) also called for a new household space, the "family room," a place "within which the members of a family will be better equipped to enjoy each other on the basis of mutual respect" and affection. Builders of the 1950s heeded this call. A family-recreation room—and, ideally, even a separate play room for children—provided additional space for the leisure-oriented lifestyle that the middle-class family was being urged to embrace.

Many people celebrated suburban life. Its predominantly white, middle-class residents aspired to economic success. Suburbia's broadly shared value system seemed, in the eyes of many observers, to bring a sense of comfort and community. Even if suburbia promoted conformity, this condition might serve as a balm for rootlessness and a cushion against the anxieties of rapid social change. Looking beyond the home and family life, many architects hailed the suburban shopping mall—the first entirely indoor, climate-controlled mall opened in Edina, Minnesota, in 1956—for creating a business-cultural center that would provide a focus for community life. The suburban mall, these planners argued, offered a streamlined, purified version of the nation's now-decaying downtown shopping areas.

Suburbia, however, produced complaints as well as compliments. Viewed as a cultural phenomenon, it became an object of caricature and derision. The folk singer Malvina Reynolds called suburban homes "little boxes made of tickytacky" and jabbed at the men who all drank "their martinis dry" and the children who all went "to summer camp and then to the university." Critics of taste snorted at the new suburbs: the monotony of the architecture; the obsession with a manicured, pesticide-enhanced lawn; and the clutter of autos, tricycles, lawn mowers, and children.

Social critics claimed that postwar suburbia promised, but often failed to produce, a sense of contentment. A new literary genre, exemplified by books such as *The Crack in the Picture Window* (1956), focused on the tensions of daily life in what one critic called "Disturbia." In this view, suburban living generated a myriad of problems. Burgeoning private housing developments often overcrowded existing public facilities and created the kind of urban-style congestion that suburbanites had hoped to escape. Payments for home mortgages, autos, and consumer goods brought financial worries. Suburban living generally meant that the distance between home and work grew longer and longer, and those who commuted in private automobiles contributed to clogged freeways and polluted air.

Meanwhile, many public planners also attacked the economic and political impact of the new suburbs. Suburban expansion, they argued, left low-income and nonwhite families in decaying central cities and drained vital tax dollars and jobs to outlying areas. Similarly, the suburban shopping malls took customers, revenues, and ultimately businesses themselves from downtown commercial areas. A mall may have promised people a new public space, but it remained under private control, an arrangement that gave its owner broad legal authority to exclude people and ideas deemed disruptive. Legal battles broke out over whether malls could exclude political activists who had the right to use downtown streets.

Women's Work and Domesticity

The baby boom and suburban lifestyles may have placed a new emphasis on the home as a woman's proper place, but the number of women employed outside the home rose steadily during the 1950s. Historically, a large percentage of women from blue-collar families and women of color had always participated in the paid labor force; for women from these groups, employment trends of the 1950s represented little change. By 1960, however, more than one-third of *all* the women of working age were employed, and nearly one-third of all wives worked outside of the home. For many families, the extra income contributed by women sustained the middle-class lifestyle so celebrated during the 1950s. The rising level of personal consumption rested, in part, on the growing number of women who joined the paid labor force.

Women found the greatest job opportunities in areas that had become designated as "women's work": clerical and secretarial jobs, teaching positions, and the lower-paid sectors of retail sales. Women's work during the 1950s carried distinguishing markers. Jobs were often part-time; held after the age of thirty-five or forty, when children were no longer at home during the day; and not oriented toward a long-term career. In addition, employment for women was generally low paying, on the theory that a woman's income was always a secondary one, providing niceties, but not necessities, for a family. Although women were attending college in unprecedented numbers, few received graduate degrees, and the number of women employed during the 1950s in many professions, including college teaching, actually dropped from that of earlier decades. Women's employment, while becoming widespread, retained the stigma of being low paying and conferring low status.

Despite the rising numbers of working women, the ideal of female domesticity nonetheless persisted during the 1950s. Psychologists tended to diagnose signs of women's discontent as a failure to adjust to their "natural" passive and subordinate role. Popular magazines even featured articles that equated happiness with intellectual mediocrity: A *Good-Housekeeping* column advised that a woman with a grade-point average of "C" was "more likely to succeed" than a woman of great intelligence because she had a greater chance for a lasting marriage and a contented family. If a woman showed concerns about issues related to equal rights or feminism, such an interest likely reflected some deep-seated neurosis or social maladjustment, most psychologists claimed. A national poll in 1957 reported that 80 percent of the respondents believed that people who chose not to marry were sick and immoral. Even institutions of higher education emphasized marriage and family. College presidents and campus speakers stressed how higher education would prepare women to marry and serve the nation by raising virtuous, industrious sons and dutiful, domesticated daughters.

Images of domesticity in the 1950s became linked, more than ever before, to women's roles as consumers. Advertisers geared most of their campaigns to women. *Better Homes and Gardens,* a women's magazine (edited by men) with a circulation of millions, exemplified the trend. Advertisements took up far more than half the space, and the remaining pages contained tips on how to consume efficiently and "scientifically"—how to plan quick meals, determine which washing machine to buy, keep a family budget, and so on. Both the ads and the articles often emphasized saving money, but even these pieces were designed to stimulate consumer tastes and pitch new products. Women's magazines of the 1950s, always projecting a white, middle-class lifestyle as the universal norm, both reflected and reinforced the link between domesticity and consumption.

Along with this emphasis on more "scientific" housekeeping techniques came advice on "scientific" childbearing and child-rearing practices. Prior to World War II, the majority of births had not taken place in hospitals; many were supervised by a midwife. During the postwar era, more and more women had their children in hospitals, relying on male physicians who employed a variety of painkilling methods. Childbearing became safer but also more institutionalized and impersonal. Meanwhile, sales of commercial baby food soared, and women shifted in massive numbers from breast- to bottle-feeding. In child-rearing practices, outside expertise was also exalted. Dr. Benjamin Spock's *Baby and Child Care* (first published in 1948) rivaled the Bible in sales and stood next to it as a guide to appropriate conduct in most middle-class homes. Although Dr. Spock cautioned mothers against becoming too tied to their children, he nonetheless saw full-time motherhood as the most desirable role for women and essential to a child's physical and emotional health.

Although much of the popular culture of the 1950s glorified the role of mother and homemaker, recent studies emphasize that other messages about women's proper roles circulated as well. Women's magazines regularly praised women who held jobs outside the home or who served as public officials. Women were often urged to take more active roles in public affairs. Similarly, the popular media sympathetically covered problems encountered by wives and mothers, frequently addressing the burdens of housework and the frustrations of child-rearing.

Moreover, although the dominant media generally portrayed feminist activism as outmoded and deviant, women associated with the strong prewar women's rights movements continued to address political issues. Members of the National Woman's Party consistently lobbied Congress on behalf of an Equal Rights Amendment. Groundbreaking studies in women's history included Mary Beard's *Woman as a Force in History* (1946) and Eleanor Flexner's *Century of Struggle* (1959). Zora Neale Hurston continued her ethnographic writing on African American women. And the sociologist Mirra Komarovsky published her classic work on behalf of gender equality, *Women in the Modern World* (1953). These and similar efforts helped to establish the intellectual basis for a revitalized women's movement during the 1960s.

Organization Men and Women

Despite the era's family ideal, large corporate organizations often intruded into the lives of many during the 1950s. The person whom the writer William H. Whyte described in *The Organization Man* (1956) established his primary roots not in a particular town or region but within a corporate structure. The business corporation provided the setting in which he defined himself and gauged his status. He did, of course, withdraw from the corporate world to his home and family each day, but this retreat occupied only a few evening and weekend hours. Sociological studies claimed that success as a husband and father and occupational advancement usually varied inversely. Home and office were seen as separate and competing spheres, and the organization would often win out as the primary frame of reference.

The economic growth that spurred the rapid occupational mobility of the 1950s reinforced corporate loyalty. A young executive who displayed dedication and moderate talent could generally rise through the corporate hierarchy. But career advancement could also require moving around the country at the company's behest. "We never make a man move," one company president explained. "Of course, he kills his career if he doesn't. But we never make him do it." This kind of geographic mobility strengthened the bond between employee and company, for it hindered development of strong ties to a geographic community and could bring the organization into the family circle as an important decision-maker. Popular culture of the 1950s featured dramas that explored the conflict between organizational and familial loyalty.

The relationship of women to the large business organization was quite different. To some young women, a position in the corporate world may have initially promised excitement and independence. However, during the 1950s, most corporations generally hired women only for positions as secretaries or typists, jobs in which pay was low and a woman was called a "girl" no matter what her age. Consequently, commitment to the corporation generally did not transcend dollars and cents, and younger women often deserted such jobs for domestic life, if it became economically possible to do so. This turnover phenomenon bolstered the claim that large businesses needed to recruit men, and ignore women, when it came to staffing the top-levels of their corporate hierarchy.

Meanwhile, the wives of corporate executives also became organization women, deriving income and social status from their husbands' jobs. A wife's identity often came through her husband, and the model corporate wife was supposed to feel devotion to the business world that she seldom saw. However, this obligation of loyalty, together with the husband's unfamiliarity with his spouse's domestic routine, drove subtle wedges between married couples in their search for family "togetherness." *The Man in the Gray Flannel Suit,* a popular book and motion picture of the mid-1950's, focused on such tensions.

Sexual Politics

Behind the promotion of the family ideal often lay fears of uncontrolled sexuality. In mainstream culture the threat posed by sexualized women was often compared to the destructive effects of uncontrolled atomic energy. Women who expressed their sexuality became typed as "bombshells," and the brief bathing suit introduced during the 1940s became popularly known as the "biki-ni," after the site of an atomic explosion. As historian Elaine Tyler May has shown, the foreign-policy crusades of the cold-war period often had their domestic counterparts in the battle to "contain" sexuality.

The policing of sexuality targeted teenagers. With so many teenagers getting married, the high-school years, more than ever before, seemed a crucial time for warnings about the dangers of premarital sex, especially when many states regulated birth control and virtually all prohibited abortions. High schools required classes in health education, which used films with titles such as *What to Do on a Date* and *Dating Do's and Don't's* as a means of portraying proper sexual behavior.

The nation's moral guardians supplemented warnings about promiscuity with the promotion of peer-oriented rituals that might help to channel a teenager's sexual energies. High schools sponsored clubs, sock-hops, and other social events as a means of gaining influence, if not control, over the leisure activities of students. Meanwhile, a growing bevy of experts on teenage sexuality endorsed the practice of "going steady." A relatively new turn in boy-girl relationships, high-school (and even junior-high) students were expected to pair off in couples. Going steady became popularized in such teen anthems as The Five Satins' "To the Aisle" and Ricky Nelson's "I Believe (You're Going Steady with Nobody Else but Me)." Commercial entrepreneurs supported this relationship with a wide variety of rings, pins, bracelets, and other trinkets that could serve as signs that two teenagers had forged a one-to-one relationship—a dress rehearsal for the kind of stable marriage idealized during the postwar era.

Teenagers, however, received mixed messages. As early as 1944, when *Seventeen* magazine first appeared, the advertising industry had begun to recognize young people as a special audience with, as one observer put it, "a sense of identity, of purpose, of belonging." During the 1950s, teenage girls became a growth market for the fashion and cosmetics industries. According to one estimate, teenage girls devoted nearly one-fourth of their total expenditures to cosmetics and other beauty products. Thus, at the same time that young women were hearing warnings about the dangers of uncontrolled sexuality, they began to be targeted through sexualized images of beauty. The Barbie doll (introduced in 1959) and the latest bevy of Hollywood starlets celebrated a slim-waisted, big-breasted ideal. Young women were not only confronted with a set of conflicting messages about sexuality, summed up in the phrase "naughty but nice," but expectations of beauty that only a very few could hope to achieve. In contrast to a popular TV show of the 1970s that depicted the 1950s as a series of "Happy Days," historian Wini Breines entitled her 1992 memoir-social history *Young, White, and Miserable.*

The era's dominant emphasis on monogamous relationships, within an idealized nuclear family, existed alongside other powerful centrifugal forces. Dr. Alfred Kinsey of the University of Indiana published studies in 1948 and 1953 on sexual behavior in the United States. Kinsey's research—which has come under critical scrutiny in recent years for making broad generalizations on the basis of limited, randomly collected evidence—claimed that people were engaging in a wider range of sexual practices, more often, and with more partners than anyone had ever thought. Despite almost antiseptic prose, Kinsey's studies on the sexual behavior of men and women became best-sellers and their suspect data widely popularized.

FIGURE 4–2   Beauty and Success

Ads for cosmetics, which filled popular
magazines, suggested that both women and
men could purchase sex appeal.

The greatest popularizer of new attitudes toward sexuality, at least among men, was not the scholarly Dr. Kinsey, however, but the flamboyant (or pathetically juvenile, according to his critics) Hugh Hefner. During the late 1940s and early 1950s, laws aimed at sexually explicit publications had been facing greater scrutiny from the courts. The First Amendment to the Constitution, civil libertarians argued, should prevent governmental censors from writing their own sexual mores into law. Although legal definitions of what was obscene or pornographic remained unsettled, there was enough liberalization for entrepreneurs like Hefner. In December 1953, he published the first edition of *Playboy,* heralded as "entertainment for men," and tested the boundaries of First Amendment protection for sexually oriented literature.

Hefner used *Playboy,* which highlighted an unclothed "playmate next door" in every issue, to expound his philosophy of a "liberated" lifestyle based on mass consumption and sexual experimentation. The *Playboy* philosophy, as Hefner explained it during the 1950s, also stressed liberation, for men, from all of those restraints, both sexual and financial, associated with the cold-war ideal of family "togetherness." A monogamous marriage and the nuclear family were traps that ensnared men and robbed them of money that could be spent on hi-fi equipment, sports cars, and attractive young women. *Playboy's* philosophy, according to historian Barbara Ehrenreich, was part of a "male revolt" against the dominant model of home life in which the husband earned the bulk of his family's income and his wife made the major decisions (though in a spirit of togetherness) about what to buy and how to raise the children. Hefner did not advise a "playboy" to abandon his career or to stop making money; he should simply forget about sharing his paycheck with a wife and family. Any man who wanted to enjoy the freedom that the cold-war United States supposedly promised, *Playboy* concluded, should remain sexually active and resolutely single.

Mixed messages also emerged about homosexuality. The 1940s and 1950s represented, in some ways, a period of liberation for gay men and lesbians. The familiarity of military life during World War II had provided new opportunities for single-sex relationships, and postwar life allowed homosexuals to gather, away from the glare of small-town scrutiny, in a growing urban subculture. Whereas most large cities had a number of bars catering to gay men, lesbians generally preferred to seek companionship through more private "friendship networks." Nevertheless, the results were the same: a growing sense of individual and group identity.

The issue of homosexuality gained considerable visibility from the Kinsey Reports. They claimed that people with "homosexual histories" could be found "in every age group, in every social level, in every conceivable occupation," and in virtually every part of the country. Kinsey's findings, on the one hand, helped to empower homosexuals by suggesting that homosexuality was not limited to the fringes of society. On the other hand, the idea that homosexuals could be anywhere increased the fears of people who were already opposed to homosexual lifestyles.

In the dominant culture, homosexuality came to be depicted as another of those "diseases" that, like communism and juvenile delinquency, threatened the nation and needed to be contained. Anti-Communists even claimed that homosexuals, if they were not already inclined toward communism because of their own "alien" lifestyles, could prove particularly susceptible to blackmail by Soviet agents. In 1953, the Eisenhower administration endorsed this theory with an executive order that prohibited homosexuals from holding government jobs. This kind of blacklisting at the national level energized local "purity crusaders." Police departments and district attorneys could cite the example of the national government and anticommunism when unleashing their own campaigns against gays and lesbians.

COMMERCIAL CULTURE

In the relatively prosperous 1950s, the notion of freedom generally connoted the liberty to choose from an ever-expanding array of cultural and entertainment products. By 1950, consumers were already spending twice as much money on entertainment as on rent or mortgage payments, a total expenditure equal to one-seventh of the GNP. Throughout the decade, leisure-time activities further exploded.

Travel and Sports

The travel industry rapidly expanded after World War II. To those who could afford the price, travel agencies marketed package tours to Europe. In only two weeks travelers could absorb the culture of the "Old World." For those who lacked the money, or who had already toured the Continent, the United States provided its own new vacation spots. Freshly built motels, their quality certified by motor clubs or franchise owners, began to replace the old, independently owned tourist cabins that *film noir* portrayed as centers of sin. When travelers reached Southern California, Las Vegas, or Miami Beach, they found luxury resort complexes that offered nightclubs for adults, recreation for children, and kennels for family pets.

Professional sports, which had suffered reduced schedules during the war years, quickly regained, and then surpassed, earlier levels of attendance. Major League Baseball welcomed back the stars, such as Joe DiMaggio and Ted Williams, who had served in the armed forces and dropped the lesser talents and fading veterans who had filled out team rosters during World War II. The late 1940s and early 1950s proved to be the last hurrah for baseball's old minor-league system. Many cities and smaller towns, before television hijacked customers, supported professional baseball. With only sixteen major-league clubs, there was a surplus of talented players to stock the minors.

In the context of the cold war, baseball promoted itself as a symbol of the openness and equality of American society. Publicists celebrated it as an integral part of the American way of life. One prominent writer-broadcaster, Bill Stern, invented uplifting stories about the national pastime. A dying Abraham Lincoln, Stern once solemnly claimed, had told an aide to "keep baseball going; the country needs it." To accept baseball's claim of being a leader on racial and social issues, however, required ignoring crucial aspects of "the game." In 1947 Jackie Robinson had become the first player of African descent to play in the major leagues since the nineteenth century, but only exceptionally talented black and Latino athletes found spots in the newly integrated teams of the

For a **NEW** kind of vacation...take a Greyhound Expense-Paid

AMAZING AMERICA TOUR!

two days to two months of pre-planned pleasure ...
with reservations, sightseeing included at one low price!

GREYHOUND'S thrilling *Amazing America Tours* are complete pleasure trips planned in advance by experts — and including hotel accommodations, itineraries, and sightseeing side trips. Choose from hundreds of tours like these:

PAUL BUNYAN CIRCLE
7 Days from Minn'pls $38.75
YELLOWSTONE NATIONAL PARK
Three Days $44.75
NEW ENGLAND CIRCLE
8 Days from New York $54.55
LOS ANGELES
Six Days $24.65
EVERGREEN CIRCLE
3 Days from Seattle $21.85

MEXICO CITY
Eight Days $65.15
WASHINGTON, D. C.
Four Days $19.75
NIAGARA FALLS
Three Days $11.75
MACKINAC ISLAND
Four Days $35.80
GREAT SMOKIES
Four Days $60.50
COLORADO SPRINGS
Five Days $35.60
NEW YORK CITY
Five Days $25.05

To these Tour prices, add Greyhound round-trip fare from your home. U.S. tax extra. Prices subject to change.

FREE! "AMAZING AMERICA" VACATION TOUR FOLDER
Greyhound Information Center, 105 W. Madison, Chicago 2, Ill.—Send me a free illustrated folder telling all about the tour in which I am interested.

MY TOUR PREFERENCE

NAME

ADDRESS

CITY_____STATE_____ A7-50

Giant statue of Paul Bunyan and his Blue Ox at Bemidji, Minn.

GREYHOUND

FIGURE 4–3 Amazing America Tour!

The travel industry boomed during the 1950s, promoting tourism by planes, trains, automobiles—and the Greyhound Bus.
Source: "Amazing America Tour." Item #: T2753. Ad*Access. 1999. Rare Book, Manuscript, and Special Collections Library, Duke University. [http://scriptorium.lib.duke.edu/adaccess/]. The Trademarks are Registered Trademarks of Greyhound Lines, Inc. Used with Permission.

1950s. Positions such as second-string catcher or reserve infielders and out-fielders invariably went to players of European descent. Moreover, everyone who played professional baseball, including the top stars in the major leagues, remained tied to a monopolistic business system in which teams could contractually "reserve" a player's services forever. Owners enjoyed absolute power to trade a player from team to team. Conversely, even a star player possessed little bargaining leverage, and major-league salaries lagged behind comparable pay in the rest of the entertainment industry.

Professional boxing, plagued by underworld domination, lacked baseball's reputation but still attracted large crowds. Joe Louis, who had symbolized that sports could become an avenue of opportunity for African-American men, finally concluded his long reign as heavyweight champion. Ray Robinson, another black fighter from Detroit and the first of several "Sugar Rays," lost only one of nearly one hundred bouts between 1943 and 1951 and won acclaim as the greatest fighter, "pound for pound," of all time. A stocky Italian-American, Rocky Marciano, bulled through forty-nine opponents before retiring in 1955 as the undefeated heavyweight champion. A bout for a world championship (limited to one in only eight weight divisions during this era) and club fights in neighborhood arenas all made money. Professional boxing became a prime-time staple of network television. Meanwhile, though, the image of the penniless, punch-drunk ex-boxer became more than a popular cultural cliché. Even Louis and Robinson, among the highest paid entertainer-athletes of their day, retired with only a fraction of the money they had earned.

Professional wrestling and Roller Derby, pseudo-sports that dated back to the 1930s, also reached prime-time television. Carefully contrived and scripted in advance, professional wrestling (as distinguished from the amateur sport) offered simple morality plays: A villain, often claiming to be from Germany or Japan, abused a long-suffering hero until some dramatic reversal sealed the bully's fate. Justice and the American Way of Life ultimately triumphed. A variety of different gambits and a flexible catalog of "rules" allowed promoters to vary scenarios and lure fans to upcoming matches. Only Roller Derby, with two teams of skaters careening around a banked, wooden track, offered a comparable blend of feigned mayhem and cultural symbolism. According to Roller Derby's publicity, "two [recent] impacts have hit the American public—the atom bomb and the Roller Derby—and it appears the latter will have the most permanent effect."

Roller Derby rapidly faded away, but virtually every other (male) sport thrived during the 1950s. Bowling, golf, and tennis attracted growing crowds to professional tournaments and matches, and millions of amateurs took to the lanes, links, and courts. Professional hockey and basketball, which had established firm roots only in the Northeast by World War II, slowly gained national audiences in the postwar period. Professional basketball achieved needed continuity and stature with the gradual formation, and racial integration, of the National Basketball Association (NBA). Football remained the premier sport on college campuses, and the professional version made great strides. The Cleveland Browns and the Los Angeles Rams, both of which featured African-American players, became the dominant powers in a revamped National Football League (NFL). By the end of the 1950s, the NFL stood ready to challenge major league baseball as the nation's leading spectator sport.

The Hollywood Motion Picture Industry

Meanwhile, the Hollywood film industry struggled. In 1946, weekly attendance had averaged nearly ninety million people, and people spent nearly ninety cents of every entertainment dollar at the movie theater. Then, Hollywood began to lose ground. By 1953, the weekly audience had been nearly cut in half, and revenues suffered accordingly at the box office. Although conventional wisdom blamed television for this decline, many other forces were at work. In 1948, the major Hollywood studios settled a longstanding antitrust case and agreed to end the practice of owning motion picture theaters. By producing, distributing, and showing films, federal prosecutors had argued, Hollywood monopolized the movie business. Forced to sell existing theaters and prohibited from building new ones of its own, Hollywood lost valuable sources of revenue. More important, the growth of other leisure activities during the 1950s provided Hollywood with considerable competition for the entertainment dollar. People were spending money on a variety of other recreational and leisure activities, including gardening, golfing, and in-home, do-it-yourself projects.

Director Billy Wilder's *Sunset Boulevard* (1950) bade a cynical good-bye to the old Hollywood. This classic *noir* begins with a corpse floating in a Beverly

FIGURE 4-4   Roller Derby.

This popular form of sports-entertainment attracted live and TV audiences.
Source: Minnesota Historical Society.

Hills swimming pool, and the dead man, a second-rate screenwriter, narrates the remainder of the flash-backed story. Norma Desmond, a middle-aged silent film star played by Gloria Swanson, lives under the illusion that she will triumphant-ly return to the silver screen in a biblical epic. A hopeful call from her old studio turns out to be merely a request to use her antique automobile as a prop, and she drifts even further into a fantasy world. The final sequence reveals that the actress has killed the screenwriter and gone completely mad. *Sunset Boulevard* suggests that mid-century Hollywood, like Norma Desmond, sustained itself on illusions while madly seeking to recapture its faded glory. One prominent studio head, en-raged by the film's portrayal of the industry, urged that Wilder be blacklisted.

Hollywood itself experimented with ways of luring people to half-empty theaters. First, the major studios drastically cut the number of films they pro-duced, and the classic B-picture, which had served since the 1930s as the sec-ond half of nearly every theater's double feature, became an early casualty. Even the B-western—the genre that had turned cinema cowpokes like Gene Autry, Roy Rogers, and Dale Evans into national heroes—disappeared

While many western stars and other B-film stalwarts, such as Ronald Rea-gan, were galloping over to television, Hollywood tried to redirect the savings gained from its slimmed-down production schedule. One strategy was to target a specific clientele, such as the fans of *film noir,* rather than a mass audience. Similarly, studios revived the kind of "adult film" that had prompted the Hollywood Production Code of 1934. By addressing subjects such as impotence, adultery, and nymphomania, Hollywood portrayed itself, on these issues at least, to be in the forefront of a fight for free expression. Lurid lobby cards and advertising copy proclaimed that Hollywood dealt with subjects "too daring to film until now." Another stratagem was to produce big-budget blockbusters that offered the kind of "quality entertainment" unavailable on television. Biblical epics, such as *The Ten Commandments* (1956), and films based on classic novels, such as *Around the World in 80 Days* (1956), became staples of the 1950s.

Hollywood also introduced new ways to see films. In 1953, the industry unveiled the 3-D cycle, a string of movies filmed in a three-dimensional process that gave the illusion of onscreen projectiles hurtling toward the audience. The flimsy 3-D glasses needed to view these films proved a marketing liability, and this craze quickly passed. Hollywood found more success with the drive-in theater. In 1947, there had been fewer than 600 of these in the country; by the end of the 1950s, there were nearly 5,000. Drive-ins, which were initially aimed at the family audience, revived the double feature—and even the triple bill; they also offered snack bars, playgrounds for children, and laundry facilities. In addition, Hollywood unveiled a wider screen for all theaters during the 1950s, and processes like Cinemascope, Vista Vision, and Panavision made the old, square screen a quaint relic. Finally, Hollywood introduced even larger screens for seeing its blockbuster films, including Todd-AO (for movies such as *Around the World in 80 Days*) and Cinerama (for novelties like *This is Cinerama*).

Hollywood could not avoid cold-war politics. Avowedly anti-Communist films, one-dimensional jeremiads such as *My Son John* (1952), flopped at the box office, but those that could deliver their messages more obliquely gained wide acclaim. *On the Waterfront* (1954) allowed screenwriter Budd Schulberg and director Elia Kazan, former members of the Hollywood left who had cooperated with anti-Communist investigative committees during the blacklisting era, to defend people who inform on former friends and allies. Filled with Christian imagery, *On the Waterfront* features Marlon Brando as a former prizefighter who testifies against a corrupt union boss, Johnny Friendly (Lee J. Cobb). Critics of the blacklist denounced the film for simplifying complex moral and political issues, while its supporters praised it for portraying the kind of individual integrity on which, they insisted, democratic government ultimately rests. Hollywood's establishment rallied behind the movie, which garnered eight Academy Awards. *On the Waterfront* remains a contested symbol of the movie industry's uneasy relationship with cold-war politics.

Relentlessly in search of patrons, Hollywood experimented with offbeat films that eschewed Tinseltown glamour. Orson Welles, long scorned by the major studios as too quirky and independent, returned to direct and star in *A Touch of Evil* (1959), a movie that simultaneously celebrates and mocks the conventions of *film noir.* Racial tension provided the backdrop for several films, the most popular being *The Defiant Ones* (1956), a chain-gang story in which interracial brotherhood triumphs over bigotry. The cold-war climate did not chill all critical expression, and *Paths of Glory* (1957) indicts military leaders for corrupt values and portrays war as anything but a glorious enterprise. The film did poorly at the box office but won its youthful director, Stanley Kubrick, considerable acclaim.

Directors in the mold of Welles and Kubrick were attracting attention during the 1950s as the *"auteur"* approach to film criticism gained currency. Imported from France, *auteurism* singled out directors who could supposedly surmount the bureaucratic restraints of Hollywood and use their films, much like authors of a novel or an essay, to make personal statements. Reviewers in the *auteur* vein often singled out directors, such as Douglas Sirk and Samuel Fuller, whose work ordinarily merited scant critical attention. As the giant Hollywood film factories struggled, directors such as Alfred Hitchcock could use *auteurism* as a way to obtain greater personal control over their movies. In turn, the revamped studios began marketing films on the basis of the reputation of *auteur* directors such as Hitchcock and John Huston.

Television

During the 1950s, television thrived. TV sets not only appeared in homes but in various public places, especially neighborhood taverns. Bar-owners rearranged their establishments so that the TV set became the focus of attention. A few even introduced theater-style seating to facilitate watching sporting events. In 1945, only a few people had ever seen television. By 1960, nearly 90 percent of families owned at least one set. In little more than a decade, television replaced movies and radio as the primary medium for representing everyday life and transmitting cultural and political values across generations.

Picture tubes expanded, up to 21 inches, and manufacturers encased them in finely finished wooden cabinets. These sets—"handcrafted and hand rubbed," proclaimed the advertisements—were to complement the decor of any middle-class living room. Although the electronics industry would soon introduce less expensive and less bulky TV sets, which could be plopped down in every room in the house, television viewing during the 1950s generally revolved around a large, wooden cabinet, a kind of "electronic hearth" that was designed to attract the entire family to its warm (though still black-and-white) glow.

The TV set was only one of the new products that television spawned. To allow families to watch without a meal-time interruption, the TV tray and the frozen TV dinner provided alternatives to the dining room table and a prepared-from-scratch meal. Soon, a variety of TV snacks, "munchies," arrived to help viewers sustain themselves during an evening's schedule. Television also inspired the recliner chair. According to most advertisements, this nearly horizontal TV command post was generally reserved for Dad.

Commercial advertising, of course, was the engine that drove "free" television. As had been the case in network radio, early TV shows often carried the name of their sponsor—the "Colgate Comedy Hour," the "General Electric Theater," or the "Hallmark Hall of Fame." More commonly, in contrast to the later practice of selling 15- or 30-second commercial spots to different advertisers, a single sponsor would often underwrite an entire season of a single program, as Texaco did with television's first smash hit, "The Milton Berle Show." This arrangement obviously gave sponsors considerable leverage over a program's content. In the case of TV drama, for example, this translated into a preference for story lines and imagery that showed people working their way up the ladder of success by buying more and better products. An early genre, now called "TV *noir*," attracted relatively few sponsors and gave way to sunnier-looking fare.

Many TV programs joined the commercials that sustained them in extolling mass consumption. A familiar theme in early TV situation comedies found blue-collar families trying to move from older, Depression-era values of thrift and careful saving to postwar consumerism. Story lines on shows such as "The Life of Riley," which focused on a working-class family in Los Angeles, or "The Goldbergs," which featured a Jewish-American family in New York City, suggest that the road to happiness could be paved by the purchase of consumer goods and leisure-time activities rather than by faithfulness to ethnic rituals and traditions. Non-European ethnic groups were almost invisible except on "Amos 'n Andy," a show that angered civil-rights organizations and frightened away corporate sponsors because its representations of African-American life seemed outdated stereotypes.

By the mid-1950s, network programmers were shelving shows such as "The Life of Riley" in favor of ones that featured more affluent families who were more firmly anchored in the culture of mass consumption. "The Adventures of Ozzie and Harriet" came to television with "The Goldbergs" but lasted nearly two decades longer. Still carried on some cable-TV outlets, Ozzie and Harriet's "adventures" included frequent shopping forays, extensive leisure time, and even a live-in rock star, their son Rick Nelson. Industry executives aggressively pushed family images. Many popular shows featured those now-legendary TV families—the Andersons, the Cleavers, the Ricardos—and their never-ending familial conflicts, such as the good-natured tussles between Wally and Theodore (Beaver) Cleaver. So that everyone could better watch Ward and June Cleaver save the day, television executives urged viewers to convert their living rooms into centers of family—and TV—culture. One TV advertisement from the 1950s advised parents that their children needed the tube "for their morale as much as they need fresh air and sunshine for their health."

Most critics of "taste" denounced television for both the content of programming and its effect on cultural values. The quiz-show scandals of the 1950s came to symbolize the deceptive images and corrupt principles that supposedly dominated televisual culture. Quiz show producers, uneasy about programs that they could not completely script, gradually found that rigging the results gave them a crucial measure of control. They also discovered that, by manipulating the outcome of quiz contests, they could transform unknown contestants into instant (and relatively inexpensive to employ) celebrities. In the most notorious case, Charles Van Doren, a Columbia University professor who had thrilled more than 50 million TV viewers week after week by answering questions on virtually every subject, admitted that his entire performance had been rehearsed. Producers provided the answers and hints for making his replies seem as dramatic—and, therefore, as "real"—as possible. Quiz shows seemed to offer tests of mental power that were every bit as genuine as the tests of physical power in professional wrestling, and they temporarily vanished from the air. As a means of recovering from the quiz-show scandals, network executives devoted more time to public-affairs programming in hopes of refurbishing their own, and their medium's, image.

Rock Around the Clock: The Cultures of Youth

Fears about television seemed mild when compared to dire warnings about the cultural passions of young people. Youth-oriented motion pictures, comic books, hot-rod cars, and rock-and-roll music all gained the ire of a growing group of self-styled experts. Denouncing the leisure-time activities of young people and explaining "juvenile delinquency" became growth industries during the 1950s. The award-winning journalist Harrison Salisbury claimed that delinquency stretched from the nation's worst slums to its most affluent suburbs. In an age of increasing world tensions, this "shook-up generation" even constituted "a matter of national security," Salisbury (with apparent seriousness) concluded. A song written for Elvis Presley, "All Shook Up," subsequently parodied Salisbury's title.

Worries about delinquency joined concern about commercial culture. Motion pictures such as Marlon Brando's *The Wild One* (1953) and *Rebel Without a Cause* (1955), which rocketed James Dean (who had died in a car crash only a few days before the film's release) to stardom, showed how Hollywood could attract a new youthful audience. However, the relatively sympathetic portrayal of rebellious youths in films such as these alarmed observers of juvenile delinquency. Ostensibly marketed by Hollywood as explorations of juvenile delinquency, this new genre of "teen pics" struck many social observers as dangerous guidebooks for young people. Far too many motion pictures, these critics complained, featured images of juvenile misbehavior.

Comic books provided another convenient target. During the early 1950s, the comic-book industry marketed a billion books every year. This flood tide included familiar characters from other media, such as Bugs Bunny, Donald Duck, and various detective and western heroes. It also contained, however, new genres that featured stories of horror and exaggerated violence. In addition to offending genteel standards, such comics became linked to a restless, allegedly violent youth culture. In one of the widely cited examples of gruesome comic art, ghouls played baseball with various parts of a dissected human body.

Hot-rod cars became another contested cultural symbol. In fact, automobiles of all kinds, especially the increasingly common second car, provided young people with mobility, status symbols, entertainment, and makeshift bedrooms. They provided transportation to teenage gatherings, out of parents' sight, and with the freedom of privacy. The most frightening symbol of the youth-oriented car culture was the souped-up hot rod, with its noisy, dual exhaust system, raked body, and rolled-and-pleated interior. For many young men, the process of transforming one of Detroit's stereotyped products into a special, personal creation may have represented a subtle, though tangible, revolt against the mass-produced world of their parents. Although only a small proportion of men actually owned such a creation, the "Kandy-Kolored Tangerine-Flake Streamline Baby," to use writer Tom Wolfe's phrase, provided a prominent symbol of rebellious youth.

Rock-and-roll music also triggered concern. To people who considered Frank Sinatra as animated as a pop music star should ever get—and even to those who were embracing avant garde trends in postwar jazz, such as be-bop—rock appeared to be merely gratuitous noise, wild "jungle" sounds that accompanied frenzied new dance crazes. Moreover, the sexual innuendos in many songs seemed another dangerous incitement to deviance. The fact that rock grew out of rhythm-and-blues, a musical style popularized by urban African Americans, alerted segregationists to the possibility of some plot, perhaps by subversive communists, to sway young people toward integration.

Rock-and-roll thus had to grow, as ragtime had done at the turn of the twentieth century, outside the major channels for producing and distributing popular music. Rock artists, such as Chuck Berry and Carl Perkins, generally wrote their own material, and maverick producers, such as Sam Phillips of Sun Records in Memphis and Leonard and Phil Chess in Chicago, began to market aggressively what the major labels hesitated even to record. During the mid-1950s, Phillips unveiled the now legendary figures of early rockabilly—Perkins, Johnny Cash, Jerry Lee Lewis, and Elvis Presley. The Chess brothers, who had been featuring rhythm-and-blues artists such as Muddy Waters, introduced rock-and-roll pioneers like Berry and Bo Diddley during the mid-1950s. Other small record producers across the country were also releasing songs by black and white artists who fell outside the mainstream of popular music. Although established radio stations and prominent radio personalities steered clear of the new rock sound, smaller stations and younger DJs hitched their futures to it.

The association of motion pictures, hot rods, comics, and rock music with rebellious youth helped to focus attention on mass culture during the 1950s. Invoking the disease metaphors that were prominent in so many discussions of the time, critics portrayed mass entertainment as a cancerous invader that threatened the nation's cultural immune system. The violence in comic books supposedly ate away at young minds and produced juvenile delinquents. Social psychologists hypothesized that the simplicity of the typical comic-book story, violent or not, hindered young people's emotional development by conditioning them to expect quick, simple solutions to life's problems. Pressure groups urged Congress to ban comic books or, at a minimum, censor their contents. Quickly responding, the comic-book industry established its own regulatory code, a step that eliminated the more controversial offerings from the store racks and drove publishers like EC Comics into retirement. (The people behind EC's offbeat brand of culture quickly regrouped and introduced the long-running satirical classic, *MAD* magazine.)

The passing of the great comic-book scare was soon followed by the taming—at least temporarily—of rock music. Alan Freed, the most enterprising and eclectic of rock's early DJs, tottered atop a burgeoning musical empire that collapsed completely when federal prosecutors indicted him for accepting money to play specific records, a practice dubbed "payola." Dick Clark, host of the long-running TV show "American Bandstand," quickly assumed Freed's place and gave the emerging rock-and-roll dance culture a national audience. Many rock "purists," however, accused Clark of dishonoring Freed's legacy by mass-producing a generation of marginally talented artists who bumbled through sterile, prepackaged material. Rock seemed to lose its rough edge, ethnic identity, and quirky spontaneity. The careers of flamboyant eccentrics such as Huey ("Piano") Smith and Jerry Lee Lewis suddenly collapsed, and the major record companies absorbed rock into the pop music mainstream that came to dominate TV programming and Top-40 radio play-lists during the late 1950s.

Meanwhile, the broader youth culture itself began to seem somewhat less threatening. As recent histories have stressed, there never had been a single "youth culture" anyway. Social and cultural trends among young people during the 1950s always varied according to race, class, ethnicity, gender, and geography. These disparate phenomena, then, could hardly have constituted a single, generational challenge to the cultural order. More important, these "youth cultures," especially those centered on automobiles and music, easily linked up to broader cultural trends that seemed increasingly compatible with dominant values of the 1950s.

Youth cultures thrived in the new suburbs, where the general affluence washed down from parents to children. As sales of the new 45-rpm records and long-playing albums exploded, for example, a collection of the latest hits and new record players became important status symbols. Corporations and advertisers discovered that the youth culture could become an even bigger business opportunity than they had imagined. By 1960, according to one estimate, teenagers were spending $10 billion a year on products targeted specially at them.

The Mass Culture Debate of the 1950s

The recognition that the youth cultures were more closely linked to consumer spending patterns than to any generational-based insurgency did not halt the critique of mass culture. For many of the elite critics of mass culture, the immediate issue was always the fate of "taste" rather than that of social order. They considered beneath contempt most of what millions of people, both the young and their parents, liked to read, hear, and see.

The commercial culture of the 1950s, from this critical vantage point, seemed another example of how a mass-production and mass-consumption economy ignored issues of quality. In contrast to works of high culture, mass-marketed books and TV programs supposedly made no effort to deepen understanding or provoke critical contemplation. The typical cultural product aimed at the millions seemed more like chewing gum than real art. It was to be consumed as rapidly as possible and then discarded. Unlike true folk culture, what critics identified as "authentic" art that preserved the communal traditions of ordinary people, mass culture was stamped out by hack writers and mediocre image-makers concerned only with meeting their assigned quota of marketable products. This kind of standardized culture constituted an affront to refined tastes and promoted a mindless conformity among "the masses."

Commercial culture, to these critics, resembled an intellectual cancer. Even talented writers and artists were succumbing to its corrupting allure and churning out only easily marketable junk. In turn, consumer tastes were becoming too vulgarized even to recognize good art. Mass culture thus carried the seeds of intellectual decay. Both high and folk cultures could eventually be totally destroyed or, at best, reduced to some grotesque mutation, such as a mindless "middlebrow culture." Worse still, as mass culture proliferated, the ability of consumers to discriminate good from bad could become so eroded that they could fail to recognize the ways in which mass culture manipulated their desires and prejudices. An important group of these critics, onetime members of the "Frankfurt School," who had fled Nazi Germany during the 1930s, did speculate on the social impact of this culture and warned that North American mass culture of the 1950s might provide the "kitsch" with which a native totalitarian movement could pacify the innocent, conformist masses.

Not every student of mass culture sounded such a bleak note. Gilbert Seldes, a longtime partisan of the popular arts, defended the culture of the 1950s as richer and more varied than that produced during earlier decades and chided the critics of taste for their elitism. Although lacking Seldes's enthusiasm for the cultural products themselves, others shared his skepticism for tracing all manner of cultural and social problems back to mass culture. Robert Warshow, a prominent film critic, sarcastically announced he would stop worrying about his son's taste for EC Comics. The kid was simply a "fan," not an "addict." Moreover, once criminologists looked more carefully at the data, popular claims about a sudden rise in juvenile delinquency seemed greatly exaggerated. Some sociologists even argued that mass culture could help people, especially children and adolescents, to negotiate an increasingly complex society. The popular children's book *Tootle the Train,* for example, showed young people the need to "stay on the tracks" and adjust to community expectations.

Perhaps the most buoyant theorist of mass culture, especially television, was Marshall McLuhan, a media scholar from Canada. Speculating on the course of TV's worldwide expansion, McLuhan foresaw a "global village," in which people of previously distinct cultures could experience a common bond of sensory awareness simply by abandoning themselves to this "cool medium." Initially hailed as a visionary, McLuhan saw his reputation plummet as subsequent media theorists came to doubt that television, as McLuhan's global theories implied, could be studied apart from its reception in specific political and cultural contexts.

The Mass Culture Debate Revisited

McLuhan's successors, analysts who had been raised on postwar mass culture, have tried to anchor their own theories of commercial culture in more precise contextual settings. By the 1980s, academics and journalists were coming to see the mass culture debate of the 1950s as a historical phenomenon to be explained, not a set of cultural judgments to be endorsed or rejected. According to one interpretation, the elitist, cold-war critics feared that mass culture, with its broad audience and eclectic creativity, threatened their own cultural authority, which was rooted in mastery of a limited range of high-culture works. The fact that the new mass culture drew on sources outside the traditions of the college-educated, white middle class—such as the music of urban African Americans, Mexican Americans, and southern whites—only underscored the elitism and cultural blinders of intellectuals of the 1950s.

In addition, subsequent students of commercial culture increasingly came to look at how people actually employed products and images to help make sense of their daily lives. Research in this vein tends to suggest that mass-produced cultural products could be received and used by consumers in ways that did not necessarily promote conformity or other mind-numbing responses. The music of Elvis Presley and Chuck Berry, which blended white and black sounds, seemed to have crossed racial boundaries and become a kind of cultural civil-rights movement. Berry's "Brown-Eyed Handsome Man" provided an early rock anthem of black pride, while his "Roll Over, Beethoven" imagined the overthrow of old cultural hierarchies. Even though male artists such as Presley and Berry generally reinforced subordinate images of women in both the lyrics of their songs and in their own performances, women entered the rock music scene during the late 1950s. Songwriters such as Carole King and "girl groups" such as the Shirelles spoke to the mixed messages that young women were receiving about sexual and gender politics. Popular songs such as "Will You Love Me Tomorrow" allowed young people, particularly women, to test their personal visions against those in rock music and, thereby, develop a critical rather than passive relationship to mass-produced cultural products. The "trashy" romance novels that proliferated in paperback form during the 1950s, one cultural anthropologist suggests, provided women with images that led them to question, at least in tentative ways, the hierarchical, male-dominated structures that shaped their lives. The mere act of sitting down to read a novel for pleasure could represent a small-scale revolt against the ethic that a woman-and-mother's work was "never done."

Finally, students of media increasingly note the diversity of cultural representations available during the 1950s. Television, many historians of the medium have come to argue, contributed to a vibrant cultural tableau. It extended the old, vaudeville-based culture—including the routines of performers such as George Burns and Gracie Allen, Groucho Marx, and Milton Berle—and, simultaneously, nurtured new forms, including the sitcom ("I Love Lucy"), the police drama ("Dragnet"), and the psychological western ("Gunsmoke"). "Amos n' Andy," later students of African-American culture argue, provided jobs for black actors and multidimensional representations of life in an all-black neighborhood. Similarly, even professional wrestling and Roller Derby, other studies suggest, portrayed working-class heroes for blue-collar audiences and offered more opportunities for participation by women than most "real" sports. An almost instinctual contempt for the commercial culture of the 1950s has never entirely disappeared, but the critique championed by the cultural elite of that decade has increasingly given way to less dogmatic and apocalyptic forms of analysis.

RACE, ETHNICITY, AND URBAN ISSUES

As newly affluent, white city dwellers moved to the suburbs, people from rural areas arrived to replace them. Many of these migrants were neither white nor middle class. For them, the 1950s did not bring affluence, and economic gains often came against a backdrop of discrimination.

African Americans

People of African descent, in search of jobs in war-related industries, had left the rural South for northern cities during World War II. Even though employment possibilities increased, many of these migrants faced harsh living conditions. With the nation's resources being poured into national defense, little money remained for housing programs. In Detroit's black neighborhoods, for example, one investigator reported that an aging, converted one-family dwelling might hold over one hundred people, one family to a room. However, such conditions did not curb the postwar flow into urban areas in the North.

In time, the northern migration advanced the economic position of most African Americans. Between 1947 and 1952, the median income of nonwhite families rose from $1,614 to $2,338, and the gap between black and white incomes narrowed slightly. In 1940, 80 percent of all black workers were employed in unskilled jobs; by 1950, the figure had dropped to 63 percent. Similarly, the life expectancy of blacks advanced from 53.1 years in 1940 to 61.7 in 1953 (compared with 64.2 to 69.6 for whites). Throughout the 1950s, the expanding economy and favorable job market helped maintain the economic gains that the war had initially stimulated.

At the start of the Eisenhower administration, in 1953, almost every area of southern life still mandated segregated facilities for blacks and whites. Segregation extended to public transportation, rest rooms, drinking fountains, even parking lots and cemeteries. Required by law and always demanded by custom, these separate, but rarely equal, facilities symbolized the inferior status that whites assigned to African Americans. The National Association for the Advancement of Colored People (NAACP) had financed a series of court challenges during the Truman years, and the decision in *Brown v. Board of Education* (1954) marked the culmination of a long legal crusade against discrimination.

In *Brown,* all nine Supreme Court justices agreed that legally sanctioned segregation of public schools violated the equal protection clause of the Fourteenth Amendment. Chief Justice Earl Warren argued that separate schools were "inherently unequal" and deprived black children of equal educational opportunities. However, this Court decision, by itself, could not produce a social revolution. Bowing to political pressure and pleas by educators, the Supreme Court later ruled (in a case that lawyers called *Brown-II*) that school desegregation could proceed "with all deliberate speed."

Most white southerners decried *Brown.* Some condemned it as an "invasion of states' rights"; others denounced it as part of a Communist plot to destroy "the white race"; and most pledged massive resistance to school integration. The Ku Klux Klan (KKK) revived, and a new organization committed to defending segregation, the White Citizens Council, sprang up across the South. Not every segregationist endorsed forcible resistance, but some did turn to violence. During the summer of 1955, two white men from Money, Mississippi, murdered Emmet Till, a black teenager from Chicago who was visiting relatives in the South, for allegedly insulting a white woman. During that same summer, at least two other African American men, who had violated segregationist norms by registering to vote, were shot to death in Mississippi.

Southerners also used legal and political stratagems to delay changes in race relations. In 1957, 101 members of Congress signed the Southern Manifesto, a protest against "federal usurpation" of states' rights, and southern senators employed the filibuster to block civil rights legislation. A segregationist image seemed linked to political survival in most southern states. After a moderate young lawyer, George C. Wallace, lost badly to a rabid segregationist, he announced that he would never be "outnigraed again."

The most spectacular example of official resistance came in Arkansas. In 1957, Governor Orval Faubus defied a federal court order to desegregate Little Rock Central High School and deployed the state's National Guard to bar black children from the building. President Eisenhower could not ignore the challenge.

Although not a personal partisan of the civil rights movement, Eisenhower headed a Republican party with a long tradition of backing African-American causes. Many office-holders from the GOP's eastern establishment had voting records on civil-rights issues that looked as progressive as those of most Northern Democrats. Eisenhower himself had received more than one-third of the (largely northern) African-American vote in his two electoral victories, and as the nation's commander-in-chief, the president could hardly ignore Faubus's open defiance, by using national guard troops, of federal authority

Washington quashed southern attempts to stop school integration through the force of law. Eisenhower placed the Arkansas National Guard under federal control, augmented it with regular army troops, and protected the small group of African American students from the hostile crowd of segregationists who surrounded Little Rock's Central High. The following year, Arkansas officials tried to block desegregation through judicial strategies. Meeting in emergency session, the U.S. Supreme Court summarily rejected Arkansas's claim that a state need not obey a federal court order. Soon thereafter, the Court declared unconstitutional the evasive tactics of closing down public schools and gerrymandering school districts, and it pressed southern school officials to devise more aggressive desegregation plans. Delaying tactics, though, remained the norm throughout the South. Ten years after the initial *Brown* decision that "ended" legal segregation, only 1 percent of black children attended integrated schools in southern states.

The drive to end racial discrimination by law in the South initially gained considerable support in the rest of the country. Fighting Nazi racism and crusading against communism had made national leaders, of necessity if not conviction, more sensitive to the issue of racial injustice at home. Policymakers, competing with the Soviets for the goodwill of Third World nations, found it too difficult to explain away legal discrimination against nonwhites in the United States. When diplomats from the new African states experienced segregation firsthand, the whole system of Jim Crow became highly embarrassing to the people who directed the nation's foreign policy. Many religious leaders and prominent scientists, who ridiculed theories of racial inferiority, also lent their prestige to the civil rights cause.

Meanwhile, the migration of northern-based corporations and industries to the South was producing important changes there. In many different ways, the South was becoming more like the North. To a new generation of white southern leaders, this process of "northernization" made old forms of racial domination, such as Jim Crow and political exclusion, seem anachronistic. Many younger, white southerners lacked a deep-seated commitment to segregation and were willing to accept change on racial issues in order to speed economic and social transformation of the South.

Changes also affected black southerners. With the rise of farming operations patterned on northern models using new agricultural techniques, the largely rural, southern black population faced severe economic pressure as old living patterns were disrupted. Slowly at first and then at a much more rapid rate, African Americans found themselves pushed off the land. Many moved to cities within the South or to urban areas in the North and West. During the 1940s and 1950s, more than 3 million African Americans left the South. This migration helped to break old deferential patterns and to encourage a spirit of militancy among youth. By the mid-1950s, new leaders and new organizations within local African American communities were spearheading the fight against discrimination.

The Montgomery bus boycott of 1956–1957 provided an example of a successful, community-based assault against Jim Crow. Rosa Parks, a seamstress who had been a longtime stalwart in the local NAACP chapter, sparked the Montgomery campaign when she was arrested for refusing to surrender her bus seat to a white man. African Americans organized a boycott of all municipal transit and refused to ride until facilities were desegregated. Lasting for more than a year, the Montgomery boycott ended in a victory for antidiscrimination forces and brought to prominence a young Baptist minister named Dr. Martin Luther King, Jr.

Dr. King, who had been raised in Atlanta and who had earned a doctorate from Boston University before moving back to the South, quickly gained recognition as a charismatic presence and a skilled strategist. He was still in his twenties when he joined the Montgomery boycott. King's tactics of nonviolent civil disobedience and economic pressure became the civil rights movement's primary weapons during the 1950s. Citing the success of Mahatma Gandhi's passive resistance in India, King preached the importance of laying one's body on the line and of loving one's enemy. "If we are arrested every day . . . if we are trampled over every day, don't ever let anyone pull you so low as to hate them. We must use the weapon of love." In 1957, King and other black ministers formed the Southern Christian Leadership Conference (SCLC), which became the most active civil rights organization in the South.

King and the SCLC relied on African American churches and drew their greatest support from middle-class blacks. The son of a prominent Atlanta minister, King spoke in the measured cadence of the black preacher, the person who traditionally led the black community. He also moved white audiences with his message of Christian love. Whether he sought the role or not, the media identified King as the symbolic leader of the nation's entire black population. Such a position gained him the emnity of angry whites and, eventually, of more militant activists.

Puerto Ricans

Thousands of Puerto Ricans moved to New York City during the decade after World War II and transformed that city's ethnic makeup. New York's Puerto Rican community grew by over half a million in twenty years, from 70,000 in 1940 to 613,000 in 1960. A variety of circumstances contributed to this massive migration. Throughout the 1940s, Puerto Ricans had experienced increased contact with the U.S. mainland through mass media, advertisements, and military life. (Sixty-five thousand Puerto Ricans served in the U.S. armed forces during World War II.) Life in the United States, especially to younger Puerto Ricans, proved alluring. New York's unemployment rate was lower than Puerto Rico's, and its social services network was superior. The administration of Luis Muñoz Marin in Puerto Rico encouraged migration hoping to raise Puerto Rico's per capita income by reducing the island's population. Comparatively inexpensive air service between San Juan and New York, which had begun in 1945, facilitated migration, as did mainland businesses, where Puerto Ricans were recruited for work in agriculture and in the garment trades. In time a sizable Puerto Rican community formed in New York and other East-Coast cities and generated its own growth through a high birthrate and additional migration by friends and relatives.

Puerto Ricans laid down roots in East Harlem and then in other neighborhoods throughout the five boroughs of New York City. Studies showed that the newcomers generally had a higher level of education and job skills than the Puerto Ricans who remained behind, but their Spanish language and close ties with the island left them outside the mainstream of city life. During the 1950s, many Puerto Ricans could obtain only the lowest-paying jobs, and few entered New York City politics. Puerto Ricans suffered the fate of other people who lacked economic power and political muscle: discrimination, deteriorating schools, overcrowded housing, and governmental indifference. Every year, around 30,000 people returned to the island, but New York City's Puerto Rican population still continued to grow rapidly throughout the 1950s. By 1960, it was one-hundred times greater than it had been twenty years earlier.

Mexican Americans

Before World War II, most Mexican Americans had lived in rural areas, but by 1960, 80 percent resided in cities. According to the 1960 census, more than 500,000 Mexican Americans lived in the greater Los Angeles area. Large Spanish-speaking neighborhoods also existed in El Paso, Phoenix, and other Southwestern cities; and northern industrial centers—such as Chicago, Detroit, Kansas City, and Denver—attracted growing numbers of Mexican-American workers. City life and the favorable job market from World War II through the 1950s raised the overall living standards of most Mexican Americans. By 1960, Mexican Americans in California and throughout the Southwest had constructed what one historian calls a "parallel society," a vibrant, growing infrastructure of small businesses, owner-occupied homes, entertainment facilities, and media outlets that reflected the cultural influence of Mexico. Many Mexican Americans believed, however, that discrimination limited what they and their communities might accomplish.

The U.S. government continued to welcome additional migrants from Mexico under the *bracero* (farm worker) program. The executive agreement between the United States and Mexico that had initiated the *bracero* program in 1942 had been intended to augment the work force temporarily during World War II. Under pressure from large agricultural enterprises, Congress continued to authorize migration of farm laborers long after the war. Throughout the 1950s, the number of incoming Mexican workers climbed each year, reaching almost 1 million in 1959 alone. Mexican migrants provided low-paid, unorganized labor to harvest seasonal crops from Texas to Montana. Growers reaped enormous profits. By the mid-1960s, however, the rising unemployment rate among Americans, combined with anti-Mexican prejudice, convinced Congress to discontinue the *bracero* program. Over the protests of large growers, but to the satisfaction of labor unions, which feared competition from low-paid workers, the *bracero* program was ended, although illegal immigration of undocumented workers from Mexico, often stigmatized as "wetbacks," continued.

Meanwhile, the Eisenhower administration stepped up deportations of illegal immigrants in a program called "Operation Wetback." In a five-year period, the government claimed to have deported nearly 4 million people back to Mexico. The operation contributed to a climate of fear in Mexican-American communities and helped justify discrimination by employers.

In the midst of discrimination and threats of deportation, however, new political movements took shape during the 1950s. Several Mexican American organizations sought equality in legal and political rights and greater access to economic resources. Drawing strength from the broader antidiscrimination efforts of the 1950s, the League of United Latin American Citizens (LULAC) and the Unity League forced desegregation of some public facilities and schools, worked against discrimination in housing and employment, and helped elect the first local Mexican-American officeholders in the Southwest. In El Paso, Texas, political mobilization among Mexican-Americans, who made up one-half of that city's total population, swept Raymond L. Telles into office in 1957 as the nation's first Mexican-American mayor. The limited gains and gradualist strategies of the 1950s, however, led other groups to press for change more forcefully than LULAC. A more militant organization, Asociación Nacional México-Americana (ANMA), before it became a casualty of FBI surveillance and harassment, backed drives for labor union organizing and protested the mass deportation of Mexicans under the McCarran Act. The FBI and agricultural processors also used anticommunism as a justification to undercut labor unions that had large Mexican-American memberships.

American Indians

The mobilization effort during World War II had encouraged many Indians, women as well as men, to leave their reservations, and the federal government's policies in the postwar era increased the pace at which Indians moved to the cities. During the 1940s, the number of Indians living in urban areas had nearly doubled. After World War II, the Truman administration began efforts to streamline the Bureau of Indian Affairs, the governmental agency that dealt with both the tribes and individual Indians. It had also supported the creation of an Indian Claims Commission, which was to settle outstanding financial disputes between the national government and various tribes. These measures, which aimed at reducing Washington's role in Indian affairs, eventually merged into a broader, longstanding policy of inducing more Indians to leave the reservations and to assimilate into American life.

The Eisenhower administration, with support from Congress, built on the programs of the Truman era. The goal, as one policy document put it, was to end Indians' "status as wards of the United States, and grant them all of the rights and privileges pertaining to American citizenship." The new policy, called "termination," aimed at ending the old relationship between Indian tribes and Washington and at ending the reservation system. The first bills of termination, applying to tribes that supposedly no longer needed a special relationship with the federal government, passed Congress in 1954. Eventually, 109 tribes and bands were terminated, and more than 10,000 people lost more than a million acres of land.

While pursuing termination, the government also set up a Voluntary Relocation Program (later called the Employment Assistance Program) to coax more Indians into urban areas. Begun in 1952, this program of relocation encouraged Indians to move to one of ten cities with local relocation offices. It then paid living expenses until the first paycheck arrived. During the next decade, more than 60,000 (approximately one of every eight) Indians would migrate from reservations to urban centers. The number of Indians living in cities more than doubled during the 1950s.

The policies of termination and relocation disrupted tribal life. Some terminated tribes, after becoming subject to state tax requirements, fell on hard times. Others sold tribal lands to private developers. Indians who moved to the cities sometimes found the transition from a semi-communal, rural existence to the isolation of urban life very difficult. Federal officials had claimed that termination and relocation would assimilate Indians into the American mainstream and end federal outlays to support them, but assimilation proved to be a complicated social and cultural process, not simply a geographical move. The Bureau of Indian Affairs estimated that 35 percent of all relocated Indians eventually returned to the reservations, and other studies suggested that about 75 percent would probably have returned had the reservations offered more job opportunities.

As the consequences of termination and relocation became clear, even Indians who had initially favored the theory behind the policies came to denounce the results. Protests against the breakup of reservations and the destruction of Indian culture mounted. Despite being labeled as pro-Communist by proponents of termination and relocation, the National Congress of American Indians (NCAI) waged a vigorous legal and political resistance. Although the Eisenhower administration never officially abandoned termination, it pledged not to press it on unwilling tribes. In 1960, both the Democratic and Republican parties repudiated this discredited policy and promised to develop new economic opportunities on reservations rather than to force Indians to leave them. (Even so, the Kennedy administration still signed, in 1962, the final termination order for the Northern Poncas.)

Despite hardships, the number of people of American Indian descent grew rapidly during the 1950s. Between 1950 and 1960, the Indian population increased by nearly 50 percent; some tribes, particularly the Navajo who enjoyed relative isolation from infectious disease, experienced an even greater increase. American Indians were concentrated in relatively few states: Arizona, New Mexico, Oklahoma, Montana, Minnesota, South Dakota, North Dakota, Washington, Wisconsin, and New York. The increase in population would have been even greater had it not been for an infant death rate among Indians that was nearly two-and-one-half times as great as that for any other ethnic group.

In 1955, the same year that the federal government compiled statistics on the infant mortality rate, a thirty-five-year-old Indian, Ira Hayes, a member of the Pima tribe, died of alcoholism and exposure along a roadside in Arizona. Hayes had been a much-celebrated hero of World War II, but by the 1950s his equally publicized failure to readjust to postwar life had made him a symbol of the difficulties faced by other American Indians during the postwar era. His life became the subject of a popular song, "The Ballad of Ira Hayes," and a Hollywood motion picture.

Urban Life and the "Invisible Poor"

Although the term "urban crisis" did not become a cliché until the 1960s, most American cities confronted upheaval during the 1950s. Most cities rapidly expanded outward. Sprawling across the landscape, urban areas became more fragmented than ever before. After studying cities along the eastern seaboard, a French geographer called this new form of social organization the "megalopolis." "We must abandon the idea of the city as a tightly settled and organized unit in which people, activities, and riches are crowded into a very small area clearly separate from its nonurban surroundings," wrote Jean Gottman. A city would spread out "far and wide around its original nucleus" until it melted into the suburban neighborhoods of other cities.

Many people, particularly in the West, saw no problem with this kind of cityscape. Cities in California eagerly pursued rapid geographical expansion. Between 1945 and 1956, Los Angeles County added nearly 40,000 lots each year for new single-family homes. Adjacent Orange County could claim only about 200,000 residents in 1950. During the Eisenhower era, an explosion in housing projects, shopping centers, and business enterprises allowed Orange County to emerge as a rival to Los Angeles itself. When Disneyland opened near Anaheim in 1955, Orange County became the epicenter of the nation's mass-culture explosion. Further north, San Jose was in the midst of an expansion process that would swell the size of the city from only 11 square miles in 1940 to 137 square miles by 1970.

The pace of geographical expansion worried many urban planners. They argued that cities would pay a price for unregulated development. Despite the introduction of planning boards and zoning commissions during the early twentieth century, the private decisions of business leaders continued to exert the greatest influence on the direction and pace of urban change. The needs of business enterprises largely determined what land would be used, how it would be developed, and what groups would pay the highest social costs. As metropolitan areas grew larger, the idea of developing coherent, centralized administrative systems, the dream of many experts on urban policy, became more difficult. The resultant decentralization of governance, according to most urban planners, left less affluent areas in the center of most cities saddled with poor schools, inadequate public services, and too little money to address social problems. Urban sprawl seemed to make people feel like transients rather than members of a community. As long as more affluent urbanites could commute from their jobs to their suburban homes, it was claimed, they would hesitate to commit themselves or their tax dollars to projects that addressed urban problems.

Some governmental attempts to deal with urban issues seemed counterproductive. Significant federal aid for construction of low-cost housing rarely reached central cities during the 1950s. The goal of building 810,000 public housing units by 1955, the target of the Housing Act of 1949, would not be achieved until the end of the 1960s. Worse, by that time, many planners had already concluded that massive housing projects, such as the giant Pruit-Igoe complex in St. Louis, were too large, too sterile, and too costly to maintain. These large-scale, high-rise housing experiments, once the great hope of urban designers, failed to provide the kind of stable, desirable living environment that planners of the 1950s had expected.

Meanwhile, urban renewal—another program authorized in the Housing Act of 1949—was actually reducing the number of dwellings available to people with low and moderate incomes. In theory, urban renewal allowed local governments to use federal funds to replace dilapidated buildings with new public housing units or with other projects, anything from new cultural complexes to concrete parking garages. In practice, the Eisenhower administration allowed planners and private developers to evade the responsibility of replacing or increasing the supply of affordable, urban living units.

New York City's Robert Moses epitomized the postwar approach to urban issues. Moses, who dominated building and planning in the nation's largest city from a variety of appointive positions, ridiculed critics of his grandiose schemes. "When you operate in an overbuilt metropolis, you have to hack your way with a meat ax," he once claimed. Moses taunted opponents that he was "just going to keep on building. You do the best you can to stop it." Moving low-income people as if they were disposable commodities, Moses held fast to his build-at-any-cost vision of urban progress. For those who "like things as they are," Moses offered this advice: "Keep moving further away. [New York] is a big state, and there are other states . . . go to the Rockies." Even though most of New York City's postwar residents owned no automobiles, Moses's expensive freeway projects cut through, around, and above the urban landscape.

The vast network of multilane expressways in New York City and elsewhere brought paradoxical changes to urban life. They did allow affluent commuters to live even farther from urban centers and to travel to work in the privacy of their automobiles rather than on public transportation. This only accelerated urban sprawl. Freeways also contributed to the decay of existing mass transit facilities and worked against construction of new ones. The stream of cars creeping to and from the central cities also increased air pollution, without noticeably speeding the pace of urban commuting. Finally, the new expressways destroyed even more old buildings and further contributed to the fragmentation of urban life. By 1960, urban problems seemed so pressing that the presidential candidates of both major parties promised to support the creation of a new cabinet-level office to coordinate federal assistance to urban areas.

Still, most of the people who lived in central city neighborhoods during the 1950s were probably better off than many of those in the rural United States. As the larger farm operators mechanized and streamlined their operations, they needed more land. Throughout the rural Midwest, young people left family farms during the 1950s rather than try to compete with larger enterprises. In Appalachia, a million-and-one-half people abandoned unproductive patches of land. The elderly farmers who remained were often those least able to cope with mechanization and changing markets. By 1954, nearly 60 percent of total agricultural sales came from about 10 percent of the larger farm operators, and this imbalance would continue to grow. Unemployment accompanied this agricultural revolution, and a new kind of rural poverty became a major, if often unnoticed, problem. Whether a person was an African-American tenant farmer in Georgia, an American Indian on an isolated reservation, a white farmer in the hills of Appalachia, or a migrant worker, hard times dominated his or her life.

A new kind of economic inequality emerged, claimed author Michael Harrington, who coined the term "invisible poor." During the 1950s, television

Cecelia Tichi, *The Electronic Hearth* (1991); Lynn Spigel and Denise Mann, eds., *Private Screenings* (1992); Glenn C. Altschuler and David I. Grossvogel, *Changing Channels* (1992); Karel Ann Marling, *As Seen on TV: The Visual Culture of Everyday Life in the 1950s* (1994); Nina C. Leibman, *Living Room Lectures: The Fifties Family in Film and Television* (1995). For an overview of theoretical approaches to TV texts, see the various essays in Robert C. Allen, ed., *Channels of Discourse, Reassembled* (rev. ed., 1992).

The literature on music continues to grow. Greil Marcus, *Mystery Train* (rev. ed., 2001) and Charlie Gillet, *Sound of the City: The Rise of Rock and Roll* (rev. ed., 1996), are two classic, and now updated, studies. See also Ed Ward, Geoffrey Stokes, and Ken Tucker, *Rock of Ages: The Rolling Stone History of Rock & Roll* (1986); Nelson George, *The Death of Rhythm and Blues* (1988); Peter Guralnick, *Lost Highways: Journeys and Arrivals of American Musicians* (rev. ed., 1999); Steve Waksman, *Instruments of Desire: The Electric Guitar and the Shaping of American Musical Experience* (1999); and Jim Miller, *Flowers in the Dustbin: The Rise of Rock and Roll, 1947–77* (1999). There is a huge, still expanding literature on "the King." See, for example, Peter Guralnick's *Last Train to Memphis: The Rise of Elvis Presley* (1994) and *Careless Love: The Unmaking of Elvis Presley* (2000); Karal Ann Marling, *Graceland: Going Home with Elvis* (1996); Erika Doss, *Elvis Culture: Fans, Faith, and Image* (1999); and Michael T. Bertrand, *Race, Rock, and Elvis* (2000). On the diversity of the youth culture, see William Graebner, *Coming of Age in Buffalo: Youth and Authority in the Postwar Era* (1989).

On religious trends see Christopher Owen Lynch, *Selling Catholicism: Bishop Sheen and the Power of Television* (1998); Robert Wuthnow, *After Heaven; Spirituality in America since the 1950s* (1998); James Gilbert, *Redeeming Culture: American Religion in the Age of Science* (1997); John R. Stone, *On the Boundaries of American Evangelicalism: The Postwar Evangelical Coalition* (1997); Douglas Jacobson and William Trollinger, *Reforming the Center: American Protestantism from 1900 to the Present* (1998); Joel A. Carpenter, *Revive Us Again: The Reawakening of American Fundamentalism* (1997); and Wade Clark Roof, *Spiritual Marketplace: Baby Boomers and the Remaking of American Religion* (1999).

On social issues, see Michael Harrington's classic, *The Other America* (1962), and his later work, *The New American Poverty* (1984); James T. Patterson, *America's Struggle Against Poverty, 1900–1980* (1981). On African Americans and the civil rights movement, see Doug McAdam, *Political Process and the Development of Black Insurgency, 1930–1970* (1982); Pete Daniel, *Lost Revolutions: The South in the 1950s* (2000); Dean J. Kotlowski, *Nixon's Civil Rights: Politics, Principle, and Policy;* Harvard Sitkoff, *The Struggle for Black Equality* (1983); Tony Freyer, *The Little Rock Crisis* (1984); David Garrow, *Bearing the Cross: Martin Luther King, Jr., and the Southern Christian Leadership Conference* (1986); the relevant chapters of Earl Black and Merle Black, *Politics and Society in the South* (1987); Jack Bloom, *Class, Race, and the Civil Rights Movement: The Political Economy of Southern Racism* (1987); David Garrow, ed., *The Montgomery Bus Boycott and the Women Who Started It: The Memoir of Jo Ann Gibson Robinson* (1987); Taylor Branch, *Parting the Waters: America in the King Years, 1954–1963* (1988); Steven J. Whitfield, *A Death in the Delta: The Story of Emmett Till* (1988); Herbert Haines, *Black Radicals and the Civil Rights Mainstream, 1954–1970* (1989); Nancy J. Weiss, *Whitney M. Young, Jr., and the Struggle for Civil Rights* (1989); Kevin Gaines, *Uplifting the Race; Black*

Leadership, Politics, and Culture in the Twentieth Century (1996); Henry Hampton, ed., *Voices of Freedom: An Oral History of the Civil Rights Movement* (1990); Robert Weisbrot, *American Crusade: A History of the Civil Rights Movement* (1990); Chana Kai Lee, *For Freedom's Sake: The Life of Fanny Lou Hamer* (1999); Armstead L. Robinson and Patricia Sullivan, eds., *New Directions in Civil Rights Studies* (1991); the relevant chapters of Jacqueline Jones, *The Dispossessed* (1992); Vicki Crawford, Jacqueline Anne Rouse, and Barbara Woods, eds., *Women in the Civil Rights Movement* (1990); David L. Chappell, *Inside Agitators: White Southerners in the Civil Rights Movement* (1993); Mark V. Tushnet, *Making Civil Rights Law: Thurgood Marshall and the Supreme Court, 1936–1961* (1993); James F. Findlay, Jr., *Church People in the Struggle: The National Council of Churches and the Black Freedom Movement, 1950–1970* (1993). On Asian-Americans, see the relevant chapters of Ronald Takaki, *Strangers from a Different Shore: A History of Asian-Americans* (1989). On Latinos, see Mario Garcia, *A History of Mexican-Americans: 1930–1960* (1989); Ricardo Romo, *East Los Angeles: History of a Barrio* (1989); David G. Gutierrez, *Walls and Mirrors: Mexican Americans, Mexican Immigrants, and the Politics of Ethnicity* (1995); Ruben Donato, *The Other Struggle for Equal Schools: Mexican-Americans During the Civil Rights Movement* (1997); Andrés Torres, *Between Melting Pot and Mosaic: African Americans and Puerto Ricans in the New York Political Economy* (1995); Manuel Alers-Montalvo, *The Puerto Rican Migrants of New York* (1985); Joseph P. Fitzpatrick, *Puerto Rican Americans: The Meaning of Migration to the Mainland* (2nd ed., 1987). On American Indian issues see Larry Burt, *Tribalism in Crisis* (1982); Donald L. Fixico, *Termination and Relocation: Federal Indian Policy, 1945–1960* (1984); Kenneth R. Philp, *Termination Revisited: American Indians on the Trail to Self-Destruction, 1933–1953* (1999); and Thomas Cowger, *The National Congress of American Indians: The Founding Years* (1999).

5

The Promise and Perils of the 1960s

The title of a best-selling book by an aide to John F. Kennedy lamented that "Johnny We Hardly Knew Ye." The phrase was unintentionally revealing. Kennedy's partisans tried to obscure the darker side of both his private life and his presidency and to deflect any critical assessment of his character and accomplishments. More recently, historians have peeked through the veil of adulation behind which former associates and friendly chroniclers shrouded the thirty-fifth president. Revisionist views have had little effect, however, on Kennedy's popular image: When a cross-section of the citizenry is asked to name the "greatest" president, Kennedy still ranks near Abraham Lincoln. At the same time, Kennedy has become more than a political figure from the past. As with Marilyn Monroe, the actress romantically linked to him and his brother Robert, JFK remains very much alive as a celebrity-icon in contemporary media culture.

THE PRESIDENT WE HARDLY KNEW

John F. Kennedy, according to his admirers, followed a storybook path to the presidency. His wealthy father, active in Democratic party politics, had dreamed that one of his four sons might gain the nation's highest office. He sent John Kennedy to an elite prep school and then to Harvard. Young John pursued beautiful women; refined his social graces; and, while at his father's side, gained an insider's view of public affairs. When his older brother died during World War II, John, also a war hero, was there to fulfill his father's dream. Early on, Kennedy displayed intolerance for those without his tough-minded approach to politics. People who could not say what they had to say quickly, especially those who moralized while they digressed, irritated him. How could people who could not get to the point ever do great things? Kennedy surrounded himself with quick-witted, ambitious young people who shared his distaste for sentimentality. The public Kennedy—idealistic, inspirational, and sometimes emotional—was very different from the hard-nosed, calculating politician who began to pursue the presidency during the mid-1950s.

The Rise of John F. Kennedy and the Election of 1960

Kennedy's narrow victory over Richard Nixon in the presidential race of 1960 capped a rather unimpressive political career. In 1946, JFK won election to the House of Representatives and six years later to the U.S. Senate. Kennedy always found the tradition-bound Senate to be slow-moving and, often, simply boring. He usually supported fairly generous expenditures for domestic-spending programs and enthusiastically championed an anti-Communist foreign policy—but he sponsored no important legislation. While in Congress, he married Jacqueline Bouvier, whose youth and social prominence proved to be important political assets. With the help of ghostwriters he authored a prize-winning book, *Profiles in Courage*. Between 1956 and 1960, Kennedy took full advantage of the new era of jet travel by courting the Democratic party hierarchy and accumulating political debts that he could cash in during the 1960 campaign. He put together a smooth-running organization that included his younger brothers, Robert and Ted, and a coterie of university professors. Skilled in new polling techniques, his team also excelled in old-fashioned, political arm-twisting, seeming to know just how much leverage to use and exactly where to apply it.

Kennedy dominated the presidential race of 1960. His speeches rehashed standard postwar themes—the cold war with the Soviet Union, economic growth at home, and sacrifice for country—but they were cleverly phrased and, after some speaking lessons, effectively delivered. Kennedy gave particular attention to the criticism, by economists and military strategists, of the New Look policies of Dwight Eisenhower. The decision to emphasize his Roman Catholic background during the Democratic primary contests, rather than waiting for his opponents to raise the question, helped Kennedy defuse religion as a central issue. Unlike Adlai Stevenson, who had let the Democratic convention choose his running mate in 1956, JFK made a carefully calculated choice: Senate Majority Leader Lyndon Baines Johnson of Texas. Johnson appealed to party regulars and also to white southern Democrats, who had been restive since the 1948 election because of the party's support for civil-rights measures. Meanwhile, Kennedy's own youth and supposed vigor contrasted with that of his predecessor, the much older, more deliberate Dwight Eisenhower.

Richard Nixon, Eisenhower's vice-president and the Republican presidential candidate in 1960, planned to counterpose his supposed maturity and experience in government against Kennedy's alleged immaturity and insubstantial legislative record. This strategy exploded during the widely heralded opener to a series of presidential debates. People who listened on radio generally reported that Nixon had bested Kennedy, but TV *showed* a very different contest. It made the sharp-featured Nixon, then recovering from illness, appear old and tired at the age of forty-seven, whereas it accentuated the best qualities of Kennedy, only four years younger. The harsh TV lights also high-lighted Nixon's famous five o'clock shadow, reminding viewers of the old car-icature of him as "Tricky Dick," the "guy from whom you would never buy a used car." Most important, Kennedy's confident manner during the crucial first debate undercut Nixon's claim about his opponent's inexperience.

The election of 1960 was very close: Kennedy won by only 120,000 popu-lar votes, and small shifts in several large states—such as in Illinois, where the Democratic machine mobilized enough phantom voters in Chicago to give Kennedy a statewide victory—would have made Nixon president. An unusual-ly high percentage of the eligible electorate, nearly 64 percent, turned out to vote. Although Nixon scrupulously avoided any hint of anti-Catholicism, some of his supporters did not. This apparently mobilized Catholic voters, who tend-ed to be Democrats anyway, and JFK piled up large Catholic majorities in most northern states. Kennedy also ran better among African American voters than Stevenson had in 1956, and a high turnout among blacks plus the political clout of Lyndon Johnson allowed the Democratic ticket to carry the crucial state of Texas. Johnson's presence also apparently helped the Democrats pull out victories in several other southern states.

The New Frontier: Camelot

Although Kennedy could hardly claim a popular mandate, his publicists quick-ly built an imposing image for his administration—the "New Frontier," the successor to the New and Fair Deals. JFK assembled his version of Franklin Roosevelt's brain trust. He appointed his brother and campaign manager, Robert Kennedy, attorney general; Robert McNamara, president of Ford Motor Company, became secretary of defense; Harvard's McGeorge Bundy assumed the important role of national security adviser to the president; and Dean Rusk, the head of the Ford Foundation, received the coveted position of sec-retary of state. Even the secondary jobs claimed top individuals. (Henry Kissinger, outgunned in such fierce competition, took over Bundy's courses at Harvard and awaited an administration that would better appreciate his tal-ents.) Vice-President Johnson left the first cabinet meeting dazzled by the in-tellect that Kennedy had assembled. "You should have seen all those men," he told House Speaker Sam Rayburn. "Well, Lyndon, you may be right and they may be every bit as intelligent as you say," replied Rayburn, "but I'd feel a whole lot better about them if just one of them had run for sheriff once."

Kennedy's White House advertised itself as a center of art and culture. (Later accounts would highlight another side of White House life: alleged assig-nations with paramours, a supposed reliance on amphetamines and other drugs, apparent connections with organized crime figures, and a successful effort to hide the president's physical infirmities.) Jacqueline Kennedy, a well-educated woman who spoke several languages, became the special guardian of culture. She invited classical musicians to perform at the White House, redecorated the old mansion, hired a French chef, and even conducted a tour of the White House for TV viewers. The Kennedy parties were lavish productions in the grand style; I. F. Stone, the maverick journalist, complained that the atmo-sphere resembled that of "a reigning monarch's court." Such a comparison probably did not disturb Kennedy's admirers. Many of them liked to think of the Kennedy White House as a modern-day Camelot.

The New Frontier also emphasized toughness. John Kennedy's inaugural address boasted, in a jibe at the age of the outgoing Eisenhower administration, that he and his advisers were all "born in this century, tempered by war, disciplined by a hard and bitter peace." Facing a dangerous world, they could not afford to appear "soft." In defending his space program, for example, JFK bragged that Americans would accept challenges "not because they are easy but because they are hard." The Kennedy team displayed its mettle during impromptu touch football games; here, the president's brother Robert gained a reputation as a hard-nosed scrapper with little use for losers. After Floyd Patterson lost his heavyweight boxing title, the attorney general quickly removed the ex-champ's picture from his office. Kennedy's people, to some critics, seemed too anxious to find a foreign or domestic "crisis" in which they could display their grit under pressure.

In 1962, for example, Kennedy massed the full power of the national government to combat a price increase by U.S. Steel and several other large firms. JFK denounced the companies as unpatriotic and contrasted their actions with those of military officers who were already dying in Vietnam and of reservists who had been called up to meet a feared confrontation with the Soviet Union in Berlin. The president coupled this verbal offensive with a massive legal one. The justice department sought evidence of price fixing; FBI agents investigated possible illegal activities by steel corporations; the Federal Trade Commission threatened to look into the same questions; and administration sources hinted at antitrust actions against the steel giants. At the same time, the defense department refused to buy from companies that raised prices, and the Kennedy administration pressured its corporate friends to resist the lead of U.S. Steel. Confronted by this counterattack, the steel companies retreated and rolled back prices.

The steel episode became a contested symbol of Kennedy's approach to leadership. The president portrayed the short skirmish as an extension of foreign affairs; price increases, he claimed, threatened national security. This was the type of problem that required crisis management. The president's critics viewed the situation differently. Business representatives predictably denounced Kennedy for using "police state" tactics, but even some foes of large corporations wondered if Kennedy's actions suggested a dangerous "crisis mentality" and, later, a lack of consistent domestic policies. Within a year, the steel firms raised prices twice, critics noted, and the Kennedy administration did nothing.

Although JFK was more interested in foreign policy than in domestic issues, he did identify some general goals for his New Frontier at home. Some recalled Harry Truman's Fair Deal: federal aid to education, a national health program, and expansion of domestic-spending programs. Kennedy never saw his proposals on education or health care pass Congress, but he could take some credit for several pieces of domestic legislation. Congress broadened Social Security coverage, covered more people under federal minimum-wage standards, raised the minimum-wage rate itself to $1.25 an hour, appropriated more money for public housing, established a manpower training program, and passed an area redevelopment act for impoverished areas in Appalachia. These measures reflected JFK's preference for moderate, gradual change and his political caution. Nowhere was Kennedy's cautious approach more evident than on the question of legislation aimed at racial discrimination. (See pp. 135–138.)

Kennedy's presidency also coincided with a renewed interest in women's issues. In 1961, at the urging of prominent women within the Democratic party, he appointed a Presidential Commission on the Status of Women, headed by Eleanor Roosevelt, that was charged with addressing the "prejudices and outmoded customs [that] act as barriers to the full realization of women's rights." The commission's report, entitled *American Women* (1963), found discrimination in employment; inequality in legal guarantees for men and women; and minimal social services, such as child care, that limited many women to part-time, low-paid employment. It recommended action to create additional child-care services, urged more women to seek public office, and pressed the federal government to move against discriminatory practices.

One result of this new activism was the Equal Pay Act of 1963, which made it illegal for employers to compensate men and women at different rates of pay for the same job. Although this legislation did not significantly raise the economic status of working women, most of whom were employed in job categories that included few men, the issue of gender inequality had been revived as an item for public debate. *American Women* also spurred some state governments to undertake similar studies and helped to energize a new generation of women's rights activists.

The Kennedy administration tried to refine the techniques of Truman's positive-state economists. In his first state of the union address, JFK promised that the sluggish economy would soon turn around and then enter a period of steady, long-term growth. Kennedy, of course, blamed economic problems on the Eisenhower administration. The GNP had risen too slowly during the late 1950s, while the unemployment rate had climbed to around 6 percent. Although Kennedy shared Eisenhower's limited background in economics—he had received a C in his introductory economics course at Harvard—he gathered a distinguished group of advisers, including John Kenneth Galbraith and Walter Heller. According to these advocates of the "new economics," the executive branch could use its influence over federal expenditures and over monetary policy to promote economic growth and "fine-tune" the economy.

The Kennedy administration adopted a number of economic strategies. Increased government spending pumped new funds into the economy and brightened the long-range picture on growth, Kennedy's economists claimed. In 1962, the White House persuaded Congress to give business firms a 7 percent tax credit for investments in new machinery and plants. At the same time, the administration granted one of the business community's key requests, a readjustment in the depreciation schedules for corporate taxes. This change in the tax code was designed to encourage the purchase of new equipment by allowing businesses to write off assets against their tax liabilities more quickly. Taken together, the investment tax credit and the revised depreciation schedule reduced business taxes and theoretically increased corporate spending by about $2.5 billion; the total tax cut amounted to almost 12 percent.

Advocates of the new economics urged further steps to boost production and employment. Galbraith, who had become ambassador to India, continued to advocate massive government expenditures for social-welfare programs.

Kennedy rejected this approach but did consider further tax cuts. Slashing taxes would expand purchasing power for both consumers and businesses, but it would also increase the federal deficit. Heller, who became head of the Council of Economic Advisers, was among those who favored further tax cuts, while advocates of a balanced federal budget, particularly Federal Reserve Board Chair William McChesney Martin, counseled Kennedy to reject this move. The president did shelve any tax-cut proposal for 1962 but unveiled a comprehensive revenue bill that included a $10 billion cut and various other changes in the tax laws the following year.

Kennedy's approach to domestic affairs reflected his core assumptions about the role of the national government. The "old sweeping issues have largely disappeared," he told Yale's graduating class in 1962. Domestic problems were now "more subtle and less simple" than those of the New-Deal era. Government now needed to help manage a complex economy, ensure increased productivity, and guarantee a rising prosperity for all citizens. The "sophisticated and technical questions involved in keeping a great economic machinery moving ahead" required "technical answers—not political answers." Clear-thinking bureaucrats, rational technicians who could manage complex institutions, held the key to effective government. Although his brief tenure in office tempered some of his early optimism about implementing this vision, John Kennedy died confident that his view of government remained correct and that Camelot's bright young managers could handle the nation's domestic problems.

Assassination

John F. Kennedy's presidency ended violently on November 22, 1963. A presidential motorcade was winding its way past unexpectedly friendly crowds in Dallas when a volley of shots—some claimed three, others, four or five—raked Kennedy's open-topped limousine. John Connally, the Democratic governor of Texas, was seriously wounded. One shot ripped away the back of Kennedy's head. Within an hour, doctors at Parkland Hospital pronounced the president dead; the thousand days of Camelot were over. Aboard Air Force One, Vice-President Lyndon Baines Johnson took the oath of office as the new chief executive.

The president's death brought several days of similarly stunning events, all of which were shown live on the "cool medium" of television Kennedy had mastered during his political life. For several days, people watched an elaborate, televised memorial to John F. Kennedy. Pictures of Kennedy's coffin, of a riderless horse that symbolized the fallen president, and of his grieving family clashed with scenes from Kennedy's past. Images of a vibrant JFK—sailing off Cape Cod, laughing with his children, or working in the Oval Office—made his violent death seem even more tragic. The Kennedy mystique grew exponentially during these few days.

Yet, this TV spectacle also raised troubling issues. Shortly after the president's shooting, Dallas police officials claimed that they had captured the president's killer, Lee Harvey Oswald. A former Marine who had briefly lived in the Soviet Union, Oswald proclaimed his innocence. On Sunday, November 24, while Dallas police were transferring Oswald to a new jail, TV viewers witnessed the assassination of Kennedy's alleged assassin. Jack Ruby, a local nightclub operator who (like Oswald himself) had vague ties to organized crime figures, fatally shot Oswald at close range, right in the Dallas police station.

Oswald's bizarre death raised doubts about his role in the Kennedy assassination. Could one gunman, whose skills as a marksman seemed unremarkable, have killed a president with an inexpensive rifle purchased through a mail-order catalogue? Might not Oswald be part of (or even the patsy for) some larger conspiracy? Was Kennedy's death somehow tied to pro- or anti-Castro forces? Was Ruby a hit man sent to silence Oswald? Might the Dallas police, the FBI, or even the CIA be involved? Was it possible that members of organized crime, who disliked Kennedy and his brother Robert, had ordered a "hit" on the President?

Lyndon Johnson, wanting to squelch rumors, persuaded Earl Warren, the chief justice of the United States, to head an official inquiry. After a ten-month investigation, the Warren Commission declared Oswald the lone assassin and rejected all notions of a broader plot. Conspiracy buffs, however, were already offering an amazing variety of scenarios, and the Warren Commission's *Report* merely gave them twenty-six volumes of evidence to piece through. More sober critics pointed out serious flaws in the Commission's hastily researched and sloppily documented *Report*. Americans gradually came to dismiss its version of what happened in Dallas.

Proponents of alternative conspiracy theories received some vindication in 1979. A special committee of the House of Representatives concluded, on the basis of additional (but debatable) evidence, that the Warren Commission had failed to account for all of the shots fired at Kennedy's motorcade. JFK had "probably" fallen victim to some kind of plot, possibly involving organized crime figures, the committee speculated, but it offered scant evidence to bolster its theory.

The controversy over Kennedy's death, which never receded from popular memory, revived following the release of Oliver Stone's film *JFK* in 1991. *JFK* recounted the story of Jim Garrison, who had tried unsuccessfully to prosecute an alleged conspiracy while a district attorney in New Orleans during the mid-1960s. Stone's docudrama merged contemporary film footage, including Abraham Zapruder's famous home movie of Kennedy's motorcade encountering a hail of gunfire, with Hollywood recreations of the events of November 22, 1963. Moreover, *JFK* supplemented the cast of bizarre characters who had been drawn into Garrison's failed prosecution with a fictional governmental official who claimed that responsibility for Kennedy's assassination extended into the highest levels of power in Washington.

Stone's film tapped popular skepticism about the Warren Commission's theory and initiated a new drive to reopen the case. Critics of the Commission charged that vast quantities of evidence about Kennedy's death remained inaccessible to independent scrutiny. As a result, Congress created a blue-ribbon commission and charged it with ensuring that evidence about the Kennedy assassination would be preserved and declassified for future researchers.

Nearly fifty years after John F. Kennedy's rise to prominence, both his life and death remain topics of sharp historical debate and of tabloid-style speculation. The problems and tragedies suffered by other members of his family, such as the 1999 plane-crash death of John F. Kennedy, Jr., kept "the Kennedy story" alive. The desire to know more about Kennedy and the days of Camelot seems to have grown more, rather than less, intense with the passage of time.

THE GREAT SOCIETY

Controversy also continues to swirl around Kennedy's successor, Lyndon Baines Johnson. Two of the most emotion-charged events in postwar history, the ambitious set of domestic programs that Johnson called the Great Society and U.S. involvement in the Vietnam War, dominate the story of his presidency.

LBJ

Lyndon Johnson, except for being another wealthy Democrat, appeared to have little in common with the cool, urbane Kennedy. Johnson, in contrast to JFK, had loved the Senate, and during the 1950s he had dominated that body as the Democratic majority leader. But despite his many years in Washington, Johnson remained "a good old boy" from the hill country of Texas. During his early White-House days, Johnson liked to show a homemade film of deer mating on his ranch and contribute his own ribald soundtrack.

The whiff of scandal surrounded Johnson's career in Washington. Critics snickered about "landslide Lyndon's" suspicious eighty-six-vote triumph in a 1948 senatorial primary in Texas; about his close association with Washington influence-peddlers; and about questionable financial dealings throughout the Southwest. Johnson came to Washington as a Depression-era crusader during Roosevelt's New Deal; he left as a former president and a multimillionaire. To some people, LBJ looked too much like Jay Gatsby in a Stetson hat.

Johnson constantly worried about his public image. People would not give him "a fair shake as president," he often complained, "because I am a southerner." But even Johnson realized that his problems lay deeper. "Why don't people like me?" he asked visitors to the White House. One elderly caller, who felt that his advanced years protected him, replied honestly: "Because, Mr. President, you are not a very likable man." Defensive about his roots in rural Texas and perhaps still burdened by the conflicting childhood demands of his rough-edged, hard-drinking father and his refined, intellectual mother, Johnson seemed to require constant reassurance.

He also demanded unswerving loyalty. Johnson could fly into sudden rages, publicly berating his aides and summoning them for meetings at all hours of the night. He appeared to need the LBJ brand on everything. (His wife inherited the name Lady Bird, but LBJ christened his daughters Lynda Bird and Lucy Baines and even called his dog Little Beagle.) White-House aides worried about having to be the bearer of bad news, and those who did often quickly dropped from favor. Critical reporters could expect the "Johnson treatment"—a private audience during which the president conducted a nonstop monologue on his own glories.

Johnson smoothly handled the transition from the Kennedy administration. Tapes of his telephone and office conversations from late 1963 and 1964, many of which became available through the Johnson Presidential Library during the 1990s, suggest an energetic, confident leader. LBJ could effortlessly switch attention from topic to topic and simultaneously deal with an array of problems, personal as well as political. He could also change what he claimed to be his own position on an issue just as quickly. He could reassure a critic of

Kennedy's policies, for example, that his support for their enactment was dictated by practical politics, not personal commitment; minutes later, when talking to a supporter of Kennedy's initiatives, he could take the opposite tack. LBJ kept copies of public opinion polls, the earliest ones testimonies to his popularity, close at hand.

After 1964, however, Johnson watched his standing in these polls steadily decline. He often blamed the media for his "credibility gap," and unflattering stories about Johnson's vanity and duplicity probably did color popular perception. Most reporters had liked Kennedy and pigeonholed unfavorable stories about his personal life. Johnson considered himself the target of unfair reporting by journalists who compared him unfavorably with the still untarnished image of JFK as well as with the vigorous reality of the Kennedy family. President Kennedy's youngest brother, Ted, had won election to the Senate from Massachusetts in 1962, and two years later, Robert Kennedy gained a Senate seat from New York. Members of the Kennedy entourage hardly concealed their distaste for Johnson. Many Washington reporters expressed more sympathy for "Camelot-in-exile—the intellectuals and politicians who swarmed around Bobby's home at Hickory Hill, Virginia, and the Kennedy family compound on Cape Cod—than for the embattled Johnson administration. Toward the end of his presidency, as controversy over the Vietnam War engulfed the White House, what might be called Johnson-bashing became a national political pastime.

Lyndon Johnson and his presidency continue to attract passionate critics and, increasingly, some equally passionate defenders. A host of questions remain up for debate. How could a person seemingly so skilled in politics wound his own party and deplete his own political capital in such a short time? What is the legacy of his Great Society and how did it affect social policy making? Why did Johnson, the consummate political horse trader for most of his political life, appear incapable of brokering some deal to extricate the United States from Vietnam?

The Johnson Program and the Landslide Election of 1964

In the wake of Kennedy's death, Lyndon Johnson began to break what legislative activists had long called the "stalemate" in Congress. During LBJ's first year as president, Congress approved a tax bill, a civil rights law, federally sponsored recreation activities, funds for urban mass transit, and the Economic Opportunity Act, the measure that signaled the beginning of the War on Poverty that Johnson would later officially declare.

Johnson also moved to fulfill JFK's promise to promote economic growth. The economy, aided by the tax reductions enacted in 1964 (which Kennedy had proposed) and by increased federal spending (particularly for the expanding war in Southeast Asia), built on the gains begun during Kennedy's administration. Between 1960 and 1964, the Gross National Product increased by 24 percent while corporate profits went up by 57 percent; the next year the GNP climbed by almost 7 percent and corporate profits by 20 percent; and by 1965 the nation reached what most economists considered full employment, an unemployment rate less than 4 percent. The boom lasted through Johnson's second term. The unemployment rate never exceeded 4 percent, and the GNP expanded at a rate of almost 5 percent a year. The median family income, measured in constant dollars, increased from $8,543 in 1963 to $10,768 in 1969.

The Kennedy-Johnson boom did not impress everyone. Conservative economists warned that the expansion was occurring too rapidly and that the Johnson administration was ignoring the threat of inflation. Observers to the left of Johnson, such as Harry Truman's former economic adviser Leon Keyserling, contended that the tax cuts of 1964 tilted too much toward the wealthy. According to Keyserling's calculations, the average taxpayer in the $10,000-per-year-income bracket received only a 3.5 percent increase in disposable income; someone who earned $100,000 enjoyed a boost of 16.5 percent; and those in the $200,000-plus category, got a 31.1 percent windfall. Keyserling and other economists concerned about inequality also contended the rise in corporate profits during the Kennedy-Johnson years indicated that large corporations seemed the primary beneficiaries of the high-growth policies of the new economics.

Lyndon Johnson, who claimed to be "president of all the people," saw the situation differently. Of course, wealthy individuals and large businesses benefited from economic expansion, but so did ordinary workers and budding entrepreneurs. Moreover, galloping prosperity would enable the country to advance beyond the goals of the New Deal, the Fair Deal, and Kennedy's New Frontier. Buoyed by his early successes, LBJ claimed "a broad, deep and genuine consensus among most groups within our diverse society" on behalf of programs aimed at helping people who were struggling on the most meager of incomes during a period of general affluence.

If only everyone would "sit down and reason together," Johnson argued, the United States could realize what he was coming to call the "Great Society." Speaking during the spring of 1964 before an outdoor crowd of nearly 100,000 people, LBJ heralded the coming of a time in which "the meaning of our lives matches the marvelous products of our labor" and a place "where men are more concerned with the quality of their goals than the quantity of their goods." The measures passed during his first year in office, in other words, were merely the prelude to the Great-Society programs that people could expect if he were elected president in 1964, Johnson claimed.

Republicans virtually handed Lyndon Johnson the presidency in 1964. Militant conservatives, most of whom lived in the rim states from southern California to Florida or in small Midwest towns, had gained control of the GOP following Nixon's defeat in 1960. Wanting to offer the nation "a choice, not an echo," they nominated Senator Barry Goldwater of Arizona for president. The hero of these conservatives, Goldwater struck too many other people as an injudicious extremist. During a series of bitter primary campaigns, some of his overzealous supporters reinforced this image by personal attacks on Goldwater's Republican opponents, particularly New York's Nelson Rockefeller. When Rockefeller rose to address the GOP's 1964 convention, Goldwater's delegates shouted him down. Goldwater's own acceptance speech only increased doubts about his intentions. "Extremism in the defense of liberty," he challenged his critics, "is no vice. . . . Moderation in the pursuit of justice is no virtue." A likable, unpretentious person, who enjoyed a good personal relationship with most Democrats, including Johnson, Goldwater never understood why so many people distrusted his conservative political ideas.

Goldwater ran squarely against Johnson's brand of liberalism. Ever since the New Deal, Republican candidates had ritualistically denounced the government in Washington, but Goldwater really seemed to mean it. His strategists claimed that a militantly conservative campaign would bring millions of alienated people to the polls and attract a backlash vote from southern whites who were angry about the civil-rights movement. A Goldwater administration, the senator from Arizona appeared to say, would sweep away all the programs established since the New Deal: agricultural subsidies, protection for labor unions, civil-rights measures, and all of the other "socialistic" laws. "I will give you back your freedom," he promised. On several occasions he even mused about making Social Security voluntary, an off-handed comment that Democrats falsely translated into the claim that Goldwater actually planned to abolish the system entirely. At the same time, missile-rattling asides about confronting the USSR and gaining a quick victory in Vietnam enabled Democrats to paint Goldwater as a trigger-happy Neanderthal.

Johnson won a landslide victory in November. With the moderate center of the electorate deserting the Republican party, Johnson and his running mate, Senator Hubert Humphrey of Minnesota, gathered 61.3 percent of the popular ballots and the electoral votes of all but six states. At the same time, Democrats gained 39 seats in the House of Representatives and more than 500 new seats in state legislatures across the country. Johnson celebrated his "politics of consensus," and some nervous East-Coast Republicans even feared, *very wrongly* it turned out, that the "Goldwater caper" might destroy the GOP. Certainly, the 1964 election provided Johnson with the perfect context for pushing new federal legislation. There were more Democrats in Congress than at any time since 1938, and many of the new Democratic senators and representatives enthusiastically supported the legislation on Johnson's agenda. Only during the New Deal of the 1930s would a twentieth-century congress do so much so quickly. When Johnson left Washington in 1969, his cabinet gave him a plaque commemorating the more than 200 "landmark laws" passed during his administration.

The Great Society and the War on Poverty

LBJ watched his Great Society measures speed through the Eighty-Ninth Congress. Medicare and Medicaid programs fulfilled Harry Truman's goal of providing some type of government-sponsored health-care for people over sixty-five and for those with low incomes. Two other long-debated measures, the Elementary and Secondary Education Act and the Higher Education Act, extended federal funds to schools at all levels of the educational hierarchy. The Voting Rights Act of 1965 eliminated barriers against black voters in the South. It suspended literacy tests and authorized federal inspectors to monitor precincts in which the attorney general suspected chicanery in voting procedures. In response to urban problems, Congress passed the Housing Act of 1965, which created the new Department of Housing and Urban Development (HUD), and the Demonstration Cites and Metropolitan Development Act of 1966, which provided federal money for local model city projects. Prodded by advocates of automobile safety, Congress passed several bills dealing with highway and traffic safety. One measure, the Motor Vehicle Safety Act (1966), inaugurated federal safety standards for the auto industry and established a uniform grading system for tire manufacturers. Congress also created a new cabinet-level Department of Transportation and gave its secretary the job of coordinating all of the federal programs that concerned transportation issues.

Finally, Congress passed a number of other laws that, in the context of the other Great Society legislation, seemed minor but later proved to be of major significance. There was the Immigration Act of 1965, which admitted newcomers primarily on the basis of their economic skills rather than their national origin and provided special provisions for people who already had close relatives in the United States. The law was expected to increase immigration from Eastern Europe, but the greatest beneficiaries of the changes were people who wanted to come to the United States from Asia and Latin America.

Several laws began a process in which the scope of federal regulation would inexorably, until the backlash of the 1980s, expand. The Truth in Packaging Act, which dealt with deceptive advertising practices, showed concern for consumer protection. Congress moved into another new area by creating the National Endowment for the Arts and the National Endowment for the Humanities, two agencies that would come to play significant, and controversial, roles in providing federal funding for cultural activities. In addition, the Great Society introduced important environmental legislation, including the Wilderness Act of 1964, which set aside 9 million acres of federal land for preservation from development, and a 1967 bill aimed at mandating clean air standards.

Most people initially accepted these measures. Although arch-conservatives labeled them "socialistic," they seemed part of a Johnson-inspired version of the "positive state" anticipated by the New Deal and outlined in the Employment Act of 1946. Controversies erupted over details—how much Medicare patients should pay from their own pockets or how quickly automakers should comply with safety standards—but a majority of voters accepted the broad goals of these Great Society laws. Much to LBJ's displeasure, the loudest complaints came from social activists who charged that the programs required only minimal sacrifices from wealthy individuals and corporations and provided too little assistance for truly needy citizens. Consumer advocates, for example, claimed that Detroit's auto manufacturers were blocking more stringent safety laws while using the cost of minimal improvements as an excuse to raise their prices. Federal assistance for mass-transportation systems and low-income housing, urban planners complained, remained small.

Johnson, in addition to expanding the reach of the positive state, launched a crusade of his own: the elimination and prevention of poverty. Most Americans, as Michael Harrington had tried to remind policymakers during the 1950s, had largely forgotten that nearly one-fourth of the population, mostly of European descent, still lived in substandard housing and subsisted on inadequate diets. His book, *The Other America* (1962), had helped to bring wider attention to these "invisible poor," and Johnson declared his own War on Poverty in 1965.

The array of antipoverty programs initially seemed dazzling. There were federal funds for public-works projects, particularly new highways in Appalachia; a Job Corps to train young people who lacked marketable skills; Work-Study, a program to supplement the incomes of college students; Volunteers in Service to America (VISTA), which would send young volunteers to low-income areas;

and Head Start, a program designed to provide compensatory education for preschoolers from low-income families. Although these measures went beyond any previous national effort, even the supporters of these programs conceded the traditionalist approach of the War on Poverty. In providing federal tax dollars and another Washington agency (the Office of Economic Opportunity, or OEO), the Great Society was still employing the positive-state approach of the Fair-Deal era.

One part of the War on Poverty, the Community Action Program (CAP), did suggest a possibly significant change in approach. Under Title II of the Economic Opportunity Act, Congress authorized funds for local groups, either private nonprofit or public organizations, that developed innovative, grassroots programs. Sounding a theme that conservatives would later use for a very different political agenda, President Johnson argued that CAP rested on "the fact that local citizens best understand their own problems and know best how to deal with these problems." At first, many grassroots activists hoped that CAP might provide federal funds with which to plan their own social and economic programs.

The War on Poverty brought Lyndon Johnson—and people with low incomes—few clear-cut victories. Conservative critics denounced the antipoverty effort for giving taxpayers' money to people unwilling to help themselves. ("I helped the War on Poverty," went one lame joke of the mid-1960s. "I threw a hand grenade at a bum.") Actually a good deal of the federal funds went to OEO's white-collar bureaucrats or into expensive equipment. After their stints in public service, some antipoverty workers established consulting firms that received government contracts to provide "expert" advice. Early in the fight, some social critics declared that the "poverty-industrial complex" was doing better than the people who were supposed to receive tangible assistance.

The CAP initiative also produced mixed results—and considerable controversy. Established welfare agencies and local political leaders opposed funding new community groups. When some of the CAP organizations called for radical redistribution of wealth and political power, OEO's bureaucrats rejected the entire CAP concept and began to emphasize prepackaged programs from Washington, such as Head Start, community beautification projects, and legal aid. The OEO came to see local CAP groups as administrators rather than policy-initiators.

Most important, although Lyndon Johnson would never admit it, the nation simply could not wage both a war in Vietnam and one against economic problems at home without increased taxation. As a result of Johnson's determination not to seek a substantial tax increase, the entire nation soon faced a rising rate of inflation, and low-income people saw funding for social programs begin to dry up. Although federal expenditures for social programs, measured in proportion to the country's GNP, continued to increase between 1965 and 1975, the sums appropriated never matched those that LBJ had once projected.

More than thirty years after Johnson sounded his battle cry, historians and students of public policy continue to debate the significance and meaning of the Great Society. Beginning in the late 1970s, when conservative winds began to sweep over American life, Johnson's Great Society began to attract even harsher criticism than it had received during the 1960s. Social scientist Charles Murray, in his much-discussed *Losing Ground* (1984), changed the terms of debate. Although some conservatives continued to claim that the Great Society had given aid and comfort to many "undeserving" people, "welfare cheats" and "food-stamp hustlers," Murray's book argued that low-income people themselves deserved better than the flawed Johnson programs. The Great Society provided little tangible assistance to people who needed help and actually did them considerable harm by promoting social deterioration. Enticed by higher welfare payments, Murray's study charged, many low-income people saw little need to marry, settle down, and seek permanent employment. A life on minimal governmental assistance seemed to satisfy too many. Thus, the Great Society, according to this interpretation, was both ineffective and socially pernicious.

Moreover, according to this conservative critique, the Great-Society experiment eventually choked off economic growth by fueling inflation and converting potential investment capital into wasteful governmental programs. Had ill-conceived social spending not damaged the nation's economy, *Losing Ground* concludes, virtually everyone could have found a job and a relatively affluent lifestyle. This conservative thesis, which gained wide currency in both the media and academic institutions during the last two decades of the twentieth century, saw the Great Society, at best, as an ignoble failure and, at worst, as a precipitant of the poverty and economic stagnation it was supposed to cure.

Defenders of the Great Society challenged this conservative viewpoint. Most rejected, for example, the claim that low-income people actually preferred welfare to meaningful employment. Moreover, since expenditures for Great-Society programs never approached massive levels, they could not have had the disastrous economic consequences posited in *Losing Ground.* Appropriations for OEO, the centerpiece of the War on Poverty, never amounted to more than $2 billion per year. Still, the Johnson programs of the 1960s were the first significant commitment to federal spending for domestic programs since the 1930s. Between 1964 and 1976, federal spending for social welfare programs increased from 5 percent of GNP to 11 percent.

Supporters of the Great Society have also claimed qualified successes for Johnson's efforts. Governmental programs were managed with reasonable efficiency, provided tangible benefits to recipients, and demonstrated the still untapped potential of the positive-state model. Within two decades, for example, new national legislation enabled black voters, 90 percent of whom had been disenfranchised in 1965, to cast ballots and to elect thousands of black officeholders. Similarly, Medicaid extended basic health care to many low-income people, and Medicare provided broader, albeit incomplete, coverage for the elderly. Although these and other Great-Society programs may never have fulfilled Johnson's grandiose goals, they did inaugurate more than a decade of social spending that improved the everyday lives of millions of Americans. In this view, the Great Society's faults came more from the failure to continue adequate funding than from flaws in the basic vision.

Even these positive assessments of the Great Society, it should be reemphasized, acknowledged that Johnson intended no radical assault on postwar assumptions about the role of governmental socioeconomic policy. Emphasizing the goal of creating economic opportunity, architects of the Great Society never envisioned a redistribution of wealth, income, or political power. Their solution to what they called economic "injustice" rested on the same positive-state vision as Harry Truman's Fair Deal. They hoped to adjust the existing governmental and political machinery to promote greater economic expansion and target a portion of this growth for more generous funding of social-welfare programs. The promise of an ever-growing economic pie could again eliminate discussions about what proportion of the whole might be redistributed—through a radically revised tax system, for example—to each citizen. Studies of both income distribution and of individual and family wealth showed that the gap between the very rich and the truly needy narrowed relatively little during the era of the Great Society. Johnson's program did not change the nation's basic socioeconomic structure; nor was it intended to do so. Once Johnson began fighting a lengthy and increasingly expensive war overseas, though, the hope of sustained economic growth and, consequently, rising expenditures for domestic social programs seemed increasingly out of reach.

The Warren Court and the Origins of "Liberal Legalism"

During the 1960s, the federal judiciary also confronted the difficulty of effecting rapid social change. Chief Justice Earl Warren, who had been appointed to the U.S. Supreme Court by Dwight Eisenhower in 1953, and his activist colleagues believed that they could forecast the path of social change and advance the cause of justice. The result was a flood of controversial, landmark judicial decisions, especially during the 1960s.

Long before Johnson became president, controversy had surrounded the Supreme Court and Chief Justice Warren. The famous civil rights decision, *Brown v. Board of Education* (1954), angered opponents of racial integration throughout the country. In a series of rulings handed down late in the mid-1950s, a divided Court also ruled in favor of the First-Amendment claims of alleged Communists. Anti-Communist crusaders denounced the Court, and the ultra-reactionary John Birch Society erected billboards that demanded IMPEACH EARL WARREN. However, when the Court appeared to reverse itself on several free-speech cases later in the decade, civil libertarians criticized the justices, particularly Felix Frankfurter, for allegedly caving in to popular pressure. The Warren Court thus established no clear pattern of decision making during the chief justice's first years on the bench.

During the 1960s, however, the activists within the federal judiciary gained ascendancy. The U.S. Supreme Court under Chief Justice Warren attracted the most attention, but many lower federal courts, staffed by judges appointed during the years of Democratic political dominance, proved every bit as activist in their rulings. Legal historians have come to label this era's judicial activism as "legal liberalism"—an attempt by courts to advance political policies, such as strict protection of the rights of criminal defendants, that lacked the votes to be enacted into law by legislatures. Critics charged that such judicial activism, particularly when done by five of nine appointed Supreme Court justices, flew in the face of basic principles of democracy. Supporters of the Court, in response, could counter claim that nothing could be more democratic than actively protecting individual and group rights, as federal courts were trying to do. In this view, a legislative vote against a bill expanding the rights of criminal defendants might be a case of majority rule but not necessarily a principled example of democratic governance.

The liberal legalism of the 1960s sparked a "rights revolution" that lasted into the 1970s. The decisions of the U.S. Supreme Court, in particular, signaled that a majority of justices would be sympathetic to individuals and groups who claimed a violation of their constitutionally protected rights.

To begin, this majority supported the argument that state and local governments must conform to a strict, uniform standard when they accused someone of committing a crime. The activists agreed, for instance, that the effective assertion of legal rights too often remained dependant on income and social standing. Wealthy, well-connected people could afford effective lawyers and thereby aggressively assert their rights. Low-income people rarely employed any kind of attorney and faced powerful government institutions with inadequate legal knowledge. In *Gideon v. Wainwright* (1963), the Court held that the Bill of Rights demanded that states must, in felony cases, furnish an attorney to all persons who could not afford to hire their own. Decisions such as *Gideon* expressed the Court's commitment to enforcing a single, national standard of "due process of law" and to making the right of "equality before the law" both a legal principle and a social fact.

In addition, federal courts during the Warren era attempted to align constitutional law with the political policies of the New Deal, Fair Deal, and Great Society. Beginning with *Baker v. Carr* (1962), a majority of justices held that the way in which most states laid out electoral districts deprived urban voters (more likely to be Democrats) of equal protection of the law. *Baker v. Carr*'s "one person-one vote" rule aimed at eliminating the situation in which rural districts with comparatively few people had the same number of political representatives as more populous urban ones. Hoping to encourage more vigorous scrutiny of public officials, *New York Times v. Sullivan* (1964) made it more difficult for politicians to intimidate critics with libel suits. In a series of highly controversial decisions, the majority declared that most types of Bible reading and prayer in public schools violated a policy of toleration for religious difference (or indifference) and the First Amendment's prohibition against the establishment of religion. Earl Warren was declaring God himself unconstitutional, conservatives complained. Their mood remained sour when the same Court struck down laws against obscenity on the basis of the First Amendment's protection for the right of free speech.

Despite the criticism, however, the Supreme Court's activists seemed to have consolidated their position by the mid-1960s. The Kennedy-Johnson appointees—particularly Arthur Goldberg; Abe Fortas; and the court's first African-American justice, Thurgood Marshall—appeared to ensure an activist majority for years to come. Then, after 1966, this majority began slowly to unravel, and attacks on the Court gradually escalated.

One of the Court's own decisions did considerable damage. In *Miranda v. Arizona* (1966), a majority held that, once a police investigation focused on a particular person, authorities had to inform the suspect of their constitutional rights to an attorney (including one appointed by the state) and to remain silent. *Miranda,* more than any other ruling of the 1960s, united the Court's critics around a highly emotional issue. This decision coincided with popular fears that criminals were running roughshod and that rulings of the Warren Court were handcuffing the police. Although most criminologists saw the situation as more complex than this—crime rates were rising but court rulings, including *Miranda,* seemed to play no direct role in this phenomenon—popular criticism and pressure from conservative lawyers increased. Congress considered legislation to overturn the *Miranda* decision, and conservative politicians demanded the appointment of judges who promised to "interpret the Constitution strictly." In practice, of course, this would mean appointment of judges who favored a less strict interpretation of the Bill of Rights and who opposed the political assumptions of the Warren Court's majority.

Amid growing political and legal controversy, Chief Justice Warren announced in 1968 that he would be retiring before the end of Johnson's term. Johnson wanted to elevate his confidant Abe Fortas to replace Warren as chief justice and then appoint an ally from Texas to the spot that Fortas would vacate. Hoping for a GOP victory in the 1968 election, Republicans and many conservative southern Democrats were able to block Johnson's plan when *Life* magazine uncovered evidence of questionable financial and political deals by Justice Fortas. Johnson had to withdraw his nomination, and Fortas was eventually forced to resign. Johnson's Republican successor, Richard Nixon, thus inherited two vacancies on the Court. The chief justice's post went to Warren Burger, and another Minnesotan, Harry Blackmun, replaced the disgraced Fortas.

Meanwhile, legal scholars were beginning to question the impact of legal liberalism and the rights revolution. Obviously, activist judges had established, for example, stricter standards for the law enforcement officials who applied criminal law. But these same courts lacked the means—as they always had and always will—to enforce their rulings to the letter. Police departments could learn to live with the *Miranda* warnings and still gain confessions; publicly appointed lawyers sometimes acted more as agents of the prosecutor's office than as representatives of their clients; and local pressures often made it very difficult to implement decisions on controversial cultural issues such as prayer in schools and legal protection for sexually explicit publications and films.

One study claimed that even the most activist of courts often offered a "hollow hope" when it came to promoting social change. New interpretations of the law of libel, for example, could not make every journalist into a vigorous crusader for the public interest, and reapportionment of state legislatures would not automatically produce more effective lawmaking bodies. On the most explosive public issue of the late 1960s, U.S. involvement in the war in Vietnam, the courts took no position at all and avoided ruling directly on cases that challenged the constitutionality of U.S. participation in a conflict that Congress had never officially declared to be a "war." In addition, although the federal courts played a vital role in the early days of the civil-rights movement's fight for legal and political equality, it seemed increasingly arguable that judges lacked power to order the kind of sweeping social and economic changes that militants would come to demand. When the civil-rights struggle turned away from issues involving legal discrimination to broader ones involving political and economic power, the judiciary could play only a limited role.

FROM CIVIL RIGHTS TO BLACK POWER

The campaign against discrimination had taken root during the 1950s as an effort to overturn the legal structures, primarily in the states of the Deep South, which required racially segregated public institutions. This campaign gradually broadened into a battle for greater economic opportunities, but the overriding goal remained one of providing equal access for all Americans within the existing political and economic system. By the late 1960s, however, the antidiscrimination crusade became eclipsed by a struggle to restructure, in radical ways, the nation's polity and to reimagine, in equally radical ways, the nature of racial politics.

Civil Rights: The Kennedy Years

Several groups joined forces with Martin Luther King's SCLC in the early 1960s. The Congress of Racial Equality (CORE), which had employed nonviolent civil disobedience as early as the 1940s, assumed a more prominent role in the antidiscrimination effort during the Kennedy years. A new group, the Student Nonviolent Coordinating Committee (SNCC), emerged as a result of dramatic demonstrations in North Carolina during the winter of 1960 when black college students, polite and neatly dressed, unsuccessfully tried to eat at a dime-store lunch counter. Braving hostile white segregationists—who tossed lighted cigarettes, dumped ketchup, and threw punches—the young blacks remained seated and patiently waited for service. The sit-in movement quickly spread to other kinds of public facilities, and thousands of young activists, both white and black, joined the protests. Veterans of these sit-ins, aided by Ella Baker (a charismatic grassroots organizer who had been a civil-rights activist since the 1940s), formed SNCC. While accepting the broad outlines of Dr. King's philosophy of nonviolent protest, SNCC also saw the times as ripe for a more assertive effort. The early "freedom songs" expressed this optimism:

Freedom's Comin' and It Won't Be Long

We took a trip on a Greyhound bus,
Freedom's comin' and it won't be long
To fight segregation, this we must
Freedom's comin' and it won't be long.
Violence in 'bama didn't stop our cause. . . .
Federal marshals come enforce the laws. . . .
On to Mississippi with speed we go. . . .
Blue-shirted policemen meet us at the door. . . .
Judge say local custom shall prevail. . . .
We say "no" and we land in jail. . . .

The election of John Kennedy in 1960 seemed to herald greater White House support for the civil-rights movement. During his campaign, JFK promised a new frontier in the fight against discrimination. Once in office, Kennedy appointed prominent African Americans to federal positions and filed more desegregation suits than his predecessor. He also supported a new civil-rights act that would go beyond those of 1957 and 1960, which had primarily dealt with voting rights. Kennedy proposed a measure that would ban discrimination in public accommodations and give the attorney general authority to file school desegregation suits.

Kennedy's political caution, however, influenced his antidiscrimination policy. During the 1960 presidential campaign, he had denounced Eisenhower's refusal to issue an executive order ending discrimination in federally funded housing—Ike could do this with "a stroke of the pen," claimed Kennedy—but he delayed his own order for two years. He even briefly agreed, despite his

FIGURE 5–1   "Don't Buy Where You Can't Eat."

Civil-rights pickets seek to integrate a "dime-store" lunch counter in St. Paul, Minnesota, 1960.
Source: Photo by St Paul Dispatch—Pioneer Press, Minnesota Historical Society.

party's platform, to extend the policy of termination for Indian tribes. Desiring good relations with southern Democrats, Kennedy often deferred to them on patronage questions, appointing several outright racists to the federal bench. (One Mississippi judge referred to black civil-rights workers as "monkeys" and consistently demeaned African American defendants.)

Kennedy also allowed J. Edgar Hoover's FBI to chart its own course in civil-rights cases. In effect, this meant that Hoover, no friend of civil-rights groups, would do as little as possible to help African Americans and to jeopardize his close relationship with segregationist law officers in the South. Without careful background investigations by the FBI, the Justice Department often lacked evidence to prosecute antidiscrimination cases. Meanwhile, Hoover stepped up his bureau's surveillance of African American groups and leaders. An effort to neutralize Martin Luther King, Jr., became an obsession of Hoover's, and the FBI mounted a campaign of wiretaps, surveillance, and harassment that eventually touched every aspect of the civil-rights movement, especially the personal and political activities of Dr. King.

Local events in the Deep South hastened the pace of change. In 1961, for example, an interracial group from CORE and SNCC began riding southern buses to pressure the Kennedy administration to enforce rigorously a recent

Supreme Court decision banning segregation in interstate bus terminals. These activists also hoped that such "freedom rides" would end segregated seating on interstate buses themselves. Segregationists responded by assaulting the freedom riders, and this racist violence forced Washington to respond. Attorney General Robert Kennedy dispatched troubleshooters from the Justice Department and a corps of federal marshals to protect the riders. He also asked the Interstate Commerce Commission to end segregation on interstate buses, a request that it honored in the fall of 1961.

As recent local histories make clear, this kind of grassroots activism in southern communities, much of it with origins in the 1940s and 1950s, provided an important impetus for change. The Highlander School in Tennessee had long preached the importance of community-based insurgency and had nurtured a small corps of talented organizers. Trained in the Highlander techniques, the heroic figures of the civil-rights movement included the ordinary men and women who dared to challenge a pattern of segregation that was, ultimately, supported not simply by the law but by a pattern of official and unofficial violence. Women, such as Fanny Lou Hamer and Ella Baker, were often the most reliable activists.

At the same time, the accelerating pace of grassroots activism created new questions for the larger antidiscrimination movement. Could the sit-in, which proved effective in mobilizing support for desegregating public facilities, be used to advance broader goals such as voter registration? What was the role of northerners, particularly white people, in local struggles in the Deep South? How much could grassroots activists rely on federal protection in the small southern communities in which the KKK and the local police enjoyed close, often family, ties? Perhaps most important, what was the relationship between events in the small towns and rural counties of the Deep South and the decisions that were being made in the nation's capitol?

Although "local people"—the term that one historian applies to Mississippi's grassroots, civil-rights activists—remained important, the struggle increasingly focused on events in Washington, particularly decisions to invoke the power of the national government. In 1961, the use of federal personnel to protect the freedom riders established an important pattern. President Kennedy reinforced the marshals with U.S. Army troops to quell the violence that followed the enrollment of a black student at the University of Mississippi in 1962. Kennedy's actions probably prevented bloodshed on other campuses—two people had died during disorders at Ole Miss—and a confrontation at the University of Alabama in 1963 ended differently. After symbolically "standing in the schoolhouse door," Governor George Wallace, who had championed "segregation now and forever," stepped aside and watched officers from Kennedy's Justice Department integrate the university without serious incident.

During the spring of 1963, the focus of the antidiscrimination effort shifted to the streets of Birmingham, Alabama. The drive to desegregate public facilities in this urban center marked an important turning point in the struggle for racial equality. Police violence escalated into savagery. Police Commissioner Eugene "Bull" Connor, the stereotype of a redneck southern law officer, turned fire hoses and dogs on black demonstrators, including small children. Club-swinging police rounded up thousands of protestors and threw them into makeshift lockups. White vigilantes unleashed a terror campaign that culminated in the bombing of the Sixteenth Street Baptist Church; four young girls who were at Sunday school died in the blast.

Events in Birmingham, which were covered extensively in the national media, reverberated across the country. Appalled by the violence and Bull Connor's tactics, opinion in Congress swung behind new civil-rights legislation. Equally as important, the militancy of Birmingham's young blacks gave a new urgency to efforts, in both Alabama and Washington, to calm racial conflict. Seeking to avoid further violence and bloodshed, white leaders in Birmingham's business community compromised with the less militant members of the city's African-American leadership: 3,000 imprisoned demonstrators were released, and the city's white leaders agreed to begin desegregation efforts. In Washington, John Kennedy told the nation that the "rising tide of discontent that threatens the public safety" could not be calmed by "repressive police action." It was time, he urged, for Congress to act and pass a strong civil-rights bill.

Order returned to Birmingham, but the events there presaged a change in racial politics across the country. Some people in crowded urban neighborhoods had never fully accepted Dr. King's idea of passive resistance, and a period of urban conflict, which ultimately transformed the antidiscrimination movement, began in Birmingham. The conflict there also transformed SCLC's strategy as it came to recognize that violent white responses ultimately rebounded to its benefit. While never publicly acknowledging the change, it turned increasingly toward a strategy of "nonviolent provocation" in which racist violence, which received extensive media coverage, was intended to build support for new civil-rights legislation. During its crusade in Selma, Alabama, on behalf of voter registration, SCLC embraced this approach, and racist attacks against peaceful marchers helped push Congress to enact the Voting Rights Act of 1965.

The tensions that would spark later confrontations remained hidden beneath a glow of optimism and a spirit of cooperation that climaxed in the famous March on Washington in late August 1963. Most northern media organizations praised the neat appearance, politeness, and commitment of the estimated 200,000 marchers. The unity within the movement also seemed exemplary. Youthful activists from SNCC shared the platform with older members of the NAACP and SCLC as well as with white church and labor leaders. And just when a brutal summer sun threatened to wilt the marchers, Martin Luther King, Jr., revived their spirits with his stirring "I Have a Dream" speech. This address, a carefully structured series of images and rhetorical turns, confirmed King's reputation as the movement's greatest spellbinder. With the formalities completed, civil-rights leaders adjourned to the White House in order to have coffee with the Kennedys.

The Civil Rights Act of 1964: End of an Era

Although civil-rights leaders had disliked JFK's caution, his death initially seemed a setback to their cause. Quickly, though, Lyndon Johnson, a southerner with an ambivalent record on civil-rights, helped push a stronger version of Kennedy's civil-rights bill through Congress. Recognizing that southerners within his own party would not all support the legislation, Johnson counted on members of the GOP's eastern establishment and worked hard to win over moderate northern Republicans, particularly Senate's minority leader, Everett Dirkson of Illinois.

The Civil Rights Act of 1964, a bipartisan measure, promised significant change in the pattern of race relations in the United States. It outlawed discrimination on the basis of race, religion, and sex; discrimination in private businesses that served the general public, such as restaurants and gas stations; and discrimination in public facilities, such as swimming pools and parks. It also authorized the executive branch to withhold federal grants and contracts from institutions that practiced racial discrimination and gave the attorney general broader power to file school desegregation suits. To protect voting rights, the law established a sixth-grade education as the basic requirement for establishing a potential voter's literacy. This provision, it was hoped, would end the state "literacy tests" that had been used, especially in the Deep South, to limit the right to vote. (A white voting inspector in Alabama once rejected a black applicant because his literacy test contained "an error in spilling.")

This measure marked the end of an era. It demanded no less than destruction of the legally sanctioned racial hierarchy that had slowly emerged in the South after the formal end of slavery in 1865. Moreover, it struck down more subtly constructed patterns of discrimination elsewhere in the country. According to the act, anyone from any ethnic background could now sleep in any motel, eat in any restaurant, or sit anywhere on any bus. But these legal changes, which were vitally important and which had taken much bloodshed and political skill to obtain, required no immediate change in the nation's socioeconomic structure or in the distribution of political power.

By 1964, the battles of the 1950s and early 1960s had raised the stakes. Some activists even charged prominent civil-rights leaders with "selling out." After the troubles in Birmingham, white philanthropists, perhaps worried about violence moving northward and perhaps moved by the rightness of the cause, had pledged additional funding for the leading civil-rights organizations. The more militant activists denounced this as a payoff and Kennedy's civil-rights program as tokenism. During the March on Washington, John Lewis, the youthful head of SNCC, had been forced to rewrite a fiery address in which he had intended to criticize the Kennedy civil-rights bill. "What is there in this bill to ensure the equality of a maid who earns $5 a week in the home of a family whose income is $100,000 a year?"—and to condemn "the cheap political leaders who build their careers on immoral compromises and ally themselves with open forms of political, economic, and social exploitation." To preserve the harmony of the day, Lewis agreed to soften his rhetoric. Others boycotted the march and refused to temper their words. One person who had not even been invited to Washington asked, "Who ever heard of angry revolutionists all harmonizing 'We Shall Overcome Some Day' while tripping and swaying along arm-in-arm with the very people they were supposed to be revolting against?" The young man was Malcolm X, an advocate for political militancy and black pride.

A series of disturbing events in 1964 and 1965 made peaceful political appeals seem less attractive to some activists. In Mississippi, three civil rights workers—Andrew Goodman, James Cheney, and Michael Schwerner—were brutally murdered. That same year, 1964, an interracial group of people who had risked their lives to organize the Mississippi Freedom Democratic Party (FDP) came to the Democratic National Convention with hopes of unseating the regular delegation, composed entirely of white segregationists. A stirring speech at the convention by Fannie Lou Hamer, who detailed the violence she had endured, brought sympathizers to tears but angered Lyndon Johnson. He called an unscheduled press conference that preempted speeches by other representatives from the FDP and orchestrated a deal, promoted by Senator Hubert Humphrey of Minnesota, by which the segregationist delegates from Mississippi were to be seated at the convention and two members of the FDP were to be admitted as "delegates at large." The FDP rejected the deal. "We didn't come all this way for no two seats," Fannie Lou Hamer announced.

During the "Freedom Summer" of 1964, a SNCC-sponsored campaign to register voters and establish "freedom schools" in Mississippi, tensions within the movement itself increased. Blacks began to criticize "paternalistic" whites and "fly-by-night freedom fighters who were bossing everybody around." Sexual relationships among the young civil rights workers, especially between black men and white women, added cultural complications. As SNCC and other interracial organizations continued to test the viability of nonviolence in the South, African Americans in some Northern cities began to express their own grievances and frustrations in explosive ways.

Urban Neighborhoods Explode

Less than three weeks after President Johnson signed the Civil Rights Act of 1964, violent protests had broken out in several northern cities. Johnson, recognizing that conservatives would try to use these episodes to cripple his programs, pressured the FBI to issue a report that blamed racial discrimination alone for the outbreaks. Johnson's theory implied that federal spending would calm northern cities, but a second summer of much greater violence followed the first.

In August 1965, a clash between a white highway patrol officer and an African-American motorist touched off four days of violence near the Los Angeles neighborhood of Watts. Thirty-four people died; property losses from fires and looting reached more than $20 million; and only National Guard troops could restore order in the streets of Los Angeles. According to one of Johnson's aides, the president "just wouldn't accept it." He initially refused to look at the reports that described the escalating conflagration.

Several more years of urban disorders followed the outbreak in Watts. The worst was 1967, with trouble in 128 cities and major clashes in Newark and Detroit. In Detroit, regular army units assisted police and the National Guard; at least 43 people died; and fires and looting left permanent scars on Detroit's neighborhoods. In all of these confrontations, the vast majority of people killed were African Americans, and property damage remained largely confined to black communities. Investigations revealed indiscriminate shooting by authorities and several incidents of outright murder by police officers. These "long, hot summers," in addition to leaving behind burned-out buildings and escalating urban tensions, produced what came to be called a "white backlash" against the antidiscrimination movement. Johnson himself was reported to have asked, "How is it possible after all that we've accomplished? . . . Is the world topsy-turvy?"

What could explain the violence? Official explanations tried to steer between right-wing theories of an organized criminal conspiracy and left-wing claims of an incipient popular revolution against systematic exploitation. Investigating the Watts disorder, the McCone Commission (headed by former CIA Director John McCone) propounded what became known as the "rotten apple" or "riff-raff" interpretation. A small group of troublemakers, the McCone Report concluded, had precipitated and then fueled the violence. The "riot" was not a legitimate protest against substantive grievances but a series of "formless, quite senseless, all but hopeless" outbursts of looting and burning "engaged in by a few but bringing great distress to all." The Commission theorized that most of the rotten-apple troublemakers had recently migrated from the rural South and had not yet adjusted to urban life. Although it refused to call Watts a ghetto, because it contained mostly single-family dwellings and wide, tree-lined streets, or to concede a serious issue of police brutality, the Commission found that Watts suffered from inadequate mass transit, poor educational facilities, and badly trained police officers. After insisting that the situation required no fundamental social or economic change, the report called for greater job opportunities near Watts, more money for education, and "better understanding" between police and citizens.

Critics quickly challenged the McCone Commission. They called the disorder a political "protest" rather than a formless riot. Events in Watts, they claimed, involved a sizable portion of the community, not simply a few misfits. The protesters had lived there for some time, usually held low-paying jobs, and possessed the best education that the neighborhood's schools could provide. Disputing the idea that the violence had been senseless, these dissenters argued that protesters had tried to avoid looting black-owned businesses and had concentrated on firms that were considered especially dishonest. Much of the housing in Watts was dilapidated; many businesses took advantage of neighborhood customers and employees; and police brutality was a common occurrence. Critics of McCone's report concluded that the violence grew out of deep-seated, legitimate grievances.

This dispute between "riot" and "protest" theorists involved more than a semantic difference. The riot view pointed toward the swift suppression of disorder and gradual change within the existing system. The protest position implied a legitimate basis for the upheaval and supported the need for more sweeping social and economic transformation. Equally as important, the riot view tended to see the problem as one between good and bad people. The protest theory pointed to a deeper-seated structural crisis that made individual intentions less relevant.

As disorder continued throughout the 1960s, the official explanation changed very little. The most extensive governmental investigation, done in 1968 by President Johnson's National Advisory Commission on Civil Disorders (commonly called the Kerner Commission), rejected the claim of fundamental problems with the political-economic system. The commissioners did identify "white racism" as part of the trouble, but not before firing staff members who wanted stronger language and rejecting a more outspoken staff report entitled "The Harvest of American Racism." The commissioners' final document recommended a moderate, two-pronged approach: increased social-welfare expenditures and more effective use of force to suppress disturbances. The last solution, greater force, proved more acceptable to most members of Congress than increased social spending. Congress quickly voted additional funds to beef up local law enforcement agencies and to train the National Guard in new methods of riot control. Saddled with burgeoning expenditures for the Vietnam War, President Johnson filed away the commission's other recommendations.

Black Power

Meanwhile, militant African American leaders were citing intransigence among whites as justification for rejecting integration, the traditional goal of the civil-rights movement. The Nation of Islam, a long-established religious group popularly known as the Black Muslims, gained prominence during the early 1960s. The Nation of Islam preached the superiority of black people and black institutions, predicted eventual collapse of a decadent white society, urged the creation of separate black-controlled areas within the United States, and stressed the necessity for hard work and self-discipline. The Nation of Islam had gained converts during the 1950s, including Malcolm Little, a self-educated man with a keen intellect. Rejecting his "Christian slave name," Malcolm X became a top aide to Elijah Muhammad, the leader of the Nation of Islam, and his most eloquent spokesperson. Malcolm's fiery oratory and his conversion of boxing champion Cassius Clay, who became Muhammad Ali, gained the Nation of Islam national attention.

FIGURE 5–2   Muhammad Ali, London, 1966.

After becoming heavyweight champion, boxer Cassius Clay converted to Islam, changed his name to Muhammad Ali, and became the world's most recognized sports icon.
Source: Getty Images Inc.

Malcolm X anticipated and helped to inspire the Black Power movement of the late 1960s. He questioned the value of nonviolence in every situation and the desirability of integration in a culture with racial hatred. Malcolm X refused to renounce violence, at least when used in self-defense, and he dismissed civil-rights leaders as "professional beggars" who were content with "handouts" from white leaders. The only sensible option, he preached, was separation of the formerly enslaved people from their former white masters. This kind of rhetoric, especially Malcolm's exhortation for community self-defense "by any means necessary," frightened both black and white integrationists. Meanwhile, though, his appeal and power base within African American communities in the North began to grow, and his speaking engagements attracted ever-larger crowds.

In time, Malcolm X began to seek new paths toward political and racial change. He broke from Elijah Muhammad and the Nation of Islam and formed his own Organization of Afro-American Unity. Although Malcolm X remained interested in political and economic issues and even tentatively sought inter-ethnic alliances with progressives, he came to place special emphasis on an African American cultural revival. If black people were to press successfully for social and economic change, they first needed to "launch a cultural revolution to unbrainwash an entire people." Although Malcolm X was assassinated in 1965, by old enemies from the Nation of Islam, his emphasis on reinvigorating African American culture and on cultivating a strong sense of individual self-identity was to live on. Younger activists eagerly read his *Autobiography* and listened to recordings of his speeches, especially a "Message to the Grass Roots." According to one of the architects of the emerging Black Power movement, "Black history began with Malcolm X."

In 1966, racial politics in the United States reached a crossroads. The march toward legal and constitutional change, the traditional project of the civil-rights movement, seemed stalled. Resistance to enforcement of the Civil Rights Act of 1964 and the Voting Rights Act of 1965 produced further bloodshed in the South. To some blacks, the urban disorders in the North suggested the possibility that violent protests might bring more rapid change than nonviolent civil disobedience. In May 1966, SNCC, still officially committed to integration, urged blacks "to begin building independent political, economic, and cultural institutions that they will control and use as instruments of social change in this country." Later that summer SNCC joined other civil-rights groups, including the SCLC and CORE, in a protest march through Mississippi, an effort that widened divisions within the antidiscrimination movement. Stokely Carmichael, SNCC's new head, seized the media spotlight from Martin Luther King, Jr., who was often absent. Carmichael vowed that he would never peacefully go to jail again and declared that "every courthouse in Mississippi ought to be burned down to get rid of the dirt." In the most publicized event of the march, he coined the movement's new slogan: "Black Power!"

Activists within SNCC and CORE were also coming to believe that the goals of the 1950s and early 1960s needed to be reformulated. Integration, wrote Stokely Carmichael, "reinforces among both black and white, the idea that 'white' is automatically better and 'black' is by definition inferior." Continuing the search for equal political and legal rights now seemed less important than seeking economic and political power. Black people, it was argued, had to control their communities and expel what became known as the "white power structure"—the "dishonest" businesspeople, the "rent-gouging" landlords, and the "crooked" politicians. And as a means of stimulating black pride and cultural nationalism, militants demanded community control of neighborhood schools. Where this was not immediately possible, they sought separate black studies courses taught and administered by African Americans.

There were many variations on the themes of Black Power and cultural revival. Some people, identifying with dark-skinned peoples in the postcolonial countries of Africa and Asia, viewed African Americans as colonized people subject to the domination of alien white masters. Others adopted a Marxist framework, seeing blacks as the most exploited group in an exploitative capitalist society. Violent revolution, a few extremists even suggested, offered the only means of redressing grievances. But even most activists warned against open confrontations with the overwhelming firepower of the national and state governments and sought to build bases of local support before pressing the movement for peaceful, but significant, social change.

The history of the Black Panthers, a relatively small organization dominated by young men that attracted intense media interest during the late 1960s, revealed the tensions generated by debates over Black Power and cultural insurgency. Formed in Oakland, California, the Black Panthers gained the media spotlight primarily through a shootout with local police and the success of *Soul on Ice* (1968), a manifesto-autobiography by one of the group's leaders, Eldridge Cleaver. Outfitted in paramilitary garb, the Panthers frightened many people, and law enforcement officials denounced the organization as a clear and present danger. The Panthers demanded a guaranteed income for all citizens, exemption of blacks from military service, government funds for cooperative housing facilities, reparation payments "as retribution for slave labor and mass murder of black people," release of all black prisoners "because they have not received a fair and impartial trial," and use of all-black juries to try African American criminal defendants. Such demands borrowed from black nationalist ideas, but they also owed much to a curious blend of Marxism and American constitutional law. (Huey Newton, a Panther leader, carried a stack of law books in his car.)

The Panthers found it difficult to articulate a coherent political strategy. Should they ally with white activists, or should they avoid cross-racial ties and go it alone? The Panthers finally did seek ties with both white and black insurgents, a course that helped to divide the party's already small membership. Meanwhile, many people, black as well as white, charged that its social programs, such as running soup kitchens in low-income neighborhoods, were simply a cover for more violent, ganglike activities, including dealing illegal drugs. The Panthers themselves, their critics charged, directed as much violence against their opponents within African-American neighborhoods as the police directed against them and were primarily the creation of a sensation-seeking media.

The Civil Rights Act of 1968 indicated the ambivalent response of Congress to the new turn in the antidiscrimination movement. Title VIII of this law prohibited discrimination in the advertising, financing, sale, or rental of most homes and charged the executive branch with acting "affirmatively" to achieve integrated housing. Together with state open-housing laws, this act pointed toward gradual desegregation of the postwar suburbs. If coupled with more generous funding for inner-city housing projects, it also promised a greater supply of homes and apartments for people with low incomes. The urban violence, it seemed, had produced some positive responses, in the form of congressional legislation and bureaucratic attention, from the politicians.

This same Civil Rights Act of 1968, however, also indicated a growing backlash against militancy. Congress made it a crime to use the facilities of interstate commerce "to organize, promote, encourage, participate in, or carry on a riot; or to commit any act of violence in furtherance of a riot." In approving this seemingly vague provision, which had been pushed by Senator Strom Thurmond of South Carolina, most members of Congress knew exactly what they wanted: a federal law that would stop the activities of people such as H. Rap Brown, who had succeeded Stokely Carmichael as head of SNCC. This so-called Rap Brown section of the 1968 law gave national authorities a catchall statute to use against nation-wide organizing efforts of people whose political activities prompted confrontation.

The Black Power movement signaled an important change in African American politics. Most African Americans, according to public opinion polls, still supported the goals of the civil-rights movement: desegregation, equality of opportunity, and legal rights. At the time of his death in 1968, Martin Luther King, Jr., remained the preeminent black leader, but a backlash against the civil-rights movement and the positive messages of the Black Power crusade were helping to change the African American agenda.

In one sense, efforts still proceeded as if there were no fundamental conflict between integration and renewed ethnic pride. Black politicians, gaining crucial votes from white progressives and other people of color, built their own power base within urban communities and won elective office in a number of cities during the late 1960s and early 1970s. At the same time, the average income of black families rose, and the gap between the average yearly income for whites and blacks began to narrow. African Americans who possessed job skills and educational credentials found it easier to pursue the dream of integration that King had sketched in his famous speech of 1963.

In another sense, though, the new spirit of racial pride and self-identity helped to produce movements that would challenge the ethos of the early civil-rights movement. Although the more radical political demands of the Black Power movement faded from the agenda, many of its cultural initiatives did take root. The African American renaissance of the 1960s extended from the angry verses of the Last Poets to the sweet soul music of Sam Cooke, from the multifaceted Black Arts movement to the macho posturing of singer James Brown, from the precisely crafted sounds of Miles Davis to the contradictory imagery of "blaxploitation" films such as *Superfly* (1972) and *Foxy Brown* (1974). It also became evident that there was not simply a black culture—and, indeed, there never had been merely one—but many different African American cultures. African American feminists, for example, were finding their own voices and denouncing not only racism but also the sexism that they found embedded in institutions and social practices, both white and black, that were dominated by men. These feminists were unwilling to allow men alone, even African American men, to define racial struggles in ways that papered over gender issues.

More broadly, the transition from civil rights to Black Power had a significant impact on American politics and culture. Between 1954, when the Supreme Court struck down school segregation in the *Brown* case, and 1968, when Dr. King was gunned down in Memphis, the crusade against racial discrimination affected the entire nation. Although the first civil-rights battles focused on African Americans and segregation in the South, the struggle eventually expanded. Other ethnic groups, which had long been part of antidiscrimination efforts, moved from the shadows of what the dominant political and media story had generally framed as a white versus black confrontation. Groups asserting the cause of Mexican Americans, of Puerto Ricans, and of other groups became prominent parts of the fight against discrimination. Women's groups and organizations representing people who were elderly and/or disabled stepped forward to fight discrimination and to make claims on behalf of their rights. Very quickly, there were many different antidiscrimination movements, all searching for legal protection and for political and cultural empowerment. (See Chapter 6.)

Finally, as the struggle against discrimination proceeded, the nature of the issues changed. The early civil-rights movement had attempted to eliminate the burden of legalized racism and to open up the political process to black voters. Although legal and political battles remained to be fought, the Black Power movement heralded new concerns, cultural as well as political, about empowerment. The issues first raised in the 1960s were to become even more important in the decades to come. Indeed, in an age in which visual images could be preserved and reproduced for mass distribution, as in the "Eyes on the Prize" TV series, or recreated in docudrama form, as in Luis Valdez's *Zoot Suit* (1981) or Spike Lee's *Malcolm X* (1992), cultural imagery would increasingly help to shape the complex politics of antidiscrimination efforts.

The Kennedy and Johnson years brought a flood of domestic legislation, several civil-rights laws, and important Supreme-Court decisions. But the promise of the early 1960s faded as familiar political rhetoric, carefully drafted legislation, and elegantly reasoned court opinions seemed to address only some of the riddles of social policy and discrimination. At the same time, problems in foreign affairs increasingly limited the tangible resources and political capital available for addressing domestic issues.

KENNEDY'S FOREIGN POLICIES

John F. Kennedy had promised new activism in the cold war. In the presidential campaign of 1960, he charged that the Eisenhower-Nixon team had allowed a dangerous "missile gap" to develop between the United States and the Soviet Union and had not tried to eliminate Castro. (Neither charge was true.) Once in the White House, Kennedy tried to fulfill his pledge to wage the cold war in a more determined way. He advocated a policy of "flexible response," which would challenge communism on every level by enlarging atomic capabilities, forging new "counterinsurgency units," exerting economic pressure, and broadening covert-action capabilities.

New Programs

The Soviet Union and the Chinese Communist government both supported "wars of national liberation" in the Third World, often aligning their brands of communism with nationalist aspirations in areas desiring to throw off the yoke of colonialism. The Kennedy administration realized that it had to compete for grassroots support against communism by rivaling the Communists' nationalist and reformist appeal.

General Maxwell Taylor, army chief of staff, told Kennedy, "We must show the Russians that wars of national liberation are not cheap, safe, and disavowable but costly, dangerous, and doomed to failure." Believing that ground-war capabilities were essential, even in the era of atomic power, Taylor and his staff sketched a heady new mission for the army called "nation building." Highly trained elite forces, such as the Green Berets, were to teach local troops the techniques of counterinsurgency warfare against guerrilla fighters and instruct them in twentieth-century technology and liberal democracy. For Kennedy even more than for John Foster Dulles, the front lines of the cold war were everywhere. Capitol Hill enthusiastically funded Taylor's programs, and Kennedy involved himself in the smallest details of the new Green Berets, helping select distinctive uniforms and pouring over the special design of their tennis shoes. Adlai Stevenson, whom Kennedy's youthful and vigorous staff considered a too-cautious old-timer, bemoaned the new president's circle as "the damndest bunch of boy commandos running around."

Others in the new administration stressed using America's wealth to promote stability through what was called "modernization." In their fervor of can-do activism, these individuals talked about short-circuiting the poverty and sense of helplessness that fueled Communist appeals in the Third World. Ironically, while Kennedy found it difficult to secure congressional approval for reform at home, Congress authorized a number of new departures in foreign aid, such as the Alliance for Progress and the Peace Corps.

The Alliance for Progress, a "ten-year plan for the Americas," was signed at Punta del Este, Uruguay, in August 1961 by all nations of the Western Hemisphere except Canada and Cuba. In it, the United States promised new loans and private investment that were supposed to finance social programs, such as health care, housing, and education; boost local rates of growth by 2.5 percent annually; and encourage industrial diversification and land reform. Advocates calculated that these measures would thwart radicalism in Latin America and encourage moderate, reformist leaders while breaking oligarchic or anti-American regimes. The Agency for International Development (AID), operating on a smaller scale in all Third World areas, also promoted anti-Communist programs aimed at modernization.

An even more imaginative program, the Peace Corps sent volunteers to willing nations throughout the world. Functioning primarily in rural areas, it worked to improve health, education, and economic efficiency. Its director, R. Sargent Shriver, expected no dramatic results, only "cumulative years of goodwill among the common folk." By 1963, volunteers were working in over forty countries as teachers, crop specialists, and construction supervisors.

Although both programs reflected the New Frontier's confidence in its ability to shape the world, they also showed the limits of such ambitions. The Alliance for Progress never fulfilled its vision. Reform stalled, and promises outran growth. Latin American nations that had been the greatest recipients of Alliance for Progress loans grew more debt-ridden and, ironically, less economically stable. As the prospect of social improvement dimmed, advocates of radical, anti-American change grew stronger rather than weaker. The Peace

Corps often made welcome contributions in education and health care, but even its seemingly benign objectives could come under attack. Bolivia, for example, expelled volunteers after charges that they cooperated with the involuntary sterilization of Indian women. Overall, the Peace Corps may have transformed the lives of its idealistic, young volunteers, who became acquainted with new languages and cultures, more than it changed the communities in which it operated.

Cuba

Kennedy's foreign policy focused initially on Cuba. The Eisenhower administration had given the green light to a CIA project to invade Cuba with a small force of anti-Castro expatriates, and Kennedy decided to follow through on this plan. The disgruntled population of Cuba, American intelligence predicted, would welcome these rebels as liberators.

On April 17, 1961, two days after CIA operatives had attacked Cuba's air bases with B-26 bombers, approximately 1,400 Cuban exiles waded ashore at the Bay of Pigs. Stumbling from their boats that were wrecked on coral reefs that CIA planners had not detected, the brigade was soon surrounded by Castro's forces, numbering 20,000. Although members of the brigade fought bravely, the supply ships carrying signaling equipment, food, and ammunition did not get through. Most of the unit's members were captured within a few days. A ship carrying a battalion of additional troops was grounded away from shore and never met up with the invasion party.

Although some in the State Department and military urged full-scale intervention, Kennedy held to his earlier insistence that the U.S. military was not to become directly involved. Reluctantly, he accepted the failure of the mission. Now realizing that many planners had mistakenly assumed that, if the invasion faltered, Kennedy would be forced to authorize a direct, U.S.-led attack, the president commented, "How could I have been so stupid?" Nevertheless, he publicly took responsibility for the fiasco. "Victory has a hundred fathers," he said, "but defeat is an orphan." Oddly, the American public seemed to sympathize with the new president, and his approval rating rose ten points to 83 percent. Apparently "the worse you do, the better they like you," remarked Kennedy.

The Bay of Pigs disaster greatly embarrassed the new administration. U.S. leaders had publicly denied the first news reports of U.S. involvement in its planning and then had to retract the denials. In the UN and around the world, the Soviets denounced U.S. aggression. Moreover, the attempted overthrow only tightened Castro's control in Cuba, reinforced his dependence on the Soviet Union, and loosed yet another round of Yankeephobia throughout Latin America. The debacle also raised Kennedy's anxiety about being perceived as weak-willed and thus increased his determination to get tough in future showdowns. Quietly, the Kennedy administration stepped up its covert anti-Castro efforts in Operation Mongoose, a plan of assassination plots, sabotage, and economic sanctions. Many documents from this period suggest policies to "get rid of" or "eliminate" Castro, and at least three assassination plots proceeded as far as delivery of a weapon to an assassin.

Before Washington officials could recover from this setback, another confrontation loomed. Perhaps hoping to gain concessions from an inexperienced president, at an informal summit meeting in Vienna in June 1961 Khrushchev proposed reuniting the divided city of Berlin, incorporating it all into Soviet-dominated East Germany. He hinted at war unless the United States agreed to abandon support for West Berlin. Determined to uphold America's credibility, Kennedy mobilized the National Guard, accelerated arms production, tripled draft calls, and traveled to West Berlin to reassure its citizens of America's commitment. Khrushchev blustered about "thermonuclear holocaust" but acted much more cautiously. Using barbed wire and then a wall of cement blocks, the Soviet and East German governments sealed off West Berlin from the rest of East Germany, ending an embarrassing flow of defectors to the West (some 3 million since 1945) and cutting off a black market in goods and currencies. The Berlin Wall, which would finally be hacked down by citizens when the cold war ended in 1989, became the very symbol of cold-war distrust and tension.

Khrushchev, rebuked by domestic critics for his posturing over Berlin and challenged by Chinese leader Mao Zedong for leadership of the Communist bloc, sought to demonstrate geopolitical gains elsewhere. When Castro asked the Soviet Union for military hardware and firmer protection against U.S. plots, Khrushchev agreed to provide sophisticated weapons, including missiles armed with atomic warheads.

On the morning of October 16, 1962, Kennedy learned that American U-2 surveillance aircraft had reported Soviet missile launching sites being erected in Cuba. The president's first response was personal. "He can't do that to me!" he declared. Kennedy called a meeting of top advisers to decide upon a

FIGURE 5–3 The Cuban Missile Crisis.

Fears of nuclear confrontation with the Soviet Union brought handfuls of protesters into the streets during the 1950s and early 1960s. This small group demonstrated against JFK's policies in Cuba.
Source: Photo by St Paul Dispatch—Pioneer Press, Minnesota Historical Society.

response. Afraid to be perceived as weak, the president initially leaned toward removing the missiles through a military strike. His 1960 campaign, after all, had charged Eisenhower with tepid cold-war responses and had pledged a tougher posture. In a televised address on October 22, 1962, Kennedy vowed that "the United States will not compromise its safety," and he ordered the Strategic Air Command to full alert. During the course of his high-level, daily meetings, however, he came to realize that a strike might kill Soviet personnel and provoke a Soviet response that could quickly escalate toward nuclear war. Robert Kennedy later remembered his growing alarm at the proposed "tough" responses. "Many times I heard the military take positions which, if wrong, had the advantage that no one would be around at the end to know," he recalled.

Finally, the president decided to order the navy to "quarantine" Cuba, sending ships to turn away any Soviet merchant ships carrying missiles. The word "quarantine" was carefully chosen because the word "blockade" would have signaled a formal act of war under international law. Tensions mounted as Soviet radar in Cuba picked up a U-2 surveillance plane overhead, and it was shot down. Then Soviet fighters chased another U-2 that had inadvertently strayed over Russian territory. Clearly, events could have easily spun out of control. Alarmed, Khrushchev wrote that if people did not "show wisdom" they would "come to a clash, like blind moles, and then reciprocal extermination will begin."

Behind the scenes, as Soviet and American ships approached each other in the waters off Cuba, both Kennedy and Khrushchev began searching for a compromise. Complicated secret messages between the Kremlin and the White House soon confirmed an agreement: The Soviet Union would recall its ships and terminate the placement of nuclear weapons in Cuba; the United States would publicly pledge not to attack Cuba again and would privately remove its obsolete Jupiter missiles from Turkey. CIA operations continued to harass Castro's Cuba, but superpower confrontation there was over. Recently declassified documents show that Kennedy even began some tentative discussions aimed at improving relations with Castro, a move that was cut short with the president's death.

This Cuban missile crisis highlighted the perils of cold-war diplomacy. The swiftness of nuclear escalation frightened both sides; mutual blackmail, if miscalculated, could easily bring disaster. Leaders mellowed their rhetoric. Khrushchev talked of "peaceful coexistence," and Kennedy called for "mutual tolerance." During the summer of 1963, the two countries set up a "hot line," a direct telephone link between their capitals. On July 25, 1963, America, Britain, and the Soviet Union initiated a nuclear test-ban treaty that ended all except underground atomic explosions. (Soviet fears that on-site inspections might learn too much about its industrial potential made a total ban impossible.) These measures did little to lessen rivalry between the two superpowers, but they did indicate a mutual desire to avoid nuclear confrontation.

Although tensions with the USSR eased a bit, the Kennedy administration nonetheless redoubled its efforts to fight communism. Policymakers believed that with wealth, power, and determination the United States could surely build nations in the Third World like itself: prosperous, democratic, and anti-Communist. Nurtured by this self-confidence and armed with theories about how to "modernize" poorer countries, the Kennedy administration fatefully expanded the American role in Vietnam.

THE STRUGGLE IN VIETNAM

Hoping to refurbish the nation's credibility while pushing back a Communist liberation movement in Southeast Asia, the Kennedy administration tested its new ideas about counterinsurgency, nation building, and the other tactics of flexible response. Presidential foreign policy adviser Walt Rostow insisted that the United States needed "not merely a proper military program of deterrence but programs of village development, communications, and indoctrination." Kennedy was convinced that, in the words of a crucial 1961 report, defeat in Vietnam would signal the loss not "merely of a crucial piece of real estate, but the faith that the United States has the will and the capacity" to fight communism.

Billions of dollars, tons of sophisticated weapons, and 16,000 American support and combat troops reached the Vietnamese countryside by 1963 in an attempt to support the government of Ngo Dinh Diem and defeat the National Liberation Front (NLF) in South Vietnam. At first, the Communist effort wavered, seeming to justify the Pentagon's tactics. Then Hanoi increased its aid to the NLF, and Kennedy increased American intervention to include covert actions against North Vietnam. Meanwhile, aid pouring in from Washington brought jolting corruption to Saigon and hindered normal operations of state. Land reform collapsed. More and more aid was requested. Kennedy had presciently remarked that once Americans became involved it would "be like taking a drink. The effect wears off, and you have to take another." Diem's regime slowly became addicted.

In May 1963, Diem (a Catholic) tried to shore up his government by stepping up persecution of his Buddhist critics. The Catholic archbishop even forbade the carrying of Buddhist flags. Forced either to abandon some religious practices or to face charges of treason, Buddhists organized massive demonstrations, which culminated on June 16, 1963, when a priest martyred himself by setting fire to his gasoline-soaked robes. More and more people paraded in the streets of Saigon and prayed at pagodas for Diem's downfall. More self-immolations and the growing violence of student strikes convinced Diem and his brother, Ngo Dinh Nhu, that only strong measures could restore order. On August 21, detachments from American-trained special-forces units attacked Buddhist sanctuaries in Saigon, Hue, and most provincial capitals. This repression, coupled with political arrests, prompted another, even more violent, cycle of protests and autocratic responses. Intellectuals and the urban middle class abandoned the Diem regime, which was now consumed in its own self-destruction.

No one in Washington knew what to do. One obvious option was to get rid of the unpopular Diem. The internal chaos of his regime enervated the war effort against the Communists and mocked hopes for a democratic example for the Third World. Religious persecution bothered Americans, including the president, himself a Catholic. During the fall of 1963, several Vietnamese generals suggested plans for a coup to the American ambassador, Henry Cabot Lodge, Jr. They received an encouraging reply. If Diem did not reform, Washington cabled its ambassador, "we must face the possibility that Diem himself cannot be preserved." The CIA also began to work toward Diem's replacement. In October, the Kennedy administration unexpectedly canceled the commercial-import program that financed Diem's government and publicly criticized its corruption. Although, at the last minute, Kennedy began to fear that a coup would only increase instability and cabled Lodge that "we should discourage them from proceeding," the generals were already wheeling into action. On November 1, Vietnamese battalions near Saigon captured administrative centers and surrounded Diem's palace. The man whom Americans had vainly tried to turn into the George Washington of a non-communist Vietnam died that night, murdered while trying to escape from his country. That same month, on November 22, President Kennedy died in Dallas, victim of an assassination.

Anxious to maintain continuity and not to look weak in the upcoming presidential election, Lyndon Johnson did not challenge the growing U.S. involvement in Vietnam. Although several advisers predicted that victory would be almost impossible and Johnson himself believed that escalating the war effort was probably a mistake, the president rejected the idea of withdrawal. Many advisers suggested that the United States must repel Communist insurgencies in Southeast Asia lest other friendly countries question America's willingness and ability to protect them against subversion. A Pentagon expert once explained that repelling Communist aggression in Asia was "only 10 percent" of America's purpose; the war was being fought primarily to reassure allies that the U.S. would keep its commitments. Johnson also feared a domestic political backlash if South Vietnam fell to the North. After a month-long inspection tour, Secretary of Defense Robert S. McNamara and Chief of Staff Maxwell Taylor had reported on October 2, 1963, that the United States could probably begin pulling out its troops by early 1964. The opposite occurred.

A Vigorous Beginning, 1964–1965

America began steps toward a full-scale Indochinese war during the winter of 1964–1965, responding to growing chaos in South Vietnam. A revolving door of military juntas undermined the anti-Communist effort on the battlefield and aggravated Diem's legacy of corruption and malaise. The NLF rapidly filled the political vacuum in the countryside. The NLF, supported by military aid from Hanoi, began preparations for a major assault on provincial capitals. Considerably frightened at this prospect, Pentagon officials drew up plans for an air war against North Vietnam. No other option seemed feasible, short of an embarrassing disengagement, but escalation required legal, if not moral, justification. The White House drafted a congressional resolution authorizing air attacks and waited for an opportunity.

It came almost too quickly. In early August, a confrontation developed in the Gulf of Tonkin, where North Vietnam patrol boats fired upon the U.S. spy ship *Maddox*. Two days later, the *Maddox* and another destroyer, the *C. Turner Joy*, returned to the Gulf of Tonkin. In the midst of a storm on the night of August 4, anxious naval captains and malfunctioning sonar equipment reported an attack. By afternoon, the commander of the *Maddox* wired that there had been no visual sighting and that freak weather effects may have explained the sonar and radar signals. The Johnson administration, seeking an excuse for retaliation, chose to believe the first reports of an attack.

Denouncing "unprovoked aggression" during a nationally televised speech, President Johnson ordered reprisal raids against North Vietnamese naval bases. The temporary feeling of crisis prompted Congress to pass the so-called Gulf of Tonkin resolution. Its open-ended phraseology authorized Johnson "to take all necessary measures" to repulse Communist advances. Unaware of the dubious nature of Hanoi's attacks and, like the chief executive himself, ill informed about Vietnamese complexities, the Senate adopted the resolution, which was later used as a de facto declaration of war, eighty-eight to two. Only Senators Wayne Morse and Ernest Gruening voted against this potentially unlimited commitment.

During his 1964 presidential campaign, Johnson had presented himself as a peace candidate, firmly rejecting prescriptions from critics, such as retired Air Force Chief of Staff Curtis Lemay, for "bombing Hanoi back into the Stone Age." After the 1964 election, however, Johnson launched a sustained air assault. Pentagon officials argued that no government in Saigon could reform itself as long as the insurgency, supplied from the North, continued. Bombing strikes against the North and elite U.S. counterinsurgency operations in the South, they concluded, would be necessary to win the war and restore America's global credibility. However, popular discontent with the Saigon regime, together with carefully cultivated affinities between Vietnamese communism and Vietnamese traditionalism, continued to fuel the NLF's success.

More and more, the problem of Vietnam preoccupied Washington's planners. The treadmill of escalation continued. Just a little more aid, just a few more soldiers would supposedly turn the tide. Victory always seemed so close. Johnson himself hoped that a steady, predictable escalation would avoid intervention by China or Russia and at the same time convince the NLF and Hanoi that they would not win.

Escalation, 1965–1967

The war slowly intensified. Sustained bombing of North Vietnam began on February 15, 1965, ostensibly in reprisal for an NLF mortar attack against a Marine Corps base at Pleiku. That spring, American combat troops began to aid Vietnamese army units under fire. Johnson authorized the first search-and-destroy missions—independent sweeps involving large numbers of GIs—in June 1965, several miles northwest of Saigon. Most military experts estimated that victory would require a one-to-ten ratio against NLF-North Vietnamese troops, but the enemy, then recruiting the bulk of its troops within South Vietnam itself, even at this ratio, more than matched Pentagon escalations.

Against a backdrop of Johnsonian rhetoric about "winning the hearts and minds of the Vietnamese people," U.S. advisers crisscrossed the countryside. AID officials offered health care and new agricultural techniques. Combat units built hospitals, schools, and orphanages. Government subsidies assured farmers high prices for their crops but low prices for consumers. The junta in Saigon periodically deployed urban volunteers to counteract the work of Communist cadres. Such nation building, however, barely touched Communist strength in rural areas. By 1967, frustrated officials adopted still another device for rural pacification: the strategic-hamlet program. To protect villagers from NLF attack and ensure their loyalties to Saigon, American soldiers garrisoned many

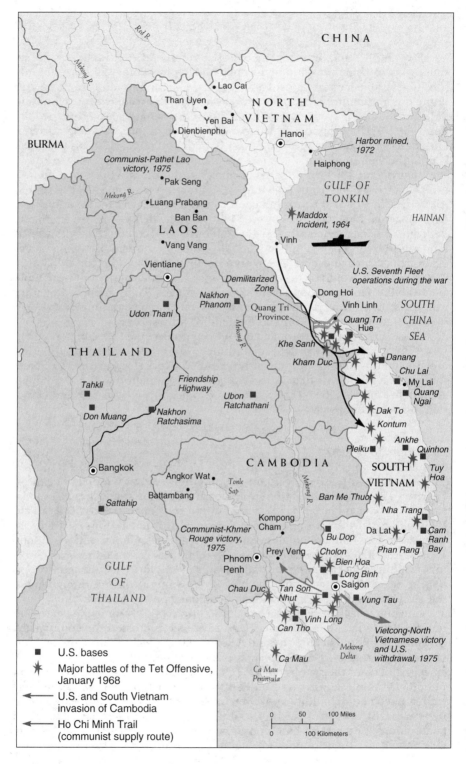

FIGURE 5–4 The War in Indochina.

The war that began in Vietnam spread throughout Indochina.

rural towns, often erecting makeshift forts. Herded into barbed-wire enclosures and living under American machine guns, the peasants were expected to continue their agrarian way of life. Such fortified camps did achieve their military purpose, but they alienated farmers, now separated from land and tradition.

Bewildered and angered by the failure of their good intentions, Americans came to rely on more Draconian tactics. Perhaps bombs, artillery, and rifles could kill so many enemy soldiers that eventually the NLF and North Vietnamese could not replace them, given their relatively small population base. To many American soldiers, both enthusiastic volunteers and uneasy draftees, the war often seemed waged against the Vietnamese themselves. Search-and-destroy missions created a misconception that only "body count" and improved "kill ratios" mattered. Some officers, realizing that careers depended on numbers, lied to superiors about enemy dead; GIs tortured NLF suspects, matching the tactics of their foe. The U.S. command in Saigon charted free-fire zones, huge areas in which helicopter gunships could strafe anything that moved. Chemicals defoliated the earth, and bombers pulverized North Vietnam's industry and South Vietnam's farms. Some devices may have limited Communist freedom of movement, but they also destroyed American prestige. In a traditional society whose members valued their ties to ancestral lands and to village communities, terror and free-fire zones steadily discredited the American cause.

The United States miscalculated badly, but few officials admitted it. Middle-level civilians and field officers reported what higher officials in Saigon wanted to hear; America's ambassadors and generals further refined the stylized ritual. We are winning the war, they wired Washington, but send us more money, more men. For many in the Johnson administration, displaying toughness became not a means but an end in itself. A militant stand ensured approval as a "realistic appraisal," and giving assurance of victory garnered points in bureaucratic infighting. Having shoe-horned the conflict into America's global strategy, Johnson isolated himself completely from Vietnamese complexities and vowed, "I will not be the first president to lose a war."

Such unrealistic calculations scuttled opportunities for compromise. Johnson and his advisers used diplomacy either to justify further escalation or to attempt to secure an American victory. When U Thant, secretary-general of the United Nations, suggested in July 1964 that the Geneva Conference reconvene, Johnson righteously refused: "We do not believe in conferences called to ratify terror." However, nine months later as the war firmly escalated, the president told an audience at Johns Hopkins University that the United States would discuss peace. He even offered American capital to rebuild "a peaceful Southeast Asia." Yet his accompanying demand for a non-Communist regime in Saigon was tantamount to a Hanoi-NLF capitulation. The enemy routinely rejected such efforts to achieve at the bargaining table what military force had not won in the field. Every rebuff, the president chided his critics, proved Communist perfidy.

Escalation continued. During a thirty-seven-day period in December 1965 and January 1966, Johnson halted the Rolling Thunder bombing raids against North Vietnam and sponsored a far-flung peace initiative. His closest friends applauded his cleverness. The air war had not materially impaired Hanoi's war production, and few military targets remained. Ho Chi Minh had simply decentralized, then camouflaged his industry in the countryside. Although Ho responded to Johnson's pause with hints of a coalition or neutralist government for South Vietnam, Johnson rejected further talks. Instead, he pointed to enemy "truculence" and unleashed a new air war, this one directed against Hanoi's supply routes through Indochina's mountains and jungles. At the same time, Johnson enlarged the ground war. U.S. troop levels jumped from 150,000 in February 1966 to 550,000 at their peak in 1968.

Washington officials also tried to reform Saigon's government. Absorbed in its coups and intrigues but assured of American money, the military junta in Saigon became more dictatorial and even less effective. Johnson summoned the two most recently installed generals, Nguyen Van Thieu and Nguyen Cao Ky, to a meeting in Honolulu in February 1966. He extracted promises from the quiet Thieu and the flamboyant Ky that they would redistribute land, end corruption, and rule more liberally. Like Kennedy before him, the president had few levers to enforce these assurances. Thieu and Ky were elected president and vice-president by suspiciously lopsided victories in 1967 after a "constitutional convention," but they postponed reforms and ruled through fiat and secret police. This facade of democracy in Saigon further aggravated discontent in the countryside.

The unending war in Vietnam began to divide American citizens. A growing protest movement questioned their country's purposes. Although he had earlier guided the Gulf of Tonkin resolution through the Senate, J. William Fulbright lashed out against what he called "the arrogance of power." Head of the Foreign Relations Committee, Fulbright observed that "power tends to confuse itself with virtue." Months of generally peaceful protest marches culminated in October 1967 in a giant three-day rally in Washington, D.C. The mushrooming antiwar movement deprived Johnson of a crucial part of his natural constituency among Democrats. Ominously, the protests polarized American society into "hawks" or "doves"—those who favored pursuing victory or seeking peace through compromise.

Tet and the President's Discontent, 1968

The year 1968 became a turning point. Critics of the war doubted that the United States could ever win in Vietnam at any reasonable cost, but a majority of Americans still believed in the cause. Walt Rostow told reporters that captured documents showed a Communist collapse to be "imminent," and, indeed, the NLF was becoming exhausted and desperate. Then, in late January 1968, during celebrations for Tet, Vietnam's lunar new year, NLF guerrillas and North Vietnamese armies coordinated a massive attack against Saigon and Hue, the imperial capital of Vietnam, and nine provincial capitals. The insurgents overran much of Cholon, the Chinese section of Saigon, and even penetrated the grounds of the American embassy, killing several guards. In Hue, the rebels executed a reign of terror against their political opponents. The attacks on regional cities had the greatest military repercussions. To restore control, General William Westmoreland, the commander of U.S. forces, had to shift troops from northern South Vietnam and from rural areas. Communist cadres quickly infiltrated the now unprotected countryside, but their overall offensive had failed.

To the U.S. command, the Tet offensive confirmed the enemy's weakness. The NLF had overextended itself, exhausting months of supplies in an unsuccessful effort to end the war. "The enemy is on the ropes," Westmoreland said. "Tet was his last gasp." If only he had 200,000 more men, the American commander promised, he would crush the rural insurgency "once and for all."

Several civilian advisers, however, had for months counseled diplomatic compromise. Secretary of Defense Robert McNamara recommended a coalition government for South Vietnam and then resigned. George Ball, the undersecretary of state, repeatedly pointed out the folly of forcing a people into allegiance and had also resigned. The CIA for years had counseled against the effort. But Johnson, until now, had listened more to his generals, demanding only good news and then relying on their promises. After the Tet offensive, the president asked an old friend and much-respected confidant of Democratic presidents, Clark Clifford, to chart a fresh course.

As the new secretary of defense, Clifford soon discovered that the military numbers game was relatively straightforward. To send 200,000 men to Southeast Asia and still fulfill American commitments elsewhere, the president would have to call up the army reserves or triple already high draft quotas. Only new taxes and wide-ranging controls on an overheated economy could ensure war production at a reasonable cost and temper an accelerating inflation. Influential politicians privately told Johnson that the country would reject such steps toward a wider war. Despite the fact that Tet had been a military setback for the NLF, Clifford urged Johnson to negotiate.

The Tet offensive convinced many in Vietnam that the war could never end until the United States left. "Before the Americans came," an old man told a reporter in Saigon, "my home was on the land of my ancestors and my family was honorable. Now I live off my daughter's earnings as a hooch-girl." Morale in the U.S. Army collapsed. Helicopter pilots sometimes refused to fly during their last four weeks "in country." Some units sought escape in drugs or "fragging"—surreptitious assaults on their own officers. Others lost all restraint, as at My Lai, where American soldiers killed children, women, and old men, apparently without thought or guilt. Both Vietnamese society and the U.S. army were coming apart under the strain of a stalemated war.

Amid the pressures for peace, Johnson gradually lost control of his party. Senator Eugene J. McCarthy, an outspoken Democratic critic of Vietnam policy, nearly won New Hampshire's presidential primary. Robert F. Kennedy entered the presidential race, pledging to stop the conflict. The president, a great campaigner, could not defend himself publicly on the hustings because the Secret Service considered the security risk too great. Trapped in the White House, losing both the presidential nomination and popular respect, Johnson brooded about the war.

Finally, on March 31, 1968, Johnson told a nationwide TV audience that he had rejected Westmoreland's request for more troops. American escalation would stop. To signal his good intentions and bring Hanoi to the bargaining table, he halted bombing north of the nineteenth parallel. Then, almost as a postscript, Johnson announced that he would not run for reelection.

Yet the level of violence within South Vietnam actually increased. Thieu promised to conscript another 135,000 men, a figure that together with more Americans already in training camps nearly fulfilled Westmoreland's request.

Proscribed from attacking the North, American pilots intensified the air war in the South. Johnson was still attempting to "negotiate from strength."

Ho Chi Minh, wanting to ensure the bombing halt, took up Johnson's offer for talks, and American and Vietnamese negotiators privately worked out a practical arrangement that reflected battlefield realities. America would end all bombing if North Vietnam agreed "by its silence" not to increase support for the NLF. Both sides might then consider possible coalition governments for South Vietnam. In seeking this compromise, however, Johnson had not reckoned with his ally in Saigon. President Thieu thought that the Republican presidential candidate, Richard Nixon, could arrange better terms. "I will win the peace," Nixon had vowed. Saigon obstructed multilateral talks with the NLF, thus scuttling any deal. Thieu could challenge Washington with threats that he would quit and thereby bring on chaos. Nixon's eventual victory pleased Thieu immensely, but the new U.S. president required time to formulate specific policies. Diplomats marked time by haggling over the shape of the bargaining table. By the beginning of 1969, Nixon's Republican administration faced an extraordinarily difficult situation: stalemated war, ungovernable allies, and domestic impatience.

Soldiers

One young man who enlisted for duty in Vietnam recalled, "my grandfather went in 1917, my father went in 1942. It was my turn." Those soldiers who brought to Vietnam visions of World War II (or the representations of World War II from Hollywood films), however, found quite a different war. Draftees for World War II were drawn from all sectors of American society; the Vietnam conflict was, in historian Christian Appy's phrase, a "working-class war." World War II usually had clear battle lines; in Vietnam, nothing was clear.

Of the two and one-half million enlisted men who served in Vietnam, around 80 percent came from low-income or working-class backgrounds, the sons of factory workers, clerks, farmers, truck drivers, secretaries. One study of wartime casualties from Illinois concluded that men who came from low-income areas were four times more likely to die in Vietnam than were men from areas that were solidly middle or upper class.

Whether men had set their sights on attending college or not seemed to make a crucial difference. While some college men who confronted the draft struggled with their consciences and felt the weight of making a difficult personal decision, most other men saw military service not as a choice but as an inevitability. On college campuses, even on those where pro-war sentiment was strong, there was a supportive culture for avoiding the draft. Antiwar counselors and informal conversations taught young people how to secure deferments, argue for status as conscientious objectors, join the low-risk National Guard, or escape to Canada. In working-class communities, by contrast, military recruiters and peer pressure presented war service as unavoidable or even as a welcome opportunity for leaving the confines of home. Many men enlisted with a group of supportive friends. "There wasn't any question as to whether you were going to do it or not. It's part of life," recalled one enlistee from Long Island whose father and uncles had proudly talked of service in World War II and Korea as he grew up.

The Johnson administration encouraged low-income youth to join the military in the so-called "Project 100,000." A small part of the War on Poverty, this project promised each year to admit 100,000 men who failed the qualifying exam for the military in order to expose them to various kinds of useful training. Robert McNamara said that such men would thereby "be given an opportunity to return to civilian life with skills and aptitudes which for them and their families will reverse the downward spiral of poverty." As recruiting rose, however, training programs lagged. Of the 400,000 men admitted under this program during the four years after 1966, 40 percent were African American, and casualty rates reached twice that of other enlisted men.

Basic training for all recruits taught little about the conditions of battle in Vietnam. Soldiers learned nothing about Vietnamese culture or French colonialism. Although they learned that they were to eradicate the Viet Cong's infrastructure in the villages, few understood before they arrived "in country" that the Viet Cong would usually be indistinguishable from noncombatant civilians. In his novel *Fragments,* Jack Fuller recalled his brother cautioning about the "peaceful" villages. "People will bow, children smile. But they'll blow you away in a minute. . . . Sometimes I wonder whether it wasn't our expectation of deceit more than deceit itself that proved so corrupting." The villages—indeed all of the Vietnamese country—could seem ominously hostile.

The prevalence of land mines in and around villages proved especially frightening. According to many estimates, more than one-fifth of all U.S. casualties came from mines, those hidden explosives that instantly and impersonally claimed lives and limbs with no visible enemy engagement at all. The constant dread of mines demoralized troops and deepened their distrust of the villagers they were supposed to be protecting. American soldiers fought against tactics of concealment, as both the mines and the guerrilla enemy blended into the countryside and nullified the superior firepower and rising numbers of American troops.

As the enemy avoided confrontation, American ground troops, often exhausted by heat, dehydration, and anxiety, marched through jungles and rice paddies. The Psychological Warfare Office dropped millions of leaflets from helicopters showing cartoons of villages being bombed by American planes with piles of dead in pools of blood. The caption read "If you support the Vietcong . . . your village will look like this." But who could tell supporters from nonsupporters? Who could distinguish those whom the war was saving from those whom it was eliminating?

Especially after the Tet offensive of 1968, a deep skepticism came to pervade the U.S. ground units, and morale sharply declined. During the early 1970s desertion became a major problem in the military. One source reports that in 1965 the desertion rate was fifteen of every one-thousand men; by 1972 it had climbed to seventy, the highest rate in modern American military history. Half a million men deserted over the course of the war. Declining troop morale, together with military stalemate and growing antiwar sentiment at home, set important limits within which the new Nixon administration would try to forge policy.

FALLOUT FROM THE WAR

While the war in Southeast Asia preoccupied U.S. foreign policy, relations with the Soviet Union continued to oscillate between distrust and accommodation. The war in Vietnam both pleased and worried the Soviets. America's burgeoning commitments in Asia threatened the Soviet's rival, China, more than the Soviet Union itself. In addition, Soviet leaders presumed that the war in Vietnam might divert American attention and resources away from regions of greater interest to their country. Yet Johnson's very willingness to use force convinced Khrushchev's successors, Leonid Brezhnev and Aleksei Kosygin, that the Americans respected only military strength. Many Soviet scientists worried about the implications of NASA's (National Aeronautics and Space Administration) mammoth space rockets and plans for orbiting platforms. The Soviets consequently stepped up production of their most sophisticated missile, the SS-9, and accelerated atomic stockpiling and research on biological warfare. The United States, at the same time, expanded its own military research, developing Multiple Independent Reentry Vehicles (MIRVs), which vastly increased the payload of a single rocket, and "smart bombs," which guided themselves to their target through electronic devices.

Still, neither power wanted to let cold-war rivalry escalate beyond its control. During June 1967, Johnson and Kosygin conferred privately at Glassboro State College in New Jersey. Worried that the enormous success of Israel's just completed Six-Day War might bring on a Soviet-American clash in the Middle East, each promised to respect his rival's vital interests in this crucial region. Moreover, Washington reacted mildly to Moscow's brutal repression of Czechoslovakian reform efforts in 1968 rather than jeopardize the Nuclear Nonproliferation Treaty, finally signed in early 1969. Such tradeoffs symbolized, once again, the high priority both nations placed on avoiding atomic war.

Although consistently proclaimed as a crusade to reassure its allies, America's involvement in Southeast Asia further fragmented the Atlantic alliance. Western Europe's accelerating prosperity—in part a consequence of American spending overseas—eroded its sense of dependency. Determined to build a national nuclear force, in 1967 French President Charles de Gaulle removed France from the integrated command structure of the NATO alliance. He openly criticized U.S. policy in Vietnam and, ignoring U.S. pressure, extended diplomatic recognition to China. Many West Germans, hoping to build better relations with their neighbors, also chafed at Washington's rigid anticommunism. Even the "special relationship" between Great Britain and the United States withered a bit, as economic obsolescence pushed British leaders toward the European Common Market. Many Britons opposed America's policy in Vietnam and worried that the United States would be weakened by its costly involvement. The war, therefore, became a visible wedge that threatened to drive the Atlantic community apart.

The conflict in Southeast Asia also set the context for U.S. policies in the Third World. Determined to create an Asian consensus for his policy, Johnson did not challenge oppressive and unpopular regimes in the Philippines and South Korea as long as they supported his effort in Vietnam. Both countries sent troops to Vietnam. U.S. policymakers and the CIA also rallied to support a military oligarchy in Indonesia, after General Suharto ousted the increasingly pro-Chinese Sukarno in 1965.

Support for dictators reverberated in U.S. policies toward Latin America. Fearing the spread of Castro-style communism throughout the hemisphere, Kennedy had adopted a carrot-and-stick approach, publicly emphasizing the Alliance for Progress while privately stepping up covert action and military assistance to limit local insurgencies. Johnson, increasingly, relied solely on the stick. Downplaying support for social reform, which he feared might lead to unrealistic expectations and actually fuel revolutionary discontent, he accelerated aid to military establishments that promised stability. In 1964 in Brazil, for example, generals supported by the United States toppled the populist Joao Goulart, who was talking about the nationalization of foreign businesses.

Panicked by fears of "another Cuba," Johnson resorted to military intervention in the Caribbean. In the Dominican Republic, a right-wing coup had ousted the constitutionally elected reformist government of Juan Bosch. But when Bosch's supporters attempted to regain control, American representatives on the island reported that Communists had infiltrated Bosch's movement and requested that Johnson send the marines. Some 20,000 troops landed in mid-1965, and despite the quickly discovered inaccuracy of American reports, Johnson left the troops there until September 1966, when carefully supervised elections installed another pro-American leader, Joaquin Balaguer, as president. U.S. gunboat diplomacy and alliances with dictators complemented a flood of private investment by American corporations, which were looking to Latin America for profits but demanding political stability.

Preoccupied with Vietnam, Johnson tried to force other nations into roles as either pro-United States or pro-Communist, often ignoring, as in Vietnam, both nationalism and indigenous cultures. In this way, the Southeast Asian war shaped American foreign policies, even outside of Asia, by emphasizing above all else, the goal of fighting communism.

The 1960s had begun with Kennedy's bright promise "to get the country moving again" toward economic growth for all and toward spreading democracy abroad. Lyndon Johnson picked up the themes of his martyred predecessor, guiding his Great Society programs through Congress, endorsing new civil-rights legislation, and steadfastly refusing to lose to Communists in Vietnam. Ambition, however, overreached vision and judgment. By 1968, the society that had been summoned to be "great" watched as cities burned from racial conflict and antiwar demonstrations filled the streets. The country had been called to fight two wars—one against poverty and one against Vietnamese Communists—but both struggles brought growing discord.

SUGGESTED READING

The best study of the tensions that beset the positive-state policies of the Democratic party during the 1960s is Allen J. Matusow, *The Unraveling of America* (1984), but see also the relevant chapters of Alonso Hamby, *Liberalism and its Challengers* (1992). Gary Wills, *Nixon Agonistes* (rev. ed., 1980) and *The Kennedy Imprisonment* (1983) offers critical viewpoints, as does Thomas C. Reeves, *A Question of Character: A Life of John F. Kennedy* (1991). More favorable, though not uncritical, is David Burner, *John F. Kennedy and a New Generation* (1988). James N. Giglio's *The Presidency of John F. Kennedy* (1991) provides a reliable overview. For more detail, see Herbert J. Parmet's two volumes—*Jack* (1980) and *JFK* (1983). Seymour Hersh, *The Dark Side of Camelot* (1997) is unrelentingly critical. Journalist Richard Reeves anchors his *President Kennedy: Profile of Power* (1994) in considerable archival research. Finally, there are many sympathetic accounts of Kennedy's presidency by close associates; by far the best is Arthur Schlesinger, Jr., *A Thousand Days* (1965).

Events surrounding Kennedy's death have attracted almost as much attention as those during his brief presidency. Edward Jay Epstein's two studies, *Inquest* (1963) and *Legend* (1978), are the best of the older accounts that reject the Warren Commission's version of the assassination. Theories of the assassination itself include Henry Hurt, *Reasonable Doubt* (1988); John H. Davis, *Mafia Kingfish: Carlos Marcello and the Assassination of John F. Kennedy* (1989); and Peter Dale Scott, *Deep Politics and the Death of JFK* (1993), all of which are critical of the Warren Commission's conclusions. But also see two attempts to rehabilitate its general conclusions in David Berlin, *Final Disclosure* (1989), and Gerald L. Posner, *Case Closed* (1993). Michael J. Kurtz, *The Crime of the Century* (2nd ed., 1993), tries to offer historical grounding, and Barbie Zelizer, *Covering the Body* (1992), is a superb cultural study. Part of the political aftermath of Oliver Stone's movie *JFK* (1991) may be seen in U.S. Assassination Records Review Board, *Final Report* (1998).

Specific aspects of the Kennedy administration are covered in Grant McConnell, *Steel and the Presidency—1962* (1963); Jim F. Health, *John Kennedy and the Business Community* (1969); Victor Navasky, *Kennedy Justice* (1971); Carl M. Brauer, *John F. Kennedy and the Second Reconstruction* (1977); James Tobin and Murray Weidenbaum, eds., *Two Revolutions in Economic Policy: The First Economic Reports of Presidents Kennedy and Reagan* (1988); and Laurence J. McAndrews, *Broken Ground: John F. Kennedy and the Politics of Education* (1991).

In addition to general studies on the civil rights movement cited for Chapter 4, the following studies are also recommended: Howard Zinn, *SNCC* (1965); Elliot Rudwick and August Meier, *CORE* (1972); David Garrow, *Protest at Selma* (1980); William Chafe, *Civilities and Civil Rights* (1980); Clayborne Carson, *In Struggle* (1981); Elizabeth Jacoway and David R. Colburn, *Southern Businessmen and Desegregation* (1982); Steven Lawson, *In Pursuit of Power* (1985); Doug McAdam, *Freedom Summer* (1988); Emily Stoper, *The Student Non-violent Coordinating Committee: The Growth of Radicalism in a Civil Rights Organization* (1989); David Garrow, ed., *Birmingham, Alabama, 1956–1963: The Black Struggle for Civil Rights* (1989); John Walton Cotman, *Birmingham, JFK, and the Civil Rights Act of 1963* (1989); Kenneth O'Reilly, *Racial Matters: The FBI's Secret Files on Black America, 1960–72* (1989); Stewart Burns, *Social Movements of the 1960s: Searching for Democracy* (1990); Hugh Davis Graham, *The Civil Rights Era: Origins and Development of National Policy, 1960–1972* (1990); Raymond S. Franklin, *Shadows of Race* (1991); Richard A. Couto, *Ain't Gonna Let Nobody Turn Me Round* (1991); John T. McCartney, *Black Power Ideologies* (1992); Mark Stern, *Calculating Visions: Kennedy, Johnson, and Civil Rights* (1992); William L. Van Deburg, *New Day in Babylon: The Black Power Movement and American Culture, 1965–1975* (1992); Eric R. Burner, *And Gently He Shall Lead Them: Robert Parris Moses and Civil Rights in Mississippi* (1994); Gerald Home, *Fire This Time: The Watts Uprising* (1995); Brian Ward, *Just My Soul Responding: Rhythm and Blues, Black Consciousness, and Race Relations* (1998); Belinda Robnett, *How Long? How Long? African American Women in the Struggle for Civil Rights* (1997); Gerald D. McKnight, *The Last Crusade: Martin Luther King, Jr., the FBI, and the Poor People's Campaign* (1998); Timothy J. Minchin, *Hiring the Black Worker: The Racial Integration of the Southern Textile Industry, 1960–1980* (1999); Timothy N. Thurber, *The Politics of Equality: Hubert H. Humphrey and the African American Freedom Struggle* (1999); Louis A. DeCaro Jr., *Malcolm and the Cross: The Nation of Islam, Malcolm X, and Christianity*

(1998); William L. Van DeBurg, *Black Camelot: African American Cultural Heroes in Their Times, 1960–1980* (1997); Komozi Woodard, *A Nation within a Nation: Amiri Baraka (LeRoy Jones) and Black Power Politics* (1999); and Marshall Frady, *Martin Luther King, Jr.* (2002).

Many of the works cited on gender and family issues for Chapter 4 are also relevant here. In addition, see Susan M. Hartman, *From Margin to Mainstream: American Women in Politics Since 1960* (1989); Lauri Umansky, *Motherhood Reconceived: Feminism and the Legacies of the 1960s* (1996); Susan M. Hartmann, *The Other Feminists: Activists in the Liberal Establishment* (1998); Dennis A. Deslippe, *"Rights, Not Roses": Unions and the Rise of Working-Class Feminism, 1945–80* (2000); and the relevant chapters of Linda Gordon, ed., *Women, Welfare and the State* (1990).

On Lyndon Johnson, see Paul K. Conkin, *Big Daddy from the Perdaneles* (1986); Robert Caro, *The Path to Power* (1982), *Means of Ascent* (1990), and *Master of the Senate* (2002); Robert J. Dallek, *Lone Star Rising: Lyndon Johnson and His Times, 1908–1960* (1991) and *Flawed Giant: Lyndon Johnson and His Times, 1961–1973* (1998); Irwin and Debi Unger, *LBJ: A Life* (1999); and Michael Beschloss, ed., *Taking Charge: The White House Tapes, 1963–64* (1997) and *Reaching for Glory: Lyndon Johnson's Secret White House Tapes, 1964–65* (2001). For overviews of Johnson's presidency, see Vaughn Davis Bornet, *The Presidency of Lyndon Baines Johnson* (1983); Irving Bernstein, *Guns or Butter: The Presidency of Lyndon Johnson* (1996); and John A. Andrew, III, *LBJ and the Great Society* (1999). Doris Kearns, *Lyndon Johnson and the American Dream* (1976) remains worthwhile, as does the multivolume project, *The Johnson Years* (1987–), edited by Robert A. Divine. Joseph A. Califano, Jr., *The Triumph and Tragedy of Lyndon Johnson* (1991) is an insightful memoir.

On the Great Society and the War on Poverty, begin with the critical assessment in Matusow, *The Unraveling of America*. A much more positive view is *The Promise of Greatness* (1976) by Sar Levitan and Robert Taggert. John E. Schwarz, *America's Hidden Success* (rev. ed., 1988) is equally upbeat. The most influential analysis of Great Society liberalism from the right has been Charles Murray's *Losing Ground* (1984); for views of the Great Society from the left, see, for example, William P. Ryan, *Equality* (1982) and Richard Cloward and Francis Fox Piven, *Poor People's Movements* (1978). Marvin E. Gettleman and David Mermelstein, eds., *The Great Society Reader* (1965) remains a useful documentary collection. More recent studies include the relevant chapters of Christopher Jencks, *Rethinking Social Policy* (1992); Martha F. Davis, *Brutal Need: Lawyers and the Welfare Rights Movement* (1994); Robert C. Lieberman, *Shifting the Color Line: Race and the American Welfare State* (1998); and Michael K. Brown, *Race, Money, and the American Welfare State* (1999).

On the Warren Court and liberal reform, begin with the unabridged edition of Bernard Schwartz, *Super Chief* (1983); G. Edward White, *Earl Warren* (1982); the relevant parts of Mark Tushnet, *Red, White, and Blue: A Critical Analysis of Constitutional Law* (1988), and of Samuel Walker, *In Defense of American Liberties: A History of the ACLU* (1990). Morton J. Horowitz, *The Warren Court and the Pursuit of Justice* (1998) is an excellent brief study, and Lucas S. Powe, Jr., *The Warren Court and American Politics* (2000) is the best of recent, longer works. See also Neil McFeeley, *Appointment of Judges: The Johnson Presidency* (1987); the relevant chapters of Melvin I. Urofsky, *The Continuity of Change: The Supreme*

Court and Individual Liberties, 1953–1986 (1991); Tinsley E. Yarbrough, *John Marshall Harlan: Great Dissenter of the Warren Court* (1992); Laura Kalman, *The Strange Career of Legal Liberalism* (1996); and Charles R. Epp, *The Rights Revolution: Lawyers, Activists, and Supreme Courts in Comparative Perspective* (1998).

On foreign policy in the 1960s, see many of the general studies listed for Chapter 1, such as McCormick, LaFeber, and Ambrose. On Kennedy's foreign policy, see Thomas G. Paterson, ed., *Kennedy's Quest for Victory: American Foreign Policy, 1961–1963* (1989); Michael R. Beschloss, *The Crisis Years: Kennedy and Khrushchev, 1960–1963* (1991); Noam Chornsky, *Rethinking Camelot: JFK, the Vietnam War, and U.S. Political Culture* (1993); Richard D. Mahoney, *JFK: Ordeal in Africa* (1983); Jane Stromseth, *The Origins of Flexible Response* (1988); Lawrence Freedman, *Kennedy's Wars: Berlin, Cuba, Laos, and Vietnam* (2000); Michael E. Latham, *Modernization as Ideology: American Social Science and 'Nation Building' in the Kennedy Era* (2000); Stephen G. Rabe, *The Most Dangerous Area in the World: John F. Kennedy Confronts Communist Revolution in Latin America* (1999); Elizabeth Cobbs-Hoffman, *All You Need Is Love: The Peace Corps and the Spirit of the 1960s* (1998); and Fritz Fischer, *Making Them Like Us: Peace Corps Volunteers in the 1960s* (1998).

A huge literature on the missile crisis in Cuba includes Graham T. Allison, *Essence of Decision: Explaining the Cuban Missile Crisis* (1971); Trumbell Higgins, *The Perfect Failure: Kennedy, Eisenhower, and the CIA at the Bay of Pigs* (1989); Dino A. Brugioni, *Eyeball to Eyeball: The Inside Story of the Cuban Missile Crisis* (1991); James Blight, *Cuba on the Brink: Castro, the Missile Crisis, and the Soviet Challenge* (1993); Mark J. White, *The Cuban Missile Crisis* (1996); John C. Ausland, *Kennedy, Khrushchev, and the Berlin-Cuba Crisis, 1961–1964* (1996); Timothy Naftali and Aleksandr Fursenko, *"One Hell of a Gamble": Khrushchev, Castro, and Kennedy, 1958–1964* (1997); and Ernest R. May and Philip D. Zelikow, eds., *The Kennedy Tapes: Inside the White House during the Cuban Missile Crisis* (1997).

Johnson's foreign policies are treated in Bernard Firestone and Robert C. Vogt, eds., *Lyndon Baines Johnson and the Uses of Power* (1988); Warren I. Cohen and Nancy Bernkopf Tucker, eds., *Lyndon Johnson Confronts the World: American Foreign Policy, 1963–1968* (1994); Diane Kunz, ed., *The Diplomacy of the Crucial Decade: American Foreign Relations during the 1960s* (1994); and H. W. Brands, *The Foreign Policies of Lyndon Johnson: Beyond Vietnam* (1999). On specific issues, see Walter A. McDougal, *The Heavens and the Earth: A Political History of the Space Age* (1985); Glen Seaborg, *Stemming the Tide: Arms Control in the Johnson Years* (1987); Bruce Palmer, Jr., *Intervention in the Caribbean: The Dominican Crisis of 1965* (1989); and Richard B. Parker, *The Politics of Miscalculation in the Middle East* (1993).

There is a huge scholarly literature on the war in Vietnam. The following are good places to begin. George Herring, *America's Longest War: The United States and Vietnam, 1950–1975* (1986); Marilyn Blatt Young, *The Vietnam-American Wars, 1945–1990* (1991); Melvin Small, *Johnson, Nixon, and the Doves* (1988); Bruce Palmer, Jr., *The 25-Year War* (1985); Gabriel Kolko, *Anatomy of War: Vietnam, the United States, and the Modern Historical Experience* (1994); Larry Berman, *Lyndon Johnson's War: The Road to Stalemate in Vietnam* (1989); R.B. Smith, *An International History of the Vietnam War* (1983); Michael Hunt, *Lyndon Johnson's War: America's Cold War Crusade in Vietnam, 1945–1968* (1996); Robert Buzzanco, *Masters of War: Military Dissent and Politics in the Vietnam Era* (1996);

Robert D. Schulzinger, *A Time for War: The United States and Vietnam, 1941–1975* (1997); Robert J. McMahon, *The Limits of Empire: The United States and Southeast Asia since World War II* (1999); William M. Hammond, *Reporting Vietnam: Media and Military at War* (1998); Frederik Logevall, *Choosing War: The Lost Chance for Peace and the Escalation of War in Vietnam* (1999); Qiang Zhai, *China and the Vietnam Wars, 1950–1975* (2000); and Charles E. Neu, eds., *After Vietnam: Legacies of a Lost War* (2000).

More specific studies include Marilyn Young and Jon Livingston, *The Vietnam War: How the United States Intervened in the History of Southeast Asia* (1990); Lloyd C. Gardner, *Approaching Vietnam: From World War II through Dien Bien Phu* (1988); George McT. Kahin, *Intervention: How America Became Involved in Vietnam* (1986); James J. Wirtz, *The Tet Offensive: Intelligence Failure in War* (1991); Ronald Spector, *After Tet: The Bloodiest Year in Vietnam* (1993); David M. Barrett, *Uncertain Warriors: Lyndon Johnson and His Vietnam Advisors* (1993); David L. DiLeo, *George Ball, Vietnam, and the Rethinking of Containment* (1991); Edwin Moise, *Tonkin Gulf and the Escalation of the Vietnam War* (1996); Roger Warner, *Back Fire: The CIA's Secret War in Laos and Its Link to the Vietnam War* (1995); Richard A. Hunt, *Pacification: The American Struggle for Vietnam's Hearts and Minds* (1995); Leslie Gelb and Richard K. Betts, *The Irony of Vietnam* (1978); Paul Joseph, *Cracks in the Empire* (1981); Larry Berman, *Planning a Tragedy* (1982); the relevant chapters of Lawrence Wittner, *Rebels Against War: The American Peace Movement, 1933–1983* (1984); Mary Hershberger, *Traveling to Vietnam: American Peace Activists and the War* (1998); Andrew E. Hunt, *The Turning: A History of Vietnam Veterans Against the War* (1999); William Conrad Gibbons, *The United States Government and the Vietnam War: Executive and Legislative Roles and Relationships* (1986); John P. Burke and Fred Greenstein, *How Presidents Test Reality: Decisions on Vietnam, 1954 and 1965* (1989); Mark Clodfelter, *The Limits of Air Power: The American Bombing of North Vietnam* (1989); David M. Barrett, *Uncertain Warriors: Lyndon Johnson and His Vietnam Advisors* (1993); Stuart I. Rochester and Frederick Kiley, *Honor Bound: American Prisoners of War in Southeast Asia, 1961–1973* (1998); Lewis Sorley, *A Better War: The Unexamined Victories and Final Tragedy of America's Last Years in Vietnam* (1999); and Christian G. Appy, *Working Class War: American Combat Soldiers in Vietnam* (1993).

For cultural debates generated by the war in Vietnam, see Loren Bartiz, *Backfire: A History of How American Culture Led Us into Vietnam and Made Us Fight the Way We Did* (1985); Kathleen Turner, *Lyndon Johnson's Dual War: Vietnam and the Press* (1985); Susan Jeffords, *The Remasculinization of America: Gender and the Vietnam War* (1989); Albert Auster and Leonard Quart, *How the War Was Remembered: Hollywood and Vietnam* (1988); John Carlos Rowe and Rick Berg, eds., *The Vietnam War and American Culture* (1991); Michael Gregg, ed., *Inventing Vietnam: The War in Film and Television* (1991); David W. Levy, *The Debate over Vietnam* (2nd ed., 1995); Fred Turner, *Echoes of Combat: The Vietnam War in American Memory* (1996); Robert R. Tomes, *Apocalypse Then: American Intellectuals and the Vietnam War, 1954–1975* (1998); Keith Beattle, *The Scar that Binds: American Culture and the Vietnam War* (1998); Rhodri Jeffreys-Jones, *Peace Now!: American Society and the Ending of the Vietnam War* (1999); and Gerald Nicosa, *Home to War: A History of the Vietnam Veterans Movement* (2001).

6

Polarization and the Search for Empowerment

For nearly four decades, Americans have been arguing about the 1960s and early 1970s. People who protested against the war in Vietnam and social conditions at home wrote many of the initial accounts. Most, bearing titles such as *Democracy is in the Streets* and *The Unfinished Journey,* saw the period dominated by a youth-oriented "New Left" politics and "counterculture" and portrayed the protest movements as still relevant to the problems of American life. In contrast, other veterans of the era, while seeing similar political and cultural forces at work, dismissed protests as the fantasies of youth. The era of the New Left and counterculture, in books with titles such as *Second Thoughts,* seemed a time of romantic revolt that never had anything to do with addressing serious issues.

Subsequent studies, many by people too young to draw on personal memory, try to offer a broader view. They see the initial accounts tainted either by old political and cultural allegiances or by visceral reactions against them. Much recent writing emphasizes the extent to which developments other than political and cultural radicalism among young people mark the 1960s and early 1970s. These were the years, for example, during which large-scale institutions, both private and public, expanded dramatically. (See Chapter 8.) At the same time, this era saw a growing conservative movement—and not simply the more noticeable activism of the left. The dynamic between the New Left and the new conservatism brought a political and social polarization that not only shaped events of the 1960s and 1970s but those of the next several decades as well.

THE "YOUTH MOVEMENT"

The activities of young people on the political and cultural left provided one of the polarizing forces at work during the 1960s. Enthusiasm for John Kennedy on college campuses had initially encouraged his supporters to imagine that the decade would be dominated by his vision of a New Frontier. Many students joined older activists in the Peace Corps in order to spend several years of their lives helping other peoples and nations. Even before Kennedy's death, though, some young people were becoming disillusioned with JFK's gradualism and sought more ambitious political initiatives. The result, in a phrase popular in the media and in the earliest accounts of the 1960s, was a "youth movement."

This term may assign too much coherency and influence to a loose collection of different styles of political and cultural dissent. Members of a "New Left" sought radical solutions for what they considered the failures of the national political tradition that extended from Franklin Roosevelt's New Deal to Lyndon Johnson's Great Society. They claimed that local grassroots activism by community-based organizers could provide an alternative means to promote social and economic change and bring "power to the people." At the same time, devotees of the highly diverse counterculture embraced altered forms of consciousness and a revolution in cultural values and practices as the best antidotes for what they saw as the sterility and conformity of postwar society. The New Left and the counterculture remain important elements in any story of the era.

The Origins of the Youth Revolt

The potpourri of sources from which disaffected young people claimed insight and inspiration underscored the diversity of insurgency. Beat writers, academic mavericks, and religiously oriented movements such as the early civil-rights crusade were three of the most important sources from which young dissenters would draw inspiration.

The youthful protesters of the 1960s were beginning the school day during the 1950s by saluting the flag when writers and poets called "the Beats" were championing the cause of dissent. Jack Kerouac's novel *On the Road* (1957) glorified the drifters and rebels who resisted the temptation to settle down. The poems of Allen Ginsberg denounced materialism and middle-class morality and celebrated drugs, Eastern religions, and homosexual love. Beat poets such as Ginsberg and Gary Snyder displayed a free-flowing style that challenged restrictive forms. Hipster and huckster, Ginsberg carried the Beat movement into the 1960s, and became a revered elder-in-residence to a new generation of radicals.

While the Beats generally focused on cultural issues, C. Wright Mills, an Ivy-League sociology professor, concentrated on political ones. He cultivated his image of a maverick from Texas, wearing a leather jacket and riding a Harley Davidson. He also rejected the dispassionate stance of most cold-war academics in favor of politically committed scholarship. Mills helped to popularize theories that became some of the central tenets of the New Left: that an undemocratic "power elite" dominated American politics; that the program of the Democratic party, stressing gradual social change promoted by Washington, now bolstered the status quo; and that most journalists and academics offered rationalizations for inequality at home and knee-jerk anticommunism overseas. An activist as well as a scholar, Mills visited Cuba and praised Fidel Castro's socialist experiment. After his death in 1962, Mills became a revered academic saint for radicals.

The critique of the postwar United States received extended elaboration in the writings of philosopher Herbert Marcuse. A German-born Marxist, Marcuse attacked the sophisticated technology and economic prosperity that marked the "American way of life". The United States, according to Marcuse, was becoming a quasi-totalitarian "technocracy." Effective power increasingly rested with the "technocrats": the self-styled experts in government, business, science, and other dominant institutions who defined social policies and national priorities. In such a "one-dimensional" society, a technological imperative prevailed. The mass-production, mass-consumption economic system satisfied only "false needs"—mass-produced gadgets that provided no real sense of happiness or personal fulfillment.

Disaffected young people borrowed from dissenting academics such as Mills and Marcuse. Terms such as power elite, false needs, and technocracy became part of an apocalyptic vocabulary. The people who ran the big universities and the big government in Washington became villains. At best, they celebrated a flawed status quo; at worst, they frustrated popular aspirations with mass-mediated illusions rather than with guns and repressive policing tactics.

Work in religiously oriented causes, especially the civil-rights movement, also prompted dissent among many young people. A recent study of the University of Texas, for example, suggests that students who embraced activism envisioned their activities as part of a long tradition of religious-influenced insurgency. Throughout the South during the early 1960s, the civil-rights movement relied on college-age volunteers for time-consuming, labor-intensive jobs such as preparing leaflets, running copying machines, and canvassing neighborhoods. In time, the ways in which these tasks were divided along gender lines would encourage many women to embrace a new feminism. Initially, though, these activities brought young people together in a common cause. Traveling long distances and sleeping in makeshift accommodations, civil-rights workers saw a sense of community that seemed missing elsewhere in the United States. As one woman later wrote, the civil-rights movement was "home and family, food and work, love and a reason to live." These young idealists claimed to find personal fulfillment in a crusade that they expected would change the entire society.

Too often, civil-rights workers complained, they confronted hostile or cautious political leaders. Segregationists in Alabama and Mississippi would make no concessions, and politicians in Washington stressed the need to move slowly on racial issues. While segregationists assaulted civil-rights workers, FBI agents seemed to be looking on and taking notes. Youthful activists charged that the Kennedy administration offered Band-Aid solutions for deep national wounds. Segregation and racism were affronts to democracy that could not be tolerated.

Inventing a New Left

Not all young people protested, and the new radicals constituted only a minority of those between the ages of eighteen and twenty-five. Others remained true to the spirit of John Kennedy, voting for Lyndon Johnson and supporting a war for "democracy and freedom" in Vietnam. Another important group of young people, who were as distanced from Kennedy and Johnson as any member of the New Left, joined a new conservative movement. Most young people probably resented protestors of any kind and eagerly embraced the consumer products and the nine-to-five jobs scorned by cultural radicals. Still, younger radicals seemed to overshadow their peers and the group of older radicals who had inspired them because they captured the attention of the media and dominated politics on many university campuses during the 1960s. Critical of the direction of postwar life and convinced that they could find alternatives, the youthful rebels came to symbolize an entire generation.

What distinguished the young radicals from others of their age? Drawing on several studies of college students at elite schools, psychologist Kenneth Keniston offered an early, still intriguing explanation. The rebels were "psychological adults" but "sociological adolescents." Protestors tended to be excellent students, usually in the humanities, Keniston claimed. Coming from relatively affluent homes, they could afford to postpone settling into permanent social roles. Instead of having to choose an established career path, they could adopt that of activist for social and political change. Most important, Keniston argued, most believed that they and their parents actually shared the same ideals but that their parents were forced to compromise them in their day-to-day lives. This belief intensified the desire among young radicals to remain free from settled, adult routines.

To these young dissenters, the failures of their parents' generation seemed more important than its successes. Too many jobs looked boring and repetitive; too much of daily life appeared to lack adventure and excitement; and, too often, discrimination, rather than freedom, seemed the law of the land. Moreover, the cool, rational world of John Kennedy appeared to substitute rhetoric for change. A stance of opposition, in contrast, seemed to offer hope for immediate personal fulfillment as well as the possibility of transforming American life. Through a commitment to radical alternatives, young people might complete Paul Simon's "dangling conversations" or explore Bob Dylan's "smoke rings of the mind."

At various universities—especially the University of Wisconsin at Madison, the University of California at Berkeley, and the University of Michigan—dissident students linked scholarship with social activism. Believing that their own professors were too committed to research for research's sake, radical students saw themselves in training to be a new breed of college professor. They would awaken campus life from its stupor and reinvent radical politics. Other students took more direct action. Rebels at Berkeley joined an older generation of activists and staged mass protests against the House Un-American Activities Committee (HUAC), capital punishment, and racial discrimination. College students continued to travel to the South, helping miners fight the coal companies in Hazard County, Kentucky, and working for civil-rights organizations.

Students for a Democratic Society (SDS), one of earliest of the New-Left organizations, attracted the most attention. Its "Port Huron Statement" of 1962, largely written by Tom Hayden, imagined a new social and political system in which people "shared in those social decisions determining the quality and direction" of their lives. As an alternative to the prevailing political order—which allegedly frustrated "democracy by confusing the individual citizen, paralyzing policy discussion, and consolidating the irresponsible power of military and business interests"—SDS espoused a "participatory democracy." This kind of democracy, the Port Huron Statement argued, would be "governed by two central aims: that the individual share in those social decisions determining the quality and direction of his life; that society be organized to encourage independence in men and provide the means for their common participation." Still, SDS's 1962 manifesto sounded no call for a cultural revolution and endorsed political programs (such as civil-rights legislation) that seemed consistent with the agenda of the Fair Deal and Kennedy's New Frontier.

Initially, many in the New Left viewed community organizing, a technique pioneered during the 1940s and 1950s by Chicago activist Saul Alinsky and the Highlander School in Tennessee, as the first step toward participatory democracy. Low-income people fell victim to better-organized elites, people such as Alinsky argued, because they could not exert political pressure commensurate with their numbers. Ordinary people could best be organized, the theory went, on the basis of local, grassroots issues. Thus, members of the New Left left college campuses to launch neighborhood-based organizing campaigns. In cities such as Newark, New Jersey, they mounted drives against urban renewal projects that displaced low-income residents and in support of better housing, more jobs, and school-lunch programs. These organizers displayed a missionary zeal but discovered the difficulty, especially for young activists from affluent backgrounds, of mobilizing low-income people. Some persisted, in the face of inexperience with Alinsky-style organizing techniques and impatience with endless rounds of meetings, to help establish vibrant local groups that laid down permanent roots in urban neighborhoods. Doubts about participatory democracy, however, prompted others in the New Left to abandon community projects. Seeking a more congenial environment and embracing the issue that seemed most pressing—the Vietnam War—they returned to the college campus, the center of youth-oriented ferment.

Radical Politics: From the College Campuses to the Streets

The most publicized of the early campus protests occurred at the University of California at Berkeley. During the fall of 1964, after university officials tried to limit political activity by students, protesters charged the administration with bowing to pressure from right-wing business leaders and limiting free speech. As protests against the university's restrictions on political expression escalated, the "Berkeley student revolt" featured massive student rallies and the seizure of university buildings. A number of campus groups, not all of which embraced New-Left politics, joined under the banner of the Free Speech Movement (FSM). The FSM attacked the bureaucratic impersonality of the entire university structure and called for a campuswide student strike. FSM claimed that almost three-quarters of the student body, and a sizable portion of the faculty, supported it. The FSM agenda also included concerns that transcended campus life. As Mario Savio, one of the leaders of the FSM, put it, there were times when the social-political machinery "makes you so sick at heart . . . [that] you can't even tacitly take part. And you've got to put your bodies upon the gears and upon the wheels, upon the levers, upon the apparatus, and you've got to make it stop." By the spring of 1965, campus issues gave way to larger causes, especially the war in Vietnam.

This basic scenario repeated itself, with important local variations, on many large college campuses during the mid-1960s. Dissent might begin with a limited range of issues, expand, and grow more militant. In banding together to fight college administrators and their outside supporters—a student participant in the 1968 disturbances at Columbia University simply called them "the biggies"—young people could find a sense of community empowerment. They could also develop a kind of garrison mentality, viewing themselves as vulnerable victims of a vast power structure against which resistance seemed futile but necessary.

The modern "multiversity" such as Berkeley and Columbia provided an easy target during the early and mid-1960s. Big universities displayed what even students who were not of the New Left considered unforgivable: emphasis on large lecture classes and haphazard discussion sections, a competitive race for high grades, and bureaucratic structures. Students who had been reared in the ethos of "family togetherness," open communication, and concern for individual feelings chaffed at the multiversity's assembly-line approach to education. Students claimed to see themselves as mere numbers who were subject to the whims of computers and faceless bureaucrats. Clark Kerr, the University of California's president, did portray himself as the administrator of a large "benevolent bureaucracy," a huge enterprise that produced knowledge instead of consumer goods. "The university and segments of industry are becoming more alike," Kerr once approvingly observed.

Dissidents could also tap a strong strain of resentment against the intrusion of campuswide rules on lifestyle choices that students were coming to see as personal "rights." Women, even those who were of legal age, had to observe dress codes and dorm hours on most college campuses during the early 1960s. Men at many state universities were required to take two years of military training, and administrators routinely censored student publications. Campus administrators still tried to exercise a kind of quasi-parental role and enforce various kinds of "parietals," including the monitoring of sexual relations between consenting students. Dissidents demanded that universities abandon or relax restrictions on the lives of students, reduce the number of academic requirements, and introduce educational programs "relevant" to pressing social concerns. The rules that shaped the daily routine on campus, many students charged, needed to be overthrown

Student muckrakers found the multiversity's role in the broader community equally suspect. Professors conducted classified research for the Defense Department. Had not chemists at Harvard, after all, developed the napalm that was being used in Vietnam? Did not urban universities, seeking space for expansion, spread into neighboring areas and push out the low-income residents? To extend the indictment, big universities rarely admitted students of color; except for talented athletes and a few academic superstars. Viewed from within, the multiversity seemed to offer mind-numbing courses and senseless regimentation. Seen as part of the larger U.S. society, it appeared implicated in war and racism.

Activism was not limited to the elite colleges and the multiversities. A number of smaller state universities also spawned vigorous antiwar and campus protest cultures. Here, many of the dissidents, in contrast to those whom Kenneth Keniston had studied, came from blue-collar backgrounds and were first-generation college students. Indeed, students at Kent State University in Ohio had already organized their own campus protest movement before the Berkeley student revolt of 1964 came to dominate media attention.

All across the country, there were significant changes and a few strategic retreats by college administrators, particularly on curricular and lifestyle issues. Most colleges abolished compulsory military instruction, adjusted curricular requirements, made efforts to recruit a more diverse student body, and established ethnic studies programs. Some professors encouraged social activism by substituting community-based internships for more traditional classes. In some cases, colleges had even begun to relax lifestyle restrictions in advance of student demands. At the University of Kansas (KU), for instance, campus administrators themselves, finding the role of moral censor at odds with their image as educated professionals, had begun the process of abandoning many of their parietals, especially over issues of sexuality, even before the rise of student militancy.

Campuses and Antiwar Demonstrations

Meanwhile, many campuses were coming to play a central role in the antiwar dramas of the 1960s. They could serve as staging areas for political demonstrations, and large groups of nonstudents, who were attracted to the cultural ferment engulfing college communities, provided additional troops for both on- and off-campus protests. A radicalized university, activists began to hope, could speed social and cultural change.

The growing protest against U.S. involvement in Vietnam demonstrated both the value and the limitations of the campus milieu as a base for insurgency. The antiwar crusade did not begin on the campus, but dissent there gave it an influential forum. Early in 1965, when President Johnson escalated the bombing campaign in Vietnam, antiwar activists organized a nationwide series of campus teach-ins, town-hall style meetings at which supporters and opponents of LBJ's policies debated. Initially, organizers hoped that teach-ins, which tended to be dominated by opponents of the war, might mobilize dissenters and force Johnson to change his policies. As the struggle in Vietnam raged on, by 1966 most opponents of the war were dismissing the teach-in as a waste of time. Consequently, the antiwar movement began to desert campus lecture halls for the nation's streets.

The typical antiwar demonstration borrowed from the tactics of the civil-rights movement and the techniques of the teach-in. Beginning with a mass march in the streets, an antiwar protest typically concluded with speeches and musical entertainment at a public park. Organizers hoped that the presence of large numbers of people in the streets and parks would dramatize the strength of their movement, spread antiwar sentiment, and force Washington to change its policies. Consequently, each new demonstration had to outdo the last. Organizers struggled to attract more people and to devise new ways to lampoon the military establishment. During an October 1967 march on Washington itself, a group—which one alternative newspaper called "witches, warlocks, holymen, seers, prophets, mystics, saints, sorcerers, shamans, troubadours, minstrels, bards, roadmen and madmen"—tried to exorcize the Pentagon by hurling "mighty words of white light against the demon-controlled structure."

The politics of organizing an antiwar demonstration helped to conceal significant differences over goals and tactics. Negotiations with political officials, police chiefs, rock-music entrepreneurs, and portable-toilet vendors required time

FIGURE 6–1 Flower Power versus Police Power.

An antiwar demonstrator offers a flower to military police who are guarding the Pentagon in 1967.
Source: S. Sgt. Albert R. Simpson / National Archives and Records Administration.

and skill. Marches and demonstrations, for many people, came to serve much the same function as religious revival meetings. The faithful assembled, felt their spirits renewed, and then went back home to prepare for the next gathering. Moreover, by attracting tens and then hundreds of thousands of people to a single demonstration, antiwar leaders could reassure themselves that all was going well.

What did the teach-ins, demonstrations, and marches accomplish? Critics have claimed that they actually worked against the antiwar campaign by daring the combative President Johnson to resist compromise and to conduct more of the war in secret. Others, though, have argued that the antiwar movement achieved at least limited success. Although policymakers publicly denied that they took any notice of the protest gatherings, the demonstrations did help to convert some former hawks and to embolden doves within the government. They also may have made it increasingly difficult for Johnson—and, later,

Richard Nixon—to claim any consensus for his war policies and, once the secret side of his policies became public knowledge, to mount any new, bold escalations. Perhaps most important, defenders of the antiwar movement claim, it may have limited the violence that Washington could use to conduct the war in Southeast Asia, even if it could not immediately halt the bloodshed.

Some young people gradually drifted away from sustained protest, even when directed against the Vietnam War. In time, their antipathy toward figures of authority extended to the "peace bureaucrats" in the New Left, the people who worked so hard to organize antiwar demonstrations. They joined cultural radicals who emphasized "doing your own thing" rather than joining a political cause. San Francisco, a favorite haunt of the Beats during the 1950s, attracted another generation of cultural rebels whom the media came to call "flower children" or, more commonly, "hippies."

The Counterculture

In the mid-1960s, the Haight-Ashbury neighborhood of San Francisco became identified with a burgeoning "counterculture." "Hip" people from all over the country flocked there, seeking the "laid-back" lifestyles of the "age of Aquarius." Soon, the media became fascinated with their comings and goings. It highlighted the communal living arrangements, the liberated views on sex, the illegal drugs, and the electrified sound of folk-rock music. Hippies claimed to be emancipated from "hang-ups" such as work and clothing fashions. Attired in America's castoff clothing, including old military uniforms, they espoused a cultural agenda that stressed mystical experiences and universal love. Following the Beat writers of the 1950s, some delved into Eastern faiths such as Zen and Taoism. Others eclectically sampled psychedelic drugs. Some simply embraced slogans. "Make love, not war" and "Flower Power" became familiar parts of the hippie litany. Sociologists eagerly studied hippie culture; pop journalists such as Tom Wolfe breathlessly covered it; and middle-aged sightseers made a bus tour of the Haight-Ashbury neighborhood an essential part of their visit to San Francisco.

Haight-Ashbury soon became something other than a colorful haven for the counterculture. San Francisco's political leaders declared war on "this hippie thing." Police officers, in their search for illegal drugs, often harassed any unkempt young person. At the same time, the Haight (as the neighborhood was called) faced an invasion of petty criminals who saw hippies as easy prey. The youth culture also developed internal divisions. "Hip entrepreneurs" took control of the neighborhood's economic life, and the earliest countercultural arrivals complained of phony "weekend hippies" invading the area. Dope became big business, and pushers began to peddle stronger chemicals. The more savvy warned about the dangers—"Speed kills," proclaimed posters—but the naive became hooked on hard drugs or experienced bad "trips" on powerful hallucinogens. Some died from drug overdoses. A handbill printed in August 1967 condemned the growing commercialism of Haight-Ashbury:

> The trouble is that the hip shopkeepers probably believe their own bullshit lies. They believe that dope is the answer and neither know nor care what the question is.

Have you been raped? Take acid and everything will be groovy. Are you cold, sleeping in doorways at night? Take acid and discover your inner warmth. Are you hungry? Take acid and transcend these mundane needs.

You can't afford acid? Pardon me, I think I hear somebody calling me.

The counterculture remained a source of fascination, especially when linked to new trends in rock music. By 1966, the Beatles and the Rolling Stones were dominating rock, and Bob Dylan was augmenting his acoustic guitar with a new, amplified sound. Groups from San Francisco took the lead. Jerry Garcia and the Grateful Dead attracted a devoted following, the fabled Dead Heads. The band gradually added various kinds of light shows, and the Merry Pranksters (a group who were attracted to the novelist Ken Kesey) laced the audience with LSD. ("Can you pass the acid test?" the Pranksters slyly asked concertgoers.) The result was acid rock and a whole new genre of drug-related, "mind-blowing" sounds. Soon, something called progressive rock became a smashing success, financially as well as artistically. Although cautious programmers and disc jockeys generally excluded these new rock sounds from AM radio's top-40 play lists, progressive rock spawned its own medium, free-form FM radio. The sound of San Francisco groups—particularly the Dead, Jefferson Airplane, and Big Brother and the Holding Company (featuring Janis Joplin)—swept across the country. The union of disaffected youth, drugs, and rock music seemed to have been consummated. By the late 1960s, the counterculture extended its reach, and the media portrayed the Woodstock Music Festival of 1969 as the arrival of an incipient cultural revolution and spoke of the birth of a "Woodstock nation."

This countercultural impulse was always difficult to classify. It was variously characterized as a state of mind, as a way of life, or sometimes merely as a style of dress. It developed its own alternative, weekly newspapers, such as the *Berkeley Barb* and the *Los Angeles Free Press,* and even a Liberation News Service. Although few of these enterprises survived in their original form, the emergence of an iconoclastic, alternative media represented one of the tangible legacies of the counterculture's broad aspirations.

Abbie Hoffman and Jerry Rubin, the creators of the spurious Youth International Party or Yippies, rivaled rock groups such as The Greatful Dead as icons of the counterculture. The Yippies owed more to Groucho, Harpo, and Chico than to Karl Marx. Their political program was theater in the streets, an updated, drug-enhanced vaudeville of the radical left. In one of their most famous escapades, Yippies invaded the New York Stock Exchange, hurling currency at brokers who were busily trading their paper securities. The Yippies' penchant for playing radicalism for laughs—Hoffman entitled his treatise *Revolution for the Hell of It*—and their cultural bravado substituted for any coherent program of social change or political transformation. Rubin and Hoffman, according to their critics on both the political left and right, drew more support from the managers of the mass media than from members of the various youth movements. Once certified as hippie celebrities, though, they came to enjoy far more visibility than other, less media-savvy dissenters. Both political and cultural protests increasingly became captives of the mass media. Film, television, and the popular press helped to contain and then trivialize the youth movement, political dissenters increasingly claimed.

FIGURE 6–2   Guitarist Jimi Hendrix, 1970.

Hendrix's music became a symbol of protest, especially after the Woodstock Music Festival, where he turned the national anthem into a discordant, antiwar statement.
Source: AP/Wide World Photos.

THE NEW CONSERVATISM

The fiercest attacks on New-Left politics and the counterculture came from a renewed conservative movement, another of the important polarizing forces of the 1960s and early 1970s. This new conservatism, much like the New Left, could trace its origins back to the 1950s.

The Origins of the New Conservatism in the 1950s

William F. Buckley, Jr., who had established the *National Review* in 1955 to provide a forum for conservative writers, became a patron saint of the new conservatism. The precocious product of a wealthy Catholic family, Buckley regarded the promotion of anticommunism, at home and abroad, as a religious and patriotic duty. Buckley attacked the Democratic party's version of the positive state for threatening individual liberties at home and underestimating the Communist menace overseas. Buckley even considered McCarthyism a legitimate, if overwrought, response to a perilous situation that Democrats and even some Republicans failed to recognize fully. He proved a powerful conservative magnet and attracted many talented writers to his magazine.

Buckley shrewdly built on the work of other conservative intellectuals. Friedrich von Hayek, whose *The Road to Serfdom* (1944) had become an unexpected bestseller, condemned governmental "interference" with the "natural" workings of the economic marketplace as a major step toward totalitarianism. This Austrian-born scholar became a popular source of conservative ideas, especially about the relationship between the growth of governmental power and the threat to individual liberties. Other conservatives championed the strict construction of the U.S. Constitution, a respect for the venerable doctrine of states' rights, and the close relationship between economic and personal freedoms. Conservatives insisted that positive-state social policies violated the nation's constitutional tradition of limited government.

Conservatives aggressively joined the public-policy debates of the 1950s. The Foreign Policy Research Institute, headed by Robert Strausz-Hupe, advocated a foreign policy that not only contained but rolled back communism. Strausz-Hupe urged the United States aggressively to "carry the battle to the vital centers of communist defense." William F. Buckley took up another important conservative theme, the perilous state of higher education, in his 1951 jeremiad *God and Man at Yale*. His alma mater, Buckley charged, typified institutions of higher education in the way that its faculty championed "collectivist" ideas and derided conservative, Christian ones. Buckley and other cold war conservatives launched a concerted campaign to interject their ideas into public discourse, especially on college campuses.

This new conservatism incorporated a wide range of ideas and personalities. Russell Kirk, one of the movement's most pessimistic pundits, appeared to reject the concept of democratic government and to advocate a greater sense of deference to the nation's "natural leaders," people such as himself. Kirk lived as a twentieth-century country squire in a small Michigan town and used a converted school building to house his vast personal library. In contrast, other prominent conservatives, such as political scientist Clinton Rossiter, linked their cause with democratic values and even praised some of the Democratic party's positive-state programs, especially Social Security, for providing stabilizing influences that conservatism should favor. And whereas Kirk advised censorship of "dangerous" ideas, libertarian conservatives such as Murray Rothbard often joined left-leaning civil libertarians in urging the courts to constitutionally protect a "free marketplace in ideas."

Conservatism also began its troubled alliance with charismatic religious leaders of the TV age during the 1950s. Billy Graham had become a religious celebrity during the late 1940s when the conservative publisher William Randolph Hearst placed his media empire behind the young evangelist, and in 1950 Graham launched a weekly radio program, the "Hour of Decision." The following year he embarked on an ambitious television ministry that continued into the twenty-first century. Very quickly, evangelists well to the right of Graham, such as Dr. Fred Schwarz of the Christian Anti-Communism Crusade, followed him into the mass media and conservative politics.

FIGURE 6–3   Independence Day Parade, July 4, 1969.

Antiwar demonstrations, such as this one at People's Park in Berkeley, reflected the political and cultural polarization that helped propel the conservative governor of California, Ronald Reagan, to national prominence.
Source: Courtesy of the Bancroft Library, University of California, Berkeley.

in several Democratic primaries in 1964. Goldwater, one of a handful of congressional Republicans to have voted against the Civil Rights Act of 1964, carried five southern states in November's general election.

Wallace, who saw 1964 as merely the prelude to a career in national politics, offered conservatism a powerful, quasi-populist rhetoric. As the historian Dan Carter, Wallace's most astute biographer, observed, the Alabaman used a no-holds-barred, grassroots language that seemed to tap many ordinary peoples' deep-seated fears that the 1960s might soon spiral into chaos and that social and cultural change really meant moral corruption and degeneration. Sacred American values, particularly religious ones, and traditional institutions such as the family seemed at risk. Student protestors, black militants, arrogant intellectu-als, and uncaring governmental bureaucrats in Washington had laid siege, Wal-lace charged, to the lives of ordinary, hard-working people.

The politics of race, especially the turn toward Black Power, was only one of the issues to which Wallace's rhetoric spoke. In his standard address, he con-tended that "there's not a dime's worth of difference" between the two major parties; denounced "pointy-headed bureaucrats" who "don't know how to park a bicycle straight"; and predicted that "intellectual morons" and "theoreticians" were "going to get some of those liberal smiles knocked off their faces." Wal-lace none too subtly linked popular distaste for big government with contempt for intellectuals and the counterculture: "Our lives are being taken over by bu-reaucrats, and most of them have beards." Wallace pointed the new conser-vatism toward a strategy in which the politics of polarization promised to bring electoral victory.

THE POLITICS OF POLARIZATION, 1968

The presidential campaign of 1968 channeled the social and cultural turmoil of the 1960s into the political arena. Electoral politics, it turned out, offered a poor way to calm the waters. Few national elections have produced as much vi-olence and polarization as that of 1968.

The Fall of Lyndon Johnson

Lyndon Johnson's presidency became 1968's first casualty. After having cap-tured more than 60 percent of the popular vote in 1964, Johnson celebrated a "politics of consensus." Mired in Vietnam and assailed by critics of his Great So-ciety, Johnson watched doubts about his capacity to lead the nation grow. Trapped in the White House by the antiwar demonstrations that followed him everywhere, he hunkered down in front of his bank of TV sets. Where had he gone wrong? Why had a promising presidency become a debacle? His standing in opinion polls continued to plummet. Finally, a group of dissident Democrats, led by the mercurial Allard Lowenstein (a veteran of the civil-rights and anti-war movements), organized a "dump Johnson" effort in order to do the unthinkable—deny an incumbent president his party's nomination.

Most political observers initially considered the anti-Johnson effort a hope-less cause, especially after Senator Robert Kennedy refused to challenge LBJ for the nomination. Senator Eugene McCarthy of Minnesota, an unlikely presi-dential aspirant, eventually stepped forward. An unorthodox, aloof antipoliti-cian—his detractors called him arrogant and lazy—McCarthy promised no great society. "All we want is a moderate use of intelligence," McCarthy told supporters. A small army of college students rallied behind the only candidate in either major party calling for peace in Vietnam. When Johnson declined to campaign personally in New Hampshire's presidential primary, the media was left to focus on McCarthy's quixotic crusade, which came to dominate political reporting. Although McCarthy actually lost New Hampshire's March 1968 pri-mary to the noncampaigning Johnson, pundits claimed that he had run well enough (gaining 43 percent of the vote) to break the president's lock on the Democratic nomination. McCarthy's appeal seemed as much anti-Johnson as antiwar. When asked by pollsters about their second choice as a Democratic candidate, people who supported McCarthy often named conservative George Wallace, a committed hawk on Vietnam.

New Hampshire and the decision of Robert Kennedy to join belatedly the race for the Democratic nomination increased the pressure on the president. Facing certain defeat by McCarthy in the Wisconsin primary, a physically and spiritually exhausted Johnson retired without a fight. On March 31, 1968, he shocked all but his closest confidants by announcing that he would not seek another term. About to be relieved of the responsibilities of the presidency, Johnson abandoned the Spartan routine that his heart condition required. Within two years he would suffer a serious heart attack; within five years he would be dead.

THE NEW POLITICS AND THE ELECTION OF 1968

Hubert Humphrey, LBJ's vice-president and Eugene McCarthy's one-time Senatorial colleague from Minnesota, enjoyed the support of Democratic party chieftains in 1968. Labor leaders like George Meany, political bosses like Chicago Mayor Richard Daley and Texas Governor John Connally, and Johnson himself all endorsed Humphrey. With this kind of backing, Humphrey could simply bypass the Democratic primaries and let his political sponsors line up the many delegates who were appointed to attend the party's national convention. At first, he preached "the politics of joy," but even the ebullient Humphrey, who personified the programs of the Fair Deal and the Great Society, came to recognize the dismal political atmosphere of 1968.

Unrelenting violence mocked Humphrey's slogan. In April 1968, Martin Luther King, Jr., was gunned down in Memphis, and black neighborhoods erupted in anger. Disorders rocked more than 100 cities, 36 people died, and more than 50,000 National Guard and federal troops patrolled urban streets. Many people refused to believe that another lone gunman, this one an escaped convict named James Earl Ray, could have killed another national leader. In 1997, members of King's family met with Ray, who had been convicted of King's murder on the basis of a confession that he later recanted as coerced. They sought a formal trial and suggested that the civil-rights leader had been the target of a well-organized conspiracy that exceeded James Earl Ray's meager economic and intellectual resources. Ray died without ever receiving a jury trial. To some, King's assassination, like that of John Kennedy, remains an unsolved crime.

Meanwhile, Eugene McCarthy and Robert Kennedy attempted to woo voters by offering a "new politics." A much-abused phrase, the term minimally suggested no backroom deals with powerful interest groups, reliance on youthful volunteers, and unorthodox campaign techniques. Shaving beards and donning skirts to "come clean for Gene," many college students enthusiastically canvassed for McCarthy. (Kennedy once joked that McCarthy attracted the "A" students while he specialized in those who received "B's".) Kennedy tried to reach out beyond the antiwar issue and advocate social programs that would hopefully attract a diverse coalition that included European ethnics, voters of color, anti-Johnson Democrats, and even supporters of George Wallace. As he vigorously stumped Indiana, touting his brand of new politics, cynical reporters dubbed Kennedy's campaign train the "Ruthless Cannonball."

While Humphrey rested on a safe cushion of nonelected delegates, Kennedy and McCarthy faced off in a series of primary contests. Their only hope was to convince the Democratic power brokers now backing Humphrey that, in November, they could bring out more voters than a ticket headed by the vice-president. Although opinion polls suggested that the new politics appeared to alienate more voters than it attracted, McCarthy and Kennedy battled on. In Oregon, McCarthy became the first candidate ever to outpoll any Kennedy in an election, but a Kennedy campaign remained special. Movie stars, musicians, athletes, university professors, and even business executives dropped everything to follow the New York senator and heir apparent to the Kennedy mystique. Ignoring threats against his life, Kennedy waded into crowds wherever he went, relying on a few burly friends to shield him from danger. The night of the climactic California primary, his supporters stood helplessly nearby as Kennedy was shot at point-blank range in the kitchen of a Los Angeles hotel. Police immediately arrested Sirhan Sirhan, a lone gunman with no apparent political motive for murdering Kennedy. Minutes earlier, Kennedy had accepted congratulations for a narrow victory over McCarthy. Twenty-four hours later, he was dead. Although McCarthy promised to continue his own campaign and Senator George McGovern belatedly assumed the mantle of Kennedy's new politics, Humphrey enjoyed a clear path to the Democratic nomination.

Prior to the Democratic national convention, the Republicans gathered in Miami, amid racial violence and demonstrations that took the lives of four people. GOP delegates turned to a face from the past—former vice-president Richard M. Nixon. Although he had lost the 1960 presidential contest and had presumably retired from politics after his defeat in the California gubernatorial race of 1962, image-makers proclaimed a "new Nixon." ("There is no new Nixon," a pundit quipped. "What we have here is the old Nixon, a little older.") Nixon suggested peaceful overtures to the Soviet Union and the People's Republic of China and promised citizens of color "a piece of the action in the exciting ventures of private enterprise." He insisted he had a plan for ending the war in Vietnam.

Nixon also seemed willing to polarize, rather than bridge, political and cultural differences. He praised the "forgotten Americans, the nonshouters, the nondemonstrators"; he suggested that Americans had been "deluged" by government welfare programs that had only "reaped . . . an ugly harvest of frustrations, violence, and failure." He promised that his attorney general would "open a new front against crime." Nominated on the first ballot, Nixon surprised the convention by selecting Spiro T. Agnew, a confrontational conservative who was the governor of Maryland, as his running mate.

Events at the Democratic National convention in Chicago allowed Nixon to escalate his cry for law and order. Mayor Richard Daley expected trouble. Antiwar groups planned demonstrations, and the Yippies promised a "festival of life," an answer to what they called the Democrats' "festival of death." Abbie Hoffman talked about sending 10,000 nude Yippies wading into Lake Michigan, releasing greased pigs in Chicago's crowded downtown, and even slipping LSD into the city's water supply. Mayor Daley, who mistook Hoffman's comedy routine for a strategy, readied his police force and had the Illinois National Guard and the United States Army on alert. One alternative newspaper parodied a folk-rock anthem that had been written a year earlier about Haight-Ashbury: "If you're going to Chicago, be sure to wear armor [and not a flower] in your hair."

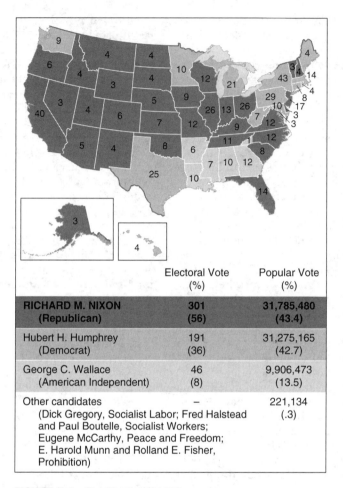

	Electoral Vote (%)	Popular Vote (%)
RICHARD M. NIXON (Republican)	**301 (56)**	**31,785,480 (43.4)**
Hubert H. Humphrey (Democrat)	191 (36)	31,275,165 (42.7)
George C. Wallace (American Independent)	46 (8)	9,906,473 (13.5)
Other candidates (Dick Gregory, Socialist Labor; Fred Halstead and Paul Boutelle, Socialist Workers; Eugene McCarthy, Peace and Freedom; E. Harold Munn and Rolland E. Fisher, Prohibition)	–	221,134 (.3)

FIGURE 6–4   The Election of 1968.

George Wallace's third party candidacy and the close contest between Richard Nixon and Hubert Humphrey nearly tossed the choice of a president into the House of Representatives.

After several days of skirmishes between antiwar protesters and the Chicago police, violence erupted. On the night delegates nominated Humphrey as their candidate for president, police officers assaulted demonstrators, bystanders, and members of the media. The presence of TV camera crews and demonstrators, chanting "the whole world is watching," failed to tame their fury. A special commission eventually labeled the disorders a "police riot," but most people apparently saw events very differently. One poll reported that nearly 60 percent of their sample blamed the demonstrators and supported the police.

Humphrey, who feared criticizing either Mayor Daley's police or the antiwar forces, found himself surrounded by squabbling Democrats. He tried to pretend that the party would pull together, but his early campaign efforts belied such optimism. Antiwar hecklers confronted Humphrey at every stop, and many loyal Democrats remained unenthusiastic about his candidacy. Finally cutting loose from Johnson's Vietnam policy in late September, Humphrey announced that he favored a bombing halt as a way of hastening peace talks. Several days before the election, President Johnson did order a temporary cessation of air raids over North Vietnam. These steps induced some antiwar Democrats, including Eugene McCarthy, to announce grudging support for Humphrey. By early November, pollsters judged the 1968 presidential race too close to call.

George Wallace, like Nixon, hoped to benefit from Humphrey's troubles. One poll, taken in the wake of the violence in Chicago, suggested that more than 20 percent of likely voters might support Wallace's presidential bid. Running in every state, on the American Independent ticket, Wallace repeated the themes that he had introduced to national politics four years earlier. Hoping to add conservative northern voters, especially blue-collar Democrats, to his solid base of support in the Deep South, he now also advocated a federal program for job training, a higher minimum wage, and new protections for labor unions. Trying to capitalize on resentment against the Democrat's allegedly "no-win" military policy in Vietnam, Wallace selected one of the country's most militant hawks, General Curtis LeMay, as his vice-presidential running mate. The choice quickly backfired when LeMay, during his first press conference, claimed that he saw no serious problem with using nuclear weapons. The growing recognition that the American Independent ticket could never out-poll either the Republicans or the Democrats, however, crippled Wallace's campaign more than LeMay's bombast. As election day neared, many northern voters who had been leaning toward Wallace began rejoining the Democratic ranks.

Hubert Humphrey fell about 100,000 votes short of victory, and Richard Nixon captured the presidency with only about 43 percent of the popular vote. George Wallace gained nearly 10 million popular ballots and 46 electoral votes in five southern states. If Humphrey and Wallace, between them, could have found only 32 additional electoral votes, Nixon would have lacked a majority, and the House of Representatives, as stipulated in the Constitution, would have decided the presidential context. By the slimmest of margins, Richard Nixon, whom the historian Garry Wills dubbed the lonely long-distance runner, finally won his big race. Nixon's victory did little to ease the tensions that the election of 1968 had exacerbated. Despite his promise of bringing people together, the first years of his presidency brought further political and cultural polarization.

THE VIOLENT YEARS, 1969–1972

In the face of Richard Nixon's talk of a plan for ending the war, the violence in Vietnam not only continued, but it accelerated. After a review of war policy, Nixon and his national security adviser, Henry Kissinger, made several crucial decisions. First, while stepping up the air war, the United States would turn the fighting over to its South Vietnamese ally and begin a gradual withdrawal of U.S.

ground forces. In addition, the United States would seek Soviet help in wringing concessions from Hanoi. In July 1969, the president placed his Vietnam policy within a grander design—the so-called Nixon Doctrine—in which the United States would continue military assistance to anti-Communist governments in Asia but would require Asians, not Americans, to do the fighting. This policy of "Vietnamization," critics charged, provided a formula for stepping up the war while defusing domestic dissent by ending the involvement of American draftees. The president promised peace but still hoped for the military victory that had beguiled and eluded Kennedy and Johnson.

Violence in Southeast Asia

Nixon looked to Henry Kissinger, rather than to members of his cabinet, to oversee Vietnamization. In fact, the foreign-policymaking process became so secretive and centralized in the White House that Secretary of State William Rogers and Secretary of Defense Melvin Laird often remained peripheral to, even uninformed of, important decisions. Kissinger, a former Harvard professor, saw world policies as a global, geopolitical confrontation between Soviet and U.S. power. America's primary duty consisted of foreclosing Soviet opportunities for expansion; conflicts anywhere in the world had to be viewed in light of how they "linked up" to this central concern of U.S. policy. This concept of linkage justified Kissinger's hopes for an early and favorable settlement in Vietnam. Kissinger hoped, he later wrote in his memoirs, to make "progress in settling the Vietnam War something of a condition for advance in areas of interest to the Soviets, such as the Middle East, trade or arms limitation."

This plan for ending the war by enticing the Soviets to pressure the North Vietnamese depended on at least two highly debatable assumptions: that the Soviets could easily influence Hanoi and that the Soviets would agree to act on America's behalf. Neither proved correct, but Kissinger and Nixon continued to pursue Vietnamization.

To buy time until South Vietnam's army became an effective force, Nixon and Kissinger accelerated the conflict while still technically honoring Johnson's bombing halt over the North. They launched a new offensive against targets in the South and accelerated full-scale combat inside Cambodia. To mask this escalation, the U.S. military talked of "accelerated pacification" and "protective reaction strikes."

Antiwar forces at home denounced the accelerating violence in Southeast Asia. The belated revelation of the My Lai massacre (which had occurred in March 1968) intensified this criticism. The story of My Lai involved an American unit that killed unarmed civilians, including women and children, until stopped, at gunpoint, by other American soldiers. After a bungled cover-up, the Pentagon finally prosecuted several officers, but only a young lieutenant named William Calley was convicted.

In May 1970, Nixon went on television to announce a U.S.-led invasion of Cambodia, technically a neutral country. Here, he ignored the advice of his secretaries of state and defense and neglected to consult (or even inform) Lon Nol, America's Cambodian ally, who less than two months before had overthrown the neutralist regime of Prince Norodom Sihanouk. North Vietnamese forces had used parts of Cambodia as a staging area for attacks in Vietnam, and

Pentagon strategists had long pressed the White House to enter Cambodia and destroy a supposed Vietnamese guerrilla headquarters. A quick strike, it was hoped, would unsettle the enemy and capture many of their supplies.

Widening the war into Cambodia proved disastrous. U.S. troops met surprisingly little resistance and never located any guerrilla headquarters. The president's defenders, nevertheless, declared the invasion a success and claimed it had disrupted the enemy's future plans. Nixon continued to wage a secret air war in Cambodia. The heavy bombing destroyed large portions of what had been a peaceful, agricultural country, created a large refugee population, and triggered a devastating shortage of food supplies. The Khmer Rouge, the native Communist guerrilla organization, transformed itself into a growing, murderous force. Lon Nol, who now seemed nothing but a U.S. puppet, could find support only in the capital city. The subsequent American defeat and withdrawal would leave Communist regimes in both Vietnam and Cambodia, ironically contributing to the domino effect the war had initially been intended to forestall.

The Cambodian invasion of 1970 also intensified antiwar sentiment at home. On college campuses, students mounted protest marches and strikes at more than 400 schools. Many colleges abruptly ended the spring semester early and simply closed their doors. At the same time, antiwar activities by former Vietnam veterans became more prominent. The largest organization, Vietnam Veterans Against the War (VVAW), which had been formed in 1967, marched across part of Pennsylvania, while staging mock search-and-destroy missions. The following year, VVAW mounted its most dramatic demonstration when veterans, some of them on crutches and in wheelchairs, hurled their war medals over a fence and into the grounds of the U.S. Capitol. After Cambodia, the conflict in Southeast Asia clearly became "Nixon's war."

Violence at Home

Paralleling the bloodletting in Vietnam was a violent turn in the radical movement at home. A small group called the Weathermen pledged to "bring the war home to Amerika" in order to help the National Liberation Front. This violent offshoot of SDS gained considerable media attention but few converts. Its much-publicized "Four Days of Rage," a protest campaign in Chicago in 1969, proved especially disastrous. After smashing some windows, the helmeted protesters were overwhelmed, beaten bloody, and arrested by Mayor Daley's police.

After this, the New Left, already in disarray, splintered into small fragments. Some radicals went underground, trying to avoid arrest for previous activities. A few mounted a senseless bombing campaign. Between September 1969 and June 1970, there were more than 170 bombings and attempted bombings on college campuses. An explosion at the University of Wisconsin killed a graduate student, and other campuses suffered nonlethal explosions. Bombers also hit other targets such as the Bank of America, the Chase Manhattan Bank, and even the U.S. Congress. Three radicals blew themselves apart when their bomb factory in Greenwich Village exploded in 1970. Few of these attacks did major damage—corporation bathrooms, the easiest place to hide explosives, suffered the brunt of the onslaught—but they contributed to an increasingly ugly mood throughout the country. As a result of the bombings and other violent activities, some radicals went underground. For the next three decades, refugees from these desperate days emerged from hiding and surrendered to authorities or were finally apprehended by law-enforcement officials.

Nixon and Agnew pledged to uphold the law. "You see these bums, you know, blowing up the campuses," the president grumbled after students protested (in most cases, nonviolently) his invasion of Cambodia. "We cannot afford to be divided or deceived by the decadent thinking of a few young people," fumed Agnew. We could, he argued, "afford to separate them from our society—with no more regret than we should feel over discarding rotten apples from a barrel."

Most of the lethal violence, however, came from authorities charged with upholding law and order. In early 1968, state troopers killed three protesting black students at Orangeburg State College in South Carolina. During a 1969 confrontation at Berkeley, state police indiscriminately dropped tear gas from helicopters and fatally shot a bystander in the back. In December 1969, Chicago police stormed the Illinois headquarters of the Black Panthers and killed two people. In May 1970, white police officers opened fire on a women's dormitory at Mississippi's Jackson State College, an all-black institution, and killed two unarmed students. In the most celebrated incident, the Ohio National Guard shot thirteen students, four of whom died, at Kent State University during the spring of 1970.

A Law-and-Order Administration

Nixon continued to preach law and order. Insurgent movements were singled out as special targets. Indeed, many Americans saw the young antiwar protesters and the other dissidents as a unified band of troublemakers. After the killings at Kent State, public-opinion polls showed that most people believed that the National Guard had fired on the unarmed students in self-defense. Confident that a new conservative tide was rolling in behind them, Nixon and Agnew continued their tough talk, and Attorney General John Mitchell strengthened the Justice Department's internal security division. Moreover, the White House, the FBI, and the CIA all continued, and even intensified, illegal activities against domestic radicals.

The FBI did not limit itself to the surveillance of groups espousing violence. It also infiltrated groups and harassed individuals who simply favored significant, but peaceful, social change. In one celebrated case, the bureau invented vicious rumors about the personal life of a prominent actress who supported insurgent causes. Similarly, some undercover agents operated as agent provocateurs and actually urged protestors to undertake the kind of violent action that could be prosecuted under state statutes and the federal "Rap Brown law" of 1968. After an investigation of COINTELPRO, one the FBI's programs to disrupt "radical" activities, a committee of the House of Representatives charged that "careers were ruined, friendships severed, reputations sullied, businesses bankrupted and, in some cases, lives endangered." COINTELPRO extended from 1956 to 1971, and the FBI terminated it only after stolen documents revealed its existence.

While conducting or condoning lawbreaking by the national surveillance bureaucracy, the Nixon administration was also mobilizing the criminal justice system against dissidents. In the Chicago conspiracy trial of 1969, the most celebrated political prosecution since the trial of leaders of the Communist party during the 1940s, Attorney General Mitchell secured indictments against eight prominent representatives of different organizations. The government charged this group—which included Tom Hayden of SDS, Bobby Seale of the Black Panthers, and Yippies Abbie Hoffman and Jerry Rubin—with conspiracy and with crossing state lines to encourage violence at the 1968 Democratic convention. Some of the defendants viewed the affair as countercultural theater rather than a legal battle, and the defendants (who barely knew one another before the trial) never mounted a coherent courtroom defense. At the end of the trial, the judge unexpectedly cited all of the defendants for contempt of court. Concluding the sorry affair, the jury rendered a compromise verdict: It acquitted all of the defendants of the more serious conspiracy charge but convicted the most famous of crossing state lines to incite a riot. After a lengthy appeal process, all of the defendants escaped jail. Similar trials, including ones involving the antiwar Catholic priests Philip and Daniel Berrigan, produced few convictions but helped to label political dissidents as "criminals in the streets." Simply by filing charges, the Nixon administration and state officials encouraged public fears of radicalism and worsened the disarray on the left.

The Violence Wanes

Richard Nixon also continued to champion the "forgotten American." During 1969 and 1970, he and Vice-President Agnew warned that New-Left "hooligans," aided and abetted by "radical liberals" in the Democratic party, threatened the country's stability. Agnew assailed the "biased liberal" media, which "slandered" the president; the "nattering nabobs of negativism," who scorned traditional American values; the "curled-lip boys in the eastern ivory towers" who thumbed their noses at ordinary people; and renegade professionals such as Dr. Benjamin Spock, who encouraged a growing "spirit of permissiveness."

Still, the Republicans made few gains in the national elections of November 1970. The GOP did add a couple of Republicans to the U.S. Senate but dropped about a dozen seats in the House of Representatives and lost eleven governorships. The Democrats, though still divided as a result of the battles of 1968, remained the majority party. Nixon's strategists consequently abandoned grand theories about "an emerging Republican majority" and began to plan a 1972 presidential campaign that divorced Nixon, as much as possible, from the rest of the Republican ticket. His image-makers left the divisive rhetoric to Agnew, planned more subtle campaign tactics for Nixon himself, and accentuated the president's role in foreign affairs.

Some of the passions of the 1960s and early 1970s slowly seeped from domestic politics. By beginning to reduce U.S. ground forces in Vietnam, pushing to end the military draft, and helping to lower the voting age to eighteen, the Nixon administration dampened three highly emotional issues. Even the media gradually lost interest in youth-oriented politics.

A few reckless radicals, seeking new inspiration and fresh recruits, turned to prison inmates as the vanguard of revolution. This move, toward a powerless group that was heavily infiltrated by police informers, proved suicidal. In 1973, a tiny group of white radicals joined with an escaped African-American prisoner to form the Symbionese Liberation Army (SLA). Their kidnapping of Patricia Hearst, the daughter of a prominent newspaper publisher, instantly converted members of the SLA into media celebrities. During the spring of 1974, six members of the group were killed in a shoot-out, carried live on local television, with the Los Angeles police. Hearst was freed but later stood trial for joining in the crimes of her SLA captors. At the beginning of the twenty-first century, authorities were still seeking one SLA fugitive and indicting several other former members for offenses committed a quarter-century earlier.

The vast majority of activists from the 1960s turned to gradualist, nonviolent strategies during the 1970s. Having discovered no magical shortcut to social transformation, they worked, generally at the grassroots level and outside of the media's gaze, to bring about the social changes for which they had once marched and demonstrated.

THE SEARCH FOR EMPOWERMENT

Although the Nixon administration's fears were exaggerated, the spirit of dissent did spread throughout American society. By the early 1970s, a number of different groups were pressing for greater empowerment. They achieved few dramatic victories, but their day-to-day activities helped spark social change and provided the basis for the "identity politics" that would be so prevalent in late-twentieth-century American life.

African American Politics

African American politics moved in many different directions. Following Martin Luther King's murder, the SCLC had lost prestige, especially when its "Poor People's March" of 1968 proved to be a disaster. This demonstration— Dr. King's final, unfinished project—aimed at making an interracial group of low-income and unemployed people, camped out in "Resurrection City" on the Capitol Mall, an ongoing presence in Washington. This tent encampment's residents, it was planned, would lobby Congress and the Nixon administration for new social legislation. But torrential spring storms turned Resurrection City into a rain-soaked mess, and its inhabitants split into squabbling factions. Later, Nixon ordered the eviction of the few remaining activists, bringing a dismal end to this era of mass-protest demonstrations.

Taking a different tack, a broad coalition of African American activists formed a National Black Political Assembly in 1972. More than 10,000 people met in Gary, Indiana, to hammer out a "Black Agenda." This militant statement, which upset some integrationists, charged that the "crises we face as black people . . . are the natural end-product of a society built on the twin foundations of white racism and white capitalism." Within months, however, fissures developed within the Black Political Assembly as Marxists tilted with liberals, integrationists with cultural nationalists. While these activists debated theories of cultural and political change, historian Manning Marable has argued, the mass of workers, students, and the unemployed generally ignored this bold effort to create a nationwide political movement aimed specifically at African Americans.

Slowly, nonetheless, African American politics began to change. Decades of migration of people from the South to northern cities (together with the flight of many whites to the suburbs) ensured the election of greater numbers of African American political leaders. In 1955, for instance, only a couple of districts in New York City and Chicago had sent African American representatives to Congress. By 1972, fifteen African Americans held seats in the House of Representatives. A number of cities—including Cleveland, Gary, and Newark—elected African American mayors, and several northern states, especially Michigan and New York, claimed growing numbers of black officials at all levels of government.

New African American officeholders struggled to alter public policy and to tackle problems that involved, but also transcended, racial issues. Once in power, they faced a dilemma: Should they direct programs toward low-income neighborhoods, or should they work with local whites and thereby gain access to public and private funds for rebuilding the larger urban infrastructure? Some African American politicians, such as Coleman Young in Detroit, seemed able to satisfy conflicting pressures, but others, such as Kenneth Gibson in Newark, found themselves entangled in competing, oftentimes incompatible demands. In Detroit spokespeople for low-income, African American neighborhoods oftentimes charged that Mayor Young (who was first elected in 1973 and who served, altogether, five terms) catered to the corporate and political elites' desire to rebuild the Motor City's business center while generally ignoring the plight of Detroit's most needy residents. Mayor Young countered that the prosperity of Detroit's citizens ultimately rested on a viable business environment and that his policies addressed the needs of the entire population. Meanwhile, cynicism about all politicians, black as well as white, set in. Despite the efforts at political mobilization during the 1960s and early 1970s, the percentage of northern blacks who bothered to register and to vote actually declined between 1964 and 1972.

The Nixon administration moved cautiously and obliquely on racial questions. Although Nixon voiced a strong stand against busing as a means of achieving school desegregation, he generally followed a circumspect course. Daniel Patrick Moynihan, a Democrat who advised Nixon on domestic issues, urged "benign neglect"—a policy of scaling down the level of promises as a means of generating less frustration over the slow pace of change.

Moynihan's proposal, whatever its merit as a public-policy decision, arguably represented a shrewd political appraisal of the nation's record on issues related to race. Change was occurring on both the economic and the political fronts, but the results were seldom dramatic. Officials in the Department of Health, Education and Welfare (HEW), citing the small numbers of nonwhites and women in the professions, began to press graduate and professional schools to take "affirmative action" and recruit a student body that was not so overwhelmingly white and male. African Americans who sought a college degree stood to gain from such pressure, but many universities hesitated to overemphasize their affirmative action programs, which critics denounced for establishing "quotas" and for denigrating "merit." Working-class blacks also encountered obstacles, especially from labor unions whose largely white memberships considered the government's efforts to increase minority employment a direct attack on their traditional seniority systems. In 1970, for example, only

3.3 percent of the nation's sheet metal workers and 1.7 percent of its tool and die makers were African American.

The Nixon administration was most active on economic issues. It promised to help find better jobs for African Americans who already possessed marketable skills and to promote more opportunities for "black capitalists." Consequently, the number of banks owned by African Americans more than doubled between 1970 and 1975. A similar expansion occurred in the small-business sector, especially with mom-and-pop stores. Citing gains such as these, Attorney General John Mitchell advised African Americans to "watch what we do, not what we say."

The Nixon administration's critics denounced what it was doing as well as what it was saying. The NAACP accused the administration of catering to the conservative, "white backlash" vote. The head of the U.S. Civil Rights Commission denounced its reluctance to enforce existing civil rights measures. Leon Panetta, head of the Civil Rights Division in HEW, resigned in protest over Nixon's opposition to school busing as a means of integrating public schools.

Nixon's record on racial issues did look mixed. His administration did little to help register African American voters in the South; its promises to push integration of federal housing programs went almost nowhere; and it even failed to provide adequate funding for its own project, black capitalism. On a broader front, the gap between black and white incomes, which had narrowed in the late 1960s, grew slightly wider during the 1970s. Meanwhile, though, the Voting Rights Act of 1965 (renewed in 1970) and pressure from black groups gradually produced some tangible results in the South. In the election of 1970 more than 100 black candidates gained office in the South, increasing the total to 700. At the same time, black voters gained more leverage in contests involving only white candidates. As a result, many southern veteran politicians, even George Wallace and Strom Thurmond, began to reach out to black voters and abandon their old image as die-hard segregationists. After several decades of steady decline, the African American population of the South began to increase, a trend that continued into the twenty-first century.

Mexican American Politics

Although developments among African Americans captured the most media attention, other groups also displayed growing militancy, while seeking greater empowerment, during the late 1960s and early 1970s. As the country's Mexican American population grew in numbers, living principally in the Southwest and in northern communities close to migrant farming jobs, it began to reach for greater political power.

Despite the development of a growing middle class, the average Mexican American child still had only a seventh-grade education during the 1960s. Many young people had to leave school to help support their families. As one teacher put it, "Our kids don't drop out; they are pushed out by poverty." The tradition of maintaining a Spanish-speaking culture and the proximity of Mexico's cultural institutions could also stigmatize Mexican Americans. In some California school districts, students could be expelled for speaking Spanish, even on the playground. Situated on the border between two cultures, Mexican Americans debated among themselves whether to build on their Spanish-speaking heritage or to assimilate within North American institutions. Older Mexican American leaders, such as U.S. Representative Henry Gonzales of Texas, urged a continuation of the cautious legal and political strategies of the 1940s and 1950s. By the mid-1960s, however, a new generation launched more militant mass movements designed to lift the economic status of Mexican Americans and to celebrate their cultural roots.

Cesar Chavez mounted a drive to raise wages among farm workers, many of whom were Mexican Americans. Chavez, who had grown up in California migrant camps during the late 1930s, recalled his family's first grape-picking job. "Each payday the contractor said he couldn't pay us because the winery hadn't paid him yet. At the end of the seventh week we went to the contractor's house and it was empty—he owed us for seven week's pay. . . . We were desperate." When the federal government's *bracero* (farm worker) program ended in 1965, Chavez began to unionize workers in the grape fields. With the flow of labor from Mexico diminished, unionization had a chance, he believed. The outlook grew even brighter when his United Farm Workers Union (UFW) attracted support from the powerful American Federation of Labor. During the grape pickers' strike in Delano, California, in 1965, Walter Reuther of the United Auto Workers joined Chavez on the picket lines, carrying a sign reading HUELGA ("STRIKE") and reminiscing about his own organizing fights during the 1930s. Robert Kennedy also visited the scene and became one of the UFW's most influential political supporters, but the growers held out, always finding enough hungry and jobless people to replace the strikers. Finally, Chavez adopted the technique that would make him famous—the nationwide boycott. Dramatizing his personal commitment, he went on a lengthy fast, an act that damaged his frail health.

Chavez's appeal to forgo grapes from California gained widespread support. Millions of people supported the boycott. (The Pentagon, however bought great quantities of grapes and sent them to Vietnam). Growers finally began to sign with the UFW, and Chavez, always a favorite of the media, became the first Mexican American to appear on the cover of *Time* magazine. Admiring reporters hailed him as a Spanish-speaking Martin Luther King, Jr. When lettuce growers signed what Chavez considered sweetheart contracts with the Teamsters Union, he organized a boycott of lettuce. By the late 1970s, however, the effect of such boycotts waned, and Chavez's victories grew fewer and fewer.

While Chavez was working to improve economic conditions among field workers, a Chicano student movement promoted educational change. In East Los Angeles in 1968, 10,000 high-school students participated in a "Blow Out," a strike against discrimination in educational institutions. Similar student strikes spread throughout the Southwest. On college campuses, students successfully pressed for Chicano studies programs and made new contributions to Mexican American history and literature. *El Grito* and *Aztlan,* the first national Chicano studies journals, and Quinto Sol Publications, the first independent Mexican American publishing house, provided new outlets for Chicano and Chicana writers and scholars.

José Angel Gutiérrez's political movement, the La Raza Unida Party (LRUP), directed its attention toward electoral politics. La Raza, which argued that any political program based on assimilation inevitably implied the inferiority of Mexican American institutions and culture, captured a majority of seats on the school board in Crystal City, Texas, in 1970. It began to remold the educational system in line with the needs of the town's largely Spanish-speaking population. Soon, La Raza gained control of other political offices in Crystal City and dreamed of spreading its influence throughout the Southwest.

Despite grassroots militancy, political officials at the national level devoted little attention to Mexican American issues. In 1969, Senator Joseph Montoya of New Mexico introduced a bill to extend the life of the president's Inter-Agency Committee on Mexican American Affairs, a group that studied conditions in the United States. The bill passed the Senate and went to the House, where it was lost. After months of delay, searchers finally found the bill, misfiled with the Foreign Affairs Committee.

Groups such as La Raza tried to make sure that this kind of oversight would end. Although there were few dramatic breakthroughs, the political militancy and cultural resurgence of the 1960s and early 1970s provided new programs, especially on the cultural front, around which to organize. In 1971, in line with the "rights revolution," federal courts ruled Mexican Americans to be a recognizable ethnic group that qualified for special protection under the nation's civil-rights laws.

American Indian Movements

The slogan of "Red power" suddenly attracted the national media on a cold November morning in 1969, when a group of American Indians seized Alcatraz Island, the site of an abandoned federal prison, in San Francisco Bay. Hundreds of supporters soon joined them and demanded that the government convert the island into an Indian cultural center and establish a "Thunderbird University." Although few political leaders took these proposals seriously, the occupation helped to spark a new, pan-Indian cultural consciousness. The Indians on Alcatraz represented tribes from throughout the United States, and Alcatraz provided a particularly appropriate symbol. Its uninhabitable buildings, bad water and sanitation, and guaranteed unemployment resembled conditions on many Indian reservations.

The vast majority of Indians had missed out on the general postwar affluence. Two-and-one-half decades after World War II, the per capita income of Indians was 60 percent that of whites; Indian life expectancy was only 47 years; half of all Indian children never completed high school; and the unemployment rate for Indians was 40 percent (on most reservations it exceeded 50 percent). Discrimination was widespread. One of the original occupiers of Alcatraz remembered the "meanness of the small towns around the reservation. Blackfoot, Pocatello—they all had signs in the store windows to keep Indians out. . . . There were Indian stalls in the public bathrooms; Indians weren't served in a lot of the restaurants; and we just naturally all sat in the balcony of the theaters." What were the effects of such treatment? "It becomes part of the way you look at yourself," she explained.

Indian activists became even more militant in the wake of Alcatraz. Ojibwas in the Minneapolis-St. Paul area organized the American Indian Movement (AIM). In 1973, AIM began protesting the disparity in law enforcement for Indians and whites. In Custer, South Dakota, officials had

FIGURE 6–5   Tribal Dancing at Mille Lacs, Minnesota, 1961.

Preservation of traditional rituals were an important part of the American Indian movements that began during the 1960s.
Source: Photo by Monroe Killy, Minnesota Historical Society.

charged a white man with second-degree manslaughter for fatally stabbing an Indian, whereas in nearby Rapid City an Indian accused of killing a white woman was held without bail for murder. AIM led protests in both cities and eventually seized a trading post at Wounded Knee, South Dakota, where the United States Army had crushed the last substantial pan-Indian resistance movement during the 1890s. AIM leaders saw this small community on the Pine Ridge Reservation as an appropriate place for launching a cultural-political revival.

AIM's occupation split the Indian community at Pine Ridge. The community's leaders condemned its members as outside agitators who were bringing physical destruction to an Indian town and attacking tribal elders. Others, including many elderly people, sympathized with AIM's opposition to tribal leaders, people who were criticized for corruption and a cozy relationship with the Bureau of Indian Affairs.

Indians also waged important legal battles in the rights revolution. Indicted for the events at Wounded Knee, members of AIM used the occasion of their trial in St. Paul, Minnesota, to have U.S. treaties with Indians (which, they contended, the government had systematically violated) admitted into evidence. After a nine-month trial, the presiding judge dismissed the indictments and charged the government prosecutors with misconduct. By the mid-1970s, other Indians were launching legal challenges to redress old grievances, especially over tribal lands that had been lost as a result of legal chicanery or outright theft. This type of legal activity had a far-reaching impact. It promoted a new pride in Indian culture, a fresh concern with preserving an ancient heritage, and a stronger determination to use the courts to enforce past promises.

The legal affairs of American Indians were complicated by a new "Indian Bill of Rights." Enacted as part of the Civil Rights Act of 1968, this bill of rights extended the provisions of the federal Bill of Rights, for the first time, to Indians who lived on reservations. Many Indians had expressed ambivalence over this measure; they feared that it might lead the national judicial system to ride roughshod over the traditional customs of individual tribes and even to undercut claims of Indian sovereignty, the legal doctrine on which many tribes relied. During the 1970s, however, new congressional legislation and several Supreme Court decisions reaffirmed the principle of tribal sovereignty. Confident of operating on a sound legal-constitutional foundation, many tribes and organizations, such as the Native American Rights Fund (NARF), used lawsuits to regain lost lands and confirm traditional fishing, water, and agricultural rights.

A New Women's Movement

A new women's movement also emerged from the ferment of the 1960s. The report of John Kennedy's Presidential Commission, *American Women* (1963), signaled a spirit of insurgency. (See Chapter 5.) This drive could not be papered over by claims, such as those prominently featured in traditional publications, that women never "had it so good" and that they were, in many ways, "much better off than men." Although a 1962 article in *Harper's*, entitled "The American Female," argued that few women responded to "the slogans of the old-fashioned feminism," it also detected a trend that it called "crypto-feminism." Many middle-class women, the article conceded, were coming to consider domesticity and motherhood, which had been so central to the official gender gospel of the 1950s, as roles that failed to challenge and fulfill the talents of most women. Other articles, such as "Our Greatest Waste of Talent Is Women," suggested a growing feminist consciousness.

Meanwhile, the daily lives of millions of women were continuing to change during the early 1960s. The number of women working outside the home rose dramatically; a growing percentage of young women remained single much longer than had their sisters during the 1950s; divorce rates increased; the number of female-headed households grew; and women played significant roles in the early civil-rights movement. The birth control pill, introduced in the 1960s, contributed to this new environment.

In 1963, Betty Friedan published *The Feminine Mystique,* a critique of the gender-role tracking that she believed channeled women, even if highly educated, into subordinate social and economic positions. From dolls and dainty ruffles through teenage dating conventions to myths of married bliss as a happy dependent, women faced a gendered mystique that limited their opportunities. According to Friedan, women should be able to move beyond the domestic sphere without suffering social stigma and should have options for self-fulfillment equal to those of men.

A new kind of organizing followed. In 1966, Friedan and other women founded the National Organization for Women (NOW). Modeled on the civil-rights movement, NOW campaigned against gender discrimination, lobbied

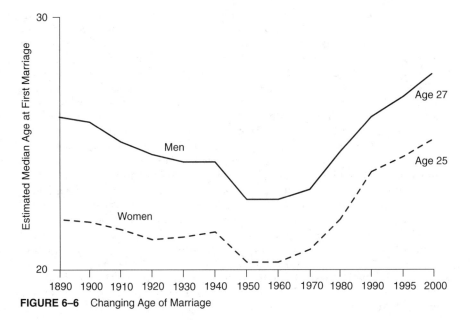

FIGURE 6–6 Changing Age of Marriage

The median age at first marriage for both men and women dropped after World War II and then rose sharply after 1970. What might be some of the causes and consequences of these trends? *Source:* U.S. Census Bureau.

for child-care centers, and publicized women's causes through the media. NOW created local chapters and eventually adopted, from other feminist groups, the idea of "consciousness raising." Consciousness-raising sessions encouraged small groups of women to vent grievances; to question prevailing constructions of gender; and, perhaps most important, to explore the political dimensions of their own personal lives. Consciousness raising, feminists hoped, would enable women to reexamine social arrangements and draw the strength needed to change society and their own everyday lives.

Meanwhile, the Civil Rights Act of 1964, enacted mainly to assist the struggle against racial discrimination, offered a somewhat unexpected legal tool for advancing women's rights. The provision of the act that prohibited discrimination on the basis of sex, as well as on race, had been pushed by women activists but was, ironically, also supported by southern representatives who hoped that it might diminish the entire bill's chances for passage. The southern strategy not only failed to derail the act but rebounded in favor of women's groups, who could use the Civil Rights Act of 1964 to attack a host of discriminatory practices. Newspapers could no longer run want ads that distinguished between men's and women's work, and the federal government strengthened its requirement of equal pay for equal work. By the late 1960s, corporations or institutions receiving federal funds had to adopt nondiscriminatory hiring practices. In the early 1970s, Washington pressed affirmative action programs as a means to recruit more women into those schools or jobs in which the number of men was far greater than the number of women.

The political insurgency of the 1960s also contributed to the new feminism. As women helped to organize against racial discrimination and the Vietnam War, they realized their own second-class status, even within supposedly progressive movements. Men monopolized positions of authority and the media spotlight; they relegated women to lesser roles. While participating in movements committed to social change, many women came to realize, for the first time, the extent of gender discrimination. As a result, struggles for women's liberation developed within the antiwar and other insurgency movements. Chicana groups coalesced within the Farm Worker's movement, and African American women expressed and organized around an ethic of "black feminism." Although the counterculture may have helped to provide some space for the renewal of feminist activism, it, like the earlier Beat movement, could also represent a "male revolt" against responsibility. Feminists charged that many of the men who dominated the radical movements of the 1960s too often viewed women as sexual conquests, rather than as equal partners in a common, democratic cause.

During the early 1970s, feminism became a widespread, but by no means unified, movement. Class, race, and ethnicity divided women even as gender united them. NOW, which was dominated by white, middle-class professionals, sought legal equality through the legislatures and the courts. More radical feminists attacked the same capitalist system in which supporters of NOW wanted to work. Cultural radicals assailed marriage, a social arrangement that they considered inherently sexist and exploitative. A new generation of writers, including Alice Walker and Toni Morrison, gave voice to the concerns of African American women. And groups of women from all ethnic backgrounds established community-based institutions to serve the needs that male-dominated structures had long ignored: rape-crisis centers, battered-women's shelters, women's health collectives, women's studies programs in colleges and universities, and support groups for clerical workers combating sexual harassment on the job. New periodicals, such as *Ms.*, and more scholarly journals, such as *Feminist Studies* and *Signs,* provided forums for feminist discussion.

As feminism expanded its base, women who recoiled at the idea of "women's lib" formed counter-organizations. Claiming that feminists were stereotyping the ordinary housewife as ignorant, useless, and exploited, these conservative women rallied around the cold-war era values of domesticity and family togetherness. They insisted that motherhood and devotion to family values remain the bedrock of true femininity. They also denounced the presence of lesbians within the feminist coalition.

One of the most bitter battles pitting women against women came over the long-proposed Equal Rights Amendment (ERA) to the Constitution. The amendment, granting equal rights specifically to women, passed Congress in early 1972 and was quickly ratified by more than half of the states. Then, the amendment's progress suddenly stalled. NOW lobbied intensely on its behalf, but vigorous opposition from conservatives such as Phyllis Schlafly and the Christian Crusade counterbalanced NOW's efforts. Opponents of the amendment charged that it would undermine the stability of the traditional family and could even threaten the constitutionality of rules on alimony payment and of laws that provided special protection to women. In response to such arguments and to the growing identification between the new conservatism and opposition to the women's movement, the Republican party reversed a position it had held for 40 years and dropped support of the amendment from its party platform in 1980. The ERA was never ratified.

Abortion became an even more controversial issue than the ERA. In *Roe v. Wade* (1973), the U.S. Supreme Court upheld a Texas woman's claim that her state's law criminalizing all abortions abridged her personal privacy by denying her the right to consult with a doctor and secure a medically safe method of terminating her pregnancy. After this decision, abortions could be legally and more safely obtained by most women during the first trimester of pregnancy. But people who supported a woman's right to make her own reproductive choices quickly recognized the limitations and ambiguities of *Roe v. Wade*. Most immediately, it fueled a powerful backlash in the form of the "right-to-life" crusade.

The right-to-life effort—which drew support from traditionalist Catholics, fundamentalist Protestants, and conservative political groups—denounced abortion as legalized murder and championed the "rights of the unborn." Calling their crusade "pro-family," opponents of abortion also condemned many other social changes of the 1960s and early 1970s, especially those related to greater gender equality. Abortion-rights advocates countercharged that antiabortion activists usually ignored most other questions involving family or right-to-life issues, especially subsidized child care and sex education, projects that seemed to offer alternatives to abortion. As public debate became more acrimonious, politicians found that abortion could overshadow all other issues, even in local elections.

By the middle of the 1970s, women's roles were continuing to undergo significant changes. Women who worked outside the home became the norm, and obvious gender barriers were toppled in nearly every occupation and profession. However, greater employment opportunities by no means brought equality at the pay window: The median income for women who worked full time was less than 60 percent of the median income for men. (The disparity actually grew larger during the 1960s and 1970s; the ratio had been 63 percent in 1956.) In addition, most men continued to expect certain supposedly male prerogatives. On the average, for example, the husbands of women who worked outside of the home did only about one-fourth of all work around the house, creating a "double day" for women who were employed in the labor market.

Changes in gender roles were associated with other social issues. Domestic violence against women appeared on the rise. (As consciousness about domestic abuse grew, this crime was probably reported more often to public authorities than it had been in the past.) Rates of divorce increased, and divorce often meant a drastically reduced living standard for newly single women. With significant numbers of unmarried women trapped in low-paying jobs or on welfare, some analysts highlighted "the feminization of poverty" as one of the most alarming trends of the 1970s.

The women's movement brought major changes to daily life. People working on college campuses and in corporate offices became more sensitive than ever before to practices and behaviors of "sexual harassment." Traditionalist women's groups such as the Girl Scouts developed a new concern for the achievement of young girls. Mainline Protestant churches began to admit women into the ministry, and previously all-male bastions such as the Rotary

Club, the Chamber of Commerce, and educational institutions embraced gender integration. The lives of millions of women were becoming very different from those of their mothers, only a generation earlier.

Gay and Lesbian Empowerment

Public debate over gender definitions and the general spirit of social insurgency boosted empowerment movements by gays and lesbians. In 1969 New York City police raided a gay bar in Greenwich Village called the Stonewall Inn. Although such police raids against homosexuals had been common for decades, the patrons of Stonewall resisted arrest and demanded the right to be free from harassment. Stonewall provided a rallying cry, and New York's Gay Liberation Front became a model for the creation of new advocacy groups around the country. Borrowing rhetoric from civil-rights causes, gay and lesbian activists urged their supporters to come "out of the closet," assert pride in their lifestyles, and demand equality.

The gay and lesbian rights movement had both a cultural and a legal agenda. Newspapers, theaters, and specific urban neighborhoods became centers of "queer" culture. At the same time, activists pressured local governments to protect their right to privacy as consenting adults and to prohibit discrimination in housing and employment on the basis of sexual preference. Although the gay and lesbian movement won significant support, especially from civil-liberties elites, it also produced a considerable backlash among those who considered homosexuality an immoral way of life. Those groups who were active in the right-to-life movement also generally fought against gay and lesbian rights.

POLARIZATION: AN AMBIGUOUS LEGACY

The years of polarization took their toll. By the mid-1970s, some veterans of the various protest movements seemed worn down by too many battles. The more radical ones always had to consider the very real danger of governmental action, both legal and illegal, against themselves and their friends. Writing after the deaths of two black students, killed during protests at Southern University in 1973, the poet June Jordan confessed

> I'm tired
> and you're tired
> and everybody's goddam tired
> tired
> students tired
> Liberals tired
> Revolutionaries tired. . . .*

Moreover, the years of polarization produced fragmentation. As feminists and black activists discovered, new strategies and tactics could lead to confrontations not only with defenders of the status quo but also with people who supported gradualist social change and with "sisters" and "brothers" who dis-

---

*Reprinted by permission.

agreed about how and where to take the next bold step toward the future. The gap between what people wanted to be done and what they realized could be accomplished rarely seemed to be closing.

Still, these years of polarization left important, if controversial, legacies. Civil-rights laws, abolition of the military draft, less-restrictive drug laws, and relaxed rules in college curricula and social life were only some of the changes traceable to the insurgent movements that emerged during the 1960s. If one takes a longer view of their impact, these insurgencies created the basis for ongoing activity by feminists, racial and ethnic groups, advocates of gay and lesbian rights, environmentalists, community-based self-help organizations, and a variety of other groups.

A second legacy of the years from 1963 to 1976 was the attack, from both the left and the right, on the positive-state programs of the Fair Deal, the New Frontier, and the Great Society. The search for empowerment by people who claimed too little had changed, too slowly, contributed to diminishing support for national initiatives. In this sense, the years of polarization cost Democrats like Lyndon Johnson and Hubert Humphrey the support of people who came to identify governmental programs with a corrupt status quo. When proponents of the "new politics" tried to move the Democratic party cautiously leftward in response to the insurgent movements of the 1960s, they risked losing the support of people who detested the protestors and who feared that they would shoulder a disproportionate share of the tax bills needed to fund new domestic-spending programs. As conservatives such as George Wallace, Richard Nixon, and Ronald Reagan realized, both the Democratic party and the GOP's eastern establishment were losing support from the people Nixon called the "silent majority."

Thus another, and perhaps most important, legacy of the years of polarization was the growing power of a new conservatism, symbolized by Ronald Reagan and his attacks on both protestors and federal government programs. The 1960s and early 1970s threw up all kinds of unusual political figures, most of whom enjoyed instant media attention and then suffered almost equally rapid obscurity. Most pundits predicted a similarly brief political career for Reagan. Despite the conventional wisdom heard from 1966 until 1980 that he was "too old," Reagan became the only prominent political figure of the 1960s to prosper during the 1980s. Reagan's curious career says a great deal about the ambiguous legacy of the years of polarization.

SUGGESTED READING

The literature on the opposition movements of the 1960s and 1970s is already immense and of widely varying quality. Several classics of the 1960's counterculture are good places to begin: Philip Slater, *The Pursuit of Loneliness* (rev.ed., 1976); Theodore Roszak, *The Making of a Counter Culture* (1969) and *Where the Wasteland Ends* (1972); and Charles Reich, *The Greening of America* (1970). Sohnya Sayers et al., *The 60s Without Apology* (1984) and Clair Albert and Stewart Albert, *The Sixties Papers* (1984) remain useful anthologies, which can be supplemented by Barbara Tischler, ed., *Sights on the Sixties* (1992). David Chalmers, *And the Crooked Place Made Straight: The Struggle for Social Change in the 1960s* (2nd ed., 1996) is an overview. Important recent works include David Farber, ed., *The Sixties: From Memory to History* (1994); Alexander Bloom and Wini Breines, eds., *"Takin' it to the Streets": A Sixties Reader* (1995); Rebecca E.

Klatch, *A Generation Divided: The New Left, the New Right, and the 1960s* (1999); Paul Lyons, *New Left, New Right, and the Legacy of the Sixties* (1996); David Burner, *Making Peace with the Sixties* (1996); and Doug Rossinow, *The Politics of Authenticity: Liberalism, Christianity, and the New Left in America* (1998).

The conservative insurgency is the subject of Mary C. Brennan, *Turning Right in the Sixties: The Conservative Capture of the GOP* (1995); Robert Alan Goldberg, *Barry Goldwater* (1995); John A. Andrew, III, *The Other Side of the Sixties: Young Americans for Freedom and the Rise of Conservative Politics* (1997); Gregory L. Schneider, *Cadres for Conservatism: Young Americans for Freedom and the Rise of the Conservative Right* (1999); Lisa McGirr, *Suburban Warriors: The Origins of the New American Right* (2001); and Rick Perlstein, *Before the Storm: Barry Goldwater and the Unmaking of the American Consensus* (2001).

Milton Viorst, *Fire in the Streets* (1981), brings to life the personal stories of some of the leading cultural radicals. See also Richard Etulain, ed., *Cesar Chavez* (2002). Marty Jezer, *Abbie Hoffman: American Rebel* (1992) and Jonah Raskin, *For the Hell of It: The Life and Times of Abbie Hoffman* (1996) look at the Yippie celebrity. In addition to work cited in the previous chapter, opposition to the war can be traced in Thomas Powers, *The War at Home* (1973); Nancy Zaroulis and Gerald Sullivan, *Who Spoke Up?* (1984); Charles De Benedetti, *An American Ordeal: The Anti-war Movement of the Vietnam Era* (1990); Melvin Small and William D. Hoover, eds., *Give Peace a Chance* (1992); Kenneth J. Heineman, *Campus Wars: The Peace Movement at American State Universities in the Vietnam Era* (1993); Amy Swerdlow, *Women Strike for Peace: Traditional Motherhood and Radical Politics in the 1960s* (1993); Tom Wells, *The War Within* (1993); Adam Garfinkle, *Telltale Hearts: The Origins and Impact of the Vietnam Antiwar Movement* (1995); and Brian Dooley, *Robert Kennedy: The Final Years* (1996).

Todd Gitlin indicts the media for speeding the fall of opposition efforts in *The Whole World is Watching* (1980). Maurice Isserman, *If I Had a Hammer* (1987), looks at the conflict between the old and new lefts. Wini Breines, *Community and Organization in the New Left, 1962–1968* (1982) and Peter B. Levy, *The New Left and Labor in the 1960s* (1993) are important studies on New Left politics. Government surveillance of radical cultural and political figures is the subject of James Kirkpatrick Davis, *Spying on Americans* (1992).

The diversity of the counterculture is evident after considering Tom Wolfe, *The Electric Kool-Aid Acid Test* (1969); Morris Dickstein, *Gates of Eden* (new ed., 1997); Joan Didion, *The White Album* (1979); Charles Perry, *The Haight-Ashbury* (1985); and Sally Banes, *Greenwich Village 1963: Avant-Garde Performance and the Effervescent Body* (1993). Abe Peck covers the underground press in *Uncovering the Sixties* (1985), and Daniel Yankelovich tries to fathom changing social values in *The New Morality* (1974) and *New Rules* (1982). The relationship between the Sixties and Seventies is explored in Bruce Shulman, *The Seventies: The Great Shift in American Culture, Society, and Politics* (2001), an important, recent overview; David Frum, *How We Got from Here: The 70s: The Decade that Brought You Modern Life (For Better or For Worse)* (2000), a breezy overview; and Stephen Paul Miller, *The Seventies Now: Culture as Surveillance* (1999), an intensive reading of several cultural texts.

During the 1980s, strong nostalgia for the 1960s began to emerge. Jim Miller, *Democracy Is in the Streets* (1987); Todd Gitlin, *The Sixties: Years of Hope, Days of Rage* (1987); Joan Morrison and Robert K. Morrison, eds., *From Camelot* to Kent State: The Sixties Experience in the Words of Those Who Lived It (1987); and Hans Konig, Nineteen Sixty-Eight: A Personal Report (1987) all express complex, though not uncritical, feelings of loss. In contrast, the former radicals who look back in Peter Collier and David Horowitz, eds., Second Thoughts (1989) have almost nothing good to say about the 1960s. This perspective is updated in Peter Collier and David Horowitz, Destructive Generation (1996). See also, Roger Kimball, The Long March: How the Cultural Revolution of the 1960s Changed America (2000). Among the attempts to gain some perspective on the decade, especially the allegedly pivotal year of 1968, see Irwin Unger and Debi Unger, Turning Point, 1968 (1988); David Caute, The Year of the Barricades: A Journey Through 1968 (1988); David Farber, Chicago '68 (1988); Douglas Knight, Streets of Dreams: The Nature and Legacy of the 1960s (1989); Lewis Gould, 1968: The Election that Changed America (1993); Dominick Cavallo, A Fiction of the Past: The Sixties in American History (1999); and Jules Whitcover, The Year the Dream Died (1997).

On the continuation of the new feminist movement, see many of the works noted at the end of Chapter 5; see also Jo Freeman, The Politics of Women's Liberation (1975); Linda T. Sanford, Women and Self-esteem (1985); Jane J. Mansbridge, Why We Lost the ERA (1986); Mary Francis Berry, Why ERA Failed (1986); Johnnetta B. Cole, ed., All American Women: Lines that Divide, Ties that Bind (1986); Catherine MacKinnon, Feminism Unmodified (1988); Susan Staggenborg, The Pro-choice Movement (1991); and N. E. H. Hull and Peter Charles Hoffer, Roe v. Wade: The Abortion Rights Controversy in American History (2001).

Sara Evans, Personal Politics: The Roots of Women's Liberation in the Civil Rights Movement and the New Left (1979) and Alice Echols, Daring to Be Bad: Radical Feminism in America, 1967–1975 (1989) seek to trace the emergence of a new feminism out of the male-dominated ethos of the New Left and the counterculture and to suggest that 1968 did not represent a sudden end to insurgent movements. See also Blanche Linden-Ward and Carol Hurd Green, Changing the Future: American Women in the 1960s (1992); Winifred D. Wandersee, On the Move: American Women in the 1970s (1988); Nancy Whittier, Feminist Generations: the Persistence of the Radical Women's Movement (1995); Catherine MacKinnon, Feminism Unmodified: Discourses on Life and Law (1988); Susan Staggenborg, The Pro-Choice Movement: Organization and Activism in the Abortion Conflict (1991); Hugh Davis Graham, Civil Rights and the Presidency: Race and Gender in America, 1960–1972 (1992); the relevant chapters of Leslie Reagan, When Abortion Was a Crime: Women, Medicine, and Law in the United States, 1867–1973 (1997); Amy Erdman Farrell, Yours in Sisterhood: Ms. Magazine and the Promise of Popular Feminism (1998); Kate Weigard, Red Feminism: American Communism and the Making of Women's Liberation (2001); Marilyn Jacoby Boxer, When Women Ask the Questions: Creating Women's Studies in America (1998); and Ruth Rosen, The World Split Open: How the Modern Women's Movement Changed America (2000).

On the gay and lesbian rights movement, see the relevant chapters of John D'Emilio and Estelle B. Freedman, Intimate Matters: A History of Sexuality in America (1988); Randy Shilts, And the Band Played On: Politics, People, and the AIDS Epidemic (1987); Steven Epstein, Impure Science: AIDS, AIDS Activism, and the Politics of Science (1996); Jeffrey Escoffier, American Homo: Community and Perversity (1998); Rodger Streitmatter, Unspeakable: The Rise of the Gay and Lesbian Press in America (1995); Paul Robinson, Gay Lives: Homosexual Autobiography from

204 POLARIZATION AND THE SEARCH FOR EMPOWERMENT

John Addingon Symonds to Paul Monette (1999); Leila J. Rupp, *A Desired Past: A Short History of Same-Sex Love in America* (1999); Lillian Faderman, *To Believe in Women: What Lesbians Have Done for America* (1999); and David A. J. Richards, *Women, Gays, and the Constitution: The Grounds for Feminism and Gay Rights in Culture and Law* (1998).

On the escalation of violence in Southeast Asia, see Seymour Hersh, *Cover-up* (1972); William Shawcross, *Sideshow* (1979); and Karl D. Jackson, *Cambodia, 1975–1978: Rendezvous with Death* (1989).

For a general theory of insurgency during these years, see Ira Katznelson's *City Trenches* (1981). See also Michael Reich, *Racial Inequality* (1981); Rufus Brown, Dale Rogers Marshall, and David Tebbs, *Protest Is Not Enough: The Struggle of Blacks and Hispanics for Equality in Urban Politics* (1984); Peter Mathiessen, *In the Spirit of Crazy Horse* (1983); George Lipsitz, *A Life in the Struggle: Ivory Perry and the Culture of Opposition* (1988); Barbara Epstein, *Political Protest and Cultural Revolution* (1991); and William H. Chafe, *Never Stop Running: Allard Lowenstein and the Struggle to Save American Liberalism* (1993).

The complexity of ethnic issues may be gleaned from Michael Novak, *Rise of the Unmeltable Ethnics* (1973); Richard Kirckus, *Pursuing the American Dream* (1976); Patricia Zavella, *Women's Work and Chicano Families: Cannery Workers of the Santa Clara Valley* (1987); William Julius Wilson, *The Declining Significance of Race: Blacks and Changing American Institutions* (1978) and *The Truly Disadvantaged: The Inner City, The Underclass, and Public Policy* (1987); Carlos Muñoz, Jr., *Youth, Identity and Power: The Chicano Movement* (1989); Jim Sleeper, *The Closet of Strangers: Liberalism and the Politics of Race in New York* (1990); Charles P. Banner-Haley, *The Fruits of Integration: Black Middle-Class Ideology and Culture, 1960–1990* (1993); and Herbert Hill and James E. Jones, Jr., eds., *Race in America* (1993).

7

Times of Turmoil: The 1970s

Richard Nixon promised political tranquility and a law-and-order administration. His presidency produced partisan turbulence and a constitutional crisis that Nixon himself never seemed fully to understand. The president's tight circle of advisers—notably his "Berlin Wall" of John Ehrlichman and H. R. (Bob) Haldeman—shielded him from dissenting views and reinforced his worst instincts, especially a penchant for secrecy and for seeing politics in highly personal terms. Nixon seemed to enjoy jousting against political opponents, so it was not surprising that his White House would have its own "enemies list" and order illegal surveillance of people whom the president distrusted.

Nixon's immediate successors, Gerald Ford and Jimmy Carter, came to the same realization as their ousted predecessor: The presidency, although a position with substantial power, could not command. The chief executives of the 1970s constantly confronted limits in their ability to achieve their policy goals. During the 1970s, many of the battles of the 1960s still raged over how to define the nation's role in the world and to shape social policy at home.

DOMESTIC POLITICS UNDER NIXON AND FORD

Richard Nixon provided inconsistent direction on most domestic issues. Playing to GOP conservatives, the president condemned the "welfare mess" and promised to get people off relief rolls and into work roles. He also talked of stocking the federal courts with conservative judges and opposed school busing to bring school integration. Despite such rhetorical flourishes, however, Nixon made no serious effort to roll back the positive state. He extended the broad out-lines of Dwight Eisenhower's version of Republicanism and located his admin-istration to the left of the positions that Barry Goldwater had staked out during the 1960s and ones that Ronald Reagan would espouse during the 1980s.

Nixon's Domestic Policies

Following the advice of Daniel Patrick Moynihan, the influential Democrat in his administration, Nixon presented Congress with a dramatic welfare-reform proposal, the Family Assistance Plan (FAP). FAP horrified conservative Re-publicans by suggesting that the federal government guarantee every American family an annual income of $1,600. Nixon and Moynihan touted FAP as a way to pare down the welfare bureaucracy and to eliminate burdensome restric-tions, including the one that denied aid to low-income families with a man liv-ing in the household. Angry conservatives, wondering if Nixon had lost his sanity, grumbled at the program's potential cost. Democrats, who also won-dered what Nixon might have in mind, denounced FAP's $1,600 guarantee as too miserly. Nixon himself never pressed vigorously for FAP's passage, and a pe-culiar coalition of conservatives and activist Democrats blocked the proposal. As one of Nixon's biographers later suggested, simply offering a plan for bold change seemed enough for the president. Once forced to steer FAP through a suspicious Congress, Nixon seemed to lose interest in his own plan.

Expenditures for social welfare programs grew during Nixon's presiden-cy. This growth was a result of the residual strength of the positive-state ideal in Congress and Nixon's own disinterest in pushing aggressively for the do-mestic agenda he had promised to conservatives. Although Nixon shut down Johnson's Office of Economic Opportunity, spending for nondefense programs increased by about 46 percent during the years between Lyndon Johnson's last budget and Nixon's 1971–1972 one.

The Nixon White House supported important changes in other areas. It backed creation of two new federal agencies, the Environmental Protection Agency and the Occupational Health and Safety Administration, which signif-icantly extended the regulatory reach of the positive state. A barrage of new laws tackled pollution problems and established new environmental regulations. (See Chapter 8.) The 1972 decision to index Social Security payments (begin-ning in 1975) to the rate of inflation meant that millions of elderly people saw their incomes remain above what the federal government defined as the pover-ty line during the inflationary period of the 1970s and early 1980s. Indexing So-cial Security, in other words, produced an effective income-support measure, albeit one targeted at only one segment of the population.

Nixon showed particular interest in a domestic initiative he called the "New Federalism." The most tangible part of this proposal was "revenue shar-ing," a concept that paralleled a goal of the failed FAP—cutting red tape. Under revenue sharing, Washington returned a portion of its tax revenues to state and local governments as "bloc grants," with relatively few federal restrictions on how these were to be spent. Revenue sharing, Nixon argued to conservatives, would take power away from bureaucrats in Washington and redistribute it, along with money, to people at the grassroots. Nixon's Democratic critics claimed that revenue-sharing would fund projects that would do little to help people who already lacked political clout at the state and local levels. Giving money to state and local governments proved popular, however, and Congress enacted a modified version of Nixon's revenue sharing in 1972.

Stagflation

Richard Nixon faced two alarming new economic trends—"stagflation," a concurrence of recession and inflation, and a growing deficit in the U.S. balance of payments.

Conventional economic wisdom held that inflation (rising price levels) resulted from an overheated economy in which demand for goods far exceeded supply. Dampening demand by inducing a mild economic downturn was supposed to reduce inflation. To attack inflation, Nixon approved policies that raised interest rates and brought more unemployment—in order to suppress demand. The downturn came. Rising interest rates nearly ended residential construction, forced businesses such as the Penn Central Railroad into bankruptcy, reduced industrial production, and raised unemployment to 6 percent. Yet, contrary to expectations, prices still galloped forward. Business and labor continued to layer higher wages and higher costs on an economy now slowing into a recession (what economists called negative growth). By 1971, economists were speaking of stagflation, an unprecedented economic condition in which unemployment and the spiral of inflation moved upward simultaneously.

After trying antiinflation measures, Nixon decided that inflationary prosperity was better than an economic slowdown that might jeopardize his 1972 presidential campaign. He endorsed policies to attack the recession he himself had earlier induced. After telling a startled group of journalists, "I am now a Keynesian," Nixon embraced a tactic supposedly only used by Democrats, deficit spending financed by government borrowing to stimulate economic growth. This dramatic about-face prompted a TV commentator to quip, "It's a little like a Christian crusader saying 'All things considered, I think Mohammed was right!'" But the stimulus of government spending scarcely dented unemployment, and prices rose even faster. Measures taken against either inflation or unemployment seemed only to make the other problem worse. Some advisers began to advocate an across-the-board, government-imposed freeze on wages, prices, and interest rates as the only way to hold down inflation, but Nixon shied away from governmental price controls.

Worrisome foreign-trade statistics soon caused the president to change his mind once again. For 80 years, the United States had exported far more than it imported, but after World War II huge military expenditures and corporate investment overseas created deficits in the balance of payments. The country paid some of this debt from its sizeable supply of gold bullion. (For the rest, foreign creditors accepted U.S. dollars, which were pegged to a constant and specific value in gold bullion.) By 1970, the Vietnam War was producing ever-larger deficits, and inflation was crippling America's ability to sell its high-priced goods abroad. At the end of June 1971, the Commerce Department announced a trade deficit, the first since 1890. Meanwhile, America's prewar hoard of gold had shrunk by half. As fears about the nation's financial solvency increased, speculators attacked the U.S. dollar, dumping vast amounts on world currency exchanges to avoid the losses that would result from its widely expected devaluation.

In August 1971, Nixon responded to the international monetary crisis and to the larger problems, including inflation and the new trade deficit, which fueled it. First, the United States ceased to peg the value of the dollar to a set price for gold. Instead, the U.S. dollar would (as it still does) "float" on the world's money exchanges, supply and demand determining its value against that of other currencies. Second, the president leveled a 10 percent tariff surcharge, which significantly reduced imports into America. Nixon later removed the surcharge in return for obtaining new world monetary agreements. The new arrangement terminated the system of fixed monetary exchange rates established at the Bretton Woods Conference of 1944, and it undercut the dollar's position as the most privileged medium of international exchange. (See Chapter 1.) By substantially altering the system of international exchange, Nixon had given U.S. financial experts more room to manipulate currency values and combat the trade deficit. He had also led the United States and the world into the uncharted waters of floating exchange rates, a system that had proven economically perilous and politically destabilizing during the 1930s.

Nixon's advisers also plotted a new antiinflation program for the domestic economy. The president froze wages and prices for ninety days, an interim measure called Phase I, while he worked on a comprehensive program to attack inflation and the trade deficit. In November 1971, the White House announced its new program, Phase II. It cut government spending and provided business with a tax credit aimed at encouraging domestic production. As a special stimulus for the automobile industry, Congress repealed the 7 percent excise tax on American-made cars. Such measures ensured higher profits for business and, together with the certainty that Nixon would not risk retrenchment in an election year, perked up the sluggish economy. Consumer spending increased. Meanwhile, a new Cost-of-Living Council attacked inflation by banning wage hikes of more than 5.5 percent and limiting retail price increases to 2.5 percent. Nixon's economic program seemed to give the economy a mild stimulus while holding down inflation through government controls. It worked just long enough to smooth Nixon's 1972 reelection.

The 1972 Election

George McGovern, a convert to the "new politics" of the 1960s, captured the 1972 Democratic nomination for president. Working with activists to move the party leftward and capitalizing on changes in the rules enacted after the chaos at the 1968 Chicago convention, the McGovern campaign lined up delegates in the nonprimary states. Meanwhile, in the states that held primaries, the South Dakota senator outlasted more centrist candidates, notably Senator Edmund Muskie and Hubert Humphrey. Overall, though, McGovern won only eight popular-vote primaries.

By the time Democratic delegates gathered in Miami for their 1972 convention, many familiar faces, including Mayor Richard Daley of Chicago, were absent. Outmaneuvered by McGovern's strategists, they watched the convention on television. One veteran labor leader who disliked the new politics complained that the gathering in Miami contained too many women, too many long-haired young men, and "too few cigars." McGovern easily captured the nomination on the first ballot, but old-line Democrats, such as Chicago's Daley and labor's George Meany, were less than enthusiastic and gave McGovern only tepid support or left him to stumble on by himself.

Stumble he did. McGovern quickly jettisoned his running mate, Senator Thomas Eagleton of Missouri, after it was revealed that Eagleton had earlier undergone electric shock treatment for nervous exhaustion. Then, several prominent Democrats (including Edward Kennedy) declined to become Eagleton's replacement. McGovern did find a running mate (Sargeant Shriver, Kennedy's brother-in-law and LBJ's ambassador to France), but he never persuaded large numbers of voters to accept his theme of "Come Home, America." His central issue, a speedy withdrawal from Vietnam, lacked the appeal of Nixon's call for an "honorable" peace. McGovern also failed to convert his stands on domestic issues into popular support. Calls for higher taxes on large inheritances and for "demogrants" of $1,000 to every citizen appeared to alienate some traditionally Democratic voters without attracting significant numbers of new supporters.

The Nixon reelection campaign, in contrast, enjoyed broad support, some of it in the form of illegal financial contributions. While wooing potential donors, Nixon's fund-raisers warned of the antibusiness tone of a McGovern administration and hinted at the advantages contributors would gain from a second Nixon administration. Not even the arrest, in mid-June 1972, of intruders at the Democratic party headquarters in the Watergate complex in Washington could slow Nixon's reelection drive. The president's press secretary quickly dismissed this illegal entry as a "third-rate burglary"—by people with close ties to the Republican campaign and the White House itself, who were updating sophisticated wiretapping equipment. The media gave the Watergate incident little attention during the campaign, and it had no discernible effect on Nixon's or McGovern's political fortunes.

Richard Nixon, dismissed only six years earlier as a political has-been, captured nearly 61 percent of the popular vote, and the Nixon-Agnew ticket won all but a handful of the Electoral College ballots. The McGovern-Shriver ticket carried only one state, Massachusetts, and the District of Columbia. Subsequent analysis confirmed what was apparent in November. People likely to vote perceived George McGovern as far outside the political mainstream, while Richard Nixon occupied a centrist position, much as LBJ had done against Barry Goldwater in 1964.

Once settled in his second term, Nixon again struggled with stagflation. He first replaced Phase II price ceilings with "voluntary" restraints. Predictably, consumer prices shot upward, compensating for the time they had been under controls. In midsummer, he again froze prices, this time for sixty days, while his advisers again debated alternatives. Finally, in April 1974, he again reversed course, canceling all government price restraints. Nixon, now immersed in Watergate difficulties, lost interest in devising any consistent economic strategy.

Nixon's mercurial policies accompanied growing hostility between the White House and the Democratic Congress. In 1973, the president vetoed nine major bills, including education and antipollution measures. He also announced that he would "impound" funds, rather than spend them, even if Congress constitutionally overrode this kind of quasi-veto by the executive branch.

Nixon's congressional opponents, and later the courts, condemned impoundment as unconstitutional. Growing personal hostilities and policy differences thus brought the two branches of government to an impasse.

After Nixon left office, economists continued to debate what had gone wrong. Inflation continued at an annual rate of nearly 10 percent, and unemployment hovered at just under 6 percent, a recession rate. After several years of battling stagflation and trade deficits, the economic situation seemed worse than ever. Inflation appeared endemic. All of Nixon's remedies had failed. Although economists and politicians differed sharply over the precise reasons for their failure, they agreed that inconsistencies of approach and scatter-gun solutions during Nixon's presidency had aggravated the nation's economic situation.

Nixon simply cared much more about foreign policy than domestic issues, and when he glanced inward, he too often seemed narrowly focused on punishing his enemies. In the end, Nixon's preoccupation with battling political adversaries and orchestrating foreign relations left too little time for tackling policy issues at home.

The Underside of the Nixon Administration: Leaks, Plumbers, and Watergate

Many of Nixon's Watergate troubles stemmed from his own fears about the reliability and loyalty of many governmental agencies and officials. The Watergate eavesdropping team first took shape in order to provide the White House with its own covert intelligence unit. The so-called Huston Plan of 1970 had proposed improving the administration's ability to coordinate the use of wiretaps, mail covers, and "surreptitious entries." Although Nixon secretly approved the outlines of such an idea, rumors about its potential scope alarmed officials in the CIA and FBI who had always monopolized such covert activities. Claiming that the Huston Plan threatened serious violations of civil liberties, J. Edgar Hoover forced the president to drop its implementation.

While the White House began to leak information to the press critical of the aging FBI director, it looked for ways of restarting the Huston initiative. Top officials finally decided to use the issue of drugs as a cover for creating a secret strike force, controlled from the White House, that could bypass the FBI and CIA, agencies allegedly "infested" with Democrats. G. Gordon Liddy, a former FBI agent, formulated plans for an antidrug squad in the Treasury Department that could undertake covert work against Nixon's enemies. If things went wrong, the claim that this unit was fighting the "drug menace" could be used as a cover for its activities. The administration began planning a mass media campaign against drugs, and a presidential declaration of a national "heroin emergency" was slated for late June 1971. However, on June 13, the *New York Times* began to publish excerpts from the "Pentagon Papers," a hitherto secret governmental history of America's involvement in Vietnam that had been prepared by the Defense Department during Lyndon Johnson's presidency.

Alarmed at this breach of secrecy, Nixon's inner circle shifted their attention from drugs to security leaks. The president's antidrug speech was canceled, and the national heroin emergency was never declared. Instead, the administration mobilized to stop further publication of the "Pentagon Papers" and to scrutinize the executive branch itself. It obtained a court injunction that barred further publication of the "Pentagon Papers." Responding to this unprecedented use of a prior restraint, government censorship in its classic form, the *New York Times* appealed to the U.S. Supreme Court. By a vote of six to three the justices lifted the injunction, holding that the First Amendment barred prior restraints in instances such as this. Many people celebrated this ruling as a victory for openness in government, but the Nixon administration was already mounting a covert crusade on behalf of secrecy.

Using personnel already assembled for the spurious antidrug effort, the White House formed its own leak-stopping crew, the self-styled "Plumbers." The group soon included Liddy, E. Howard Hunt (a former CIA agent), and several Cuban exiles with close ties to the CIA. After it became known that Daniel Ellsberg, a former analyst for the Defense Department, bore primary responsibility for leaking the "Pentagon Papers," the Plumbers began a campaign, including a burglary of the office of his psychiatrist, to harass and discredit him. The secret strike team conducted similar illegal activities against other "enemies" of the White House. With the significant addition of James McCord, another former CIA operative, this group was eventually caught with the eavesdropping apparatus inside Democratic headquarters at the Watergate in June 1972.

Nixon's defenders have subsequently contended that such activities did not start with his administration. John Kennedy, for instance, took a particular interest in expanding the executive's covert capacities, both overseas and at home, and Robert Kennedy, his attorney general, gave the FBI wide latitude in wiretapping and bugging operations.

Still, the Nixon administration, its critics have replied, significantly expanded the scope and purpose of domestic surveillance. During Lyndon Johnson's second term, for example, his attorney general had limited the use of FBI wiretaps. Despite the turmoil of the 1960s, their number declined from 233 in 1965 to only nine in 1968. The next year, Nixon and his attorney general, John Mitchell, claimed that the president could order wiretaps, without a court order, on any group or individual considered a threat to national security. (In 1972, the Supreme Court held that presidents could not order, on their own authority, electronic surveillance of purely domestic organizations.) Reports on some of these illegal taps were forwarded not only to officials concerned with national security but also to Nixon's primary political strategist, Bob Haldeman.

Haldeman's involvement in the earliest activities of the plumbers established a pattern that would lead to Nixon's downfall: the attempt to centralize so many operations of this type within the president's inner circle. As the historian Garry Wills has noted, Nixon and his close aides operated a kind of "counterinsurgency presidency." Seeing themselves as lonely defenders of the "American way of life," the Nixonites waged war not only against the New Left but also against the very same institutions that the protesters often attacked—the mainstream press, J. Edgar Hoover's FBI, and even the CIA. In the end, Nixon became ensnarled in a clumsy effort to create a secret government, one that could spy on both the demonstrators in the streets and the elites in Washington.

The same concern for centralizing control within the White House affected the conduct of foreign relations. Nixon and Henry Kissinger, his national security adviser, saw the official foreign policy agencies—including the departments of State and Defense and the CIA—as uninformed and unimaginative. Worse, Nixon and Kissinger believed, these branches of government were filled with people who would obstruct presidential initiatives or, as in the case of Daniel Ellsberg, leak sensitive and secret material to the press. As a result of these fears and the desire for greater White House oversight, Nixon and Kissinger began to conduct their own secret foreign policy—secret from the American people and from other government officials. Their decision in 1970 to begin heavy bombing of neutral Cambodia, for example, deliberately bypassed high officials in the State and Defense departments.

The media slowly learned of Nixon's secrets. Most of the early investigative reporting about the Watergate burglery during the 1972 election came from a single newspaper, the *Washington Post,* and only two of its reporters, Bob Woodward and Carl Bernstein. In developing their stories, Woodward and Bernstein relied on "Deep Throat," a still-unidentified informant (or perhaps several informants) in the governmental bureaucracy. Other journalists began to cover the scandal spreading around the Nixon administration. Using information developed by federal prosecutors and relying on leaks by anti-Nixon sources in government, other journalists gradually assumed an aggressive, adversary relationship toward the administration. Nixon and his advisers, who had been castigating the press for several years, responded with vague hints about reprisal.

Nixon found that he could not halt, or even slow, critical stories about his administration. In the late summer of 1973, rumors of wrongdoing began to envelop Vice-President Spiro T. Agnew, and in October he pled "no contest" to charges of having accepted illegal monetary kickbacks when holding office in Maryland. Following Agnew's resignation, Nixon chose Gerald Ford, the GOP minority leader in the House of Representatives, as his new vice-president. The man who held the office generally considered to be the most powerful in the world discovered his inability to control events or even employees of his own executive branch.

Nixon's Last Battle

As Nixon futily attempted to cut off the trail of criminality at members of the Watergate entry team, then at high officials in CREEP, and finally at top-ranking members of the White House staff itself, the president's pursuers pressed on. In May 1973, a special Senate committee headed by North Carolina's Sam Ervin began televised hearings into the 1972 presidential election. Ervin, a conservative Democrat who called himself a "simple country lawyer," quickly became a media celebrity, and his folksy image contributed to his panel's credibility. Throughout the summer of 1973, witness after witness offered tantalizing hints about White House involvement in a series of unseemly activities. Even Senator Howard Baker of Tennessee, a Republican loyalist, came to ask, "What did the president know and when did he know it?" Then, in mid-July, the answer to this query suddenly had a most unlikely source—Richard Milhaus Nixon.

"Nixon Bugged Himself!" proclaimed newspaper headlines. An obscure White House official named Alexander Butterfield revealed that Nixon secretly taped the bulk of his presidential conversations and phone calls. These tapes promised the "smoking gun" that Nixon's defenders had challenged his accusers to produce. The Ervin committee and a special Watergate prosecutor, Archibald Cox of Harvard Law School, immediately sought access to the tapes. Claiming an absolute executive privilege, Nixon flatly refused.

Threatened by lethal strands of audiotape, Richard Nixon struggled to survive. Although some advisers urged him to destroy the tapes, Nixon tried to battle free while still clutching the damning evidence. A veteran political club fighter, the president bobbed and weaved and occasionally even counterpunched. His opponents had the heavier weapons. In October 1973, Nixon's dramatic dismissal of the special Watergate prosecutor, Archibald Cox, for his refusal to accept the president's formula for limited access to nine of the most crucial White-House tapes backfired. Elliot Richardson and William Ruckelshaus, two of the most respected figures remaining in the Nixon administration, resigned in protest. Nixon was forced to appoint another special prosecutor, Leon Jaworski, and to surrender the nine tapes, one of which contained an 18 ½-minute gap that was later found to have been the result of a deliberate erasure.

The "Saturday Night Massacre," as the president's firing of Cox and the two resignations was called, represented Nixon's last attempt to take the offensive. Slowly, the president retreated, trying to stave off impeachment. By early 1974, after a grand jury indicted seven of his top aides, Nixon could do little more than continue his personal cover-up, hoping that miraculously he might avoid being indicted by a grand jury or impeached by Congress.

Increasingly, the fight pitted Nixon, comforted in the final days of his presidency by his immediate family and a handful of loyalists, against the combined power of the other branches of the federal government. Nixon tried one last desperate gamble. He released his own edited version of an additional forty-two taped conversations that were being sought by Jaworski and the House Judiciary Committee. These bowdlerized transcripts, repeatedly sanitized by the phrase "expletive deleted," only raised new doubts about the president's character and competence.

Nixon's defenders in Congress and his lawyers before the Supreme Court had no better luck than their chief. By early summer, the issue was not whether the House Judiciary Committee would support Nixon's impeachment but how many Republicans would join the Democratic majority and how many articles of impeachment they would vote against the president. Meanwhile, the Supreme Court, which had expedited an appeal of Nixon's refusal to obey a subpoena for additional tapes, voted unanimously to reject the president's sweeping claim that this evidence, needed for a criminal investigation, was protected by an absolute executive privilege.

At nearly the same time, the House Judiciary Committee completed its deliberations on articles of impeachment. On July 27, 1974, three days after Nixon's defeat in the Supreme Court, the committee passed, by a margin of 27 to 11, the first article of impeachment against the president. It charged Nixon with obstruction of justice for trying to impede the investigation of Watergate. Subsequently, the committee voted two other articles. One charged Nixon with abuse of presidential power by trying to use agencies such as the IRS and the FBI for partisan purposes, and the other charged him with violating his constitutional duty to enforce the law by refusing to turn over subpoenaed tapes. (The committee rejected an article that would have cited Nixon for his secret bombing of Cambodia.)

Although Nixon promised a floor fight in the House and a last-ditch battle in the Senate, his shrinking entourage was already easing him out of office.

FIGURE 7–1   Nixon Leaves the White House.

In-coming President, Gerald Ford, who had been appointed to the vice-presidency less than a year earlier, says farewell to Pat and former President Nixon as they prepare to depart from the White House lawn in a helicopter.
Source: Nixon Presidential Materials Project, National Archives and Records Administration. Photo by Oliver F. Atkins.

Even before the Supreme Court had handed down its decision on Nixon's tapes, a presidential assistant had finally found, in these very same tapes, the elusive "smoking gun." The tape of a conversation between Nixon and Haldeman on June 23, 1972, showed that the president had planned, from the very beginning, to use the CIA to halt investigation of the Watergate break-in on the spurious grounds of national security. The tape suggested that the president himself had orchestrated a cover-up, had conspired to obstruct justice, and had systematically lied about his role.

In late July and early August, aides to Nixon and to Vice-President Gerald Ford began discussing plans for terminating the Nixon administration and inaugurating a Ford presidency. Unyielding to the end, Nixon insisted that his conversation with Haldeman contained no fatal admissions. His new chief of staff, General Alexander Haig, flatly contradicted this claim and went ahead with plans for the transition to a new presidency. Once a partial transcript of the June 23 meeting became public, most of Nixon's remaining Republican support vanished. Richard Nixon gave up his lonely battle and resigned. On August 9, 1974, Gerald Ford became the nation's first chief executive who had not been elected as either president or vice-president.

After several years away from the limelight, Richard Nixon made yet another comeback. While fighting in the courts to keep additional tapes of his presidential conversations and phone calls secret, Nixon used television appearances and numerous publications to build the image of a wise, even seer-like, elder statesperson. The passage of time eliminated or mellowed many of Nixon's old critics, and a new generation of historians began to paint relatively favorable pictures of a Nixon presidency "without Watergate." Nixon's death in the spring of 1994, though, helped to spark a new round of critical commentary about the only president whose illegal activities forced his resignation from office. In 1997, after winning a court battle over access to more of Nixon's tapes, the historian Stanley Kutler published transcripts that convincingly detailed Nixon's abuses of power.

The Ford Presidency: The Wounds Remain

The failed Nixon presidency, coming so soon after the trauma of the late 1960s, fed popular cynicism about politics and government. For many voters, Watergate seemed less the personal failture of Nixon than yet another example of political disarray in Washington. Gridlock between the White House and Congress made many Americans fear that "politics" were taking precedence over "governance." According to public opinion polls, confidence in governmental officials had been declining throughout the 1960s, the years of Vietnam. This slide continued into the 1970s. In the presidential election of 1972, only 56 percent of those eligible to cast ballots did so; in 1976, the turnout decreased once again, this time to 54 percent.

Gerald Ford later remembered his brief presidency (1974–1977) as a time of healing, but political divisions continued to appear. Popular doubts about politics seemed confirmed when Ford granted Nixon an unconditional pardon, an act that shielded the former president from prosecution and contributed to Ford's defeat in the 1976 presidential race. Moreover, the Ford years brought new revelations about illegal, or at least questionable, domestic surveillance activities that had been undertaken since World War II by the FBI, successive presidents, and the CIA.

The CIA was already wounded by Watergate politics and its own internal power struggles. The agency, it seemed, could no longer keep secrets. Former agents wrote best-selling exposés, and aggressive reporters exploited leaks within the agency to reveal the CIA's domestic spying operations, violations of the agency's mandate to operate only overseas. Gerald Ford, whose penchant for falling and stumbling (in and out of helicopters and down ski slopes) remain visible in reruns of old *Saturday Night Live* sketches from the mid-1970s, blurted out one of the CIA's most explosive secrets: Before a group from the *New York Times,* Ford inadvertently revealed the agency's involvement in attempts to assassinate foreign leaders, including Cuba's Fidel Castro. Although the *Times* sat on the story, Ford's gaffe soon reached reporters who were not bound by the president's claim that his remarks had been "off the record."

Even before the CIA's secrets became public knowledge, President Ford had created a special commission, headed by his newly appointed vice-president, Nelson Rockefeller, to look into allegations of domestic spying by the agency. In time, committees in both the House and the Senate heard about a wide range of CIA "dirty tricks"—drug-testing on unsuspecting subjects, mail covers on private citizens, efforts to destabilize the economies of other nations, and several bizarre plots to murder foreign leaders. Testimony before congressional committees left no doubt that intelligence officials often considered constitutional and legal restraints mere annoyances, paper restrictions that were to be overridden by claims of national security.

As revelations of misconduct undercut public faith in government, the continued deterioration of the nation's economy added to the disillusionment. Like Nixon, Ford aimed his economic remedies alternately at inflation and then at recession, and he was left with worse cases of both.

Ford identified inflation, rather than unemployment, as the more serious economic problem. As a substitute for new legislation, the White House organized a media-dominated campaign of public pressure against price increases that Ford called WIN or "Whip Inflation Now." WIN included buttons and ballyhoo, but the country fell into its worst recession since the 1930s. Consumer demand dropped precipitously, especially in the automobile sector, where higher sticker prices and worries about gasoline prices frightened off potential buyers. Triggered by layoffs in Detroit, unemployment quickly spread. Slackening consumer demand closed more and more factories, which in turn further reduced the demand for goods.

Faced with a jobless rate averaging nearly 13 percent and with falling production almost everywhere, President Ford reversed course within a few months. In late 1974, now focusing on jobs and trying to cure the recession, Ford projected a budget deficit of some $60 billion and cooperated with Congress on tax-cut legislation. These measures, hopefully, would increase consumer spending and create new demand for manufactured goods. Meanwhile, the Federal Reserve Board eased down interest rates to 8 percent. Taken together, these moves prompted a modest economic revival during the summer of 1975. Inflation, however, also began rising, and once again reached the double-digit level. The economy continued to oscillate between recession and inflation, both worsening with each swing and both undermining America's economic position internationally.

While economic issues were the major irritants, other problems widened the gap between the Ford White House and the Democratic Congress. Energy policy became a battleground as oil prices, controlled largely by Arab states, rose sharply. Afraid that dependence on Middle Eastern oil might weaken U.S. foreign policy, Ford wanted to raise the price of domestic gasoline by boosting federal taxes and ending all price controls on oil. The marketplace, he reasoned, would "ration" gasoline and, in effect, force down consumption. Democrats countered that Ford's approach would further accelerate inflation by raising gasoline prices, unfairly hurt low-income people, and give oil companies windfall profits. In the off-year, 1974 election, held in the wake of Nixon's resignation, voters had sent many younger, Democratic representatives to Capitol Hill. A feisty, heavily Democratic Congress outlined its own energy program, and Ford vetoed measures that would have maintained price controls and allocated funds for mass transit. He denounced government-imposed gasoline rationing as unworkable. The policy deadlock and absence of any unified response to the nation's economic and energy problems illustrated the sorry state of domestic decision making during the early 1970s, many people concluded.

NIXON, KISSINGER, AND WORLD POLITICS, 1969–1976

Henry Kissinger, Nixon's national security adviser until February 1973 and thereafter Nixon and Ford's secretary of state, dominated foreign policy during the early 1970s. He viewed himself as a master of geopolitical strategy. He talked of detente with the Soviets, but his later memoirs make it clear that his detente was not a policy of passivity but a beefed-up form of containment—"a firm application of psychological and physical restraints and determined resistance to challenge." Detente, according to Kissinger, was *realpolitik*—political realism exercised forcefully, unrelentingly, and employing a variety of political, economic, and psychological methods.

The Three-Dimensional Game

Arranging America's geopolitical cards to maximum advantage involved introducing a new player—China. Triangular diplomacy, in which the United States could exploit the Chinese-Soviet rivalry, might gain substantial advantages for the United States as both sought America's support. Throughout the Nixon-Kissinger years, Americans negotiated with the Soviets and opened channels to China in what Kissinger called a "three-dimensional game" of diplomacy.

After 1969, the Soviet Union and the United States intermittently discussed nuclear arms control. In 1969, both powers pledged not to build underwater installations and agreed to begin strategic arms limitation talks (SALT) in April 1970. These negotiations required intense bargaining over intricate, technical issues as well as over broad questions of strategic balance. After mid-1971, when the United States formally accepted the principle of nuclear parity between the two superpowers, diplomats made progress.

Reassured by the progress of SALT, the Nixon administration took up a more visible but even less familiar task: normalizing relations with China. Small courtesies started a chain reaction. Nixon began to call the country the "People's Republic," rather than "Red China," and told journalists of his desire to visit "that vast, unknown land." Nervous about relations with the USSR and about Japan's surging economy, Chinese leaders reopened Sino-American talks through ambassadors in Warsaw. Nixon eased trade restrictions against China in early 1971, and the Chinese reciprocated with an invitation for a ping-pong tournament. Then, in July, Kissinger made a secret trip to Peking to arrange a presidential visit for 1972. The announcement of Nixon's trip startled political leaders in the United States and refashioned world politics. The United Nations admitted the People's Republic three months later, rejecting the American two-China proposal, which was designed to preserve membership for Jiang Jie-Shi's government on Taiwan.

On February 21, 1972, President Nixon, one of the world's most celebrated anti-Communists, traveled to Peking to shake hands and bow gently with Mao Zedong, the archetypal anticapitalist. Nixon and his wife walked atop the Great Wall, mingled with Communist dignitaries, and ate a twenty-two-course state dinner. Still, public goodwill, extensively televised, could not dissolve long-standing animosities. Although contacts continued—especially scientific exchanges, token shipments of grain from the United States, and relaxation of trade and travel restrictions—movement toward compromise on fundamental differences, particularly related to Taiwan's future, remained slow.

The prospect of Sino-American detente apparently pushed the Soviet Union into some technical concessions at SALT and toward an invitation, eagerly accepted, for Nixon to visit Moscow in the spring of 1972. There, Nixon and Soviet leader Leonid Brezhnev initialed arms control treaties, called SALT I, which terminated the development of antiballistic missile systems (ABMs) and capped the number of individual nuclear missiles that each side could deploy. The Americans and later the Soviets, however, quickly expanded their stocks of MIRV missiles, containing multiple warheads on each individual missile. Thus, both sides could abide by the treaty yet still expand their number of deliverable weapons. (The United States had a two-to-one lead in total warheads.) Although SALT I's actual results thus did little to cool the arms race, the treaty did provide a precedent for future arms control negotiations. A year later, Brezhnev visited the United States, and Nixon returned to Moscow in mid-1974. The momentum of detente continued and seemed to demonstrate the advantages of triangular diplomacy.

As the Watergate scandals unfolded, Nixon increasingly sought redemption by stressing his international accomplishments. His personal diplomacy with China and the Soviet Union rated high in domestic opinion polls, and Kissinger was the only prominent member of Nixon's inner circle who emerged unscathed from the Watergate scandals.

The End of the War in Southeast Asia

Despite the popularity of detente, the war in Vietnam threatened the president's reputation and sapped America's strength. In 1971, Nixon continued negotiations in Paris while widening the war into Cambodia and Laos to "clean out" Communist supply camps. In response to antiwar protest at home, Nixon angrily told the nation that the United States would not "become a pitiful, helpless giant." The North Vietnamese counterattacked in both Cambodia and Laos, and the American-led invaders were routed. In Laos, retreating South Vietnamese troops dangled from helicopter skids trying to escape; American advisers reported wholesale desertions.

In Paris, several months of secret diplomacy between Kissinger and North Vietnam's Le Duc Tho stalled. Leaders in Hanoi, encouraged by the U.S. misadventure in Laos and Cambodia and already planning their own military offensive, insisted that Nguyen Van Thieu and his regime in Saigon must go. The

Nixon administration, however, saw Thieu's presidency as the symbol of South Vietnam's self-determination. Slow bargaining against the luxurious setting of Parisian restaurants and elegant townhouses could not unravel the basic puzzle: If Thieu stayed on, the war would continue; without Thieu and his political organization, South Vietnam would quickly fall under Communist control, for the NLF was its best-organized opposition force.

Both sides stepped up their search for a military solution. In late March 1972, North Vietnam attacked along a broad front, capturing An Loc, a gateway city only 30 miles from Saigon. Thieu's troops fell back on all fronts, and American air power failed to check the Communist ground advance. With many in the Pentagon again predicting humiliating defeat, Nixon resumed bombing raids in North Vietnam and Cambodia and ordered the navy to mine North Vietnam's harbors, a risky move that Lyndon Johnson had avoided for fear of damaging Soviet or Chinese ships and triggering superpower conflict. With this new escalation, few military targets remained untouched, and civilian casualties and the number of refugees mounted.

The violent spring and the upcoming U.S. election of 1972 at first spurred more diplomacy. Several weeks before the end of the presidential campaign, Kissinger announced another cease-fire. "Peace," he said, "is at hand." But as happened so often in the past, U.S. leaders still believed that their sophisticated military technology could bring victory. In mid-December 1972, Nixon ordered B-52s to bomb North Vietnam twenty-four hours a day "until they are ready to negotiate." Despite heavy losses, American bombers attacked North Vietnam's factories; destroyed rice fields; and damaged schools, hospitals, and other civilian facilities. This so-called Christmas attack was the heaviest aerial bombing in history. It caused an international uproar, brought protesters back to the streets of American cities, and sparked greater determination among antiwar members of Congress to end U.S. involvement in the Vietnam conflict.

The Christmas bombing marked the last desperate gasp of Nixon's military effort. In January 1973, the United States and North Vietnam signed the Paris Peace Accords, ending formal hostilities. Washington promised to withdraw its remaining 50,000 troops, dismantle its military installations, and deactivate mines in North Vietnam's harbors. Foreign troops were to leave Laos and Cambodia, but Hanoi's forces could stay "in place" in South Vietnam. North Vietnam agreed to release American prisoners of war and to cooperate in holding national elections in the South. The accords, however, did not bring peace, only a withdrawal of U.S. troops by March, 1973. The war between the Communist North and Thieu's government dragged on, 48,000 soldiers dying during the first eighteen months of the "cease-fire." By the summer of 1974, war had again returned to most of Indochina.

Meanwhile, Hanoi's military strategist, General Nguyen Giap, was organizing a coordinated assault for the spring of 1975. Disintegration and demoralization in the South aided his plans. Thieu arrested opponents, banned opposition political parties, and closed down most newspapers. To consolidate his military position and possibly frighten the United States into sending more military hardware, Thieu withdrew his armies from the three northern-most provinces of South Vietnam. But the planned retreat turned into a disorganized rout when Giap's troops took the opportunity to attack. Deprived of U.S. air support, South Vietnamese troops raced southward. The North Vietnamese

FIGURE 7–2   Leaving Vietnam.

American servicemen, former prisoners of war, cheer as they fly out of Hanoi.
Source: National Archives at College Park.

followed, scarcely having to fight, while hundreds of thousands of civilian
refugees crowded highways. Only at the gateway to Saigon itself, the provincial
capital of Xuan Loc, did the South Vietnamese army make a stand. Thieu's
regime collapsed, however, and the Communists overwhelmed the city in less
than a week. On May 1, North Vietnamese and NLF forces entered Saigon,
just as the last American officials were frantically escaping from the U.S. embassy by helicopter.

Face-saving maneuvers followed. Military airlifts flew over 100,000 South
Vietnamese, mostly people closely identified with the United States, to new
homes in America. Meanwhile, Kissinger and the new president, Gerald Ford,
tried to counter any adverse diplomatic and psychological consequences of
the Communist victory. Quietly reassuring allies in Western Europe, the secretary of state pledged that his country would never yield to "neo-isolation-
ists" at home. The administration also successfully blocked congressional efforts
to reduce the number of American soldiers stationed overseas and to pare
down military spending. To regain an image of diplomatic initiative, Kissinger
gave a green light to a CIA project to supply and bankroll friendly forces in the
Angolan civil war. America's intervention in Angola prompted large-scale Soviet and Cuban aid to the other side. When Congress discovered and terminated this CIA operation in Africa, a Soviet-backed faction came to power in
Angola.

In Cambodia, Lon Nol's U.S.-backed government succumbed to Communist Khmer Rouge forces under Pol Pot. In late May 1975, the new Khmer

Rouge regime seized an American merchant vessel, the *Mayaguez,* and imprisoned its crew for allegedly carrying contraband within Cambodia's territorial waters. President Ford, determined to flex American muscle and rebuild his sagging popularity at home, dispatched a naval task force and some 2,000 marines to rescue the 39-man crew. Critics denounced the gunboat diplomacy that cost America 38 dead and 50 wounded, but most Americans supported the president. Clearly, although the Communist victory in Vietnam may have marked the limits of American power, the Ford administration still wanted to demonstrate its worldwide reach.

The long struggle in Vietnam proved more costly than anyone had imagined. It provoked bitter divisions at home and ended the cold-war consensus of the post-World War II period. It also heightened the government's preoccupation with secrecy. The Watergate scandals and the revelations of CIA activities gave glimpses into the secret government that had expanded its reach during the war. At the international level, the war strained the U.S. balance of payments and built up pressure on the dollar. Defeat hurt the credibility of American commitments abroad, chipping away still more at the dollar's strength. Through Vietnam, Americans discovered the consequences of power used unwisely.

For many years after the war, Americans seemingly wanted to forget Vietnam. The idea that a small Asian nation could have, after a ten-year struggle, forced the retreat of the United States, a country at the pinnacle of its power, seemed almost beyond comprehension. Unlike the returning troops of World War II, Vietnam veterans were often shunned and their needs ignored. Even the government that had ordered them into combat tried to dodge its responsibility for the Agent Orange-related disorders that afflicted many veterans. Agent Orange was a deadly defoliant used to level the jungles in Vietnam. After a long court battle, during which it was revealed that the Dow Chemical Company and government officials had known in advance about the chemical's hazards, the government established a compensatory fund. But the amount of money set aside paled in comparison to the number of veterans afflicted, and the Department of Veteran Affairs consistently sought to limit the scope of coverage.

If slightly submerged for a time, however, domestic divisions over the war and nagging questions remained. Slowly, interest in the Vietnam War rekindled, and within a few years, a battle over how to interpret "the lessons" of the struggle emerged. Not surprisingly, these evaluations tended to reflect earlier positions on the war itself.

Former hawks continued to claim that the war could have been won. Some noted the lack of a government-censored media and charged that journalists had drained the American people of the will to persevere. Some complained that the war was lost in Washington by politicians who would not commit themselves to the military measures necessary for victory. Some blamed the antiwar movement and argued that defeat took place in the streets of America. Most of these analysts argued that the military itself was not at fault but was the victim of an unsupportive domestic milieu. Even within military ranks, though, disagreements developed. One line of military analysis suggested that the war was lost because the Pentagon emphasized counterinsurgency tactics rather than the kind of conventional warfare in which U.S. forces excelled.

Wartime doubters and dissenters expanded their case that the war came in the wrong place, at the wrong time, for the wrong reasons. They argued that Vietnam had held little strategic importance for the United States and that U.S. leaders had mistakenly made South Vietnam's fate into a symbol of American honor. The North, most argued, waged a "people's war," whereas Americans came to be seen as foreign invaders, the inheritors of a colonialist tradition. Some military strategists bolstered these arguments, insisting that victory could have no operational meaning in a struggle that required the destruction of a land and its people in order to win.

From the welter of arguments on all sides emerged a central point of agreement: In Vietnam, the goal of victory over the Communist North had not matched the means available to achieve it. Military leaders warned that they would never again become the tools of a no-win policy, and most Americans wanted no more engagements that demanded an expenditure of lives and treasure for a hazy goal and a problematic assessment of U.S. national interest. In short, the United States should more carefully weigh strategic advantages against costs and not simply assume omnipotence. Americans of all persuasions, whether they had been for or against the war, would warn against getting involved in "another Vietnam."

The Middle East and Latin America

As Americans disentangled themselves from Southeast Asia, the Middle East exploded in war. In the fall of 1973, on the Jewish holy day of Yom Kippur, Egypt and Syria attacked Israel, determined to regain the territory lost in the 1967 war. Bouyed by U.S. diplomatic support and large donations from American Jews, the Israelis first weathered the assault and then drove deeply into Arab territories. Anxious to defuse Arab-Israeli hostilities, Kissinger argued that the United States could best help Israel by facilitating negotiations. For nearly two years, he shuttled back and forth between Washington and the Middle East and eventually achieved a tentative settlement: Israel would pull back from part of the Sinai, and the United States would grant military aid to both Israel and Egypt. Best of all, according to Kissinger, this "shuttle diplomacy" eased the Soviets out of playing a role in Middle East settlements.

Kissinger's efforts to jockey for geopolitical advantage and reduce Soviet influence throughout the world translated into a simple formula: Support friends and punish enemies. In pursuing this policy, Kissinger did not worry much about the character of his friends' internal policies. His *realpolitik* held that America would support countries that provided a regional bulwark and were hospitable to American economic interests. Kissinger's grand design for world stability through strong strategic allies aligned U.S. global interests with some repressive dictators—Shah Reza Pahlevi in Iran, Park Chung-Hee in South Korea, Ferdinand Marcos in the Philippines, and the military leaders of Brazil. In Africa, Kissinger's so-called tar-baby report of 1969 concluded that black African insurgent movements were not "realistic or supportable" alternatives. The Nixon-Kissinger policy therefore continued to look primarily to the white, apartheid government in South Africa (which received 40 percent of U.S. investments in Africa) for stability in the region.

U.S. military assistance and training programs fed these dictatorships. Private foreign sales of American arms also skyrocketed, reaching $10 billion by the end of the Nixon presidency. Arms sales ameliorated America's serious balance-of-payments problems and contributed to short-term stability, but they encouraged more military dictatorships. In Latin America during the Nixon years, for example, Uruguay, Chile, and Argentina experienced coups that interrupted diverse traditions of civilian democracy and brought repressive U.S.-backed military dictatorships to power.

The case of Chile demonstrated the punitive measures the United States could employ against a regime that tried to pull out of its sphere of influence. In 1970, Salvador Allende, a Marxist, was elected president of Chile, a country with a strong tradition of civilian government and an apolitical military establishment. Greatly alarmed by Allende's campaign pledges to nationalize American-owned copper companies and move toward socialism, Nixon and Kissinger met with CIA chief Richard Helms, who emerged from the Oval Office with these notes:

> One in 10 chance perhaps, but save Chile!
> worth spending
> not concerned risks involved
> no involvement of Embassy
> $10,000,000 available, more if necessary
> full-time job—best men we have
> game plan
> make the economy scream
> 48 hours for plan of action

With an unlimited budget and full authority for any maneuver to "save Chile" from its elected ruler, the CIA first attempted to arrange a military coup to prevent Allende from taking office. This plan ran up against the Chilean military's traditions and thus, at that point, failed. CIA encouragement did, however, lead to the assassination of one of Chile's most respected generals, a man who had persistently opposed a military takeover. Next, Helms urged an economic offensive: The U.S. government ceased its aid to Chile; the World Bank cooperated by dropping Chile's credit rating; private banks suspended loans; and International Telephone and Telegraph (ITT) and American copper companies, which Allende had nationalized, worked tirelessly to promote his downfall. As chaos overtook the Chilean economy—Chile had huge foreign debts because of the large loans extended under JFK's Alliance for Progress—CIA dollars helped finance a trucker's strike that brought the distribution of goods to a halt. Shortages mounted, and the middle class increasingly blamed Allende. In 1973, the Chilean military finally decided to intervene. President Allende and thousands of his supporters died in a military coup, which installed a regime whose use of torture embarrassed many in the U.S. government. Over Kissinger's protest, Congress subsequently suspended aid, and after the new Chilean government managed to assassinate Allende's former ambassador to the United States, right on the streets of Washington, D.C., relations between the two countries broke down almost completely—at least on an official level. On a private level, however, U.S. enterprise and investments again flooded Chile, attracted by its iron-fisted stability.

THE CARTER PRESIDENCY

James Earl Carter, soon to be known around the globe as Jimmy, capitalized on the popular disenchantment with secretive intelligence agencies, Watergate-associated political corruption, and economic disarray. Emphasizing his rural roots, his born-again Christianity, and his lifelong distance from Washington, the naval commander-turned-peanut farmer promised voters that he would never sail a crooked ship of state. Beginning the 1976 race for the White House in 1973, the former governor of Georgia presented himself both as a plain person of the people—"a Southerner and an American . . . a farmer . . . a father and a husband, a Christian"—and as a skillful technocrat—"an engineer . . . a planner . . . a nuclear physicist." These diverse talents, he suggested, made him the ideal person to answer the "two basic and generic questions" facing the nation: "Can our government be honest, decent, open, fair, and compassionate? Can our government be competent?"

Jimmy Carter: Compassion and Competency?

Carter's meteoric rise was aided not only by his own talents but also by his staff's ability to operate in the new political climate. Popular disillusionment during the Vietnam and Watergate eras had contributed to a decline in party identification and in voter turnout, and the upheavals of the late 1960s and early 1970s had brought significant changes in the ways the two national parties, especially the Democrats, selected delegates to their national conventions. By 1976, local party machines and prominent party leaders had lost considerable clout. Carter's strategists realized that they could appeal directly to ordinary voters, either in person or through the media, and make an end run around party stalwarts. Thus, Carter outmaneuvered more established Democrats, most of whom could not match his energy (holding no political office, Carter could devote full time to campaigning) or his shrewd, young staff. Carter campaigned successfully for the Democratic nomination and then against Gerald Ford for the presidency as an honest political manager, someone who could balance both the nation's moral accounts and its national budget.

Another outsider with plenty of time to run for office, California's former Governor Ronald Reagan, almost snatched the GOP nod away from Gerald Ford, who was even less exciting as a candidate than as a president. Had Reagan only started a little sooner or had the GOP's electoral process been as democratized as that of the Democrats, Reagan might have pushed aside Ford and captured the Republican nomination in 1976.

The new political ground rules made Carter's victory over Ford in the November 1976 election seem the product of trends that expanded democracy. In 1968, it should be remembered, Lyndon Johnson had virtually handed the nomination over to Hubert Humphrey, and in 1972 George McGovern gained the nomination after winning only a handful of presidential primaries. In contrast, Jimmy Carter survived three years of caucus battles and primary fights—what one journalist aptly labeled a political marathon—before gaining the Democratic nomination. Thus, Carter owed relatively little to the traditional power brokers and a good deal to the "new politics" of the late 1960s.

Once anointed by the voters, Jimmy Carter still needed to win over powerful interest groups. The rules by which candidate Carter captured the presidential sweepstakes might have changed, but the larger political system in which President Carter had to govern remained the same. Carter owed his position to his direct appeal to voters, while traditional power-centers largely rooted in geography and economic interest, retained much influence in Congress. Carter soon found himself under sharp attack for his allegedly weak leadership, political naiveté, and inability to understand the complexities of Washington. Many of Carter's difficulties as president grew out of the unorthodox route by which he reached the White House and his self-proclaimed status as an outsider.

Economic Dilemmas

President Jimmy Carter's first domestic proposals sounded no clarion call for social justice but stressed managerial and technical issues—reorganization of the executive branch, streamlining of existing welfare programs, and new budgetary procedures. Confounded by sharply rising oil prices, the consequence of turmoil in the Middle East, Carter did talk about the energy crisis as "the moral equivalent of war," but his "wartime" strategy followed rather conventional paths. Most important, the Carter administration's plans assumed that the familiar *deus ex machina*—economic growth—could be restored and could provide, as it had in the past, a means of avoiding a direct confrontation with economic inequity. If, through the magic of new energy-producing technologies, the economic pie could once again expand, even the smallest slices would be bigger.

The Carter administration, however, was no more successful than the Nixon or Ford administrations in promoting real economic growth. Throughout the 1970s, under Republicans and Democrats, the American economy failed to perform as well as it had in the 1960s—or even in the 1940s and 1950s. Although the United States still produced more than any other country, the gap narrowed as America's economic productivity—its output per worker—grew more slowly than that of other industrial nations. Even Britain and Italy, countries with serious economic problems, could boast higher productivity rates than the United States in the 1970s and 1980s. At the same time that productivity languished, inflation flourished as energy prices pushed up the cost of everything. In 1979, the inflation rate was 14 percent; in 1980, it was pushing 20 percent. According to one study, a family of four that had earned $13,200 in 1970 would have required an income of more than $25,000 to maintain the same standard of living in 1980. Although the salaries of upper-income professionals tended to keep pace with inflation, most American workers suffered declines in their real income.

In trying to restore the health of the economy, there seemed no conventional wisdom to which Carter—or any president—could turn during the 1970s. The economist-social critic Herman Daly, for example, spoke for many advocates of the "small-is-beautiful" approach when he urged abandoning the traditional goal of economic growth in favor of a "steady-state economy," one that aimed at "sufficient wealth efficiently maintained and allocated, and equitably distributed—not maximum production." Other social critics also advocated

FIGURE 7–3   Gas Shortages, 1973.

Even suited businessmen looked for alternative transportation during the oil crises of the 1970s.
Source: David Falconer, EPA, National Archives at College Park.

major departures from the old, positive-state economic formulas. After surveying the growing pressures on the supplies of resources in the United States and in other nations, Richard J. Barnet predicted the onset of "the lean years." He urged greater government planning, reliance on "soft" rather than "hard" energy technologies (solar energy in preference to nuclear energy, for example), and greater democratization of the national and international marketplaces. Socialist writer Michael Harrington joined Barnet in condemning the misuse of power by the giant multinational corporations. In the age of monopoly capitalism, Harrington argued, unemployment, inflation, and a stagnant economy grew out of decisions first made in corporate boardrooms and then rubber-stamped by political leaders.

Other observers offered a much different analysis. According to neoconservative theoreticians such as Irving Kristol, traditional economists such as Milton Friedman, and representatives of large business corporations, economic problems could be traced back to the national government's interference in the marketplace and to "crushing" levels of taxation, especially on businesses. They blamed government deficits, unnecessary environmental and safety regulations, and the general burden of government-required paperwork for stifling economic growth. These conservative writers promised no easy solutions. They urged significant governmental deregulation and substantial tax cuts, measures calculated to stimulate the "supply side," that is, the productive infrastructure of the economy. They also called for tighter control over the money supply and a sharp reduction of government borrowing to finance deficits, which they claimed deprived private business of necessary loans for research and expansion. They insisted that their proposals were good not only for business but also for all citizens. Conservatives did not ignore the issue of economic justice; but the problems of inequality could only be addressed, they argued, by unleashing American capitalism.

Even the more conventional economists, to whom Carter ultimately turned, offered him a variety of approaches to the key problems of productivity and inflation. Although the president endorsed the Humphrey-Hawkins proposal, a 1978 law that pledged a reduction in unemployment to 4 percent by 1982, his economic advisers focused on fighting inflation. First, they bowed toward the arguments of the deregulators and sought to lower prices by ending federal regulatory structures, such as those in the transportation industry, that supposedly impeded competition. Although the Carter administration rejected a thoroughgoing system of wage and price controls, it announced voluntary wage and price guidelines. Finally, Carter and his economic aides pursued a policy of tightening credit (thus raising interest rates) and of cooling down the economy. Carter's monetary policies did drive down the inflation rate—although it still hovered near double-digit levels—but they also generated rising unemployment and increased social tension. By the summer of 1980, the nation had slid into a recession.

Equality, Affirmative Action, and the New Right

Throughout most of the nation's history, equality seemed to mean "equality of opportunity," the chance for every citizen to join in the race for individual success. The sweetest victories and the largest rewards, it was assumed, should go to those who ran the swiftest. But everyone should have a chance to get to the starting line, and no one should have to jump hurdles while their more favored competitors sailed along an obstacle-free track. Yet equality of opportunity, although much celebrated, remained elusive. Many people, especially women, African Americans, ethnic minorities, and homosexuals, were adversely stigmatized or never really got into the contest at all. A traditional blues song summarized the way many black people saw the great American race:

> If you're White, you're all right,
> If you're Brown, stick around,
> But if you're black, O' brother,
> Get back! Get back! Get Back!

Many of the political and legal battles of the 1960s and of the 1970s aimed at preventing people from being "moved back," at rehandicapping the race, and at removing old hurdles. Thus, the demands of the civil-rights movement involved the elimination of various obstacles, such as segregation laws and discriminatory hiring practices, that prevented some people from even entering the gates of national institutions. Similarly, women's groups had channeled their energies toward passage of the Equal Rights Amendment, an attempt to end gender discrimination through legal and constitutional change.

While the struggle to eliminate obstacles to equality of opportunity was still proceeding, the victories in this area began to change the perspective of many activists. As they looked at the race-for-success ideal, these "new egalitarians" began to argue that efforts to allow everyone to enter the race and to remove the old system of hurdles were not enough. Renewed commitment to the principle of equality of opportunity would probably not change the fact that only a few people were leading the race for economic success, that many people were bunched in the middle of the pack, and that a sizable portion had fallen permanently behind. In the distribution of both income and wealth, the United States in 1980 remained a very unequal society. At the top of the scale, 5 percent of the population received 20 percent of the nation's income and owned more than 50 percent of its wealth; the lowest 20 percent, in stark contrast, gained 3 percent of the income and held less than 0.5 percent of the wealth. According to these new egalitarians, such inequality of condition and of results meant that there were all sorts of subtle and hidden handicaps in the system.

If the United States were to be a truly just society, the new egalitarians argued, there must be vigorous "affirmative" action to achieve greater "equality of condition" rather than simply equality of opportunity. Not only should students of color and women, for example, be protected from discriminatory procedures that barred them from educational institutions, but affirmative action programs should also work to ensure their admittance and graduation. In the area of employment, proponents of affirmative action urged measures to ensure that women and persons of color were not simply interviewed but were then hired and promoted on an equal basis. Proof of substantial progress was increasingly measured by comparing the percentage of women and minorities in educational or business institutions with their percentage in the total population, a process that opponents of affirmative action condemned as inevitably leading to the institution of quotas.

Efforts to achieve equality for women raised special controversy because the structure of the American family became the issue. Proposals to expand government funding for day-care centers—necessities for most women who wanted both children and a job—angered those who claimed that the state should stay out of "private" matters and those who argued that more day-care facilities would only upset an already unstable family structure. In addition, most employers displayed little enthusiasm for such ideas as flexible work hours and job sharing, arrangements that might have benefitted both men and women who wanted families and careers.

The quest for greater equality of condition involved more than pressure for affirmative action and day-care programs in educational and corporate institutions. Looking at the gross inequality of wealth and income, many egalitarians argued that the nation needed to confront the issue of income redistribution more generally. After surveying the problem in *Inequality* (1971) and resurveying it in *Who Gets Ahead?* (1979), sociologist Christopher Jencks claimed that social science data proved that attempts to equalize people's "personal characteristics," especially their educational backgrounds, was an "unpromising way of equalizing incomes." If people truly wanted a different economic order, Jencks concluded, efforts to "redistribute income itself" offered the most effective strategy.

As George McGovern discovered during the 1972 presidential campaign, however, redistributive proposals were difficult to sell to voters. Although many of Richard Nixon's "silent majority" would have benefitted from McGovern's proposed changes in inheritance laws, for example, most voters saw his ideas as too radical. "They must think they're all going to win a lottery," complained McGovern. In fact, many people viewed redistribution with suspicion. It seemed to strike at deeply rooted commitments to private property and individualism. Public opinion polls taken in the late 1970s showed that people expressed considerable pessimism about the general economic situation but a striking optimism about their own prospects. Unlike affirmative action, which became widespread during the 1970s, redistribution of wealth never became a serious public policy goal.

Opposition to the new egalitarianism became an important principle of a broader conservative coalition, often called "the New Right," that emerged during the 1970s. This new phase in postwar conservatism built on the successes of the 1960s and early 1970s. (See Chapter 5.) Conservatives had mastered the latest media and organizational techniques; some celebrities, such as William F. Buckley and Milton Friedman, had become skilled TV performers; and right-leaning foundations had begun providing funding for television programming. Conservative fund-raisers had developed direct-mail appeals for donations and, in many ways, proved more innovative in political organizing than opponents to their left. Although many conservatives in the GOP had opposed the changes in campaign financing laws that grew out of Watergate, Republican-oriented pressure groups on the political right quickly grasped the subtleties of the new measures, especially the provision allowing unlimited spending by independent "political action committees" (PACS).

The New Right also broadened its intellectual base during the 1970s. A steady flow of prominent defectors from the Democratic ranks enlivened conservative causes. Some of these former Democrats, who became known as "neoconservatives," settled into research positions at right-leaning think tanks (such as the Heritage Foundation); others occupied newly funded chairs and programs at universities and smaller colleges; and most wrote for a variety of lively scholarly and popular journals.

Neoconservatives blended the old with the new. Espousing a varient of the anti-communism that had been forged during the early cold-war era, neoconservatives denounced familiar enemies—international communism, Marxism, domestic radicalism, and mass culture. Their favorite causes—political gradualism, enlightened capitalism, economic growth, and high culture—also had been the bedrock of their ideology during the period of Truman's Fair Deal. But the leftward drift of other Democrats and the emergence of a new cultural and political radicalism during the 1960s propelled many neoconservatives rightward during the 1970s. Norman Podhoretz, editor of *Commentary* magazine, proudly pointed out that, during the early 1960s, he had nurtured a number of authors who became associated with the counterculture and had broken ranks only after realizing the "sinister" implications of that movement. The counterculture, Podhoretz claimed, was still gaining ground during the 1970s, and sober intellectuals must take a firm stand against its "irrational" ideas and "dangerous" values.

Critical of what they considered a cowardly appeasement of communism overseas and a soft-headed tolerance of cultural and political radicalism at home, people like Podhoretz, Irving Kristol, Daniel Bell, and Nathan Glazer formed the intellectual core of neoconservatism. In addition to their own numerous publications, they helped to popularize an important body of conservative social-science literature, including the work of Edward Banfield and James Q. Wilson. The resulting battles between the neoconservatives' set of academic experts and those of the left were fierce. Many of the leading neoconservative theorists possessed backgrounds in both academia and journalism, and they combined these talents to produce sprightly polemics for *Commentary* and more scholarly pieces for *The Public Interest,* an influential periodical edited by Kristol and Glazer.

Neoconservatives saw the United States—indeed, Western civilization—entering a period of profound crisis, and the specter of the new egalitarianism frightened them almost as much as did the Soviet Union. Some neoconservatives were disturbed by the new efforts to achieve the traditional goal of equality of opportunity, at least when such equality was sought by militant feminists, cultural radicals, and homosexuals. Kristol and the political scientist Walter Berns, for example, endorsed more vigorous censorship of cultural materials, and Ernest van den Haag warned that the new militancy of gays and lesbians threatened traditional values based on heterosexuality.

The attack on the new egalitarianism, however, centered on what neoconservatives denounced as "equality of outcomes." Glazer condemned affirmative action as an insidious form of reverse discrimination, a doctrine that discriminated not simply against white males but also against all people of true merit. When applied to African Americans, the political scientist Robert Sasseen argued, affirmative action really affirmed an "arrogant contempt" for blacks: It disguised a "paternalistic policy" that consigned its purported beneficiaries to "perpetual inferiority" and to a life as "special wards of the state." Midge Decter denounced militant feminism as a revolutionary attack on motherhood, as a sign of deep-seated self-hatred, and as the manifestation of the "desperately nihilistic idea" that there were no "necessary differences between the sexes." Kristol blamed most of the controversy over equality on "an intelligentsia" that despised liberal capitalism and "that is so guilt-ridden at being implicated in the life of the society that it is inclined to find even collective suicide preferable to the status quo."

The struggle over the meaning of equality was not, of course, limited to rhetorical clashes. The egalitarian currents of the 1960s and 1970s, as wary neoconservatives recognized, touched most areas of public life, especially educational and corporate institutions. Did affirmative action programs that tried to fill a specified number of classroom seats or jobs with certain minorities constitute reverse discrimination against others who claimed they were more deserving of the places on the basis of their individual merit? Should, for instance, students of color be admitted to a law school when whites with higher test scores were rejected? (Such questions became especially difficult and emotional when the persons rejected came from ethnic groups, such as Jewish- and Italian-Americans, who had once suffered from discrimination themselves.)

The controversy over affirmative action and reverse discrimination raged throughout the 1970s, and the U.S. Supreme Court finally entered the fray. In the much-discussed *Bakke* case of 1978, a deeply divided court struck down a plan that set aside a certain quota of seats at a California medical school for "minority" applicants. More significantly, however, a majority of justices also indicated that they were not willing to invalidate all affirmative action programs. The

Court upheld a private plan devised by Kaiser Aluminum to upgrade the positions of minority workers and approved a congressional requirement that 10 percent of all contracts awarded under a public-works program would go to "minority business enterprises."

The nation's economic difficulties and the sharp debates over how to advance equality contributed to the volatile political climate. In 1976, Carter had exploited the popular distrust of political institutions; as president, he became the victim, rather than the beneficiary, of popular cynicism about government. Moreover, in charting his political course, he had to deal with shifts in the structure of both political parties. Watergate had marked merely a momentary downturn for the GOP. As the Republican party regrouped behind Ronald Reagan and its conservative wing gained more power, the Democratic party splintered into even more factions than it had in the late 1960s. Carter and his strategists had successfully built their own electoral machine, but many Democrats expressed little enthusiasm for Carter's record in either foreign or domestic affairs.

Carter's Foreign Policy

Jimmy Carter's promise to encourage respect for human rights in international affairs won him votes during his campaign but, ultimately, brought him trouble as president. Forming alliances with hated despots, Carter had argued, was neither morally right nor strategically sensible. Once America abandoned its image as a benevolent power, he claimed, it lost its major strength in international affairs and its most powerful weapon in the cold war.

This human rights policy, however, proved difficult to effect. President Carter appointed a full-time officer to oversee implementation of the policy, supported the weighing of human rights records in granting foreign aid, and stopped America's role as a supplier of instruments of torture, but these abrupt changes could not help but affect America's global position. Quietly, Carter quickly assured many of America's dictator-allies that U.S. national security commitments would continue to take precedence over their internal conduct. Thus, the pro-American dictatorships in Iran, South Korea, and the Philippines experienced few punitive measures under the new human rights policy, but they did feel increasing pressure to ease up on the most flagrant violations. Other repressive regimes, such as Chile and Argentina, felt the new administration's disapproval much more dramatically.

As Carter's critics had predicted, the human rights policy gave heart to popular liberation movements in several countries and contributed to especially perplexing dilemmas over American policies toward Nicaragua and Iran. Popular uprisings swept the governments of Anastasio Somoza in Nicaragua and Shah Reza Pahlevi in Iran out of power in 1979. Despite severe pressure from domestic Republican allies of both regimes, the Carter administration, after a few attempts at compromise solutions, did not intervene to save the despots. After so many years of profiting from a close alliance with dictators in both countries, however, the United States might not have expected the new governments to be friendly. In Nicaragua, the new regime, headed by the revolutionary Sandinista movement, increasingly adopted a Marxist orientation antagonistic to the United States. In Iran, Carter faced an even more difficult situation that ultimately proved to be his administration's undoing.

After the shah's ouster, a long-exiled religious leader, the Ayatollah Khomeini, established an Islamic Republic dedicated to wiping out American influences. In late 1979, a group of Islamic revolutionaries entered the compound of the U.S. embassy and seized about sixty Americans. The Iranian government demanded custody of the shah, whom the Carter administration had allowed into the United States to undergo medical treatment for cancer, in exchange for the release of the hostages. Khomeini also talked of gaining possession of the shah's personal fortune and of placing some of the American hostages on trial for spying, using evidence captured in the embassy takeover. Despite the shah's departure from the United States and various attempts at mediation, U.S.-Iranian relations worsened. Iran cut off oil shipments to the United States; the American government froze Iranian assets, instituted full economic pressure against the ayatollah's regime, and attempted—against the advice of Secretary of State Cyrus Vance—an unsuccessful military mission to rescue the hostages. In this climate of extreme tension, even the shah's death in the summer of 1980 did not bring swift release of the hostages. Carter later recalled that the hostage crisis, which preoccupied the last 444 days of his presidency, "was a gnawing away at your guts. No matter what else happened, it was always there." He met with the families of the hostages and took responsibility for their plight.

Carter came under immense criticism at home. Many Americans across the country tied yellow ribbons to trees to symbolize the hostages' plight. The ABC television network began a nightly news program called "America Held Hostage." In the wake of Vietnam, the Iranian crisis seemed to be one more example of American weakness, and Jimmy Carter received the blame. Finally, in a frantic round of diplomacy in the closing days of the Carter administration, a deal was struck: freedom for the hostages was promised in exchange for the unfreezing of Iranian assets in the United States. The hostages returned home shortly after the inauguration of President Ronald Reagan. Some officials in the Carter administration charged that Reagan's advisers had worked to delay any earlier release of hostages, which might have helped Carter in the 1980 election; Reagan officials denied the charges. Whatever the political complexities of the release, however, relations between the United States and Iran remained poor, and Carter's opponents had successfully identified the president with weakness and failure.

Despite difficulties, President Carter's human rights emphasis redressed the previous drift of American policy and began to encourage the forces of democratization that would sweep Latin America in the late 1970s and 1980s, especially the return to civilian rule in Ecuador, Peru, Brazil, Argentina, and Uruguay. Carter also engineered rapprochement with black Africa. UN Ambassador Andrew Young, a black veteran of civil-rights struggles in the South, gained Africans' trust as had few high-ranking Americans before him. Although Young was forced to resign in 1979 after he lied to the State Department about engaging in talks with representatives of the Palestine Liberation Organization (PLO), a group with which the State Department had forbade dealings, the new look in African policy continued. For example, President Carter stood behind British efforts to force the white minority government in Rhodesia (Zimbabwe) to effect a peaceful transition to black rule, a transition that signaled the end of an important bastion of white rule in Africa.

Unlike the human rights policy, many of Carter's major foreign-policy achievements—in Panama, the Middle East, and China—were based on the prior initiatives of his Republican predecessors.

In September 1977, the United States and Panama signed two treaties covering the ownership, operation, and defense of the Panama Canal. U.S. control over the Canal Zone, a strip of 550 square miles slicing through the middle of Panama, had caused bitter resentment for years and brought serious riots in 1964. Denounced in Latin America and throughout the Third World for still holding this land acquired in the days of territory-grabbing imperialism, the United States under President Lyndon Johnson committed itself in 1965 to the negotiation of a new treaty. Talks took place over the next thirteen years. After heated debate and a full application of arm-twisting by Carter, the Senate ratified the new treaties in 1978. Under their terms, the Canal Zone ceased to exist, and Panama assumed general jurisdiction; the United States retained primary responsibility for operating and defending the canal until the year 2000 but with ever-increasing Panamanian participation; and Panama agreed that the canal should be permanently neutral—open to all vessels with no discrimination on tolls. In addition, Panama would receive a share of canal revenues and a substantial commitment of American loans.

Although critics charged that the treaties represented a rollback of America's strength, the Carter administration stressed that the aging canal was no longer the economic and strategic lifeline it had once been. Moreover, ratification would deflate anti-American sentiment in Latin America, a goal of growing importance to Carter's negotiators, as Mexico, Ecuador, and Peru were discovering new fields of petroleum.

Fresh from the battle over the Panama treaties, President Carter turned his full attention to the Middle East. Kissinger's efforts at shuttle diplomacy between Tel Aviv and Cairo had stalled after the breakthrough on partial Israeli withdrawal from the Sinai Peninsula in 1975, but Egypt's president, Anwar Sadat, surprised the world by traveling to Jerusalem. Sadat's visit to Israel indicated the economic exhaustion that ongoing confrontation had brought to both Egypt and Israel. The time again seemed right for diplomatic progress. For thirteen days in 1978, Carter, Israeli Prime Minister Menachem Begin, and Anwar Sadat remained in near isolation at the presidential retreat at Camp David, Maryland. Carter personally mastered the minutiae of issues under dispute, developed personal rapport with Sadat, and parried Begin's lawyerlike argumentation. When the leaders emerged for TV cameras, they issued an emotional three-way statement that outlined the beginnings of a negotiating process, subsequently ratified by treaty. Carter had defied all conventional wisdom that predicted failure.

The Camp David agreements provided only a framework, not the substance, of a settlement. The most difficult issue—the future of the West Bank and Gaza—remained unresolved. Israel categorically forbade any official participation by the PLO in the negotiations, even though it was the major representative of the Arab Palestinians in the West Bank and Gaza. The PLO and most Arab states charged that Sadat had negotiated matters that were not his to negotiate. The split within the Arab world widened as Israeli-Egyptian divisions narrowed. Optimists, nevertheless, argued that the importance of the 1979 agreements lay in the momentum of negotiation. Clearly, the Egyptian-Israeli peace firmly established U.S. hegemony and eliminated Soviet influence in Egypt. Carter, like Nixon, had dangled the large carrots of American aid and more arms sales to both parties.

Carter's diplomacy with China had less ambiguous results. On January 1, 1979, the United States and the People's Republic of China established formal relations, and over the next year they signed a number of cultural, scientific, and economic agreements. A joint economic committee worked to enhance trade, and the United States zoomed up to fourth place among China's trading partners. The new technocrats who succeeded to Chinese leadership after the death of Mao were bent on accelerating economic growth by borrowing from the capitalist West, and the lure of the China market once again enthralled the American business community.

Renewing the Cold War

Toward the end of 1979, the counselor for the State Department summarized the general view that had initially guided the Carter administration's foreign policy worldwide: "It is not a sign of weakness to recognize that we alone cannot dictate events elsewhere. It is rather a sign of American maturity in a complex world." Carter could immerse himself in the details of foreign policy but proved less adept in projecting an overall direction. His speeches seemed didactic, not inspirational, and he instinctively avoided evocative slogans. Negotiation, compromise, and greater attention to human rights marked Carter's early foreign policy, but an emphasis on complexity and specific context could be seen as lack of vision and strength.

External events and political pressures at home gradually led Carter to revise his foreign-policy emphasis. By 1978, policymakers talked more of larger military spending and cold-war dangers. Then in December 1979, the Soviet Union invaded Afghanistan. The Soviet action, the first armed Soviet invasion since the incursion into Czechoslovakia in 1968, probably reflected the Soviets' fear of a unified Islamic movement and their desire to solidify their shaky sphere of influence in Afghanistan. Coming at a time when Americans were exceedingly nervous about the security of Middle Eastern oil supplies because of the Iranian revolution, the Soviet invasion touched off feverish cold-war rhetoric reminiscent of the 1950s.

Critics of Carter's foreign policy denounced America's presumed weakness and clamored for a response. The Carter administration warned Americans that overreaction was as dangerous as underreaction but announced reprisals against the Soviets. Carter ordered a halt to exports of grain and high technology to the Soviet Union, began to arm Pakistan, publicly highlighted a trip to China by his secretary of defense, organized a boycott of the Olympic Games held in Moscow in the summer of 1980, withdrew the SALT treaty from the Senate, and reinstituted registration for a military draft. Despite such measures—the strongest response possible short of some type of military action—more and more Americans began to charge that Carter had presided over an erosion of American power that had opened the way for Soviet action. Neoconservative groups such as the Committee on the Present Danger pointed to signs of America's weakness: the shah's ouster in Iran, the Soviet-Cuban presence in Africa, the growing power of Soviet-aligned Vietnam in Southeast Asia, and revolutionary ferment in the Caribbean. The promise of rebuilding U.S. power became the theme of Ronald Reagan's presidential campaign of 1980, as a public opinion poll showed that 82 percent of respondents disapproved of Carter's handling of foreign policy.

Carter saw the political perils. Afghanistan, he said, shattered his previous illusions about Soviet behavior, and he promised to lead the nation in more forceful directions. A rift grew between Secretary of State Cyrus Vance, who believed more in detente and the negotiating process, and National Security Adviser Zbigniew Brzezinski, who harbored a deep distrust of the Soviets. When Carter ordered an ill-fated military mission to rescue the hostages in Iran (whose lengthening captivity had become a major political liability), the secretary of state resigned his post. Vance indicated that he was out of sympathy not only with what he considered a rash and risky military incursion into Iran but also with the new confrontational policy in general. With Republicans goading the administration about a weak defense, Carter complemented cold-war rhetoric with promises to revitalize America's strategic posture. He began refurbishing military bases throughout the world; he increased defense spending and promised more emphasis on high-technology weapons systems (satellites and lasers); and he backed a new controversial and costly missile system called the MX. His advisers even began to blur the traditional distinctions between nuclear and conventional military action, leaving the Soviets to speculate publicly that the United States no longer considered limited nuclear strikes unthinkable.

Although the new cold warriors drew alarming pictures of an expansionist Soviet Union, the Soviets were themselves feeling embattled. Suffering major economic problems, threatened by growing dissent at home, and wary of a resurgent and hostile China, Soviet leaders also faced a decline in geopolitical power. Kissinger and Carter had both outmaneuvered the Soviets in the Middle East and effectively excluded them from influence in that area. Signs of discontent in Eastern Europe—especially a successful strike by Polish workers in August 1980—highlighted strains within the Warsaw Pact.

If both American and Soviet leaders felt increasingly insecure about their global roles in the early 1980s, it was partly because much of the rest of the world was beginning to loosen the grip of bipolar alliances and to build more independent power blocs. The movement of nonaligned nations; OPEC; the Committee of 77, which represented the poorer countries in the Southern Hemisphere; the new power of Islam; the economic prowess of Japan; and a variety of regional pacts all illustrated the growing intricacy of world politics. As Americans grew worried about the taking of hostages and about Soviet moves, they feared their power was in retreat. Jimmy Carter, never charismatic in projecting either foreign or domestic messages, got the blame.

The Election of 1980

Confidence in Carter's leadership, as measured by various public opinion surveys, steadily plummeted. By the time of the Democratic convention in August 1980, only 23 percent of the Gallup Poll's sample thought the president was doing a good job. Carter's showing was even more dismal than that of Harry Truman during his final months in office or that of Richard Nixon during the dog days of Watergate.

Yet Carter amazed most political pundits and recaptured the Democratic nomination. As the nation's commander-in-chief, he ironically gained some support as a result of his own foreign-policy moves. With Iranians occupying the American embassy in Teheran and the Soviets invading Afghanistan, many Democrats rallied around their leader, even when his policies—such as admitting the shah of Iran into the United States—had contributed to some of his difficulties. Carter also benefitted from the liabilities of his major Democratic rival, Senator Edward Kennedy of Massachusetts. Kennedy's own personal problems dominated the media while he was an active candidate, and many Democrats, pollsters discovered, distrusted Kennedy more than they disliked Carter. Finally, Carter effectively (ruthlessly, claimed the Kennedy camp) used federal patronage to build local ties. Although the White House lacked clear strategies for meeting domestic ills, it did dispense federal grants, both large and small, to Democratic mayors and governors. Thus, the Democratic National Convention of 1980 unenthusiastically renominated a candidate, Jimmy Carter, who seemed a sure loser in November.

Election day proved to be a disaster for Carter and a serious setback for the Democratic party. The GOP's ticket of Ronald Reagan and George H. Bush carried forty-four states, including most of those in Carter's native South, and captured 486 electoral votes. (Independent candidate John Anderson gained 7 percent of the popular tally but failed to win any electoral votes.) The GOP gained twelve Senate seats, taking control of that body for the first time since 1954, and also picked up thirty-three seats in the House. Reagan and Bush cut into almost all of the traditionally Democratic voting blocs, especially union members and white ethnic voters. According to one survey, 25 percent of normally Democratic voters supported Reagan. The oldest person ever elected to the presidency (Reagan was only a few months short of seventy on November 4, 1980), the former governor of California even out-polled Carter among voters under thirty years of age.

In many other ways, the result of the presidential race represented more of a repudiation of Jimmy Carter than an affirmation of Ronald Reagan. Nearly half of the eligible voters did not vote for any presidential candidate, so Reagan's 51 percent of the popular vote gave him the support of little more than one-quarter of the potential electorate. Still, Reagan's Republican party showed that it had recovered from Richard Nixon and Watergate. It would continue to rebuild on the basis of the new conservative agenda.

Reagan and his inner circle of wealthy advisers came to Washington to reverse the domestic political trends that had dominated the postwar political era. In contrast to Carter, for example, Reagan pledged not to reorganize government agencies but to dismantle at least some of them. His secretary of interior promised to ignore environmental "extremists," and Budget Director David Stockman suggested that most government welfare programs should be eliminated. A master of political symbols, Ronald Reagan immediately won rave reviews for presidential image making. The lavish inaugural proceedings—generously sprinkled with designer gowns, sleek limousines, and Reagan's old Hollywood friends—recalled the early splendor of the Kennedy administration; Reagan's speeches, which called for rebuilding the American dream, suggested the self-confident optimism of Franklin Roosevelt; and the president's narrow escape from an assassin's bullet only a few months after taking office, placed him in the fearless western mold of John Wayne, a pop-culture icon often invoked by Reagan himself. With Reagan's great skills as a symbolic communicator presiding over the nation, conservative supporters hoped the cold war would be reinvigorated and talk of a new egalitarianism would be a remnant of the past.

ASSESSING THE 1970s

Despite numerous attempts to offer a comprehensive historical vision of the 1970s, scholars have come to emphasize very different facets of this complex decade. To some, it exuded a spirit of aimlessness in both public and private life. In a much-debated report prepared for the Trilateral Commission, political scientist Samuel Huntington linked this spirit to a "failure of leadership" that ultimately stemmed from "an excess of democracy." The egalitarian demands of the late 1960s and 1970s, in this neoconservative analysis, overburdened both the political and the economic systems.

Other observers also detected a sense of aimlessness but drew different conclusions. Finding a proliferation of "personal-growth" therapies, a spirit of self-absorption, and an apparent retreat from social concern among young people, Tom Wolfe (in a generally positive analysis) called the 1970s the "me decade." Pointing to similar trends, but interpreting the theme in a much less positive way, historian Christopher Lasch saw the 1970s as dominated by a "culture of narcissism."

Yet even Lasch, one of the decade's bitterest critics, could point to more positive themes as well, including a remarkable growth of community-based self-help movements. Looking back on the "splendid decade," William Braden of the *Chicago Sun-Times* called the 1970s a time of "grass-roots revival." In small ways, often far from the glare of the national media, the "me decade" may have produced as much, if not more, ferment for social change as the 1960s.

Great Society programs had encouraged ordinary citizens to participate in community projects. Some of these efforts, such as attempts to gain community control of neighborhood schools, failed to topple centralized bureaucracies, but other local efforts met with limited, sometimes even striking, success. Local arts programs contributed to a grassroots cultural revival reminiscent of the 1930s. Neighborhood clinics, legal-aid offices, and recreational and counseling services became regular features of everyday life during the 1970s. Meanwhile, community organizing developed broader goals and spread to all parts of the country and ideological spectrum.

In a dialectical process, the growth of outsized institutions and the age's economic instability encouraged local counterresponses. In a trend thoroughly representative of the decade's complex reaction to oversized institutions, small group homes, in which people who were mentally or physically challenged could be helped in a community and family setting, came to offer alternatives to the large mental-health facilities of the oversized medical establishment.

Many different groups participated in this decade's grassroots approach to social change. Some African Americans, for example, found it difficult to maintain, let alone expand on, the economic gains of the late 1960s and early

1970s. In 1978, there were twice as many blacks out of work as a decade earlier. The same year, the median income of African Americans stood at only 55 percent of the median income of whites, the same percentage as in 1965, the year LBJ unveiled his Great Society. The concentration of African Americans in decaying parts of central cities became even more intensive. By the late 1970s, more than half of the nation's black population lived in the oldest, job-starved portions of the inner cities. Meanwhile, the national black organizations and their white allies found it difficult to get significant new help from the federal government. Consequently, many concluded that the most effective strategy involved a return to their own communities and a renewed effort to develop localized institutions and a spirit of self-help. Jesse Jackson, the mercurial leader of Operation PUSH, headed one such movement in Chicago; Detroit became another city in which local organizations grew significantly; and a black-owned news service provided an alternative information network for small African American newspapers across the country.

Members of other ethnic groups adopted similar grassroots strategies. During the late 1970s, increased immigration and high birthrates swelled the Hispanic population—largely Mexican American and Puerto Rican—to about 6 percent of the nation's total. Without significant help from Washington or from local governments, many Hispanics turned to community-based institutions. Cesar Chavez continued to be the most charismatic Mexican American leader, especially in rural areas, but others, such as Ernie Cortes of Los Angeles' United Neighborhood Organizations, worked to organize urban communities, often relying on the resources and personnel of the Catholic church. American Indian leaders also eased away from dramatic clashes with white authorities, placing a new emphasis on self-sufficiency. White ethnics also mobilized through development of local neighborhood associations. According to one estimate, there were literally millions of such grassroots, self-help organizations that flourished in the 1970s.

Moreover, ferment went beyond ethnicity. Older Americans, one of the country's fastest-growing interest groups, banded together to make "gray power" a reality. Feminist groups formed collectives that attempted to restructure everything from women's health care to literary forms to small-business organizations. Some blue-collar workers organized to demand more control over their job sites, and some tried to take over plants that were being abandoned by large corporations and run them as employee-owned ventures. Consumer cooperatives also flourished. In response to pressure from cooperative supporters, in 1978 Congress created the National Consumer Cooperative Bank, a special institution that could provide loans to this new form of grassroots enterprise.

What was the larger significance of all these grassroots self-help movements? Given the political fragmentation of the 1970s, many answers were close at hand. Advocates of local activism saw such movements as tangible signs of a "new citizenship." At the backyard and neighborhood levels, people seemed ready and willing to reassert control over their lives and supplant big government, big business, and other established institutions of power. Such movements, their celebrants proclaimed, heralded the birth of new forms of community and a "new populist" spirit.

Other analysts and even participants in such movements were not so sanguine. They worried that individual organizations tended to focus on single issues and to ignore a larger vision of the entire nation's future. The successful effort by the gray-power lobby to extend the mandatory retirement age to seventy, for instance, only seemed to place another hurdle in the paths of younger women and minority workers. Similarly, pressures to raise Social Security benefits for the elderly resulted in Congress placing new tax burdens on current wage-earners. Some political observers complained that single-issue pressure groups only further fragmented the political process. In the western states, American Indian groups hesitated to cooperate with ranchers and farmers, longtime enemies, in a common stand on environmental and energy issues. Similarly, organizations of blacks and white ethnics traditionally drew a good deal of their individual energies from antagonistic rather than cooperative relationships.

Highly publicized taxpayer revolts of the late 1970s highlighted the ambiguous nature of grassroots campaigns. Gaining momentum after Californians enacted Proposition 13 (a 1978 measure that drastically cut state property taxes) and marching behind neopopulist attacks on big government, tax-cut activists advocated proposals that often adversely affected low-income people who faced cutbacks in public services. Although tax-cut proponents claimed they were simply using a grassroots democratic process to fight what they considered inequitably apportioned taxes and unresponsive government bureaucracies, the tax revolt illustrated the wider consequences of single-issue activism. In the context of the fragmented politics of the 1970s, much of the tax cutting failed to translate into any broader idea of community.

Ronald Reagan, with his individualistic vision of a new capitalism, seemed a major beneficiary of the 1970s impulse toward localism and self-help. Distrust of government institutions, especially at the national level, allowed Reagan's supporters to argue against extending, and even for dismantling, social-welfare and regulatory programs. Although many social activists continued to see local community organizing and grassroots action as the best path toward social change, the ascendancy of Reaganism at the national level would change the ways in which political and social issues would be defined during the 1980s.

SUGGESTED READING

Garry Wills, *Nixon Agonistes* (rev. ed., 1980) remains a good single-volume introduction to Richard Nixon and his place in postwar political culture. More recent entries in the Nixon bookshelf include Bruce Odes, ed., *From the President: Richard Nixon's Secret Files* (1989); Stephen Ambrose, *Nixon: The Triumph of a Politician, 1962–1972* (1989); Roger Morris, *Richard Milhous Nixon: The Rise of an American Politician* (1990); Herbert Parmet, *Richard Nixon and His America* (1990); Jonathan Aiken, *Richard Nixon: A Life* (1993); Joan Hoff, *Nixon Reconsidered* (1994); Allen J. Matusow, *Nixon's Economy: Booms, Busts, Dollars, and Votes* (1998); Melvin Small, *The Presidency of Richard Nixon* (1999); Anthony Summers, *The Arrogance of Power: The Secret World of Richard Nixon* (2000); Irwin F. Gellman, *The Contender: Richard Nixon: The Congress Years, 1946–1952* (1999); and Richard Reeves, *President Nixon: Alone in the White House* (2001).

On Watergate and the broader ethos of secret government, see Peter Schrag, *Test of Loyalty: Daniel Ellsberg and the Rituals of Secret Government* (1974); Theodore White, *Breach of Faith: The Fall of Richard Nixon* (1975); Athan Theoharis, *Spying on Americans: Political Surveillance from Hoover to the Huston Plan*

(1978); Frank J. Donner, *The Age of Surveillance: The Aims and Methods of America's Surveillance System* (1980); L. H. LaRue, *Political Discourse: A Case Study of the Watergate Affair* (1988); Stanley I. Kutler, *The Wars of Watergate: The Last Crisis of Richard Nixon* (1990) and *Abuse of Power* (1997); Michael Schudson, *Watergate in American Memory: How We Remember, Forget, and Reconstruct the Past* (1992); and Bob Woodward, *Shadow: Five Presidents and the Legacy of Watergate* (1999).

On the brief Ford presidency, see Edward L. and Frederick H. Schapsmeier, *Gerald R. Ford's Date With Destiny: A Political Biography* (1989); James Cannon, *Time and Chance: Gerald Ford's Appointment with History* (1994); John R. Greene, *The Presidency of Gerald R. Ford* (1995); and John F. Guilmartin Jr., *A Very Short War: The Mayaguez and the Battle of Koh Tang* (1995). Henry Kissinger, who directed Ford's foreign policy, offers his perspective in *Years of Renewal* (1999).

On the Carter years, see Burton I. Kaufman, *The Presidency of James Earl Carter Jr.* (1993); Betty Glad, *Jimmy Carter: In Search of the Great White House* (1980); Erwin C. Hargrove, *Jimmy Carter as President* (1988); Garland Haas, *Jimmy Carter and the Politics of Frustration* (1992); Kenneth Morris, *Jimmy Carter: American Moralist* (1996); and Anthony S. Campagna, *Economic Policy in the Carter Administration* (1995). Carter's own reminiscences are entitled *Keeping Faith* (1982). See also Charles O. Jones, *The Trusteeship Presidency: Jimmy Carter and the United States Congress* (1988); Herbert D. Rosenbaum and Alexej Ugrinsky, eds., *The Presidency and Domestic Policies of Jimmy Carter* (1994); Gary M. Fink and Hugh Davis Graham, eds., *The Carter Presidency: Policy Choices in the Post-New Deal Era* (1998). Douglas Brinkley, *The Unfinished Presidency: Jimmy Carter's Journey beyond the White House* (1998) discusses the post-presidential years.

On international issues during Nixon's and Carter's presidencies, see Paul Kennedy, *The Rise and Fall of the Great Powers: Economic Change and Military Conflict from 1500 to 2000* (1987); Walter LaFeber, *The Panama Canal* (1979) and *Inevitable Revolutions: The United States in Central America* (1983); Paul Sigmund, *The Overthrow of Allende* (1977); John Stockwell, *In Search of Enemies* (1979); Barry Rubin, *Paved with Good Intentions: The American Experience with Iran* (1980); Garry Sick, *All Fall Down: America's Tragic Encounter with Iran* (1986); Franz Shurmann, *The Foreign Politics of Richard Nixon: The Grand Design* (1987); Jeffrey Kimball, *Nixon's Vietnam War* (1998); William Bundy, *A Tangled Web: The Making of Foreign Policy in the Nixon Presidency* (1998); Penny Lernoux, *Cry of the People* (1980); Raymond Garthoff, *Detente and Confrontation: American-Soviet Relations from Nixon to Reagan* (1985); Gaddis Smith, *Morality, Reason, and Power: American Diplomacy in the Carter Years* (1986) and *The Last Years of the Monroe Doctrine, 1945–1993* (1994); Herbert D. Rosenbaum and Alexej Ugrinsky, eds. *Jimmy Carter: Foreign Policy and Post-Presidential Years* (1994); Richard C. Thornton, *The Carter Years: Toward a New Global Order* (1991); David Skidmore, *Reversing Course: Carter's Foreign Policy, Domestic Politics, and the Failure of Reform* (1996); Timothy P. Maga, *The World of Jimmy Carter: U.S. Foreign Policy, 1977–1981* (1994); Joanna Spear, *Carter and Arms: Implementing the Carter Administration's Arms Transfer Restraint Policy* (1995); John Dumbrell, *American Foreign Policy: Carter to Clinton* (1996); Robert A. Strong, *Working in the World: Jimmy Carter and the Making of American Foreign Policy* (2000); and Robert A. Pastor, *Whirlpool: U.S. Foreign Policy Toward Latin America and the Caribbean* (1992).

In addition to works cited earlier on the 1970s, especially Bruce Shulman's book, see Peter Caroll, *It Seemed Like Nothing Happened* (1983), a general history of the entire decade; Harry C. Boyte, *The Backyard Revolution* (1980); Thomas Ferguson and Joel Rogers, *The Hidden Election* (1981); Walter Dean Burnham, *The Current Crisis in American Politics* (1982); Martin P. Wattenberg, *The Decline of American Political Parties* (1984); Gillian Peele, *Revival and Reaction: The Right in Contemporary America* (1984); Theodore Lowi, *The Personal President* (1985); Mark E. Kann, *Middle-Class Radicalism in Santa Monica* (1986); and Thomas Ferguson and Joel Rogers, *Right Turn: The Decline of the Democrats and the Future of American Politics* (1987).

On the battle over the new equality, see Christopher Jencks, *Who Gets Ahead* (1979); Paul Blumberg, *Inequality in an Age of Decline* (1980); Lars Osberg, *Economic Inequality in the United States* (1984); Philip Green, *Retrieving Democracy* (1985); Charles Harr, *Fairness and Justice: Law in the Service of Equality* (1987); Jay MacLeod, *Ain't No Makin' It: Leveled Aspirations in a Low-Income Neighborhood* (1987); Peter L. Berger, *Capitalism and Equality in America* (1987); Nathan Glazer, *Affirmative Discrimination: Ethnic Inequality and Public Policy* (rev. ed., 1987); Kenneth L. Karst, *Belonging to America: Equal Citizenship and the Constitution* (1989); Sara Evans and Barbara J. Nelson, *Wage Justice: Comparable Worth and the Paradox of Technocratic Reform* (1989); Irvin Solomon, *Feminism and Black Activism in Contemporary America* (1989); Karen Hansen and Ilene Philipson, eds., *Women, Class, and the Feminist Imagination* (1990); David Allyn, *Make Love Not War: The Sexual Revolution: An Unfettered History* (2000); Iris Marion Young, *Justice and the Politics of Difference* (1990); Martha Minow, *Making All the Difference: Inclusion, Exclusion, and American Law* (1990); Herbert Hill and James E. Jones, Jr., *Race in America: The Struggle for Equality* (1993); Howard Kohn, *We Had a Dream: A Tale of the Struggle for Integration in America* (1998); Stephen Steinberg, *Turning Back: The Retreat from Racial Justice in American Thought and Policy* (1995); Howard Ball, *The Bakke Case: Race, Education, and Affirmative Action* (2000); and Clara E. Rodriguez, *Changing Race: Latinos, the Census, and the History of Ethnicity in the United States* (2000).

8

An Oversized Society Life during the 1960s and 1970s

The 1960s and 1970s brought significant growth in the scale of American economic and social institutions. President Lyndon Johnson symbolized the trend: He drove too fast; he threw gargantuan barbecues; and in one well-publicized incident, he pulled his dog's ears until the puppy yelped. Restraint seemed a quality of the past. The era throbbed with raw power and extremes. U.S. involvement in Vietnam seemed to escalate uncontrollably; both Johnson and Nixon roared at their critics; business conglomerates expanded rapidly; football replaced baseball as the national sport; and some rock singers, with the assistance of "speed" or other drugs, grew old before they turned thirty. The 1970 census reported that three of every ten homes had more than one TV set and that only three of every hundred had no television at all. The Post Office, assisted by the introduction of zip-code numbers and electronic equipment, delivered a yearly average of 400 pieces of mail to every man, woman, and child. Book publishers issued more than 35,000 titles annually, double the number put out just ten years earlier. According to one study, the average American threw away four pounds of garbage per day, and the nationwide total amounted to 150 million tons a year—enough refuse to fill three lines of garbage trucks extending from New York to Los Angeles and enough potential energy to light the United States for an entire year.

Many people found the change in the scale and pace of life bewildering. Who could understand a trillion-dollar economy, trace lines of responsibility through the sprawling federal bureaucracy, or gain redress from an impersonal, computerized corporation? As Americans experienced the ways in which computerization, more rapid communications, and greater population mobility changed their lives and culture, journalists tried to label the trend. Alvin

Toffler's best-selling book coined the popular phrase "future shock"; Kirkpatrick Sale argued that American life was losing its "human scale."

THE ECONOMY: A GATHERING OF GIANTS

In his farewell address of 1961, President Dwight Eisenhower warned of a permanent, government-supported weapons industry. No longer, he explained, did Americans mobilize civilian industries for war and reconvert them after the peace. Cold-war pressures had kept the economy on a perpetual war footing and had created "a permanent armaments industry of vast proportions." The old general—whose own administration had done little to halt this trend—now warned that "we annually spend on military security more than the net income of all United States corporations" and that this military-industrial complex held the "potential for the disastrous rise of misplaced power."

The Military-Industrial Complex

This military-industrial complex expanded during the 1960s. The national security structure consisted, at the top, of politicians, military personnel, business contractors, and university researchers and, at the bottom, of workers in defense industries. All of these groups were mutually dependent. Government grants for research and development constituted a significant portion of a major university's operating revenue; huge corporations, such as General Dynamics and Lockheed, depended almost exclusively on government contracts; in 1968, nearly 70 percent of defense spending went to the nation's top one hundred companies. If the air force wanted a new plane, then Boeing Aircraft wanted a lucrative contract, and the people of the Pacific Northwest wanted more jobs. Taxpayers who shouldered the bill had little control over spiraling costs, for few could evaluate the need for a new weapons system. Foreign policy was a beneficiary as well a benefactor: Without this complex of research, industry, and manpower, the United States could not have pursued a globalist vision of national security, which in the postwar years required large-scale and high-tech military capabilities. The Pentagon directed the largest planned economic system outside of the Soviet Union.

The end of the Vietnam War in 1975 brought little decrease in military production. Profits for defense industries had become sufficiently important that the administration of Richard Nixon sought new customers abroad. During the 1970s, U.S. arms sales to foreigners boomed, providing one of the few bright spots in a dreary picture of deteriorating trade balances. There were always customers for arms—always friends, such as the shah of Iran and the generals in Brazil, eager to beef up their military establishments. Between 1972 and 1978, the shah purchased nearly $20 billion worth of military equipment from the United States. For the United States, arms sales supposedly brought two blessings—profits and the development of strongly militarized allies who could police their particular region and relieve the United States of direct involvement in fighting Communist insurgencies.

Arms sales helped to produce the rising level of violence throughout the world. Countries in Southeast Asia, the Middle East, Latin America, and finally Africa began to engage in mini-arms races. As sophisticated weaponry saturated the world, the toll of death and destruction from regional rivalries and

Year	Spending (in billions)	Percent GDP
1945	$717	34.5%
1950	$114	4.3%
1955	$285	8.9%
1960	$273	8.0%
1965	$264	6.7%
1970	$339	7.6%
1975	$241	5.4%
1980	$245	4.9%
1985	$331	5.9%
1990	$355	5.1%
1995	$282	3.6%
2000	$270	2.9%

FIGURE 8–1 Defense Spending.

Defense spending (in 1996 dollars) and as a percent of gross domestic product, 1945–2000.
Source: Pentagon.

civil wars increased immeasurably. Even President Jimmy Carter, who had promised during his 1976 presidential campaign to curtail arms sales and encourage human rights abroad, proved unwilling to accept the consequences of canceled arms contracts, reduced exports, and discontented allies. The flow of weapons from the United States continued unabated during the Carter years, changing not its volume but only its channels. After the shah's ouster in 1979, for example, the advanced weaponry that would have been sold to Iran found buyers in Israel, Egypt, and elsewhere. In January 1980, Carter approved production of America's first armament manufactured solely for export, the FX fighter plane.

Brisk military spending also continued at home. One might have expected that a period marked by the end of conflict in Vietnam and by arms limitation talks (SALT) with the Soviets would have dampened the arms race, but the reverse was true. Expenditures in Vietnam, the Pentagon claimed, had delayed modernization, and the military had accumulated a backlog on its wish list. The lengthy SALT negotiations, which produced an interim agreement called SALT I in 1972 and the more comprehensive accord, SALT II, in 1979, actually spurred military rivalry, as both sides hurried to develop new weapons that could be traded off for concessions from the other side.

The space program—which depended on the interrelationship of university research, government funding, and industrial production—was also a child of the 1960s. Shortly after the Soviet Union launched its first Sputnik satellite in 1957, Congress had created the National Aeronautics and Space Administration (NASA), and in 1961 President Kennedy committed the nation to landing an American on the moon by 1970. The space program—often compared to the Manhattan Project, which had developed the atomic bomb during World War II—mobilized scientific and technical bureaucracies for a crash (and ultimately successful) effort to surpass the Soviet Union in space exploration. On July 20, 1969, NASA fulfilled Kennedy's promise. Neil Armstrong and Edwin ("Buzz") Aldrin planted an American flag on the moon's surface and scooped up forty-seven pounds of lunar rocks to bring back for study. More space missions followed.

Critics complained about the expense of the space program (which some called a "moon-doggle") and compared it to the building of ancient Egypt's

FIGURE 8–2   Astronaut's Leg, Foot and Footprint in Lunar Soil, 1969.

NASA developed a special lunar surface camera to document the first landing of Americans on the moon, a major goal of three presidents during the 1960s.
Source: National Archives and Records Administration, Records of the U.S. Information Agency. Photo by Neil Armstrong.

pyramids, a feat of much grandeur but little practicality. They pointed to the economic progress Japan was making by directing its research and development efforts into products that would do well in foreign markets. The space program, they argued, helped to direct U.S. efforts toward channels ultimately detrimental to its balance of trade. In order to counter such charges, NASA stressed the spin-offs of space research for civilians, such as heart pacemakers and miniature electronic components. Orbiting satellites helped to revolutionize the communication industry and to solidify U.S. domination of world radio and TV transmission.

Government-financed military research accelerated other new developments, especially in the electronics and computer industries, that transformed American life. The Pentagon considered innovation in computer hardware essential to its global anti-Communist mission. The computer became part of both the military's defensive capabilities, when used to detect Soviet missile launches, and its new offensive operations. Computer-assisted technologies for military purposes were refined during the war in Vietnam. The Internet, which would revolutionize communications during the 1990s, began from a government-funded experiment to link together scientists working on defense projects.

Business Giants

The infusion of government money into the economy during the 1960s, together with a rising level of consumer spending, helped to promote rapid business expansion and consolidation. Corporate expansion seemed the key to greater profits, and the fastest way to grow was to merge with or purchase other firms. By the late 1960s, the 200 largest U.S. companies controlled 58 percent of all manufacturing assets in the nation, and further centralization of economic power was accelerating.

The "conglomerate" was the business innovation of the era. Conglomerates rapidly bought up a variety of unrelated industries, to minimize overall economic risk by diversifying their holdings. Gulf and Western and Transamerica Corporation, two of the most dynamic conglomerates of the 1960s, acquired companies as fast as they could find them. In their heyday, before their business model proved unwieldy, they owned Hollywood studios, auto-parts distributorships, land-development corporations, insurance companies, and sports arenas.

As U.S. enterprise expanded at home, it also moved into other countries at a pace that astonished and alarmed many foreigners. A variety of incentives encouraged this globalizing trend: cheaper labor, lower interest rates, favorable tax laws, and proximity to new markets and raw materials. IBM, for example, provided 70 percent of all computers in the non-Communist world and maintained research labs in most of the developed nations; Standard Oil of New Jersey drilled and distributed oil throughout the globe; Coca-Cola sold one-half of its beverages outside the United States; and Pepsi-Cola, the traditional rival of Coke, inched its way into the usually closed markets of the Soviet Union. These global companies propelled an unparalleled outflow of U.S. investment dollars into the world.

U.S. agriculture also became, more than ever before, a multinational enterprise. Although the number of people living on U.S. farms continued to decline, the production of agricultural products, aided by increased mechanization and by new seed technologies, continued to increase. Giant "agribusinesses," such as The Cargill Company and Archer-Daniels-Midland, came to dominate the world's grain market and worked closely with agencies of the U.S. government. The U.S. rice industry, which had accounted for little more than 5 percent of world sales in 1955, controlled 20 percent of the world market in 1970.

The financial power of these multinational companies often exceeded that of the nation in which they operated. One official for the American Agency for International Development (AID) reported in the late 1960s that if the gross national products of nations were ranked with the gross annual sales of corporations, half of the top hundred would be corporations and two-thirds of these would be American-based. During the 1970s, other multinational competitors, especially Japanese companies, began to challenge U.S. enterprises, and the globalization of the world economy continued to accelerate.

Rapid business growth and new technologies changed the way Americans themselves lived. Demand for natural materials, such as wood, wool, cotton, and natural rubber, declined relative to artificial substitutes—plastics, acrylic fibers, and synthetic rubber. In 1968, the quantity of synthetic fibers surpassed the output of natural fibers. All kinds of new products flooded the marketplace. During the 1960s, drug and grocery stores stocked 6,000 new products every year; the rate for the introduction of new items nearly doubled during the 1970s. More than half of the items stocked by supermarkets in the 1970s did not even exist in 1960, and nearly half of the products available in 1960 had been withdrawn from the marketplace a decade later. Stiff competition for the buyer's dollar often made packaging and advertising more important than a product's content. Critics of the highly competitive breakfast food industry, for example, claimed that the quality of some cereals was so low that the flashy packages had more nutritional value than the overprocessed grain inside. The list of new products grew so rapidly that finding an unused brand name could be a problem. Some large companies set their computers to work providing printouts of letter combinations that sounded attractive—Exxon and Pringles were two of the results.

Entrepreneurs devised new marketing methods. During the 1960s, independently owned and operated businesses saw customers turning to large chain or franchise operations that offered greater volume at lower prices. What McDonald's did for hamburgers, Holiday Inn did for travel, K-Mart for retailing, and 7-Eleven for neighborhood groceries. Every city of any size had a "strip" nearly identical to that of every other: a string of discount stores, supermarkets, and fast-food chains. Shopping became easier when the Bank of America introduced Bank Americard (renamed Visa). This new credit card, quickly imitated by large New York banks, tempted customers to spend and borrow more and channeled large amounts of consumer purchasing through a few large financial institutions.

During the 1970s, many of the old industrial-age companies, such as the Big Three automakers and U.S. Steel, faced stiff foreign competition, especially from Japan. Newer sectors, however, boomed. Demand accelerated for consultants of all sorts; cable television became a major industry; aircraft manufacturing flourished; and sporting goods and leisure companies chalked up large gains. (In 1979, American joggers spent $400 million on running shoes and warm-up suits.) Challenging supermarkets as the source for family meals, fast-food chains also continued their growth. McDonald's alone established 4,000 new outlets during the 1970s.

The rapid rise of the computer industry symbolized this new era of growth. During most of the 1960s, IBM's giant "mainframe" computers, which were generally leased rather than sold to customers, dominated the industry. Everything from police records to life-support systems in hospitals to word-processing equipment in corporate offices began to be plugged into computer networks. Banks of file cabinets could be replaced with computerized records, while the file clerk gave way to someone trained in the new field of data entry. Perfection of the silicon chip, a tiny microprocessor that for $10 could do the work of a $100,000 computer, revolutionized electronics, opening the way for such new products as computerized cash registers and video games.

In time, most sectors of the U.S. economy entered the computer age. Continued innovations in the semi-conductor and silicon chip industries, spearheaded by new corporations such as Texas Instruments and Intel, brought smaller computers into the marketplace during the 1970s. In 1977, Apple Computer Company, an upstart competitor to IBM, introduced the first, mass-marketed personal unit for both business and home use. Meanwhile, two young entrepreneurs, Bill Gates and Paul Allen, were helping to develop new computer software that became the basis for the Microsoft empire (the company was formed in 1975) and its MS-DOS operating system.

Energy and Ecology

This breakaway economic growth strained resources and the environment. In 1970, according to one calculation, Americans constituted less than 6 percent of the human race but used 40 percent of the resources consumed worldwide each year and produced 50 percent of the physical pollution.

Inexpensive sources of energy fueled postwar economic growth. Gasoline consumption rose from 1 billion barrels in 1950 to 2.25 billion barrels in 1971; the production of electricity increased 500 percent between 1950 and 1971. By 1979, the United States was using 18.4 million barrels of oil a day, nearly half of which was imported; it was consuming nearly 30 percent of all the oil produced in the world.

New products were energy-thirsty. Aluminum, for example, an excellent substitute for steel and tin in certain cases, was dubbed "congealed electricity" because of the enormous amount of energy required to produce it. The United States processed twenty times more aluminum in 1971 than it had before World War II, and each year production figures climbed higher. Aluminum cans, aluminum pipe, aluminum siding, all treasured for their light weight and noncorrosiveness, contributed to the pressure on the environment.

Where would people find the energy required to fuel their economy in the future? Advocates of unrestricted domestic development of energy sources had some answers. Increased strip mining and relaxation of environmental regulations would enhance the nation's ability to use its enormous coal deposits. Accelerated oil drilling in offshore beds would bring new supplies hitherto blocked by environmental safeguards. Development of atomic power plants would increase America's energy self-sufficiency.

Environmental groups questioned many of these plans. In April 1970, environmentalists staged Earth Day, a carnival-like extravaganza designed to encourage the nationwide concern that civil-rights and antiwar causes had generated during the 1960s. Subsequently, scientists such as Barry Commoner, author of *The Closing Circle,* became popular on the college-lecture circuit. Commoner warned that, beyond a certain point, damage to ecological systems was irreversible. The obsession with careless material growth, he argued, was already beginning to strain the environment to the breaking point. Commoner and others popularized the word "ecology," the natural balance necessary to sustain life on this planet, and helped move the science of ecology to the center of a new environmental movement.

Toward the end of the 1970s, environmental groups increasingly focused on the issue of nuclear power. Ralph Nader and other activists argued that atomic power plants presented unacceptable risks, and the "antinuke" movement received a boost from the popularity of a film about a nuclear meltdown, *The China Syndrome* (1978). Just when the power industry was ridiculing the "implausible" premise of this reel-life drama, a real-life incident during the spring of 1979 ignited a fierce debate over the use of nuclear energy.

A malfunctioning reactor at Three Mile Island, near Harrisburg, Pennsylvania, threatened to become a major disaster. Residents living close to the facility evacuated their homes, and the confusion and conflicting reports during the following several days increased public doubt about the nuclear industry's ability to contain its potentially lethal technology. According to the industry's supporters, the incident at Three Mile Island proved that the ultimate disaster, a total meltdown, could be avoided and that even a fairly serious accident could be contained. Critics, however, pointed out the lack of established safety procedures, highlighted the escape of radiation into the surrounding atmosphere and water, and calculated the huge costs of cleanup. Subsequent reports by a special presidential commission and the Nuclear Regulatory Commission (NRC) criticized the nuclear power industry. The NRC's investigation concluded that without "fundamental changes" in the nuclear industry, "similar accidents—perhaps with the potentially serious consequences that were avoided at Three Mile Island—are likely to recur." The projected expense from new designs, more elaborate safety procedures, and lawsuits exploded claims that nuclear energy would be cheap and safe. In the wake of the Three Mile Island incident, the all-out rush to switch to nuclear energy sources slowed and then stopped.

Most people were coming to agree that the United States needed a comprehensive energy policy. But what kind? Environmentalists favored federally assisted programs to encourage decentralized production of power through solar, geothermal, or wind-generated systems. Ralph Nader and Barry Commoner argued that the energy debate involved fundamental issues of economic control, pitting decentralized, "democratic" energy sources against those that utility and oil companies could continue to monopolize and run from a centralized facility. Critics of the Nader-Commoner position, however, dismissed solar, geothermal, and wind power to be, at best, marginal sources that simply could not satisfy the nation's need for energy. They urged Washington to ease environmental regulations and open some long-delayed offshore oil developments; they continued to tout coal, synthetic fuels, and nuclear power.

Nearly everyone favored conservation. Tax breaks encouraged home weatherization; utility companies began to dispense advice on the most efficient use of energy; and consumers responded to higher prices by changing their own living patterns. Consumption of crude oil fell from 7.15 million barrels in 1979 to 6.8 million in 1980.

Environmentalists and industrialists continually clashed over the issue of pollution. The material goods that people consumed bore ecological price tags—brownish skies, strangely colored rivers, drying lakes, persistent respiratory problems, and a sharply rising cancer rate. Urban areas suffered most visibly during the 1960s; breathing New York's air for a day, one study reported, was the equivalent of smoking four packs of cigarettes. Strip mining, which doubled during the 1960s, raised the specter of the permanent destruction of land. Pro-business pressure groups and political conservatives tried to make environmentalism a dirty word. Affluent environmentalists, it was charged, opposed the economic development that would allow middle-class people to maintain their present living standard and the less affluent to improve their lives. Industrialists and their supporters emphasized two other points: Stringent regulations would put an even greater stress on America's apparently dwindling energy reserves by making it difficult to use high-pollution fuels, such as coal; and

Major Environmental Legislation, 1969–1980

National Environmental Policy Act of 1969	Required environmental impact statements
Clean Air Act of 1970	Set national air quality standards
Clean Water Act of 1972	Set national water quality goals
Federal Environmental Pesticides Control Act of 1972	Required registration of pesticides
Marine Protection Act of 1972	Regulated dumping of waste into oceans and coastal waters
Coastal Zone Management Act of 1972	Authorized federal grants to states to develop coastal zone management plans
Endangered Species Act of 1973	Protected all "threatened" and "endangered" species
Safe Drinking Water Act of 1974	Set standards on quality of drinking water
Toxic Substances Control Act of 1976	Allowed the EPA to regulate dangerous chemicals
Federal Land Policy and Management Act of 1976	Provided for management of public lands
Resource Conservation and Recovery Act of 1976	Regulated hazardous wastes
National Forest Management Act of 1976	Set standards for management of national forests
Surface Mining Control and Reclamation Act of 1977	Established environmental controls over strip mining
Alaska National Interest Lands Conservation Act of 1980	Protected 102 million acres of Alaskan land
Comprehensive Environmental Response Act of 1980	Authorized federal government to clean up "superfund" dump sites

FIGURE 8–3   Major Environmental Legislation, 1969–1980.

A remarkable number of environmental protection laws passed during the 1970s, sparking ongoing debates over the wisdom and consequences of federal regulation.
Source: Adapted from *Environmental Policy in the 1990s,* ed. Norman J. Vig and Michael Kraft (Washington, D.C.: Congressional Quarterly Press, 1990).

the cost of meeting tough environmental standards would make domestic industry uncompetitive with foreign enterprises. Environmentalists, they charged, were impractical; it was impossible to live in a risk-free society.

The government's Environmental Protection Agency (EPA) tried to steer a middle course. Established in 1970, it became Washington's largest regulatory body, employing 10,000 people and striving to enforce a host of new statutes enacted by Congress. Environmental legislation enacted during the 1970s aimed at limiting the use of pesticides; protecting endangered species of birds, animals, and fish; tightening occupational safety standards in the workplace; controlling strip-mining practices; and reducing the emission of chemical and bacteriological pollutants into the air and water.

The EPA came under sharp attack from both industrialists and environmentalists. Industry charged it with obstructing its operations and raising costs for consumers; environmentalists assailed it for too often relaxing enforcement of environmental regulations. Still, the EPA's efforts did help to improve safety in the workplace, to dissipate much of the urban smog of the 1960s, and to clean up many of the nation's waterways.

In the late 1970s new issues emerged. Requiring taller smokestacks on coal-burning plants, for example, helped eliminate urban smog but also elevated the pollutants, spread them over wider areas, and altered their chemical composition. The resultant "acid rain," which threatened croplands miles away from the smokestack source, constituted a less visible but more serious hazard than smog. Moreover, scientists began to warn about the long-term effects that industrial production might have on the global atmosphere. The depletion of the world's ozone layer portended new health hazards, and the threat of global warming raised the specter of dramatic changes in climatological patterns.

The safe disposal of toxic wastes presented another problem. People began to discover that many industries had, for years, haphazardly dumped toxic chemical wastes, some of which were capable of promoting genetic defects and cancer. Sometimes these dumps became landfill for housing projects, as was the case at Love Canal in upstate New York. Toxic effects were usually not immediately apparent. Any increased rate in environmentally caused cancer, for example, might take twenty years to detect. If the 1970s had been an "environmental decade" of new concern and legislation, the additional problems that environmentalists uncovered seemed far more complex than those that had sparked the first Earth Day in 1970.

Land and Real Estate Hustlers

A new boom in land use that began during the mid-1960s added to the concerns of environmentalists. Aggressive entrepreneurs began subdividing tracts at a rapid rate, creating more suburbs and freeways. They focused on the Sun-Belt states of Florida, California, New Mexico, and Arizona but also operated in ones that offered recreational opportunities, such as Colorado, Montana, and Maine. By the early 1970s, developers in California were buying 50,000 to 100,000 acres a year; subdivided land near Albuquerque, New Mexico, was projected to hold a population four times the size of Baltimore; and plots for sale in Colorado would have increased the state's population five times over. Many development corporations, such as the Del Webb Company that built Sun City, Arizona, created attractive planned communities with good sanitary facilities, nearby employment opportunities, and attractive recreation areas. Others simply bought large tracts of cheap land and resold it in expensive, lot-sized packages. A company in Florida, for example, purchased some swampy land for

FIGURE 8–4 Ramps to Nowhere.

As new freeways gobbled up both urban and rural land, they boosted the growth of suburbs but damaged inter-city neighborhoods.
Source: Robert Peterson.

$180 an acre and quickly resold it for $640 an acre. In order to reap this enormous profit, the company did not drain the land, build roads, or plan sanitation facilities. Instead, it hired a high-pressure sales force, ran advertisements around the country, and gave the supposed community a fancy name. In North Carolina, two people were charged with mail fraud after allegedly trying to sell over 60,000 acres of the Great Smoky Mountain National Park.

During the 1970s, the land boom expanded to the nation's central cities as conditions seemed to portend an "urban renaissance." Rising gasoline prices boosted the price of commuting to distant suburbs; the large baby-boom generation was straining the suburban housing market; nostalgia was helping to generate interest in the renovation of older houses; and a temporary decline in the crime rate boosted the image of cities. The new pollution standards made urban air bearable again, and cities also benefited from the demise of some dirty, industrial-age jobs and the rise of clean, service occupations. By 1980, for example, the largest single employer in the "steel city" of Pittsburgh was not U.S. Steel but the University of Pittsburgh. Although New York City and Cleveland hit the headlines for walking the tightrope of bankruptcy during the 1970s, many other cities found that federal revenue-sharing funds temporarily gave them a surplus. In 1969, few cities received more than 10 percent of their general revenue in the form of federal money; by 1980, many received over 50 percent in federal funds.

Such conditions encouraged urban revitalization in parts of most U.S. cities. Developers once devoted to mapping out suburban shopping centers began designing urban malls, and renovators swarmed over any edifice with a brick facade still standing. Prices shot up as speculators quickly acquired an interest in promoting historical preservation. Condominiums, a form of residential living that became popular during the 1970s, attracted young professionals and retirees who wanted the advantages of home ownership without the disadvantages of keeping up a single-family dwelling.

This process of "gentrification"—the return of the more affluent to the inner city—had its flip side. Revitalization was, after all, highly selective. "Old towns" of new-old cobblestone streets and tourist-oriented businesses might flourish where the architecture was interesting and sound, but the subsequent rise in property values and rental rates displaced low-income residents from these neighborhoods. Where were people in need of affordable housing to go? Speculators began to realize that even nongentrified areas experienced a boom in prices and brought easy profits. For people trying to get by on low, and even moderate, incomes, the inner-city renewal of the 1970s was often something to oppose and organize against. It brought rising prices, physical disruption, and the fragmentation of older communities. Most city officials, however, were slow to see the adverse results of gentrification; they were delighted by the new activity and continued to promote plans for joining public and private capital in developmental projects aimed at affluent residents and the highly courted tourist trade. The land and real estate hustlers of this era contributed to both the advantages and disadvantages of increased population mobility.

AN OUT-SIZED CULTURE

The Publishing Industry

The publishing industry, once the comfortable preserve of gentlemen-editors and small booksellers, grew and changed along with the rest of the economy. By the mid-1970s, for the first time since the early days of the silent cinema, the number of bookstores in the United States surpassed the number of movie theaters. The yearly revenues of the publishing industry even temporarily outstripped those of Hollywood. By the end of the decade, people were buying twice as many books each year as movie tickets. Although small bookstores still held their fascination, most people shopped in streamlined book supermarkets. Large-scale operations, such as the B. Dalton chain, dominated sales figures. Using their own computerized systems, book supermarkets discounted mass-market paperbacks and hardbacks from the bestseller lists, and aimed for a brisk, steady turnover. Such a sales system threatened the survival of many small bookstores and made it more difficult for readers to find shops willing to stock, or even order, volumes that lacked mass appeal.

As a consequence of the general consolidation of American business, most publishers became subsidiaries of large corporations, often "communications groups" that included newspapers, electronic media, and record companies. Some publishers conceded that before making a final commitment to publish a book, they weighed the author's potential appeal on TV talk shows. The publisher of the best-selling *Your Erroneous Zones* recalled that he had been more enthusiastic about the TV personality of the author, Dr. Wayne Dyer, than about his book. A model "media package" might span the entire communications spectrum: There could be a network TV miniseries for the domestic market, a theatrical movie for distribution overseas, a record album of the sound track, and a mass-market paperback for drugstore racks and large bookstore chains.

Veterans of the literary establishment condemned such trends. Publishing, they conceded, had never been a purely philanthropic enterprise, but never had it been so crassly commercial. The metamorphosis of the highly prestigious National Book Awards—prizes selected by prominent literary critics and by celebrated authors—into the American Book Awards—which were to be chosen by committees that included mass-market publishers and individuals from the bookstore chains—symbolized the new developments.

Similar trends affected journalism. The newspaper business, continuing a pattern that had been evident for more than half a century, became increasingly concentrated. By 1980, readers in only the largest cities could turn to competing daily papers. Financial pressures forced some papers to fold, including the widely acclaimed Chicago *Daily News,* and many more, especially in smaller cities, became the property of large newspaper chains. Although not every chain imposed a uniform editorial policy on its papers, fewer hands were coming to wield the power of the press. As a result, critics complained, journalists were becoming too complacent and, lacking competition, found little incentive to dig out fresh material on local affairs. Reluctance to probe into the dark corners of public and business life reflected the close, interlocking relationships between newspapers and powerful local interests.

Critics of the press also noted an intensification of "celebrity journalism." Newspapers, especially those that followed the tabloid tradition, had long featured stories about prominent personalities. However, in response to a media environment in which most people were using television as their primary source of information, newspapers increasingly emphasized features on popular culture, living styles, and prominent celebrities. Celebrity journalism also spawned new magazine ventures, including the very successful *People,* which was devoted to the rise and fall of celebrities and was distributed only at magazine counters and supermarket racks.

Although consolidation and celebrification reflected dominant trends in publishing during the 1960s and 1970s, other forces were at work as well. Many of the publications that had dominated magazine journalism during the 1940s and 1950s by pursuing a general, family-oriented readership—such as *Look, The Saturday Evening Post,* and *Life*—either folded or underwent drastic overhauls during the 1960s and 1970s. Meanwhile, more specialized journals of opinion— such as the *National Review* on the political right and *The Nation* on the left— gained circulation and prestige. This kind of specialized publishing expanded in other areas. *Sports Illustrated,* which had made its debut during the 1950s, became increasingly profitable during the next two decades and provided the model for publications that targeted a particular audience.

Even in the newspaper business, some diversity survived. Most of the countercultural papers of the 1960s, including the famous *Berkeley Barb,* disappeared, but alternative journalism sometimes took root in the form of community-based newspapers and entertainment-oriented weeklies. The going was always rough for these publications, but many journalists, especially younger ones who could not find other jobs in a glutted market, were willing to make the sacrifice. In some cases, these smaller papers provided the kind of critical, investigative reporting that the larger dailies hesitated to pursue.

The political polarization and fragmentation of cold-war orthodoxies during the 1960s and 1970s sparked considerable public debate over the role of media. Many journalists liked to think that criticism by the media, especially of the Vietnam War and the Nixon administration, contributed to a healthy, critical spirit in public life. People who believed in the war and Richard Nixon's brand of conservatism, however, charged that left-leaning journalists systematically distorted coverage of public events. Antiwar forces and Nixon's opponents, by contrast, often saw the media as too slow to challenge people in power and too reliant on government-generated briefings. Meanwhile, the entire publishing industry came under greater scrutiny by specialized, watch-dog publications such as the *Columbia Journalism Review*. The growing scrutiny, from all sides, of the publishing industry stood in stark contrast to the smug complacency that had prevailed during the early cold-war era of the 1940s and 1950s.

The Motion Picture Industry

Significant changes also affected the motion picture industry during the 1960s and 1970s. For more than four decades, filmmaking and the huge Hollywood movie factories had been synonymous. Using their sprawling back lots and deploying vast armies of stars and contract players, the major studios nourished the dreams of millions of moviegoers. Young men dueled alongside Errol Flynn or Clark Gable; women floated through the glamorous world of Barbara Stanwyck or Lana Turner. During the 1950s and early 1960s, however, the giant studios transformed their operations. Challenged by television and other competitors for entertainment dollars, Hollywood's box-office receipts declined steadily. Seeking to reduce production costs and to bring new realism to the screen, many filmmakers abandoned the Hollywood sets and shot on location, often outside the United States. By the late 1960s, most of the old stars of Hollywood's golden age had either died, retired, or switched to cameo roles; their heirs apparent, stars of the late 1950s such as Rock Hudson and Doris Day, discovered that their names alone no longer guaranteed a film's financial success.

By the mid-1960s, filmmakers had found new audiences, especially among young people, with movies that were very different from the classics of Hollywood's studio era. Consciously working against Hollywood's standard promilitary frame, Stanley Kubrick populated the national defense establishment with morons and lunatics in *Dr. Strangelove* (1963); he later explored the mystical science fiction of Arthur C. Clarke in *2001: A Space Oddysey* (1968) and looked at the issues of violence and behavior modification in *A Clockwork Orange* (1972). While traditionalists denounced new films such as these, movie executives recognized that films aimed at the family audience rarely made money. The box-office success of Dennis Hopper's *Easy Rider* (1969), an inexpensively made film about two hippies who used a drug sale to finance a motorcycle trip across the southwestern United States, wove together many themes of this "new Hollywood"—social criticism, sex, and violence—and inspired a number of (much less successful) films about the counterculture, including the documentary *Woodstock* (1970). Meanwhile, African American directors offered a highly successful series of pictures, derided by critics as "blaxploitation" films, set in violence-filled, corporate-controlled, inner-city neighborhoods, the kinds of places through which Gene Kelly had danced in films of the late 1940s and early 1950s.

Perhaps the most interesting series of films to span the late 1960s and the entire decade of the 1970s focused on an oversized society of burgeoning institutions and increasingly powerless individuals. The result, in the words of one historian, was a cinema of loneliness and alienation. Many of these same films also rebelled against the old genres, the tight forms—such as the war movie or the western film—that had marked Hollywood's classic studio system. Robert Altman's *M*A*S*H* (1970) mocked the standard war picture, and his *McCabe and Mrs. Miller* (1968) and *Buffalo Bill and the Indians* (1976) debunked the historical images in which Hollywood's western films had long been grounded. In *The Long Goodbye* (1973), Altman portrayed Philip Marlowe, the detective hero who had been played by Humphrey Bogart in *The Big Sleep* (1946), as a confused loser, a patsy who could not even find his own cat. Going even further, Francis Ford Coppola's *The Conversation* (1974) offered a chilling, almost despairing view of a culture based on surveillance.

Although some of these films gained more support from critics than from ticket-buyers, many did attract huge audiences. Francis Ford Coppola's *Godfather* sagas reworked the classic gangster genre while also exploring the theme of alienation. *The Godfather* (1972) and *Godfather II* (1974) presented a searing critique of American society and American history. The only refuge from corruption, the film seems to suggest, is the close knit, patriarchal family, a place of apparent warmth and safety, dominated by a ruthless but protective godfather (played by Marlon Brando). Inexorably, though, the godfather's role as a crime boss—which overlaps with his business and political connections—begins to corrupt the family circle. One by one, family members fall. At the end, in the America of the 1970s, the new godfather (Al Pacino) is left alone: isolated, lonely, alienated, an outcast from both society and his own family.

Toward the end of the 1970s, this cinema of loneliness and alienation lost touch with popular tastes. Altman's only commercial success came with *M*A*S*H* at the beginning of the decade, and Coppola's ambitious plans to create his own studio collapsed due to the lack of box-office hits. Challenging the cinema of loneliness was a new cycle of motion pictures from film-school graduates who had reverentially studied Classical Hollywood's image-making machinery. Steven Spielberg updated the monster genre with *Jaws* (1975), and George Lucas surpassed Spielberg's epic with *Star Wars* (1977).

Star Wars quickly became credited with (or blamed for) ushering in the era of the Hollywood "blockbuster," the expensive, action-oriented film that aimed at attracting a mass audience both at home and overseas. *Star Wars* drew images and plot situations from familiar Hollywood genres—especially the war film and the western—but also introduced the kind of computer graphics that would soon become standard, blockbuster fare. In contrast to films in the loneliness-and-alienation cycle, *Star Wars* seemed to make militarism fun once more. It also prompted a multimillion dollar business in product spin-offs, such as Darth Vader and Luke Skywalker "action figures," and successful sequels. Although some critics decried the blockbuster film for sublimating character development and story lines to violence-filled action, Hollywood moguls defended it as a logical response to the rising costs of marketing and the need to attract a broad audience, both within the United States and overseas.

Even people who criticized Hollywood's infatuation with the blockbuster recognized that film culture, in many ways, grew stronger during the 1960s and 1970s. Increased popular attention to film styles and themes, for example, reflected the popularization of more sophisticated types of cinematic criticism. During the 1970s, most urban areas still supported a least one retrospective house—a commercial theater that specialized in previously released film classics—and there was growing business at theaters that featured foreign-made movies and motion pictures once dismissed as noncommercial "art films." More people were coming to take the motion picture itself seriously. The study of movies produced by Hollywood became a part of most university and many high-school curricula. Specialized publications devoted to movie criticism, cinematic theory, and film history proliferated as more and more people came to appreciate the subtle, complex connection between the world of the movies and everyday life. Toward the end of the 1970s, film-viewing expanded rapidly with the introduction of pay-for-view channels on cable TV (CATV) and the videocassette (VHS) format.

Sports

Sports also exemplified the expansive trends in American life during the 1960s and 1970s. There were more fans, more teams, and more TV coverage. At the beginning of the 1960s, big league baseball still dominated the sports scene; the two major leagues expanded into new cities during the 1960s and 1970s. Despite expansion, the national pastime lost ground to other spectator sports, particularly to the faster-moving, more violent games of football, basketball (a noncontact sport only in theory), and ice hockey. Professional football's Super Bowl replaced baseball's World Series as the sports world's most-talked-about annual attraction. Cities competed vigorously for almost any type of professional franchise; lucrative TV contracts and generous tax write-offs made ownership of a team especially alluring to wealthy business owners and corporations.

Always seeking additional forms of competition to sell, promoters aggressively marketed new sports attractions. They expanded the number of golf tournaments (women's as well as men's), imported soccer, tried (unsuccessfully) team competition in tennis, and even formed short-lived "major leagues" for slow-pitch softball and volleyball. Similarly, the growing popularity of women's sports produced the first women's professional basketball league and superstar-status for women's tennis and golf. Predictions that the energy shortage was ending America's love affair with the automobile did not cool sports fans' ardor for all types of auto racing. The Indianapolis 500 rivaled the Super Bowl as sports' biggest one-day event, and stock-car racing retained its great popularity in the South.

Professional boxing, once considered on the ropes because of the taint of fixed fights, staged a vigorous comeback. The dominant figure was Muhammad Ali, the three-time heavyweight champion. Ali modestly claimed that he was the best-known person on the planet, and there seemed little reason to doubt him. Certainly, he made boxing a worldwide enterprise. In 1964, he made his first title defense before a handful of people in a hockey rink in Lewiston, Maine; when he retired, he could boast that he had fought before millions of people from Malaysia to Zaire. Ali noted accurately that governments, and not simply promoters, bid for his services. His success in the ring, however, was tempered by a dramatic decline in his personal health, a condition aggravated by his long boxing career.

Sports figures remained America's special heroes. Some, like football's Jim Brown, retired in favor of full-time acting; others, such as Joe Namath, found it more profitable to hop back and forth between stadium and sound stage. Many sports celebrities discovered that business ventures could handsomely supplement their athletic contracts. During the heady 1960s, some even challenged Colonel Sanders and McDonald's in the highly risky, franchise-food business, but most contented themselves with a safer course, product endorsements. After breaking Babe Ruth's lifetime home-run record, Hank Aaron ushered in the days of multimillion dollar endorsement deals by signing a $5 million pact with Magnavox.

Inevitably, politicians tried to tap the glamour that surrounded big-time sports celebrities. Richard Nixon assiduously cultivated his image as the nation's number-one sports fan. (He even contributed a trick play to the 1972 Super Bowl; perhaps a bad omen, it lost 13 yards.) Presidential candidates rushed to sign up prominent athletes for their campaign squads, and some, including former star quarterback Jack Kemp and pitcher Jim Bunning, successfully ran for political office themselves.

Most of the professional team sports went through considerable legal turmoil during the 1960s and 1970s. Players achieved at least partial emancipation from the once dictatorial control of their owners. Professional athletes had long complained that they received a disproportionately small share of the profits; but, through the 1950s at least, the laws applying to sports tilted toward the side of capital. A new generation of athletes, armed with union advisers and spurred on by the sight of burgeoning revenues, changed this slant. Hockey, basketball, and football players made some gains when rival leagues began to bid for their services in the late 1960s and early 1970s, but not until the mid-1970s were their victories, and new breakthroughs by baseball players, written into law. In 1970, baseball's owners narrowly escaped defeat when the Supreme Court, after considerable internal squabbling, finally voted five to three to reject a suit challenging the national pastime's reserve clause as an unconstitutional form of involuntary servitude.

The owners' victory was short-lived. By 1980, other legal decisions had given athletes in every major professional sport, including baseball, the freedom to play out their options to their old team and to auction off their services as "free agents" in the marketplace. The result was hefty inflation in the salary structure of professional sports. In 1979, Nolan Ryan, owner of baseball's fastest fast ball, became the sport's first million-dollar-a-year player when he switched his allegiance from Gene Autry (the cowboy-star owner of the California Angels) to the Lone Ranger (the cowboy hero who symbolized the home state of Ryan's new team, Houston). Although some fans grumbled—especially when highly paid players failed to deliver on the field or court—most owners found that steadily rising revenues and generous tax breaks could cover the new salaries.

Sports and legal questions became intertwined with gender issues. Critics condemned big-time sports for promoting sexism—pointing, for example, to the emphasis on female cheerleading squads that resembled Las Vegas chorus lines—and urged inclusion of more women into the world of athletics. Colleges and universities, mandated by Title IX of the Civil Rights Act of 1964 to achieve equality in sports activities, faced difficult decisions about how to finance and promote women's sports. In sports where professionalism prevailed, such as tennis and golf, the trend was unabashedly toward emulating the male model: Prize money, endorsement contracts, and media coverage for women all steadily increased after the mid-1970s.

The growing commercialization of big-time sports, even at the collegiate level, also provoked lively debate. Traditionalists continued to defend amateur sports as character-building enterprises and joined with fans in celebrating the vicarious thrill of watching highly skilled professionals perform their special magic. But, writing in a different vein, the historian-social critic Christopher Lasch spoke for many when he argued that corporate promoters had trivialized athletic contests into prepackaged spectacles which were often tainted with corruption and suffused with nearly criminal violence. A fascination with violence was especially evident in the growth of professional hockey, the revival of boxing, and the curious renaissance in professional wrestling.

Television

Television played an important role in boosting sports. During the 1960s, professional football steadily gained a larger viewing audience on Sunday afternoons; at the beginning of the 1970s, it invaded Monday night's prime-time schedule and, to the surprise of most sports and media experts, immediately dominated that evening's ratings contest.

During the 1970s, the air time devoted to sports by the three major networks more than doubled. The reason was simple. Sports brought "good numbers" in the form of high ratings; these good numbers produced another set of happy figures—increased advertising revenues. Taken together, these two numerical sets translated into greater corporate profits for ABC, CBS, and NBC. Between 1970 and 1975, the percentage of NBC's advertising take from sports nearly doubled, and higher TV revenues from sports inevitably meant higher payments for the privilege of carrying sporting events on television. In 1976, the rights to telecast the 1980 Montreal Olympics cost ABC $25 million; four years later, the same network paid more than $200 million dollars more for rights to the 1984 summer games.

The symbiotic relationship between sports and television helped to solidify television's position as the most popular of the popular arts. Television attracted a mass audience, not only in the United States but throughout most of the world. According to a study published in the mid-1970s, nearly half of the U.S. population ranked watching television—as opposed to seeing motion pictures, reading, playing cards, talking with friends, or any other activity—as their favorite pastime. Surveys also showed that people were spending more and more time with their sets. In 1961, respondents indicated that they watched television slightly more than two hours a day; by 1974, the figure had jumped to more than three hours a day. By the time a child graduated from high school, it was estimated, he or she had spent more time with TV than with a twelve-year supply of teachers.

The need to attract this mass audience helped to shape the content of network television. Throughout the 1950s, some people had continued to hope that television would find time for symphony concerts, sophisticated dramas, and in-depth news analysis. When some corporations underwrote the cost of an entire show, such as the "Hallmark Hall of Fame," their image-makers often considered the acclaim of highbrow critics to be as important as the attention of a mass audience. As network television changed its sponsorship base so that the thirty-second, individually sold commercial advertisement became the key element in network programming, the number and type of people tuned to a particular show became all important to both sponsors and programmers. Few advertisers wanted to buy commercial time on a TV program with a small audience or on one with a viewership made up largely of people with small disposable incomes. Television programmers came to focus more and more on the bottom line: They were in the business of attracting the largest possible segment of the American population and then reselling this audience to corporate sponsors, at the highest possible rate.

Network executives, who faced the nearly impossible task of predicting what a diverse audience might want to watch, came to rely on a relatively small group of programming specialists and on tried-and-tested formats. People who had developed and packaged one successful show gained an inside track. During the 1970s, for example, Aaron Spelling began his prolific career in network television. Beginning with "The Mod Squad," a program about youthful crime fighters who supposedly expressed the countercultural values of the 1960s youth generation, Spelling developed a string of crime series that ended with "Hart to Hart," a show that featured a wealthy couple with the upscale consumer tastes of the late 1970s. Every one of his shows ranked (for at least one year) among the twenty-five most popular programs, and Spelling, who dismissed his own creations as "mind candy," epitomized the successful television auteur. He offered viewers predictable plots; likable, uncomplicated, characters; lush scenery; a good deal of action; and reassuring endings. Most important, he provided ABC with consistently high ratings and left himself with a backlist of shows that could be sold for syndication outside of the prime-time viewing period.

Network TV did break some familiar genres and molds during the 1960s and 1970s. CBS's "Sixty Minutes," the first TV newsmagazine, eventually entered the Nielsen's Top-Ten rankings. "The Mary Tyler Moore Show," a variety of programs produced by Norman Lear (including "All in the Family"), and "M*A*S*H" won plaudits for bending hackneyed TV formulas. Because of the emphasis these programs gave to character development and ensemble playing—rather than focusing on a show's headliners or weekly guest stars—viewers could find a continuity missing from most TV shows. With Hollywood's film archives almost depleted, TV executives also began to produce their own made-for-television films and longer miniseries, including the much-discussed "Roots" (1977). Meanwhile, TV comedy broke new ground in the 1970s with "Saturday Night Live" and "SCTV," two ensemble shows that specialized in satire directed not only at political and social events but also at the TV medium itself.

By the 1970s, viewers could also select a highbrow alternative to network television, though few actually did so. Public television, authorized by Congress in 1967 and expanded (with the help of corporate and foundation grants) during the 1970s, attracted only about 5 percent of the viewing audience for its most popular adult shows. (Children's programs, such as "Sesame Street" and "Mr. Rogers' Neighborhood" did considerably better.) But the Public Broadcasting System (PBS) produced considerable controversy. In 1972, Richard Nixon tried to block its appropriations because of the allegedly left-liberal bias of its public affairs offerings. Private broadcasting interests complained bitterly about the steadily increasing federal subsidies. Public television's most popular programs, other critics liked to point out, were purchased from British television rather than produced by PBS's own staff. Finally, noting the large number of programs bankrolled by oil companies, some pundits claimed that PBS stood for the Petroleum Broadcasting System.

Most people who touted television's potential ignored both the networks and PBS; instead, they claimed that new technologies unveiled in the 1970s seemed the best hope for innovation and greater diversity. Minicams and new videotape equipment greatly increased television's mobility and the speed with which it could relay images back to viewers. The new communications satellites allowed live transmissions from most parts of the world. Introduction of cable TV systems (CATV) during the mid-1970s gave millions of subscribers new options, including channels reserved for public access programming. The subsequent arrival of videocassette recorders (VCRs) allowed viewers to record programs for replay at their convenience, a step toward breaking the tyranny of the network schedules.

The Popular Music Industry

The pop music industry also expanded at a rapid pace during the 1960s and 1970s. Many stars surpassed TV personalities and sports figures in popularity and wealth. Performers received huge fees for concert appearances and staggering royalties from album sales. Some of the superstars of the 1960s—Janis Joplin, Jimi Hendrix, and Jim Morrison, for example—lived at a frantic pace, spending money wildly while killing their talent and ultimately themselves with drugs and alcohol. When Morrison succumbed to a heart attack at the age of twenty-seven, physicians reported that his internal organs resembled those of a person in his fifties. Other stars displayed more concern about their health and their financial balance sheets. Bob Dylan, the Beatles, and Mick Jagger became multimillionaires. Even the Grateful Dead, a group closely associated with San Francisco's counterculture movement, came to concentrate on cash flows and tax write-offs as much as on musical arrangements. In 1973, the business magazine *Forbes* estimated that at least fifty rock superstars earned between $2 million and $6 million a year. "The idea all along," explained Alice Cooper, "was to make $1 million. Otherwise the struggle wouldn't have been worth it." As one writer put it, "rock and roll was here to pay."

In addition to obtaining great financial rewards, rock musicians were gaining serious critical attention. The success of the Beatles and Dylan helped rock escape its juvenile image, and both rock and folk-rock became widely accepted as serious forms of artistic expression. The poetic lyrics of Dylan and Paul Simon, it was said, gave voice to the frustrated dreams of restless youth, their concern about the "sounds of silence" ("people talking without listening"), and

FIGURE 8–5   Beatles Press Conference.

The Beatles not only performed music but issued public pronouncements on a wide range of issues.
Source: Photo by Sully for the St. Paul Dispatch—Pioneer Press, Minnesota Historical Society.

their outrage against the persistence of social injustice. Young composers blended various types of musical styles into the rock idiom. Traditional folk music, black blues, jazz, and country-western music all influenced the progressive rock of the 1960s.

Throughout the 1960s, much of rock music intersected with political and cultural trends, offering a kind of running commentary on each new turn. In 1966, the Beatles released both their much-celebrated psychedelic album, *Sgt. Pepper's Lonely Heart's Club Band,* and John Lennon's "All You Need Is Love." Juxtaposed with the outpouring of feeling against U.S. involvement in Vietnam, violence in inner cities, and the rising fervor of the New Left, the Beatles appeared to be urging young people to take a break from politics and immerse themselves in the pleasures of the counterculture. As if in reply, Bob Dylan's *John Wesley Harding* avoided psychedelic trappings and adopted a philosophical-religious tone, with songs like "All Along the Watchtower" and "I Dreamed I Saw St. Augustine." The following year, as the political atmosphere became more explosive, the Rolling Stones issued "Street Fighting Man," a new rock anthem that expressed both anger at the political establishment and a deep ambivalence about the role of rock-and-roll millionaires in the so-called youth revolution.

The Stones' *Sympathy for the Devil* (1968) presaged the music of the 1970s, which replaced songs of community and hope with ones of individualism and decadence. In contrast to the communal spirit of the late 1960s, much of the music of the 1970s highlighted the cult of rock stars as lonely, isolated artists, people set apart from the larger community—except from those communities expected to buy singles, albums, and T-shirts. Beset by personal and artistic difficulties, the preeminent symbol of a rock community, the Beatles, released their final collaborative album in 1970. By then, the high-tech, decibel-breaking sound of heavy-metal contrasted vividly with the folk-rock of the 1960s. Designed largely for audiences of working-class males who gathered in cavernous urban auditoriums, heavy metal seemed calculated to drown out all sense of feeling and to mimic the screeching noise of industrial life. Heavy metal groups, such as Kiss, explored another popular theme of the 1970s-style rock: decadence. Rock artists of various persuasions became symbols of spiritual exhaustion and the single-minded pursuit of pleasure. The Rolling Stones, always alert to changing consumer trends, easily slipped from a revolutionary stance to a carefully calculated pose of decadence.

At the same time, many other pop music entrepreneurs, seeking a cleaner image, began to distance their products from rock-and-roll. The big business of making and distributing music was returning to a kind of pre-rock standardization, critics of the industry charged. Recording companies, which surpassed the Hollywood film industry in yearly revenues during the 1970s, emphasized expanding their incomes. Competition among record executives, who were paid to anticipate not only the next new musical fad but the following one as well, encouraged corruption and discouraged innovation. The major labels, now generally owned by giant multinational corporations, were more than eager to package the latest trend, subsidizing journalistic puffs for the rock magazines and concert tours for the latest products of their hit-making machinery. They were more reluctant to underwrite significant new directions in music.

A similar situation eventually characterized the radio industry. The expansion of FM stations during the 1960s and early 1970s had broken the tyranny of the old top-40 playlist. Formats became freer, the range of music expanded, and local and regional artists received airplay. By 1980, though, the introduction of radio-programming services had again narrowed the musical spectrum. Relying on sophisticated survey data, these programming services carefully packaged each minute of air time, eliminated the discretion of disk jockeys, and emphasized the music that their data said would appeal to a client's desired audience. They ignored artists and musical styles that did not fit their survey results. Local talents lost out to national recording stars, and individuals on the smaller record labels lost out to artists being promoted heavily by the majors.

Corporate domination also affected the production of music by African American artists. During the 1960s, James Brown became a symbol of both independent black capitalism and cultural innovation. "The hardest working man in show business," Brown broke rock and rhythm-and-blues molds to feature soul music and its later variant, funk. From the late 1960s through the mid-1970s, Aretha Franklin, with her gospel-inspired readings of soul, broke through the male-dominated genres that had epitomized rock music. Brown, Franklin, and the various artists who recorded for Stax, a small record label based in the

South, all tried to avoid the kind of mainstream dance records that many music critics associated with the Detroit-based "Motown Sound." But the money that could be made from soul and from its African American consumers eventually attracted the attention of both the Harvard Business School—which did a study for CBS in 1971—and the major record labels. By 1976, Stax had been absorbed into CBS, and other multimedia conglomerates were working to assimilate soul into various crossover formats, such as disco.

Meanwhile, country and country-rock music, which had once been centered in Nashville and the "Grand Old' Opry," suddenly became a national, increasingly corporate-based phenomenon. During the 1950s and most of the 1960s, northerners who had wanted to hear country music on their radios had to wait until evening when they could pick up high-beaming stations from the Deep South. By 1980, though, every metropolitan area had several country music stations, and many country artists were crossing over to the pop and rock stations. Singers such as Kris Kristofferson, Dolly Parton, and Willie Nelson (the first country artist to "go platinum" by selling 1 million copies of a single album) became nationwide celebrities with TV and movie careers.

Critics debated the widening appeal of country music. Some claimed that people were drawn to its simplicity and honesty, its stories of broken hearts and faded loves—"Your Cheatin' Heart Will Tell on You." Others were attracted, it seemed, by the music's nostalgic overtones, its celebration of rural life and simple virtues—"My Heroes Have Always Been Cowboys." For people buffeted by many different kinds of change, country music also spoke about the pain of moving on—"Lost Highway"—and to the hope of finding some secure resting place—"No Place Like Home."

Religion

During the 1950s, many observers had noted that Americans seemed increasingly attracted to religion. Church membership climbed; President Eisenhower spread "piety along the Potomac"; and the Reverend Norman Vincent Peale's popular *The Power of Positive Thinking* seemed to carry faith and optimism to Protestants throughout the land. Skeptics warned that signs such as these did not necessarily measure religious commitment and charged that the religiosity of the 1950s emphasized form over substance, fund-raising over worship. But at least the sanctuaries were full, and most churchgoers seemed content with the way things were.

Religious institutions, however, did not escape turmoil during the 1960s— the search for new forms of spirituality, the splits over social issues, and the growth in sheer scale. By the end of the decade, established churches were racked by factionalism, were losing membership, and were being challenged by newer sects and religious movements.

Merger movements became almost as fashionable in religion as in business. Mainstream Protestant denominations seemed preoccupied with consolidation and centralization. Lutherans, Methodists, and Congregationalists each approved important mergers arranged by their national decision-making bodies and accepted by most local congregations. Greater centralization crept into other functions as well. More and more, national boards set church policy, raised funds, budgeted money, and directed missionary and social efforts.

The umbrella organization for Protestant churches, the National Council of Churches, revamped its structure in the mid-1960s to further the centralized direction of policy. But the interjection of national-level decisions into affairs of local churches often exacerbated tensions within individual congregations.

When national church bodies, which were fairly progressive politically, began to express themselves on controversial issues, such as civil rights and the war in Vietnam, factional disputes within local congregations became severe. Some people wanted their church to remain aloof from social issues; others pressed for it to take an even more activist stance. The split over the role of the church was basic, and it was bitter. Church attendance declined markedly during the 1960s, and the drop was most evident in the mainline denominations.

The Catholic church faced a number of difficult issues. There was not only turmoil over political questions such as the Vietnam War—Catholics were bitterly divided between a deep-seated cold-war conservatism and the left-radicalism of antiwar priests such as Daniel and Philip Berrigan—but also over church doctrine. The Second Vatican Council of 1962–1965 ushered in a period of change by substituting English for Latin in the liturgy. Subsequently, demands for greater changes accelerated. While traditionalists recoiled, some Catholics pressed for liberalization of rules concerning priestly celibacy, the role of women in the church, and birth control.

Jewish synagogues and temples confronted a problem even more baffling than divisions over doctrinal and social policies—maintaining their members' very identity as Jews. Economic success within the Jewish community and the decline of overt anti-Semitism, ironically, presented serious challenges for Judaism in the United States. Large numbers of young people were failing to pursue Hebrew-school lessons; they had forgotten that giant business, educational, and professional organizations had once discriminated against Jews; and many were marrying gentiles. With more and more American Jews still identifying themselves with "Jewish culture," while belonging to no synagogue or temple, students of Jewish life engaged in a heated debate. Were Jews becoming "assimilated" into American life—and thus losing their unique identity—or were American Jews simply becoming more "acculturated" to non-Jewish institutions and social practices?

Meanwhile, an evangelical Protestant spirit swept the country during the 1960s. Prominent revivalists such as Billy Graham and Oral Roberts headed huge bureaucracies relying on the mass media and the latest advertising techniques, but their sermons attracted people by appealing to personal religious values and traditional social virtues. Their message provided an anchor for many Americans who felt buffeted by the pace of change. During the 1960s, some popular preachers, such as Billy James Hargis and Carl McIntire, linked Christianity, anticommunism, and ultra-right-wing politics. Hargis charged that equal rights for women would bring the nation to the brink of hell, and his organization carried on a well-funded campaign against feminist causes. McIntire joined Hargis in attacking the environmentalist movement, charging it with rejecting Christianity and assisting communism.

In contrast, Roberts and Graham became important establishment figures. Roberts financed his own university in Oklahoma and used the school's successful basketball team as a promotional device. (During one stretch the squad lost only 19 of 134 games.) He also built a huge media empire, which rivaled that of Graham, who continued to be the nation's most revered religious leader. Graham took his crusades around the world, preaching to crowds of over 100,000 people. He also became an important spiritual counselor to President Nixon, often leading prayer breakfasts at the White House. Year after year, he stayed near the top of the list of most admired Americans.

Other types of religious movements blossomed. The Bahai faith built several breathtaking temples in the United States and gained numerous converts. Members of the Hare Krishna sect, with their shaved heads and robes, appeared in larger cities; various communally oriented groups—denounced by their detractors as "cults"—attracted young people who were willing to renounce their families and adopt a new life and loyalty. Religiosity took on other dimensions as well. Americans became fascinated with spiritualism, mysticism, and transcendental mediation. Bookstores expanded their sections on religion and the occult. Many people of all ages and political persuasions, it seemed, were seeking a spiritual refuge from a bureaucratic, centralized, and oversized society.

Many of the religious trends of the 1960s continued through the 1970s. Although attendance at Catholic masses leveled off after the decline of the 1960s, mainline Protestant and Jewish congregations continued to lose members. At the same time, all of the major denominations still struggled to heal internal divisions, especially those involving the role of women in the church. By the 1970s, feminists in major religions argued that women should participate more fully in nearly all phases of spiritual life. The Roman Catholic Church reaffirmed its opposition to such changes—including papal bans on female priests and on artificial methods of birth control—but most Protestant denominations agreed to modify at least some patriarchal practices. The situation in Judaism was complicated by the division among the Orthodox, Conservative, and Reform movements. Although Conservative and Reform congregations changed some traditional rituals and doctrines, the Orthodox movement, the only wing of Judaism to gain members during the 1970s, held firm. Finally, the evangelical and fundamentalist revival of the 1960s gained momentum in the 1970s. Even though mainline Protestant denominations lost members, the total number of Protestants attending church remained constant because of the growth of evangelical and fundamentalist congregations.

The growth of evangelical and fundamentalist movements could be measured in watts, in dollars, and in political power, as well as in church attendance. Radio and TV ministries remained central forces in this surge of Protestantism, and hundreds of other media preachers joined Graham and Roberts. The most prominent included Robert Schuller, who preached an updated version of Norman Vincent Peale's positive thinking from his splendid Crystal Cathedral in California; Jerry Falwell, a Baptist fundamentalist who began building a media empire based in Virginia; the gospel-singing Jimmy Swaggart, who played the piano in a manner that resembled the styles of his first cousins, country-rock stars Jerry Lee Lewis and Mickey Gilley; and Pat Robertson, a corporate-lawyer-turned-evangelist, who hosted the "700 Club," a religious version of the familiar TV talk show.

Although the major TV networks refused to sell religious broadcasters prime-time slots, the media preachers used their burgeoning bank accounts to purchase time from local stations and even to establish their own networks. Robertson's Christian Broadcasting Network (which later merged with The Family Channel) boasted of its own satellite system and of its ability to reach hundreds of stations and cable-TV systems on an around-the-clock basis. By the end of the 1970s, there were more than 1,400 radio stations and 30 TV outlets that specialized in religious broadcasting.

Some of the media preachers actively entered politics during the late 1970s. After supporting Jimmy Carter in 1976, both Robertson and Falwell turned rightward. Falwell's political lobby, the Moral Majority, campaigned against homosexuals, federal involvement in education, the Equal Rights Amendment for women, and liberalization of abortion laws. The Moral Majority also ran workshops on political organizing and rated members of Congress on the basis of their adherence to Moral-Majoritarian positions. By 1980, the right wing of the Republican party actively sought support from conservative media preachers such as Falwell and Robertson.

Meanwhile, the world's largest religious faith, Islam, developed a more visible presence in America. Students who came from Muslim countries to study in the United States after World War II created in 1965 the first significant Muslim organization—the Muslim Student Association (MSA). The MSA quickly sprouted various associated professional branches, which provided a community for the many well-educated, middle class professionals who decided to seek jobs and settle in North America. In 1981, the creation of the Islamic Society of North America (ISNA) provided a new umbrella organization for the growing number of specialized Islamic groups. Dedicated to educating Muslims and to presenting Islam to non-Muslims, it became the most important national organization of immigrant Muslims, and began, among its other services, a mutual aid fund and a variety of professional journals. The Islamic Center of Southern California and the Muslim Community Center in Chicago also both expanded to achieve status as national organizations.

Some African American leaders had begun to turn to Islam even before World War I, arguing that Christianity was a religion of whites and that Islam would be more consistent with pride in their African heritage. Conversion to Islam grew rapidly in association with the black power movement of the 1960s and 1970s, and the Nation of Islam under Elijah Muhammad became a significant force in some African American communities. With the death of Elijah Muhammad in 1975, his son, Warith Deen Muhammed, assumed leadership, directed the organization toward more orthodox Muslim beliefs and practices, and changed its name to the American Muslim Mission in 1980. When he instructed his mosques to integrate with other Muslim communities, some leaders such as Louis Farakhan refused and, instead, sustained the name of the original Nation of Islam.

In 1980 the number of Muslims in America was estimated at 3.3 million or 1.5 percent of the total population. Most lived in three states, New York, California, and Illinois, and nearly one-third were African Americans. Immigration would soon enlarge Muslim communities and bring them to other regions of the country.

In this era, controversy also swirled around the power and influence of "cults," a term that covered very different types of religious movements. The Unification Church, headed by South Korea's staunchly anti-Communist Reverend Sun Myung Moon, used sophisticated techniques to gain followers and the latest corporate management practices to handle its growing wealth. Young people claimed to find a new sense of community and a renewed religious faith when they joined the "Moonies." Moon's church also gained the endorsement of prominent supporters, including some conservative academics who shared Moon's political outlook. Moon preached conservative politics, laissez-faire capitalism, and a hard-line anti-Communist foreign policy. During the early 1970s, the Unification Church illegally funneled a considerable amount of money—much of it coming from young people selling flowers on street corners—to various groups supporting Richard Nixon. These activities resulted in a jail term for Moon himself.

The People's Temple, a religious-political movement based in San Francisco, provided an example of a different kind of "cult." Led by a charismatic and increasingly paranoid preacher, the Reverend Jim Jones, the People's Temple appealed to the very poor, those who could find no secure place in the oversized society. Jones, who could claim vague ties to political groups on the left, promised both religious salvation and social progress. He gained a sizable following, especially among low-income African American families, and many of these people moved with him to Guyana in South America. There, in 1978, nearly a thousand members of the People's Temple died in a mass-suicide ritual.

The Educational Labyrinth

Pressure from the baby-boom generation and demands of a rapidly expanding economy had brought enormous changes to America's educational establishment during the postwar era. Thousands of new schools had to be built and equipped, and corporations stood ready to sell the latest in instructional devices. During the 1960s, under Lyndon Johnson's Great Society programs, federal funds became available for expanding and upgrading educational facilities and introducing new teaching methods. Many of the instructional techniques sought to involve students as active participants rather than as passive listeners. In some schools, architects eliminated walls, creating an open and airy environment in which students would, it was hoped, become more expressive.

Change involved course content as well as teaching techniques. The "new math" and the "new English" aimed to substitute analysis and attention to concepts for traditional categories and extensive memorization. The "new social studies" emphasized evaluation of primary documents and "value-clarification" exercises rather than the regurgitation of names and dates. Under pressure from women's organizations and minority groups, elementary schools began to replace the white, middle-class characters of "Dick and Jane" with a more diverse cast of characters. Supporters of these new approaches claimed that they would produce students who could think, evaluate, and make critical judgments. Even sympathetic critics, however, charged that methodological innovation outstripped changes in educational personnel and that many veteran teachers became confused by and resentful of the innovations. Approaches that worked in a laboratory school did not always succeed in an ordinary classroom. Some pupils easily adapted to the new math, but others graduated from high school without being able to balance a checkbook. After two decades of experimentation, critics of the new techniques contended that "Johnny still can't read, and he can't add, either."

Another innovation of the 1960s was to offer more education outside of the traditional system. Some parents who disliked the top-down structure of traditional public schools sent their children to experimental "alternative schools." Head Start, a key Great Society program, sought to provide educational experiences for preschoolers from disadvantaged backgrounds so that they could enter kindergarten on a par with those from more privileged circumstances. Innovators also touted educational television as a way to reach preschoolers, dropouts, adults, and even school-aged children themselves with educational material ranging from U.S. history to language instruction to guitar playing.

PBS, in conjunction with the Children's Television Workshop, developed the most successful venture in educational programming—"Sesame Street." Colorful and fast-moving, "Sesame Street" had viewers reciting numbers, letters, and difficult words (some in Spanish) before they entered kindergarten. Although "Sesame Street" captivated children, traditionalists thought that its flashy graphics and rapid visual cuts emphasized style over substance. Some even charged that the "Sesame-Street aesthetic," which borrowed from that of TV commercials, best prepared students to become consumers of media imagery.

Many schools also saw important changes in the nature of their student bodies. Educational planners, especially in rural areas, worked to consolidate smaller schools into larger, better-equipped ones. As a result, the size of educational institutions increased dramatically. In 1950, there had been more than 86,000 school systems in the country, averaging about 300 students each; by 1965, there were fewer than 30,000 systems, averaging 1,400 students each. Most children no longer knew all their classmates or teachers, and many students were bused to a school miles away from their home. The undeniable educational gains of consolidation came at the expense of nearby facilities and a feeling of community.

The baby-boom generation also strained the resources of colleges and universities during the 1960s. Higher education contended not only with the natural population increase but also with a rising percentage of youths who chose to go to college. In 1955, only 27 percent of college-aged people had attended schools; by 1965, the figure had risen to 40 percent. The flood of new students stemmed from postwar affluence, governmental-assistance programs, young men's desire to avoid the draft by staying in school, and a huge influx of young women. Graduate schools also boomed. By the mid-1960s, there were about a quarter of a million full-time graduate students, three of every five receiving some form of financial support. Half of all the Ph.D. degrees granted in the United States between 1861 and 1970 were earned during the 1960s. A researcher writing in 1971 accurately predicted that the graduate education and research establishment in American universities was about 30 to 50 percent larger than could be effectively employed during the coming decades.

The debates of the 1960s—over the size and structure of schools, over philosophies and techniques of instruction, and over the content of the curriculum—became more bitter and complex during the 1970s. The declining birthrate of the 1960s finally caught up with education: For the first time in several decades, students were not crowding the educational labyrinth. School officials at the elementary and secondary levels—faced with rising costs, declining revenues, and mandates for racial desegregation—responded by consolidating additional schools and closing down others. Neighborhood schools would not be nearly as close to most people's homes as they had been during the 1950s and early 1960s. School busing, ordered by federal courts to accomplish desegregation, also sparked controversy and a surge in enrollments at private schools. Moreover, public schools, which had to depend on tax dollars, faced growing protests against higher property taxes and new school-revenue bonds. As a result, school districts throughout the country began to slash educational staffs, instructional programs, and extracurricular activities. The problem was most serious in large cities, where shrinking tax bases and escalating costs added to difficulties produced by reluctant taxpayers.

The problems of American education transcended issues of teaching method, financial strain, and consolidation. There were more subtle forces contributing to what appeared to be a growing backlash against a strong commitment to education of the young. Put simply, more and more people saw public schools, especially in urban areas, as educational and social failures. In some schools, traditional discipline problems—truancy, smoking in rest rooms, scuffles on the playground—seemed trivial when compared with the everyday reality of hard drugs and violence against both teachers and students. At the same time, educational results as measured by standardized tests steadily dropped. Between 1966 and 1976, the average score on the verbal portion of the Scholastic Aptitude Test (SAT) dropped from 467 to 429. The hope that school integration would introduce children to a heterogeneous environment began to fade as more affluent families, from all ethnic groups, left for the suburbs or sent their children to private schools. The vast majority of urban public schools came to serve children from primarily low-income families. In Pasadena, California, for example, more than 35 percent of white parents removed their children from public schools after court-enforced busing went into effect. Nationwide, it was estimated that 40 percent of middle-class African American parents sent their children to private schools.

Although colleges and universities also began to face the necessity of contraction, they enjoyed greater flexibility than primary and secondary schools. They, unlike the lower-level schools, could create students. Colleges and universities increasingly sought "the nontraditional student." Foreign students and adult scholars—individuals (especially women) slightly or considerably older than the traditional eighteen- to twenty-two age group—became obvious targets. Four-year institutions also began to compete more actively with two-year, community colleges for students. Of course, colleges and universities also vied with one another to attract a steady number of students from a shrinking pool of high-school graduates. Admissions offices became recruiting centers that relied on consultants to provide their college with an attractive image and an effective set of recruiting tools. A number of smaller colleges gave up and closed their doors.

Meanwhile, at all levels, people continued to debate the traditional, and still central, questions: What should students learn and how should they be taught? In response to the continuation of trends begun during the late 1960s, which tried to open up new subject areas and introduce more flexible methods of instruction, a back-to-basics movement emerged. At the postsecondary level, traditionalists began to regroup and to seek a rollback of changes they believed were eroding educational excellence. A movement to reinstitute requirements, to establish core curriculums (or at least core courses), and to limit the spread of programs in areas such as women's and minority studies slowly took shape.

Much of the historical writing about the 1960s and 1970s focuses upon the rise and decline of political protest and cultural experimentation. Certainly these trends did mark the two decades, but an equally important theme is the rapid expansion in both the scope and scale of American economic and social institutions. Although some U.S. industries, such as steel and auto making, downsized due to international competition, other industries—particularly in communications, entertainment, and computers—consolidated rapidly and were coming to dominate the national and international marketplace. Meanwhile, large-scale organizations and greater centralization also changed the ways in which people purchased products, spent their leisure time, worshiped, and received their education. The growth in the scale of daily life affected politics, providing the cultural backdrop for a president, Ronald Reagan, who would address the new milieu with conservative appeals to return domestic life to the rhythms of an older, less complex America.

SUGGESTED READING

Changes in the scale of institutions during the 1960s and 1970s are analyzed from varying perspectives in W. Lloyd Warner, *The Emergent American Society* (1967); Arthur Selwyn Miller, *The Modern Corporate State* (1976); Morris Janowitz, *The Last Half-century* (1978); Christopher Lasch, *The Culture of Narcissism* (1978); Kirkpatrick Sale, *Human Scale* (1980); Theodore Lowi, *The End of Liberalism* (rev. ed., 1979); John Tirman, ed., *The Militarization of High Tech* (1984); Donald Worster, *Rivers of Empire* (1985); Louis Galambos, *The New American State: Bureaucracies and Policies Since World War II* (1987); Paul Kennedy, *The Rise and Fall of the Great Powers* (1988); Juliet B. Schor, *The Overworked American* (1991); and Ann Markusen, et al., *The Rise of the Gunbelt: The Military Remapping of Industrial America* (1991).

On economic and demographic developments, see Seymour Melman, *Pentagon Capitalism* (1970); Richard J. Barnet and Ronald Muller, *Global Reach* (1974); Dan Morgan, *Merchants of Grain* (1979); Samuel Bowles, David M. Gordon, and Thomas Weisskopf, *Beyond the Wasteland* (1983); Charles P. Kindleberger, *Multinational Excursions* (1984); Lester Thurow, *Dangerous Currents* (1984); the relevant portions of Lewis Mandell, *The Credit Card Industry: A History* (1990); Raymond Mohl, ed., *Searching for the Sunbelt* (1990); Mike Davis, *City of Quartz: Excavating the Future in Los Angeles* (1990); Daniel Yergin, *The Prize: The Epic Quest for Oil, Money, and Power* (1991); Thomas I. Palley, *Plenty of Nothing: The Downsizing of the American Dream and the Case for Structural Keynesianism* (1998); Kathleen Barker and Kathleen Christensen, *Contingent Work: American Employment Relations in Transition* (1998); Jefferson Cowie, *Capital Moves: RCA's Seventy-Year Quest for Cheap Labor* (1999); Alejandro Portes and Alex Stepick, *City on the Edge: The Transformation of Miami* (1993); Robert J. Samuelson, *The American Dream in the Age of Entitlement, 1945–1995* (1996); Ross Miller, *Here's The Deal: The Buying and Selling of a Great American City* (1996); Roger E. Bilstein, *The American Aerospace Industry: From Workshop to Global Enterprise* (1996); Steven P. Dandaneau, *A Town Abandoned: Flint, Michigan, Confronts Deindustrialization* (1996); Ruth Milkman, *Farewell to the Factory: Auto Workers in the Late Twentieth Century* (1997); Judith Stein, *Running Steel, Running America: Race, Economic Policy, and the Decline of Liberalism* (1998); and Charles Noble, *Welfare as We Knew It: A Political History of the American Welfare State* (1997).

On the computer revolution see James W. Cortada, *The Computer in the United States: From Laboratory to Market, 1930–1960* (1993); Paul N. Edwards, *The Closed World: Computers and the Politics of Discourse in Cold War America* (1996); Randall E. Stross, *The Microsoft Way* (1996); Arthur L. Norberg and July O'Neill, *Transforming Computer Technology: Information Processing for the Pentagon, 1962–1986* (1996); and Janet Abbate, *Inventing the Internet* (1999).

On environmental issues, begin with several classic studies that helped raise public consciousness: Rachel Carson, *The Silent Spring* (1962); Barry Commoner, *The Closing Circle* (1971); Amory Lovins, *Soft Energy Paths* (1977); Richard J. Barnet, *The Lean Years* (1980); and Michael Brown, *Laying Waste* (1980). Historical works include Samuel P. Hays, *Beauty, Health, and Permanence* (1987) and *Explorations in Environmental History* (1998); Joseph Morone and Edward Woodhouse, *The Demise of Nuclear Energy? Lessons for Democratic Control of Technology* (1989); Thomas Raymond Wellock, *Critical Masses: Opposition to Nuclear Power in California, 1958–1978* (1998); the relevant portions of Anna Bramwell, *Ecology in the Twentieth Century* (1989); Thomas Huffman, *Protectors of the Land and Water* (1994); Kirkpatrick Sale, *The Green Revolution: The American Environmental Movement, 1962–1992* (1993); Craig E. Coltren and Peter N. Skinner, *The Road to Love Canal: Managing Industrial Waste before the EPA* (1996); Michele Stenehjem Gerber, *On the Home Front: The Cold War Legacy of the Hanford Nuclear Site* (1996); Terence Kehoe, *Cleaning Up the Great Lakes: From Cooperation to Confrontation* (1997); Hal K. Rothman, *The Greening of a Nation? Environmentalism in the United States Since 1945* (1997); and Scott Hamilton Dewey, *Don't Breathe the Air: Air Pollution and U.S. Environmental Politics, 1945–1970* (2000).

On education, see the conflicting interpretations in the following: Herbert Gintis and Samuel Bowles, *Schooling in Capitalist America* (1976); Hugh Davis Graham, *Uncertain Triumph: Federal Education Policy in the Kennedy and Johnson Years* (1984); Ira Katznelson and Margaret Weir, *Schooling for All* (1985); Lois Weis, ed., *Class, Race, and Gender in American Education* (1988); Allan Bloom, *The Closing of the American Mind* (1988); Roger L. Geiger, *Research and Relevant Knowledge: American Research Universities Since World War II* (1993); and Hugh Davis Graham and Nancy Diamond, *The Rise of the American Research Universities* (1996).

On commercial culture, many of the works cited for earlier chapters cover developments during this period. In addition, see Robert Lipsyte, *Sportsworld* (1975); Geoffrey Stokes, *Star-making Machinery* (1976); Robert Venturi, Denise Scott Brown, and Steven Izenour, *Learning from Las Vegas* (rev. ed., 1977); Robert Sklar, *Prime-time America* (1980); Ben Bagdikian, *The Media Monopoly* (1983); Jon Weiner, *Come Together: John Lennon and His Time* (1984); Herbert Schiller, *Who Knows? Information in the Age of the Fortune 500* (1984) and *Culture, Inc: The Corporate Takeover of American Expression* (1989); Todd Gitlin, *Inside Prime Time* (1985); Benjamin Rader, *In Its Own Image: How Television Has Transformed Sports* (1985); Helen Baehr and Gillian Dyer, eds., *Boxed In: Women and Television* (1987); John Fiske, *Television Culture* (1987); Robert Kolker, *Cinema of Loneliness* (rev. ed., 2000); Stuart Ewen, *All Consuming Images: The Politics of Style in Contemporary Culture* (1988); Michael Ryan and Douglas Kellner, *Camera Politica: Politics and Ideology in Contemporary Hollywood Cinema* (1988); Ethan Morden, *Medium Cool: The Movies of the 1960s* (1990); Peter Lev., *American Films of the 70s: Conflicting Visions* (2000); Marsha Kinder, *Playing with Power in Movies, Television, and Video Games* (1991); Neil Postman, *Technopoly: The Surrender of Culture* to *Technology* (1992); Cecelia Tichi, *High Lonesome: The American Culture of Country Music* (1994); Deidre Boyle, *Subject to Change: Guerrilla Television Revisited* (1997); Steven Watts, *The Magic Kingdom: Walt Disney and the American Way of Life* (1997); Karal Ann Marling, *Designing Disney's Theme Parks: The Architecture of Reassurance* (1997); Mike Budd, et al, *Consuming Environments: Television and Commercial Culture* (1999); and Janet Wasko, *Understanding Disney: The Manufacture of Fantasy* (2001).

On religious trends see Martin E. Marty, *The New Shape of American Religion* (1978); Marshall Frady, *Billy Graham* (1979); David Harrell, *All Things Are Possible* (1974), *Oral Roberts* (1985), and *Pat Robertson* (1987); Charles Shepard, *Forgiven: The Rise and Fall of Jim Bakker and the PTL* (1989); Randall Balmer, *Mine Eyes Have Seen the Glory: A Journey Into the Evangelical Subculture of America* (1989); Garry Wills, *Under God* (1990); Bryan V. Hillis, *Can Two Walk Together Unless They Be Agreed: American Religious Schisms in the 1970s* (1991); Michael Lienesch, *Redeeming America: Piety and Politics in the New Christian Right* (1993); Martin E. Marty and R. Scott Appleby, *Fundamentalism and the State: Remaking Politics, Militance, and Economies* (1993); James Hunter, *Smile Pretty and Say Jesus: The Last Days of PTL* (1993); R. Laurence Moore, *Selling God* (1994); Martin E. Marty, *A Short History of American Catholicism* (1995); Gerald Sorin, *Tradition Transformed: The Jewish Experience in America* (1997); Joel A. Carpenter, *Revive Us Again: The Awakening of American Fundamentalism* (1997); and Richard Brent Turner, *Islam in the African-American Experience* (1997).

9

A Conservative Turn, 1980–1992

Any discussion of the years between 1980 and 1992 must begin with Ronald Wilson Reagan. His movie-star image dominated politics and touched culture as well. Reagan admittedly ignored the details of governance in favor of pressing a few basic ideals and trusting his subordinates to follow his broad aims. He promised to rekindle faith in the nation's future and to derail the positive-state agenda of the Democratic party. Government is "the problem, not the solution," Reagan famously proclaimed. He made "big-government liberal" a label from which most Democrats and all Republicans fled. Admirers of Reagan saw him arriving in office determined to transform the country and leaving a conservative legacy for his successor, George H. Bush (1989–1993).

DOMESTIC POLITICS DURING THE REAGAN YEARS

Ronald Reagan's image was his greatest political asset. His Hollywood-honed charm provided presidential charisma, a quality absent during the Nixon, Ford, and Carter years. After Nixon's scowl, Ford's stumbling, and Carter's solemnity, Reagan offered an easy smile, Hollywood-style grace, and quick one-liners. Gaffes in policymaking and questionable activities by associates all failed to stain Reagan's image. Ronald Reagan was a "Teflon president"—nothing stuck to him—a prominent Democrat complained.

What might have stuck to Reagan's image? Critics charged that the president, especially during his second term, seemed cheerfully ignorant of what subordinates were doing and rarely studied domestic and foreign-policy issues himself. Reportedly, he "prepared" for a disarmament conference by reading

Tom Clancy's novel, *Red Storm,* rather than intelligence briefings. If historians credit Dwight Eisenhower with running a "hidden hand presidency," in which a former military commander skillfully delegated crucial tasks to others, one scholar mused, might historians see Reagan's presidency as one in which others delegated trivial tasks to a former movie actor? Such a harsh judgment, Reagan's defenders contend, forgets that his strength never lay in setting the details of policy but in establishing broad priorities and then skillfully articulating them.

Presidential Style and the Conservative Turn

Reagan's presidency recalled the glamour of John Kennedy's Camelot. The singer-actor Frank Sinatra, briefly part of Kennedy's entourage and a close friend of Nancy Reagan, again became welcome at the White House. The First Lady, a former actor herself, proved fiercely protective of the president's image and insisted that aides never call on him to explain complex issues or to take rigid stands on social controversies such as abortion. Ronald Reagan came to Washington with a clear agenda—economic recovery, military rearmament, and bureaucratic retrenchment. Opinion polls showed that most people, even if they did not support him, could identify his goals. The "Great Communicator," gliding effortlessly through political scripts and scenarios, made the portrayal of upbeat, self-confident images seem more important than the engagement with specific policies.

The consummate media politician, Reagan tapped popular dreams and national ideals. One set of images dated from the early days of the cold war. Reagan portrayed a world populated by good guys (including "freedom fighters" in Central America and Afghanistan) and bad guys (Communists, except the Chinese, and "terrorists," a new threat that had emerged during the 1970s). He depicted foreign policy in stark, one-dimensional terms. The USSR was an "evil empire," and the U.S. crusade against it justified extraordinary expenditures on national defense. In domestic policy, Reagan's symbols evoked an America of wide, tree-lined streets, limited government, and hardworking people. Even as economic distress ravaged family farms and small towns during the early 1980s, Reagan extolled a small-scale republic in which "the American people," not governmental "bureaucrats," were in control. After eight years of living at 1600 Pennsylvania Avenue and presiding over the largest budget deficits in the nation's history, Reagan could still denounce "those big spenders in Washington."

The conservative political turn, of course, predated the presidency of Ronald Reagan. He had entered politics as a spokesperson for Barry Goldwater in 1964, and the conservative surge of the 1970s took him from the governorship of California, which he held from 1967 to 1975, onto the national political stage. Initially dismissed as too old for the White House, Reagan crisscrossed the country preaching the need for "getting government off our backs" to people who felt pressed by taxes, inflation, and bureaucratic regulations. Democrat Jimmy Carter had also run for the White House, it should be recalled, as a Washington outsider and apostle of small-town virtues, and his successful 1976 campaign garnered the support of religious conservatives such as

FIGURE 9–1 Ronald Reagan Saddles Up.

The conservative turn of the 1980s built upon Reagan's image as a movie hero often associated with western themes.
Source: National Archives and Records Administration.

Pat Robertson and Jerry Falwell who later backed Reagan. After Carter's administration floundered, Reagan's 1980 presidential campaign picked up some of Carter's own antiestablishment themes.

In both 1980 and 1984, Reagan's personality, more than his programs, proved decisive. Lingering memories of Carter's presidency always aided Reagan. In 1980, as one of Reagan's speechwriters observed, "there was no Reagan without Carter." Four years later, Reagan's reelection benefited from the blandness of his Democratic challenger, Carter's former Vice-President Walter Mondale, who unwisely attempted to revive the old Democratic vision of "tax and spend," as Reagan ridiculed it. Despite Reagan's 1984 landslide, the GOP remained in the minority in both the Senate and House of Representatives. Exit polls suggested that 20 percent of those who voted to reelect Reagan harbored "serious" doubts about his domestic policies and that another 20 percent cared little about his stance on specific issues.

Although Reagan's presidency accelerated the conservative turn, he was never a captive of the New Right's agenda. In return, the New Right never fully embraced Reagan but accepted him as the most conservative political figure with the best chance to capture the presidency. Fundamentalist and evangelical religious groups, with their old Democratic ties, lacked deep loyalties to either the GOP or Reagan himself. Militant conservatives such as North Carolina Senator Jesse Helms, himself a former Democrat, criticized the president's policies as insufficiently conservative, especially on halting abortion, injecting religious values in public schools, and waging cultural warfare. The New Right saw the Reagan administration pushing few of its social proposals through Congress or implementing them through the federal bureaucracy. The movie-land background of both Reagans made them less rigid, White-House insiders claimed, on social issues, particularly abortion, than their party's ultraconservative wing. Culturally, the tone at Reagan's White House suggested Hollywood more than any conservative tradition. When the First Lady invited the Beach-boys, Republican supporters of the president, to sing at the White House, many on the New Right were dumbfounded. If the Democratic party remained splintered, as it had been since the 1960s, over questions of race and the legacy of the "new politics," the Republican party was itself divided throughout Reagan's presidency.

Reaganomics: The Eventual Boom

Reagan immediately turned to his campaign pledge of revitalizing the economy. First, the White House promised to stimulate production, reduce inflation, cut taxes, and balance the federal budget. Invoking the theory of supply-side economics, it claimed that targeting corporate producers and giving them incentives would flood the market with consumer goods and thereby halt inflationary pressures. Next, the Reagan administration proposed the largest budget reduction in U.S. history on the theory that governmental expenditures also generated inflation. All of the budget cuts, including possible ones in social security, were slated for the domestic side because military expenditures were to increase substantially. Finally, the administration advocated radical reductions in federal taxes. According to supply-siders, the bounty produced by a revived economy would more than offset the revenue lost through reducing prevailing tax rates. (In a 1981 interview, however, White House Budget Director David Stockman conceded the implausibility of their theory and admitted that huge tax cuts primarily provided a covert way to shrink funding for domestic programs.)

"Reaganomics" debuted to a mixed reception. Partisan battles over Reagan's proposed budget, which most Democrats claimed would harm people with low incomes and anyone who relied on federal programs, produced ad hoc compromises between different factions in Congress and in the Reagan White House. After Reagan himself rejected any changes in Social Security, the White House picked up congressional support from the so-called "Boll Weevils," conservative, largely southern Democrats. The final Omnibus Budget Reconciliation Act of 1981 did eliminate about 300,000 public-service jobs, which had been funded under Carter through the CETA program, and reduced expenditures for others, such as AFDC and job training. Still, spending cuts were far less drastic than either the budget's Democratic critics or its Republican supporters claimed. Staunch conservatives such as David Stockman saw the budget battle as a defeat for their cause. In virtually every case, the Reagan administration only trimmed, rather than dismantled, domestic programs.

In contrast, the Economic Recovery Tax Act of 1982 (ERTA), again passed with the support of Boll-Weevil Democrats, brought the largest revenue cut in U.S. history. It called for tax rates to fall by 5 percent in 1981 and by another

10 percent in both 1982 and 1983. Although businesses, particularly those connected to the oil industry, received significant reductions, ERTA aimed most of its tax cuts at individuals, especially those with large incomes who paid the bulk of the federal taxes.

The White House predicted signs of economic revival by early 1982. Instead, every indicator signaled the worst depression since the 1930s. The official unemployment rate soared to nearly 11 percent during 1982. Industrial output plummeted to the lowest figure, 68 percent of capacity, since 1948. The rate of business failures, especially for smaller family-run farms in the Midwest, rose significantly. The nation's GDP declined—or, in the language of economics, "grew at a negative rate"—while the federal government's budget shortfall, rather than its revenues, skyrocketed. The budget deficit topped the $200 billion mark, and the accumulated national debt passed the trillion-dollar barrier. Reagan himself optimistically urged the need to "stay the course" with his remedies and insisted that the economy simply needed more time to recover the "nonstop binge" of Democratic spending. Noting that inflation had declined by 1982, his supply-side advisers predicted that Reaganomics would soon drive inefficient producers from the marketplace and push down labor costs, thus producing both a recovery and a more competitive economy. Voters seemed ambivalent. During the congressional elections of 1982, the Republicans lost twenty-six seats in the House of Representatives, but exit polls suggested that most voters still held the Democratic policies of Jimmy Carter, rather than those of Reagan, primarily responsible for current economic woes.

A number of forces, which came together in early 1983, ushered in the promised recovery. Most businesses had by then adopted energy-saving measures to blunt the impact of the oil-price increases of the 1970s and had found more efficient ways to produce products and deliver services, especially by cutting "middle-management" positions. The Federal Reserve Board (FRB), under Carter appointee Paul Volker, increased the amount of money in circulation as a spur to economic activity. At the same time, the initial tax cuts of 1981 finally appeared to work, although most economists saw their impact being felt in the form of renewed spending by consumers rather than increased savings and investment, as supply-side theorists had predicted. As supply-siders lost influence, others within the administration worked with Congress to replace the previously scheduled cuts with modest tax increases in 1982, 1983, and 1984.

Perhaps most important, Reagan's massive expenditures for defense, which ignored his promise of a balanced federal budget, provided constant economic stimulus. Congress passed the Gramm-Rudman-Hollings Act of 1985, which tried to limit budget overruns, but the U.S. Supreme Court declared it an unconstitutional invasion of executive authority. Although Congress eventually passed a substitute measure that limited the size of federal deficits, called simply Gramm-Rudman, congressional Democrats generally joined the White House in ignoring both the annual budget shortfalls and the long-term federal deficit they fueled.

Economic indicators improved substantially over a 92-month period; the Reagan boom lasted through Reagan's presidency and the first years of George Bush's. Between 1983 and 1990, the GNP grew by 32 percent, and the economy added 18 million new jobs. Unemployment figures dropped, as did the rate of inflation. The stock market soared. By 1987, the Dow Jones Industrial Average stood at its high of more than 2,700. Even the "Black Monday" crash of October 19, 1987, which saw the Dow Jones set another record by plummeting 508 points or nearly 23 percent in a single day, failed to dampen either confidence in the Reagan boom or the stock market. Economic expansion continued, and Wall Street rebounded quickly. During Reagan's presidency, the S&P stock index rose by nearly 300 percent.

At the beginning of the Reagan boom, *Newsweek* invoked a popular cultural symbol of the economic, and political, turn-around and dubbed 1984 the "Year of the Yuppie." A young, upwardly mobile, urban professional, the Yuppie supposedly had abandoned the hippie-style protests of the 1960s for Reagan-era lifestyles. Popular films such as *The Big Chill* (1983) and *Wall Street* (1987) represented these former baby boomers as consumption-hungry profit maximizers, crass materialists who calculated the impact of Reaganomics on their own, rather than governmental, budgets. In addition to career- and resume-building, a Yuppie allegedly focused on health spas, cholesterol levels, foreign-built sports cars, trendy restaurants, and upscale boutiques. Just as affluent suburbanites had symbolized the Eisenhower era of the 1950s, Yuppies denoted the Reagan period. At their 1988 National Convention, Democrats expressed contempt for eight years of Reagan with buttons that said, "Die Yuppie Scum."

The Reagan-era economy also became associated with a culture of extravagance (rather than one of mere Yuppie affluence). "Lifestyles of the Rich and Famous," a popular TV program of the 1980s, showed how movie stars and corporate CEOs spent their vast wealth. A real-estate mogul from New York City became an all-purpose celebrity. Donald Trump lent his name to an office tower, a gambling casino, an apartment palace, an autobiography, and even a board game. Malcolm Forbes, publisher of the financial magazine bearing his name, motorcycled with Hollywood stars, threw his own multimillion-dollar birthday bash in Morocco, and published an annual tally of the nation's 400 richest individuals, a Reagan-era counterpart to *Fortune* magazine's list of the top 500 corporations. The job of being a tycoon, or an "entrepreneur," once again seemed in fashion.

Reaganomics: The Debate

Critics thought otherwise. Labor leaders charged the White House with "union-busting." When PATCO, the union that represented governmental air traffic controllers, went on strike in 1981, the Reagan administration quickly fired the strikers and hired replacement workers. Conservative appointees to the National Labor Relations Board (NLRB), the national agency that adjudicated labor-management disputes, adopted a decidedly anti-union tilt, and the federal courts, restocked with Reagan-nominated judges, showed little inclination to support organized labor's legal claims. Meanwhile, the decline of the nation's old industrial infrastructure, especially the steel industry, inexorably eroded labor's traditional base, and organizers made slow progress in unionizing the growing service sector. By 1988, only about 15 percent of U.S. workers belonged to a union. As a result, pro-union economists complained, the economic expansion under Reagan produced millions of jobs, but mostly nonunionized, low-paying ones.

Critics of Reaganomics also questioned the stability of the nation's corporate and financial structures. Had not "junk bonds," securities without the kind of backing required of more traditional commercial paper, financed many corporate mergers? The junk-bond craze, in fact, did not survive George Bush's presidency. Ivan Boesky, one of the 1980s most celebrated merger moguls, plea-bargained a reduced jail term by agreeing to testify against his associates. In 1990, the giant financial institution of Drexel Burnham Lambert, which had orchestrated the junk-bond phenomenon, declared bankruptcy, and one of its principal architects, Michael Miliken, went to prison.

Problems in the savings-and-loan (S&L) industry dramatized the underside of corporate growth during the Reagan boom. S&Ls, financial institutions that specialized in home mortgages and were subject to different government regulations than ordinary banks, staggered during the 1970s. Federal regulations, dating from the Depression Decade of the 1930s, limited the amount of interest that they could pay to savings-account depositors, and people withdrew money from low-interest S&L accounts in order to seek higher rates of return during a time of inflation. In an attempt to revive the industry, the Reagan White House and Congress lifted a variety of restrictions on S&Ls, permitting new kinds of riskier lending. After briefly benefiting from this deregulation and from the general economic recovery, the entire S&L industry began unraveling. Many S&Ls, especially in Sunbelt states such as Texas, overindulged on junk bonds and high-risk business ventures. Others squandered money in old-fashioned ways, such as fancy living by extravagant owners. Only unprecedented assistance from Washington, it finally became apparent, could prevent a meltdown within the S&L industry. The largest corporate bailout plan in U.S. history, hastily enacted by Congress in 1989, propped up the S&L system, at a cost of at least $3,000 to every taxpayer in the country.

The specter of insolvency, critics claimed, threatened to spread beyond the savings-and-loan industry. During the 1980s both corporations and family businesses, along with ordinary consumers, increased their debt load. Businesses relied on complex debt-restructuring deals, and ordinary consumers counted on credit cards, as the number of cardholders increased by more than 30 percent. Commenting on these trends, *Business Week* magazine talked of a "debt binge" and dubbed "Charge It!" the battle cry of the Reagan era. Critics also noted, not surprisingly, that the number of bankruptcy proceedings was steadily increasing. Both ordinary wage-earners and former wheeler-dealers, such as former Texas Governor John Connally, declared bankruptcy and conceded that their personal boom had ended.

The most passionate debates involved the impact of Reaganomics on peoples' well being rather than on business balance sheets. Although the severe inflationary pressures of the 1970s subsided and employment figures steadily increased, "real" income (what people earn after adjusting for inflation) continued to decline, though at a relatively slower rate, during the Reagan boom. Between 1978 and 1988, the average wage, when adjusted for inflation, failed to keep pace with the cost of living. Women's earnings continued to lag behind those of men, workers of color behind those of whites. Many young wage-earners, including those from two-income families, struggled to enter the home-buying market. For the first time since World War II, the percentage of people owning their own homes dropped. Even the everyday life of the salaried Yuppie was not all fern bars and BMWs. Young professionals complained of working long hours, worrying about debts, and juggling too many responsibilities.

The Reagan boom had its defenders. One historian, seeking to characterize the economic milieu of the Reagan era, adapted a familiar line from Charles Dickens: If the 1980s were not the best of times, they were not the worst. Despite the junk-bond and S&L debacles, the nation's corporate and financial structure remained fundamentally sound. If the total amount of indebtedness rose, the accelerating value of business and personal assets meant that the overall ratio of debts-to-assets looked much better in 1990, after ten years of Reaganomics, than it had in 1980. The remarkable economic boom of the 1990s largely silenced those who had looked with envy at Japan's and Germany's economies during the 1980s and undercut claims that Republican administrations had allowed the nation's business and financial systems to fall into decay. Although figures on individual real income did register a slight decline during the 1980s, the average worker's total compensation package, which included fringe benefits and bonuses rather than simply wages and salaries, actually increased during the 1980s. Moreover, as more married women entered the job market and average family size decreased, the real income of households (as opposed to that of individuals) also rose, once the depression of 1981–1982 passed.

Reaganomics and Fairness

Reaganomics recast the "fairness" question that had been so central to the equality debates of the 1970. Republicans argued that the Reagan-Bush economic revival eventually did reduce the number of people living in poverty, if only by a few percentage points. Similarly, they noted that budget cuts never eliminated aid for the "truly needy" and that what Reagan called the social "safety net" remained in place. If virtually every study showed that *relatively* little of the economic growth generated between 1983 and 1990 reached people living below or near what governmental statisticians defined as the poverty line, celebrants of Reaganomics downplayed these findings. Emphasizing opportunity for individuals over equality of results, they insisted that economic and social policies that rewarded people who were morally and economically successful would eventually "trickle down" the social-economic structure. Moreover, conservatives continued to insist that the welfare system itself actually produced, rather than ameliorated, economic distress and urged simply junking it. A few programs, most notably AFDC, did see reductions in funding, but the continued clout of congressional Democrats and pro-Democratic lobbying groups, such as The Children's Defense Fund, actually brought a slight increase in the total amount of federal spending for social programs during the Reagan and Bush presidencies.

The economic boom clearly made the already wealthy even wealthier. The earnings of an average corporation CEO reached nearly 100 times that of an average worker; the comparable gap was 25 times in Germany and only 17 in Japan. According to one study of pre-tax income shares, the annual portion going to the richest 20 percent of the population increased by about $44 billion between 1980 and 1985, whereas the remaining 80 percent saw their share decrease by about the same amount. A 1991 study by the Census Bureau found that net worth of the richest 20 percent of households increased substantially during the late 1980s while that of the remaining 80 percent hardly changed at all. Even the staunchly conservative *Business Week* asked if the apparently growing wealth and income gaps might eventually become a serious national problem.

Economists identified several reasons for these trends. The flood of baby boomers into the workforce, together with the rising percentage of women who worked outside the home, swelled demand for entry-level jobs. Tax revision primarily benefited people in the top-income levels. According to one study, the wealthiest 1 percent of the population watched their taxes decrease by 25 percent during the 1980s, whereas those in the bottom 40 percent saw virtually no tax relief at all. Budget cutbacks, although never as drastic as many Republicans in Congress desired, did take a toll. Programs to fund public-sector employment and job-training, which had never been extensive, were either eliminated or scaled back. This reduction meant that, as jobs in the old, industrial-manufacturing sector disappeared, workers could not easily gain the skills needed for comparable-paying jobs in other areas. At the end of the 1970s, a male college graduate, on average, earned about 50 percent more than a high-school friend who had bypassed higher education. By the early 1990s, this figure stood at nearly 85 percent.

Economic trends reshaped the relationship between ethnicity and income in the United States. At a time when a college degree was becoming increasingly important to economic success, college-completion rates for European and Asian Americans were rising steadily. Among students from African-American and Spanish-speaking backgrounds, the picture was mixed. Even though high-school completion rates were increasing, the percentage of low-income African Americans who went on to college dropped by nearly 10 percent during the early and mid-1980s; the comparable figure for Latinos fell by about 7 percent. After 1986, college and university enrollments among African American and Hispanics did increase, largely as a result of increased enrollment by students from middle-income families, especially at private institutions.

Short-term trends portended long-term consequences. They signaled that African American and Latino college graduates would provide the basis for growing middle-class communities but also meant that other members of those same ethnic groups lacked the higher education increasingly needed for economic mobility. The Reagan-Bush era, in other words, provided the basis for an income structure, left intact during the 1990s, in which disparities *within* non-European ethnic groups—especially within the African American community—would become as great as ones between people of European and non-European descent. While observers noted an expanding African-American middle class, for instance, economic statistics showed that the number of children from African-American families whose income fell below the official poverty line was also growing.

Millions of people, then, glimpsed the economic boom from afar. People who could not afford permanent housing dotted big city streets. Some members of this "homeless" population were individuals with drug-dependency and/or mental problems. Releasing mentally impaired individuals from institutions, a "reform" of the 1970s, often substituted bus terminals and subway stations for state-run hospitals. But even families who had been pushed out of the job and housing markets sometimes found themselves on the streets or in temporary shelters. Of the more than 30 million people officially classified as "poor" according to governmental statistics, more than one-third—13 million—were children. Nearly a half-million children were estimated to be among the homeless by the late 1980s.

The 1980s also recalled Michael Harrington's earlier observation of how a generally affluent economy could conceal inequality. As social workers recognized, low-income people lived not only in clearly marked "ghettos" but also in other communities, the most segregated of which were defined by ethnicity or by age. One study, which tracked African American men during the early 1980s (before AIDS and crack cocaine made conditions much worse), found that "black men in Harlem were less likely to reach the age of 65 than men in Bangladesh," one of the poorest countries in the world. The infant mortality rate in the United States remained higher than in any other industrial country, and New York City's rate (which had declined during the 1960s and 1970s) actually rose during the 1980s because of inadequately funded health and social-service facilities and increased use of crack cocaine among women. Although the worst rural problems, farm foreclosures and small-town business failures, had eased by the end of the 1980s, the fact that many farm families continued to rely on food stamps and surplus commodities remained one of the grim ironies of the 1980s. Critics complained that the media rarely covered such issues of poverty in any depth.

The "feminization of poverty" persisted. According to some studies, about half of the people living below the poverty line also lived in families headed by women. The combined value of AFDC and food stamps could not buy enough to lift a family of three, the average size of a household receiving welfare, above the poverty line. Without job-training programs, however, women who had never held a steady position could feel psychologically unprepared for work. As one mother who wanted employment explained, "I get so nervous and scared going out looking for a job . . . I never know how to talk." Yet the welfare system, unlike most low-wage jobs, did provide coverage of basic health-care needs through Medicaid, an essential consideration for women with small children.

Different frameworks for viewing social-policy issues, each employing its own set of labels, competed with each other to shape the discussion of political priorities policy issues. Those who had espoused the "new egalitarianism" during the 1970s found Reagan using his presidential pulpit to label them as "big spenders" who were clinging to the "failures of the past." In response, they tried to claim that the Reagan administration's characterization of Great Society-era policies still unfairly "blamed the victims" of inequality and wrongly indicted governmental programs that, if adequately funded, would address complicated, structural problems. A dwindling number of congressional Democrats continued to support this analysis and vote for increased spending for welfare programs.

Many other members of Congress and policy analysts at the White House explained inequality differently, employing a popular analysis that talked of "the underclass." In this view, many of the unemployed and welfare recipients were rootless, criminally and sexually deviant, socially disorganized people who had never embraced values such as work, commitment, and responsibility. Theories of the underclass also claimed that parents from this social stratum transmitted their aberrant cultural values to children, who in turn, dropped out of school, used drugs, and evaded responsibility. Conservatives continued to blame the welfare system, particularly AFDC payments, for encouraging unmarried women with children to stay on welfare rather than to seek work. The problem of the underclass, in this view, stemmed from a failure of individual character and a decline in cultural values that could be traced back to the broader failure of the positive-state vision of social policy.

Another prominent theory, associated with the sociologist William Julius Wilson, spoke of "the truly disadvantaged." Agreeing in part with the new egalitarianism, it noted structural problems: Businesses were taking jobs from low-income neighborhoods, population shifts were draining tax dollars to new suburban areas, and governmental policies were failing to rebuild community infrastructures. The absence of adequately paid jobs at the entry level, the lack of training programs, and the paucity of child-care facilities made welfare payments seem to be the rational alternative for many poor women. Yet, the truly disadvantaged formulation also agreed with the underclass theory in seeing low-income communities suffering from individualized problems, such as a lack of positive role models. Conservative policymakers eagerly embraced only the second half of the truly disadvantaged framework. Rejecting structural solutions, such as intensive job-training programs, they pressed remedies that would target individual behavior by strengthening criminal sanctions, particularly for drug-related offenses, and would curtail the existing welfare system that supposedly encouraged deviant behavior and values.

Lawmakers from across the political spectrum came to agree on the need to revamp welfare but differed on how to do it. Even many Democrats who had long supported expansion of welfare programs such as AFDC reluctantly conceded that the newly conservative political climate made it unlikely that Congress and state legislatures would vote increased funding. Consequently, debate centered on cutting welfare rolls by encouraging the unemployed, particularly women on AFDC, to obtain the training and the skills needed to secure steady employment. One approach, anchored in the new egalitarianism of the 1970s, emphasized job-training provisions that were linked to creation of actual jobs. The more popular alternative, pushed by conservative think tanks such as the Heritage Foundation and Cato Institute, gave top priority to eliminating welfare itself. At a time of growing conservatism, proposals by Republicans and their Democratic allies, such as provisions in the 1982 budget act designed to push women off AFDC, seemed politically more popular than calls to train workers and create jobs.

Finally, in 1988, a bipartisan congressional coalition passed the Family Support Act (FSA). A compromise measure, FSA required states to implement their own versions of "workfare," new employment requirements for welfare recipients, and to help women currently receiving AFDC attain job skills. It also mandated that states make provision for child-care and health-care needs of people who were to be moved off welfare. Because the FSA lacked clear federal guarantees, especially for job creation, advocates of the new egalitarianism saw it as a largely symbolic, ill-conceived attack on people who needed welfare programs to survive. Most strong conservatives also viewed FSA, since it retained much of the existing system, as more symbol than substance. However, the more pragmatic legislators, moderates and conservatives alike, who accurately forecasted the political climate of the 1990s, viewed FSA as an important step toward ending the existing welfare system.

Drugs, AIDS, and Abortion

When covering social issues, the media emphasized drugs, AIDS, and abortion, all of which became the focus of emotional debate. Both Ronald Reagan and George Bush pledged all-out war against drug dealers and drug use. Nancy Reagan spearheaded a much-publicized campaign to "Just Say No" to drugs. Bush appointed tough-talking William Bennett, who had been Reagan's spokesperson on higher education, as "drug czar" and charged him with stopping the flow of illegal drugs into the country and confronting the violent gangs that distributed them. Yet only a few blocks from the White House, drug dealers continued to peddle their wares, relatively free from official interdiction.

No community escaped drug dealing and substance abuse, but people who dealt with these issues every day complained that members of the media and politicians too often sensationalized problems and offered unrealistic solutions, especially more Draconian laws. Between 1986 and 1991, for example, the number of men of African descent in prison for drug-related offenses increased by 430 percent while the comparable figure for women rose by more than 800 percent. The gap between these numbers and those for other ethnic groups, criminologists argued, did not reflect differences in drug use and trafficking as much as different approaches to enforcing anti-drug laws and sentencing offenders. Suburbanites convicted of cocaine-related offenses invariably received lesser penalties than inner-city residents connected to the traffic in crack cocaine.

A dangerous new threat—AIDS—affected every ethnic group and social strata. AIDS, or acquired immune deficiency syndrome, actually designated several types of fatal viruses that were usually sexually transmitted but could be spread in other ways as well. Throughout the decade, both the unknown and the celebrated died from AIDS—Hollywood's Rock Hudson, the Old Right's Roy Cohn, the New Right's Terry Dolan, the fashion world's Halston, and tennis's Arthur Ashe were among the prominent people who succumbed.

Everything about AIDS seemed controversial. Initially, the disease primarily affected gay men, and this pattern inclined conservatives to downplay efforts to fight, or even to publicize, its spread. Similarly, the association of AIDS with people from Africa and the Caribbean encouraged both misinformation and prejudice. Even scientists pursuing a cure became embroiled in nasty disputes over how AIDS was spread, which people were at greatest risk, and what team of scientists deserved the credit (and the money) for isolating its probable viral source. Meanwhile, activists complained that Washington was moving far too slowly to encourage and license drugs that promised to at least slow the effects of AIDS.

Gay and lesbian issues continued to generate controversy. Faced with what they saw as intransigence and delay on the AIDS issue, some gay activists charged the Reagan administration with kowtowing to the New Right by initially dismissing AIDS as a "special-interest" issue. Most gay leaders urged "safe sex" and monogamous relationships. Others, however, worried that this kind of advice implicitly embraced the kinds of sexual strictures favored by the New Right. Although right-wing libertarians such as Barry Goldwater condemned governmental interference with gay and lesbian lifestyles, most religious conservatives denounced homosexuality as sinful and urged criminal penalties, a stance supported by a majority of the U.S. Supreme Court in *Bowers v. Hardwick* (1986).

Reagan's own Surgeon General, C. Everett Koop, enraged the New Right by acknowledging the reality of sexual relationships outside the bounds of heterosexual marriage and promoting condom use as a sensible precaution against sexually transmitted diseases (STDs)

The furor over abortion overshadowed the politics of AIDS. Here, New Right activists continued to preach a blunt message: The government must say no to abortions. Fearing any compromise, some refused to make exceptions for rape or incest. Although opinion polls suggested that most people favored legal abortions in a variety of circumstances, the anti-abortion forces pressed their case through direct action, including the kind of civil disobedience pioneered by the civil-rights movement of the 1950s and 1960s, and aggressive political lobbying.

The anti-abortion, or pro-life, coalition increasingly hoped that the Supreme Court would overturn the *Roe v. Wade* decision of 1973. In the fall of 1987, though, the pro-choice forces joined with civil liberties groups in successfully blocking Reagan's nomination to the Court of Robert H. Bork, an outspoken opponent of the rights revolution that had produced *Roe*. By a 58–42 margin, the Senate rejected Bork, who many expected would provide the crucial vote needed to overturn *Roe*. This decision energized the New Right, who charged critics with misrepresenting Bork's legal positions and "Borking" their nominee. Others blamed the White House, sardonically claiming that Bork's nomination would have sailed through Congress "if Reagan were still alive." The Senate subsequently confirmed Anthony Kennedy, a Reagan-style conservative from California.

Bork's failed nomination further polarized abortion politics. Justice Kennedy did provide a key anti-abortion vote in the *Webster* case (1989), a 5–4 decision that upheld a Missouri statute that severely limited women's access to legal abortions and opened the door for restrictions in other states. However, in this and subsequent cases, Justice Sandra Day O'Connor refused to join the four-justice bloc ready to overturn *Roe v. Wade*. As a result, both pro-choice and pro-life forces mobilized, all across the country and even in U.S. territories such as Guam. Groups associated with the New Right, such as "Operation Rescue," organized sit-ins outside of abortion clinics and picketed the offices and private homes of physicians who staffed them. Women found it more difficult than any time since *Roe* to gain access to safe and legal abortions.

The Culture of Sleaze

As the Reagan administration was preparing to leave office, a widely respected GOP leader asked, "For God's sake, are we not entitled to hope that the next administration will be a little less sleazy?" Indeed, "sleaze" became a much-noticed side effect to a time of renewed affluence.

The media, as if warming up for the exposure crusade of the Clinton era (see pp. 328–332), began to uncover sleaze everywhere. The religious wing of the New Right offered a ready political target. Jimmy Swaggart, who headed a vast TV and religious publishing empire, fell into disgrace and (even worse for an evangelical preacher) media oblivion when a rival minister revealed Swaggart's patronage of prostitutes. Oral Roberts, a longtime leader of the electronic church, confronted falling TV ratings and declining revenues after a sleazy fund-raising campaign in which he claimed that the Lord might strike him dead if donors failed to fill his coffers. Perhaps the biggest sleaze spectacle of the 1980s took down Jim and Tammy Bakker, a husband and wife evangelist team, who lost their religious theme park, TV network, personal fortune, and each other following revelation of a sex and money-skimming scandal.

The pursuit of sleaze paid dividends for the media. CBS's "60 Minutes" used stories about scams and schemes to reach Nielsen's top ten, and ABC's "Nightline" garnered its highest ratings when featuring the problems of the Bakkers. By the middle of the 1980s, imitators such as "Hard Copy" and "A Current Affair" flooded TV's syndication market with stories and formats considered too sleazy to meet network standards. Going one step further, TV "talk" shows such as "Geraldo," in which verbal excess became standard fare, found a niche on independent stations and provided the prototype for the CATV shows, such as "Geraldo Live," that marked the 1990s.

Even Ronald Reagan's Teflon coating began to look stained. Most people regarded Reagan as personally honest but increasingly felt he had paid too little attention to the sleazy behavior of his subordinates. More than one hundred members of his administration were either convicted of crimes or cited for ethical violations by governmental watchdog bodies. Several top-ranking officeholders, including two cabinet officers, resigned while under fire. The Department of Housing and Urban Development (HUD) paid generous "consulting" fees to prominent Republicans and channeled scarce housing and redevelopment funds into a series of questionable projects. Political appointees in the Pentagon pleaded guilty to accepting bribes, and investigative journalists claimed that $2.2 trillion worth of defense expenditures included huge cost overruns on faulty products and expenditures for vastly overpriced spare parts. After Reagan had been out of office a year, opinion polls showed his approval rating below that of another former president, Jimmy Carter, the person whom he had handily out-polled a decade earlier.

Reagan's Democratic adversaries also had their troubles. During the 1988 presidential primaries, journalists discovered presidential aspirant Gary Hart, who presented himself as a "family man," sailing off the coast of Florida and sneaking around Washington with a woman who was not his wife. Other prominent Democrats—including Jim Wright, who was Speaker of the House of Representatives—were forced to leave office in the wake of stories, pressed by both journalists and Republican activists, about questionable financial dealings.

The Independent Counsel Act, part of the broader Ethics in Government Act of 1978, helped make the search for sleazy behavior a permanent part of national politics. This law grew out of the wars of Watergate and aimed at preventing a repetition of the so-called Saturday Night Massacre of 1973, when Richard Nixon dismissed Archibald Cox, who was investigating his administration. It established complex procedures by which the attorney general or, sometimes, a special three-judge panel (in instances when it seemed that the attorney general had a conflict of interest) could appoint a special independent counsel to investigate alleged misdeeds by high-ranking members of the executive branch. The president could not fire this independent counsel.

The law itself remained controversial. Lawyers in Reagan's administration, particularly attorney general Edwin Meese, thought it unconstitutional because it mingled the work of the executive and judicial branches of government and thus violated the separation-of-powers principle. The U.S. Supreme Court, however, upheld the law, and five special independent counsels—two of whom investigated allegations of wrongdoing by Meese himself—were appointed during Reagan's presidency and several others during George H. Bush's. The institutionalization of an independent counsel arrangement—used previously only in extraordinary instances, such as the Truman-era scandals and Watergate—marked an important turn in both governance and partisan politics.

THE NEW COLD WAR, 1981–1987

During the presidential campaign of 1980, Ronald Reagan portrayed Jimmy Carter as a weak leader presiding over the erosion of American power abroad. Reagan promised to restore respect for the United States by aggressively confronting the Soviet's "evil empire" in every part of the world. Returning to the rhetoric of the early cold war and portraying the world as simply a bipolar battleground between the forces of good and evil, Reagan's foreign policy initially stressed unilateralism, militarism, and anticommunism. During his first term, the president launched a military buildup, abandoned detente with the Soviets, delayed arms-control negotiations, installed new missiles throughout Europe, pulled out of the UN Educational, Scientific, and Cultural Organization (UNESCO), beefed up the CIA, sent troops to Lebanon and Grenada, funded a mercenary army to fight the Marxist government of Nicaragua, and funded anti-Marxist troops in Angola, Afghanistan, and elsewhere. After the nation's defeat in Vietnam and the hostage crisis with Iran, Reagan seemed to tap a desire to assert American power aggressively and globally.

A New Anti-Communist Offensive

A massive military buildup, unprecedented in the absence of a war overseas, dominated Reagan's foreign policy. Massive new expenditures, accompanied as they were by tax cuts, tripled the national debt, increased the government's share of the GNP to over 25 percent, and transformed the United States from the world's principal creditor into its largest debtor. Critics charged that such large deficits undermined the nation's economic health, but Reagan requested deeper and deeper cuts in domestic social programs to compensate. He refused to acknowledge what David Stockman later conceded: that reduction of social spending could never come close to bridging the gap between expenditures for the military buildup and tax cuts.

In Reagan's vision, activism by the federal government was appropriate in the area of military expansion, but not in social welfare. The "Reagan revolution" required curtailing the government's domestic regulatory and welfare functions while expanding its national security sector. The administration aimed at enlarging both nuclear and conventional military capabilities. It ordered more of the controversial MX missiles and B-1 bombers and enlarged its force of Trident submarines. Over grassroots protests throughout Europe, America's NATO allies agreed to deploy U.S.-made Pershing II and cruise missiles in Western Europe. Billions of dollars went for the military payroll and the modernization of equipment and bases.

During his first term, Reagan used arms-control talks primarily to help fuel this defense buildup. As a candidate, Reagan had condemned Carter's SALT II accords, which Congress never ratified but which both the United States and the USSR unofficially observed. As president, Reagan opened new negotiations, which he relabeled START (Strategic Arms Reduction Talks), and then argued that only enlarged military budgets and an arms buildup could bring these talks to a successful conclusion. Arms control, however, proved politically popular at home, and a rapidly growing movement that urged a freeze on nuclear weapons criticized the administration for its apparent opposition to slowing the arms race. Documents made public in 2001 showed that the FBI conducted illegal surveillance against these domestic dissenters, including some members of Congress.

Carrying military competition to outer space became the most important—and most controversial—part of Reagan's military agenda. In 1984, after several private meetings with Dr. Edward Teller, the "father of the H-bomb," Reagan surprised even close advisers by proposing a Strategic Defense Initiative (SDI), a space-based system that would supposedly shield the United States from incoming warheads. Widely called "Star Wars," SDI would theoretically provide more protection than the traditional policy of deterring attack by the threat of "mutually assured destruction" (MAD).

Controversy over SDI mounted as scientists and politicians calculated its staggering costs and weighed its practicality. Many scientists warned that the computer software needed to operate a comprehensive space defense could never be made reliable. The dependability of advanced space technology became an even larger issue after the spring of 1986, when the space shuttle Challenger—whose mid-morning launch had been scheduled to take advantage of well-publicized, live television coverage—exploded in midair, killing all seven of its crew. Moreover, some strategic analysts pointed out that a missile defense system would only prompt the Soviets to build more technologically elaborate missiles, thereby greatly escalating the arms race without improving national security.

SDI divided the scientific community. Some scientists pledged to accept no government work for SDI, whereas others welcomed the new pipeline of lucrative contracts. The SDI proposal became a major obstacle to arms-reduction agreements with the Soviets and dominated foreign policy and budget debates for several years. Research money for SDI was appropriated during the Reagan years and then was gradually reduced for a decade after Reagan left office. Space-based defenses, however, would reappear as a major issue in American politics in the late 1990s.

The Reagan administration showed its readiness to deploy military power. In 1982, Israeli forces invaded Lebanon to destroy and disperse the Palestine Liberation Organization (PLO). Lebanese Muslims, allied with Syria and backed by the Soviet Union, fought both the Lebanese Christians and the Israeli occupiers. After arranging Israeli withdrawal, the Reagan administration dispatched 1,600 U.S. troops to Lebanon as part of a multinational force, but Lebanese Muslims renewed the struggle, now against forces from the United States. After a suicide commando mission in October 1983 killed 241 American troops, domestic criticism of Reagan's policy in Lebanon mounted. The U.S. military presence had aggravated, not lessened, violence and factionalism in Lebanon. Early in 1984, an election year, U.S. troops withdrew, and Syria consolidated its influence over Lebanon. The Reagan administration's hope to limit Syrian gains and stabilize Lebanon through military power collapsed.

Moreover, the perception among many Arabs that U.S. policy in the Middle East was almost identical to Israel's brought additional problems. Some Palestinian groups, fragmented and further radicalized after their expulsion from Lebanon, stepped up their use of terrorism and gained support from Libyan leader Muammar Qaddafi. As Qaddafi railed against Zionism and the United States, Reagan denounced the Libyan leader as a terrorist and a "flake." In the spring of 1986, Reagan ordered the bombing of Libya as part of a broader plan to eliminate Qaddafi from the scene. The bombs did considerable damage and killed Qaddafi's daughter, but his government survived. In the meantime, negotiations to end the spiraling bloodshed among Israel and its neighbors stalled for lack of any resolution on the Palestinian question.

Violence elsewhere in the Middle East mounted. Iran and Iraq engaged in a prolonged and devastating war, and militant Islamic groups seized a number of hostages from Western countries that they viewed as enemies. Publicly, Reagan pledged not to negotiate for the release of the hostages for fear of encouraging more kidnappings. Secretly, however, the administration began to arrange a deal to sell arms to Iran in exchange for the safe return of American hostages.

Meanwhile, the president's advisers found less risky places to assert U.S. military power. In counterpoint to the unsuccessful application of force in Lebanon, Reagan raised his ratings in opinion polls when he invaded the tiny Caribbean island of Grenada in October 1983. Justified as necessary to safeguard American medical students who were allegedly endangered by a leftist, revolutionary regime, the invasion really aimed at overthrowing an unfriendly government that looked to Castro's Cuba for ideas and material support. With a Pentagon-imposed blackout on news coverage delaying reports of unnecessary casualties, bungled intelligence gathering, and an uncoordinated battle strategy, the U.S. attack seemed a total success. Reagan's popularity soared. His supporters seemed eager to forget the Lebanese fiasco and to bask in what the administration proclaimed as a clear-cut military triumph closer to home.

In Africa, Reagan's anticommunism brought a stepped-up commitment to rebels seeking to overthrow the Marxist government in Angola and a more sympathetic policy toward white leaders in South Africa. His administration sided with the South African government in denouncing the African National Congress (ANC) as Communist-led, even though it was the oldest black political organization in South Africa and enjoyed widespread support internationally and among African Americans in the United States. Reagan's assistant secretary of state for African affairs called his South African policy "constructive engagement," arguing that U.S. support for the white South African government would promote change in its racial policies faster than punitive measures.

Constructive engagement provoked mounting controversy. South African Anglican Bishop Desmond Tutu, winner of the Nobel Peace Prize in 1984, charged that Reagan's sympathy toward white South Africans significantly worsened the situation for blacks and called for a change. Meanwhile, street protests throughout the United States, smaller-scale versions of the civil-rights and antiwar marches of the 1960s, pushed Congress and then the president into adopting some limited economic sanctions against South Africa. In 1985, an executive order curtailed loans to the South African government, prohibited importation of South African gold coins (krugerrands), banned most transfers of nuclear technology, and forbade export of some computers.

The Reagan administration made Nicaragua a central battleground of the new cold war. Determined to oust Nicaragua's Sandinista government because of its Marxist leanings and pro-Cuban stance, Reagan's advisers employed the by-now classic techniques of covert action. An economic offensive induced shortages and discontent; a propaganda campaign portrayed the Nicaraguan government as nothing but a Soviet or Cuban client; and support and training for a counterrevolutionary army, called "the contras," kept the Nicaraguan government under siege. Meanwhile, the administration expanded the U.S. military presence in neighboring Honduras and conducted ominous training exercises throughout the Caribbean, threatening an invasion of Nicaragua.

Congressional opposition and adverse public opinion, however, restrained the Reagan administration. Domestic opposition to its campaign against the Nicaraguan government intensified after revelations that the United States had mined Nicaraguan harbors (technically an act of war) without congressional assent. When the World Court supported Nicaragua's claim that the U.S. action violated international codes of conduct, the Reagan administration responded that the court lacked jurisdiction in the matter. In 1984, the U.S. Congress, after considering the mounting evidence of terrorist tactics and corruption by the contras, weighed in by cuting off military (though not humanitarian) aid to forces opposing the Sandinistas.

Undeterred, Reagan's policymakers stepped up economic destabilization measures against Nicaragua and pressed foreign governments and ultraconservative millionaires in the United States to secretly fund the contras' military efforts. In 1986, this fund-raising effort took a bizarre turn. Lieutenant Colonel Oliver North, who was directing the secret fund-raising and arms-supplying effort to the contras, offered to sell weapons to Iran in exchange both for the release of American hostages in the Middle East and for funds that could then be diverted to the contras. The head of the CIA, the national security adviser, and other top officials apparently knew of the scheme. Oddly, it was Reagan's close adviser and attorney general, Edwin Meese, who inadvertently revealed the peculiar connection between North's Iran and contra projects during a news conference.

When the Iran-contra scheme became public knowledge, it even seemed as if Ronald Reagan's own Watergate might be on the horizon. (The media dubbed the affair "Irangate.") News about the plan, gradually emerging in televised congressional hearings during the summer of 1987, discredited Reagan's foreign policy. First, North's plan violated the spirit of the congressional ban against military aid to the contras. Second, it contradicted Reagan's strong public stands both against negotiating with terrorists for hostages and militarily assisting Iran in its ongoing war with Iraq. The Reagan administration's private policy seemed to contradict its public posture. Third, the whole approach to foreign policy raised serious questions about presidential leadership. As details of the plan emerged, Reagan first seemed to deny any knowledge of the deals but later accepted responsibility without seeming to comprehend the legal ramifications and policy contradictions of his doing so.

The Iran-contra affair marred Reagan's image. Throughout lengthy investigations by Congress, by a presidential panel, and by a special independent prosecutor, the public increasingly glimpsed an administration that was fragmented and secretive. North, his immediate superior, National Security Adviser John Poindexter, and several other officials were convicted on criminal charges related to the affair. (Appellate courts overturned the convictions of North and Poindexter, and George H. Bush pardoned six other members of the Reagan administration linked to the Iran-contra deal during the closing days of his administration.) Then well into his seventies, Ronald Reagan suddenly looked old, confused, and barely in charge.

Surprisingly, to his critics as least, Reagan's most substantial foreign-policy feat still lay ahead of him. This was a positive, and surprising, achievement— concrete steps toward ending the cold war.

The Cold War Suddenly Thaws

During the last year-and-a-half of Reagan's presidency, the new cold war, which the president had heightened with inflamed rhetoric and hard-line policies, suddenly thawed. In a dramatic turn, the White House reversed course and took unprecedented steps toward detente.

In 1987, the administration that had launched the biggest military buildup in history signed a major arms-control treaty. A year earlier, at a summit conference in Reykjavík, Iceland—the first summit of Reagan's presidency—the Soviets had advanced the surprising proposal that both countries cut their nuclear weapons by half. Negotiations over such dramatic cuts, however, had stalled over the issue of SDI, Reagan's pet project that the Soviets wanted to end. Finally, in December 1987, a treaty reducing intermediate-range missile forces (IMF) was approved at a summit held in Washington, D.C. The agreement only slightly altered the overall strategic balance but carried immense political and symbolic significance. Both sides agreed to eliminate short- and medium-range missiles from Europe (including those that the Reagan administration had earlier pushed so hard to install) and approved on-site verification procedures, safeguards the Soviets had previously resisted. IMF signaled a major shift away from the arms race of the cold war.

What triggered this sudden thaw? For both countries, the reasons were much the same: grassroots pressure to redirect government priorities; top leaders who began to take a more pragmatic, less ideological, approach to policy; and urgent domestic economic problems.

In the United States during 1987, several trends jolted the Reagan administration into its reorientation of foreign policy. Growing concern over nuclear weapons made both citizens and political leaders increasingly sensitive to the danger of superpower conflict. The Iran-contra scandal dramatized the excesses of secret governments and the dangers of a heavily ideological, do-anything-necessary-to-win attitude.

Moreover, new advisers gained Reagan's ear. By the end of 1987, many of the officials who had shaped policy during the early Reagan years had departed and others had mellowed. New appointees, particularly former senator

Howard Baker, were less committed to anti-Communist crusades and less beholden to the GOP's New Right, which viewed a militant foreign policy as some solace for Reagan's failure to war aggressively against domestic social programs.

In this more pragmatic atmosphere, economic problems increasingly worried the business and public-policy elite and eroded support for Reagan's large defense budgets. Taken together, the yawning budget deficit and the adverse balance of trade portended a national security threat greater than communism: long-term economic decline. Academic publications and the public press trumpeted dire warnings about the end of the "American age." A scholarly study, *Rise and Fall of the Great Powers* by historian Paul Kennedy, became an unlikely bestseller and popularized a theory of "imperial overreach." Historically, wrote Kennedy, heavy military spending had caused the decay of powerful nations, and this seemed to be the fate awaiting the United States in the late twentieth century. The *New York Times Magazine,* in an issue that featured Paul Kennedy and other prophets of America's decline, pictured the United States as an aged, balding eagle, supported by a cane. Such economic worries, combined with the Democratic victories in the 1986 elections, eroded congressional support for weapons systems such as SDI. The Soviets believed they could now negotiate arms limitation without insisting on formal assurances of SDI's termination. As the public and policy elites became increasingly concerned over the deficit and trade balance, support for detente and arms control became more evident.

The most important causes of the thaw, however, stemmed from changes in the Soviet Union. Mikhail Gorbachev came to power in the USSR as part of a younger generation committed to major structural transformations in the Communist system. Announcing policies of *glasnost* (a more open society) and *perestroika* (economic restructuring and liberalization) at home, Gorbachev also championed arms control and detente. His initiatives brought him sympathetic coverage from the world press. As the image of "Gorby," a forward-looking international leader took hold, the Reagan administration did not want to risk being portrayed as captive to an old and dangerous cold-war mindset.

Gorbachev's policies, of course, were as much the result of changes in the Soviet Union as their cause. By the late 1980s, the Soviet economy was in chaos; environmental damage was widespread; and the USSR simply could no longer afford the expense of maintaining the cold war and managing an increasingly restive empire. In Eastern Europe, deteriorating economic conditions and the advancing age of the Soviet-bloc leadership portended a coming crisis for Communist regimes. Moscow's attempt to install a client government in neighboring, largely Muslim Afghanistan proved so costly and unpopular that Gorbachev finally withdrew Soviet troops, and the USSR's other international commitments also came under review. Moreover, Gorbachev and his advisers realized that the integration of Western Europe's economies, projected for 1992, could leave the Soviet Union and its Communist allies further and further behind in economic development. Restructuring (*perestroika*) needed to begin immediately, or the USSR's economic and imperial decline might be irreversible.

Leaders in both the United States and the Soviet Union finally acknowledged that the world was no longer, if it had ever been, rigidly bipolar. The robust economies of Japan and Germany, the projected economic integration of Western Europe, and rapid development in Pacific rim areas such as Korea and

Southeast Asia reshaped geopolitical and strategic thinking. The idea of a U.S.-Soviet cold war seemed an outmoded concept in a rapidly changing world, and domestic and foreign policies appeared in need of substantial readjustment. Governments seemed to chase transformations as much as they led them.

THE PRESIDENCY OF GEORGE H. BUSH

The thaw in the cold war, beginning shortly before the presidential election of 1988, muted debate over many questions. Ronald Reagan's legacy seemed to belong on every side of foreign policy issues, and Democrats lacked firm ground from which to criticize his policies. Most Democrats neither wanted nor were able to outflank Reagan in cold war crusading. Yet progress on arms control and the waning of the Soviet threat allowed the Reagan administration to claim credit for detente and a safer world. Both George Bush and Democratic nominee Michael Dukakis, the governor of Massachusetts, tried simultaneously to project "toughness" in foreign policy and to endorse the easing of the cold war. On domestic policies, Democrats, after two successive defeats to Reagan, could not offer another positive-state agenda similar to the one proposed by Walter Mondale in 1984.

The Election of 1988

The presidential election of 1988 turned more on personalities and symbols identified with the individual candidates than on specific policy differences. Michael Dukakis, an uninspiring campaigner in the mold of Walter Mondale, hinted at reversing Reagan's animus against social programs but offered few specific proposals. Instead, he presented himself as a skilled, bureaucratic manager who could bring greater economic growth. He claimed to have nurtured a "Massachusetts miracle" while governor. George Bush, while stressing his loyal service as vice-president, cautiously broke with the Reagan administration by promising a "kinder, gentler America" that would come through a new spirit of voluntarism, symbolized by his image of "a thousand points of light." Fine-tuned by Lee Atwater, the first major party leader talented enough to have played rock guitar professionally, Bush's media-savvy campaign portrayed Dukakis as big on taxes, soft on crime, and beholden to special interests, such as pro-choice feminists and his former rival for the nomination, Jesse Jackson. Bush pledged "no new taxes" and stressed his reverence for national symbols, particularly the right to bear arms and the Pledge of Allegiance to the flag.

Bush's media managers excelled in the art of TV advertising. Their ads invariably bathed Dukakis in gloomy shadows and captured his face while contorted in a frown. In contrast, they filmed the vice-president with strong backlighting and enveloped him in a warm, Disneylike glow. The most infamous ad of 1988, which received more air time when replayed on public-affairs talk shows than when originally broadcast, linked Dukakis to a sexual assault committed by an African American prisoner named Willie Horton, who had fled a Massachusetts institution while on a furlough program. Slow to fathom the emotional impact of this issue, Dukakis initially talked about how many furloughed prisoners had returned without incident. As one political consultant quipped, this apparent lack of emotion allowed the Bush forces to make it seem as if Willie

Horton, rather than Texas Senator Lloyd Bentson, were Dukakis's running mate in 1988. Bush and his own vice-presidential selection, J. Danforth Quayle, a young senator from Indiana who was a favorite of the New Right, won the election by a comfortable margin—426 electoral votes to 112 and 40 states to 10.

Bush's Domestic Policies

On domestic issues George Bush's administration generally staked out centrist positions that often angered the New Right. Its partisans saw Bush as less conservative than Reagan. They rejoiced when Bush vetoed a 1990 civil rights law, for allegedly mandating quotas for the hiring of women and people of color, but complained when he agreed to the very similar Civil Rights Act of 1991. A broad coalition of advocacy groups supported this measure, whose major innovation allowed employees to sue employers in order to recover damages for "sexual harassment," a legal remedy long championed by lawyers representing the feminist movement.

George Bush enthusiastically supported another important civil-rights measure passed during his presidency, the Americans with Disabilities Act (ADA) of 1990. The ADA would cover, its supporters estimated, more than 40 million people, the largest "minority" in the nation and one with the greatest number of Republicans. Recalling the "new egalitarianism" of the 1970s, the ADA required special workplace accommodations for people with disabilities, banned discrimination against physically and mentally challenged workers, and mandated removal of barriers to wheelchair access in all public facilities and places.

Bush's attempt to nudge the U.S. Supreme Court further rightward produced mixed results. Ronald Reagan had appointed three conservatives—Sandra Day O'Connor, Antonin Scalia, and Anthony Kennedy—to the Court, but David Souter, Bush's first nominee, kept his distance from the conservative bloc headed by Scalia and Chief Justice William Rehnquist. Bush's second nominee, Clarence Thomas, held legal and social views that pleased the New Right, but his nomination hearings before the U.S. Senate angered many women, including ones who normally voted Republican. (See pp. 312–313.)

Conservatives ultimately judged Bush by his campaign pledge: "Read my lips. No new taxes." Economic problems immediately threatened this anti-tax promise. As the unemployment statistics steadily rose and the rate of economic growth leveled off, the national government's budget deficit soared. Bush's advisers decided that the White House could not oppose a congressional economic package that did include increased tax rates, and in 1990, the president agreed to "tax revenue increases." Bush discerned a difference between "tax revenue increases" and "new taxes," but angry conservatives could read the president's lips. Bush's reversal on taxes widened divisions among Republicans that Reagan's two terms had successfully muted.

Economic issues, in general, dogged Bush's presidency. Even when the unemployment rate neared 8 percent, the administration made no aggressive response. Although the economy showed signs of recovery toward the end of 1992, this upswing did little to help George Bush. According to one poll, three-fourths of respondents still saw the economy in poor shape. The president's approval

**Percent of total population
below poverty level:** **12.5**
18 years and over 10.8
65 years and over 10.6
Related children under 18 years 17.1
Related children under 5 years 19.7
Related children 5 to 17 years. 16.1

FIGURE 9–2   People Below the Official Poverty Level, 2000.

Source: U.S. Census Bureau, Demographic Surveys Division, Created: June 28, 2001.

rating, which had once stood at more than 80 percent, steadily plummeted, and he received especially low marks as an economic manager. More broadly, people complained of "gridlock" in Washington, a political stalemate in which neither a Republican White House nor a Democratic Congress seemed able to agree on legislation to address economic recovery, rising health-care costs, or welfare and urban policies.

Events finally forced Bush to confront urban issues. Jack Kemp, secretary of housing and urban affairs, initially championed new inner-city policies. A free-market conservative, Kemp urged job-creation efforts targeted at low-income urban neighborhoods and proposed new programs, including one to allow tenants in public housing complexes to purchase their units. Kemp, who had formerly represented an urban congressional district, also hoped to bring more people from non-European ethnic groups into the GOP. When violence convulsed South Central Los Angeles in April 1992, after a jury acquitted four white police officers who had been charged with beating an African American motorist, Rodney King, the president himself turned toward urban issues. The "Rodney King riots," the worst urban conflagration since the 1960s, killed 53 people, left thousands injured, and produced property damages totaling more than $1 billion, the largest in U.S. history until the terrorist attacks on the World Trade Center on September 11, 2001. When calm returned to Los Angeles, Bush visited South Central and other low-income urban areas to promise increased governmental spending, but neither the White House nor Congress produced any programmatic innovations during Bush's presidency.

Foreign Policy under Bush

George Bush, a former ambassador to China and the UN and once the head of the CIA, focused more on foreign than domestic issues. He had hardly settled into the Oval Office before a chain of dramatic events reshaped international affairs. For at least two years, it had been obvious that the cold-war order was changing, but no one, anywhere in the world, forsaw how rapidly Communist governments would fall.

In late 1988, Soviet Premier Mikhail Gorbachev had, in effect, repudiated Leonid Breshnev's doctrine forbidding any nation in the Soviet sphere of influence from renouncing communism. "Freedom of choice is a universal principle," Gorbachev declared. Beginning in the summer of

1989, Eastern Europeans quickly tested his words. Poland ousted its Communist government in favor of one influenced by the popular, non-Communist labor movement, Solidarity. East Germans dismantled the Berlin Wall, forced their Communist government to resign, and moved quickly toward reunification with West Germany. Czechoslovakians, Hungarians, Romanians, and Bulgarians all mounted massive street demonstrations, tossed out their Communist rulers, and then struggled to establish new systems with market economies and parliamentary governments. A few months earlier, movements for change had swept across China, but the Chinese government abruptly halted them, killing some one thousand student protestors in Tienanmen Square in Beijing and tightening its grip over social and economic life.

People in the United States seemed dazzled by the pace of events. "No one was expecting the Eastern bloc to go out of business in a month," one State Department official exclaimed. "It's as though there is a fire, and we are chasing the trucks to the scene." Some saw opportunities: McDonald's quickly opened restaurants in Budapest and then in Moscow. *Playboy* became the first American magazine sold in Hungary.

The abatement of the cold war reverberated throughout the world. In Africa, tensions in some trouble spots had already eased. Lengthy negotiations finally brought independence to Namibia and the beginning of the withdrawal of Cuban troops from Angola, both areas in which cold-war tensions had exacerbated and prolonged disputes. Early in 1990, the South African government finally recognized the African National Congress (ANC), the black nationalist group it had long labeled as Communist, and released its most prominent leader, Nelson Mandela, from prison. Another startling thaw came in Nicaragua, where the Sandinista government, which the United States had long tried to undermine, held a free election and was voted out of power. The new government and the Sandinistas both worked toward national reconciliation. Clashing interests and ideologies remained in all of these places, but local rivalries no longer shaped themselves according to cold-war allegiances.

Soviet leaders became increasingly preoccupied with internal matters. The Baltic states of Latvia, Lithuania, and Estonia, which had been dominated by Moscow since World War II, declared independence. Then the major provinces that had made up the USSR itself sought self-government. The president of the new state of Russia, Boris Yeltsin, defiantly and successfully resisted a countercoup by hard-line Communists in August 1991, and his popularity rapidly eclipsed that of Gorbachev. Yeltsin championed the establishment of a new Commonwealth of Independent States. On December 12, 1991, the Parliament of Russia ratified such a plan, and eleven ex-Soviet republics followed suit. The Soviet Union no longer existed, and the United States suddenly faced the task of opening new embassies and developing diplomatic relations with more than a dozen new nations.

The Bush administration tried to shape a new foreign policy for this post-cold-war world. The secretary of defense projected a slowed pace of military spending, and members of Congress began to talk hopefully about a "peace dividend." Still, if the former Soviet threat seemed to be diminishing, Bush's policymakers pointed to new foreign dangers, and Pentagon planners charted new missions. Future actions, they suggested, would probably involve rapid, targeted strikes, perhaps against those nations that sponsored and harbored terrorists. Bush also turned to the military to fight the war against drugs that he had promised to wage during the election campaign.

Panama became an example of a new style of post-cold-war military action. Its government, under dictator General Manuel Noriega, carried on drug trafficking. The Reagan administration had legally indicted Noriega for drug dealing and tried to force him from power through economic pressure. Although Reagan's tactics crippled the Panamanian economy, Noriega only tightened his own political grip and denounced U.S. interference in Panama's affairs. Despite fears that Noriega, who had once worked closely with the CIA, could embarrass the United States by exposing intelligence secrets, the Bush administration decided to take military action. It wanted a friendly government with which to complete the transfer of the Panama Canal to Panamanian sovereignty. U.S. marines landed in Panama on December 20, 1989, and by the first week of January 1990, Noriega surrendered for extradition to the United States, where he stood trial, was convicted, and imprisoned. Not only did U.S. intervention gain Bush wide popularity at home and create a pro-United States government in Panama, it also seemed a warning to other drug dealers in the hemisphere.

Other U.S. military actions against drugs, such as a blockade of the coast of Colombia to interdict drug shipments and aerial destruction of coca fields in Peru, became increasingly controversial. Some leaders of Latin American countries, especially those who had to deal with the problems of drug production and crime within their borders, pointed out the futility of simply blaming foreign nations for the upsurge in drug use in the United States. They urged the United States to adopt antidrug policies more attuned to the law of supply and demand: to reduce drug consumption at home and build incentives for coca producers in Latin America to shift to other cash crops.

Environmentalists argued that post-cold-war foreign policy should focus on the dangers that seemed to loom on every front. Scientists documented the deterioration of the life-protecting ozone layer. Human practices that made desert out of productive land spread famine in Africa and elsewhere. Rain forests, which are needed to clean and produce oxygen for a healthy planet, suffered accelerating destruction. Water systems and animal habitats were coming under attack from acid rain and chemical poisons. Perhaps most ominously, experts debated whether or not the planet was beginning to experience the onset of a "greenhouse effect"—a general global warming aggravated by the heat from industrial processes that could alter climate patterns and disrupt habitat and livelihoods throughout the world. No less a figure than George Kennan, the "father" of the cold war's containment doctrine, saw environmental degradation as the most pressing threat to national security in the 1990s and called for a major national commitment. In April 1990, Earth Day II, a star-studded, twentieth anniversary of what had been a small consciousness-raising festival held in 1970, became an elaborate global media event. International drug problems and environmental hazards, however, were quickly overshadowed as the Bush administration turned its attention to trouble in the oil-rich Persian Gulf.

The Persian Gulf War

On August 2, 1990, President Saddam Hussein of Iraq invaded Kuwait and an-nounced that it would become his nation's nineteenth province. Although Hussein had been massing troops on the Iraq-Kuwait border and denounc-ing Kuwaiti oil producers, his bold move surprised U.S. officials. Anxious not to underestimate Hussein's ambitions a second time, intelligence experts now warned that Saudi Arabia, the Middle East's largest oil exporter and a longtime ally of the United States, might be Iraq's next target. George Bush compared the territorial ambitions of Saddam Hussein to those of Adolf Hitler.

Bush skillfully organized an international response. He convinced Saudi Arabia, initially reluctant to allow Western troops to enter its devoutly Muslim culture, to accept U.S. military installations. Only four days after the Iraqi in-vasion of Kuwait, he announced operation "Desert Shield" and ordered 230,000 troops to the Middle East. After consulting with Western European leaders and Moscow, the president approached the UN, which denounced the invasion of Kuwait, imposed economic sanctions against Iraq, and issued an ultimatum for Iraqi withdrawal. The United States deployed 200,000 additional U.S. troops in the Middle East, while allied countries agreed to bear 80 percent of the oper-ation's economic cost.

Bush's domestic critics feared a protracted war, "another Vietnam," against Iraq's supposedly battle-hardened army. They warned that such a conflict might only produce greater instability in the Middle East. In addition, some charged Bush with blatant economic imperialism in order to preserve the West's access to cheap oil.

In response to antiwar sentiment, the president asked Congress for a res-olution supporting the use of force in the Persian Gulf. Although debates were heated and the pro-war resolution passed the Senate by a mere five votes, Bush could claim a mandate for military action. The United States, he argued, had a moral obligation to sustain Kuwait's independence, and he also emphasized the economic peril that Iraq might pose to the West's supply of inexpensive oil. Secretary of State James Baker bluntly summarized what the ordinary U.S. citizen had at stake in Kuwait: "Jobs." As the UN's January deadline approached, Saddam Hussein promised a long, bloody war. He hinted about unleashing deadly new weapons, perhaps with chemical, bacteriological, or even rudi-mentary nuclear warheads.

The United States launched a new kind of war. Dubbed "Desert Storm" by the Bush administration, the Gulf War fit the routines of network television and the aesthetics of the small screen. The initial bombing assault on Iraq was timed so that it coincided with the evening news programs in the United States, and journalists from CNN covered the opening U.S. salvos from hotel rooms in Baghdad. Both Iraqi and U.S. officials tuned to CNN for information about what the other side was doing. Journalists, whose movements were carefully controlled by the U.S. government as they had been in Panama, cooperated with the military and generally reported only what the Pentagon wanted viewers to see. Charismatic military leaders, such as Generals ("Stormin'") Norman Schwarzkopf and Colin Powell, and the military's super-sophisticated arsenal of post-Vietnam weaponry were on prominent display. In video game fashion, TV

FIGURE 9–3   Preparing for War in the Persian Gulf, 1990.

President George Bush eats Thanksgiving dinner with U.S. troops deployed in advance of the 1991 war.
Source: George Bush Presidential Library and Museum.

screens showed "smart bombs," explosive devices equipped with complex guidance systems, hitting their targets with supposedly surgical precision and "Patriot" missiles supposedly intercepting Iraq's Scud attacks. After the war had ended, critical scrutiny of this Pentagon-managed imagery drastically deflated claims about the accuracy of the smart bombs and success rate of the Patriots. No Iraqi missile, it was finally determined, had ever been intercepted.

On February 24, 1991, the United States began a ground offensive against Iraq, and it took only four days of heavy pounding to end the war. Controlling the skies with air power, the United States kept its casualties to fewer than 150 battlefield deaths, whereas Iraqi military casualties were estimated at 100,000 deaths. Before retreating, Iraqi forces torched more than 500 of Kuwait's oil wells, producing a black inferno that required many months to extinguish. The brief war devastated the economic, transportation, and communication infrastructures of both Iraq and Kuwait. Although some officials wanted to continue the assault on Iraq and topple Saddam Hussein himself, Bush feared the uncertain consequences of such moves, which lacked the support of the United Nations, and pulled back the U.S. military.

The Gulf War represented a strong show of force by the United States and the United Nations. It undermined Saddam Hussein's prestige and his pretensions to leadership of an anti-Israeli, anti-Western bloc in the Middle East.

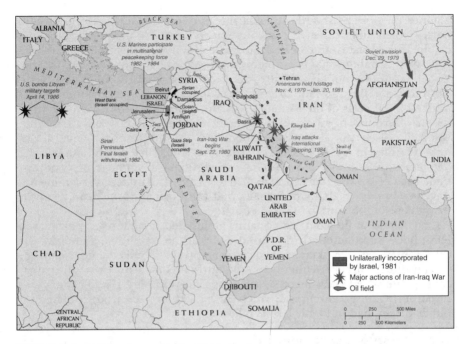

FIGURE 9–4   U.S. Involvement in the Middle East.

Oil, ethnic rivalries, and growing Islamic fundamentalism fuelled conflicts centered around Israel, the hostage crisis with Iran, and Iraq's attempted annexation of Kuwait in 1990.

In an effort to curtail Saddam Hussein's future power, the United States enforced "no-fly zones" in northern and southern Iraq, depriving Saddam Hussein of control over his own air space; leveled economic sanctions against the regime; and supported inspections to preclude the making of weapons of mass destruction in Iraq. The end of the Gulf War somewhat eased tensions throughout much of the Middle East and provided the backdrop for historic negotiations between Israel and the Palestine Liberation Organization. In August 1993, the PLO recognized Israel's right to exist in return for its acceptance, in principle, of Palestinian authority over the Gaza Strip and Jericho on the West Bank. These "Oslo Accords" provided a first step toward self-rule in these Israeli-occupied areas. President Bush had laid the basis for this Middle East peace process while still strongly supporting Israel.

Although the conflict in the Persian Gulf temporarily boosted George Bush's prestige as a world leader, the president failed to draft a clear foreign policy blueprint. He did have some successes. The international economic picture gradually improved. Huge debts, which Third World nations owed to U.S. banks, had threatened to shake the entire American banking system during the mid-1980s, but most were renegotiated by the end of the decade. New free-market economies began to evolve in ex-Communist states, and Western Europe planned major steps toward economic integration. Bush also made progress toward a North American Free Trade Agreement (NAFTA) that would join Canada, the United States, and Mexico into the largest free-market zone in the world.

New instabilities and problems, however, overshadowed these international economic policies. Civil turmoil convulsed several of the ex-Soviet provinces, and the transition to a private property, free-market economy proved difficult in all parts of the former USSR and in the formerly socialist states of Eastern Europe. Yugoslavia disintegrated, and Serbia embarked on a brutal campaign of territorial aggrandizement and "ethnic cleansing" against Muslims in Bosnia. In Asia, American officials complained that unfair business practices contributed to Japan's economic strength and to a dangerously adverse trade balance between Japan and the United States. In Africa, severe famine produced so much instability in Somalia that Bush ordered American troops to help establish humanitarian relief efforts.

The end of the cold war certainly eliminated some foreign-policy problems, but it simultaneously destroyed many of the traditional guideposts for what constituted U.S. national security. The president talked about shaping a "new world order," but neither he nor his advisers could explain how this broad concept translated into concrete goals or specific priorities. The policy of standing strong against communism, which Bush had followed throughout his long public career, had suddenly lost its relevance.

THE CULTURE INDUSTRY 1980–1992

During an era in which one president excelled in image-making and another struggled to do so, the importance of images and symbols—and of the process that produced them—assumed larger and larger significance in American culture. A burgeoning culture industry remained an arena of conflict.

The Reagan Boom and the Culture Industry

With a former movie star dominating politics, it seemed only appropriate that Hollywood, which had staggered through the 1970s, would prosper. The world market for movies, still dominated by Hollywood, more than doubled in size during the 1980s. At the same time, as European countries switched from state-run to commercial television systems, Hollywood-produced films and TV shows became sought-after commodities. By 1990, there were more television sets in Europe, primarily tuned to programming from the United States, than in North America.

Hollywood declared a truce in its battle with the video and CATV industries, which were expanding rapidly both in the United States and overseas. Filmmakers recognized the profits to be made from the rental and sale of their films and acknowledged that home-taping off TV, which the Supreme Court allowed in a 1984 decision, was a minor issue. Between 1980 and 1990, the number of VCRs in the United States rose from less than 2 to 62 million—more than two-thirds of U.S. homes owned at least one—and the sale of pre-recorded videos soared from 3 to 220 million units. Although Hollywood's receipts from theater box offices actually declined, those from CATV and from video sales and rentals increased substantially, a clear signal that more people were now watching

Hollywood movies at home than in theaters and that distinctions between the motion-picture and television industries had all but disappeared.

Hollywood moguls talked about "synergy," the capacity of a hit movie to spin off other products into non-film markets. Musical soundtracks, now marketed in CD format, remained a staple, but many other products, often tied in with marketing campaigns by other businesses, became part of a film's overall "package." A "Happy Meal" at McDonalds, for example, might include a replica of a popular character from Disney's *Little Mermaid* (1989) and prompt Burger King to counter with a movie tie-in of its own. *Jurassic Park* (1993) even included a sequence, within the movie itself, that showed the T-shirts and lunch boxes, which could be purchased in the theater lobby once Steven Spielberg's blockbuster had run its two-hour course.

Jurassic Park typified the kind of "high concept" film that came to dominate North American and world markets. Borrowing from the made-for-TV films and early blockbusters such as *Jaws* (1975) from the 1970s, a high-concept movie offered a pared down story line that could be captured through a 30-second TV commercial or even an eye-catching billboard. Characters, like stories, became simple and straightforward, as in *Die-Hard* (1985), in which an off-duty New York police officer (Bruce Willis) fights a multinational gang of terrorists who have seized a Japanese-owned office tower in Los Angeles. With minimal dialogue and maximum action, high-concept films such as *Jurassic Park* and *Die-Hard* easily generated sequels and did at least as well in non-English-speaking markets overseas as in the United States. Expanding the process of saturation booking, first used for *Jaws*, Hollywood simultaneously released its high-concept films in theaters across the country and flooded the media with glossy advertisements. George Lucas and Steven Spielberg, filmmakers raised on the TV and movie fare of the 1950s, followed their successes of the 1970s with ultraexpensive, high-concept movies about monsters, rock-and-roll, alien empires, and powerful heroes. In two of the three *Indiana Jones* thrillers, the Lucas-Spielberg hero even fought those most familiar of cinematic villains, Adolph Hitler's Nazis.

Male heroism, in the "hard body" mold of *Die-Hard*, did big business in the domestic and overseas markets. Sylvester Stallone's Rocky Balboa, a club-fighting journeyman boxer in his 1976 film debut, gains the heavyweight championship and in *Rocky IV* (1985) even battles the "evil empire" by fighting a Soviet superman. Stallone's cycle of Rambo films, violence-filled epics about an embittered Vietnam vet, also flourished during the Reagan era. Although Stallone himself had never served in Vietnam, his Nautilus-tuned character announces that defeat in Indochina—which Rambo's version of history attributed to journalists and cowardly politicians—could be avenged by an unencumbered superhero. Stallone's Rambo joined an entire platoon of heavily muscled, tight-lipped vigilantes and macho avengers (such as those played by Arnold Schwarzenegger) who blasted their way through the high-concept films of the 1980s and early 1990s. Off-screen, Willis, Stallone, and Schwarzenegger supported the GOP, an unusual political allegiance for younger Hollywood celebrities.

The new Hollywood offered few leading roles for women. Major distributors considered motion pictures that focused on independent women particularly risky ventures. Hollywood's moguls preferred women who stood by their men and stood up for traditional values, as they did in *Tender Mercies* (1982) and *Country* (1984). Women who stepped out of narrowly drawn gender boundaries risked becoming the butt of cruel jokes—or worse. An antifeminist backlash emerged in the new genre of "slasher" films, in which knife-and-chain-saw artists pursued potential female victims, and in mainstream films such as *Jagged Edge* (1985) and *Fatal Attraction* (1987). In the high-concept *Batman* (1989), Jack Nicholson's antihero, "the Joker," also casually brutalized women. Successful, mass-market films that touched on women's issues generally soft-pedaled their messages. Jane Fonda's *Nine to Five* (1980) leavened its images of feminist politics in the workplace with over-the-top slapstick humor. *Tootsie* (1982), in some ways the most daring "feminist" film of the 1980s, cast a cross-dressing Dustin Hoffman in its leading "female" role. During the early 1990s, the Oscar-winning Fonda abandoned Hollywood filmmaking in favor of doing exercise videos for the lucrative VCR market.

Despite persistent charges of corruption, what was becoming called "the sports-entertainment business" flourished during the Reagan-Bush presidencies. The media revealed players betting on games, continued drug use, and even fixed games and point shaving. Organized baseball's commissioner banned Pete Rose, one of the game's greatest hitters, from the sport—and eligibility for the Hall of Fame—for ties to gambling. In this atmosphere, professional wrestling, which had traditionally limited signs of treachery and double-dealing to clearly defined villains, thrived by introducing story lines in which one night's hero, even a super-hero like Hulk Hogan or Steve Austin, could suddenly become the following evening's villain. Despite rumors of rampant drug use by grapplers and back room corruption by promoters, particularly Vince McMahon of the World Wrestling Federation (WWF), wrestling became a billion-dollar enterprise.

Basketball, which had struggled during the 1970s, also rebounded. The NCCA's college tournament, the "Countdown to the Final Four," became one of the biggest attractions in North American sports. Three charismatic players—Ervin (Magic) Johnson, Larry Bird, and Michael Jordan—dominated a revived National Basketball Association (NBA). The Olympics first accepted NBA players at its 1992 games, and the U.S. "Dream Team," led by Jordan, avenged the 1988 failure to win a gold medal. Jordan, who earned far more money from product endorsements than from his multimillion dollar salary, reigned as an international celebrity in the way that Muhammad Ali had done during the 1970s.

Reprising the Past

A desire for products and images from the late 1940s to the early 1960s became an important cultural theme, often associated with the Reagan era of the 1980s. The popular board game *Trivial Pursuit* rewarded players who could recall the kind of shirts worn by the Beach Boys or the name of Ann Margaret's first motion picture. A special edition allowed baby boomers to revel in memories of their youth. Television also reprised the past. Prime-time soap operas, the hottest network products of the 1980s, transferred long-familiar daytime formats to nighttime viewing. "Dallas" (1978–1991), "Dynasty" (1981–1989), and "Colbys"

FIGURE 9–5   Michael Jordan.

Professional basketball boomed, and Michael Jordan provided a new model
for world-wide sports marketing.
Source: Rick Stewart/Allsport.

(1985–87) featured outsized characters, such as oil tycooon J.R. Ewing (played
by Larry Hagman) and Alexis Carrington Colby (Joan Collins), who ostenta-
tiously displayed their Reagan-era affluence. These soaps also found roles for
one-time Hollywood stars such as Charleton Heston, Rock Hudson, and Jane
Wyman, Ronald Reagan's first wife. Just as these series were running their

course, Fox introduced "Beverly Hills 90210" (1990–2000), a prime-time soap aimed at a younger viewing audience, in which the Walsh family abandons Walter Mondale's Minnesota for Ronald Reagan's sunny California, the home to 1950s TV families such as the Nelsons.

CATV, steadily wooing viewers away from network programming, also reprised tested formats. ESPN initially introduced unfamiliar TV sports, such as Australian-rules football and table tennis, but increasingly beamed a steady diet of Big-time football, baseball, and basketball. CATV channels—particularly HBO, Showtime, USA, and Nickelodeon—did underwrite some original productions but relied on older products, drawn from the vast archives of Hollywood and the TV industry, to fill their programming needs. "Leave It to Beaver," "I Love Lucy," "Father Knows Best," and other black-and-white artifacts from the 1950s became CATV staples, while Ted Turner's TNT, and later TCM, drew on his company's vast holdings of Hollywood films. As a result, the products in studio vaults became worth several times the market value they had carried only a decade earlier.

Much, though certainly not all, popular music invoked popular memory. All across the country, radio stations switched to "oldies" formulas. In larger markets, every decade from the 1940s to the 1970s claimed at least one spot on the radio dial. Advertisements for tapes and CDs that featured the "hits of yesteryear" dominated late-night television. Risking once again the hazards of the road, the hit-makers of yesteryear mounted nationwide, and even lengthy international, tours. The Who and the Rolling Stones attracted the most attention and money, but many other middle-aged rockers, now sans drugs and young groupies, retraced paths of former glories. The standard contract for a Stones concert required promoters to provide a pinball machine, video games, and health foods. Bob Dylan, the folk-rock minstrel of the 1960s, toured virtually nonstop not only through the 1980s but the next decade as well. The top-selling African American artist of the period, Michael Jackson, bet much of his personal fortune on memories of the past when he purchased the rights to most of the Beatles' catalog of music.

The memory boom helped to revive the genre of popular history and to ignite a trend that lasted into the twenty-first century. Virtually every form of media participated. Public television featured "The American Experience" series that offered glossy, fast-moving documentaries about events and individuals from the nation's past. On a grander scale, documentary filmmaker Ken Burns gained acclaim for a PBS series, "The Civil War" (1990), which seamlessly integrated still photographs, a third-person narration, dramatically recreated audio sources, and "talking head" scholars to create a vibrant new form of visual history. Subsequent offerings by Burns, such as a nine-part history of baseball, added motion picture footage to this mix. The CATV channel A&E found such an enthusiastic audience for the historical entries in the long-running "Biography" series that it spun-off an entirely new "History Channel" (1994), which featured enough programs on World War II to allow comics to dub it "the Hitler channel." The giant chain bookstores, particularly Barnes & Noble, devoted entire sections to VHS versions of A&E's "Biography" series and to histories that focused on popular memory, especially of the Second World War. The prolific historian Stephen Ambrose produced a string of best-sellers.

Reworking the Past

The impulse to look backward could take peculiar twists. Music critic Nelson George coined the term "retronuevo" to characterize pop music that borrowed older forms as a means to create fresh new sounds. Retronuevo, according to George, appreciated and reworked, rather than simply reprised, the musical heritage. Artists such as Prince and Michael Jackson wove numerous traditions into their novel productions. Hip-hop music gave the old rock anthem "Roll Over Beethoven" (1955) an entirely new meaning by "sampling," borrowing notes, from a wide range of songs, including ones by artists as different as Chuck Berry and Mozart, himself the subject of a high-concept movie, *Amadeus* (1984, 2002).

Back to the Future, 1985's top-grossing film, sparked both popular and academic discussion over the relationship between Ronald Reagan's popularity and the many cultural products that invoked cold-war memories. Through errant technology, Marty McFly, a Hill Valley teenager from a strife-torn, downwardly mobile family of the 1980s, time-travels back to the 1950s. There, he finds his mother, still a vivacious eighteen-year-old, more attracted to him than to the bumbling rube who is supposed to become his father. After successfully uniting this unlikely couple, by introducing them and their high-school classmates to rock-and-roll, Marty (played by Michael J. Fox, who was then portraying the Republican son of old hippie parents on the TV series "Family Ties") scrambles back to "the future," Ronald Reagan's 1980s. In the process, he leaves an imprint on his parents' past and reconstructs their own present for the better. Marty thus answers the taunt, made earlier in the film that "no McFly ever amounted to anything in the history of Hill Valley" and fulfills his own promise that "history is gonna change."

Back to the Future generated conflicting interpretations. Reagan, invoking its images of high-tech solutions, borrowed a line from the movie for his 1986 State of the Union address. "Where we're going, we don't need roads." The film also seemed to contain another Reaganlike message—the faith that technology and optimism alone could solve complex, deeply rooted problems. Other critics, though, saw the movie expressing disquietude about both the present and the past. Rather than simply evoking memories of the 1950s, *Back to the Future*'s elaborately constructed narrative, in this view, challenged Reagan's central message by suggesting both the need for a significantly different present and that past mistakes, made during the heyday of Eisenhower Republicanism, still affected the 1980s.

Cleverly constructed cultural products, which imaginatively reworked the past, became identified with "postmodernism." This ill-defined, much-discussed cultural style, which had begun to take shape during the 1970s, gained force as consumers and critics embraced cultural forms that seemed to borrow, shrewdly and ironically, from previous ones. Devotees of postmodernism, who were especially attracted to the products of commercial mass culture, hailed its ability to recast the familiar in new and unusual ways.

Postmodern architects rejected the so-called international school, with its sleek, straight-lined, steel-and-glass skyscrapers, that had dominated the urban building boom of the 1950s and 1960s. Dismissing these "glass boxes" as soulless and pretentious monuments to industrial and financial elites, postmodern architects now embraced familiar forms from everyday life—highway billboards, Las Vegas casinos, and almost anything with elaborate ornamentation. In designing New York City's AT&T building the architect Philip Johnson abandoned the international style and designed a whimsical structure that resembled a nineteenth-century grandfather clock, topped by ornamentation that recalled Chippendale furniture of the eighteenth century.

Postmodernists, both approving and hostile observers agreed, blurred and often parodied elite cultural forms. Woody Allen's *Zelig* (1983) blended grainy film footage from the 1920s with new (though perfectly matched) scenes from the 1980s and created a pseudo-documentary about a fictional celebrity whom historians had supposedly forgotten. It showed Allen's character playing baseball alongside Babe Ruth and talking about literature with F. Scott Fitzgerald. Michael Moore's iconoclastic, postmodern-inspired documentary, *Roger and Me* (1989), delivered an anticorporate message through sly humor rather than moral strictures.

Devotees of postmodernism constantly sought new cultural forms. Artists used the types of copying machines found in any college library to create new works. Others "painted" images with computers and even fax machines, rather than the traditional brushes and easels. Simultaneously stretching traditional artistic boundaries and mocking the repetitive culture of advanced capitalism, these kinds of cultural productions parodied the classic TV commercial that asked viewers to decide, "Is it live? Or is it Memorex?"

Some critics even proclaimed the arrival of postmodern programs that reworked, generally in clever parodies, popular memories of TV's own brief history. "The Simpsons" (1987-) offered a cartoon version of a strife-ridden, off-center version of the nuclear family. Recalling "Father Knows Best" and classic cartoon families such as "The Flintstones," this show found a spot on a rival fourth network, Fox Broadcasting. Ridiculing, while it was recycling, traditional sitcom motifs, "The Simpsons"—and its more controversial Fox network counterpart, "Married with Children" (1987–1997)—parodied the New Right's "underclass" gospel in which suburban families transmitted proper values and built good character.

The constantly self-transforming MTV, which debuted as a CATV network in 1981, seemed at the forefront of innovative television during the 1980s and early 1990s. Its initial format, twenty-four hours of nothing but rock videos and youth-oriented commercials, raised the stakes for the music business. A "heavily rotated" video joined a gold record, a platinum album, and a movie soundtrack as a marker of musical success. Early on, MTV featured "New Pop" groups from Britain such as Duran Duran and WHAM! By the mid-1980s, North American-based heavy metal replaced New Pop as the dominant genre, but other types of music and musicians increasingly appeared on MTV. In 1984, Tina Turner lacked a record contract; the following year, after several videos featuring the rock veteran ran on MTV, she could claim a Grammy award and a hit album, *Private Dancer.* The rise of Madonna and Michael Jackson, who used MTV to become international mega-stars, was even more spectacular. Their video work, including "Like a Prayer" and "Thriller," respectively, prompted extensive commentary and helped music videos become an influential form of musical production. By the mid-1980s, even country music, the most traditional sector of the music industry, played on two national CATV channels modeled on MTV.

MTV intrigued both its targeted youth audience and a new generation of cultural critics. Its willingness to experiment with innovative media imagery and interest in postmodern aesthetics were on display in the Cars "You Might Think," reportedly the first music video to gain inclusion in the collection of an art museum. Even the network's animated promotional inserts, which featured innovative computer-generated imagery, won acclaim for their artistry. "Miami Vice" (1984–1989), an otherwise familiar police show, gained attention and high ratings by transferring the "MTV-look" to network television. Soon, both TV and motion picture productions, rapidly cutting from shot-to-shot and scene-to-scene, moved more quickly, relied increasingly on special effects, and employed the kind of dark lighting and nonlinear narratives once identified almost solely with *film noir.* During the 1950s, the average Hollywood film had contained about 600 individual shots. Adopting the sprightlier MTV look, most movies by the early 1980s contained about 1,000, and Bruce Willis's fast-paced *The Last Boy Scout* (1991) included nearly 2,000 individual shots.

While MTV was helping to change styles, cultural production, and distribution of music, it was changing its own format. Augmenting its continuous flow of visual imagery, MTV began devoting specific time slots to different musical genres, especially "grunge" and rap. Moving beyond music, MTV experimented with a game-show parody, "Remote Control," rapidly paced documentaries that gained awards for journalistic excellence, and "The Real World" (1992-), an early example of the "reality" genre that finally arrived on network TV toward the end of the 1990s.

The Politics of Cultural Confrontation

Some cultural products overtly challenged the political agendas of Ronald Reagan and George Bush. The alliance of the 1960s between music and social activism assumed new forms in the age of satellite broadcasting, as in the "Live-Aid" concert for famine relief in Africa and the recurring "Farm-Aid" productions on behalf of challenging the way in which Washington's economic policies affected rural America. These high-tech spectacles aimed at a "feel good" spirit, but other new cultural trends of the 1980s prompted sharp debate.

"Hip hop," which had emerged among African American and Spanish-speaking youth in New York City during the late 1970s, became an arena for cultural conflict. Hip-hop featured flamboyant clothing, frenetic break dancing, and graffiti art on walls and subway trains. In addition, popular disk jockeys became neighborhood celebrities by using powerful amplifiers to sample different musical backdrops, taken from a broad variety of musical styles, for break dancers and graffiti artists. These DJs soon took their amplifiers into local clubs and added new technical twists like "scratching," manipulating record turntables to produce hip-hop's unique urban sound. More important, hip-hop DJs added "rappers," young performance artists who recounted dramatic, often angry, stories about urban life over the sound of the music. Rap thus merged older traditions—including preaching, storytelling, and street-corner boasting—with postmodern electronics to provide a means by which young people could protest against urban conditions.

Rap, hip-hop's most lucrative product, immediately produced controversy. It graphically gave voice to the concerns of young people, especially of

African American men. Rap quickly rivaled heavy-metal music in its use of misogynist lyrics. Even those who admiringly recognized rap's roots in older cultural forms complained that its lyrics tended to represent the worst elements in contemporary life. Critical references to Jewish-owned businesses angered Jewish American groups, and "gangsta rappers" infuriated law enforcement officials by their "bad attitude"—a term denoting everything from fashion styles to "obscene" language to social outlook—and the violence that seemed to envelop rap culture. Conservative watchdog groups pressured record companies to censor rap lyrics, and some legal officials prosecuted rappers, such as 2 Live Crew, for obscenity.

In 1980, The Sugar Hill Gang's "Rapper's Delight" became rap's first million seller, and rappers from outside New York City, such as Miami's 2 Live Crew and LA's NWA, soon achieved prominence. MTV brought rap onto its play list and eventually created "Yo! MTV Raps," a program devoted entirely to this musical form. Hollywood embraced rap more quickly than it had rock music during the 1950s. Rappers such as Ice-T became film stars, and rap provided both the soundtrack and the subject matter for a number of successful motion pictures. Women had been part of the larger hip-hop culture from the outset, and women rappers eventually made their mark. Artists like Queen Latifah brought antimisogynist and feminist themes into rap. Some of rap's original admirers worried that "crossover" acts such as Vanilla Ice and M.C. Hammer portended its commercialization and loss of its critical edge, but rap managed to retain its connection to neighborhood communities and social issues. Some rap artists, recalling the politics of Black Power, supplemented songs about sex, drugs, and violence with "Proud to Be Black" and "Fight the Power."

Spike Lee's film *Do the Right Thing* (1989), which featured a rap and hip-hop soundtrack, sparked especially bitter debate. Its cinematic images of a racially diverse, conflict-ridden neighborhood in Brooklyn paralleled noncinematic conflict in cities such as New York, Miami, and Boston. Although Lee claimed he was simply using cinema to highlight widely acknowledged urban problems, especially ethnic tension and economic stagnation, conservatives charged his film advocated violence as a solution for social ills. Hollywood's Academy Awards completely bypassed *Do the Right Thing* and named *Driving Miss Daisy* (1989)—a picture featuring an elderly southern white woman and her loyal African American chauffeur—as the best motion picture of 1989.

The controversy over sexually explicit works cut across many different media and political alliances. What kinds of expression, lawyers and lay people asked, qualified as pornographic? Did porn merit First-Amendment coverage as legally protected speech? The fact that sexually explicit works could be exhibited on an art gallery's wall as well as on a magazine rack did not spare artists from charges of trafficking in pornography. When the prestigious Cochrane Gallery in Washington, D.C., canceled an exhibition of sexually explicit, homoerotic photographs by Robert Mapplethorpe, some in the artistic community sympathized with the gallery's apparent fear of jeopardizing its funding, especially from public sources. Others saw the Cochrane bowing to the sensibilities of the New Right and engaging in self-censorship. Sexually explicit commercial products—XXX-rated magazines, books, and videos—prompted recurring contention and sometimes strange political alignments. The "antiporn" wing of the feminist coalition argued that sexually explicit material had little value in celebrating erotic themes and mostly contributed to exploiting, degrading, and endangering women. By spearheading a campaign for new legal restraints against pornography, it saw itself pursuing the feminist conviction that "the personal is political." Other veterans of the insurgent culture of the 1960s and 1970s, now raising families in urban neighborhoods of the 1980s, also joined with antiporn feminists and members of the New Right in opposing dissemination of sexually explicit materials. The padlocking of businesses that dealt in "porn" could become part of grassroots crusades to rekindle a spirit of neighborhood uplift and community building.

The antipornography movement confronted an equally diverse opposition. Many feminists hesitated to legislate against sexually explicit images and thereby stand culturally alongside the antifeminist, antiabortion New Right. Was not this kind of censorship, although it was framed in terms of protecting women, part of a broader conservative crusade to revive small-town, Main-Street values, including narrow notions about the social roles into which women should be contained? Rallying around the banner of free expression, so-called pro-porn feminists joined with groups such as the American Civil Liberties Union (ACLU) in condemning antipornography initiatives as violations of constitutionally protected speech. Censorship of pornography, the ACLU and its allies feared, would only embolden cultural and political conservatives to push for additional controls over expression, including sexually explicit works by feminists themselves.

Other culturally charged battles, especially those involving "multiculturalism" and "political correctness," also sparked ongoing national debate. A broad coalition of educators and veterans of the cultural insurgency of the 1960s began pressing schools and colleges to represent the nation and its history more broadly in order to show a multiethnic and multicultural country. They urged historians to underscore the role of women and non-European ethnic groups and teachers of literature to supplement the traditional "canon," works generally authored by the so-called dead white men, with texts by a more diverse set of authors and perspectives. Many school districts and institutions of higher education established guidelines for multicultural, gender-fair education, and some drafted "speech codes" to help teachers and students deal with ethnic and gender differences in classrooms and on college campuses. These new educational initiatives, their defenders argued, acknowledged the reality of cultural diversity and that words, when maliciously or carelessly spoken, could produce harmful consequences. In response, opponents condemned them as part of an impulse toward political correctness, or simply "PC." The multicultural and PC debates increasingly intersected as they spread from educational institutions, to the mass media, and finally, to national politics.

The politics of multiculturalism generated intense passion during the late 1980s and early 1990s. Members of the Reagan administration, especially William Bennett and Lynne Cheney, denounced the movement for educational change as an effort by feminists and other radicals to demean the cultural heritage of the West and politicize education. Allan Bloom's surprise best-seller, *The Closing of the American Mind* (1987), linked the multiculturalism of the 1980s to the counterculture of the 1960s and criticized educators for abandoning time-honored works of "western civilization."

Such attacks escalated, as conservative philanthropic foundations and think tanks funded authors and organizations that opposed multiculturalism and political correctness. (Ironically, supporters of multiculturalism, in a playful spirit of self-criticism, had initially coined the terms political correctness and "PC," but opponents effectively made them their own.) To its critics, "PC" signified an impulse toward narrowly conceived thought, behavior, and attitudes, particularly on ethnic and gender issues. In this view, educators wanted to indoctrinate students with trendy works while ignoring more valuable texts from the literary canon. Worse, it was charged, "the PC police" insisted students read classic works such as Shakespeare's plays in terms of "contemporary political concerns" such as gender relationships. Teachers who did not toe the line, according to the critics of PC, risked having PC colleagues or disruptive students undermine them. What had begun as an attempt to open up the educational environment became characterized, by anti-PC writers such as the feminist celebrity Camille Paglia, as an attempt to stifle freedom of expression and to impose rigid standards on student life.

Debates over multiculturalism and political correctness became especially confrontational when the focus turned to race. While running for president in 1988, Reverend Jesse Jackson's call for a multicultural politics won support on many college campuses. At the same time, though, Jackson had refused to break with more controversial African American leaders such as Minister Louis Farrakhan of the Nation of Islam. By the early 1990s, Jackson's "Rainbow Coalition" was in tatters, while Farrakhan seemed a rising cultural and political force, merging the teachings of the Nation of Islam with calls for "Afrocentric" education. Afrocentrism touched all levels of culture, from African American studies programs at colleges and universities to the music of some rappers. Afrocentrism celebrated the accomplishments of a black cultural tradition that was often traced back to ancient Egypt. Some of its proponents seemed to jettison multiculturalist premises when they argued for the superior values of an African-derived culture that, in the view of some, had been deliberately undermined by people of European descent.

The Senate Judiciary Committee's 1991 televised hearings on George Bush's nomination of Clarence Thomas, a prominent African American conservative, to the Supreme Court dramatized some of the controversies around multiculturalism and political correctness. Anita Hill, another African American lawyer and Republican, charged Thomas with having harassed her with sexually explicit innuendos when both had served in the Reagan administration. Their confrontation raised a host of issues. Thomas, who had long portrayed himself as a traditional conservative with a "color-blind" view, confronted Hill's charges by appealing to the cultural politics of race. He pictured himself as a victim of racism and denounced the all-white Senate Judiciary Committee for conducting a "high-tech lynching." Meanwhile, even people who opposed Thomas's conservative legal agenda felt that Hill's allegations had little to do with his qualifications for the Supreme Court. Would any nominee of Euprean descent, they argued, have had his or her private life so ruthlessly scrutinized?

Hill's supporters saw the issues quite differently. Feminists accused Thomas's GOP supporters on the all-male Judiciary Committee with engaging in sexual harassment themselves while cross-examining her. The author Toni Morrison complained that Hill's interrogators had "dressed [her] in the oppositional costume of madness, anarchic sexuality, and explosive verbal violence." Conservative journalists, particularly David Brock (who subsequently revealed that his allegations about Hill's private life had been fabricated), assailed Hill's motives and sexual history. The Hill-Thomas confrontation, which concluded with Thomas being confirmed by a narrow vote, reverberated throughout the political culture. Feminist organizations, distributing buttons proclaiming "I Believe Anita Hill," made the episode part of a nationwide political-organizing effort that resulted in more women, including two new Democratic Senators, being voted into Congress in the November 1992 elections.

The Thomas-Hill episode became one of the many topics that enlivened talk-radio and tabloid-style TV shows, important new sites for the conduct of cultural politics during the Reagan-Bush years. Supplanting the New-Right religious preachers, a group of moralizing, though entirely secular, commentators denounced political correctness, multiculturalism, and any individual or group who espoused them. Rush Limbaugh, a former sports publicist and radio disk jockey, built a multimillion dollar multimedia empire. Only a handful of radio and TV talk shows adopted a tone sympathetic to feminist and multicultural issues. The vast majority—which included programs hosted by G. Gordon Liddy, Oliver North, and Alan Keyes—followed Limbaugh's conservative path. When Limbaugh's popularity was at its height during the early 1990s, bars and restaurants created "Rush Rooms," places in which fellow conservatives could lunch to the sound of his daytime radio program.

The cultural controversies of the early 1990s generated greater militancy within the right wing of the GOP. Outspoken cultural conservatives, such as Patrick Buchanan and Pat Robertson, challenged the older "paleoconservatives," such as William F. Buckley, who had reshaped conservatism during the 1950s, and the "neoconservatives," such as Irving Kristol, who had joined the Republican ranks during the 1970s. Buchanan called for all-out war against multiculturalism and political correctness, and he denounced George Bush's approach to cultural politics as too moderate and restrained.

A clearly conservative turn marked the period from 1980 to 1992. The Republican administrations of Ronald Reagan and George Bush could claim substantial successes, especially in foreign policy. Reagan's hard-line, anti-Communist foreign policy put the Soviet Union on the defensive and seemed to restore the "credibility" of the United States in the wake of the Vietnam War and Jimmy Carter's problems with Iran. Reagan's confident performance in the White House, despite the problems that marked his final years in office, helped to restore the image of the presidency. His successor, George Bush, easily returned the GOP to the White House in 1988 and skillfully orchestrated a multination campaign to roll back Iraq's invasion of Kuwait in 1991.

Lacking Reagan's charisma, however, Bush struggled to lead his party and the nation. The federal budget deficit yawned alarmingly, and sectors of the economy, particularly family farming and rust-belt industries, experienced severe dislocation. While the conservative turn coincided with greater prosperity for many people, those without job skills, especially persons living in rural areas and inner-city neighborhoods, faced dismal prospects. Disparities in wealth and income widened, and the recession of the early 1990s highlighted the inequities. Furthermore, as economic polarization grew, so too did conflicts over social and cultural issues. These culture wars divided people on a broad range of issues, from abortion rights to educational policy.

As Bush sought a second term in the White House, he confronted the GOP's angry New Right, led by Patrick Buchanan and Republican House leader Newt Gingrich. Meanwhile, an ambitious group of "New Democrats," including Bill Clinton and Al Gore, argued that the last three presidential elections had discredited their party's old positive-state agenda. They sought an opportunity to, themselves, take control of the conservative turn before it moved even more decisively rightward.

SUGGESTED READING

A good place to begin looking at the 1980s is in the census data. See Andrew Hacker, ed., *US* (1983). For a controversial, provocative interpretation of the nation's place in the world, see Paul Kennedy, *The Rise and Fall of the Great Powers* (1988).

Interpretations of Ronald Reagan include James E. Combs, *The Reagan Range: The Nostalgic Myth in American Politics* (1993); Stephen Vaughan, *Ronald Reagan in Hollywood* (1993); Lou Cannon, *Reagan* (1982); Robert Dallek, *Ronald Reagan and the Politics of Symbolism* (1984); Michael Rogin, *Ronald Reagan: the Movie* (1987); Garry Wills, *Reagan's America: Innocents at Home* (1987); Sidney Blumenthal, *Our Long National Daydream: A Political Pageant of the Reagan Era* (1988); Robert E. Denton, Jr., *The Primetime Presidency of Ronald Reagan: The Era of the Television Presidency* (1988); Jane Mayer and Doyle McManus, *Landslide: The Unmaking of a President, 1984–1988* (1988); Kathleen Hall Jamieson, *Packaging the Presidency: A History and Criticism of Presidential Campaign Advertising* (3rd ed., 1996); William Pemberton, *Exit with Honor: The Life and Presidency of Ronald Reagan* (1997); Peggy Noonan, *What I Saw at the Revolution: A Political Life in the Reagan Era* (1997); and Dinesh D'Souza, *Ronald Reagan* (1997). For a more general view of twentieth century conservativism in America, see Lee Edwards, *The Conservative Revolution: The Movement that Remade America* (1999).

Attempts to assess the broad impact of the Reagan years also include Sidney Blumenthal and Thomas Byrne Edsall, eds., *The Reagan Legacy* (1988); Ryan J. Barilleaux, *The Post-modern Presidency: The Office After Ronald Reagan* (1988); William F. Grover, *The President as Prisoner: A Structural Critique of the Carter and Reagan Years* (1989); Richard O. Curry, *Freedom at Risk* (1989); Harold H. Koh, *The National Security Constitution: Sharing Power After the Iran-Contra Affair* (1990); Michael Schaller, *Reckoning with Reagan* (1992); Daniel Wirls, *Buildup: The Politics of Defense in the Reagan Era* (1992); Bruce Nesmith, *The New Republican Coalition: The Reagan Campaigns and White Evangelicals* (1994); and William C. Berman, *America's Right Turn: From Nixon to Bush* (1994).

Economic and social welfare policies are the subject of Michael Boskin, *Too Many Promises: The Uncertain Future of Social Security* (1986); William Greider, *Secrets of the Temple* (1987); James Tobin and Murray Weidenbaum, eds., *Two Revolutions in Economic Policy: The First Economic Reports of Presidents Kennedy and Reagan* (1988); Martin Anderson, *Revolution* (1988); Dennis Swann, *The Retreat of the State: Deregulation and Privatization in the UK and the US* (1988); Roger E. Meiners and Bruce Yandle, *Regulation and the Reagan Era* (1989); James K. Galbraith, *Balancing Acts: Technology, Finance, and the American Future* (1989); Kenneth R. Hoover, *Conservative Capitalism in Britain and the United States: A Critical Appraisal* (1989); Otis L. Graham, Jr., *Losing Time: The Industrial Policy Debate*

(1992); Christopher Jencks, *Rethinking Social Policy* (1992); Michael A. Bernstein and David Adler, eds., *Understanding American Economic Decline* (1993); Anthony S. Campagna, *The Economy of the Reagan Years* (1994); Barry D. Friedman, *Regulation in the Reagan-Bush Era: The Eruption of Presidential Influence* (1996); and John W. Sloan, *The Reagan Effect: Economics and Presidential Leadership* (1999).

Foreign policies are discussed in Walter LaFeber, *Inevitable Revolutions: The United States in Central America* (1983); Strobe Talbot, *Deadly Gambits: The Reagan Administration and the Stalemate in Nuclear Arms Control* (1984); William M. LeoGrande, *Our Own Backyard: The United States in Central America, 1977–1992* (1998); Thomas Walker, ed., *Reagan versus the Sandinistas* (1987); James A. Bill, *The Eagle and the Lion: The Tragedy of American-Iranian Relations* (1988); Roy Gutman, *Banana Diplomacy: The Making of American Policy in Nicaragua, 1981–1987* (1988); H. Bruce Franklin, *War Stars: The Superweapon and the American Imagination* (1988); Frances Fitzgerald, *Way Out There in the Blue: Reagan, Star Wars, and the End of the Cold War* (2000); Coral Bell, *The Reagan Paradox: American Foreign Policy in the 1980s* (1989); Theodore Draper, *A Very Thin Line: The Iran-Contra Affairs* (1991); Donald R. Baucom, *The Origins of SDI, 1944–1983* (1992); John Lofand, *Polite Protesters: The American Peace Movement of the 1980s* (1993); Christian Smith, *Resisting Reagan: The U.S. Central America Peace Movement* (1996); and Beth A. Fischer, *The Reagan Reversal: Foreign Policy and the End of the Cold War* (1997). Bruce Franklin, *M.I.A. or Mythmaking in America* (1992) critically dissects the claim that many U.S. prisoners of war were left behind in Southeast Asia.

Other issues of the Reagan presidency are covered in Elder Witt, *A Different Justice: Reagan and the Supreme Court* (1986); C. Brant Short, *Ronald Reagan and the Public Lands: America's Conservation Debate, 1979–1984* (1989); Raymond Wolters, *Right Turn: William Bradford Reynolds, the Reagan Administration, and Black Civil Rights* (1996); and Diane Vaughan, *The Challenger Launch Decision: Risky Technology, Culture and Deviance at NASA* (1997).

On social issues, many of the works cited for the two previous chapters are relevant. In addition, see Robert Bellah et al., *Habits of the Heart: Individualism & Commitment in American Life* (1984); Mark Friedberger, *Shake-out: Iowa Farm Families in the 1980s* (1989); Barbara Ehrenreich, *Fear of Falling: The Inner Life of the Middle-Class* (1989); Fred Harris and Roger W. Wilkins, eds., *Quiet Riots: Race and Poverty in the United States: The Kerner Report Twenty Years Later* (1989); William Julius Wilson, *The Ghetto Underclass* (1989); Russell Ferguson et al., eds., *Out There: Marginalization and Contemporary Cultures* (1990); Michael Omi and Howard Winant, *Racial Formation in the United States: From the 1960s to the 1990s* (1994); Andrew Hacker, *Two Nations: Black and White, Separate, Hostile, Unequal* (1992); Toni Morrison, ed., *Race-ing Justice, En-Gendering Power: Essays on Anita Hill, Clarence Thomas, and the Construction of Social Reality* (1992); Cornel West, *Race Matters* (1993); Manthia Diawara, ed., *Black American Cinema* (1993); Robert Gooding-Williams, ed., *Reading Rodney King* (1993); Robert C. Smith, *Racism in the Post-Civil Rights Era; Now You See It, Now You Don't* (1995); Roger Waldinger, *Still the Promised City? Afro-Americans and New Immigrants in Postindustrial New York* (1996); Mattias Gardell, *In the Name of Elijah Muhammed: Louis Farrakhan and the Nation of Islam* (1996); Jennifer L. Hochschild, *Facing Up to the American Dream: Race, Class, and the Soul of the Nation* (1995); Elaine Bell Kaplan, *Not Our Kind of Girl: Unravelling the Myths of Black Teenage Motherhood* (1997); Dallas A. Blanchard, *The Anti-abortion Movement* (1994); Randy Shilts, *And the Band Played* on: *Politics, People, and the AIDS Epidemic* (1988); Neil Miller, *In Search of Gay America: Women and Men in a Time of Change* (1989); Steven Epstein, *Impure Science: AIDS, Aids Activism, and the Politics of Science* (1996); and James Coates, *Armed and Dangerous: The Rise of the Survivalist Right* (1989).

On the cultural battles of the 1980s, see Charles Jencks, *Post-modernism: The New Classicism in Art and Architecture* (1987); E. Ann Kaplan, *Rocking Around the Clock: Music Television, Postmodernism, and Consumer Culture* (1987); Linda Hutcheon, *A Poetics of Postmodernism* (1987); David Harvey, *The Condition of Postmodernity* (1989); Mark Poster, *The Mode of Information* (1990); James Davison Hunter, *Culture Wars* (1991); Timothy Corrigan, *A Cinema without Walls* (1991); Marsha Kinder, *Playing with Power in Movies, Television and Video Games* (1991); Susan Willis, *A Primer for Daily Life* (1991); Mimi White, *Teleadvising: Therapeutic Discourse in American Television* (1992); Celeste Olalquiaga, *Megalopolis: Contemporary Cultural Sensibilities* (1992); Lawrence Grossberg, *We Gotta Get Out of this Place: Popular Conservatism and Postmodern Culture* (1992); Henry Jenkins, *Textual Poachers: Television Fans and Participatory Culture* (1992); Andrew Goodwin, *Dancing in the Distraction Factory: Music Television and Popular Culture* (1992); Carol J. Clover, *Men, Women, and Chain Saws: Gender in the Modern Horror Film* (1992); Elizabeth G. Traube, *Dreaming Identities: Class, Gender, and Generation in 1980s Hollywood Movies* (1992); Simon Frith, Andrew Goodwin, and Lawrence Grossberg, eds., *Sound & Vision: The Music Video Reader* (1993); Jim Collins, `Hilary Radner, and Ava Preacher Collins, eds., *Film Theory Goes to the Movies* (1993); Wayne Munson, *All Talk: The Talkshow in Media Culture* (1993); Anne Friedberg, *Window Shopping: Cinema and the Postmodern* (1993); Susan Jeffords, *Hard Bodies: Hollywood Masculinity in the Reagan Era* (1994); Russell A. Potter, *Spectacular Vernaculars: Hip-Hop and the Politics of Postmodernism* (1995); Michael Eric Dyson, *Between God and Gangsta Rap: Bearing Witness to Black Culture* (1996); Ambrose I. Lane, Sr., *Return of the Buffalo: The Story Behind America's Indian Gaming Explosion* (1995); Raymond Tatalovich, *Nativism Reborn? The Official English Language Movement and the American States* (1995); Jane Feuer, *Seeing Through the Eighties: Television and Reaganism* (1995); Alan Nadel, *Flatlining on the Field of Dreams: Cultural Narratives in the Films of President Reagan's America* (1997); Henry A. Giroux, *Channel Surfing: Race Talk and the Destruction of Today's Youth* (1997); Joseph Turow, *Breaking Up America: Advertisers and the New Media World* (1997); Fred Goodman, *The Mansion on the Hill: Dylan, Young, Geffen, Springsteen, and the Head-On Collision of Rock and Commerce* (1997); Rennard Strickland, *Tonto's Revenge: Reflections on American Indian Culture and Policy* (1997).

On the Bush presidency, see David Mervin, *George Bush and the Guardian Presidency* (1996); John Podhoretz, *Hell of a Ride: Backstage at the White House Follies 1989–1993* (1993); Charles Kolb, *White House Daze: The Unmaking of Domestic Policy in the Bush Years* (1994); Lawrence Walsh, *Firewall: The Iran-Contra Conspiracy and Cover-Up* (1997); Charles Kenney, *Michael Dukakis: An American Odyssey* (1988); and Herbert S. Parmet, *George Bush: The Life of a Lone Star Yankee* (1997).

On foreign affairs, see John L. Gaddis, *The United States and the End of the Cold War: Implications, Reconsiderations, Provocations* (1992); Michael J. Hogan, ed., *The End of the Cold War: Its Meanings and Implications* (1992); Paul Kennedy, *Preparing for the Twenty-First Century* (1993); Cynthia Enloe, *The Morning After: Sexual Politics at the End of the Cold War* (1993); Raymond Garthoff, ed., *The Great*

Transition: American-Soviet Relations and the End of the Cold War (1994); William G. Hyland, *The Cold War Is Over* (1995); Robert L. Hutchings, *American Diplomacy and the End of the Cold War: An Insider's Account of U.S. Policy in Europe, 1989–1992* (1997); Ezra Vogel, *Living With China: U.S.-China Relations in the Twenty-first Century* (1997); Allen Hunter, ed., *Re-Thinking the Cold War* (1998).

On the Gulf War, see Lawrence Freedman and Efraim Karsh, *The Gulf Conflict, 1990–1991: Diplomacy and War in the New World Order* (1993); Bob Woodward, *The Commanders* (1991); Rick Atkinson, *Crusade: The Untold Story of the Persian Gulf War* (1994); Michael R. Gordon and Bernard E. Trainer, *The General's War: The Inside Story of the Conflict in the Gulf* (1996); Dilip Hiro, *Desert Shield to Desert Storm: The Second Gulf War* (1992); Hamid Mowlana, George Gerbner, and Herbert I. Schiller, eds., *Triumph of the Image: The Media's War in the Persian Gulf* (1992); T. M. Hawley, *Against the Fires of Hell: The Environmental Disaster of the Gulf War* (1992); Douglas Kellner, *The Persian Gulf TV War* (1992); Richard Hallion, *Storm Over Iraq: Air Power and the Gulf War* (1992); Susan Jeffords and Lauren Rabinovitz, eds. *Seeing Through the Media: The Persian Gulf War* (1994); and Frank N. Schubert and Theresa L. Kraus, *The Whirlwind War: The United States Army in Operations Desert Shield and Desert Storm* (1995).

10

New Democrats, A New Economy, and New Americans

During the last decade of the twentieth century, both the Democratic and Republican parties encountered a turbulent political culture that had shattered the dominance of the Democrats and boosted Ronald Reagan's Republican party. Could Democrats, long identified with programs to expand the reach of the national government, develop candidates and policies that responded to the popular desire, nurtured by Reaganism, to cut back Washington's role? Might a "new Democrat" be able to update and alter familiar visions of the Fair Deal-Great Society tradition of the positive state? Would the Republicans seek to consolidate Reaganism, push further rightward, or move toward the center? How might the U.S. economy and foreign policy be reshaped—and by whom—to respond to a post-cold-war world? These questions accompanied significant demographic shifts, as new immigration and other population changes altered who Americans were and where and how they lived.

POLITICS AND CULTURE DURING THE CLINTON PRESIDENCY

In 1992, the candidacy of William Jefferson Clinton, the governor of Arkansas, challenged traditional Democrats as well as conservative Republicans. A gregarious extrovert, who emphasized his baby-boomer roots, Bill Clinton presented himself as a "new" kind of Democrat. He demonstrated considerable dexterity as a campaigner, but controversy grounded in the intersection of politics, culture, and law dogged his eight-year presidency.

1992: The Election of a "New Democrat"

George H. Bush's difficulty in articulating both his foreign and domestic policies, along with an erratic economy, proved politically fatal. During the GOP primaries in 1992, the conservative journalist-activist Patrick Buchanan challenged the more centrist president. Buchanan criticized the Gulf War—because, he claimed, it advanced no national interest—and Bush's failure to wage cultural warfare at home against the "Woodstock values" of the 1960s. The president easily won every primary contest but, in a conciliatory gesture, allowed Buchanan's supporters to set the tone for the party's National Convention. Buchanan himself declared "a religious war" for "the soul of America." Other speakers disparaged homosexuality and "welfare queens"; decried affirmative action; denigrated the pro-choice movement; and denounced the values and character of Clinton and his wife, Hillary Rodham Clinton.

With Republicans seemingly veering to the right, Clinton steered toward the middle of the political spectrum. Born in 1946, he embraced two of his generation's fallen heroes: John F. Kennedy, another Democrat with a controversial private life, and Elvis Presley, another poor southern white attracted to African-American culture. A Rhodes Scholar at Oxford, a graduate of Yale Law School, and a governor of Arkansas at thirty-two, Clinton conceded, albeit grudgingly, his political liabilities. He admitted to having smoked (but not inhaled) marijuana, having avoided the draft during the Vietnam War, and having participated in antiwar demonstrations while at Oxford. He and his wife also acknowledged a history of marital discord.

Clinton's character and behavior became major campaign issues. Although most Republicans abhorred Clinton's personal style—Bush himself denounced Clinton for lacking patriotism and even for likening himself to Elvis—other voters saw flirtation with sex, drugs, and rock-and-roll hardly unusual for a baby boomer. Rather than ducking his "bad-boy image," Clinton used it as a political asset. He donned dark glasses and played the saxophone on a late-night TV show popular with African-American viewers and appeared before youthful audiences on MTV. Although Tipper Gore, wife of Clinton's running mate, Senator Albert Gore of Tennessee, had crusaded against rock-music lyrics, MTV unofficially endorsed the Clinton-Gore ticket.

Clinton also broke familiar Democratic molds on issues of domestic policy. Joining with other members of the Democratic Leadership Council, who wanted to move their own party to the moderate right, he rejected the Great Society tradition. Clinton spoke of jettisoning the welfare system "as we know it" by requiring job-training programs, pursuing men who avoided financial responsibility for their children, and limiting the time that people could draw welfare payments. He also promised strong anticrime measures, a stance bolstered by his consistent support, while governor of Arkansas, for the death penalty. On one occasion, he interrupted his campaign schedule to preside over the execution of an African-American inmate whose mental capacity was at issue.

At the same time, Clinton courted traditionally Democratic voters. While initially distancing himself from familiar faces such as Jesse Jackson, he embraced other prominent people of color, including Vernon Jordan, a civil rights activist turned Washington insider; Ronald Brown, the African American attorney who headed the Democratic National Committee; and Federico Peña, the mayor of Denver. In the November 1992 election, nearly 90 percent of black and 65 percent of Hispanic voters supported Clinton. Hillary Rodham Clinton's work on women's issues, especially child-care legislation

FIGURE 10–1   Clinton Wails Sax.

Newly inaugurated Bill Clinton, the first baby-boomer president, joined the band at the D.C. Armory Ball in January, 1993.
Source: Diana Walker, TimePix.

and abortion rights, helped Bill Clinton capitalize on the gender gap that remained a problem for Republicans. Clinton carried a solid majority of women voters in the November 1996 election.

Most pre-election signs, particularly statistics that suggested any economic recovery would come slowly, pointed to a Clinton victory. By charging Bush with mismanaging the economy and by frustrating the president's plan to pillory him as a "big-spending liberal," Clinton could distance himself from the last three losing Democratic presidential candidates. Meanwhile, an unorthodox, independent campaign by billionaire entrepreneur Ross Perot, which focused on the federal budget deficit, hurt the incumbent Bush more than the Democratic challenger. Initially sustaining his quest for the White House by frequent appearances on CNN's "Larry King Live" and other TV talk shows, Perot subsequently spent nearly $40 million of his own money on a fall media blitz. Although Perot suffered a shutout in the Electoral College, he attracted nearly 20 million popular votes, compared to almost 45 million for Clinton and 39 million for Bush. Clinton garnered 370 electoral votes by carrying 32 states and the District of Columbia.

The 1992 election represented a stunning repudiation of George Bush, who only eighteen months before had basked in the glory of his Gulf War triumph. Taken together, the anti-Bush vote, for both Perot and Clinton, totaled more than 62 percent of the ballots cast. Bush carried a majority among only one of the major voting blocs, white Protestants in the South. Some voters seemed positively eager to repudiate the once popular president: More than 55 percent of eligible voters cast ballots, an unexpectedly large turnout that reversed thirty-two years of steady decline in voter participation.

The First Clinton Presidency: Domestic Politics

Clinton announced a domestic agenda befitting his New-Democrat label. Appointees to his administration reflected his diverse electoral coalition and included three women cabinet officers. In addition to changes in anticrime and welfare policies, he called for fresh approaches to health-care policy, educational issues, environmental regulation, and economic development. He promised to shrink, not expand, both the federal deficit and bureaucracy. A report on "reinventing government," *From Red Tape to Results* (1993), announced that the new Democratic vision, like that in corporate enterprise, should "insist on customer satisfaction" and "create incentives that drive" governmental officials "to put customers first."

Clinton himself put economic, rather than social, issues first. He pressed Congress to formulate a budget that reined in spending, while raising taxes on higher incomes, and made a start toward reducing the federal deficit. Buoyed by declining interest rates during 1993 and by rising consumer confidence, the economy built on the cautious recovery that had begun toward the end of Bush's presidency. The unemployment rate, which had been over 7 percent in 1992, fell to under 6 percent by late 1994. The annual rate of economic growth reached nearly 4 percent in 1994, without triggering a rise in prices. Even the federal deficit began to fall, reversing the recent trend of growing government borrowing.

Clinton sponsored several social and economic initiatives. He ended the Reagan-era ban on abortion counseling in family-planning clinics and steered the Family Medical Leave Act (FMLA) of 1993 through Congress. The FMLA required businesses with 50 or more employees to grant up to 12 weeks of *unpaid* leave to workers whose family was having or adopting a baby or facing a serious illness. The much more controversial Brady Handgun Control Law, which required a five-day waiting period for the purchase of handguns, inaugurated Clinton's anticrime plan. New legislation mandated tougher sentencing guidelines, placed more police on the streets, and banned most assault weapons. Small, pilot programs to provide college tuition assistance, in return for national service, and to expand youth-training programs received limited funding. Expansion of the earned income tax credit in 1993, the most important economic move of Clinton's first term, rivaled the 1972 decision to index Social Security payments as an income-support measure. By reducing the effective tax bill for low-income workers with families, the earned income provision provided tangible assistance to people who might otherwise have faced greater economic distress.

Clinton temporized on his campaign pledge to end the military's ban on homosexuals and tried to accommodate opposition from the Pentagon. Under a compromise policy—called "don't ask, don't tell"—recruiters were not to inquire about the sexuality of prospective service personnel and thus allow gays and lesbians who kept quiet to have military careers. Neither the military establishment nor gay and lesbian activists were pleased. This patchwork solution suggested Clinton's willingness to amend social and cultural goals that he had once endorsed.

A sweeping overhaul of the nation's much-criticized health-care system, Clinton expected, would highlight his domestic agenda. Hillary Rodham Clinton headed a special task force that designed new health-care arrangements intended to cover all Americans and, simultaneously, to check rising costs. The task force's proposal, unveiled in late 1993, contained several controversial features.

Health care would be delivered through large private organizations, similar to the existing health maintenance organizations (HMOs), which would seek customers within a system of governmentally "managed competition." Conservative critics charged that governmental regulation would mean that bureaucrats, rather than doctors and patients, controlled crucial medical decisions and that this plan substituted another costly and confusing system for the existing one. Critics on the left advocated the "single-payer" system, on the model of Medicare, which would be administered uniformly through direct government reimbursement.

Conflict over financing quickly engulfed the Clinton health-care proposals. In theory, contributions by employers, who would have to pay the premiums to ensure "basic coverage" for employees, and additional revenue sources, such as higher taxes on cigarettes, would fund the new system. This arrangement generated numerous questions, especially by the National Federation of Independent Business (NFIB), a highly effective lobbying group. Could smaller businesses afford to pay for employee health coverage? How would the proposed payment provisions work in the case of part-time employees? Would not the cost of covering currently unemployed and uninsured people, especially if mental health care were part of "basic" coverage, be far higher than the task force projected? Such questions and an effective counter-campaign, spearheaded by organizations representing small businesses and waged through innovative advocacy advertisements on television, derailed the task force's plan. Clinton eventually abandoned his health-care initiative altogether. This episode helped to mark Clinton as an unfocused president who could not put his bold-sounding ideas into practice.

Health-care overhaul remained an issue throughout the 1990s. Ironically, a trend toward the consolidation of health care into large, competing, managed-care bureaucracies accelerated during the decade and produced a system—without the governmental regulation—that resembled Clinton's own plan. His presidency would end with Congress and the White House still wrestling with proposed federal guidelines to protect the interests of both physicians and patients in safeguarding basic standards of care—the question of a "Patients' Bill of Rights."

Clinton also gained a reputation for ducking divisive issues, a trait that could be construed either as unprincipled or politically astute. He abandoned several of his own nominees when their selection immersed his administration in controversy. He also passed over better-known but potentially polarizing nominees and selected Ruth Bader Ginsburg to replace Thurgood Marshall on the Supreme Court. Although Ginsburg appealed to feminist organizations, because of her antidiscrimination work as a lawyer, her record as a "centrist" judge satisfied most Republican senators. Clinton also bypassed more controversial choices for his second High-Court appointment, Stephen Breyer, an expert in the intricacies of administrative law.

Clinton's Earliest Legal Battles

Militant conservatives almost immediately declared warfare against Clinton and launched a legal campaign against him. Their visceral hatred of Clinton, which surfaced during the 1992 campaign, deepened the longer he remained in office. To these conservatives, Clinton's behavior and character epitomized the "excesses" of 1960s and represented ongoing affronts to the dignity of the presidency.

The initial legal skirmishes focused on Bill and Hillary Rodham Clinton's careers in Arkansas. Both Clintons had invested in a fraud-plagued real estate development, called Whitewater, during the 1970s. In early 1994, Republican pressure led the president to ask his attorney general, Janet Reno, to secure the appointment of a special independent counsel to investigate claims that the Clintons themselves had engaged in illegal activities. Several months later, Paula Corbin Jones, ultimately aided by a conservative group connected to the antiabortion movement, sued Bill Clinton for sexual harassment that had allegedly occurred while he was the governor of Arkansas and she was a state employee. This kind of *private* lawsuit against a sitting president was unprecedented, and Clinton's lawyers tried to settle the case or at least delay his testimony if it continued. The U.S. Supreme Court eventually ruled, unanimously, that litigation could go forward while Clinton held office. The Jones suit increasingly distracted the White House, especially after Kenneth Starr became head of the Office of the Independent Counsel (OIC) charged with investigating Whitewater. A former federal judge, Starr had served in the first Bush administration and had also consulted with the legal team representing Paula Jones.

Conservative legal organizations, such as Judicial Watch, closely shadowed the Clinton administration. They filed their own lawsuits and informally assisted Starr's OIC, which received authority to conduct multiple investigations of the Clintons. Going beyond land deals in Arkansas, Starr looked into allegedly illegal activities connected to the White House's travel bureau and to the mysterious disappearance, and reappearance, of legal files sought by the OIC. Recalling the Nixon era, these episodes became known as "Travelgate" and "Filegate."

The Clintons saw these investigations as a right-leaning counterpart to the "liberal legalism" that groups on the political left had been long using to achieve their political goals. (See pp. 132-134.) The Jones lawsuit employed both the feminist-inspired concept of sexual harassment and the time-tested idea of civil-rights litigation. Although Jones had technically let the time period for filing a sexual-harassment claim lapse, her suit could go forward under the alternative claim that Clinton had violated her federally protected "civil rights." The well-organized and well-funded opposition to Bill Clinton eventually developed an ongoing campaign of litigation that might be called "conservative legalism."

The Clinton administration faced very different kinds of battles with "patriot groups" on the ultra-extreme right. People drawn to this kind of politics claimed that the national government—and many states—had been taken over by people with un-American ideas and goals. Beyond this central article of faith, these "patriots" disagreed on most other issues. Many came from farming areas and small towns that had been hit hard by the economic changes of the 1970s and 1980s. Some embraced racist and anti-Semitic explanations for their problems. Others invoked Biblical prophecy to account for the nation's, and their own, troubles and espoused apocalyptic visions of the near future. Members of the "militia movement" advocated armed resistance and set up their own, extra-legal "common law courts," claiming that both federal and state tribunals, especially under people like Bill Clinton and Janet Reno, could not be trusted.

Several violent incidents marked the contest between patriot groups and the federal government. In April 1993, agents from the FBI and the Bureau of Alcohol Tobacco and Firearms (AFT), under direct orders from Attorney General Reno, made an ill-planned, armed assault on the fortified stronghold of the Branch Davidians, a religious group that had been charged with violating federal gun laws. Seventy-eight members of the Branch Davidians, including many children, perished when fire swept through their fortresslike compound in Waco, Texas, during the AFT raid. Groups sympathetic to the antigovernment stance of the Branch Davidians charged the Clinton administration with committing murder in Waco as well as in Ruby Ridge, Idaho, where two members of a "Christian patriot" group had been killed while resisting arrest by FBI agents.

In 1995, apparently as revenge for the conflagration in Waco, a powerful, homemade bomb tore apart the Alfred P. Murrah Federal Building in Oklahoma City, killing 169 people. Two men with ties to far-right groups, Terry Nichols and Timothy McVeigh, were later convicted of the bombing, and federal authorities executed McVeigh in 2001. The Clinton administration and Congress responded with the Anti-Terrorism and Effective Death Penalty Act of 1996. This measure, opposed by civil libertarians, extended the reach of the death penalty in cases of terrorism and, more controversially, restricted the appeals process in cases where federal inmates were on death row and awaiting execution.

The Contract with America (1994) and the Clinton Resurgence (1996)

The 1994 elections highlighted Clinton's vulnerability. Conservative Republicans, led by Representative Newt Gingrich of Georgia, rallied behind a "Contract with America." This set of proposals included specific term limits for members of Congress, a rollback of tax rates, a balanced federal budget, tougher anticrime laws, and increased spending on defense. More ambitiously, it hinted at cutting the federal bureaucracy by eliminating domestic programs from the Great-Society years and, perhaps, even the New-Deal era as well. Running on this Contract, Republicans swept the November elections. For the first time in 40 years, they secured control of both houses of Congress. They also gained new governor's mansions and made significant strides in state and local races all across the country. Clinton looked like another one-term president.

Conservative Republicans correctly calculated the appeal of their proposals but badly overestimated the impact of their political triumph. Newt Gingrich hoped for a quick, direct legislative assault on the Clinton administration and began pushing some of the Contract, such as budget reduction and anticrime measures, through Congress. After the first 100 days of the Republican-controlled One-hundred-and-fourth Congress, Speaker of the House

Gingrich assumed the prerogative of a president and addressed the nation with a prime-time television speech. Within a year, though, as Clinton began co-opting the most popular parts of the Contract with America for his own agenda, Gingrich's approval ratings began lagging well behind those of the president. As a New Democrat, Clinton had no trouble with policies such as a balanced budget and reduction of the federal bureaucracy. "I hope you're all aware," he reportedly told his aides, "we're all Eisenhower Republicans . . . . fighting the Reagan Republicans."

Clinton's Republican adversaries pressed the fight. Welcoming a deadlock with the president over details of the federal budget, the Republican-controlled Congress allowed the federal government to run out of operating funds, a situation that briefly shut down many operations during the fall of 1995 and the winter of 1995–1996. (The first shutdown meant that a twenty-two-year-old intern named Monica Lewinsky, unsupervised by salaried staffers, would be working near the Oval Office.) The GOP's strategy backfired. Most people held the Republicans in Congress, rather than the Democrat in the White House, responsible for the budget impasse and the unpopular shutdowns.

The federal judiciary provided strong support for a conservative agenda during the 1990s. The U.S. Supreme Court could mobilize a five-judge majority—Justices Sandra Day O'Connor, Anthony Kennedy, Antonin Scalia, Clarence Thomas, and Chief Justice William Rehnquist—that opposed most of the liberal legalism and rights revolution of the 1960s and early 1970s. Much as the Supreme-Court majority of the 1960s had tilted toward policies associated with the Democratic party and its positive-state approach, the Court of the 1990s leaned toward positions associated with the conservatism of the 1970s and 1980s. This meant sympathy for constitutional doctrines that limited the power of the national government and that promoted those of the individual states. In 1995, for example, the Court struck down a federal law that made areas around local school buildings "gun-free zones," and two years later invalidated part of the Brady Handgun Control Law. Subsequently, the Court declared that employees of state governments could not sue under the Americans with Disabilities Act (ADA) and held the Violence Against Women Act of 1994 to be an unconstitutional extension of federal power. Although the Court's majority showed less sympathy than the Warren and Burger Courts for civil-rights claims, it generally sided with litigants, particularly Christian religious groups and commercial advertisers, who asserted First-Amendment rights. With Justice O'Connor joining Justices Ginsburg, Breyer, John Paul Stephens, and David Souter, however, the Court upheld, much to the displeasure of religious conservatives and the Court's four dissenting members, the key abortion-rights decision of *Roe v. Wade*.

Conservative legal groups such as the Federalist Society pressed for more sweeping legal rulings, such as one overturning *Roe*. Seeing a federal judiciary that was staffed, top to bottom, with judges generally sympathetic to conservative ideas, one of the founders of the Federalist Society, whose members included Justices Scalia and Thomas, hoped for a "revolutionary" legal transformation. Conservative-dominated federal courts at the district and appellate levels appeared more activist than the Supreme Court and issued rulings, particularly in cases involving the rights of criminal defendants, directly aimed against those of the Warren Court. Perhaps the most tangible legacy of the Republican victory of 1994, then, was the barrier it created to Clinton's hope of appointing judges in the mold of Justices Ginsburg and Breyer to the lower federal courts. The Republican-controlled Senate blocked a number of the president's judicial nominees and thereby preserved the conservative cast that the Reagan and Bush administrations had given the federal judiciary.

Some constitutional scholars saw the Supreme Court itself, more cautious than many lower courts, inching rightward through a strategy they called "constitutional minimalism." This first meant that the Court radically limited the number of cases on which it formally ruled. It also suggested that the Court chipped away at the reach of precedents from the rights-revolution era, such as *Roe,* without directly overruling them. Justices O'Conner and Kennedy, for example, clearly rejected the reasoning of *Roe* but feared that baldly reversing it would mark the Court as an overtly partisan body. Similarly, the Court, over the dissents of Justices Scalia and Thomas, reaffirmed *Miranda v. Arizona,* the Warren-Court ruling on the rights of criminal defendants; but it did recognize, in another case, the constitutional authority of police officers to stop and arrest motorists on the basis of only a suspected seat-belt violation.

With Congress and the federal judiciary unsympathetic to his agenda, President Clinton's strongest ally in Washington was Federal Reserve Board (FRB) Chair Alan Greenspan. Head of the Council of Economic Advisers under Gerald Ford and appointed to lead the FRB by Ronald Reagan, the Republican Greenspan insisted that the central bank remain independent of day-to-day political pressures. Clinton, recognizing this, subtly courted the FRB chief, whom he reappointed. As Greenspan announced that inflation was in check, that the budget deficit was declining, and that new technologies were improving worker productivity, the FRB kept interest rates low, a stimulus to the economy. The Clinton administration's emphasis on economic matters seemed to be paying off. By 1996, both the unemployment and inflation rates were dropping, as was the number of families living below the government's official definition of the "poverty line." The median family income, which had been stagnating or dropping since the early 1970s, actually began to increase slightly by the mid-1990s.

Such statistics boosted Clinton's political capital. Drawing on advice from other new Democrats and even some Republican strategists, he adroitly outmaneuvered Gingrich and the Republican right. Using his 1996 state of the union address to declare that "the era of big government is over," the president called for the reversal of his party's course, charted over nearly six decades, of consistently supporting expansive (and expensive) federal welfare programs. Although positive-state Democrats and ultra-conservative Republicans denounced this move, for very different reasons, Clinton and other new Democrats joined with Republicans to pass The Personal Responsibility and Work Opportunity Reconciliation Act (PRWORA) of 1996, a follow-up to the Family Support Act (FSA) of 1988.

PRWORA mandated a sweeping, complicated overhaul of the nation's welfare system. First, it tried to streamline existing programs, such as collecting child-support payments from "dead-beat dads," but its major change was a more dramatic one. PRWORA jettisoned Aid for Families with Dependent Children (AFDC), the controversial program that had long anchored the federal government's welfare effort, in favor of something called Temporary Assistance to Needy Families (TANF). TANF provided a system of block grants to individual

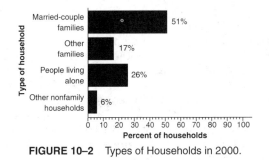

FIGURE 10-2   Types of Households in 2000.

Source: U.S. Census Bureau, Census 2000 Supplementary Survey.

states, which could design, under flexible federal guidelines, their own welfare systems. TANF limited people to no more than five years of welfare over their lifetimes and gave individual states the power to deny public assistance to anyone who had not found employment within two years. This meant that Washington would no longer fund an income maintenance program, AFDC, that enabled women to remain unemployed with children, but would press mothers to work outside of their home.

TANF divided experts in public policy. Supporters claimed that it would allow individual states to experiment with programs, including innovative public-private partnerships, that could move people off the welfare rolls and on to payrolls. Some states, such as Wisconsin, were already claiming success in their efforts to convert welfare recipients into wage earners. Although few policy experts defended the old system, those with longstanding ties to the Democratic party feared that job-creation efforts would prove inadequate and that many people, especially children, would suffer from the eventual cutback in welfare assistance. This plan, they argued, might eliminate the "safety net" that even Ronald Reagan had always pledged to retain.

Neither Bill Clinton nor his Republican opponents wanted to talk about complicated, long-term issues in 1996. Continued economic expansion reduced unemployment, helped to shrink welfare rolls in nearly every state, and provided an optimal climate for joint, public-private ventures that aimed at generating more new jobs. Linking his presidency to the popularity of "welfare reform" and taking credit for the nation's prosperity, Clinton watched his political fortunes rebound just in time for the 1996 election.

Clinton and Al Gore defeated the Republican ticket of Robert Dole and Jack Kemp by about the same margin by which they had bested Bush and Quayle in 1992. Running on his record at home and abroad, Clinton again proved to be a formidable campaigner. In contrast, Dole's effort suffered, initially, from lack of money and, always, from lack of issues. As the Republican majority leader in the Senate, Dole had actually helped Clinton pass the welfare overhaul. Even after resigning from the Senate in hopes of shedding his image as a "Washington insider," Dole found it difficult to suggest a compelling reason for making a change at the White House. Opinion polls suggested broad support for the president's domestic and international priorities. Dole's key proposal, a substantial tax cut, appealed almost exclusively to voters and groups already solidly Republican. The Republican challenger's biting wit and barbed sarcasm, which played well on TV talk shows, made him seem cynical and mean-spirited on the campaign trail. Dole thus hesitated to criticize the president's character or personal life, clearly his greatest liabilities. The GOP's hope for a last-minute bombshell, an indictment by Kenneth Starr's OIC against a close presidential aide, or even the Clintons themselves, never materialized.

Both major parties could claim victory in 1996. Democrats not only retained the presidency, the first time since 1964, but a majority of seats in state legislatures around the country. Despite the GOP's failure to topple Clinton, 1996 was still a good election for Republicans. For the first time since 1928, the GOP kept control of both the Senate and the House of Representatives. It picked up several new governorships and made modest gains in state and local elections, particularly in the South. As a result of the 1996 election, partisan conflict seemed certain to intensify.

A Culture of Exposure and Clinton's Continuing Legal Battles

The continued political warfare between Clinton and his Republican adversaries took place against the backdrop of an increasingly intense culture of "exposure" which blurred the boundaries between public and private, law and politics. This type of conflict traced its legal legitimacy to the Independent Counsel Act of 1978, which had provided the basis for several investigations of Ronald Reagan's presidency. (See Chapter 9.) Lawrence Walsh, who was appointed to investigate allegations of involvement by high-ranking members of the Reagan administration, including George Bush, in the Iran-contra affair, subsequently complained that the media largely ignored his effort. This indifference allowed Republicans to build, in Walsh's phrase, a "firewall" around Bush's presidency during the early 1990s. Although Clinton and his firefighters threw up wall after wall of their own, they confronted an uncontainable inferno.

Clinton's wounds were (*partly* according to supporters, *entirely*, according to critics) self-inflicted. The president persistently lied—to family, close aides, and the public—about his brief sexual relationship with the young intern Monica Lewinsky. Clinton also deceived his lawyers about Lewinsky when giving a deposition in the Paula Jones civil suit. Ultimately, DNA evidence of a sexual encounter with Lewinsky forced Clinton to recant earlier denials. He still insisted that he had committed no illegal acts, and that his sins remained purely private ones. Clinton's critics rejected both claims, and the logic of the culture of exposure meant that nothing about Clinton's life, even its sexual side, could remain private if some legal issue seemed at stake.

Exposure, of course, had long been part of U.S. political culture. On some occasions, as in the case of Grover Cleveland's fathering of a child out of wedlock (widely discussed during the 1884 presidential election campaign), private matters could become public issues. Invariably, though, the settled rules of political life, particularly during the post-World War II era, included a line between a public person's public and private life. John F. Kennedy's presidency confirmed that the mainstream media would respect this distinction. Even if tabloid-style publications such as the *National Enquirer* occasionally crossed the line, especially with stories about Kennedy after his death, there was little change in public discourse on radio or television or in daily publications such as the *New*

York Times or *Washington Post.* Unless a politician's own public behavior exposed a sexual encounter, as one powerful Democrat did during the 1970s by drunkenly frolicking with a stripper in Washington's Tidal Basin, the media would give private indiscretions a free pass.

During the 1980s, however, aspects of a public person's life that would have once remained private had slowly become ripe for widespread exposure throughout the media. A style of journalism, which could be called "sexual investigative reporting," aimed at revealing sexual dalliances by prominent public figures. Televangelists Jim Bakker and Jimmy Lee Swaggert (see Chapter 9) and Democratic presidential hopeful Gary Hart became early targets. Scattered incidents such as these, though, remained the exception. Bakker and Swaggert implicitly invited exposure, reporters claimed, by sheltering their gaudy lifestyles with false piety, and Hart had explicitly challenged the media, never expecting they would accept, to find sexual infidelity in his private life. Even the new tabloid-style TV programs of the late 1980s, such as "Hard Copy," dealt with public controversies, such as the activities of avowed white supremacists or alleged pornographers, and stayed clear of the private lives of political figures.

This all changed during the 1990s. The syndicated TV shows of Jenny Jones, Sally Jessy Raphael, and Jerry Springer exposed the private lives of ordinary people, preferably members of the same family, who were fighting over issues such as "revealing attire," "wild teens," "love triangles," and "cheating spouses." These shows encouraged on-camera "guests" to confront one another and, then, implicitly invited the viewing audience to pass judgment on the controversy. In their highly judgmental tone, programs such as the "Jerry Springer Show" overlapped with the more overtly trial-like programs, such as "Judge Judy" and "Divorce Court," and both genres turned private disputes into public entertainment.

This "blurring of boundaries," as the media scholar Bill Nichols characterized it, appeared everywhere. "Cops" exposed the daily routine of law enforcement officers, and "America's Funniest Home Videos" got people to reveal their *own* private lives. MTV's "Real People," which debuted in 1992, provided the model for other "reality" shows, such as CBS's sensationally successful "Survivor." The proliferation of videotape cameras, in literally every nook-and-cranny of life, made it all the easier for the media to blur boundaries. After the 1997 death of Britain's Princess Diana, killed in a car crash while trying to elude camera-wielding journalists in Paris, slow-motion footage from a surveillance camera provided the last glimpses of her life, while a computer game allowed the curious to simulate various crash scenarios that might have preceded her death. Internet sites that specialized in coverage of a single person or event intensified this culture of exposure.

Shortly before Clinton's troubles, the intermingling of public and private realms had dominated the media in a series of legal trials. The case of O.J. Simpson, a former football hero charged with killing his ex-wife and one of her friends, sustained a media spectacle that featured race, sex, and wealth. No legal event had ever captured so much media attention for so long. Virtually every aspect of Simpson's own life, and that of anyone connected to him, became fair game for the 24-hour cable stations, the so-called 7/24 outlets. Scrambling to catch up with the Simpson phenomenon, network TV disrupted regular afternoon program schedules and gutted the ratings for successful, long-running soap operas such as "Another World" (which eventually had to be canceled in 1999). Simpson's criminal trial, televised live, every weekday, for nearly nine months, became a mini soap opera of its own. It ended with a largely African-American jury rendering a "not guilty" verdict, a decision that sparked several additional months of cable-TV retrospectives about the relationship between law and race. Then, just when it seemed that the OJ saga might fade away, a subsequent civil trial brought by relatives of the two murder victims provided an acceptable sequel. It concluded with another jury, primarily composed of people of European descent, declaring Simpson "legally responsible." During these two trials, cable TV developed a formula that pundits called "All OJ, All-the-Time."

The Clinton presidency seemed to fit this new media template. Media-savvy pundits from both the anti- and pro-Clinton camps clamored to debate the president's mounting problems on shows such as "Geraldo Live." Almost anyone with a law degree became a "constitutional expert." The result, one journalist noted, resembled a form of "media ambulance chasing." Virtually any charge, including one about a Clinton-directed conspiracy to murder Vincent Foster, a member of his own administration, seemed open for debate. Four separate investigations, including one by Starr's own OIC, found Foster's death a tragic suicide, but a well-funded conservative effort to uncover wrongdoing by the Clintons, called the "Arkansas Project," raised enough new allegations to support further rounds of Clinton-centered contention on cable-TV shows. Anti-Clinton investigators also passed information to Starr's OIC, which was now interested in the president's personal conduct in the Oval Office. A freelance conservative activist, promoting possible book deals, obtained the next best thing to a surveillance video: illegally recorded audio tapes of Monica Lewinsky telling a friend of her dalliances with Clinton.

The media frame quickly shifted from financial lapses to sexual liaisons. The OIC and several journalists learned of the so-called Lewinsky tapes. In January 1998, a right-leaning Internet site, the *Drudge Report,* charged *Newsweek* magazine with refusing to print a story, by a reporter who had once exposed Jim Bakker, about a "sex relationship" between the president and a still anonymous intern, subsequently revealed to be Lewinsky. Within hours, the once-staid Sunday-morning, network news programs such as "Face the Nation" were discussing the president's sexual life. Within days cable-TV was featuring "All Bill and Monica, All-the-Time." Recalling coverage of Princess Diana, TV shows put several seconds of footage, which showed Lewinsky and Clinton briefly chatting at a public, White House event, into the "heavy rotation" mode that the early MTV employed for rock videos.

Clinton's troubles, in contrast to Richard Nixon's during the Watergate era, involved more than a single newspaper and several federal prosecutors. A vast network of exposure—which included print publications, network news programs, cable outlets, and Internet sites—peered at the Clinton White House. Was the Lewinsky "affair" Clinton's only sexual indiscretion? Most important, had Clinton committed some public offense, perhaps perjury, in the attempt to conceal his private life? When Democrats complained that scrutiny of Clinton amounted to "sexual McCarthyism," the media found this charge just another issue to be thrown into the 7/24 mix. On one occasion, the network news anchors abandoned their coverage of the Pope's historic visit to Communist

Cuba and rushed back to Washington, just to be near the unfolding Clinton saga. In several other cases, when the president ordered missile strikes overseas against a terrorist network that had bombed U.S. embassies, critics noted how closely his actions followed the story line in the movie *Wag the Dog* (1997), a political farce in which a philandering president stages a phony military intervention to stave off impeachment. Could President Clinton continue to govern effectively in this media-saturated environment? Rumors of a Clinton resignation intermittently swept through the vast media matrix.

Republicans and many members of the media seemed perplexed by the public response to Clinton's problems. Despite the so-called blurring of public and private, most Americans generally drew a clear distinction in Clinton's case. Although polls revealed disenchantment with Clinton's personal activities, this hardly affected ratings of his performance as president. After Clinton delivered his state of the union address in January 1998 and announced that the federal budget would be in balance for the first time in decades, his approval rating reached an all-time high. Moreover, when Clinton's job rating was compared to that of Republican leaders, Kenneth Starr's OIC, and the news media itself, the president came out substantially ahead. Although Starr's supporters applauded how he had obtained evidence from Lewinsky, a majority of people saw the independent counsel as an overzealous, partisan crusader obsessed with Clinton's sex life. Even if many people now shared the conservative critique of Clinton's character, the vast majority rejected its judgment about the illegitimacy of his presidency. Most people continued to rate Clinton as a better-than-competent chief executive.

The Culture of Exposure and Clinton's Final Legal Battle

Some Republicans, incredulous over Clinton's still-high approval rating, nonetheless expected his problems to bring the GOP another smashing off-year electoral victory in 1998. Newt Gingrich, as in 1994, orchestrated the Republican campaign. Defying opinion polls and dissenting Republicans, he made Bill Clinton's behavior the central GOP issue. Two months before the election, Kenneth Starr's OIC sent the House of Representatives a lengthy report, spiced by repeated, graphically detailed descriptions of trysts between Clinton and Monica Lewinsky and capped by four possible articles of impeachment. Speaker Gingrich immediately released the *Starr Report* and much of its accompanying materials about Clinton's conduct, all compiled by someone by now widely (if unjustly) seen as the reigning Puritan of American law and politics. The House Speaker also dumped millions of dollars into TV ads that attacked Clinton's character, a theme that still failed to resonate with political independents. The 1994 Contract with America, parts of which were now on Clinton's agenda, seemed ancient history. The GOP gained no seats in the Senate in 1998 and managed to lose five in the House, an excellent showing for an incumbent president under any circumstances and a stunning victory for one as embattled as Bill Clinton.

For a brief time, the culture of exposure turned away from Clinton. Under fire by Republicans for his political miscalculations, Gingrich watched the media reveal his own long-term, extra-marital affair with a congressional aide (whom, after a divorce, he married). Gingrich quickly resigned from

Congress, and Larry Flynt, the self-proclaimed "scumbag" who publishes *Hustler* magazine, gleefully offered to pay for evidence of similar affairs by other Republicans. Flynt eventually exposed Gingrich's heir apparent as House Speaker, who also resigned after his own sexual history became public. Even Henry Hyde, the septuagenarian Chair of the House Judiciary Committee who was seeking Clinton's impeachment, faced humiliating revelations of a decades-old extra-martial affair of his own.

By November 1998, virtually everyone in Washington agreed that there were simply not enough votes in the Senate to remove the president from office, and insiders from both parties worked to sidetrack an impeachment. Why, then, did William Jefferson Clinton become the first president to face an impeachment and a trial in nearly 150 years?

The interconnection among the culture of exposure, conservative legalism, and partisan politics made Clinton's impeachment an attractive option for conservative Republicans. In contrast to 1974, when the pursuit of Nixon seemed a "constitutional crisis" that eventually produced a bipartisan coalition that eased the divisive president from office, Clinton's case remained an overtly partisan affair. Few Republicans, or Democrats, worried that a Clinton impeachment would bring the nation to a constitutional impasse or confront them with a serious challenge from the opposing party. More than 200 House incumbents, running in one-party districts, had faced only token opposition or *no* opponent at all in the November 1998 elections. Invoking a familiar basketball analogy, one constitutional scholar has argued that a vote for Clinton's impeachment seemed a "no harm, no foul" situation for most Republicans. More important, many Republicans saw a vote against impeachment risking a political challenge, not from pro-Clinton Democrats but from anti-Clinton activists on the far right of their own party. Thus, many Republicans in the House, who might personally have been willing to let Clinton "go in peace," feared the political consequences of not hurling a final legal bombshell his way. The GOP's highly partisan core constituency, although only about 30 percent of the nation's total electorate, demanded the continuation of efforts to expose Clinton's character to the glare of the media.

On December 19, 1998, Republican members of a Congress about to go out of business voted two articles of impeachment. They charged Clinton with committing perjury and with obstruction of justice while covering up his relationship with Monica Lewinsky. Only five Democrats supported the more serious perjury article, and only five Republicans opposed it. Although Clinton's tortured testimony could have sustained fairly specific articles of impeachment, Republicans hastily drafted ones that, as the outvoted Democrats noted, even failed to indicate on what issues Clinton had allegedly committed perjury. The culture of exposure, Republicans seemed to believe, had so clearly revealed Clinton's fabrications that legal precision seemed unnecessary. Even if Republicans from the House, who served as prosecutors (or "managers"), could not remove Clinton, they could still use the law of impeachment to expose, from the floor of the U.S. Senate, his perfidy to a national TV and radio audience. To this end, they wanted "live witnesses," including Monica Lewinsky, to testify in person.

On the issue of witnesses, as on every other that threatened to extend and sensationalize the trial, key Republican and Democratic senators rebuffed the managers. Lacking anything like the "smoking gun" tapes that had doomed Nixon, the managers, none of whom had tried a jury case in years, proved no match for Clinton's court-toughened defense team. Opinion polls, which were taken daily during the nearly month-long trial, showed overwhelming, even growing support for the president's acquittal. On February 12, 1999, ten Republicans joined every Democratic senator in rejecting the perjury count by a 55 to 45 margin, and five GOP senators from the Northeast voted with the Democrats on the obstruction of justice allegation, producing a 50–50 tie vote.

THE "NEW ECONOMY"

Virtually everyone, including those who sought Clinton's impeachment, attributed his popularity to the state of the U.S. economy. Political advisers in 1992, urging Clinton to focus on the unpopular budget deficits, tax increases, and unemployment of the Bush years, had posted a sign in his campaign headquarters saying "It's the Economy, Stupid." The economy, indeed, remained central to the success of the Clinton presidency. The longest economic expansion in American history, which began just before Clinton's election, rested on broader forces than those the president himself controlled. Still, Clinton enjoyed the prosperity—and even the excesses—of what came to be called the "New Economy." In a way, the optimistic and ever-excessive Clinton, the poor-boy-made-good, perfectly symbolized this side of the 1990s.

Economic Boom

Just as the economic downturn at the beginning of the 1990s had doomed George Bush's presidency, the boom that carried into 2000 helped sustain Clinton's. After years of high unemployment rates, stagnating wages, and antiunion policies, workers in the industrial and service economies generally saw moderate increases in real wages. Other factors also contributed to Americans' growing purchasing power. The easy availability of consumer credit and frequent opportunities for overtime and "moonlight" work helped stretch incomes. Indeed, during the 1990s, workers in the United States could claim, after passing those in Japan, to be the hardest-working people in the world. Americans who were employed full-time worked more than forty-nine weeks a year, three-and-half per year more than Japanese workers and twelve-and-half more than those in Germany. Most American families used a second or third income to boost their consumption. By 2000, over 60 percent of married woman worked in the labor market, while more high school and college students, particularly women, worked than ever before. According to one survey, more than 60 percent of U.S. teenagers were employed, a figure three times greater than the average in all other industrial countries. Because jobs, particularly in fast-food chains and retail stores, were readily available in upper- and middle-income neighborhoods, young people from relatively affluent households were more likely to work than ones from low-income families. Economists estimated that, during the mid-1990s, teenagers alone were spending about $100 million a year, a figure nearly half the size of the nation's defense budget.

FIGURE 10–3 A High-Tech Taxicab in San Francisco, 1999.

The pioneering internet company, Yahoo!, partnered with Luxor Cab Company to offer passengers internet access during taxi rides. The internet boom of the late 1990s brought many such high-tech hybrids—some successful and some not.
Source: AP/Wide World Photos.

The post-World War II vision of ever-expanding economic growth now seemed the norm. Consumers took advantage of lower prices from the discount chains such as Walmart; other manufacturers and retailers also kept prices down and profits up because their own innovative forms of organization and management produced greater efficiency. Higher worker productivity—that is, greater hourly output per worker—meant that businesses could increase wages and salaries without generating significant price rises or triggering an inflationary surge within the economy. The FRB's Alan Greenspan, declared in mid-1998 that the "combination of strong growth and low inflation" made the U.S. economic performance "as impressive as any I have witnessed in my near half-century of daily observation of the American economy."

The surging economy meant that the federal government's yawning budget deficit narrowed, disappeared, and then turned to surplus. Tax revenues soared, and Congress could fund new transportation projects and underwrite a variety of targeted tax cuts. The stock market, enjoying the longest boom ever, prompted some economists to see a "new economic paradigm," fueled by new technologies, which would guarantee economic growth well into the future. The New York Stock Exchange's Dow Jones Industrial Average (DJIA) nearly doubled between 1996 and 2000 and reached the 12,000 level. A best-selling book, by extrapolating this number over time, predicted that DJIA would reach 36,000 in the relatively near future.

Technological innovation helped to drive this "new economy." A wave of corporate mergers mobilized resources for expanding existing firms, while "venture capitalists" financed the start-up of thousands of new businesses, many of which took advantage of wireless technology and the Internet. Enterprises that depended on the Internet, the so-called dot-com businesses, came to symbolize economic innovation during the 1990s. Internet firms such as Yahoo, E-Bay, and America On-Line (AOL) became the darlings of Wall Street, as did the "high tech" firms, such as Cisco and Sun Microsystems, that provided the infrastructure for the World Wide Web. Companies that built and marketed computers (such as Dell and Gateway) or devised and sold software (particularly Microsoft), fledgling operations during the 1980s, joined the list of the nation's leading companies during the 1990s. Telecommunications became another area of rapid growth, as analog and then digital cell phones inexorably replaced telephone booths. Similarly, satellite TV challenged cable television, a relatively new industry itself. In a move symbolic of the 1990s, America On-Line (AOL) pulled off the largest merger of the dot-com era when, in January 2000, it acquired Time-Warner's sprawling media empire, which was still working out its own recent consolidation with Ted Turner's multimedia enterprise. The FRB's Greenspan, who still wrote his own memos by pen, lent his considerable prestige to this new economy. Although an offhand 1996 remark about the stock market's "irrational exuberance" temporarily sent prices tumbling, Greenspan generally expressed optimism about the long-term consequences of innovation.

Economic expansion brought higher living standards to most people. Between 1990 and 2000 education levels climbed: The percentage of Americans with high school degrees rose from 75 to 82 percent; and with bachelor's degrees from 20 to 25 percent. Nine of every ten households owned at least one automobile, while nearly 20 percent owned three or more vehicles. The average house size grew larger, and homeowners often refinanced (more than once) their mortgages, using the equity obtained from rising real-estate values to increase their consumption. Restaurants and recreation-oriented businesses prospered. The Disney company opened a new theme park dedicated to the lifestyles of California, the world's fifth largest economy. One best-selling book talked of "the millionaire next door." The high-flying world of dot-coms not only produced many of these new millionaires but a host of billionaires, most notably Microsoft's Bill Gates.

Economic expansion, however, did not touch everyone equally. The gap between the very rich and those with chronically low incomes widened during the 1990s. Despite energetic organizing efforts, particularly in the government sector, labor unions seemed to be losing political clout, particularly among new Democrats like Clinton, and failed to increase their overall membership rolls during the 1990s. Still, economic growth cut into the official "poverty rate." By the end of the decade, 13 percent of the population lived below the official poverty line, set at $16,600 for a family of four. Nearly one in five children under the age of eighteen years also lived below this standard. Both figures were the lowest since 1979. (There were significant variations according to region.) The South, although displaying remarkable economic growth and a consequent decline in poverty rates, remained the poorest region in the country.

Meanwhile, statistics for families headed by single women, including ones who had recently joined the labor force, showed virtually no improvement, even during the years of greatest economic expansion, 1995 to 1999.

Critics of the welfare overhaul blamed the changes of 1996 for these figures. During the final years of the old welfare system, the so-called safety-net programs had reduced the percentage of families headed by mothers in the work force that fell below the poverty line. Then, when benefits began to shrink, paychecks, even in an era of low inflation, simply could not make up for cuts in supplemental governmental payments. Supporters of the 1996 measures counseled that the changes in welfare law were not an immediate antipoverty program. In time, as people relatively new to the job market acquired additional skills and training, they could expect to move on to better-paying jobs. Critics remained unconvinced. What might happen to people, particularly children, once supported by income maintenance programs, if the economy stopped producing jobs as effectively as it had done during the late 1990s?

FASHIONING POST-COLD-WAR FOREIGN POLICY

Clinton faced the task of fashioning foreign policies relevant to the post-cold-war environment. His greatest challenge involved weighing whether or not to become involved in potential military interventions around the world. Generally, he tried to ease away from the Reagan-Bush focus on military shows of strength, while emphasizing involvement in various multilateral peacemaking and peacekeeping activities.

In 1992 President Bush had ordered American troops, as part of a UN mission, to help move food and relief supplies to alleviate famine in Somalia. Gradually, however, the UN force became involved in factional fighting there, and, after U.S. troops suffered well-publicized casualties in the fall of 1993, Clinton ordered a complete pullout in the spring of 1994. The next year, bruised by criticism over the casualties in Somalia, Clinton refused to support a UN effort to stop a genocidal civil war in Rwanda, in which half a million people died. Human rights activists subsequently assailed the Clinton administration's lack of action.

During the 1992 presidential campaign, Clinton had vowed to help reestablish the elected government of Haiti, whose leader, Jean-Bertrand Aristide, lived in exile in the United States. In September 1994, U.S. troops landed in Haiti to convince the nation's military to step aside and restore electoral processes. Subsequently, UN forces took over responsibility for helping reconstruct civil order in Haiti, a task that met with little success.

The former Yugoslavia raised similarly complicated questions about when, why, and where to intervene militarily. Serbian troops carried out a murderous campaign of "ethnic cleansing" against Bosnian Muslims. The United States, working with NATO, threatened air strikes and advanced diplomatic initiatives. In U.S.-brokered accords signed in Dayton, Ohio, in 1995, agreements were reached for a cease-fire and peace-building process supervised by NATO (including U.S.) troops. Although tensions remained high and NATO became entangled in a longer-term mission than was expected, most of the killing in Yugoslavia stopped. Serbian President Slobodan Milosevic then shifted his attention to "cleansing" Albanian Muslims in the Serbian province of Kosovo. In

March 1999 a 78-day NATO bombing campaign against Serbia damaged so much of its capital city, Belgrade, and its industrial infrastructure that Serbia withdrew its forces from Kosovo. Ethnic Albanians who had tried to flee Milosevic's terror returned to an uneasy peace, supervised by NATO troops. In the fall of 2000, Serbs ousted Milosevic and subsequently sent him to stand trial before an international tribunal in the Netherlands for crimes against humanity. In all of these interventions, the Clinton administration's supporters generally applauded the president's flexibility and involvement; critics discerned a lack of overall strategic vision and tended to distrust multilateral "peacekeeping" and "nation-building" commitments of uncertain duration.

Terrorism and drug trafficking continued to claim Washington's attention. Terrorist bombs exploded in New York City's World Trade Center in 1993, U.S. embassy buildings in Kenya and Tanzania in 1998, and a U.S. battleship docked in Yemen in 2000. The Clinton administration tried to investigate, arrest, or retaliate against those involved. Tracking responsibility to an anti-American network of Islamic militants headed by Osama bin Laden, who ran training programs and received protection from the Taliban faction in Afghanistan, U.S. officials attempted an air strike and then a covert operation to eliminate him. Neither succeeded. The Clinton administration also expanded its predecessor's war on drugs in Latin America. The U.S.-funded, often military-style action against cocaine growers and traffickers seemed only to shift, rather than reduce, the output of drugs. Clinton asked, however, for ever-rising levels of military assistance, especially to Colombia, to stave off the civil instability that drug money generated. The administration introduced new measures to help identify terrorist or drug networks, but Republicans in Congress blocked regulatory legislation forcing international banks to provide greater public disclosure of possible terrorist and money-laundering transactions.

In yet another facet of his post-cold-war foreign policy, Clinton tried to mediate long-standing conflicts. Mediation promoted a fragile accord in Northern Ireland between warring Catholics, who desired independence from Britain, and Protestants, who wished to remain under British protection. In a high profile, but ultimately unsuccessful, attempt to force a settlement between Israel and the Palestine Liberation Organization, Clinton personally conducted negotiations at Camp David in 2000 and devoted the final days of his presidency to trying to broker difficult issues such as the mix of sovereignties in the Holy City of Jerusalem. The Clinton administration similarly struck a posture emphasizing international cooperation on global issues related to climate change, the crisis of AIDS, limitations on agents of chemical and biological warfare, and nuclear proliferation.

While trying to limit unilateral military missions and promote various international accords, Clinton focused on enlarging global trade and investment. The process called "globalization," Clinton argued, would generate growth and improve living standards everywhere. Building on the Reagan-Bush effort to lower trade barriers and expand markets, Clinton consummated several trade agreements. He strongly backed NAFTA, despite opposition from labor unions and other groups in the traditional Democratic coalition. After adding a few safeguards on labor and environmental issues, in December 1993 Clinton muscled NAFTA through Congress in a close vote that rested on strong Republican support. He completed trade agreements with nations of the Pacific Rim and, in February 1994, normalized trade with Vietnam. Reversing a campaign position, he continued Bush's policy of granting "most favored nation" (MNF) status to China, despite that country's record of human rights abuses. Then, after difficult negotiations in the final so-called Uruguay Round of GATT (General Agreement on Tariffs and Trade) in early 1995, GATT was replaced by a new World Trade Organization (WTO), an organization that would implement new trade agreements and settle trade disputes. Clinton agreed to support China's entry into the WTO, arguing that helping China link its economy to the global capitalist market would create incentives for democratization of the Chinese polity.

The Clinton administration aggressively intervened to stabilize market conditions around the world. When Mexico experienced a financial crisis in early 1995, Clinton extended $20 billion in credits from America's Exchange Stabilization Fund to help that country avoid economic collapse. This move was as controversial as it was unprecedented. Within just three years, though, Mexico stabilized its economy and repaid the emergency loan with interest. When an even more severe financial crisis hit economies throughout Asia in late 1997, Clinton again pledged emergency credits, this time in conjunction with the International Monetary Fund.

Clinton claimed that these economic moves—along with the emergence of market economies throughout Eastern Europe, Asia, and Latin America—would stimulate economic growth in both the United States and the global economy. Not everyone agreed with this prediction. Labor union activists argued that globalization allowed U.S. companies to lower wages and weaken environmental and labor standards at home by threatening to move their operations elsewhere in the world. Unless labor and environmental practices were internationally monitored, they charged, highly mobile capital and freer trade could create a "race to the bottom," as countries competed to offer the cheapest labor market and least restrictive corporate environment. Protestors against unregulated globalization—backed by labor, environmental, and many student organizations—revived the tactic of massive street demonstrations. At Seattle in 1999, the number of people protesting the new WTO surprised delegates and temporarily overwhelmed local police. Similar demonstrator-police confrontations became a regular feature of subsequent high-profile international economic meetings around the world.

Governmental secrecy, which had expanded significantly during the cold war, came under review. Endorsing greater openness, the Clinton administration began slowly modifying guidelines for the declassification of information. Its initiatives led in several directions. The Department of Energy released formerly secret documents showing governmental complicity in cold-war testing of the effects of radioactivity on humans. In the wake of controversy following Oliver Stone's movie, *JFK*, a massive project made available information about the assassination of President Kennedy. The CIA pledged to open historical files on a number of covert actions of the 1950s and 1960s, a promise that the agency later retracted.

Several high-level spy cases reminded Americans that espionage did not end with the cold war. In the spring of 1994, a highly placed CIA official was arrested and convicted of being a "mole," the kind of spy who for years had been simultaneously passing KGB "disinformation" to CIA analysts and U.S.

intelligence secrets to the Soviet Union and Russia, causing the death of a number of U.S. agents. Five years later, a top FBI employee (who, ironically, had spied on Americans considered security risks during the Reagan years) was discovered to have sold more high-level intelligence to Russia than any other spy in U.S. history.

Clinton's foreign policy received mixed reviews. His defenders lauded his internationalist vision: working with the UN and NATO, putting his prestige behind negotiations in historic trouble spots, advocating greater globalization of trade and investment, endorsing a variety of efforts to further international cooperation related to environment, health, and nuclear issues. Critics, however, charged the Clinton administration with a lack of overall vision and too much deference to internationalist groups. Republicans generally endorsed his free-trade emphasis but were suspicious of internationalist and peacekeeping involvements.

GOP stategists shaped a more nationalist foreign-policy agenda on which to run in 2000. Candidate George W. Bush, son of the former president, promised to back away from international environmental agreements and arms control treaties, to reduce U.S. peacekeepers in Bosnia, to take a tougher stand against the still-Communist states of China and North Korea, and to avoid involvement in Israeli-Palestinian disputes, while continuing support for Israel. Foreign policy never became a major issue in the 2000 campaign. Although the Republican critique of the Clinton administration provided clues about the priorities that the Bush administration would pursue after it took office in 2001, both parties tried to minimize their differences on foreign policy in order to focus on domestic issues.

NEW AMERICANS

The 2000 census revealed significant changes in who Americans were and how they were living. During the 1990s, the population increased by nearly 33 million, the largest ten-year increase in U.S. history. The percentage increase, just over 13 percent, fell short of that of the 1950s but roughly matched that of the 1960s, two decades in which the baby boom had swelled the population. Americans also were becoming older, and more were residing in the West and South. Fewer lived in rural areas or in "traditional" families than ever before. More than one in every ten Americans was foreign-born, the largest share of the total population since the 1930s.

Population Trends

The nation's population continued, as it had since 1975, to grow older, a phenomenon that trend-watchers called "the graying of America." In 2000, the median age, 35.3 years, was the highest in U.S. history, rising from just under 33 years in 1990. There were many reasons for this trend. The baby boom generation, that population bulge born between 1944 and 1964, reached middle age. Just as these "boomers" had once been associated with a youth movement, they now became linked to mid-life concerns such as health-care coverage and retirement planning. At the same time, the birthrate sank to its lowest level, except during the depression-ridden era of the 1930s, in American history.

Birthrates usually directly shadow trends in marriage, and people were increasingly delaying or forgoing marital vows. Between 1960 and 2000, the median age at which men married rose from 23 to 27; for women, it rose from 20 to 25. More and more women were not marrying at all. There was also a climb in divorce rates and in the numbers of mothers who worked outside the home, factors that provided disincentives for childbearing in a nation that offered little childcare assistance.

The "sunbelt" regions of the South and West experienced 90 percent of the nation's growth between 1970 and 2000. The West grew by nearly 20 percent during the 1990s, while the South increased by more than 17 percent. In contrast, the Midwest and Northeast saw their populations grow by less than 8 and 6 percent, respectively. Nevada, California, Florida, and Arizona grew the fastest, and by the beginning of the twenty-first century more than one in every ten Americans lived in California. This regional shift brought political change. In the 2000 reallocation of seats in the House of Representatives, California gained eight and Florida six. New York, by contrast, lost five. National electoral politics thus focused more than ever before on the South and West, as the old power structure, based in the Northeast and Middle West, continued to weaken.

In whatever region they resided, Americans overwhelmingly dwelled in cities or suburbs. Although the rural and small-town populations grew a bit during the 1990s, small-scale farmers continued to sell out to larger operations and the tiny farming communities that once dotted America's landscape dwindled. During the 1990s, counties dominated by agricultural economies in the Great Plains states lost as much as 10 percent of their population. In stark contrast, counties that included the region's leading cities, such as Sioux Falls, South Dakota, and Lincoln, Nebraska, registered sizable gains. By 2000 even the few Americans who still lived in rural areas often commuted to metropolitan areas to work or shop.

By 2000 even the most traditionally rural group of Americans—American Indians—primarily lived in cities. However, some rural Indian reservations did experience a remarkable revival, as lawyers successfully pressed legal rights derived from old treaties. In 1988 the Supreme Court ruled that states could not prohibit gaming operations on tribal land, and Congress subsequently passed the Indian Gaming Regulatory Act to allow casino operations. Gaming boomed, and Indian casinos became big business, often enriching the tribes that owned them. The small band of Pequot in Connecticut, for example, parlayed profits from its huge Foxwoods casino to finance various projects of cultural renewal: powwows, museums, and language preservation. Many casinos also financed better schools and health care on reservations. As whites moved out of many small communities, particularly on the Great Plains, American Indians became a significant percentage of the total rural population and sought to reclaim aspects of their cultures.

The largest areas grew the fastest. Metropolitan New York City's population surpassed the 20 million mark, while that of Los Angeles topped 16 million. These two metro areas, taken together, contained more than 13 percent of the nation's entire population. Not surprisingly, cities in the West led the way. Las Vegas grew more rapidly than any other metropolis, by a staggering 83 percent, during the 1990s, and Provo, Utah, the tenth fastest-growing metro area, increased by about half this much. Central cities generally grew more slowly than

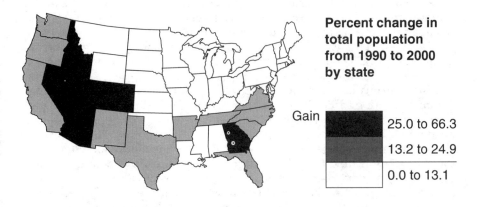

**Percent change in
total population
from 1990 to 2000
by state**

Gain

	25.0 to 66.3
	13.2 to 24.9
	0.0 to 13.1

FIGURE 10–4   Which States Had a Population Boom in the 1990s?

Source: U.S. Census Bureau.

their surrounding suburbs, but eight of the ten largest increased their population during the 1990s. Philadelphia and Detroit were the exceptions.

Metropolitan landscapes continued to sprawl into lengthy suburban cor-
ridors, extending out from, and reaching in between, cities. New "downtowns,"
consisting of business parks and automobile-friendly shopping complexes,
formed the centers of what one journalist called "edge cities." Places like Bloomington near Minneapolis or Tysons Corner near Washington D.C. lacked the
name recognition of the nearby core city but held populations and economic
enterprises (such as Bloomington's successful "Mall of America") that rivaled
or surpassed them.

Not every suburban area prospered during the 1990s. Places that one urban
specialist called "off-the-edge cities," for example, showed that jobs and economic opportunities did not always follow new housing developments. Consequently, people living in far-flung suburbs often had to drive two or even three
hours to work and send their children to overcrowded and under-funded public schools. During the late 1990s, stressful living conditions in the distant LA
suburb of Palmdale, California, generated rates of suicide and domestic abuse
that were among the highest in the nation.

Core cities themselves also changed dramatically during the 1990s. The
economic boom brought new office towers, residential developments, and complexes for sporting events and the arts to many, though certainly not all, central cities. Some people who had perhaps raised families in the new postwar
suburbs moved to upscale, urban housing developments to take advantage of
the vibrancy of downtown living, and many young, single professionals also preferred an urban scene. Even though laws required new urban developments to

contain a certain percentage of "affordable" units, people with low incomes encountered rising rents and a severe shortage of available units. A United Nations report, done in the early 1990s, claimed that the ratio between the wealthiest and the most needy resident of Los Angeles and New York City was "comparable to [that in] Karachi, Bombay, and Mexico City."

Civil libertarians talked of a growing "urban cold war." Within core cities, public and private police forces tried to keep still-growing homeless and low-income populations away from areas used by more affluent residents and tourists. Persons of color increasingly complained about "racial profiling." Criminal-justice statistics showed police stopping and detaining dark-skinned motorists and pedestrians more often than those from any other group, thus creating an offense critics called "DWB," or "driving while black or brown." Law-enforcement officials denied systematic discrimination and cited crime statistics to justify their patrolling patterns as being in line with prudent police procedures, but critics saw profiling as a new "rights issue." Even if a person were subsequently released, the fact of detention seemed to be a serious, ethnically related affront to the right of personal dignity. The nation's increasingly diverse population made profiling an explosive issue not only in metropolitan areas but along the vast United States-Mexican border.

Immigration

A growing stream of immigration also transformed American life. The Immigration Act of 1965 had terminated immigration quotas based on the national origins of current residents, a practice that had given preference to Europeans. Instead, the act shifted the balance toward applicants, from any nation, who possessed special skills or qualified as refugees. Skilled professionals from Latin America and Asia, areas long restricted under the old quotas, began to arrive in great numbers, joining the anti-Communist refugees from Castro's Cuba. After the end of the Vietnam war, refugees came from Cambodia and Laos. People left the chaos in the Soviet Union and Eastern Europe after the end of the cold war, and refugees fleeing troubled areas of Africa came during the 1990s. Meanwhile, rates of illegal immigration, especially from nations in the Western Hemisphere, mounted. The Immigration Reform and Control Act of 1986 granted legal residency to workers who had lived in the United States illegally since 1982. Another Immigration Act in 1990 further raised the total number of immigrants that could be admitted on the basis of needed job skills. The booming economy of the 1990s acted as a magnet for immigrants and helped individuals and ethnic enclaves prosper. Professional people, many from India and other parts of Asia, often found lucrative work in the high-tech sector. Meanwhile, unskilled workers began small businesses or found minimum wage jobs in the burgeoning service sector. Statistics showed that income disparities *within* various immigrant groups were often greater than those between immigrants and nonimmigrants.

The influx of immigration, together with a higher birth rate among non-European populations, altered the ethnic and national make-up of America. In 2000, one of every ten Americans had been born outside of the country. Nearly one in every five people over the age of five spoke a language other than English at home. The Census of 2000 reported (in what everyone agreed was an undercount) 30.5 million foreign-born residents, 44 percent of whom had arrived during the 1990s. Spanish-speaking people and people from Asia constituted the fastest growing groups.

From 1990 to 2000 the Hispanic population increased by 58 percent to 35 million, constituting 12.5 percent of the total U.S. population (even excluding Puerto Rico). Beneath the umbrella designation of "Hispanic," which the U.S. Census began using in 1980, however, lay great diversity. In 2000, Mexican Americans constituted nearly 60 percent of the Spanish-speaking population in the United States, with 90 percent living in the Southwest, especially Texas and California. By the 1970s, more Puerto Ricans lived in New York City than in San Juan, Puerto Rico's capital, and sizable communities also grew in Chicago and around industrial areas of New England and Ohio. By 2000, 10 percent of all Hispanics on the U.S. mainland were Puerto Rican, and the mainland population totaled three-quarters of that on the island itself. Cuban Americans had first come to Florida as refugees during the 1960s, fleeing Castro's Cuba. Generally well educated and skilled, this first wave of Cuban Americans tended to adopt a conservative political orientation because of their strong anti-Castro leanings. In Miami they formed an ethnic enclave that developed cradle-to-grave Cuban-owned services. By 2000, about half of the population of Miami was of Cuban descent. Although Mexicans, Puerto Ricans, and Cubans constituted the largest of the Spanish-speaking groups, immigrants from the Dominican Republic and Central and South America also established a significant presence in many American cities. By 2000, the number of Spanish-speaking people in the United States totaled more than in all but four countries of Latin America. In California, the most populous state in the union, people classified as "non-Hispanic whites" had constituted 80 percent of the population in 1980. By 2000 they constituted less than half. In the 1990s the most popularly used boy's name in California and Texas was "Jose."

The category of Asian American likewise grew, by nearly 50 percent to 10.2 million. Chinese Americans constituted the largest group, followed by Filipinos and then by Asian Indians, who came to the United States in large numbers during the 1990s because of the need for their skills in high-tech fields. Vietnamese, Korean, and Japanese Americans also had substantial numbers, with Japanese Americans being the only one of the major Asian nationality groups whose population in the United States actually declined between the 1990 and the 2000 census. The category "Asian American" provided an umbrella term for those who wished to encourage a pan-Asian identity consciousness among disparate groups in the United States. From the late 1970s on, for example, "Asian-American Studies" programs took shape at universities on the West Coast; many activist groups employed the word "Asian American"; and the Census also adopted the term.

"Asian Americans" had even less in common than "Hispanics," who at least shared a language. Affluent émigrés from Hong Kong, who purchased luxury high-rises in some urban centers and were fluent in English, had little in common with, say, Hmong refugees from Laos, whose agricultural background and inexperience with any written language complicated their entry into American life. Figures from the Los Angeles area suggested that "Asian Americans" from the Philippines had twice the income as those from Cambodia. Relatively recent antagonisms between Japan and both China and Korea,

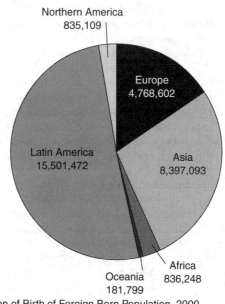

FIGURE 10–5 Region of Birth of Foreign Born Population, 2000.

Source: U.S. Census Bureau.

dating from Japanese atrocities during World War II, spilled over into the politics of their respective hyphenated groups in America. Chinese-Americans and Korean-Americans, for example, often made wartime issues with Japan an important part of their own identity-building activities during the 1990s. In response to complex political pressures, the Census Bureau designated "Asian or Pacific Islanders" as a single category but also provided specific ethnic categories and even an "other Asian" category to accommodate people of mixed-Asian heritage.

Ethnic diversity also brought greater religious variation to American life. Demographic predictions suggested that, even without any new Muslim immigration, Islam would soon replace Judaism as the second largest religion in the United States. Muslims, however, were far from homogeneous. In the late 1990s, demographers estimated that perhaps 40 percent of Muslims were African American converts and the rest had emigrated from many different regions of the world, especially South Asia, Arabic countries in the Middle East, Iran, Africa, and Southeast Asia. For some Muslims, tensions between what some individuals might hold to be Islamic law and U.S. secular law raised puzzling questions. How should antidiscrimination law, for example, deal with the issue of women who cover themselves with a *hijab* if that practice runs against workplace regulations, such as uniformed dress codes or safety requirements banning head scarves? How do rituals associated with prayer and fasting, medical treatment, and burial harmonize into an America that has little understanding of Islam and which, in the eyes of some Muslims, presented a culture that failed to nurture their ideas of morality and decency?

Cultural, linguistic, and religious diversity presented obvious dilemmas for schools and social services. A majority of school children in Los Angeles, for example, lacked proficiency in English, and as many as 80 different languages were spoken in homes. Newcomers began to transform politics as well. Orange County, California, for example, had once been the stronghold of Goldwater conservatives of Northern European descent. In 1996, however, one of the most conservative members of Congress, Robert Dornan, lost his once safe, Orange-County seat to a woman of Hispanic background. Asian American politicians also began winning a number of offices, especially in California, during the 1990s, and both political parties began to court recently naturalized citizens.

THE ELECTION AND EARLY PRESIDENCY OF GEORGE W. BUSH

The presidential election of 2000, between Democratic candidate Vice-President Al Gore and Republican George W. Bush, ended in a virtual dead heat and produced yet another spectacular, made-for-TV legal battle. Gore won the popular contest by about a half-million vote (or a margin of about one-half of one percent), and might have won the electoral vote if all disputed ballots in the crucial state of Florida could have legally been counted. As contested votes in Florida were being tallied and Bush's slim lead was slowly dwindling, a 5–4 majority of the U.S. Supreme Court issued an order temporarily halting any further recount. Three days later, the same one-vote majority declared, in *Bush v. Gore,* that the recount in Florida must cease, a decision that effectively made Bush the president of the United States. How did this unlikely, highly controversial scenario come about?

A Close Election

No candidate ignited great enthusiasm among the electorate in 2000. Two prominent personalities who ran as alternatives to Bush and Gore—Patrick Buchanan, as the standard-bearer of the Reform party, and Ralph Nader, the candidate of the Green party—together received less than four percent of the popular vote. (Ross Perot's half-hearted, Reform-party effort of 1996 had gained more than twice that total.) Targeting environmentalists and labor union members, Nader's campaign may have cost Gore some votes but likely not the election. The normally animated Buchanan, slowed by bitter divisions within the Reform party and his own poor health, largely disappeared during the fall politicking. The turnout among eligible voters continued to decline, after the sudden increase of 1992 and barely reached 50 percent in 2000.

Vice-President Gore's greatest asset, service in Bill Clinton's impeachment-marked administration, was also his greatest liability. Simultaneously hoping that voters would identify him with the Clinton-era economic boom and yet see him as "his own man," Gore kept the president, still popular among most Democrats and many independents, at arm's length. His running mate, Senator Joseph Lieberman, who practiced Orthodox Judaism, emphasized the Democratic party's commitment to multiculturalism. Gore himself, in contrast to Clinton, could never escape his "smart kid" image, and attempts to high-light his intellectual range and grasp of difficult issues only made him seem pretentious and an easy target for TV satire. The Vice-President even studied tapes of "Saturday Night Live" sketches in order to understand how his public persona lent itself to caricature. Gore's campaign, controlled by the candidate and a small inner circle, seemed to lurch from tactic to tactic, strategy to strat-egy. At times, Gore sounded the new Democratic themes of the Clinton ad-ministration but on other occasions trumpeted a brand of Democratic populism that recalled the losing efforts of Jimmy Carter and Walter Mondale.

George W. Bush, son of the former president and governor of Texas, re-mained "on message." He survived a series of bitter primary battles against Ari-zona Senator John McCain, whose support of campaign-reform legislation positioned him as a "moderate" Republican, by emphasizing his own conser-vatism. Bush, often called "W" to distinguish him from his father, promised sub-stantial tax cuts, a stance that conservatives understood to mean Washington would have less money to spend on social programs. He also appealed to those who fondly recalled the 1980s by choosing the Reagan stalwart, Dick Cheney, a Washington insider-turned-Texas-oil-executive, as his vice-presidential running mate. To satisfy voters who worried that a Bush-Cheney administration might seek drastic cuts in federal assistance to the truly needy, Bush called himself a "compassionate conservative" and claimed that he had effectively compromised with Democrats while governor of Texas.

Perhaps most important, Bush won over the religious right, something his father had never done. Here, the younger Bush effectively used a simple story, in both personal appearances and postings on the Internet, about his relatively re-cent life as a "born-again Christian." (Gore could claim the same religious ground-ing but never made it a prominent part of his campaign.) Bush's narrative helped to defuse concerns about his "wild," pre-conversion lifestyle, his self-admitted in-tellectual limitations, and a public presence every bit as bland as that of Al Gore. The story of Bush's religious pilgrimage helped transform potential personal and political liabilities into tangible assets during the fall presidential campaign.

On election night, several of the major TV networks, after interviewing people leaving the polls, initially declared that Gore would carry Florida and, hence, capture a majority in the Electoral College. A variety of circumstances—including ancient voting machines, confusing ballots, and befuddled voters—threw thousands of votes into the "disqualified" and "uncertain" categories. African Americans intending to vote for Gore encountered particular difficul-ty, but later investigations could not unequivocally substantiate the claim that racial discrimination prompted these obstacles. For more than twenty-four hours, the vote count in Florida remained in doubt, until Bush emerged with a lead of about 900 votes. Florida's elected officials, a solidly Republican pha-lanx that included Bush's own brother Jeb, the state's governor, would stead-fastly maintain that Gore had lost their state's electoral votes and refuse to extend the recount process. Meanwhile, Florida's supreme court, dominated by judges who had been appointed by Democrats, ruled that recounts should continue beyond the statutory deadline for reporting results.

The two rival political camps ritualistically condemned the other for "bringing in lawyers," while each busily augmented its own litigation staff. With-in days, at least 50 different lawsuits appeared on court dockets. The legal strategy of the Gore team seemed no clearer than its electoral one. Bush's lawyers, veterans of numerous lawsuits against the Clinton administration and the outgoing president himself, stayed focused. With Republican electoral officials in Florida ready to certify GOP victory, the Bush legal team steadfastly insisted that the recount then underway violated the rule of law and the U.S. Constitution. Opinion polls, suggesting growing popular disgust with the media spectacle (largely orchestrated by conservative activists) accompanying the recount effort in Florida, bolstered their claim that Democrats were trying to "steal" Bush's "victory." In this atmosphere of conflicting arguments, the presidential election of 2000 became a matter for the Supreme Court.

The five conservative members of the Supreme Court accepted Bush's arguments about the recount. They held that Florida's supreme court had provided no uniform standard by which to judge disputed ballots and that Article II of the U.S. Constitution gave the Florida legislature, not its judicial branch, final authority to make decisions involving U.S. presidential elections. Most constitutional commentators despaired of defending these legal justifications—which the five justices and their clerks had stitched together in a matter of hours—but citizens generally accepted the decision in *Bush v. Gore* as a pragmatic way of terminating the contested election. Out of legal options, by the margin of a single judicial vote, Gore and his advisers saw their political ones close as well.

The Presidency of George W. Bush

The Bush presidency began against the backdrop of economic uncertainty and continued partisan conflict. The White House immediately warned of a coming recession and urged significant tax reductions as the best response. Democrats charged that this proposal primarily benefited taxpayers in the highest brackets and would eliminate the Clinton-era budget surplus that might be used to bolster health and social-security programs. Similar debates surrounded energy policy. After a presidential task force urged a focus on accelerated energy production, Democrats charged it with ignoring conservation, scuttling environmental protections, catering to oil interests, and tilting toward large suppliers and traders. As energy company profits and rates soared, particularly in California which had adopted successful conservation strategies but suffered from its own flawed deregulation plan, Republican-appointed federal regulators insisted that the marketplace should determine prices. Meanwhile, the president pressed an ambitious overhaul of the nation's educational system. He called for a federally supported voucher program, which would help parents shift their children from "failing" public to private schools, and for mandatory annual testing of students.

Bush's domestic agenda—cutting taxes, boosting energy production, and promoting educational changes—met mixed success. The White House managed, in June 2001, to secure congressional approval of a modified tax package. It gave most taxpayers an immediate rebate, to stimulate the economy, and scheduled substantial cuts, especially in the higher brackets, over the next ten years. Democrats viewed these future cuts as endangering the long-run solvency of social security, but the White House saw the scaling back of taxes as crucial to economic growth.

Bush's energy and educational measures confronted stronger opposition than his tax proposal. First, Republican Senator James Jeffords of Vermont formally bolted the GOP and, as an independent, allowed the Democrats to regain control of the previously deadlocked Senate and deny Vice-President Dick Cheney his tie-breaking vote. Then, the White-House goal of immediately boosting energy production lost its urgency when the economic slow-down slackened demand and temporarily reduced energy prices. Moreover, critics effectively assailed Bush's energy task force for consulting industry representatives but not scientific or environmental experts. The non-partisan Congressional Budget Office sued the White House to learn exactly how much access private interests had enjoyed. This controversy coincided with investigations, by Congress and law-enforcement agencies, into the accounting irregularities which preceded the bankruptcy of Enron Corporation, a Texas-based energy company with close ties to the president and, apparently, to the White-House task force. Finally, stiff opposition forced Bush to defer the idea of vouchers; but, in an unlikely alliance with Senator Ted Kennedy, he did secure an education bill that provided for mandatory student testing.

Foreign crises came to dominate the president's and the nation's attention. Early in the morning of September 11, 2001, nineteen suicide comman-

FIGURE 10–6   At the Scene of the World Trade Center Disaster in New York, September 14, 2001.

President George W. Bush stands with firefighters and rescue workers as he addresses a crowd and promises a campaign against terrorism.
Source: Win McNamee / Reuters, TimePix.

dos took over four commercial airliners, filled with flammable jet fuel, in hopes of using them as hi-octane bombs. Two planes sliced through the twin towers of the World Trade Center in New York City; a third plowed into the Pentagon in Washington, D.C. Courageous passengers on a fourth plane, after learning of these events, confronted the hijackers who had seized their airliner's cockpit, and it crashed to the ground in rural Pennsylvania. The first attack on U.S. soil since December 7, 1941, the airplane bombings of "9/11" stunned the nation. More than 3000 people, including several hundred airline passengers and an even larger number of fire fighters and police officers in New York City, lost their lives. The World Trade Center, which had been bombed by Islamic extremists in 1993, could not withstand the burning jet fuel, and its iconic towers collapsed into rubble. The shock of 9/11 had not yet abated when, during mid-September, some members of Congress and several journalists received mail containing anthrax spores. Hundreds, primarily postal workers and congressional employees, received treatment for anthrax exposure, and five people died after inhaling the deadly spores. Although evidence subsequently pointed to a domestic, rather than a foreign, culprit in the anthrax mailings, an anxious nation braced for additional assaults on its population and sense of security. Many people avoided airline travel, and those who did fly confronted tightened security measures. Uncertainty shook the already troubled economy and a nervous stock market.

George W. Bush, who became Commander in Chief, suddenly presided over a world-wide military effort. Virtually every nation, including almost all of the Islamic states, condemned the bombings, and most supported the U.S. desire for a vigorous response. American officials immediately traced the attacks of 9/11 to Al Qaeda, the terrorist network headed by Osama bin Laden. An Islamic militant from a wealthy Saudi family, bin Laden had begun planning strikes at American targets in retaliation for the introduction of non-Muslim troops into Saudi Arabia during the Persian Gulf War and had been training commando units in Afghanistan, in cooperation with the Taliban, a fundamentalist Islamic group in power there. Bush soon announced a long-term, global campaign against all terrorist groups such as Al Qaeda, any nation that "harbored" terrorists, and other states (especially Iraq) that he labeled as "evil." Later called the Bush doctrine, this declaration translated into a military operation, in late 2001, when U.S. forces helped a coalition of Afghani factions topple the Taliban regime and put bin Laden's forces on the run.

Bush enjoyed bi-partisan support after 9/11. With only one dissenting vote, Congress supported his military response. It also enacted legislation, once blocked by conservative Republicans, that allowed Washington to scrutinize international financial networks in order to track how terrorist organizations such as Al Qaeda transferred and laundered money. In an effort to safeguard the home front, Bush created a new Office of Homeland Security, and Congress passed the "Patriot Act," which expanded fifteen existing laws and allowed the government broader authority to detain aliens and conduct surveillance operations. Although civil libertarians saw constitutional problems in the detention and surveillance procedure, members of Congress supported these measures as an appropriate way to shore up national security.

The Bush doctrine eventually encountered dilemmas that a simple pledge to fight terrorism and evil could not cover. Although Republicans had earlier criticized Clinton's efforts at "nation-building" and "peacekeeping" in Haiti and the Balkans, the Bush administration needed a stable, pro-American government in Afghanistan. It divided, however, over the precise role that the United States should play in reconstructing and nurturing the new Afghan state, beset by warlord rivalry and economic distress.

Other divisions, often revealed by leaks to the press, emerged over where next to take the campaign against terrorism. Some advisers, such as National Security Adviser Condeleeza Rice, supported the president's instinct to go where his father had stopped and topple Saddam Hussein's regime in Iraq. The Iraqi threat turned on Saddam Hussein's expulsion of international inspection teams that, under the agreement following the Persian Gulf War of 1992, were to ensure that Iraq was not developing biological, chemical, or nuclear weapons. One faction in the Bush administration suggested that Iraq's resistance to inspections meant that the question became when, not if, the United States would move toward Baghdad. Other advisers, particularly Secretary of State Colin Powell, worried about the foreign-policy consequences of unilaterally launching a war that might have unpredictable consequences.

The dilemmas over how to respond to terrorism, increasingly complicated by growing anti-American sentiment among Arabs and much of the Muslim world, loomed even larger when a new cycle of violence hit the Middle East during the spring of 2002. Palestinian suicide bombers attacked Israeli civilians, and the Israeli military rolled into Palestinian cities in early April. President Bush, who criticized Clinton's earlier attempt to fashion a Middle East settlement and strongly backed Israel, scrambled to forge a policy that would quell the violence and satisfy moderate (and oil-rich) Arab states.

Although partisan debate was more muted than before 9/11, differences on issues unrelated to the war on terrorism remained embedded in the political culture. Both opponents and supporters of the president honed their political strategies. Bush himself seemed determined to avoid his father's fate and gain a second term. He sought better relations with Mexico, a policy in part aimed at courting Hispanic voters in the United States. Contradicting his own free-trade policies, he accommodated pressure groups in political swing-states by imposing tariffs on some foreign steel and Canadian lumber imports. He used the occasion of the war against terrorism to gain congressional funding for a highly controversial space-based antimissile system, an updated version of Reagan's SDI initiative. Confronting a president with an approval rating that oscillated between 80 and 90 percent in the months after 9/11, Democrats moved cautiously. Somewhat emboldened by the collapse of Enron and indications that its accounting firm, Arthur Anderson, had been helping to cook the company's books, Democrats charged both firms with trading their large political contributions for exemption from regulatory oversight. As a result, congressional Democrats finally secured enough Republican votes to pass a campaign finance law that the president's supporters had been blocking. Bush unenthusiastically signed this measure, co-sponsored by Republican John McCain. The law, which opponents called an unconstitutional abridgement of political speech, banned "soft money" contributions to political parties and required greater disclosure of the source of campaign advertising.

Meanwhile, economic uncertainty prevailed. After surveying economic data, experts including the redoubtable Alan Greenspan sent confusing messages. Certainly, the bubble of unrealistic stock valuations for dot-com and "new-economy" companies had burst; some firms such as K-Mart faced bankruptcy; the stock market retreated sharply from the stratospheric levels reached during Clinton's last year in office; industrial production fell; and unemployment rose. Inflation, however, remained low; consumers continued to buy goods and services; defense spending primed the pump, and the real-estate market, buoyed by low interest rates, continued to soar. By the time economists finally adjusted the statistics for 2001, they reported only one quarter in which the overall economy had failed to grow, a finding that did not meet the technical definition of a recession. There was little agreement, even among professional economists, whether conflicting statistical indicators pointed toward recovery, recession, or drift.

RETROSPECTIVE

Any historical era represents a culmination of previous ones, but the 1990s, more than most, seemed a watershed. With George H. Bush's defeat and Bill Clinton's victory in 1992, the World War II generation passed from the political scene. Younger leaders, with their roots in the baby-boom generation, came into major positions of power. That generation had matured within the fierce social and political struggles of the 1960s and early 1970s. The polarization of this decade—over the nature of cultural, gender, and racial politics; the proper use of military force overseas; and the appropriate reach of governmental power at home—continued to produce tension within both public and private life. How would this profound generational shift help to set the nation's new agenda? What new visions might inspire the country? The future, as always, would be what people could make of it.

SUGGESTED READING

A journalistic overview of the Clinton years is Haynes Johnson, *The Best of Times* (2001). On the political background of the Clinton presidency, see Kenneth Baer, *Reinventing Democrats: The Politics of Liberalism from Reagan to Clinton* (2000); Stephen Gillon, *The Democrats' Dilemma: Walter F. Mondale, and the Liberal Legacy* (1992); Thomas Byrne Edsall and Mary D. Edsall, *Chain Reaction: The Impact of Race, Rights, and Taxes on American Politics* (rev. ed., 1992); Jack W. Germond and Jules Witcover, *Mad as Hell: Revolt at the Ballot Box, 1992* (1993); Theodore Lowi, *The End of the Republican Era* (1995); Ronald Radosh, *Divided They Fell: The Demise of the Democratic Party, 1964–1996* (1996); and Kenneth S. Baer, *Reinventing Democrats: The Politics of Liberalism from Reagan to Clinton* (2000).

   Economic issues are covered, from different perspectives, in Robert Kuttner, *Everything For Sale: The Virtues and Limits of Markets* (1997); Gwendolyn Mink, *Welfare's End* (1998); William Greider, *One World, Ready or Not* (1997); Paul Krugman, *The Age of Diminished Expectations: U.S. Economic Policy in the 1990s* (3rd ed., 1997); Daniel Yergin and Joseph Stanislaw, *The Commanding Heights: The Battle between Government and the Marketplace That Is Remaking the Modern World* (1998);

Bob Woodward, *Maestro: Greenspan's Fed and the American Boom* (2000); and Robert J. Shiller, *Irrational Exuberance* (2000).

On politics and foreign policy, see David Halberstam, *War in a Time of Peace* (2001); Bruce Cumings, *Parallax Visions: Making Sense of American-East Asian Relations at the End of the Century* (1999); Frederick W. Mayer, *Interpreting NAFTA: The Science and Art of Political Analysis* (1998); Eric Alterman, *Who Speaks for America? Why Democracy Matters in Foreign Policy* (1998); Robert Kumamoto, *International Terrorism and American Foreign Relations, 1945–1976* (1999); Michael T. Klare, *Resource Wars: The New Landscape of Global Conflict* (2001); General Wesley K. Clark, *Waging Modern War: Bosnia, Kosovo, and the Future of Conflict* (2001); and Ahmed Rashid, *Taliban: Militant Islam, Oil, and Fundamentalism in Central Asia* (2001).

The origins of cultural-political clashes of the 1990s may be found in many of the works cited in previous chapters. In addition, see James R. Lewis, ed., *From the Ashes: Making Sense Out of Waco* (1994); Stuart A. Wright, ed., *Armageddon in Waco: Critical Perspectives on the Branch Davidian Conflict* (1995); James D. Tabor and Eugene V. Gallagher, *Why Waco? Cults and the Battle for Religious Freedom in America* (1995); Sara Diamond, *Roads to Dominion: Right-Wing Movements and Political Power in the United States* (1995); Morris Dees with James Corcoran, *Gathering Storm: America's Militia Threat* (1996); Catherine McNicol Stock, *Rural Radicals: Righteous Rage in the American Grain* (1996); Edward T. Linenthal and Tom Engelhardt, *History Wars: The Enola Gay and Other Battles for the American Past* (1996); Gary B. Nash, Charlotte Crabtree, and Ross E. Dunn, *History on Trial: Culture Wars and the Teaching of the Past* (1997); Stephan and Abigail Thernstrom, *America in Black and White: One Nation, Indivisible* (1997); David Shipler, *A Country of Strangers: Black and White in America* (1997); Orlando Patterson, *The Ordeal of Integration* (1997); James Risen and Judy L. Thomas, *Wrath of Angels: The American Abortion War* (1998); Cynthia Gomey, *Articles of Faith: A Frontline History of the Abortion Wars* (1998); Edward J. Blakely and Mary Gail Snyder, *Fortress America: Gated Communities in the United States* (1997); Richard Moe and Carter Wilkie, *Changing Places: Rebuilding Community in the Age of Sprawl* (1997); Justin Watson, *The Christian Coalition: Dreams of Restoration, Demands for Recognition* (1997); Richard A. Serrano, *One of Ours: Timothy McVeigh and the Oklahoma City Bombing* (1998); Adolph Reed, Jr., ed., *Without Justice For All: The New Liberalism and Our Retreat From Racial Equality* (1999).

On Bill Clinton and his troubled presidency, begin with Theodore Lowi and Benjamin Ginsburg, *Embattled Democracy, Politics and Policy in the Clinton Era* (1995); the journalistic accounts of Elizabeth Drew, *Finding His Voice: Clinton's Ambitious and Turbulent First Years* (1994), *Showdown* (1997), and *Whatever It Takes: The Real Struggle for Political Power in America* (1997); and Bob Woodward, *The Agenda: Inside the Clinton White House* (1994) and *The Choice* (1996). See also, Robert F. Denton and Rachel Holloway, *The Clinton Presidency: Images and Communication Strategies* (1996); James B. Stewart, *Bloodsport: The President and His Adversaries* (1996); Richard Reeves, *Running in Place: How Bill Clinton Disappointed America* (1996); Stanley Renshon, *High Hopes: The Clinton Presidency and the Politics of Ambition* (1996); John Hohenberg, *Reelecting Bill Clinton: Why America Chose a "New Democrat"* (1997); Greil Marcus, *Double Trouble: Bill Clinton and Elvis Presley in a Land of No Alternatives*; Steven E. Schier, ed.,

The Postmodern Presidency: Bill Clinton's Legacy in U.S. Politics (2000); Jeffrey Toobin, A Vast Conspiracy: The Real Story of the Sex Scandal That Nearly Brought Down a President (2000); Martin A. Levin, et al., eds., Seeking the Center: Policy and Policymaking in the New Century (2001); and Joe Conanson and Gene Lyons, The Hunting of the President: The Ten-Year Campaign to Destroy Bill and Hillary Clinton (2001).

On the election of 2000 see Richard A. Posner, Breaking the Deadlock: The 2000 Election, The Constitution, and the Courts (2001) and Jeffrey Toobin, Too Close to Call (2001).

For studies on American Indians see Nancy Shoemaker, American Indian Population Recovery in the Twentieth Century (1999); Joy A. Bilharz, The Allegany Senecas and Kinzua Dam: Forced Relocation through Two Generations (1998); Joane Nagel, American Indian Ethnic Renewal: Red Power and the Resurgence of Identity and Culture (1996); John Williams Sayers, Ghost Dancing the Law: The Wounded Knee Trials (1997).

On immigration see Wendy F. Katkin, Ned Landsman, Andrea Tyree, eds., Beyond Pluralism: The Conception of Groups and Group Identities in America (1998); David Hollinger, Post-Ethnic America: Beyond Multiculturalism (1995); Merry Ovnick, Los Angeles: The End of the Rainbow (1994); Nathan Glazer, ed., Clamor at the Gates: The New American Immigration (1985); Michael D'Innocenzo and Josef P. Sirefman, eds., Immigration and Ethnicity (1992); Alejandro Portes and Ruben G. Rumbaut, Immigrant America: A Portrait (1996); Norman L. Zucker and Naomi Flink Zucker, Desperate Crossings: Seeking Refuge in America (1996); David M. Reimers, Unwelcome Strangers: American Identity and the Turn against Immigration (1998).

On Latinos, see Manuel G. Gonzales, Mexicanos: A History of Mexicans in the United States (1999); Carlos Muñoz, Jr., Youth, Identity, Power: The Chicano Movement (1989); Juan Gonzalez, Harvest of Empire: A History of Latinos in America (2000); John R. Chavez, East Side Landmark: A History of the East Los Angeles Community Union, 1968–1993 (1998); Michael Jones-Correa, Between Two Nations: The Political Predicament of Latinos in New York City (1998); Jose E. Cruz, Identity and Power: Puerto Rican Politics and the Challenge of Ethnicity (1998); Roberto Suro, Strangers Among Us: How Latino Immigration is Transforming America (1998); Mike Davis, Magical Urbanism: Latinos Reinvent the US City (2000); Maria Cristina Garcia, Havana USA: Cuban Exiles and Cuban Americans in South Florida, 1959–1994 (1996); Vicki L. Ruiz, From Out of the Shadows: Mexican Women in Twentieth-Century America (1998).

Other specific immigration studies include Mary Patrice Erdmans, Opposite Poles: Immigrants and Ethnics in Polish Chicago, 1976–1990 (1998); Yvonne Yasbeck Haddad and John L. Esposito, Muslims on the Americanization Path? (1998); Paul James Rutledge, The Vietnamese Experience in America (1992); Valerie O'Conner Sutter, The Indochinese Refugee Dilemma (1989); Luciano Mangiofico, Contemporary American Immigrants: Patterns of Filipino, Korean, and Chinese Settlement in the United States (1988); Pyong Gap Min, Caught in the Middle: Korean Merchants in America's Multiethnic Cities (1996); Barbara Posadas, The Filipino Americans (1999); Padma Rangaswamy, Namaste America: Indian Immigrants in an American Metropolis (2000); and Benson Tong, The Chinese Americans (2000).

Websites

The Internet offers a wealth of on-line resources for students and teachers who wish to consult documentary material. Three outstanding general sites that provide access to specialized documents and photo collections include those maintained by the National Archives, *www.nara.gov/*, the Smithsonian Institution, *www.si.edu/*, and the American Memory section of the Library of Congress, *http://memory.loc.gov/ammem/ammemhome.html*. Presidential libraries, run by the National Archives and accessed through its general site, provide on-line photos and documents relevant to the political history of each presidential administration. Examples of individual states that maintain on-line photo collections, with key word searches, include the On-Line Archive of California, *http://sunsite2.berkeley.edu/oac/*, and the "visual resources" at the Minnesota Historical Society, *www.mnhs.org*.

For program transcripts and valuable associated materials related to Public Broadcasting's "American Experience" programs see *www.pbs.org/wgbh/amex/*. See especially the extensive material on the Vietnam War.

For foreign policy and national security, there are large documentary collections of recently declassified materials maintained by the nongovernmental National Security Archive, *www.gwu.edu/~nsarchiv/*, and by the Historical Office of the Department of State, *www.state.gov/www/about_state/history/frus.html*. The CIA's Center for the Study of Intelligence presents declassified assessments of the Soviet threat and other intelligence materials at *www.odci.gov/csi/books/coldwaryrs/* and *www.odci.gov/csi/books/princeton/index.html/*. Historical documents at the Kennedy library are at *www.cs.umb.edu/jfklibrary/guide.html*. Copies of the controversial Venona documents are located at *www.nsa.gov/docs/venona/*.

Historical documents on law and diplomacy are available through the Avalon Project at Yale University, *www.yale.edu/lawweb/avalohn/avalon.htm*.

On American society and culture, consult the Census Bureau's extensive website, *www.census.gov*, for current and historical demographic information. On film, the internet movie database, *www.imdb.com*, is the place to start. On television history, see *www.tvhistory.tv*. The Duke University library maintains an excellent array of on-line collections, including documents from the Women's Liberation Movement, *http://scriptorium.lib.duke.edu/wlm/*, and advertising images of consumer products, *http://scriptorium.lib.duke.edu/adaccess/browse.html*. On Civil Rights, see especially the Civil Rights Documentation Project at *www.dept.usm.edu/~mcrob/* and the Martin Luther King Papers Project at *www.stanford.edu/group/king/*, and *www.sitins.com*.

To locate on-line reviews of recent books in history, consult H-Net's book review archive at *www2.h-net.msu.edu/reviews/*.

INDEX